Management Under Differing Value Systems

Editors: Günter Dlugos and Klaus Weiermair

Management Under Differing Value Systems

Political, Social and Economical Perspectives in a Changing World

Editors:
Günter Dlugos and Klaus Weiermair
in Collaboration with Wolfgang Dorow

W DE G

Walter de Gruyter · Berlin · New York 1981

Proceedings of the International Conference, Toronto, October 1980

Prof. Dr. Günter Dlugos, Fachbereich Wirtschaftswissenschaft, Fachrichtung Unternehmungspolitik, Freie Universität Berlin, Berlin (West)

Prof. Dr. Klaus Weiermair, Faculty of Administrative Studies, Department of Economics, York University, Toronto, Ontario, Canada

Dr. Wolfgang Dorow, Fachbereich Wirtschaftswissenschaft, Fachrichtung Unternehmungspolitik, Freie Universität Berlin, Berlin (West)

CIP-Kurztitelaufnahme der Deutschen Bibliothek

Management under differing value systems:
polit., social and econom. perspectives in a changing world;
[proceedings of the internat. conference, Toronto, October 1980]/ed.:
Günter Dlugos and Klaus Weiermair in collaboration with
Wolfgang Dorow. – Berlin; New York : de Gruyter, 1982.
ISBN 3-11-008553-4
NE: Dlugos, Günter [Hrsg.]

Library of Congress Cataloging in Publication Data

Management under differing vlue systems
Proceedings of an international conference held in Toronto, Oct. 1980
Includes index.
1. Industry-Social aspects-Congresses.
2. Comparative management-Congresses.
3. Social values-Congresses.
4. Industrial relations-Congresses.
I. Dlugos, Günter. II. Weiermair, Klaus, 1939 – III. Dorow, Wolfgang.
HD60.M36 658.4'08 81-15081
ISBN 3-11-008553-4 AACR2

 Printing: Karl Gerike, Berlin. – Binding: Dieter Mikolai, Berlin. – Printed in Germany.

Preface

Research in Philosophy and various Social Sciences disciplines has recently received new impetus from a general recognition that human action and behavior is largely determined by prevailing social values and norms. The relationship between social values and human behavior therefore becomes an important explanatory variable in the analysis of varying interests and needs across societies with differing value systems and, as such, also serves as the explanation and prediction of secular changes in basic human goals and human behavior.

The enterprise sector, as one of the main determinants of social and economic development obviously represents in this regard a key social subsystem with interrelationships to social values and social value changes in the product and factor markets, particularly the market for labour and the ensuing system of industrial relations. To the present, research into changing values, while concentrating on the special phenomena of western industrial society, also has emphasized the relative importance of the enterprise sector.

So far there has been no attempt at a comprehensive analysis of the interdependencies between value systems and the structures, processes and efficiencies of the enterprise sector in different societies, on the one hand, and the impact of the sector in changing value systems on the other hand.

This serious research gap, a shared interest in the field of value research and the existence of research results on enterprise related value analysis, were among the motives for the Faculty of Administrative Studies at York University, Toronto, and the Faculty of Enterprise Policy at Free University, Berlin, to organize an international conference in Toronto on

"Management Under Differing Value Systems". The conference was facilitated by the presence and active interest of a large number of social scientists engaged in value research who sought to exchange information with regard to competing paradigms and approaches and who had become interested in closer collaboration.

Among the topics of the conference were fundamental problems with the applicability and interpretation of general social value research, enterprise specific value research, questions of research design, interdependencies between social value systems, the employment relationship and managerial values, and the contextual and structural leeway accorded to them. These analyses, adapted to North American and Western European conditions, were supplemented by comparisons with conditions prevailing in Eastern Europe and Japan.

Publication of the papers should promote an overview on the state of the arts in value research as it relates to the enterprise sector, and to stimulate greater research efforts in this area for the purpose of expanding scientific collaboration. During the conference, discussion was also sought with representatives of companies, a dialogue which we would like to deepen and explore and which was a further motive behind this publication.

We are grateful to all participants of the Toronto Conference for their earnest cooperation, especially to the chairmen, speakers and discussants, and the submission of revised and largely publishable papers. As for overcoming the inevitable residue and helping with translation, we thank Hilde Karge, Helga Prouty, David Antal, and Dipl.-Kfm. Hans-Georg Lilge, all residing in Berlin, as well as Filomena Otto and Diane Plumridge in Toronto.

The realization of our desire to publish the conference papers was accommodated most generously by the publishing house of

Walter de Gruyter, Berlin - New York, whom we should like to thank for diverse favors, and the speedy publication of this research.

A necessary precondition for the realization of the conference in Toronto has been the generous support of our project by both universities involved and a grant from the Social Sciences & Humanities Research Council of Canada. We are particularly grateful to Reemtsma Cigarettenfabriken GmbH., Hamburg, Siemens AG., Zentrale Berliner Leitung, Volkswagen AG., Wolfsburg, Imperial Oil, Gulf Canada, and the Ontario Government for filling the remaining financial gaps.

The Editors

Contents

B. Industrial Relations

C. Industrial Democracy and Quality of Worklife

D. Social and Economic Rationale of Organization-Internal Labour Markets

Part IV
Values and Management Process - Cross-National Comparisons

Programme Committee

Prof. Dr. Klaus Weiermair
Faculty of Administrative Studies
Department of Economics
York University, Toronto, Ontario
Canada

Prof. Dr. Günter Dlugos
Dr. Wolfgang Dorow
Dipl.-Kfm. Jochen Wondracek
Fachbereich Wirtschaftswissenschaft
Fachrichtung Unternehmungspolitik
Freie Universität Berlin, Berlin (West)

Chairmen

Borins, Sandford, York University, Toronto
Dimick, David, York University, Toronto
Jick, Todd, York University, Toronto
Proudfoot, Stuart, York University, Toronto
Read, William, York University, Toronto
Schwan, Gesine, Free University Berlin, Berlin (West)
Spender, J. C., York University, Toronto
Thompson, Donald, York University, Toronto
Tryfos, Peter, York University, Toronto
Weiermair, Klaus, York University, Toronto
Wolf, Bernard, York University, Toronto

Discussants

Courtney, Alice, York University, Toronto
Crispo, John, University of Toronto, Toronto
Glaubrecht, Helmut, Reemtsma Cigarettenfabriken GmbH., Hamburg
Jain, Harish C., McMaster University, Hamilton
Lazar, Fred, York University, Toronto
Manzer, Ron, University of Toronto, Toronto
Meltz, Noah M., University of Toronto, Toronto
Michalos, Barbara, Woods Gordon Management Consultant, Toronto
Murray, Victor, York University, Toronto
Packmohr, Horst, Siemens AG, Berlin (West)
Simmie, Patricia, York University, Toronto
Simmons, Harvey, York University, Toronto

Part I
Fundamental Problems and the Epistemology of Value Research

Fundamental Values of Western Democracies

Alexander Schwan

ABSTRACT

This article deals with the spiritual, economic, and social crises in highly industrialized societies which are rapidly becoming problematical for western democratic nations, too. On the one hand, the democracies require a strengthening of their capacity for government, and on the other, a co-responsibility of the citizenry if these problems are to be solved. One of the most important preconditions for this would seem to be the development of a common ethos in a pluralistic society, orientated by the fundamental values inherent in our democratic constitutions. The following guiding fundamental values are described in this paper: dignity of man, liberty, life, equality, social justice, solidarity, and plurality. These values are closely related and mutually explanatory. Not one of these fundamental values can be isolated from the rest and become absolute. Political decisions orientated by these values gain in legitimacy, but they are subject to constant scrutiny, critique, and revision. The binding common ethos of pluralistic democracy, at the same time, permits the development of particular ethics for the individual and for the social subsystems. While these ethics are autonomous in themselves, they must not appear to be antagonistically opposed to the pluralistic public ethos.

Crises and Prospects of the Pluralistic Democracy

The western democracies at present must overcome some severe crises. These crises have been experienced to a different extent by the citizens of these countries, but they have been particularly acute for the young generation. Their roots are situated in material and spiritual problems which, for the most part, are phenomena resulting more from the highly industrialized and technological life of today than from special characteristics of the pluralistic society and the democratic state. The ecological problems, the scarcity of raw materials, the pressing difficulties of the world economy, especially the imbalance of the world monetary system, are international factors taking priority on our political agendas. Since the analyses and prognoses of the Club of Rome, the limits, the dangers, the possibilities, and the necessities of material growth have been intensively discussed. These structural difficulties of economy and ecology induce social and spiritual weaknesses involving the labor market and the maintaining of security in society; a great many people have lost their professional and social orientation; finally, a deep crisis over the sense of living (called "Sinnkrise" in Germany) is becoming more apparent.

All these factors have created worldwide problems in the structural and intellectual existence of modern civilization, problems which cannot simply be attributed to any particular political system. Nevertheless, they endanger the foundations and the functioning of the pluralistic democracies. In fact, only in these democracies have these problems been frankly discussed; the political system can be criticized publicly and (for the most part wrongly) be called responsible for them. Herein lies one of the reasons for the acute doubt in the competence and the capability of democratic states to continue to govern and find convincing solutions.

Indeed, the process of developing consciousness of the problems and carrying out decisions concerning them needs much time in the pluralistic democracy to be acknowledged, elaborated, and improved, and often it retains many deficiencies. But only the relatively high elasticity and stability of pluralistic democracy has good prospects for creating the potential to pose and solve the problems fairly, through free insight and public examination, by allowing individuals in the society to establish a general consent based on their own well-understood interest. Despite all its difficulties, this political system in the long run is thus more effective than any other system, especially the autocratic and bureaucratic type. The answers given by the adherents of authoritarian regimes are unacceptable for reasons of principle and practicality. They offer no real alternatives to the pluralistic democracy.

Pluralistic democracy today needs an increase of the government's capability for acting and a stimulation of constructive cooperation of citizens, social groups, and institutions. The long term policy of public authorities and the civil service will have to be more effective. At the same time, more diversification and decentralization of the different levels for political actions seems desirable, at least in most of the European countries. That would be in the interest of an active participation by the people. All individuals, groups, and organizations must assume responsibility if the vitally important attempt is to succeed in mastering the crises in a manner that combines just distribution of unavoidable burdens with security and further development of individual and political liberty.

Challenges

There are some challenges that must be responded to. In future the improvement of the quality of life for all individuals will become more important than the mere increase of material prosperity. That demands that the population must change its outlook on life. A crucial condition for improving the quality of life is the restoration and preservation of human resources (in the widest sense), which are both within man's ability through care for health, for neighborly social relations, for a humane and secure worker's situation, for an intelligent organization of leisure time, for the value of relaxation and so on. Yet an effective economy, large-scale industrial investments, a sufficient supply of energy, adequate nutrition, and many other things are equally important for a qualitatively satisfying individual and social life. Last but not least, the continual improvement of the education system is essential to the enrichment of life because that gives the chance to each member of the society to realize a relatively independent self-reliant life. But all these and many other required social accomplishments demand great effort on the part of citizens; the commonwealth can distribute to the citizens only the sum of their own individual and collective work.

It is not the purpose of this chapter to continue the outline of the problems and challenges indicated above. But it is clear that the democratic society of the near future can no longer be a hedonistic and egoistic society. It will and must be a rather ascetic and joint society, a society of solidarity yet also of freedom; that is the feat. There are no simple solutions for these complex modern tasks; there exists only a troublesome way of difficult decisions with long-term effects, most of which must connect a variety of strategies. Today's single interest groups often overlook that point, even though the special perspectives they emphasize are sometimes very useful for public discussion. But political practice in general is responsible for handling the complex of social duties, and decisions must be based upon competence and courage to take far-reaching action on behalf of the common good. They are mostly judgments in conflicting situations, often made in "tragic conflicts" between goods and values which are of equal importance in securing the quality of modern life. On these grounds political decisions can never satisfy everyone and can never claim general validity; on the contrary, there are always relative decisions under uncertain and diverse conditions, especially in the present society. This fact, however, does not diminish but it enlarges the intellectual, moral, and political demands on politicians and the population to find the readiness and strength for active participation.

The Importance of a Common Ethos

In the interest of a humane society--not only of society and mankind as such, but of free society and free mankind, the sole interesting quality of survival--the reflection on the fundamental values of the pluralistic democracy is a crucial issue. It is important that the ethical standards of the free social life of individuals, groups, and organizations are recognized and adopted. It should not only be regarded as up-to-date to accommodate social goals to the changing subjective requirements of individuals and groups; at the same time, these subjective requirements ought to be scrutinized to determine whether they are justified as supporting liberal politics in the pluralistic democracy or not.

There is a necessary framework of free society, and this framework has distinct intellectual and moral roots. For this reason, the focus on "fundamentals" (Grundwerte) in the discussion that has been going on in some of the western countries for several years is noteworthy and pleasing. In the Federal Republic of Germany, the discussion was initiated by the programmatic change of the Social Democratic Party (SPD, Bad Godesberg, 1959) which abandoned its Marxist tradition to follow a new direction of democratic socialism. Intense controversies between the parties, the churches, and other groups about various aspects of the political reforms since 1969 (Reformpolitik) have reanimated the discussion. A similar discussion has arisen in the Anglo-Saxon countries through John Rawls' eminent "Theory of Justice", through Daniel Bell's important research on the constitutional structures and changes of consciousness in the "postindustrial society", and through many other scholars. The discussions in both parts of the western world are contributing to a "reconstruction of political philosophy", a Philosophy of Practice, evaluating it against the present domination of analytical, Marxist, or linguistic--in general, the scientifically orientated--social theories. I sympathize with and participate in these efforts.

But does pluralistic democracy have any compelling ethical standards bearing on fundamentals? Is there not just the indifference of an unbounded plurality in which each single position seems to be autonomous and isolated? Without any basis will not the whole collapse into a thousand pieces? Indeed, to the pluralistic, free, and open society belongs a plurality of the ethics, legitimately practised in it, too. The different types of roles, groups, subsystems, forms of socialization, and kinds of communication in this society have a partial autonomy that gains its secured and limited validity within the state's order. Each of them, however, has its own ethos. In pluralistic society and democracy there is not the single, absolute, commanding authority of norms and rules. This is precisely the essential cause of grave difficulties that individuals and groups experience when orientating themselves within the society when forming their identity, and when finding a sense of purpose. Its absence is not a burden only, however; it also implies a sort of relief, a chance for an individual life-style. It is the prerequisite for a free and self-reliant development of the citizens, although again not a guarantee. The plurality of norms and rules, too, is in the modern world of life an unalterable and desirable thing; it is not an aim in itself, but rather a necessary means to an end--that of free moral self-realization of the individuals.

At the same time, the pluralistic society needs, and has, a basic standard of a common ethos if it is to recover or preserve that consistency and that order which are the conditions of the ability to overcome the crises in freedom. This basic standard of a common ethos lies in the fundamental values as they are fixed in or combined with the democratic constitutions. According to the American "founding fathers", the constitution of the commonwealth not only means a structure of government but, above all, a declaration of rights and a definition of the basic conditions and essential form of public morality. In this meaning, the constitution results from a fundamental consensus of the citizens or groups or various forces in the founding generation, a consensus, specifically, on the fundamental values of communal life, too. This basic consensus must be revived, renewed, deepened, and enlarged constantly by later generations, for as long as the democratic society and the democratic constitution exist.

Though the constitution in a free society is of particular importance, it is not the sole absolute authority for all ethics but only for that basic standard of a common ethos that must direct public life and politics in the pluralistic society. In this capacity, it directs all citizens and groups, too. Thus the practice of the pluralistic society's citizens and groups is formed by it to a large extent, but without a total determination and without elimination of their partial autonomy.

The Fundamental Values

What are the fundamental values fixed in model democratic constitutions like the Constitution of the United States, the Grundgesetz of the Federal Republic, or the unwritten British constitution elaborated by common law and precedent? The basis of these kinds of constitutions is the dignity of man as the indisputable and inviolable foundation of common life. From this concept, unalterable rights of men are derived, binding not only on all political power, but on all citizens, groups, and social organizations. These rights give a direction, a standard, and a set limit for the actions of individuals and social forces. Hence, it is understandable and logical that a main issue in the present struggle over the Canadian constitution is the question of which authority is to define the fundamental rights and how. The discussion involves the question of consensus on the fundamental values of public life.

The dignity of man is the dignity of each human being, the absolute importance of each individual--not arrived at through subjective assessment, or sympathy, but with the objective postulate in the strict sense of Immanuel Kant that the humanness in each person shall be handled not only as a means but also as an end in itself always.[1] The dignity of the individual therefore does not depend on how society values his achievements. On the contrary, the immutability, the inviolability, and the inalienability of the dignity and rights of men indicate truths which are not in the domain of the society, of the state, or even of the individual himself. They are essential, basic anthropological data of ontological quality. The dignity of man would actually not exist if it depended on the decisions of the individuals.

The other fundamental values founded in the democratic constitutions, liberty, life, equality, justice, solidarity, and plurality, are derived from these basic data, and are essential and necessary. They all belong together; they require and involve each other, they define each other and cannot be isolated; one cannot be amplified to the neglect of the others, or be interpreted in an extreme sense. It is the crucial principle of these democratic values that none of them can claim an extraordinary, or predominant, validity. They are only understandable and practicable as interconnected and, therefore, as strictly "relational" (not precisely as "relative"), qualities.

For example, the liberty granted and guaranteed by the democratic constitution is no mere license, no limitless arbitrary action, no total emancipation of all liability and order. It is a freedom tied to the rights of other individuals, to the acceptance of duties in communal life, to the recognition of a social order, to the acknowledgement of moral law. This liberty is not only a liberty <u>from</u>, but also a liberty <u>for</u>. It is liberty from unlawful power, that is, from any arbitrary limitation of individual action by the state or by other social forces. It is a liberty for choice, for decision-making, and for self-government and thus a liberty to participate, to cooperate, and to assume responsibility in the commonwealth. The citizens' political liberty is, as was known by the founding fathers of the American Constitution, not "freedom from the law, but by the law fixed of their own responsible making."[2] This fundamental value requires protection and, at the same time, completion in the form of a free order dividing and balancing the legislative, executive, and judicial powers of the state. It is, therefore, connected with representative democracy, while all approaches to anarchy will fail to achieve liberty and lead only to illegitimate dictatorship of biased social forces.

Concerning the present German discussion it must be said that the (critical) loyalty to the democratic constitution not only signifies a limitation of liberty, but also a kind of sensible fulfillment. There is a similar relation to the value of <u>life</u>. Its protection can be regarded as a condition, a limitation, and a part of the realization of liberty. The large controversies about abortion show how difficult it is to find the right balance in the "tragic" conflict between the values of protecting unborn life and the values of self-determination (which is part of liberty). The relationship between the fundamental values demands more mutual tolerance and understanding from the opposing partners.

Furthermore, the fundamental value of <u>equality</u> is intensively connected with liberty. Equality is not to be understood as an absolute, either. It does not mean a total, monotonous equalization of personal nature and individual behavior, but rather a parity of all citizens under the law, and the fundamental equivalence of all men is dignity and liberty. Basically, everybody possesses the dignity of free, responsible, self-determination in the same way, regardless of sex, descent, race, language, homeland, social antecedents, faith, or religious and political beliefs (as the German Grundgesetz says). In general, equality as a fundamental democratic value must be interpreted as the equal liberty of all citizens.

Hence, social justice is what makes equality credible in communal living as equal liberty of the citizens. This fundamental value holds that each member of the society has the right to material and cultural goods according to his own contributions and accomplishments. The viewpoint of individual accomplishment is an important aspect in the idea of distributive justice. But justice is compensatory, too. The dignity of each free individual requires that the interest of the citizens in a democratic commonwealth never be assessed only or primarily according to their accomplishments. The value of justice as a fundamental of the pluralistic democracy outweighs a crude justice of accomplishment. At least two perspectives still belong to it. The first is that policies following the postulate of justice steadily attempt to offer approximately equal opportunities of life (opportunities for self-actualization, for participation, and for working) to the individuals, especially to the underprivileged, as chances to guard and to realize their equal liberty; the second perspective is that these policies grant various rights of contribution to the individuals in those parts and subsystems of society where they work.An individual's interest in an opportunity to achieve real liberty is thereby combined with the society's interests (and those of all individuals in the whole) in an effective and successful functioning of, say, the economy and science. The experiences of the last decade reveal many severe problems, at least in Germany, when policies try to incorporate these important postulates of justice connecting the other fundamental values.

Solidarity and plurality are the last two fundamental values. Solidarity does not refer to partisans fighting for particular social perspectives and movements, it refers to the objective link between all individuals in a commonwealth as partners, and to the recognition of it. To further each individual's self-direction, and free yet well-informed decision-making, solidarity demands that one not only tolerate and respect the fundamental rights of other citizens, but also actively and positively take care of one's fellow citizens without ruling over them, or submitting to them. Solidarity is mutual help with a final goal of self-help. It never intends to impose uniformity. On the contrary, it asks for a plurality of individual and collective intentions, endeavors, and accomplishments that respects the necessary unity, order, and observes the standards defined by political rights and moral duties.

These fundamental values are the essential and final parts of a democratic constitution that determines the common practice of a pluralistic society's citizens, groups, and state. On the basis of these values, the constitution provides opportunities, limits, structures, challenges, instructions, and rules for common practice. The values last as long as the pluralistic democracy lasts, regardless of how particular wishes, requirements and fashions may change. Surely there is considerable leeway in how to interpret and apply them, and each decision demands a steady, careful consideration of the different aspects of these values and their complexity. There should be choices involving relative and reversible priorities. Here the controversy about the adequate and opportune realization of the fundamental values is possible and useful. But generally, the fundamental values of democratic society in modern times are in principle identical with the irreversible foundations of a humane communal life. They are necessary ethical postulates that must be practiced tentatively at all times, if communal and public life is to develop in the interests of man's dignity. Their necessity and their possibility are due to a simultaneous weakness and greatness of man.

The fundamental values have little to do with popular sovereignty. Hannah Arendt estimated that one of the greatest and most far-reaching achievements of the American revolution was the eradication of the idea of sovereignty of the people or of any other power, since in human matters sovereignty would eventually only lead to the despotism of a tyrant, wherever he came from.[3] Indeed, in the founding history there was no one constituency; there was by origin the plurality of territorial and social forces. It was the same in the new Germany when after the Second World War the Grundgesetz was established.

The idea of popular sovereignty can be, and has been, misunderstood in the sense of an absolute disposition about all rights and values in a democracy itself. That would be a radical democracy in stark contrast to pluralistic democracy. Radical democracy and the absolute sovereignty of the people are potentially self-destructive. The philosopher Karl Jaspers asked and answered in a very reasonable manner:`But what if a nation doesn't want its freedom, rights, or democracy? That seems impossible under conditions of clear volition and possible only by the smokescreening of exigencies and passions. This is where the continual inquiry on liberty originates. Everybody has to take care of liberty. Since that most precious good is never simply given, and doesn't atuomatically preserve itself. It can only be retained where there is a consciousness of liberty, and an ardent responsibility for it.[4]

If the fundamental values of pluralistic democracy are really to be valid and effective, they must be accompanied by corresponding virtues like frankness, civil courage, regard, tolerance, moderation, willingness to compromise, self-discipline, fairness, commitment, and the faculty of constructive criticism. It is a sophisticated task of education and of ethical politics to favor the exercise of these virtues and to confirm adequate patterns. Yet the virtues are not to be considered as ends in themselves. They ask for a substantial orientation by aims presented in the fundamental values.

Pluralism and Particular Ethics

The individuals in the pluralistic society cannot live exclusively with the ethos which is constitutive of, and obligatory for, pluralism itself. It is quite necessary and legitimate for them to refer to numerous particular ethics. They need peer groups and other social relationships which teach them ethical models. The socialization patterns of families, schools, and other social subsystems, of professional fields like science and economics, of the pressure groups, political parties, unions, and other associations, of informal living communities, and, last but not least, of the churches, all advocate their own particular ethics based on their special aims, interests, or duties. They assess an individual according to his capacity for integration and orientation. Thus individuals are accustomed to living in a kind of graduated ethical "network" which is not identical to the official binding ethics of the commonwealth. To everybody, the graduation presents itself in a particular way, depending on its personal character and its faculty to appropriate and to mold the aims. The pluralistic democracy, whose function is to protect liberty, expressly refrains from subordinating all these particular ethics to a collective ethos. Instead, family, religion, science, economy, and all other elements of human society having a socialization pattern shall be free to follow their own norm and rules. The structural principle of pluralistic democracy therefore cannot be transferred schematically to the social subsystems described so far.

However, to ensure its existence, and to fulfill its necessary functions, the pluralistic democracy must require from the numerous groups, forces, and subsystems that their particular ethics be consistent with pluralism, or at least that they not fight it in an antagonistic and militant way. Pluralistic democracy even asks them to support and live up to its fundamental values of man's dignity, liberty, life, equality, justice, solidarity, plurality, and the corresponding virtues.

If science, for example, follows the ethics of objectivity, of intersubjective communication, and of confidence in methodology, it thus expresses its autonomy in terms that contradict political restrictions of "partiality". Its performances, nevertheless, shall not destroy the fundamental values of pluralism cited above. That is why the state can require of the scholar a critical loyalty to the constitution guaranteeing an order of liberty. The scholar can also be required to refrain from amplifying his particular ethics into exclusiveness and from imposing it on society as a whole, that is, from measuring society and its politics by the criterion of his science. Otherwise, pluralistic politics would be delivered into the hands of false authorities who have no democratic legitimacy. That could subject the aims and methods of politics to the ideology of total objectivity (die Ideologie der Sachzwänge), or to totalitarian theories of history. The consistency of politics could be sacrificed to the changing games of hypotheses and experiments. The system of science and scholars must avoid the twofold danger of isolating themselves irresponsibly from the pluralistic society and of abusing it. But within the boundaries of these two dangers, they are not to be subjected to any political restriction in the pluralistic democracy.

According to Aristotle, the first tenet in political ethics is "that all things representing a value of some kind are innately destructible because of the too-much, or the too-little, in them." However, to find the right measure and the "middle" (μέσον) between extremes is "most difficult" (ἄκροσ χαλεπόν). That is why this "middleness" (μεσότης) and moderation (σωφροσύνη) are far from mediocrity. They are "top form" (ακρότης) or practice. "Therefore, proper practice is rare; it is praiseworthy and it is noble."[5]

BIBLIOGRAPHY

1. Immanuel Kant, Werke, ed. Wilhelm Weischedel. Frankfurt a. M., 1964, vol. IV, p. 61: "Handle so, daß du die Menschheit, sowohl in deiner Person, als in der Person eines jeden andern jederzeit zugleich als Zweck, niemals bloß als Mittel brauchest." (Grundlegung zur Metaphysik der Sitten)

2. Willi Paul Adams, The First American Constitutions. Republican Ideology and the Making of the State Constitutions in the Revolutionary Era, Chapel Hill: 1980, p. 159. (Original German edition: Republikanische Verfassung und bürgerliche Freiheit. Die Verfassungen und Ideen der amerikanischen Revolution. Darmstadt-Neuwied, 1973, p. 153)

3. Hannah Arendt, Über die Revolution, München, 1963, pp.1-

4. Karl Jaspers, Vom Ursprung und Ziel der Geschichte. Frankfurt a. M. - Hamburg, 1955, p. 164

5. Aristotle, Eth. Nic., 1106 a 24 ff

The Explanation of Values. Problems and Approaches

Karl-Dieter Opp

ABSTRACT

This paper is concerned with the question: nder which conditions do which values emerge? Values are defined as expectations about what should or must be the case. An evaluation of existing theory and research on values leads to the result that a fruitful general theory explaining the emergence of values is missing. It is argued that a fruitful strategy of stating such a theory is to look for general orienting statements being applied in the diverse writings on value formation. It turned out that authors of very diverse orientations assume - often implicitly - that the costs and benefits being associated with values are conditions for their emergence. This suggests that utility theory may be applied as a starting point for the formulation of a fruitful theory of value formation. It is argued, that utility theory has to be supplemented by at least one other theory which can explain preferences. Such theories are stated by social psychologists. Furthermore, according to research results of social psychology and sociology preferences and restrictions have to be taken into account which are ignored by economists. Whether such a strategy is fruitful is examined by suggesting a theory which explains the evolutionary formation of values. These are values emerging step by step without bargaining and without the influence of institutions.

INTRODUCTION

The literature about norms and values - we shall use these terms synonymously for reasons to be mentioned later - is concerned with three questions: The first is purely descriptive: In which countries or groups (delinquent gangs, young people, lower class people, etc.) do which values prevail? The bulk of the literature deals with this question. The second question reads: What effects do existing values have? Especially economics offers detailed answers to this question. The least effort has been devoted to answer the third question: Under which conditions do which values emerge?

In the following we will only deal with this question. At the outset it seems useful to stipulate what will be understood by "values", because this concept is used in an unclear and inconsistent way. In the second part we shall be concerned with an evaluation of the state of research on the formation of values. This discussion serves as a starting point for the last two parts. There we first deal with the strategy one may adopt in order to state hypotheses about value formation which are superior to the existing ones. We shall argue that an extended economic approach seems best suited for stating such hypotheses. Then we suggest some hypotheses about evolutionary value formation. This type of value formation has been neglected in the literature. So the formulation of such hypotheses may be a test for the fruitfulness of the economic approach.

CONCEPTUAL PROBLEMS

As is well known, the problems with a theory of value formation begin with the concept of values. The attempts at defining and classifying values are legion.[1] At the outset of every conceptual effort with regard to the value concept it seems useful to remember that definitions cannot be wrong or true, but only more or less useful for certain purposes. A basic weakness of discussions of the value concept is that the authors usually do not indicate which purposes the concepts they propose purport to serve. Since we are concerned with the explanation of values, we need a concept which is theoretically fruitful. The problem with this criterion is that it cannot be decided a priori, whether a definition fulfills it. Even if a theory is stated, severely tested and confirmed, the respective value concept can only provisionally be regarded as theoretically fruitful. The reason is that even a well corroborated theory may be falsified by future research and, thus, the value concept used may prove not fruitful.

In the present situation it is advisable to use as a working definition a comparatively broad concept (so that a relatively broad class of phenomena can be explained) and a concept which does not diverge too far from common usage in hypotheses aiming at an explanation of values. Accordingly, we will adopt the following definition: Values are expectations about what should or must be the case. We do not think that it is fruitful to distinguish between norms and values, if - as it often happens - values are designated as rather general rules or standards which do not - contrary to norms - refer to specific actions. It seems more useful to discern more or less general values, and not to stipulate a dichotomy which seems very difficult to define precisely. Thus, we designate as values standards of any generality. That such a variable is useful will be apparent from the hypotheses to be presented later on. If we speak of the emergence of values we mean the (mostly verbal) expression of now normative statements, i.e. the announcement of a certain new kind of observable behavior, or a change in the degree of acceptance (internalization in the sociological sense of such statements. Thus, if we explain the emergence of values, we explain why normative statements are expressed or why they are internalized. These conceptual stipulations are in need of clarification, but they are sufficient for our present purposes.

Since values are defined as standards and not as preferences, we shall not discuss theories dealing with the formation of preferences, although preferences are one variable which influences value formation, as will be shown later.[2]

THEORIES OF VALUE FORMATION. SOME REMARKS ON THE PRESENT STATE

In the following we want to evaluate the present state of theory and research on value formation. Every evaluation applies criteria. Since we think that these criteria should be stated explicitly, we first want to mention the criteria which we deem relevant for an evaluation of value theory and research.

Firstly, in our opinion a theory should not only explain certain kinds of values, for example, values about the distribution of outputs. Such theories are too specific. Secondly, theories should not only explain that in certain situations there will emerge some values without being able to specify which values. Accordingly, a hypothesis which simply asserts that in situations of unsecurity values emerge, would be unsatisfactory, because the theory does not answer the question: Which kinds of values do emerge? Thus, such a theory is too unspecific. An ideal theory would be able to explain exactly the specific values which emerge.[3]

A theory should not only inform us in detail about the norms which emerge. It should also be applicable in any situation, that is, it should not be restricted to certain types of situations. If a theory is only applicable in small groups or even only in dyads, it would be unsatisfactory. We may express this postulate in the following way: An ideal theory of value formation should have an unrestricted range of application.[4]

Let us specify this criterion. One may distinguish three types of situations, where values may emerge. First of all, there may exist institutions being legitimized to state norms. Examples are parliaments, bureaucracies, and the boards of firms or voluntary associations. If institutions stipulate values, we speak of institutional value formation. The question arises: Under which conditions do institutions state which values? Values may also emerge by voluntary agreements. People may negotiate with each other and reach a collective decision. We may call this process voluntary value formation. In both kinds of situations values are explicitly stated, that is to say, value formation is planned. The question to be answered reads: Under which conditions do people reach which decisions?

Many values arise in another way. Carl Menger (1883: 161 - 83, 271 - 87) already emphasized that rights, language, the state, money, and the market are the "unreflected result of social developments" (164, translated by KDO). That means, many values emerge without planning in a stepwise process. Accordingly, we may speak of evolutionary value formation. Under which conditions do such values emerge? A theory of value formation should be able to explain institutional, voluntary and evolutionary value formation.

Obviously, a criterion for the evaluation of a theory is, how far it corresponds to the facts. If empirical research is lacking, one can only ask, whether a theory seems plausible. That is, one may try to identify kinds of situations, where the theory may not hold.

How far do the existing theories of value formation satisfy these criteria? Let us, first of all, deal with hypotheses from sociology and social psychology. Let us - as a starting point - enumerate some hypotheses which are typical. A hypothesis which can be found in a great many writings, reads: "Norms are learned by individuals in social intercourse with others - that is, in the process of socialization" (Williams, 1968: 205). This learning is accomplished by means of sanctions (see especially Scott, 1971: 71 and passim). In such a process the values transmitted may be modified (Blau, 1964: 233). We call this hypothesis the transmission thesis. Another hypothesis which may be called the relief thesis and which is frequently put forward in the literature reads that in situations of insecurity values emerge, because, one may add, insecurity is depriving and values reduce the insecurity (see, for example, Davis, 1966: 105, 109).[5] Thibaut and Faucheux (1965) suggest the following hypothesis: "... when power differentiation exists in a group, whose members have a background of high interdependence and highly convergent interests, the introduction of both external and internal threats to the continued viability of the group creates the conditions for the emergence of norms which to a significant degree reduce the disruptive consequences of the threats" (89; see also Thibaut, 1968, Thibaut and Kelley, 1959). The authors define the variables of this hypothesis and present research results which confirm the hypothesis.

There are a great many other hypotheses on value formation in the sociological and social psychological literature.[6]

For our purposes it is not necessary to go into further details. The other hypotheses as well as those described before demonstrate that the criteria mentioned are quite inadequately realized. First, there is no single theory which explains exactly all kinds of specific values. For example, the transmission thesis is too unspecific: It only says that some values emerge. The same holds for the relief thesis. Other theories are too specific if they explain, for example, only norms of distribution (see Tallman and Ihinger-Tallman, 1979).

With respect to the second criterion - desirable is an unrestricted range of application - the existing sociological and social psychological theories are also not satisfactory. Take the hypothesis of Thibaut and Faucheux: It is only applicable to groups with high interdependence etc., i.e. in a very specific type of situations. Other hypotheses refer to specific organizations. Examples are hypotheses about the formation of subcultural values of inmates in prisons or the formation of values of delinquent gangs. With regard to the three types of values there is no theory which explains each of them. It seems that the transmission thesis and also the relief thesis is concerned with evolutionary value formation, whereas the hypothesis of Thibaut and Faucheux explains voluntary value formation. Other hypotheses, especially an extensive group of writings in the sociology of law, deals with institutional value formation.

Let us turn to the third criterion: For some hypotheses there is empirical evidence, for example for the hypothesis suggested by Thibaut and Faucheux. For many other hypotheses, however, research results are not consistent. This holds, for example, for hypotheses on the formation of values of inmate subcultures, on the formation of delinquent values and for hypotheses on law making in the sociology of law. Furthermore, some hypotheses seem very unplausible. This holds for the relief thesis: Some situations of uncertainty are rewarding (games or journeys) and presumably there will not develop any values.[7]

Up to now we asked, among other things, what the existing hypotheses actually explained. It is, however, possible that the explanatory power of a theory is not exhausted. This may happen, if a general theory is applied from which hypotheses about value formation are deduced. Thus, even if we argue that the existing hypotheses about value formation are too unspecific, one may object that it is possible to derive more specific hypotheses, but that this has not been accomplished so far. So we may ask: Is the explanatory potential of the hypotheses discussed greater than it seems to be according to our preceding analysis?

A necessary condition for answering this question in the affirmative is that a general theory is applied. This in fact occurred only in the work of exchange theorists to whom Thibaut, Faucheux, and Kelley pertain. The general theory applied is a variant of utility theory. Accordingly, we may ask: Is this theory appropriate to deduce, together with other assumptions, more fruitful hypotheses than those formulated so far? This question can best be answered by presenting such hypotheses. This can be accomplished by looking at the economic theory of property rights.[8]

What economists designate as "property rights" are in fact values in the sense defined above, provided that these values are connected with sanctions. In order to explain the emergence of "property rights" or values, utility theory and other assumptions are applied. This theory specifies in general, how the evaluation (i.e. reward value, costs and benefits) of events and cognitions (i.e. expectancies, subjective probabilities) - one may say weighted costs and benefits - influence behavior.

By applying this theory to explain value formation further hypotheses (assumptions) are introduced specifying the kinds of preferences and restrictions which seem empirically relevant. Technically speaking, these assumptions are the initial conditions or conditions which are empirically correlated with the initial conditions.[9]

An example may illustrate this procedure. Demsetz (1967) explains the emergence of property rights in a group of Indians by showing that at a certain time externalities[10] caused by hunting increased. Externalities may be internalized by introducing values, i.e. certain restrictions in the use of resources. But these restrictions are only introduced, if the benefits of internalization are greater than the costs. Demsetz presents some evidence in his example that at a certain time the benefits of internalization and, accordingly, of the introduction of values seemed to become greater than the costs and that at the same time property rights developed.

How specific are the values economic theory can explain? In principle utility theory can explain each kinds of norms in the sense of expressions of normative statements. In the Demsetz example one would predict: Those norms will emerge which internalize the externalities with lowest costs and highest benefits. In fact in the economic literature there are many hypotheses explaining all kinds of norms such as patent rights, ownership rights, property rights on the job etc.

Economic theory can also be applied to explain values in every situation. If the preferences and restrictions are identified, utility theory can be applied to deduce the respective consequences. There exist hypotheses about voluntary value formation. Examples are works of the contractarians (see, for example, Buchanan, 1975) and the theory of public goods, especially Olson's book (1971). This theory can explain the formation of values as far as they are public goods. There is also a bulk of hypotheses about institutional value formation. Modern political economy explains political processes by means of economic theory. Since governments, parliaments, and bureaucracies stipulate values, the work of modern political economists can be regarded as a contribution to institutional value formation. What about evolutionary value formation? Some authors note, to be sure, that not all values are explicitly stated (see, for example, Demsetz, 1967), but there are no explicit hypotheses about evolutionary value formation.

With regard to the empirical evidence of the economic theory of property rights there are many studies, consisting mostly of descriptions of historical developments of concrete laws which are explained. These materials have mostly illustrative character and, thus, lend some plausibility to the hypotheses. Severe tests are missing. However, economic hypotheses about property rights are not without flaws. For example, certain kinds of preferences and restrictions are not taken into account. Furthermore, some authors who aim at explaining cost-benefit relations do not apply general hypotheses. Their theorizing is entirely ad hoc.[11]

So we may conclude that economic theory is, as it stands, not the ideal theory we are looking for.

ON THE STRATEGY OF DEVELOPING A THEORY OF VALUES

If the diagnosis of the present situation sketched in the preceding part of this paper is accepted, the question arises: How can we develop a more fruitful theory of values which satisfies the criteria mentioned (and perhaps other criteria) to a greater extent?

The first step may be to search for some basic ideas or, in the terminology of Robert K. Merton, for some general orientations which may guide the formulation of more fruitful hypotheses about value formation.

How may we proceed to find the orienting statements we are after? An admittedly conservative strategy is to analyse the diverse writings about value formation for ideas which most (or all) of them have in common. If such an analysis is carried out, the result is rather surprising. Sociologists of whatever orientation (marxist, interactionist, functionalist, behavioralist), social psychologists and economists assert - often implicity, often in different terms - that the emergence of norms depends on the costs and benefits which are associated with them. This is asserted, if authors write that the emergence of values depends on the "gains" people get (Berger and Luckmann, 1969: 57, 60 - 61), or on the satisfaction of certain needs (Davis, 1966: 109).

If in fact so many authors advance this idea, one may adopt the following strategy: We start with utility theory and ask: Can this theory serve as a fruitful point of departure for a theory of value formation? In our opinion the answer must be a qualified "yes": We want to argue that utility theory has to be supplemented by at least one other theory which can explain preferences. Furthermore, variables have to be taken into account which are compatible with utility theory, but which have been neglected so far.

The test of this thesis is an extensive research programme. This should particularly answer the following two questions: 1. Is it possible to explain existing hypotheses about value formation or to show that these hypotheses must be modified? In general, a theory is particularly fruitful, if it corrects existing knowledge and if the respective deductions are empirically confirmed. 2. Is it possible to deduce new hypotheses which can be empirically confirmed?

Obviously, it is not possible to answer these questions in this paper. As a first step it may be meaningful to examine, whether utility theory and other hypotheses are applicable to generate some new hypotheses. As we mentioned already, there are no hypotheses explaining the process of evolutionary value formation. So we want to ask: Under which conditions do such values emerge? An attempt to answer this question seems to be meaningful as a first step in testing our thesis, since authors have perhaps not dealt with evolutionary value formation because of some difficulties in stating such hypotheses. An attempt to formulate such hypotheses may also demonstrate, in what way utility theory has to be modified or supplemented in order to yield fruitful hypotheses.

MODELS OF EVOLUTIONARY VALUE FORMATION

It seems that there are several processes leading to the evolutionary formation of values. In the following sections we will deal with one such process rather extensively. Another process will be sketched only. The two sets of hypotheses are called - as is usual in economics - "models".[12]

Recurrent Behavior and Value Formation

Let us start with a hypothesis which is often mentioned in the literature: An action which is repeatedly performed becomes a value. Homans (1974, 98) expresses this hypothesis concisely: "What is, is always becoming what ought to be."

However, not each recurrent behavior becomes a value. An example may illustrate this: In a prisoner's dilemma situation the parties involved behave in a way that the most favorable payoff for the participants is not achieved. That is, the players would be better off, if they behaved differently. If the prisoner's dilemma situation is repeated, recurrent behavior emerges. But there will not develop a value claiming that such an unfavorable behavior should be performed. Since not each recurrent behavior leads to the formation of the respective value, it is meaningful to ask: Under which conditions does recurrent behavior brings about values?

The most interesting situation seems to be the evolutionary emergence of norms in large groups. We denote a group as "large", if the single member does not perceive a possibility to bring about a value by means of negotiation or by means of other actions.

The Emergence of Recurrent Behavior

If it is asked, under what conditions regularities of behavior lead to the formation of values, it is presupposed that the behavior already occurs. For the following hypotheses, however, it is significant to ask: Which conditions do lead to regularities of behavior? We want to identify two kinds of situations which lead to regular behavior in a large group.

1. It may be possible to decompose a society into smaller units consisting in the extreme cases of single persons or of large sub-groups. Each of these units may be in a similar situation. This means, for each unit the same behavioral alternatives may have a higher expected utility than other actions. For example, for each person it may be most beneficial to open an umbrella, if it is raining. All parents of a society may reinforce the same behaviors of their children so that there emerges regular behavior of the children. This is an example for a situation where within small groups - independently of other small groups - behavior patterns are created which lead to regular behavior of all or the most members of the large group.

2. In the class of situations described in the preceding paragraph behavior is reinforced "directly". The second pos-

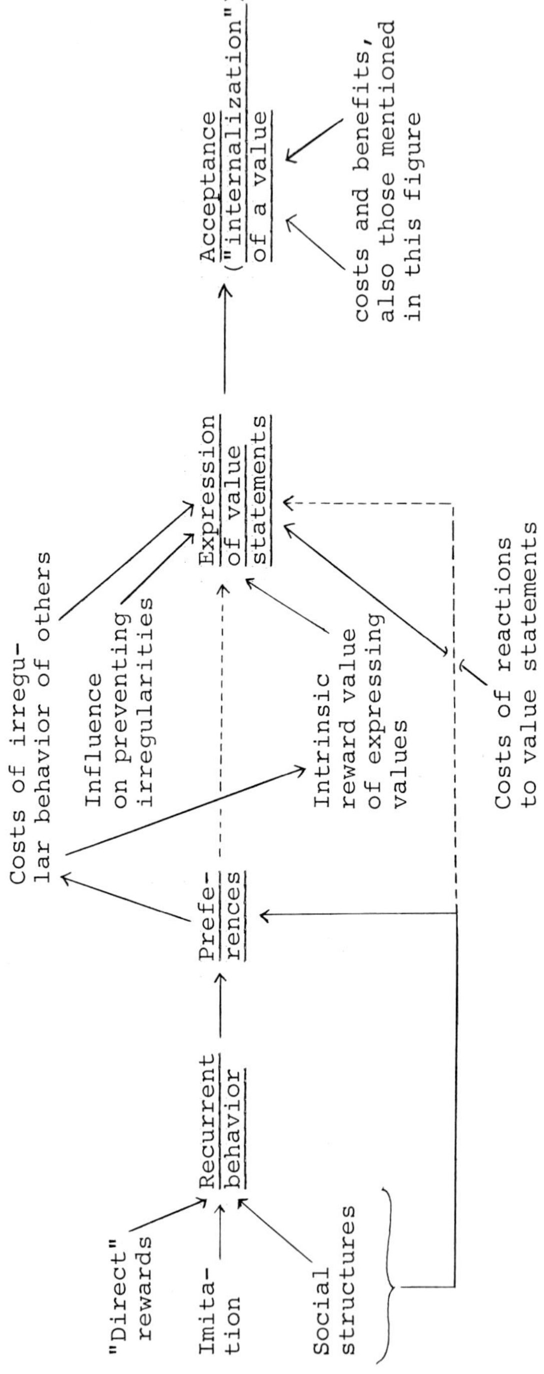

Legend: Solid arrows symbolize direct, dashed arrows symbolize indirect causal effects

Figure 1: Conditions for Evolutionary Value Formation

sibility of acquiring new behavior is by imitation. During the socialization process children are reinforced, if they match the behavior of others. One may distinguish between two kinds of imitation: Firstly, if a model (i.e. another person who is observed) is reinforced for emitting a behavior, the observer performing the same actions is often also reinforced. Thus, people learn to imitate the behavior of successful models. Secondly, reinforcement is given for imitating certain kinds of persons, for example, people who are prestigeful, attractive, and competent regardless of the success of their behavior (Bandura and Walters 1963: 107). Thus, parents of the lower class may reinforce a child, if his behavior matches the behavior of people pertaining to the upper class. A consequence is that the imitation of certain kinds of people will become intrinsically rewarding.[13]

Let us apply these hypotheses to the explanation of behavioral regularities. Departing from the first hypothesis (successful models are imitated) a behavioral regularity emerges, if a subset of the members of a group perform actions which are rewarded and if these actions are observed. Furthermore, if according to the second hypothesis (about the emergence of intrinsic reward values of imitating certain kinds of individuals) people with high status perform certain actions (or change their behavior) others will imitate them and, thus, recurrent behavior will emerge.

A sociologist aiming at an explanation of behavior would take into account social structures. By this term we mean social relationships which are defined over a set of individuals.[14] The foregoing considerations suggest that in fact particular social structures influence the emergence of recurrent behavior. Assume, certain behavior has developed in the upper class. The diffusion will be impeded, if there is no flow of information between the different strata. But if the individuals are connected by communication channels so that each person can reach - directly or indirectly - each other person or if there are at least connections between different groups so that a communication can spread from one group to another, the emergence of regularities will be furthered. Thus, the more "connected" a communication structure is, the more likely is the existence of behavioral regularities.

We suggested that the imitation of attractive models is especially rewarding. Now assume that a subset of members of a group regularly performs particular actions. If in a group the degree to which people feel sympathy for each other is high, or, in other words, if the cohesion of a group is high, many rewards are distributed for matching behavior. So we know that in highly cohesive groups homogeneity is relatively high. Accordingly, regular behavior will be performed by more people then in groups with low cohesion.[15]

These considerations indicate that social structures influence the emergence of behavioral regularities. For limitations of space we must confine ourselves to the two structural hypotheses mentioned: The more connected the communication structure of a group and the more cohesive a group, the more likely behavioral regularities arise.[16]

In sum, then, recurrent behavior can be explained by three kinds of factors which are supposed to have an additve effect: "Direct" rewards, imitation, and social structures. The assumption of the additive effects of the factors implies: Recurrent behavior may emerge, if one or two factors have the value zero. This means, for example, that recurrent behavior may be caused only by imitation or also only by direct rewards.

From Recurrent Behavior to the Formation of Preferences

The next step to the evolutionary emergence of norms is the formation of preferences. There are several social psyhological theories which can be applied to explain preferences. In the opinion of this author the most fruitful theory is the theory first advanced by M. Fishbein in 1963.[17] It is worth noting that this theory has a striking similarity to utility theory, as Fishbein himself notes. In short, the theory hypothesizes: The attitude (preference) toward an object o (which may be an activity) - symbolized by A_o - depends on the number of properties of o which a person ascribes to this object, on the evaluation (e) of each property, and on how certain the person believes that the object has these properties (b). More formally:

$$A_o = \sum_{i=1}^{N} b_i e_i$$

A_o = Attitude toward an object o

b_i = belief that an object has a property i

e_i = evaluation of the property i

According to the theory a value has to be assigned to each property associated with an object (or an action). The value expresses the evaluation and belief connected with the property. The values are multiplied for each property. Then the products are summed up. The higher the sum, the more positive the attitude.

Let us apply this theory to explain the formation of preferences for a behavioral regularity. If such a behavior is connected with many beneficial and few costly events (or behavioral consequences), compared with other behavioral alternatives, then the attitude toward this behavior will be relatively positive. Put in other terms: The higher the net utility of a recurrent behavior pattern - compared with the net utility of other behavioral alternatives, the greater is the intrinsic reward value of this behavior or, equivalently, the stronger are the preferences with regard to this behavior. Thus, if a behavior is connected with large direct benefits, if its imitation is highly rewarding and if there are structures providing further rewards, intense preferences for a behavioral regularity develop. Accordingly, the direct rewards etc. have a direct causal effect on the performance of behavioral regularities and on the formation of the preferences.

From Preferences to Value Statements

The next step in the process of evolutionary value formation is the occurence of normative statements. Under which conditions do the members express such statements? We suggest the following hypothesis: If members of a group observe or expect that others do not perform the recurrent behavior, the occurrence of normative statements (and, accordingly, by definition, the emergence of values) is the more likely, the higher the preferences for the regularities are and the more the members believe that the expression of normative statements maintains or restores the status quo. A short discussion of this hypothesis must be sufficient here.

First, the hypothesis presupposes that the occurrence of regularities for which preferences have developed is preferred to the state where some people deviate or are expected to deviate in the future. Is this assumption correct? Obviously, many regularities can be enumerated where deviations of others are costly, for example, if people break the night rest (the regularity is not to cause noise) or if a train does not arrive at the scheduled time. But also unusual dresses deviating from the prevailing fashion are aversive.

Are there examples that preferences develpoped, but that people are indifferent, if others depart from the respective regularities (or that departures are even approved of)? Take the utilization of umbrellas, if it rains. Even in this case we surmise that everybody who himself prefers to utilize umbrellas would also prefer that others do so. This seems plausible, if there is a general preference for being able to predict correctly what others do or for being not disappointed if a cognitive expectation with regard to regular behavior of others exists. So we hypothesize: The more intense the preference for a behavior, the higher the costs of irregular behavior of others.

Let a person perceive or expect that others behave irregularly. Is it plausible to assume that the announcement of normative statements such as "you should not do this" or "you should do that" is perceived as a behavioral alternative in such a situation? The expression of this kind of statements is the least costly way (i.e. it requires the least resources) to convey the information that one does not desire certain actions of others or that one wants to impose restrictions on others. Thus, a verbal normative statement seems to be the easiest strategy for informing others about what a person wants the others to do. Furthermore, this strategy seems to be commonly perceived.

Even if normative statements are in the behavioralrepertoire of most or all persons, this need not have the consequence that they are expressed. Let us state the conditions for the expression of normative statements by using the following equation:

(1) $N = p_r U_r - C_r + U_n$

N = net utility of expressing normative statements minus net utility of not expressing such statements

p_r = subjective probability of maintaining or restoring regularities by means of expressing normative statements minus subjective probability of maintaining or restoring regularities by <u>not</u> expressing normative statements

U_r = utility of maintaining or restoring regularities minus utility of irregularities

C_r = costs of expressing normative statements

U_n = intrinsic reward value of expressing normative statements

which is a transformation of utility theory.[18] Assume a person perceives the alternatives to express or not to express a normative statement. The degree to which the net utility of expressing a norm exceeds the net utility of not expressing a norm (N) depends on the following facts. 1. The more the subjective probability to restore or maintain the regularity by means of expressing normative statements exceeds the respective probability if no normative statements are expressed (p_r), the higher the net utility of expressing values (more precisely, the higher N). 2. The more an individual values the maintenance or restoration in comparison with behavioral irregularites (U_r), the higher will be the net utility of expressing normative statements.

One may formulate thesetwo hypotheses more simply in this way:

The more people think that they can influence the maintenance or restoration of behavioral regularities by means of announcing normative statements <u>and</u> the higher the utility of the status quo in comparison with the irregularities (that is, the higher the costs of irregular behavior of others), the more likely they will express normative statements.

It is worth noting that the terms "p_r" and "U_r" are multiplied. That means: If people do <u>not</u> believe they can influence the occurrence of regularities ($p_r = o$), then even a high evaluation of the status quo (compared with irregularities of behavior) does not affect the expression of normative statements. Furthermore, if the status quo and irregularities are valued equally ($U_r = o$), even a high perceived influence by means of expressing normative statements does not affect behavior.

We mentioned already that the costs of expressing normative statements are low regarding the required resources to be expended. But there may be other costs: One may expect negative (i.e. costly) reactions of the recipient of a normative statement. These reactions may reach from verbal behavior questioning the legitimacy of the normative claim to executing "dissidents" in dictatorships.

We surmise, that the expression of normative statements in situations where others "deviate" has also an intrinsic reward value. There even seems to exist a norm of the kind that one should tell people if they do not behave "adequately". But this norm seems only to hold if the "deviation" is a serious one, that is, if it is very costly for those affected. Thus, we hypothesize: The higher the costs of irregularities, the higher the intrinsic reward value of expressing normative statements.

Normative expressions are not only directed toward those performing irregularities. In everyday life all kinds of unusual events are the topics of conversations. The more costly these events are, the more likely they are discussed. This has the effect that many or most members of a group recognize the existing regularities for the first time consciously as regularities which <u>should</u> occur.

From the Expression to the Acceptance of Values

It often happens that norms are verbally stated, but that they in fact are not accepted. An accepted norm is called <u>"internalized"</u>. This means that conforming to a norm is a motive or, put otherwise, intrinsically rewarding and deviating from the norm is intrinsically costly. Under what conditions will a norm be more or less strongly internalized?

We may again apply the Fishbein-theory to answer this question. Assume, a norm is stated verbally (or people have thought about a norm). The statement of normative assertions is a kind of behavior and if, according to Fishbein, relatively many events which are positively evaluated and expected with relatively high certainty are connected with this behavior, there will develop relatively positive attitudes towards the value. That means, the value will be internalized. Thus, the higher the reward value of the events (including the preferences for regularities) connected with a value, the more intensely it will be internalized.

The theory developed so far may explain a process leading to the internalization of values referring to behavioral regularities. The theory may be applied to explain specific norms which emerged in particular groups at certain points in time. So we may explain concrete processes of norm formation. Furthermore, since the theory is a multi-level causal model, derivations are possible referring to indirect effects, as figure 1 illustrates. For example, if the cohesion of a group increases and if the other variables of the model do not change, the number of norms will increase. Other derivations are possible, if one departs from particular values of the variables in the model.

Value Generalization: The Diffusion of Values

The theory developed in the previous section presupposes that behavioral regularities develop as a first step in the process of value formation. However, there may be other conditions leading to the evolutionary formation of values. In the following we shall sketch in a very rough and preliminary way the outlines of another model.

Let us start with a concrete example. Assume that in families a hierarchical order exists and that there are values stipulating that such an order should exist. Such norms - we call them inequality norms - also exist in organizations and in teams carrying out surgical operations where one physician has to decide what to do during an operation. Thus, there are three different situations where inequality norms are accepted.

Assume now that these norms change in one of the situations: It becomes widely accepted that in families a hierarchical order is "bad".

Two consequences may emerge. Firstly, the change of values in one type of situation may be confined to this situation. Secondly, the change of values in one type of situations may bring about a change of values in at least one of the other types of situations or at least an attenuation of the values in the sense that they are less strongly accepted. For example, in organizations the members may claim "codetermination" or such a postulate will become the program of political parties and unions. Under which conditions will which consequence occur? In the following only some variables will be mentioned which might influence the "transfer" of the values.

Assume, there are advocates for (or against) a generalization of a value such as politicians or party leaders or union leaders. The more individuals identify themselves with these persons, or, to put it otherwise, for the more individuals imitation of these models is rewarding, the more the value will spread. This hypothesis is suggested by hypotheses about imitation.

Hints at other variables may be taken from the psychology of learning. If a certain kind of behavior is often rewarded in a certain type of situation, it holds: The more similar other situations are, the more often this kind of behavior will be emitted in these other situations. Accordingly, one will suggest that values will be generalized (or transferred) to other situations, if these are perceived as similar. The question arises: Under which conditions will situations be regarded as similar?

Assume, the changed values in the family are considered to be associated with high benefits and almost no cost. Furthermore, let men experience deprivations in their work situations which are in their opinion due to the exercise of power of their superiors and their submissive behavior which is expected. Furthermore, they think that the outputs are worse than they would be in more egalitarian situations. In general: The other situations are regarded as similar in the sense that similar activities (no exercise of power, no submissive behavior, codetermination) are expected to yield similar and high rewards. Thus, people think that they will be better off in other situations if certain patterns of activities will change. According to the Fishbein-theory there will develop positive attitudes toward egalitarian behavior patterns. In order to realize them people will, among other things, demand these patterns, that is, values develop.

Such demands will also arise if <u>general values</u> develop and if people believe that certain factual situations are not compatible with these values. For example, if there exists a general "trend toward equality" and if people think that situations in orgnizations "contradict" this value, they will postulate a value change. The general values attach, in terms of utility theory, costs to certain kinds of situations.

CONCLUDING REMARKS

The preceding hypotheses illustrate how an "economic framework" may be utilized for stating new and modifying existing hypotheses about the formation of values. If utility theory is applied, it seems necessary to take into account preferences and restrictions which are apparently relevant according to research results of psychology and sociology. Economists usually ignore such research results. In particular, we should explicitly take into account social structures. They can be regarded as variables which are certain distributions of preferences and/or restrictions or which are empirically related to them.

Thirdly, we applied a general theory in order to explain preferences. The explanation of preferences is sometimes considered significant by economists, but general theories are not applied. Perhaps one will not be content with only utilizing the Fishbein-theory. One should utilize theories which can explain subjective probabilities. One should also utilize theories which can explain the influence of existing preferences on other preferences. For example, if we hypothesize that high costs of irregular behavior lead to a high intrinsic reward value of expressing value statements, one may ask, how such a relationship may be explained. Perhaps cognitive theories (balance theory, dissonance theory) may be applied.

These remarks together with our considerations in the preceding sections may suggest a fruitful way how to proceed to improve the theory of value. Such improvements will consist of the formulation of new hypotheses, of the confrontation of existing hypotheses with derivations from hypotheses of the economic approach and of conducting empirical research to test the stated hypotheses.

BIBLIOGRAPHY

Alchian, A. A., H. H. Demsetz (1973). The Property Right Paradigm. In: Journal of Economic History 23: 16 - 27

Bandura, A., R. H. Walters (1963). Social Learning and Personality Development, London etc.: Holt

Bandura, A. (1969). Principles of Behavior Modification, New York etc.: Holt

Bandura, A. (1971). Psychological Medeling. Conflicting Theories, Chicago: Aldine Atherton

Barnes, S., M. Kaase, et al. (1979). Political Action. Mass Participation in Five Western Democracies, Beverly Hills and London: Sage

Berger, P. L., Th. Luckmann (1969). Die gesellschaftliche Konstruktion der Wirklichkeit, Stuttgart: S. Fischer (Original English edition: The Social Construction of Reality, New York 1967)

Biddle, B. J., E. J. Thomas (Eds.) (1966). Role Theory. Concepts and Research, New York etc.: Wiley

Blau, P. M. (1964). Exchange and Power in Social Life, New York etc.: Wiley

Blau, P. M. (Ed.) (1975). Approaches to the Study of Social Structure, New York and London: Free Press

Buchanan, J. M. (1975). The Limits of Liberty. Between Anarchy and Leviathan, Chicago and London: The University of Chicago Press

Davis, K. (1966, first 1949). Social Norms. In: Biddle and Thomas, 105 - 112

Demsetz, H. (1974, first 1967). Toward a Theory of Property Rights. In: Furubotn and Pejovich 29 - 42

Doreian, P. (1970). Mathematics and the Study of Social Relations, London: Weidenfeld and Nicolson

Eichner, K. (1980). Die Entstehung sozialer Normen, unpublished Habilitation, Hamburg

Ellwein, Th., H. Stachowiak (Eds.) (1981). Bedürfnisse und sozialer Wandel, München: Fink

Fishbein, M., I. Ajzen (1977). Belief, Attitude, Intention and Behavior, Reading etc.: Addison-Wesley

Furubotn, E., S. Pejovich (1972). Property Rights and Economic Theory: A Survey of Recent Literature. In: Journal of Economic Literature 10: 1137 - 1162

Furubotn, E., S. Pejovich (Eds.) (1974). The Economics of Property Rights, Cambridge, Mass.: Ballinger

Furubotn, E., S. Pejovich (1974a).Introduction: The New Property Rights Literature. In: Furubotn and Pejovich, 1 - 9

Haferkamp, H. (1980). Herrschaft und Strafrecht. Theorien der Normentstehung und Strafrechtssetzung, Wiesbaden: Westdeutscher Verlag

Homans, G. C. (1975). What Do We Mean by Social "Structure"? In: Blau, 53 - 65

Homans, G. C. (2nd ed. 1974). Social Behavior. Its Elementary Forms, New York etc.: Harcourt

Hummell, H. J., K.-D. Opp (1971). Die Reduzierbarkeit von Soziologie auf Psychologie, Braunschweig: Viehweg

Inglehart, R. (1977). The Silent Revolution: Changing Values and Political Styles Among Western Publics, Princeton: Princeton University Press

Inglehart, R. (1979). Value Priorities and Socioeconomic Change. In: Barnes and Kaase, 305 - 342

Korthals-Beyerlein, G. (1979). Soziale Normen, München: Fink

Menger, C. (1969, first 1883). Gesammelte Werke, vol. II, Untersuchungen über die Methode der Sozialwissenschaften und der Politischen Ökonomie, Tübingen: Mohr-Siebeck

Olson, M. (2nd ed. 1971). The Logic of Collective Action, Cambridge, Mass.: Harvard University Press

Opp, K.-D. (1979). The Emergence and Effects of Social Norms. A Confrontation of Some Hypotheses of Sociology and Economics. In: Kyklos 32: 775 - 801

Opp, K.-D. (1981). Die Entstehung sozialer Normen. Eine Diskussion einiger Thesen der ökonomischen Theorie der Eigentumsrechte. In: Ellwein and Stachowiak (in print)

Popper, K. (4th ed. 1971). Logik der Forschung, Tübingen: Mohr-Siebeck (English edition 1959)

Posner, R. A. (1972). Economic Analysis of Law, Boston and Toronto : Little, Brown

Riker, W. H. , P. C. Ordeshook (1973). An Introduction to Positive Political Theory, Englewood Cliffs, N. J.: Prentice-Hall

Scott, J. F. (1971). Internalization of Norms. A Sociological Theory of Moral Commitment, Englewood Cliffs, N. J.: Prentice-Hall

Tallman, I., M. Ihinger-Tallman (1979). Values, Distributive Justice and Social Change. In: American Sociological Review 44: 216 - 235

Thibaut, J. W. , H. H. Kelley (1959). The Social Psychology of Groups, New York: Wiley

Thibaut, J. W., C. Faucheux (1965). The Development of Contractual Norms in a Bargaining Situation under Two Types of Stress. In: Journal of Experimental Social Psychology 1: 89 - 102

Thibaut, J. C. (1968).The Development of Contractual Norms in Bargaining: Replication and Variation. In: Journal of Conflict Resolution 12: 102 - 112

Williams, R. (1968). Norms. In: International Encyclopedia of the Social Sciences 11: 204 - 208

NOTES

1. An informative overview is given in Korthals-Beierlein, 1979.

2. The work of R. Inglehart (1977, 1979) deals with preferences which he designates as values. This is perfectly legitimate, but we confine our attention to values in the sense defined above.

3. Stated more technically: The consequent of the theory should have a relatively high empirical content. On the concept of empirical content see Popper, 1971: Chapter IV.

4. Put more technically: The empirical content of the antecedent of a theory should be low. Again see Popper, 1971: chapter VI.

5. For an explication and critique of these hypotheses see Opp, 1979.

6. Further references can be found, for example, in Eichner, 1980, and Haferkamp, 1980. See also sociological and social psychological textbooks which usually contain a chapter about values.

7. For other weaknesses of the relief thesis, see Opp, 1979. For a more extensive review and critique of hypotheses on value formation in sociology and social psychology, see Eichner, 1980.

8. See especially Furubotn and Pejovich, 1972, 1974. As an introduction, see also Posner, 1972: Chapter 2. Basic theoretical works are: Alchian and Demsetz, 1973; Demsetz, 1967; Pejovich, 1972, 1976.

9. With regard to value formation the procedure of applying utility theory is sketched by Furubotn and Pejovich 1974: 2-3.

10. "Externalities" are, very roughly, defined as benefits or costs which are caused by actions of other individuals. "Internalizing" negative (i.e. costly) externalities means that the costs are borne by those who cause them. The example usually mentioned for a negative externality is pollution. An internalization would occur if, for example, those polluting compensate those being damaged by the pollution.

11. For a more detailed criticism of the Demsetz theory mentioned above, which other authors also seem to accept, see Opp, 1981.

12. An extended version of the following section of this paper will be published in the British Journal of Social Psychology, special issue on "Social Psychology and Economics", June 1982.

13. On further hypotheses and research results on imitation, see, in particular, Bandura, 1969, 1971; Bandura and Walters, 1963.

14. On this concept, see,for instance,Doreian, 1970: 38, Homans, 1975; Hummell and Opp, 1971: 38-42.

15. For other hypotheses on the consequences of cohesion, see, in particular, Homans, 1974; Thibaut and Kelley, 1959.

16. The reader may follow our discussion more easily by looking at Fig. 1.

17. Fishbein has described this theory in many of his writings. For a concise account, see Fishbein and Ajzen, 1977: 28-31.

18. For a derivation of this equation, see Riker and Ordeshook, 1973: 55. These authors do not apply this equation to the explanation of value formation.

Taking on Ayres.
Values: On the Possibility of a Convergence Between Economic and Non-Economic Decision-Making

H. T. Wilson

Is industrial society at a dead end, or running down a steep precipice into oblivion, as so many people seem to fear? Committed as we are to the life of reason, are we therefore, as both scientists & theologians seem to think, spiritually crippled? Is it true that the modern mind, nourished on science, is therefore spiritually sterile? Are all our efforts to improve our lot short-circuited by the impossibility of knowing in what direction improvement lies?

Clarence Ayres
Toward a Reasonable Society

Where in the world is a metaphysical subject to be found?

Ludwig Wittgenstein
Tractatus Logico-Philosophicus

In this paper I want to address the idea and concept of value as problematic precisely because we are so often sure we have its meaning and significance well in hand when we employ it in economic, sociological, or commonsense discourse. A focus on value, or values, is, after all, central to the argument that a convergence between economic and non-economic modes of decision-making is in fact taking place. I shall suggest further on that this convergence is indeed occurring, but that a strong case can be made for viewing its distinct possibility in a radically different light from contemporary institutional understandings. In short, it seems to me that a number of the arguments promoted in recent theoretical work in the field of economics display a manifestly sociological bias regarding their concepts, categories and ideas. I go on to argue that the analysis and even muted critique often found in such attacks on more conventional economic ideas can be better carried out where theory and theorizing is understood to be analytic and reflexive as well as hypothetical and generalizing in its ambit. Such theorizing argues for, while simultaneously seeking to display, the need for critical as well as traditional theory in economic and sociological research.

The points I wish to make suggest that the increasing recognition of value systems different from our own found in both economics and the social and behavioural sciences cannot end-run the following questions.

> What are the real motives for this effort at understanding? Are there many different and conflicting motives at work within advanced industrial societies reflecting divergent interests or ultimately do one or a few basic interests prevail?
>
> Can there be any other ultimate objective in the study of differing value systems than a convergence favourable to our own?
>
> Are our efforts in this direction really the "other side" of certain inexorable features of the economic and technological development process rather than a counterweight to them?
>
> Assuming the above to be the case, do our values, and collectively our culture-as-civilization, still possess the absorptive power that even the most repentant economist, anthropologist, or social scientist generally assumes?
>
> Finally, does our commitment in these subjects to disciplined observation and neutrality and objectivity show the limits of theoretical and practical possibility within our own culture-as-civilization rather than constituting a powerful but humane instrument for bringing order and welfare into the world? Here I am addressing our uniqueness: the only culture that denies this label while observing and analyzing everything and everyone else, then applying the label to them alone.

In what follows I shall cite and discuss several issues bearing on value, rationality and decision in philosophy, economics and the social sciences. Naturally, the paper constitutes a sketch of more detailed presentations already worked out or soon to appear. This would seem more suitable for a conference like ours, with its emphasis on discussion and dialogue. Of at least equal significance is the opportunity for me to take account of competing claims and other points of view. This conference appears to me to reflect the emergence of a new set of concerns on the part of economists and social scientists, and my objective will be to argue that these concerns cannot be effectively realized within the established conceptual and theoretical boundaries dictated by scientism and unreflexive disciplined observation.

(1) The concept of value has always been a central "objective" category in the conceptual and theoretical armoury of economics as a discipline. Political economy since Locke (if not Aristotle) had been committed to treating value as an objective category correlated with labour. It is its consummate expression in the labour theory of value, first with Locke, and thereafter in the work of Ricardo, which became a cause celebre for Marx. Regardless of how certain we may be that we have buried or superseded Marx, the disjunctions he noted with respect to the relation between the labour theory of value and capitalist economic development still haunts economic theory as a sub-discipline.[1] These disjunctions become all the more significant when we look at the ideological influence of Marxian thought not so much on the Soviet Union as on the so-called Third World.

Only in the latter case do we really have a commitment to Marxian influences not necessarily coloured by Soviet orthodoxy, and therefore of far greater consequence for Western industrial societies. Leaders in these countries treat the conventional ideological distinction between West and East as it is posed on both sides of the Oder/Neisse line with considerable skepticism. From the standpoint of their needs, problems and constraints it makes much more sense to speak of Northern rationalism relative to the large majority of developing countries found south of the 20°N line of latitude.[2] While unique culturally and in other ways, these countries do in fact possess a similar set of problems in large part generated by processes of economic and technological development, and military intervention, sponsored by the superpowers, by the European Economic Community and Comicon, and by Japan.

Returning to Marx, he claimed to have demonstrated through his materialistic method of theoretical analysis that there was indeed a dialectic of capital[3] whose future pattern of development had already begun to challenge the labour theory of value on which political economy had originally so much depended. Only as the result of the revolution that the experience of a thoroughgoing capitalist development process was to bring into being could this theory of value begin to hope for its ultimate triumph. Even today, when we are certain that the likelihood of revolution as Marx (not Engels) understood it is confined to developing countries, the question whether present realities and future trends can realize this same objective peacefully looms large. Looked at globally then, the possibility of revolution is still a real one and the developed countries remain directly or indirectly involved in this possibility.[4]

While an emphasis on differing value systems takes clear account of the existing and emerging global economy, it tries to do so without acquiescing in Marx's view that ultimately every transaction in the developed countries has zero-sum implications for someone else, someplace else. At the same time these concerns do appear to acknowledge what recent events demonstrate unambiguously: that there are more and more important effects of a zero-sum character on developed countries as a result of the values, policies, and activities in the international arena of developing countries. Yet nothing could be clearer than the paradoxical process whereby Third World countries come to consciousness of their own status and significance as a consequence of their interaction with advanced industrial societies, then use their very monopoly of resources, location, or influence on which these latter societies depend to assert themselves by industrializing, urbanizing and inevitably secularizing themselves. One is tempted to conjecture long-term developmental processes for given countries in which the very things being used to underwrite such development will be more and more needed at home.

Our concern in this conference with value or values thus points necessarily to differences between Western industrial societies, state socialism and the Third World. More importantly, however, it asks whether the convergence that takes place will synthesize West and East, North and South, in any given instance or whether only one side of the convergence will disappear.[5] Both Ricardo and Marx saw the need to comprehend value as a central objective category of political economy, along with price and capital, and both as a consequence considered political economy to be a key discipline, Ricardo for realizing it in tandem with the emerging process of capitalist development, Marx for underscoring the gap that must necessarily arise between the labour theory of value properly understood and this very process. The concept and theory of labour and value found in _Capital_ and elsewhere has great moral force in many Third World countries, and while that may not (as I shall show) have much importance for us in our own settings, it is a highly significant point in dealing with developing countries.[6]

(2) Economics is the stepchild of political economy in a very real sense precisely because of the way in which the initial emphasis on rank-ordering desired ends given scarce means has been gradually displaced by a professionalistic and scientistic approach which treats ends or values as either given or unproblematic and focusses instead on what can only be labelled technical rationality -- the efficient utilization of means given ends.[7] In my own work, I have had occasion to be astonished at a parallel intellectual development in the study of invention and innovation. It is the notion that slack resources are a prerequisite for innovation rather than fundamentally the result of innovative activities which reveals the extent of our dependence on organizational modes of rationality and thinking. At the very least, a distinction should be enforced between innovations which create slack resources and those which live off or presuppose them.[8]

The point for economics in particular is that the emphasis on technique to the exclusion of concern about ends is problematic first because it turns its back on the discipline's origins as a moral science and second because this leads it to downplay or ignore altogether what must necessarily remain one of the discipline's most fundamental concepts along with price, capital and value -- scarcity. It is precisely the failure to retain this concept in contemporary theories of innovation dependent on organizational and managerial modes of thinking which augurs badly for the future of many industrial societies. While the issue of value and values has come to the forefront in much economic thinking, this has occurred in tandem with the displacement of the ends/means distinction by more recent concerns about system, structure and function from sociology and cultural anthropology.[9] The bias of these concepts reflects the contemporary concern with order which has always been central to the social and behavioural sciences in explicit contrast to economics as a discipline. Far from being descriptive, the main function of these concepts -- if I may be forgiven the liberty -- is normative and prescriptive.

Reflection on the bias of function -- and concepts do have biases -- reveals that the clear preference for order, even if it is the sort of dynamic equilibrium prescribed for "open" systems, tends to shift attention away from ends to the means of maintaining existing interdependencies.[10] Even if we accept the idea that societies have indispensable "functional prerequisites" which must be maintained if the society is to survive, this in no way argues for the indispensability of the structures presently performing them.[11] Yet this is all too often exactly what disciplines committed to the priority of the so-called problem of order are led to presume. I am arguing that the more that economics loses touch with its original values, purposes, and objectives, the more dependent it must necessarily become in the contemporary context upon values, purposes and objectives favouring an emphasis on order. From the standpoint of present realities in Third World countries, such a posture seems to me problematic, even more problematic in fact than a return to or resuscitation of a more individuated ends/means focus.

This conference is important because it simultaneously seeks such a return or resuscitation, yet wants to do so within certain social-scientific categories which need to be subjected to intensive critical scrutiny rather than being presumed to correspond to the empirical reality of advanced industrial societies. I have argued elsewhere that it is not only possible, but unavoidable (following Mannheim) for disciplines to falsely reflect the central realities of the societies that invent and nurture them precisely because they are functioning ideologically as legitimizing or rationalizing agents. Political economy clearly performed this role during early capitalist development in the West and the social, behavioural and administrative/managerial disciplines seem to be doing it now for advanced industrial societies.[12] From some of the recent literature I would even go so far as to argue that a similar development is occurring in Eastern Europe and the Soviet Union, where Marxist orthodoxy is increasingly honoured more in the breach than in the observance in matters relating to industry, science, and technology.[13] It is the central role of disciplined observation -- an overly detached and disembodied observation function -- which is central to these disciplines and will be discussed further on as part of the problem as well as a possible agency for helping to resolve it.[14]

(3) Something very important happened to the concept of value when it began the long process by which it gradually lost its objective content in economics. My references throughout the presentation thus far to both value and values suggests a development of overarching significance: the gradual subjectivization of the concept of value to the point where it mainly becomes the individualized property of the subject-as-object so central to Society, thus to disciplined observation.[15] Perhaps our emphasis here on differing value systems is more indebted to this subjectivization process than we may want to admit in the sense that we are now actually seeing cultures, as cultural anthropology has for decades, as individualized subjects of interest and concern. The central role of disciplined observation in this process is no more readily deniable than it was in the case of the original process of subjectivization of the concrete individual which occurred in concert with the rise of market rationality and was thoroughly anticipated by Adam Smith in his Theory of Moral Sentiments, published in 1759.[16]

What in effect made value less valuable with this process of subjectivization into values was the way its status declined relative to the rise of its other, allegedly more objective, side, namely FACTS. Thus my concern about our motives for being interested in differing value systems as a managerial and an organizational problem. As collective "persons" other cultures are dealt with as individuals whose internal similarities relative to the advanced societies must necessarily have to outweigh the clear "individual differences" which we simultaneously argue are so important in dealing with social issues in our own countries.[17] In any case the process of initial subjectivization occurs in philosophy, and became a conceptual cornerstone of German idealism first with Kant, Fichte and Schelling and later on in German sociology thanks to Schmoller, Rickert and especially Max Weber. For reasons I have stated elsewhere, I do not believe that either Schopenhauer or Wittgenstein belong on this list.[18]

The point about the fact/value distinction is the way it encourages the disciplined observer to attribute objectivity to the facts as a consequence of attributing subjectivity to values. In effect, values become less valuable than facts, except when they themselves become facts for disciplined observers. At the same time, however, the very reference to values far more than to value implies that transcendence or transvaluation of value first noted by Nietzsche. The presence of values in the world makes them a fact for the disciplined observer, whose Archimidean point allegedly "outside" everything else allows him to indulge the supreme fiction --

that there could possibly be a metaphysical subject existing in any world invented by disciplined observation.[19] Wittgenstein, following Schopenhauer, put the matter most concisely when he asked, rhetorically to be sure: "Where in the world is a metaphysical subject to be found?"[20] What cannot help but emerge out of an examination of the difference between value and values is the way that the objectivity of value, however historically and culturally conditioned the idea of objectivity may be, has fallen to the fact/value distinction implicit in its subjectivization.

It is not simply the way that facts acquire objective status vis a vis values, but the way that values themselves become central facts for the disciplined observer. His objectivity resides in his nonparticipant status, the fact that he must all too often be thoroughly ignorant of the lived experience of his individual (or cultural) "subjects" if he is to acquire knowledge of them. It is essential that we continually remind ourselves of the way that subjects inevitably become objects as a consequence of this "subjectivization" process. One way of taking serious account of what this means would require us to trace these key dichotomies back to their joint source in market rationality and modern experimental science, as well as to take note of their clear interdependence with one another. Another key point is to remember that it is not dichotomization itself, but rather the unreflective process by which dichotomies become empiricized and one-dimensionalized which is the problem.[21] It is as a consequence of the activity of a disembodied observation function which has effectively unhinged itself from thought and reflexivity, then, that we fail to take account of the origin of key dichotomies like values and facts, ends and means, subject and object, even mind and body, in the man/nature distinction -- now thoroughly detopicalized under the empirical convention so central to Western rationality.[22]

(4) A case in point of which many people are aware is that of Max Weber. I am particularly concerned with Weber's theory of social action because of the central significance of his thinking for virtually all social science disciplines, including organizational and managerial disciplines.[23] In the course I have taught in the Faculty of Administrative Studies for the past twelve years, titled "The Value Framework of Administrative Decision-Making," Weber is one of the central figures. In a book three years ago I cited him as one of the three central intellectual forces, along with Durkheim and Karl Popper, in the emergence of what I called there "the American ideology." Perhaps what I have to say on a small part of Weber's work will help explain why I feel this way.

Max Weber, writing around the turn of this last century, thoroughly anticipates the displacement of the ends/means schema so central to economics' origins as the science of scarce means by system, structure and function when he addresses the failure of value-rational or principled action in particular to make the transition from his typology of action into his typology of authority.[24] Weber's overarching concept of RATIONALIZATION comprehends that aspect of functional rationality which would later become problematic for Mannheim whether or not systemic integration is realized in any particular case.[25] Principled action, for Weber increasingly the property of the subject-as-object who resists the rationalization process, is explicitly accorded the status of rational action in his scheme rather than being consigned to the non (or irr) rational status of affectivity and emotion. When he points to its failure to make the transition to legal-rational authority as one of the three "legitimate" types, and the one which is clearly most central to Western capitalism in the Twentieth Century, he is addressing the way that rationalization imperils an emphasis on principles of all kinds in favour of one on organized functions and tasks.

I say principles of all kinds not only because inherent in rationalization as a process is the de-enchantment of the world, with its consequences for certain principles or values more likely to be associated with resistance to these developments than anything else.[26] There is also the threat that rationalization as Weber comprehends it poses to the goal-rational behaviour of individuals who refuse to accede reason to Society, organization, and function. Individual goal-rational behaviour, in short, is no less suspect than explicitly principled actions, and may even turn out to be more dangerous to the desired societal and organizational monopoly. After all, it will be easier to "reduce" principled action's claims to affectivity and emotion than it will be to deal with those whose resistance includes specific reference to ends, goals, objectives and the concern about putting means together to realize them, however scarce the means may be. It is this aspect, at least as much as the fate of value rational action, which tempts Weber to question the ultimate reasonableness of the rationalization process itself.[27]

Weber, as I have argued elsewhere, wants a sociology of scarcity where the categories and concerns of political economy and economics still loom large.[28] This is clearly reflected, I think, in the way he accuses the rationalization process as it takes shape in the emergence of system, structure, and function of a violation of the "concrete" requirements for judging an action as rational. It is the way that rationalization obliterates the unavoidably individual character of the calculations originally demanded by the ends/means schema in political economy, shifting the focus to societal, organizational and functional collectives as the relevant units of analysis, which motivates Weber's attack on emanationism and collective concepts in the opening sections of <u>Theory of Social & Economic Organization</u> and elsewhere.[29] The point here is that it is as a consequence of precisely this shift that individuals with goals at variance with given collectives gradually acquire the status of non - or irrational subjects exhibiting poor socialization and/or deviant personalities requiring rehabilitation and "understanding." I would strongly argue that here we have a clear parallel to that attitude so central to disciplined observation as it views the differing value systems of Third World countries. According factual status to values in both instances points to such a convention as a possible prelude to integration rather than real convergence.

It is the way that Weber accedes to social-scientific conventions, restricting himself to critique from within the process of rationalization that creates these disciplines and gives them their mission, which constitutes the core of his social science of scarcity. He accepts the factual status of values in his own work, and the corollary decline of the individual subject into an object for disciplined observation, as something to employ in attempting to lay out the problem of a possible disjunction between reason and Western rationality, rather than something to be addressed critically and directly.[30] While he often alludes in his work in political economy to the decline of value into values with the rise of society, and its intellectual correlate sociology, his sociological work is remarkably free of any direct assaults on the way that rationalization, de-enchantment, and a concern for socialization actually help bring this about. I have argued elsewhere that Weber's greatest limitation lays precisely in that conception of duty which required him to deny in the strongest possible terms any approach to the problems of "objective possibility" predicated on reflexive and dialectical modes of analysis and thought. The fate of values for Weber is given in the factual status they acquire as problems of integration (not convergence) for the disciplined observer, and the fate of disciplined observers ambiguous about their own values as objects of their own subjectivity and subjects of their own objectivity is perfectly captured in the life of Weber himself.[31]

(5) A related point of considerable significance for the role of disciplined observation in the study of differing value systems is Weber's parallel failure to fully resolve that emphasis on a generalizing objective and an individualizing method which was so central to his temporary resolution of the _methodenstreit_ at the German sociological association meetings of 1908.[32] In this case it is the two-faced warrant given to disciplined observation which cannot help but be relevant to contemporary concerns about the nature of social-scientific knowledge. Note for example the tension between value freedom or neutrality and that allegedly prior awareness of and sensitivity to value-relevance found in his discussion of action, reason, _verstehen_ and ideal-typification.[33] A methodologically convenient "rationalistic bias" may dictate that sociology acknowledge both value neutrality as an objective and value-relevance as a fact. But it is the centrality of the concrete individual actor, once again, which lies at the heart of type construction, confirming Loewith's point that Weber's devotion to this unit of analysis has (to use Weber's own dichotomy) substantive rather than simply methodological significance.[34]

Of at least equal importance is the way that Weber establishes and defends the status of his concrete individual as a rational actor. Judgment in any particular instance, argues Weber, ought not to be based on the success of any particular effort to realize some goal or value by planfully calculating appropriate available means to this end. Instead, the disciplined observer must accede to the actor's intent to act rationally in any given circumstance, regardless of the outcome of these efforts.[35] Not only does this serve to underscore the priority of the actor over his possible or actual disciplined observer, and life over sociology's rendition of life, thereby reaffirming the lived experience of the concrete individual as a real subject. It also directs the assessment of rationality toward value-rational action, where the commitment to ultimate values and principles is usually reflected in the actual behaviour as its own justification rather than as a means to some external end or goal.[36] The separation between ends and means exemplified in goal-rational action is far less possible to maintain in the case of principled action, as for instance (to use Weber's example) where the captain decides to go down with his ship.[37]

Implied in the foregoing is the presence (ideally) for Weber of an independent end-determining activity for the individual. Nothing could more readily underscore his ultimate pessimism on these matters, however, than the way in which this activity increasingly is carried out by individuals resisting emergent developments involving rationalization, de-enchantment, and the organization of society both in spheres of activity (society; formal organization; "normal" division of labour) and in spheres of thought (science; technology; sociology). In effect, rationality ceases to really exist for Weber at all when it becomes coincident with the reproduction of properly socialized individuals who manifest their individuation as functionaries in pre-formed and organized divisions of function. After all, Durkheim's "new men" are nothing else but Weber's "last men," and the type of behaviour and legitimate authority in which Society must ultimately come to reside is the only truly collective category in his two typologies: traditional behaviour and traditional authority.[38] Rationality becomes a "tradition" once its boundaries become coterminous with Society itself, and properly socialized allegedly rational subjects as objects come to "reflect" their socialization as "individuals" whose goal rationality harmonizes with system interests and objectives. The result: agreement or acquiescence in system goals, with differences confined to the means to achieve them, that is organizational, administrative or functional rationality for employees and what we earlier termed technical (as opposed to economic) rationality for economists and social scientists.

Such detailed attention to an individual who is often rendered antediluvian by being thanked for his "classical" contribution is justified not simply because Weber tried to encounter and deal with most if not all the conflicts and issues affecting the transition of Western capitalist societies from their early entrepreneurial and market basis to their later organizational and managerial phase. It is also the present relevance of many of Weber's substantive concerns (bureaucracy, managerialism, sociology, science and technology, legitimacy, capital accounting practices, the financing of public bodies) and methodological interests (typification, comparative method, verstehen, action vs behaviour, value neutrality and value relevance, causal vs functional and teleological modes of reasoning and explanation) which clearly justifies the time I have taken here with him. Finally, there is the not-so-obvious parallel I have sought to establish between his defense of the concrete individual as a goal-rational and autonomously valuing subject and our present concerns for the differing value systems of cultures who are treated, at least in theory, as collective persons. I hope that our concern for convergence does not act as a cover for what really turns out to be a commitment to cultural integration. On the other hand, I would be less than candid if I did not complete this argument by admitting that my own position probably constitutes a far clearer version of Weber from the standpoint of his values than that of many or most of the people in this room.

(6) Let me now attempt to clarify my argument against what I call scientism as it relates to theorizing in particular in economics and the social sciences. I have argued that the displacement of the ends/means schema in economic thinking in favour of an emphasis on system, structure, and function effectively supplants real individualism with a pale substitute. This latter is achievable through the sort of occupational recognition which all too often fails to rise above the satisficing level where performance and innovativeness are concerned.[39] At the same time what I have called economic rationality as perhaps the key element in decision-making is effectivly displaced by one or another variation on technical rationality--the efficient utilization of means where ends are given or unproblematic. To the extent that even that residue of the ends/means distinction found in technical rationality is ignored or forgotten, we are able to judge just how far societal, organizational and administrative predefinitions of collective life have gone in the advanced societies.

This only serves to underscore the need for some alternative capable of filling the gap left by the collapse of individualism as a force standing against earlier societal predefinitions of reason and rationality. Looking at North America in particular, it is poignant to realize just how dependent we were on this individualism to overcome pre-capitalist and pre-industrial traditional residues over the past 150 years. This point can be made with even greater force in the case of Western Europe. What we have to recognize today is the extent to which we have fetishized Society, treating it simultaneously as the best possible form of collective life and the only one "available" to us.[40] In effect we refuse to acknowledge that Society is a culturally and historically specific form of collective life. This cannot help but have serious consequences for prevailing understandings of reason and rationality, function and innovation, and decision-making. Nowadays one is tempted to argue that even "individual differences" are best comprehended as societally and organizationally produced effects rather than autonomous agencies posing real alternatives to the existing order. This is what Weber meant when he stated that the rationalization process creates irrationalities "with the certainty of a fate."[41] Rationality becomes distended from the individual and is increasingly seen to repose in organized structures and functions which over time unavoidably acquire a traditional presence and a set of continuous rather than discontinuous vested interests in the prevailing order of things.

It is only in the context of such an established order that Karl Popper's injunctions against reflexivity as a basis for social theorizing make any political sense at all.[42] What, after all, is presupposed in any argument which claims that incremental and piecemeal reforms, what Golembiewski called the "low road," are not only the necessary but the sufficient vehicles for social change?[43] What structural reference would have to be present and be presumed valid in principle for "tinkering" to be touted as the only approach really needed? It is the insufficiency of precisely this type of thinking, underwritten by the collapse of individualism, which suggests both the paradoxical character of Western capitalist development and the need for an innovative conception of individualism. Capitalism creates its opposite by adherence to its ground rules, it would seem. The reality of established and emerging structures of public and private power in the advanced societies simply underscores the fact that the piecemeal approach is not sufficient wherever it seeks to legislate thinking about society and the economy, and that it is in this realization that our new value-set regarding a constructive individualism must take its point of departure.

I am not arguing either that incrementalism is no longer necessary in practical matters or that a reformist approach can be jettisoned in either thinking or practice. I am saying that such an approach is insufficient for our needs, and reveals how hostaged to a now traditional anti-intellectualism North Americans in particular still are.[44] By scientism in social theorizing I mean essentially the self-satisfied demand that thought and thinking subordinate itself to what is thought to be a scientific model of theorizing. Here it is the demand for testable/falsifiable hypotheses which decomposes the structure of thought and thinking often in the name of a specious attack on holism.[45] That the proverbial baby goes down the drain with the bath water in such "operational" thinking is only underscored by noticing how much freer the so-called hard sciences are to engage in this sort of theorizing activity without criticism or blame.[46] There is also the distinct lack of progress in social and economic thinking, evident in the way we all too often become the prisoners of dichotomies we have created to try to make sense of the problem of social conflict and social choice in the so-called real world.[47] It is extremely disconcerting for anyone interested in the history of the social sciences to take what he thinks will be a nostalgic wander through the key journals of the 1930's as I recently did. There you discover discussions of the fact/value distinction and the value question which are never even cited in the vastly inferior renditions presently coming across my desk as an editor of a major journal in the philosophy of the social sciences.

Any argument that the "three I's" of incrementalism, interventionism and instrumentalism are no longer sufficient where economics and the social sciences are concerned must not simply replace one set of disciplinary approaches, with their explicit or implicit defense of vested interests, with another.[48] Instead our association between a more wide-open view of thought and theorizing and a constructive and innovative individualism must begin by recognizing that reason is a human faculty distributed throughout societies and cultures whose differences are mostly a matter of chance environmental opportunities, temporary ideological advantages, and the institutional modes of cultural training and certification built up out of them.[49] As we encounter various cultures and people of the so-called Third World, we must not fail to be reflexive, by which I mean to imply constructively and innovatively individualistic, about our own culture-as-civilization, and what the essence of our uniqueness really is. Weber's institutional focus was on the right track but failed to draw attention to disciplined observation and the truncated view of thought and theorizing _vis a vis_ method and data accumulation which science, capitalism, bureaucracy, and the rule of law all have in common. My point is not to attack disciplined observation as unnecessary, any more than it was to attack reformism and incrementalism as unnecessary. I want to situate disciplined observation relative to thought in the interests of practice, and to argue that an unhinged observation function free of its reflexive moment is simply not objective enough.[50] This and related points have been made with great force by the cultural anthropologist Pierre Bourdieu in his _Outline of a Theory of Practice_, and I strongly commend his analysis of Third World practices and beliefs to you.

Wittgenstein, in his "Remarks on Fraser's _Golden Bough_," has a lovely passage where he points up just how hostaged to "rationality" we are when we make sport of peoples who, we think, actually believe that rain dances cause rain or that propitiations in advance make the sun rise. The fact that rain dances only occur during the rainy season and that these propitiations occur as the sun is rising draw attention to the distinctly non-rational and ceremonial character of these activities.[51] This leads me to two other points, which are an almost unavoidable upshot of my proposal for opening out what is considered legitimate thinking in economics and the social sciences, and in social and organizational life as well. First there is the urgent need for us to see our disciplines and our mode of information production and dissemination in management schools and elsewhere as part of the socio-economic and political reality of our cultural life rather than simply a neutral means of making objective sense of this reality at a distance from it. To say that this latter remains a valid perception is to point to the way disciplined observation embodies, even as it underwrites, what is essentially an empirical convention with its emphasis on causality, correspondence rules and a view of the whole as abstract and "its" parts as concrete.[52] A second point would argue that we often learn more about ourselves from reflexive scrutiny of our concepts and categories than we do about those "others" who become topical for our needs and interests, as both Wittgenstein's observations about cultural anthropology and the fate of economic and political "development" theory make abundantly clear.[53]

(7) As you can see, I am much more concerned here about the issue of cultural convergence-become-displacement than about the relatively "local" problem of whether there is a convergence occurring between economic and non-economic modes of decision-making in the advanced societies, or whether such a convergence is either possible or desirable. The way I would like to conclude my remarks here would be to first address the difference between the two modes of decision, what this difference signifies from the standpoint of value and values, then end by returning to the title of the essay, in order to point up the insufficiency of a straight institutional response to the reality of "differing value systems." By institutional here I of course mean institutional economics as a macro-structural and philosophical counterweight to the more scientific, professional and technical activities of the mainstream of economics as a discipline. This counterweight is represented most obviously in the North American case by Thorstein Veblen, John Commons and Clarence Ayres.[54] What we shall discover in this latter case are a number of overwhelming similarities in style to Weber's thinking, including both his pessimism and his refusal even in the face of such pessimism to endorse theoretical reflexivity in the social and economic disciplines.

It is institutional economics' refusal to address the first principles implicit in their critique of capitalist society in the West which makes it virtually impossible for it to sanction theoretical reflection as I have discussed it, as well as the bias favouring open communicative interaction which it presupposes. In effect it is really an inverted instance of the same professionalism and scientism often found in mainstream economics and the social, behavioural and administrative sciences. In common with the latter disciplines, it too turns its back on the fact that such intellectual, technical and professional activities are first and foremost forms of social interaction rather than ways of studying it neutrally and disinterestedly. By comparison with their status as socially produced cultures within a culture, their badge of neutrality and objectivity can be seen for the convention, the form of life, that it really is.[55] A consideration of some import in what follows will be whether and to what extent the vaunted "value question" so central to European and North American sociological, psychological, anthropological and economic disciplines can itself stand up to scrutiny as an objectively comprehended problem or dilemma.

I want first to state my belief that we must distinguish carefully between economic decision-making, economic rationality, economic progress and the idea of an economy when we ask whether a convergence between economic and non-economic decision-making is occurring.[56] There are, for example, clear points of difference in economics as to whether decisions either made by certain specific institutions or addressed to certain specific institutional concerns in the larger society are ipso facto "economic" at all. This would seem to be mainly a problem of definition, yet great ideological significance attaches to which side of the fence you find yourself on. When one considers how difficult certain economic and social and political realities like the modern corporation are to "fit into" theories which still carry considerable weight with members of the profession, one wonders just how far theoretical structures ought to be allowed to go in refusing to reflect these realities.[57] In this case it is the tension once again between individualism and collectivism, the entrepreneur and the vested interests which often make his life difficult if not impossible, which is at issue.

Forgetting for a moment the fact that many viable corporate structures in the West today are the collective fulfillment of an earlier entrepreneur's efforts, the badge of his success, we can note just how central this individual aspect is in discussing economic and non-economic (or socio-economic) types of decision. Diesing, for instance, argues that we ought to treat the idea of a non (or socio) economic decision as a decision which is addressed to value conflicts where the ideal is mutual adjustment.[58] His basis for non-economic decision making is to be discovered in the application in each case at hand of three principles concerned with the possibilities of change, the definition of the problem, and the approach to its solution. In the first case, it is the relevant system's openness or flexibility as it relates to the introducibility and the acceptability of change which is central. Diesing suggests that we select "the easiest possible relevant changes" in the light of these factors. In the case of the definition of the problem, Diesing argues that we must "select a problem-area that is independent enough for its context to sustain a separate solution against outside pressures." Finally, as regards solutions, he states that "one should begin a solution in such a way that expansion of the solution is possible."[59]

The impact of functionalist social theory of the Parsonian variety is evident throughout Diesing's analysis.[60] His is an attempt to apply to allegedly less concrete and less easily definable issues some form of method, however vague and unspecific it may be. Clearly the decision-maker, at least in a democratic and rule of law social system, is not only likely to be some collective or institutional "person," but this in fact seems unavoidable. Perhaps more compelling is the fact that individualized models of decision-making taken from psychology and adopted to economic analysis are often found wanting precisely because of the absence of a structural or institutional and collective dimension.[61] It appears to this reader that, hard as he tries to resist it, Diesing is put in the unenviable position of treating economic, as opposed to non (or socio) economic decision-making as both more empirically concrete and individuated and increasingly residual as a social and cultural fact. Here the bias favouring individualism as a value resolves itself into Weber's conceptual nominalism and constructivism, as economics as a discipline effectively severs its substantive bias in favour of the individual altogether.[62]

This may not appear significant at first glance, but is if only because it serves to underscore the formal character of individualistic models of economic decision-making in the highly structured and organized confines of advanced industrial societies.[63] Indeed, I have argued elsewhere that the only place these models really belong at all, the notion of economic organizations as collective legal "persons" notwithstanding, is in the analysis of individuals as consumers (as well as entrepreneurs) in the market, not as producers or employees in the firm.[64] But notice in the following statement how Diesing shifts the burden away from the issue of whether the decision is individual or collective to whether or not we have to deal with scarcity as a factor.

> All decisions dealing with the activities of a single person or a single group -- "selfish" decisions -- are either economic, or social, or a combination of the two. Economic decisions attempt to maximize the achievement of given ends (goals, desires, interests, needs) through the careful use of available means, in a situation where not all ends can be fully achieved. The means can be used in a number of alternative ways, and decision consists of a selection of one of these alternatives. A decision is reached by (1) estimating the probable effects on the ends of each alternative, (2) estimating the degree of probability of each effect, (3) estimating and comparing the value of each effect on a single scale, either money or utility, or preference indifference, and (4) choosing the alternative which has the greatest probability of producing the greatest value. This type of decision may be called

> a "maximizing" decision, since it consists of a search for that action alternative which has maximum value, or minimum loss, on some scale.[65]

(8) Two points impress themselves upon the careful reader at this point. The first one is that the so-called value problem central to non (or socio) economic decision-making is not really addressed or confronted at all in this passage. Values may, as noted, become facts for the disciplined observer, in this case Diesing, but the issue of decision or choice is nonetheless essentially sidestepped. Maybe this is evidence of its ultimate irreducibility to real factual status after all. We are not helped by Diesing's suggestion that "we select the easiest possible relevant changes," since this totally ignores the reality of interests and interest groups in society. Indeed, a posture of thoroughgoing value disinterestedness would have to be present in such cases. Even if such a posture were in fact "available" to a disciplined observer, there is the real question whether it would be in the least bit relevant to the way that economic decisions really are made.[66] Consider further the suggestion that we select "a problem-area that is independent enough from its context to sustain a separate solution against outside pressures," but "begin a solution in such a way that expansion of the solution is possible." What this only underscores is the absurdity of a neutral and disinterested pose if only because what is given in making such a posture "operational" is in fact the very top-down asymmetrical power structure which violates not only democratic values but to a lesser extent even the actual operation of democratic social systems.[67]

The other point relates to the allegedly more empirically concrete referrent of economic decision-making. Diesing shifts the burden ever so subtly away from the actual rank-ordering activity by which given individuals in the market, either as consumers or as entrepreneurs, <u>actually do decide</u>, preferring to focus instead on <u>"the achievement of given ends"</u> (emphasis mine). This constitutes first recognition of the collective and corporate character of such "concrete" decisions, where conflicting values and interests going into the process are only heightened by the different perceptions of significant parties concerning what the problem is and how important it is relative to others.[68] Needless to say, even if we admit to the reality of value-conflict in the rank-ordering of ends by concrete individuals, the problem can be far more readily resolved and in fact is so resolved. As for the notion of the household in both economic and non (or socio) economic decision-making, we must acknowledge the essentially metaphorical character of its concreteness both at the level of the family and at the level of Society understood as an economy, in favour of a focus on the individual in the first case and the collective in the second.

Notice finally how Diesing acts as if he had achieved specificity in the case of economic decisions by reference to the four estimations which must be made in order to realize a maximizing decision. There is something very disheartening about such a process of decision precisely because it requires individuals allegedly uninterested in any values themselves, save as facts for analysis and "selection." Of course this is really not the case at all, and the problem really becomes Arrow's dilemma, i.e. that there is simply no way to move from individual tastes to social preferences in the absence of "interpersonal utility comparisons" save through imposition or coercion.[69] If Monod is correct when he argues that at base we in fact do not really choose our values at all,[70] then what is the point of trying to expand the notion of taste outward from "discrete" tastes so that it comprehends what have been recently labelled "conceptual tastes" as well. The only point would be to address the need for reflexivity and communicative interaction between social and economic scientists and their subjects as objects as a counterweight to treating (discrete) tastes as nothing more than the information summarized in indifference curves.[71]

The point of this exercise has been to address the limited significance of the distinction between economic and non- (or socio) economic decision-making from two or three perspectives. Except as a self-defining distinction based on whether economists or non-economists formulate the problem or suggest the solution, it seems difficult to sustain. Perhaps a better point would be the argument that there is in fact a difference in method between an economic and non-economic decision. This too would address disciplinary differences rather than argue for the distinctiveness of the decision's referrents or "effects." At the same time, it would appear to go substantially beyond the specious issue of disciplinary proprietorship. But I have suggested that something very important happened when economics had to sever its bias for the individual in favour of collective structures. What happened in fact was brilliantly anticipated by Coase in his seminal article "The Nature of the Firm."[72] In the tension between the market and the firm as means of maximizing and accumulating capital, the organized producer gradually gained the lion's share of attention. This dilemma will very quickly need to be resolved if we are to seriously and realistically encounter "differing value systems" in the Third World.

The fact that this has begun to take place suggests the increasingly central role of non- (or socio) economic decisions, rationality, even progress in a world system where economic organizations have become more "global" in their reach than most states or societies. At the same time, there can be little doubt that the "value" of a reflexive and communicative model like the one I have outlined not only can but must be extended to the Third World, where the ideal of constructive individualism is no less important than in the advanced societies. Thus there probably is a place for the distinction between economic and non-economic decision-making, so long as the emphasis is placed on (1) the method or nature of the process rather than (2) the origin or source of the problem, solution or decision (3) the locus of its major (or entire) effect, or (4) the nature of the subject matter involved. In the case of these latter three bases for distinguishing economic from non-economic decisions, the terrain of the real world has undergone changes so overwhelming and substantial in the past 40 years as to effectively undermine their "value" in this regard.

(9) Could what we have just described really constitute evidence for a convergence, or is the type of integration really more akin to a displacement? Equally as significant is the issue of what direction (if any) this convergence or displacement is coming from? A final point at the outset would argue that a significant basis for the claim of difference between economic and non-economic decision-making has fundamentally to do with the question/answer, problem/solution fix itself. Are we ready to address these dichotomies in a way which focusses on their importance as process rather than outcome? This is surely one of the key values presupposed in my emphasis throughout this paper on communication and interaction, especially where economics and the social sciences in their relation to society, government and its work organizations is concerned.

It seems to me that an approach to society predicated on what is essentially a notion of problem-solving from mathematics and technology is problematic precisely because it is unavoidably biased in favour of outcome rather than process. That is to say, it tends toward the identification of a problem solving approach with final solutions.[73] My point is not simply to argue that in collective life there are no final solutions, but to underscore the reason why this is the case and to suggest why it should not lead us to pessimism or cynicism. Instead of focussing on relational and other forms of "complexity" or "structure" in isolating reasons for why this is the case,[74] we must once again remember that it is the unique duplex character of the human sciences which makes such disciplines a part of society and a form of social interaction at the very time that they are going about theorizing, researching, and engaging in the disciplined observation of Society.

Indeed, if there is any goodness, any value, in an emphasis on interaction and process then this value should ideally be reflected in the activities of the social sciences, not as mere "social technologies" whose theorizing must be confined to traditional non-critical modes, as Popper has argued,[75] but as enterprises whose essence is interaction under an adequacy postulate of competent communication. The phenomenologist Alfred Schutz formulated the postulate of adequacy in a way that readily allows us to see why the social and economic sciences should be engaging in critical as well as traditional theorizing and how this can be seen as a model for the way we should ideally approach the differing value systems of other cultures. "Each term used in a scientific system referring to human action must be so constructed that a human act performed within the life world by an individual actor in the way indicated by the typical construction would be reasonable and understandable for the actor himself, as well as for his fellow man."[76]

Schutz takes off from precisely the assumption of reason and rationality as substructural human properties and attributes that seems to me so essential for any honest encounter with social and cultural difference, here or elsewhere. He only underscores our argument for a reflexive moment favouring communication and process in social science research procedures when he states: "What makes it possible for a social science to refer at all to events in the life-world is the fact that the interpretation of any human act by the social scientist might be the same as that by the actor or by his partner."[77] My objective in promoting such an "anti-method" in the social sciences is not to displace traditional modes of theorizing and research, but rather to make it possible for such activities to both address the problem of value and values while encountering the goodness of difference through open communication.[78]

Finally, and in closing, however attractive a distinction like Daniel Bell's between the economizing and the sociologizing mode in problem-solving may be, it is wrong from the standpoint of our own values to argue that the latter mode should displace the former one. One is reminded of the impact on Third World countries of the aristocratic pronouncements of the Club of Rome, which often appeared to amount to the argument that the industrialized countries had effectively foreclosed growth for everybody as a consequence of their unreflective exploitation and environmental insensitivity.[79] The question whether this is the case is an open one, and the attempt to argue for a strict social accounting posture, as Bell is tempted to do, is even more problematic when applied to different cultures and value systems in the Third World than it is when applied to the industrialized nations. In effect, in trying to be sensitive to "dumb nature," we systematically exclude eighty per cent of the world's population from the deliberation and decision, to be sure with the best possible intentions.[80] There is considerable irony in this process of collective self-deprecation as it is being carried on today.

To be sure convergence and synthesis as an ideal in the interrelations of economic to non-economic considerations and decisions in the industrialized countries is a prototype for more global forms of convergence. In this case, only an economizing mode supplemented (not displaced) by a critical and reflexive mode in the social sciences and in social organization can realize an honest and open encounter with differing value systems, not in order to displace or annihilate difference but to see its goodness. Institutional economics would be correct in viewing such a process-centred "solution" as the resuscitation in our thinking of the institutional vis á vis the technological and transformative.[81] In the context of our relations with the Third World in particular it would allow us to stand once again in support of the objective concept of value which has always united Marx and the political economists.

SUMMARY OF ARGUMENT (WILSON)

(1) Value was originally an objective category in the conceptual armoury of political economy correlated with labour. Here capital and technology were seen to extend rather than contradict labour. Thus any "substitution" needed to be "rational" by reference to this theory of value,not in opposition to it. The first dent in this is found in Smith's The Wealth of Nations. The later rupture between Marx and the political economists needs to be seen in terms of the contradiction for Marx between the labour theory of value and the actual process and trajectory of capitalist industrial development.

(2) Lately, economics has begun to reorient itself as a result of the infusion of concepts from sociology and cultural anthropology like system, function and structure. These concepts are biased toward order in line with their disciplinary sources, in contrast to economic's original focus on the individual rather than collective structures. Indeed, economizing behaviour has itself been redefined to downplay or ignore the value aspects of decision implicit in the activity of rank-ordering ends given scarce means in favour of focussing on technical rationality -- the efficient utilization of means where ends are given or unproblematic.

(3) This reflects an earlier development which occurred first in philosophy -- the subjectivization of the concept and idea of value with the rise of the subject/object distinction in idealist philosophy -- and thereafter of the value/fact distinction in sociology. In the first case we probably have a reflection in philosophy of the impact on the individual of actual industrial developments, while in the second we see the consequences of turning value into values as the property of a "subject" who necessarily becomes an object with the rise of the disciplined observer. Values become associated with the non (or ir) rational baggage of an observed subject as FACTS become more valuable than anything else. This too reflects real social and economic conditions, as well as the fact that the source of disciplined observation is to be found in market rationality and experimental science.

(4) This necessitates what I call constructive individualism, a combination of the revival of the individual-centred focus of political economy and an expanded conception of thought and thinking premised on reflexivity as a sine qua non for true objectivity, in contrast to disciplined observation on its own. A strategy for reforming social science research procedures premised on radicalizing Alfred Schutz' postulate of adequacy and making it at

least an available option for researchers in social and economic sciences promises to meet legitimate requirements for competent communication while achieving important changes in social practices and values. It also updates Durkheim's understandable concern about a moral code for social scientists by making the research process part of the social structure in potentially constructive ways. (See references for work in progress.)

(5) The convergence of economic and non-economic decision-making reflects economics' dominant tendency in its analysis of production toward severing its disciplinary bias in support of the individual in favour of treating collective structures as "persons" or entities. The ends/means utility schema is effectively supplanted by one favouring system, function, and structure as noted. Scarcity and an objective conception of value must be retained if an individual-centred focus is to achieve environmental objectives while not closing off growth for developing countries. The communication model cited above is the way to realize a process-based dialogue both in the advanced societies and with the developing countries.

(6) Our interest in differing value systems needs to be understood as implying a convergence issue which parallels the absorption of economic into non-economic decision models already noted. But Bell's preference for a "sociologizing" over an "economizing" mode sidesteps the real problem of process and the role of individuals in it. Neither can institutional economics on its own provide an alternative, since it too refuses to address the consequences for "differing value systems" of our being a culture which values disciplined observation and organizational/functional and technical conceptions of rationality.

REFERENCES

1. Karl Marx, Capital, 3 Vols (Moscow: Foreign Languages Publishing Co., 1961); V.S. Vygodski, The Story of a Great Discovery: How Marx Wrote 'Capital' (Tunbridge Wells: Abacus Press, 1974); Marx, Grundrisse: A Contribution to the Critique of Political Economy (Moscow: Progress Publishers, 1970).

2. Patrick Marnham, Fantastic Invasion (London: Jonathan Cape, 1980).

3. Kōzō Uno, The Principles of Political Economy: Theory of a Purely Capitalist Society (Harvester Press, forthcoming), including an appendix by Thomas Sekine "Essay on Uno's Dialectic of Capital"; Thomas Sekine, "Uno-Riron: A Japanese Contribution to Marxian Political Economy," Journal of Economic Literature, Volume 13 (1975), pp 847-877. Also see Maurice Godelier, Rationality & Irrationality in Economics (London: Monthly Review Press, 1972).

4. Krishan Kumar, "Revolution and Industrial Society", Sociology Vol 10, No. 2 (May 1976), pp 245-269.

5. See H.T. Wilson, The American Ideology: Science, Technology & Organization as Modes of Rationality in Advanced Industrial Societies (London: Routledge, 1977), Chapter 1.

6. André G. Frank, Capitalism & Underdevelopment in Latin America (N.Y.: Monthly Review Press, 1967); Paolo Freire, Pedagogy of the Oppressed (N.Y.: Herder & Herder, 1971); Freire, Education for Critical Consciousness (N.Y.: Herder & Herder, 1972).

7. See generally John Dewey, Theory of Valuation (Chicago: International Encyclopedia of Unified Science, 1939); Clarence Ayres, Toward a Reasonable Society (Austin: University of Texas Press, 1961); Ayres, The Theory of Economic Progress (N.Y.: Schocken Books, 1962); Paul Diesing, Reason and Society (Urbana: University of Illinois Press, 1962); and Gunnar Myrdal, Value in Social Theory (N.Y.: Harpers, 1958), especially pp 206-230. For an analysis from the standpoint of critical as opposed to traditional theory, Max Horkheimer, The Eclipse of Reason (N.Y.: Seabury Press, 1974), originally published in 1947.

8. H.T. Wilson, "Innovation: the Practical Uses of Theory," in Social Change, Innovation and Politics in East Asia, edited by Y.S. Yim, H.T. Wilson and Richard W. Wilson (Hong Kong: Asian Research Service, 1980); and H.T. Wilson, Tradition and Innovation: Weber and Wittgenstein on Civilization as Culture (forthcoming)

9. For example, Walter F. Buckley (ed), Modern Systems Research for the Behavioural Scientist (Chicago: Aldine Publishing Co., 1968); and Buckley, Sociology & Modern Systems Theory (Englewood Cliffs, N.J.: Prentice Hall, 1967).

10. But see my argument against associating "sense of function" with "functional rationality" in H.T. Wilson, "Functional Rationality and 'Sense of Function': the Case of an Ideological Distortion," in International Yearbook of Organization Studies, edited by David Dunkerly and Graeme Salaman (London: Routledge, 1981) forthcoming.

11. See Young C. Kim, "The Concept of Political Culture in Comparative Politics," Journal of Politics, Vol 26 (1964), pp 313-336, and compare to I.L. Horowitz, "Sociology & Politics: The Myth of Functionalism Revisited," Journal of Politics, Vol 25 (1963), pp 248-264.

12. Wilson, The American Ideology; and "The Meaning & Significance of 'Empirical Method' for the Critical Theory of Society," Canadian Journal of Political & Social Theory, Vol 3, No. 3 (Fall, 1979), pp 57-68.

13. Here I am thinking particularly of the clear respectability accorded to narrowly positivistic, and decidedly "technological," conceptions of reason and rationality found in social scientific studies in the Soviet Union & Eastern Europe. But see Kmica, Jerzy and Nowak, Leszek, "The Rationality Assumption in Human Sciences," Polish Sociological Bulletin, No 1 (1970), pp 43-70.

14. Wilson, **Tradition and** Innovation, op cit; and Knowledge & Totality: A Critical Analysis of the Causal Principle in Science & Life,**unpublished manuscript.**

15. The idea and practice of disciplined observation both reflects and anticipates subjectivization. For the origin of the modern doctrine, C.B. Macpherson, The Political Theory of Possessive Individualism (London: Oxford University Press, 1962).

16. New York, Augustus Kelly Booksellers, 1966 (reproduction).

17. Marnham, op cit; Marion Levy, Modernization: Latecomers and Survivors (N.Y.: Basic Books, 1972).

18. Wilson, Knowledge & Totality.

19. Frederic Nietzsche, Beyond Good & Evil (London: Allen & Unwin, 1967). See Frederic Jameson, "The Vanishing Mediator: Narrative Structure in Max Weber," New German Critique, Vol 1 (1973), pp 52-89.

20. Ludwig Wittgenstein, Tractatus Logico - Philosophicus, edited by D.F. Pears and B. McGuinness, from the original English translation by Bertrand Russell (London: Routledge, 1961), 5.633.

21. Wilson, Knowledge & Totality; and **Tradition and** Innovation.

22. Horkheimer, op cit; William Leiss, The Domination of Nature (Boston: Beacon Press, 1974); Clarence Glacken, "Man Against Nature: An Outmoded Dichotomy," The Environmental Crisis, edited by Harold Helfrich (New Haven: Yale University Press, 1970), pp 127-142; Wilson, The American Ideology, Chapter 3.

23. Max Weber, Theory of Social & Economic Organization, translated and introduced by Talcott Parsons (Glencoe: Free Press, 1947), pp 87-123.

24. Ibid, see pp 112-118, 324-329.

25. Karl Mannheim, Man & Society in An Age of Reconstruction (London: Routledge, 1940), especially pp 49-60. Compare to Weber, "Science as a Vocation", in From Max Weber, edited by H. Gerth & C. Wright Mills (N.Y.: Oxford, 1946), pp 128-156. I have attempted to explicate this feature of Weber's thinking and his differences with Mannheim in "Reading Max Weber: The Limits of Sociology," Sociology, Vol 10, No. 2 (May 1976), pp 297-315. Also see Karl Loewith, "Weber's Interpretation of the Bourgeois Capitalistic World in terms of the Guiding Principle of Rationalization," in Max Weber, edited by Dennis Wrong (Englewood Cliffs, N.J.: Prentice Hall, 1970), pp 101-122.

26. Weber, "Science as a Vocation," op cit.

27. Thus the well known statement "And this you call Reason?", which is found in Weber's introduction to The Sociology of Religion (N.Y.: Scribners, 1952).

28. See Weber, Methodology of the Social Sciences, translated by Harold Shils and Henry Finch (Glencoe: Free Press, 1949), especially the detailed table of contents, references to scarcity, value, ends and means, and economics vis a vis sociology (pp 63-72). Also Wilson, "Reading Max Weber," op cit, **reference** no. 50. On values in sociological inquiry, see Howard Becker, Through Values to Social Interpretation (Durham: Duke University Press, 1950).

29. See Theory of Social & Economic Organization, pp 101-104.

30. See The American Ideology, Chapters 2,6 & 7.

31. Karl Loewith, op cit.

32. Werner Cahnman, "Max Weber and the Methodological Controversy," in Sociology & History, edited by Werner Cahnman and Alvin Boskoff (N.Y.: Macmillan/Free Press, 1964), pp 103-127.

33. Weber, Methodology of the Social Sciences & Theory of Social & Economic Organization pp 87-123 (passim)

34. Loewith, op cit: Wilson, "Reading Max Weber," op cit.

35. Theory of Social & Economic Organization, pp 87-93, 184-186.

36. Ibid., pp 115-117. See Talcott Parsons, "The Place of Ultimate Values in Sociological Theory," International Journal of Ethics, Vol 45 (1934-35), pp 282-316; and Gunnar Myrdal, Value in Social Theory, op cit. Also see Abraham Maslow (ed), New Knowledge in Human Values (N.Y.: Harper & Ross, 1959).

37. Theory of Social & Economic Organization, pp 115-117.

38. Ibid, pp 115-116, 328,341-358; Wilson, **Tradition and** Innovation, Chapter 5. On Weber's pessimism and Durkheim's optimism, see Weber, The Protestant Ethic & the Spirit of Capitalism (N.Y.: Scribners, 1952), 5 concluding paragraphs; and Emile Durkheim, The Division of Labour in Society (N.Y.: Macmillan/Freé Press, 1952), conclusion and preface to second edition.

39. Herbert Simon, Administrative Behaviour, 2nd edition (N.Y. Macmillan/Free Press, 1957), and my critique in "Rationality & Decision in Administrative Science," Canadian Journal of Political Science, Vol 6, No. 3 (June 1973), pp 271-294.

40. Theodor Adorno, "Society" in The Legacy of the German Refugee Intellectuals, edited by Robert Boyers (N.Y.: Schocken Books, 1969), pp 144-153; Wilson, The American Ideology, chapter 8.

41. See Loewith, op cit.

42. Karl Popper, The Poverty of Historicism (London: Routledge, 1957); Everett Knight, The Objective Society (N.Y.: George Braziller, 1959); Wilson, The American Ideology, especially chapter 5; and Wilson, "Capitalism, Science & the Possibility of Political Economy: A Reply to Popper & Wiles" (Unpublished paper). The most substantial volume addressing the so-called positivismusstreit, also known as the "Popper-Adorno Controversy," is The Positivist Dispute

in German Sociology, edited by Glyn Adey & David Frisby (London: Heinemann, 1975). This volume contains the contribution of the original disputants - Adorno & Popper - from the German Sociological Association meetings of 1961, to which Adorno added an equally significant debate between Jurgen Habermas and Hans Albert, as well as extant remarks by Dahrendorf, Pilat, and two of his own essays written under other circumstances. For analysis, H.T. Wilson, "Science, Critique & Criticism: The 'Open Socety' Revisited," in On Critical Theory, edited by John O'Neill (N.Y.: Seabury Press, 1976), pp 205-230.

43. Robert Golembiewski, Men, Management & Morality (N.Y.: McGraw Hill, 1965), introduction and chapter 1.

44. Richard Hofstader, Anti-Intellectualism in American Life (N.Y.: Random House, 1962).

45. Wilson, "The Meaning & Significance of 'Empirical Method' for the Critical Theory of Society," op cit.

46. See in this regard David Bohm, Wholeness and the Implicate Order (London: Routledge, 1980); and Rupert Hall, "Scholar & Craftsman in the Scientific Revolution," in The Rise of Science in Relation to Society, edited by Leonard Marsak (N.Y.: Macmillan, 1964).

47. Thomas Schelling, "On the Ecology of Micromotives," The Public Interest No. 25 (Fall, 1971), pp 59-98. See reference No. 21, for sources on dichotomization.

48. Wilson, "Social Science & Social Change: An Analysis & Critique of some Methodical Practices and an Alternative," **(forthcoming)**

49. See Wilson, "Rationality & Decision in Administrative Science," op cit. Also, see generally Adolph Lowe, On Economic Knowledge (N.Y.: Harper & Row, 1965).

50. Wilson, **Tradition and** Innovation, Chapter 3. Bourdieu's book is in English translation by Cambridge University Press, published in 1976.

51. Ludwig Wittgenstein, "Notes on Fraser's Golden Bough," The Human World, Vol 3 (1971), pp 18-41, originally written in 1930-31 and 1936-37.

52. Wilson, Knowledge & Totality

53. Wilson, "Notes on the Achievement of Communicative Behaviour and Related Difficulties," Dialectical Anthropology (forthcoming).

54. Thorstein Veblen, Theory of Business Enterprise (Boston: Huebsch, 1904); Veblen "The Place of Science in Modern Civilization," American Journal of Sociology, Vol II(1906) pp 585-609; Veblen, The Instinct of Workmanship (Boston: Huebsch, 1914); Clarence Ayres, The Industrial Economy, Its Technological Basis and Institutional Destiny (Boston: Houghton Mifflin, 1952); Ayres, Toward a Reasonable Society (Austin: University of Texas Press, 1961); and Ayres The Theory of Economic Progress (N.Y.: Schocken Books, 1962).

55. Ludwig Wittgenstein, Philosophical Investigations (Oxford: Blackwell 1953).

56. Compare the three references to Ayres in No. 54 to Paul Diesing, Reason and Society (Urbana: University of Illinois Press, 1962), particularly chapters 1 & 2 on technical and economic rationality. Also see generally, Lowe, op cit, parts 1, 2 & 4.

57. Schelling, op cit; Daniel Bell, "The Corporation & Society in the 1970's," The Public Interest, No. 24 (Summer, 1971), pp 5-32; and Charles Lindblom, Politics and Markets (N.Y.: Basic Books, 1977).

58. Paul Diesing, "Non Economic Decision-Making," Ethics, Vol 66, No. 1 (1955), pp 18-35; Diesing, "Socioeconomic Decisions," Ethics, Vo. 69, No. 1 (1958), pp 1-18. Also see Diesing, Reason & Society.

59. Diesing, "Noneconomic Decision-Making," op cit, pp 22, 25 & 27.

60. See ibid, p. 21, and Wilson, The American Ideology, Chapter 8.

61. Harold Wilensky, Organizational Intelligence (N.Y.: Basic Books, 1967), particularly his comments on the role of urgency and crisis in improving the quality of decision-making, in contrast to the argument put forward in James March and Herbert Simon, Organizations (N.Y.: John Wiley, 1958). Also see Wilson, "Rationality and Decision in Administrative Science," op cit for a discussion of the strengths and weaknesses of the "structural" position.

62. See Diesing, Reason & Society pp 1-64, and compare to the relevant sections of Weber's Methodology of the Social Sciences on this score. Also see Weber, Theory of Social & Economic Organization, pp 87-123.

63. Robert Presthus, The Organizational Society, 2nd edition, (N.Y.: St. Martins Press, 1978).

64. Wilson, The American Ideology, Chapter 6.

65. Diesing, "Socioeconomic Decisions," op cit, p. 1. But see Social Research, Vol 44, No. 4 (Winter 1977), titled "Rationality, Choice & Morality," for valuable contributions to this discussion.

66. See Wilensky, op cit, for a discussion of the impediments that are placed in the way of good decisions by specializations as forms of vested interest, particularly the part of his Chart (appendix) focussing on "Structural blockages." Needless to say, too much time can be a problem when it mainly allows all or most vested interests to get into the act.

67. Wilson, "Social Science & Social Change," op cit.

68. See Theodore Caplow, "Organizational Size," Administrative Science Quarterly, Vol 1 (March, 1957), pp 484-505; and Richard Hall, "Organizational Size, Complexity, and Formalization," American Sociological Review, Vol 33 (1968), pp 903-912 for discussion of the relationship between size, complexity and structure.

69. Kenneth Arrow, Social Choice and Individual Values, 2nd ed. (N.Y.: Wiley, 1963).

70. Jacques Monod, Chance & Necessity (London: Collins, 1972).

71. Steven Scheffrin, "Habermas, Depoliticization & Consumer Theory," Journal of Economic Issues, Vol 12, No. 4 (December 1978), pp 785-797.

72. R.H. Coase, "The Nature of the Firm," Economica, New Series, Vol 4 (1937), pp 386-405.

73. Schelling, op cit; Wilson, "The Paradox of Liberalism," Philosophy of the Social Sciences Vol 10, No. 2 (June 1980), pp 215-226. In the case of collective life it must be clear that outcomes are simply a rationale for process and that the goodness or value must be seen to lie in both the commitment to and the activity of problem-solving. My differences with Popper op cit appertain to the role of reflexivity as an essential moment of human rationality in the world which is essential to this process rather than inimical to it. In effect, what makes thought and scholarship so indispensable in this process is precisely the fact that such activities are not "value free" and are more than simply "value-relevant."

74. See No. 68. Also Conrad Studnicki-Gizbert, "Complexity, Structure and All That" (unpublished paper).

75. Popper, op cit; Wilson, "Capitalism, Science & the Possibility of Political Economy."

76. Alfred Schutz, "The Problem of Rationality in the Social World," in Schutz, Collected Papers, II, Studies in Social Theory (The Hague: Martinus Nijhoff, 1964), pp 64-88 at p. 85. Also see Harold Garfinkel, "The Rational Properties of Scientific & Commonsense Activities," in Garfinkel, Studies in Ethnomethodology (Englewood Cliffs, N.J.: Prentice Hall, 1967), pp 262-283; and Wilson, "Rationality & Decision in Administrative Science," op cit.

77. Schutz, op cit, pp 85-86.

78. Wilson, "Social Science & Social Change," op cit; Wilson, "Anti-Method as a Counter Structure in Social Research Operations: Critique as Subversion of Established Professional Practices" (unpublished paper).

79. Bell op cit; D.L. Meadows, The Limits to Growth (Cambridge, Mass: MIT Press, 1973). This pattern of thinking is nicely reflected in the view of Northern preservationists that in order to safeguard African wildlife all human beings must be kept out of certain "parks" and "reserves." Who could **possibly** have a greater commitment to any conceivable "balance of nature" in a given area than those human beings whose food supply is totally dependent upon it? See Marnham, op cit.

80. See Levy, Modernization: Latecomers & Survivors; and Marnham, op cit.

81. Veblen, op cit; Ayres, op cit.

ADDITIONAL BIBLIOGRAPHY

(Relevant Materials which were not cited in the text)

Adorno, Theodor, "Veblen's Attack on Culture," in Adorno, Prisms (London: Neville Spearman, 1967).

Andreski, Stanislav, Social Sciences as Sorcery (London: Andre Deutsch, 1973).

Becker, Gary, Human Capital (NY: Columbia University Press, 1964).

Becker, Howard, "Whose Side are We On?" Social Problems, Vol. 14 (Winter 1967), pp. 239-247.

Beer, Stafford, Decision & Control (London: Wiley, 1966).

Blackburn, Robin (ed), Ideology in Social Science (London: Fontana/Collins, 1972).

Boulding, Kenneth, The Image: Knowledge in Life & Society (Ann Arbor: University of Michigan Press, 1956).

Churchman, C. West, The Challenge to Reason (NY: McGraw Hill, 1968).

Coase, R.H., "The Market for Goods and the Market for Ideas," American Economic Review, Vol. 64 (May 1974).

Commons, John, The Economics of Collective Action (Madison: University of Wisconsin Press, 1970).

Dewey, John, Human Nature & Conduct (NY: Holt, 1922).

Dreitzel, Hans P., "Social Science & the Problem of Rationality," Politics & Society, Vol. 2, No. 2 (Winter 1972), pp. 165-182.

Elster, Jon, Logic and Society (London: Wiley, 1978).

Gouldner, Alvin, "Anti-Minotaur: The Myth of a Value-Free Sociology," in Sociology on Trial, edited by Maurice Stein & Arthur Vidich (Englewood Cliffs, NJ: Prentice Hall, 1963).

Gouldner, Alvin, "The Sociologist as Partisan: Sociology & the Welfare State," The American Sociologist, Vol. 3, No.2 (May 1968), pp. 103-116.

Habermas, Jürgen, "Toward a Theory of Communicative Competence," in Recent Sociology, No. 2, edited by Hans P. Dreitzel (NY: Macmillan, 1970).

Habermas, Jürgen, Toward a Rational Society (London: Heinemann, 1971).

Habermas, Jürgen, Legitimation Crisis (Boston: Beacon Press, 1975).

Habermas, Jürgen, Communication & The Evolution of Society (Boston: Beacon Press, 1979).

Hesse, Mary, In Defense of Objectivity (London: Proceedings of The British Academy No. 58, 1972).

Jonas, Hans, "The Practical Uses of Theory," in Philosophy of the Social Sciences: A Reader, edited by Maurice Natanson (NY: Random House, 1963).

Knight, Frank, Risk, Uncertainty and Profit (Boston: Houghton Mifflin, 1921).

Knight, Frank, On the History & Method of Economics (Chicago: Univ. of Chicago, 1956).

Kosik, Karel, Dialectics of the Concrete (Dordrecht: Reidel, 1976).

Kotarbinski, Tadeusz, Praxiology (Oxford: Pergamon Press, 1965).

Kroeber, Alfred, Configurations of Culture Growth (Berkeley: University of California, 1944).

Lepley, Roy (ed), Value: A Cooperative Inquiry (Westport, Conn: Greenwood Press 1970, 1949).

Lindblom, Charles and Cohen, David, Usable Knowledge (New Haven: Yale University Press, 1979).

Loring, L. M., Two Kinds of Value (NY: Humanities Press, 1966).

Lynd, Robert, Knowledge for What? (Princeton: University Press, 1940).

Machlup, Fritz, "Are the Social Sciences Really Inferior?" in Philosophy of the Social Sciences: A Reader, edited by Maurice Natanson (NY: Random House, 1964).

Madge, Charles, Society in the Mind (London: Faber and Faber, 1964).

March, James, and Simon, Herbert, Organizations (NY: Wiley, 1958).

Marcuse, Herbert, One Dimensional Man (Boston: Beacon Press, 1964).

Marcuse, Herbert, Negations (Boston: Beacon Press, 1968).

Marx, Karl, The Poverty of Philosophy (NY: International Publishers, 1963).

Marx, Karl, Early Texts, edited by David McClellan (London: Heinemann, 1965).

Marx, Karl, and Engels, Friedrich, The German Ideology (London: Lawrence & Wishart, 1965).

Mattick, Paul, Critique of Marcuse (London: Merlin Press, 1972).

Mills, C. Wright, The Sociological Imagination (NY: Grove Press, 1959).

Pepper, Stephen, A Digest of Purposive Values (Berkeley: University of California Press, 1947).

Pepper, Stephen, The Sources of Value (Berkeley: University of California Press, 1958).

Rex, John, Sociology & the Demystification of the Modern World (London: Routledge, 1973).

Schopenhauer, Arthur, The World as Idea and Representation, 2 Vols (Indian Hills, Colorado: Falcon's Wing Press, 1958).

Simon, Herbert, Models of Man: Social & Rational (NY: Wiley, 1957).

Veblen, Thorstein, The Place of Science in Modern Civilization and Other Essays (Boston: Huebsch, 1919).

Veblen, Thorstein, The Vested Interests & the Common Man (Boston: Huebsch, 1919).

Wiles, Peter, "The Necessity & Impossibility of Political Economy," History and Theory, Vol. 11 (1972), pp 3-14.

Wilson, H.T., "The Significance of 'Instrumental Reason' for the Critical Theory of Society" (unpublished paper).

Wilson, H.T., "Science, Technology & Innovation: The Role of

Commonsense Capacities," **(forthcoming)**

Wittgenstein, Ludwig, On Certainty (Oxford: Blackwell, 1973).

Zipf, George Henry, Human Behaviour and the Principle of Least Effort (Boston: Addison-Wesley, 1949).

Znaniecki, Florian, The Social Role of the Man of Knowledge (NY: Columbia University Press, 1940).

Part II
Societal and Political Perspectives of Value Change

Value Change in the Uncertain 1970's

Ronald Inglehart

ABSTRACT

This article tests the hypothesis that postwar affluence led to an intergenerational shift from Materialist to Post-Materialist values among Western publics, and analyzes the consequences of the economic uncertainty prevailing since 1973. The young emphasize Post-Materialist values more strongly than the old. Time series data indicate that this reflects generational change far more than aging effects, but that the recession of the mid-1970's also produced significant period effects. As Post-Materialists aged, they moved out of the student ghetto and became a predominant influence among young technocrats, contributing to the rise of a "New Class". This group apparently furnishes the ideologues and core support for the Environmentalist, Zero-Growth and Anti-Nuclear Movements.

Survey evidence from the United States, a dozen European countries and Japan indicates that the younger members of these societies are far likelier than older ones to endorse Post-Materialist priorities.[1] Indirect evidence and some time series data support the interpretation that this phenomenon reflects a process of intergenerational value change among the publics of advanced industrial societies.[2] The rise of Post-Materialist values seems to have had a variety of significant political consequences, contributing to the student protest of the late 1960s and early 1970s, among other things. Theoretically, this process of value change is due (in important part) to the exceptionally high levels of economic and physical security that prevailed during the postwar decades.

But in recent years these nations have experienced severe economic uncertainty, as well as a certain erosion of the East - West detente. Taken together with the fact that student protest has disappeared, should we assume that the Post-Materialist phenomenon has dwindled away? A review of cross-national survey evidence gathered during the period 1970-1979 indicates that the distribution of Post-Materialist attitudes has changed in important ways, with the student-age population becoming somewhat less Post-Materialist at the end of the Seventies than it was at the start; but with the general publics of most Western nations actually becoming more Post-Materialist than they were in 1970. Thus, Post-Materialism has become less of a student phenomenon than it was when it first became noisily manifest in the 1960s, but it has achieved a significant penetration into the ranks of young technocrats, professionals and political elites. As a consequence of this, and of the changing macropolitical context, the style of Post-Materialist political behavior has been modified; but, as we will demonstrate in this paper, it remains a major factor in Western politics.

Value change among Western publics is invisible and has gone largely unnoticed. But its consequences manifest themselves in a variety of ways. One example seems to be the growing emphasis on protecting the environment against pollution, highway construction or nuclear power plants. Another consequence is evident in attitudes toward work: it is no longer enough that one earn a good salary--there is increasing emphasis on interesting and meaningful work. Similarly, there is a growing tendency for women to seek opportunities for self-realization outside the traditional sex-role division of labor.

The rise of middle-class political protest in recent years seems to be a further consequence of a shift from Materialist to Post-Materialist value priorities. Normally, one expects (and finds) the highest levels of satisfaction with the established social and political order among relatively prosperous groups. But within the postwar generation, it is among the relatively prosperous strata that one finds the most intense dissatisfaction with the kind of society in which one lives--and the greatest willingness to use unconventional means to bring about change. On closer examination, this paradox becomes intelligible. For insofar as postwar prosperity has led to a gradual shift in value priorities, it has given rise to a Post-Materialist group that evaluates their society by different standards from those prevailing generally--and tends to find that society inadequate. Before presenting empirical evidence concerning the ongoing process of value change among Western publics, let us briefly outline the reasoning that led us to look for indications of such change.[3] We started with two key hypotheses:

1) A Scarcity Hypothesis. An individual's priorities reflect his socioeconomic environment: one places the greatest subjective value on those things that are in relatively short supply.

2) A Socialization Hypothesis. The relationship between socioeconomic environment and value priorities is not one of immediate adjustment: a substantial time lag is involved for, to a large extent, ones basic values reflect the conditions that prevailed during one's pre-adult years.

Both hypotheses are essential to a theory of value change. One of the most pervasive concepts in social science is the notion of a basic personality structure that tends to crystallize by adulthood, with relatively little change thereafter. Early socialization seems to carry greater weight than later socialization. In keeping with this hypothesis, as we will see shortly, we find substantial differences between older and younger groups in their relative emphasis on economic and physical security.[4]

The Scarcity Hypothesis is similar to the principle of diminishing marginal utility, in economic theory. A complementary concept--Abraham Maslow's theory of a need hierarchy underlying human motivation--helped shaped the design of the questionnaire items we used to measure value priorities.[5]

In its simplest form the idea of a need hierarchy would probably command almost universal assent. The fact that unmet physiological needs take priority over social, intellectual or esthetic needs has been demonstrated all too often in human history. Starving people give top priority to obtaining food, and people deprived of water will go to almost any lengths to obtain it. Directly related to physiological survival, a set of "safety" needs exist that seems almost equally basic, except for the fact that starving people will risk their lives in order to obtain food. The rank ordering of human needs becomes less clear as we move beyond those needs directly related to survival. Needs for affiliation seem to be basic and virtually universal, perhaps because human survival depends on being cared for by others as an infant, and in varying degrees may depend on membership in a group even as an adult. But the social needs also include a whole spectrum of goals such as prestige and self-esteem that have only a remote relationship to survival. Accordingly, they play an important role in the behavior of some individuals, but seem relatively minor concerns to others. The hierarchy proposed by Maslow seems plausible, but there is little empirical evidence in support of any detailed ordering among the social needs. What does seem clear, however, is that there is a basic distinction between immediate personal needs for psychological sustenance and safety, on one hand, and the needs for self-expression, intellectual and esthetic satisfaction, on the other hand. The recent economic history of advanced industrial societies has significant implications, in the light of the Scarcity Hypothesis. For these societies, unlike any other large polities in modern history, are not pervaded by almost unversal want. This fact seems to have led to a gradual shift, in which latent needs for belonging, esteem and intellectual and esthetic satisfaction become more prominent. While economic development is conducive to this change, it is not a process of simple economic determinism. Instead, it seems that the influence of economic factors (after rising in the early stages of industrialization) reaches a point of diminishing returns. As a society approaches a state of widespread affluence, there is a gradual shift in the goals and values of its people. The richer you get, the less riches count.

Testing our hypotheses is not easy. To do so experimentally would require that given individuals be deprived of basic human needs, while others' needs were gratified; and that this treatment be continued throughout the subjects' formative years.[6] While theoretically possible, such a laboratory experiment seems unfeasible as well as undesirable. We will utilize instead the natural experiment performed by recent history, interviewing samples of the publics of Western nations and comparing the responses of those who have undergone different formative experiences.

It is difficult to measure basic values directly. But their presence can be inferred from a consistent pattern of emphasis on given types of goals (for present purposes, we are interested in societal goals). Moreover, we were interested in the individual's priorities among desirable goals, not simply whether he considered a given goal good or bad. Accordingly, we asked representative national samples of the publics of several countries to indicate what they personally considered the most important goals, among the following list:

A. Maintain order in the nation
B. Give people more say in the decisions of the government
C. Fight rising prices
D. Protect freedom of speech
E. Maintain a high rate of economic growth
F. Make sure that this country has strong defense forces
G. Give people more say in how things are decided at work and in their community
H. Try to make our cities and countryside more beautiful
I. Maintain a stable economy
J. The Fight against crime
K. Move toward a friendlier, less impersonal society
L. Move toward a society where ideas count more than money

Our earliest survey (in 1970) utilized only the first four of the above items, in the six nations that were then members of the European Community. The full twelve-item battery was first used in 1973 in surveys carried out in the nine-nation European Community and in the United States.[7] Both the four-item battery and the twelve-item battery have been administered in several subsequent cross-national surveys. Items A, C, E, F, I and J above were designed to tap emphasis on economic and physical security ("Materialist" goals); we expected that these items would be given high priority by those who had experienced economic or physical insecurity during their formative years. The remaining items were designed to tap emphasis on various "Post-Materialist" goals, such as self-expression, a sense of belonging, and intellectual and esthetic satisfaction; we expected that they would be more heavily emphasized by those raised under relatively secure and prosperous conditions.

The survey results supported these expectations. In the first place, there was a clear tendency for those who gave top priority to one Materialist goal to give high priority to the other Materialist goals as well. Conversely, the Post-Materialist items tended to be chosen together. Hence we were able to classify our respondents as pure "Materialists" (those whose top priorities were given to Materialist goals exclusively); as pure "Post-Materialists" (those whose top priorities were Post-Materialist items in every case); or as belonging to various Mixed types.

The expected relationships with social background were confirmed strikingly. Within any given age group, those who had been raised in relatively prosperous families were more apt to emphasize Post-Materialist items than those raised in less secure circumstances. And the pattern across age groups showed the expected shift, from Materialist to Post-Materialist emphasis. Figure 1 depicts the pattern observed among the pooled sample of six West European publics interviewed in our earliest survey, in 1970 (only the two "pure" types are shown here: the balance of the sample falls into the various intermediate or "mixed" types). These surveys sampled representative cross-sections of the publics of Great Britain, France, West Germany, Italy, Belgium and the Netherlands. Although interesting cross-national differences were found, the basic pattern is similar in each nation and can be summarized as follows: Among the oldest groups, the Materialists decline and the Post-Materialists increase. A major transition point distinguishes the postwar generation (those aged 15 to 24 years in 1970) from all other age groups. Materialists are still more than twice as numerous as Post-Materialists among the next older group; but as we move across the World War II threshold, the balance shifts, with Post-Materialists becoming more numerous than Materialists. In short, the young--and particularly the postwar generation--are far more likely to emphasize Post-Materialist priorities than the older groups.

Does this pattern reflect intergenerational change or life cycle effects? Is the youngest group markedly more Post-Materialist than all the others because it is the postwar generation--or simply because its members were relatively <u>young</u>

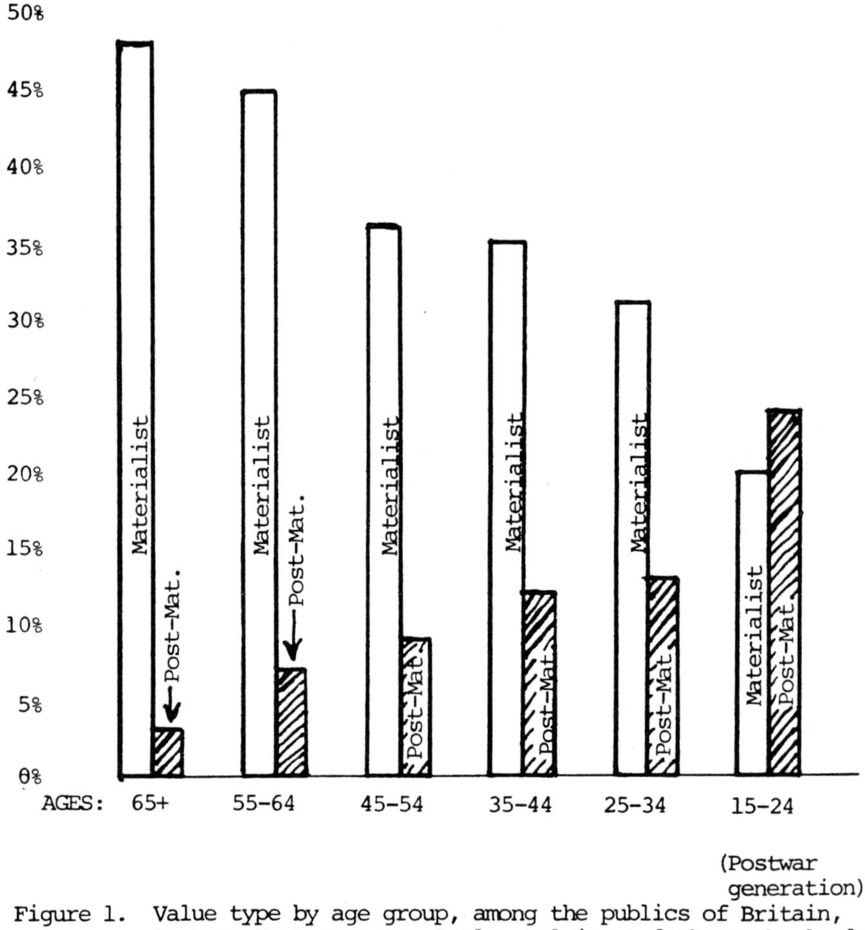

Figure 1. Value type by age group, among the publics of Britain, France, West Germany, Italy, Belgium and The Netherlands in 1970.

at the time? Though we hypothesize the existence of historical change, a life cycle interpretation is by no means implausible. After one reaches twenty-five years of age, one is likely to marry, start a family, begin one's permanent career--all of which might conceivably be conducive to a more Materialistic outlook.

It is impossible to distinguish between life cycle effects and generational effects with data from a single time point. But data are now available from surveys carried out from early 1970 to late 1978. They enable us to determine whether we are dealing with a "postwar generation" effect or an "age 25 and older" effect. They also enable us to learn something about the impact of a major economic recession. For our hypotheses imply that prosperity is conducive to the emergence of Post-Materialist values. Logically, the converse should also hold true: economic decline should lead to an increasing emphasis on Materialist values. And it happens that the most severe economic recession since the 1930s took place during the time period covered by these surveys. The Arab oil embargo of late 1973 was followed by a period of extremely high inflation, rising unemployment and negative economic growth. By 1974 or 1975, consumer confidence indices reached the lowest points on record in many Western countries. Such conditions would, presumably, tend to reverse the trend toward Post-Materialism. The crucial question is, "How quickly?" If our survey items really do tap an individual's basic value priorities, they should be reasonably resistant to short-term forces. Table 1 shows the distribution of value types among the American public, as measured in four national surveys carried out from 1972 through 1976.[8] Though these surveys cover a span of only four years, they include readings taken before and after the Recession of 1974-1975. The results run counter to any expectation that this period of economic adversity brought about the collapse of Post-Materialism among the American public. We observe only very modest shifts from one year to the next. Furthermore, while the pure Materialist type outnumbered the Post-Materialist type by 25 percentage points at the start of this period, the margin had shrunk to only 21 points by the end of 1976: if anything, there seems to have been a slight shift toward Post-Materialism. Further analysis of these data reveals an interesting phenomenon, however: the youngest segment of the American public (those 18 to 24 years of age) was somewhat less Post-Materialist in 1976 than in 1972--a shift that was more than offset by a countervailing shift among the rest of the American public. This finding parallels a similar phenomenon among the publics of Western Europe, for whom the available data base extends over a considerably longer time span, together with a much larger number of cases. Let us examine these data in more detail. Table 2 shows the distribution of value types in the six West European countries for which we have data from as early as 1970.

Table 1

DISTRIBUTION OF VALUE TYPES: United States, 1972-1976*

	CPS, 1972	Gallup, 1973	ISR 1974	CPS, 1976
Materialist	35%	35%	28%	31%
Mixed	55	55	58	59
Post-Materialist	10	10	14	10

*Source: Representative national surveys of the American public, consisting of the CPS post-election surveys of 1972 and 1976, a survey sponsored by the European Community and carried out by the Gallup Organization in April, 1973, and the American component of the Political Action survey, carried out by the ISR in August, 1974.

Table 2

CHANGES OVER TIME IN DISTRIBUTION OF VALUE TYPES*

(Based on four-item index used in 1970, 1973, 1976, and 1978)

	Britain				Germany				France			
	1970	1973	1976	1978	1970	1973	1976	1978	1970	1973	1976	1978
Materialist	36%	32	37	34	43	42	41	38	38	35	41	31
Post-Materialist	8	8	8	8	10	8	11	11	11	12	12	16
	Italy				**Belgium**				**Netherlands**			
	1970	1973	1976	1978	1970	1973	1976	1978	1970	1973	1976	1978
Materialist	35	40	41	44	32	25	30	31	30	31	32	28
Post-Materialist	13	9	11	10	14	14	14	12	17	13	14	22

*Data are from European Community Surveys carried out in February-March, 1970; September, 1973; November, 1976; and May and November, 1978 (the latter two survey results are combined to produce the figures for 1978).

The overall picture is one of remarkable stability. In contrast with the calamitous shifts in consumer confidence observed during this period, our value priorities indicator shows surprisingly little change. In most cases, the shifts from one survey to the next fall within the range of normal sampling error, so that if we had data from only two adjacent points, we could not be sure that any real change was taking place at all. Across this period of nearly nine years however, certain patterns are apparent. During the post-1973 Recession, industrial production reached a low point in 1975 in each of these countries--and we find a modest but significant overall downward trend in the ratio of Post-Materialists to Materialists from 1970 to 1976. By 1978, this trend had been reversed. The pattern varies from nation to nation: Britain and Belgium show virtually no net change from 1970 to 1978. West Germany, France and the Netherlands show substantial shifts in a Post-Materialist direction. For The Netherlands, the figures are -13 for 1970 and -6 for 1978, a seven-point shift toward Post-Materialism; for France, the figures are -27 and -15, a twelve-point shift in the same direction. In Italy, on the other hand, both economic and political conditions remained troubled, and the trend is in the opposite direction: we observe a net shift of twelve points toward the Materialist pole. For the six nations as a whole, however, the dominant trend of 1970-1976 had reversed itself and the proportion of Post-Materialists stood at an all-time high in 1978. Responses to the twelve-item value priorities battery administered in 1973 and 1978 confirms this finding: there was a net shift toward Post-Materialism during this five-year period.[9]

But different age groups responded at different rates to changes in the socioeconomic environment. One of our two key hypotheses holds that the value priorities of younger people are relatively malleable. Accordingly, we would expect them to show more change than older groups. This is precisely what we do find, as Table 3 indicates. Combined results from the six-nations indicate that the overall distribution of value types changed only slightly from 1970 to 1976. But this net result conceals two underlying processes that largely offset each other: on one hand, a long-term process of population replacement; and on the other hand, the influence of current economic conditions. The consequences were that (1) the youngest age group became five points more Materialist and four points less Post-Materialist--a net shift of nine points toward the Materialist pole from 1970 to 1976. No other age group shows such a sizeable shift; as hypothesized, the young seem more affected by current conditions. (2) The next youngest age group moved in the opposite direction! Formerly composed entirely of persons born before 1945, population replacement had brought large numbers of people from the postwar generation into its ranks by 1976.

Table 3

VALUE SHIFTS FROM 1970 TO 1978, BY AGE GROUP

(combined results from the six European nations shown in preceding table)

	1970:		1973:		1976:*		1978:**	
Ages	Mat.	Post-Mat.	Mat.	Post-Mat.	Mat.	Post-Mat.	Mat.	Post-Mat.
15 - 24	20%	24%	21%	20%	25%	20%	23%	23%
25 - 34	31	13	28	13	29	16	25	18
35 - 44	35	12	35	9	35	11	37	12
45 - 54	36	9	39	7	39	8	38	10
55 - 64	45	7	43	6	47	6	40	9
65 and over	48	3	45	4	52	5	48	6
Total:	35	12	34	10	37	12	34	14
Percent Difference Index:	-23		-24		-25		-20	

* Barometer 6 results.

** Barometer 9 + Barometer 10 combined.

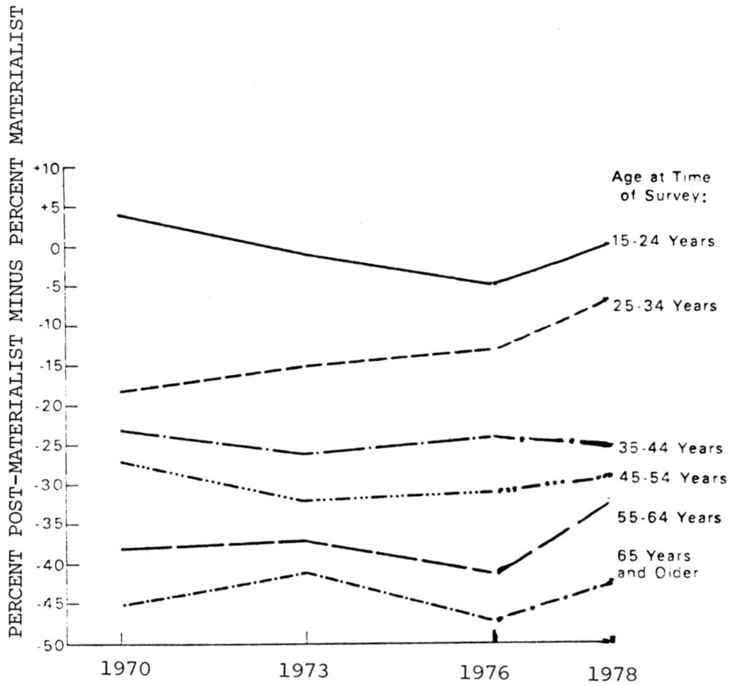

Figure 2. Change in Value Priorities, 1970-1978: Age Group Comparison.

Based on results from combined six-nation sample.

Accordingly, the 25 to 34 year old age group shows a net shift of five points toward the Post-Materialist pole. The four older groups were relatively unchanged by the recession. Thus, from 1970 to 1976, the process of population replacement largely offset the short-term effects of the recession. From 1976 to 1978, the two processes reinforced each other: the two youngest age groups both show an upward shift, which largely accounts for the overall increase in Post-Materialist emphasis in these six nations.

Figure 2 shows these value shifts in graphic form. It reveals a phenomenon of considerable theoretical significance. In 1970, by far the largest gap lies between the 15 to 24 year old age group and those 25 to 34. By itself, this finding might well be interpreted as reflecting life-cycle effects: it is only natural to "settle down" to a Materialist outlook as one passes through this stage of the life-cycle, it might be argued. But as Figure 2 demonstrates, by 1978 the largest gap fell between the 25 to 34 year old group and those 35 to 44 years old: the two youngest groups had become relatively close. Among the 15 to 24 year old group in 1978, the ratio of Post-Materialists to Materialists had not regained its 1970 level. But among the 25 to 34 year old group, the balance had shifted dramatically: in 1970 Materialists were two and one-third more numerous. In 1970 one could, with some oversimplification, speak of a "generation gap" that mainly distinguished between students and members of the adult work force. By the late 1970s, this gap had dwindled in importance; the most important distinction lay between those in their mid-thirties or younger, and those who were approaching middle age. It is almost impossible to reconcile this change of pattern with a life-cycle interpretation--but it fits perfectly with our emphasis on the distinctive experiences of the postwar generation. For, by 1978, both of the two youngest groups were composed almost entirely of people born in 1945 or after. During the years from early 1970 to late 1978, the World War II watershed had shifted from a point between ages 24 and 25, to one between ages 33 and 34.

For a more precise illustration of this point, let us turn to Figure 3, which shows the results of an age-cohort analysis, based on one's year of birth, rather than one's age at the time of the given survey. Here, the relative volatility of the youngest group is again apparent--but at all four points in time, the largest gap remains that between those born before or during World War II, and the postwar cohort. World War II seems to have established an enduring watershed that applies to progressively older groups as time goes by, but retains a fixed relationship to whether one was born before or after 1945. This watershed must be due to historical change, rather than life-cycle effects. Figure 3 also gives

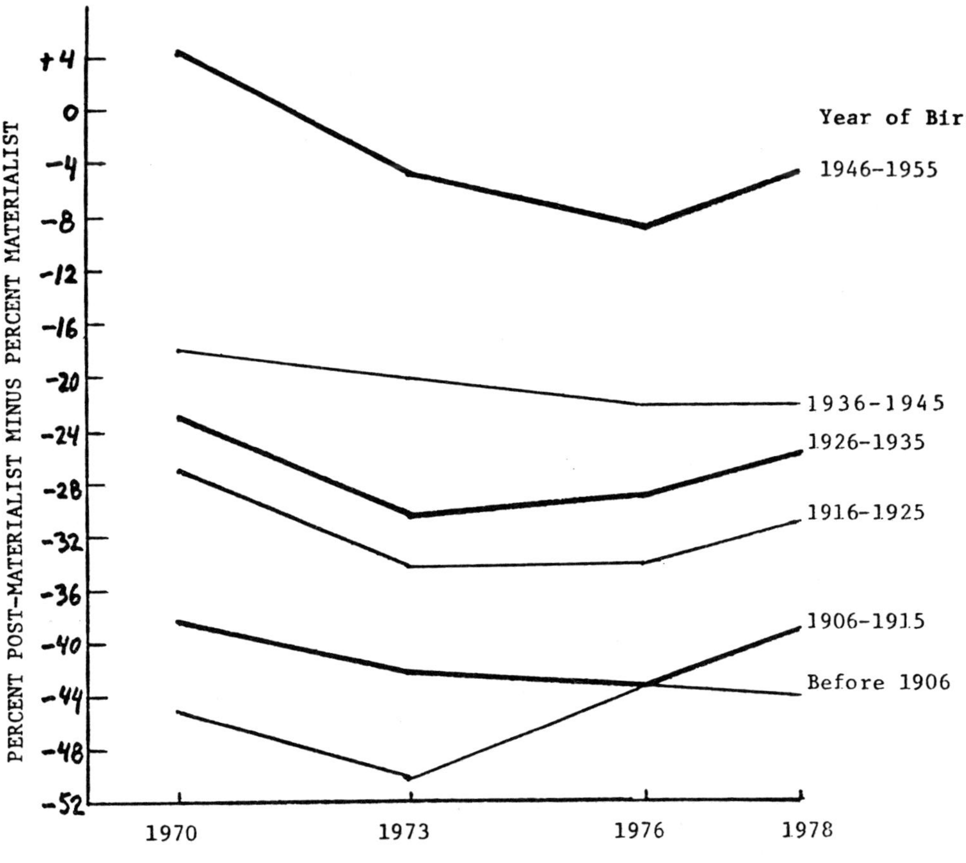

Figure 3. Changes in Value Priorities, 1970-1978: Age-cohort comparison. Based on results from combined six-nation sample.

some indication of the existence of a secondary watershed that may be linked with World War I: at most (though not all) points in time, the second largest gap between age cohorts falls between those born by 1915 and those born afterward. Finally, the data hint at a tendency toward convergence between the two oldest cohorts--a phenomenon that might be expected as the oldest members of the pre-1906 cohort die off.

These data cover a span of less than nine years. While this would be an extensive time series for some purposes, it remains a rather modest one for the analysis of intergenerational change. The pattern suggests that short-term effects are, indeed, present: the recession of the mid-1970s seems to have diminished the ratio of Post-Materialists to Materialists among the youngest age cohort. But as economic recovery took place, an upward trend was visible, with short-term effects and population replacement working in the same direction.

We cannot predict the economic future of Western Europe. But other things being equal, it seems likely that as younger, relatively Post-Materialist cohorts replace older, more Materialist ones in the adult population, one might expect increasing emphasis on Post-Materialist priorities among West European publics. Already, the process of population replacement seems to have changed the nature of the Post-Materialist phenomenon, from one linked distinctively with youth, to one penetrating well into the age-group in their thirties.

Thus the period around 1970 was an era of "Student Protest." At that point in time, the pure Post-Materialist type had attained numerical parity with the Materialists among the 15 to 24 year old group; and because of their disproportionate concentration among the more affluent and better educated, Post-Materialists were the dominant influence in the student milieu (and almost nowhere else in society). A decade later, the student-age population was somewhat less Post-Materialist than it had been in 1970--but, through the process of population replacement, all of the <u>older</u> groups (and the population as a whole) were <u>more</u> so. Post-Materialists had become especially numerous among the ranks of young professionals, journalists, civil servants, Congressional staffers and young technocrats in general. Among those elected to the European Parliament in June, 1979, Materialists outweighed Post-Materialists by only a few percentage points.[10] In the European Community as a whole, among professionals under 40 years of age, Post-Materialists were slightly more numerous than Materialists.[11] Today, social analysts no longer speak of student protest but of "The New Class"-- with reference to a technocratic elite that seems to be reshaping society.[12] The "New Class" tends to be explained in terms of its high information and educational levels--attributes that it undoubtedly does possess. But this explanation seems incomplete: highly educated groups have existed for a long time, but in the past have tended to be politically conservative. The New Class of the 1980s seems distinctive not only in how much it knows, but in what it wants and values. Quite frequently, its members seem interested in fundamental changes in the prevailing model of advanced industrial society.

Values are, theoretically, a relatively stable, deep-rooted and central part of one's worldview. We have just seen some evidence that the Materialist/Post-Materialist items tap a reasonably enduring aspect of a given age-group's outlook. How central are they?

They have a surprisingly widespread set of attitudinal ramifications, relating to a broad range of responses, many of which have no obvious similarity in terms of face content. When asked what is the most important to them in a job, for example, the vast majority of Materialists give top priority to "a good salary" or "no risk of unemployment;" among Post-Materialists, an overwhelming majority emphasize "a feeling of accomplishment" or "working with people you like."[13] If the proportion of Post-Materialists in the work force has been rising in recent decades, the motivating power of salary alone has probably been declining. The growing concern with reorganizing work in ways that provide a greater sense of personal achievement seems well-founded.

Post-Materialist values are associated with a distinctive outlook in a variety of other ways. Despite their relatively favored economic status, Post-Materialists are likelier than Materialists to perceive poverty around themselves--and more apt to blame it on society than on the individual.[14] Furthermore, Post-Materialists are likelier to support "trying to even out differences in wealth between people: "in both Western Europe and the United States, Post-Materialists are roughly twice as likely to rate this goal as "very important" as are the Materialists.[15] (The various intermediate types fall between the two pure types here, as with virtually every attitude measured.) This support for egalitarianism seems to reflect concerns for social justice or solidarity, rather than direct economic self-interest, since Post-Materialists tend to have incomes well above average and would have relatively much to lose through a more even distribution of wealth. The emphasis on equality extends to sexual equality as well: Post-Materialists (males as well as females) are far likelier than Materialists to emphasize "guaranteeing equal rights for men and women."[16]

Furthermore, Post-Materialists are relatively apt to have a cosmopolitan, rather than parochial, sense of identity. It seems that as long as an individual is preoccupied with needs for sustenance and safety, he or she has little energy available to deal with more distant concerns. The Post-Materialists, on the other hand, are relatively free to identify with remote political objects.

Partly for this reason, we would expect Post-Materialists to have a relatively high potential for political action--particularly of an elite-challenging kind.

The reasons why we expect this can be summarized as follows:

1. Materialists tend to be preoccupied with satisfying immediate physiological needs and their derivitaves; Post-Materialists feel relatively secure about these needs and have a greater amount of psychic energy to invest in more remote concerns. This may lead to involvement in a wide variety of activities, among which politics is one possibility.

2. As a recently-emerging minority whose highest priorities tend to be slighted, Post-Materialists are apt to be relatively disaffected with the established order and relatively supportive of social change.

3. The disruption and property damage that sometimes result from unconventional political action seem less negative to Post-Materialists, since they threaten things they value less than Materialists do.

In short, the Post-Materialists have a larger amount of psychic energy available for politics; they are less supportive of the established social order; and subjectively, they have less to lose from unconventional political action than Materialists. But while the first point might be conducive to higher rates of participation in any kind of political action, the second and third points are particularly conducive to unconventional political action, or political protest. We would, therefore, expect Post-Materialist values to give some impetus to conventional participation but to have their greatest impact on unconventional political action.

One of our central theses is that Post-Materialists tend to be relatively change-oriented and consequently ready to engage in unconventional political protest. Is this empirically true?

A first indicator of Post-Materialist support for change is the fact that--despite their relatively high socioeconomic status--they tend to vote for the political parties of the Left. In the nine European Community countries as a whole, 43 percent of the Materialists voted for the Left in the late 1970s, as compared with 53 percent of the mixed type and 71 percent of the Post-Materialists.[17] The strength of this relationship varies considerably from one national setting to another, reflecting the fact that the positions taken by given candidates and parties at given times can drastically affect the electoral relevance of Materialist or Post-Materialist values. Interesting though it is, voting behavior can provide only an indirect test of our hypothesis that Post-Materialists tend to be less supportive than Materialists of the social and political arrangements that prevail in their societies.

A more direct measure of whether one is relatively favorable to social change (regardless of political party loyalties and the stance taken by party elites in a given setting) has been standard feature of the European Community surveys for the past several years. Representative national samples of the publics of the European Community countries have been asked:

"On this card are three basic kinds of attitudes toward the society we live in. Please choose the one which best describes your opinion.

1. The entire way our society is organized must be radically changed by revolutionary action.

2. Our society must be gradually improved by reforms.

3. Our present society must be valiantly defended against all subversive forces."

These three alternatives might be described, in short, as Revolutionary, Reformists and Conservative (or even Reactionary). In the current West European context, Revolutionaries are a distinct minority, constituting about 7 percent of those answering the question in the seven European Community surveys carried out from 1976 through 1979 (weighted according to the population of each country).[18] The proportion is appreciably larger in France and Italy (where Revolutionaries comprised 11 percent and 10 percent of the population, respectively) and notably smaller in West Germany (where the option was endorsed by only 2 percent). The Conservative option is also a minority position, though a stronger one, being supported by 30 percent of the European Community public as a whole (and 48 percent of the German public) in the late 1970s.

Table 4

ATTITUDE TOWARD SOCIAL CHANGE BY VALUE TYPE
AMONG WEST EUROPEAN PUBLICS, 1976-1979*

	Respondent supports:			
	Revolutionary Change	Gradual Reform	Defending Present Society	N
Value type:				
Materialist	4%	57%	38%	(18,292)
Mixed	8	62	30	(26,694)
Post-Materialist	17	69	14	(6,098)

*Percentages are based on all respondents choosing one of the three options, among the publics of the nine European Community countries, weighted according to size of each nation's population. Based on pooled data from Euro-Barometer surveys from 1976 through 1979 (Barometers 6 through 12).

The Reformists constitute a clear majority--63 percent of those responding--in the European Community as a whole. And this holds true for all value types: it would be a gross error to equate Post-Materialists with Revolutionaries.

Nevertheless, there is a pronounced difference between the attitudes of Materialists and Post-Materialists toward social change. Table 4 shows the relationship between value type and attitudes toward social change, among the publics of the European Community as a whole. Among the Materialist type only 4 percent endorse the Revolutionary option; nearly ten times as many (38 percent) support the Conservative option. Among the Post-Materialists, by contrast, the Revolutionary option draws <u>more</u> support than the Conservative one. In both cases, the Reformist option is the leading choice--but the Post-Materialists are only about one-third as likely to hold Conservative views as are Materialists, and about four times as apt to seek radical social change.

Very well. Despite their relatively advantaged social status, Post-Materialists tend to support the parties of the Left--and they do so, quite often, even when they come from families that favored the Right.[19] Moreover, they are markedly more favorable to Social Change than are other value types.

But does this go any deeper than lip service? Just how far are the Post-Materialists willing to go on behalf of their values?

A central feature of an eight-nation survey carried out during 1974-1976 was a scale designed to measure an individual's potential for participation in political protest activities.[20] This scale is based on the respondent's expression of approval and readiness to carry out acts ranging from petitions (at the low end of the scale) to occupation of buildings and disruption of traffic. Tested and applied in eight countries, the scale has remarkably good technical characteristics and seem to measure, in a straightforward and meaningful way, just how far the individual is willing to go in order to carry out his or her beliefs.

Do the Post-Materialists show a relatively high propensity for unconventional political activities as measured by the Protest Potential Scale?

On one hand, it has been argued that Post-Materialist responses tap nothing more than a form of radical chic.[21] If so, the answer would presumably be no.

But if our typology reflects basic differences in societal priorities, the answer should be yes. For the Post-Materialists not only tend to emphasize goals at variance with those that have shaped their societies, but are theoretically less constrained than the rest of the population by concerns to maintain economic and physical security. Conversely, the Materialists should be relatively at home with the existing social pattern, and substantially more alarmed by activities that seem to disrupt the normal functioning of advanced industrial society.

The Protest Potential Scale was developed, in part, to test whether Post-Materialist values go no deeper than lip service to currently fashionable goals, or whether they have behavioral implications. The answer is unequivocal.

Table 5 shows the relationship between Protest Potential and value type in each of the nations surveyed in 1974. We have selected a score of "3" as the cutting off point for this table. Those scoring below this level are (at most) willing to circulate petitions or march in peaceful demonstrations: a good many of them are not willing to do anything at all. Thos scoring "3" or higher are willing to go still farther--to take part in rent strikes, illegal occupation of buildings or to block traffic.

As Table 5 makes clear, one's value priorities have a strong relationship with one's level of Protest Potential. In Great Britain (where the relationship is weakest), only 21 percent of the Materialists are willing to engage in boycotts or go beyond them in protest against some form of perceived political injustice; among the Post-Materialists, 55 percent are willing to do so. The linkage between values and Protest Potential is particularly strong in The Netherlands, where we find only 27 percent of the Materialists ranking high on Protest Potential--as compared with 74 percent of the Post-Materialists. In all countries for which we have data, the Post-Materialists are far readier to engage in political protest than the Materialists.

In multivariate analyses controlling for the effects of age, education, income, and one's level of ideological sophistication, a strong relationship persists between Post-Materialist values and Protest Potential.[22] A relatively high potential to use unconventional and mildly disruptive techniques in order to intervene in the political process, seems to be

Table 5

PROTEST POTENTIAL BY VALUE TYPE*

	The Netherlands	Britain	United States	Germany	Austria	Italy	Switzerland	Finland
Materialist	27%	21%	38%	23%	17%	20%	17%	20%
Mixed (Materialist)	38	30	46	30	19	34	23	30
Mixed (Post-Materialist)	47	33	50	43	24	42	32	38
Post-Materialist	74	55	72	74	48	69	61	58
gamma:	.342	.200	.234	.323	.244	.354	.321	.238

* Percentage scoring "3" or higher on protest potential scale. For details of index construction and a report of findings from five of these eight nations, see Samuel H. Barnes, Max Kaase, et al., Political Action (Beverly Hills: Sage, 1979).

closely linked with the Post-Materialist outlook, and not merely a spurious correlate, resulting from the fact that Post-Materialists tend to be young and well-educated.

But this seems to involve a paradox. On one hand, we have seen that the economic uncertainty of the 1970s did not cause Post-Materialist to disappear--on the contrary, its ranks seem to have increased slightly, in most Western countries. On the other hand, the dramatic political protest movements of the late sixties and early seventies have long since disappeared: why did this happen, if a relatively high protest potential characterizes the Post-Materialists?

The main answer is that people don't protest in a social vacuum. The Post-Materialists did not protest for the sake of protesting--they responded to specific issues, above all the war in Indochina. The fact that there no longer is a war in Indochina (or, at least, no American war) makes a big difference. Almost nothing can compare with war, in terms of violence, drama and human tragedy, and nothing on the current scene can command sustained mass attention in the way the war did. In the absence of any political cause fully comparable to the war in Vietnam, it is only natural that much of the attention and energies of Post-Materialists have been diverted into other channels. For some, this means seeking self-actualization through development of the inner self, rather than through social action. For those who remain politically oriented, such a turning inward seems like desertion of the Cause; in bitter disappointemnt at their contrast with the relatively politicized youth of a decade ago, the current crop of youth has been characterized as "The Me Generation." There is some truth and a large measure of misapprehension in this view: as we have seem, at the close of the 1970s, the 15 to 24 year old group was somewhat more Materialistic than their counterparts of 1970 had been--but the difference was marginal. If their potential for political protest remained only a potential in most cases, it was because none of the current causes were as compelling as the causes of the earlier decade. Nevertheless, causes did exist, and the most important new movements on the current scene--the Environmentalist Movement and the anti-nuclear movement--seem rooted in Post-Materialist values. Both of these movements involve questions of whether one gives top priority to economic growth, or to the quality of the environment and the quality of life more generally. Until quite recently, it was taken as self-evident that economic growth was inherently good; though there were sharp disapreements on how its benefits should be allocated, the pro-growth consensus embraced both labor and management, capitalist and communist. Only quite recently has this assumption been called into question, with the Environmentalist Movement in general holding that economic growth does not always justify the impact it makes on the environment; and with important segments of the movement arguing that economic growth is now becoming either undesirable, or even impossible because of the scarcity of natural resources. Environmental protection need not inevitably raise questions of environmental quality versus economic growth, but insofar as this tradeoff is involved, it pits Post-Materialist priorities squarely against Materialist ones. Thus in 1977, among the Materialists in the European Community publics, 36 percent expressed a "very high opinion" of the Environmentalist Movement--while 53 percent of the Post-Materialists did so; and while 3 percent of the former claimed to be members of some environmentalist group, 7 percent of the Post-Materialists did so.

One of the most significant features of the current energy crisis is the fact that the Environmentalist Movement has not collapsed, in the face of severe strains on Western economies due to skyrocketing energy costs that exacerbate inflation while simultaneously draining away immense sums of capital and thereby hindering investment that might lead to fuller employment. In 1980, the United States is expected to transfer $90 billion to the OPEC nations for imported oil (as compared with less than $4 billion a decade earlier); for West Germany, the capital outflow in 1980 will be around $50 billion. Despite this crisis, environmental protection standards have not been relaxed; on the whole, they have become considerably more stringent since the energy crisis first manifested itself in 1973. Similarly, opposition to nuclear power plants has not died away--on the contrary, it has brought the development of nuclear power to a halt in the United States and several other countries.

Nuclear power could conceivably play a major role in meeting this country's energy needs during the next few decades; it is equally conceivable that it could play almost no role at all. From 1968 to 1978, production of electricity from nuclear power rose from providing less than 1 percent to providing nearly 13 percent of all electricity consumed in the United States. Since 1978 this development has ceased: in 1979 nuclear sources produced only 11 percent of U.S. electrical output. In some other settings (West Germany and Austria, for example) development of nuclear power is also at a standstill; but in others, it is moving ahead rapidly. By 1985, nuclear sources will supply about 35 percent of Sweden's electricity and over half of France's electrical needs. The difference in outcomes reflects technical problems to some extent, but it is primarily a political question. In both Sweden and Austria, present policy was decided by national referenda; and in all cases, public pressures play a crucial role.

Like the Environmentalist Movement, the struggle over nuclear power reflects a clash of worldviews. For Materialists, the use of nuclear energy is likely to seem desirable insofar as it seems linked with economic growth and full employment. Among Post-Materialists, nuclear power is apt to be rejected not only because of its potential dangers but because it seems linked with big business, big science and big government--bureaucratic organizations that are evaluated negatively because they are inherently impersonal and hierarchical, minimizing individual self-expression and one's sense of meaningful human contact. Tables 6 and 7 show the relationship between value type and support for developing nuclear energy among candidates for the European Parliament.[23] In every case, Materialists are far more favorable to developing nuclear energy than are the Post-Materialists: among the nine publics sampled, a majority of the Materialists support the development of nuclear power in every country but one; while a majority of the Post-Materialists oppose it in every country but one. The differences are even more pronounced at the elite level, where a majority of Materialists supports nuclear power and a majority of Post-Materialists opposes it in every one of the nine E.C. countries. The percentage spread between Materialists and Post-Materialists is at least 46 points in every country but one--Italy, which is an exceptional case, in that nuclear power has not become a major political issue.

One of the most striking features of the nuclear power controversy is the extent to which well-informed members of the public, and even competent experts, when exposed to the same body of information, draw totally different conclusions from it.[24] We believe that this phenomenon reflects a process of cognitive screening in which given facts are retained and weighted in accordance with the individual's basic values. Though support or opposition to nuclear power is usually justified in terms of objective costs, benefits and risks, a key factor underlying it is a clash of competing worldviews. Materialists take it for granted that a high level of economic growth is crucial and weigh the costs and risks of nuclear energy against the costs and risks of alternative energy sources. Post-Materialists take economic security for granted; or tend to weigh the costs and risks of nuclear power against various no-cost alternatives--among which, reduced material consumption seems not only acceptable but, in some respects, actually desirable: insofar as it seems to lead to a more decentralized, less impersonal society that allows freer play for individual self-expression, it has a very powerful image. Thus, the debate over nuclear power is based on differing visions of the good society, with pronuclear and antinuclear advocates talking past each other because their arguments are implicitly based on different value priorities. To a considerable degree, each side seems insensitive to the values of the other.

Table 6

SUPPORT FOR DEVELOPMENT OF NUCLEAR POWER
AMONG WEST EUROPEAN PUBLICS, BY VALUE TYPE*

(Percentage "agree" or "agree strongly")

Question: "Could you tell me whether you agree or disagree with each of the following proposals?" . . ."Nuclear Energy should be developed to meet future energy needs"

	Britain	France	Germany	Belgium	Italy	Luxem-bourg	Ireland	Nether-lands	Denmark
Materialist	79%	77%	69%	56%	57%	53%	52%	59%	41%
Mixed	75	64	58	57	47	59	45	36	40
Post-Materialist	52	44	46	46	45	36	35	27	20

*Source: European Community survey (Barometer 11) carried out in April-May, 1979.

Table 7

SUPPORT FOR DEVELOPING NUCLEAR POWER

AMONG CANDIDATES TO EUROPEAN PARLIAMENT, BY VALUE TYPE*

(Percentage "agree" or "agree strongly")

	France	Germany	Britain	Italy	Belgium	Ireland	Luxem-bourg	Denmark	Nether-lands
Materialist	95%	98%	77%	55%	100%	54%	71%	86%	64%
Mixed	85	65	54	54	40	29	25	14	35
Post-Materialist	49	40	24	44	24	0	0	9	5

*Source: European Elections Study survey of 742 candidates for the European Parliament, interviewed in Spring, 1979; respondents' value type is based on top two priorities selected from the twelve-item Materialist/Post-Materialist battery. The question about nuclear energy included an "In-between" option (not proposed to the mass publics) that was selected by from 6 to 26 percent of given national samples: only in the Netherlands, Denmark and Luxembourg were pluralities opposed to developing nuclear energy.

Thus, despite the passing of student protest, the clash between Materialist and Post-Materialist worldviews remains a major component of political conflict. This clash no longer manifests itself primarily as student protest because the Post-Materialists are no longer primarily students: the student-age group has become somewhat less Post-Materialist, on one hand; and on the other, Post-Materialists have attained influential positions in the professions, government and the mass media. It seems unlikely that they have taken over the command posts of Western society, but they do seem to have achieved an impressive penetration among the younger elites. In our sample of candidates to the European Parliament, Post-Materialists are almost as numerous as Materialists (with mixed types holding the balance of power); among those less than 50 years of age, Post-Materialists substantially outweigh Materialists. Insofar as the European Parliament can be viewed as a sampling of the West European political class, Post-Materialists has become a major factor among the elites.

NOTES

1. See Ronald Inglehart, The Silent Revolution: Changing Values and Political Styles among Western Publics (Princeton: Princeton University Press, 1977); Nobutska Ike, "Economic Growth and Intergenerational Change in Japan," American Political Science Review 67, 4 (December, 1973), 1194-1203; Alan Marsh, "The 'Silent Revolution,' Value Priorities and the Quality of Life in Britain," American Political Science Review 69, 1 (March, 1975), 21-30; Peter Kmieciak, Wertstrukturen und Wertwandel in der Bundesrepublic Deutschland (Göttingen: Schwartz Verlag, 1976); Kendall Baker, Russell Dalton and Kai Hildebrandt, Germany Transformed (Cambridge: Harvard University Press, forthcoming); Helmut Klages and Peter Kmieciak (eds), Wertwandel und Gesellschaftlicher Wandel (Frankfurt: Campus Verlag, 1979); and Max Kaase and Hans Klingemann, "Sozialstruktur, Wertorientierung und Parteiensysteme: Zum Problem der Interessenvermittlung in Westlichen Demokratien," in Joachim Matthes (ed.), Sozialer Wandel in Westeuropa (Frankfurt: Campus Verlag, 1979).

2. See Inglehart op. cit., Chapters 2 and 3; of Russell Dalton, Was There a Revolution? A Note on Generational versus Life Cycle Explanations of Value Differences," Comparative Political Studies 9, 4 (January, 1977); Inglehart, "Value Priorities and Socioeconomic Change," in Samuel H. Barnes, Max Kaase, et al., Political Action: Mass Participation in Five Western Democracies (Beverly Hills: Sage, 1979); and M. Kent Jennings, Klaus R. Allerbeck and Leopold Rosenmayr, "Generations and Families: General Orientation," in Barnes, Kaase, et al., op cit., and Thomas Herz, "Der Wandel von Wertvorstellungen in Westlichen Industriegesellschaften," Kölner Zeitschrift für Sozialpsychologie 31, 2 (July, 1979), 282-302; and Inglehart, "Zusammenhang zwischen sozioökonomischen Bedingungen und Individuellen Wertprioritäten," Kölner Zeitschrift für Soziologie und Sozialpsychologie 31, 4 (January, 1980).

3. For a fuller presentation of the theoretical framework relating to value change, and a mass of supporting evidence, see Ronald Inglehart, Silent Revolution, op. cit., Chapter 2.

4. The Socialization Hypothesis complements the Scarcity Hypothesis in another significant respect: it provides an explanation for the finding that experimental tests of the need hierarchy model reveal no positive correlation between satisfaction of a given need at time 1 and increased emphasis on the next higher need at time 2. (See Peter Kmieciak, Wertstrukturen und Wertwandel, op cit, pp. 163-65.) For these experiments are based on an implicit assumption of short term changes in an individual's priorities. If, as hypothesized, an individual's basic value priorities are largely fixed by the time he reaches adulthood, we would not expect to find much short-term change of the kind tested for.

5. See Abraham Maslow, Motivation and Personality (New York: Harper and Row, 1954). For political applications of this concept, see James C. Davies, Human Nature and Politics (New York: Wiley, 1963); Amitai

Elzioni, The Active Society (New York: Free Press, 1968); Robert Lane, Political Thinking and Consciousness (Chicago: Markham, 1970); and Jeanne M. Knutson, The Human Basis of the Polity (Chicago: Aldine, 1972).

6. It does seem possible to induce reversion to emphasis on basic biological needs in a relatively short time by inducing severe psychological deprivation. In a relevant experiment, a conscientious objector progressively lost his interest in social welfare and thought about, spoke about and even dreamed about food, after a number of weeks on a semistarvation diet. See Davies, op. cit., p. 13. But it seems easier to force people down the need hierarchy than up it: even a saint continues to need nutrition; whereas a confirmed glutton will not necessarily shift his focus to spiritual concerns, given an ample supply of food: the psychological needs are primary, in this sense.

7. These surveys were sponsored by the Commission of the European Communities, under the direction of Jacques-René Rabier. Data and codebooks are available from the Inter-University Consortium for Political and Social Research, Ann Arbor, Michigan, the Zentralarchiv fur empirische Sozialforschung, Koln, the Belgian Archive for the Social Sciences (BASS) at Louvain-la-Neuve, and other national survey data archives.

8. The values index used here is based on responses to the four-item values battery (which later became a subset of a broader 12-item battery). It consists of items A, B, C, and D above. Those who gave top priority to the two Materialist items (A and C above) were coded as pure Materialists; those whose top priorities consisted of the two Post-Materialist items (B and D above) were coded as pure Post-Materialists; those who chose any other combination of these items were coded as "mixed" types.

9. The pooled results from the nine European Community publics surveyed in September, 1973 and November, 1978 are shown in Table 2A. On the 12-item battery, overall rankings of the six Materialist items declined and emphasis on the five Post-Materialist items increased. A sixth item ("More Beautiful Cities") proved to have neutral polarity. For a dimensional analysis of these items, see Inglehart, Silent Revolution, op. cit., pp. 40-51.

10. This was based on interviews with 742 candidates for seats in the European Parliament (including 62 percent of those who were actually elected). Fieldwork was carried out in Match through May, 1979, and included interviews with the following number of candidates from each country: Belgium, 40; Denmark, 41; Germany, 150; France, 128; Ireland, 26; Italy, 158; Luxembourg, 12; The Netherlands, 47; United Kingdom, 140. For details of fieldwork see Inglehart, Jacques-Rene Rabier, Ian Gordon and Carsten Lehman Sorenson, "Broader Powers for the European Parliament? The Attitudes of Candidates," European Journal of Political Research 8 (1980), 113-32. Weighted in proportion to the number of seats each nation and each party holds in the

Table 2A

GOALS OF WESTERN PUBLICS, 1973-1978

(Percentage choosing given goal as 1st or 2nd most important out of twelve goals, among publics of nine European Community countries)*

Goal:	1973		1978		
Fight rising prices	43%	137%	30%	131%	Materialist goals
Economic growth	25		26		
Fight crime	24		29		
Stable economy	23		21		
Maintain order	17		19		
Strong defense forces	5		6		
More beautiful cities	6		5		Neutral polarity
Less impersonal society	16	57%	19	63%	Post-Materialist goals
More say on job	13		14		
More say in government	11		14		
Protect free speech	11		14		
Society where ideas count	6		5		

*Each national sample is weighted according to population: thus, the pooled sample is representative of the European Community as a whole.

European Parliament, 35 percent of our sample are Materialists, 34 percent are mixed and 32 percent are Post-Materialists. This classification is based on each respondent's top two choices among items A-L above; Materialists are those whose top two priorities are both given to Materialist items (A, C, E, F, I, or J); Post-Materialists are those whose top two priorities are given to items B, D, G, H, K, or L.

11. Based on the cumulative results of the nine-nation European Community Survey of 1973 plus Euro-Barometers 3, 4, 5, 6, 7, 8, 9, 10, 11 and 12 (nine-nation survey carried out from 1975 through 1979). Total N=104,331.

12. The literature on the "New Class" in Western societies has grown rapidly. See Bruce-Briggs, The New Class? (New Brunswick: Transaction Books, 1979).

13. See Inglehart, Silent Revolution, op. cit., pp. 54-57.

14. Based on analysis of data from Euro-Barometer #5 (the May, 1976 European Community survey).

15. See Inglehart, "Value Priorities and Socioeconomic Change," in Barnes, Kaase, et al., op cit.

16. Ibid.

17. Analysis of cumulative data from the nine-nation European Community surveys carried out from 1973 through 1979.

18. Analysis of cumulative data from Euro-Barometers 6 through 12.

19. See Inglehart, "Political Action: The Impact of Values, Cognitive Level and Social Background," in Barnes, Kaase, et al., op cit., pp. 348-350.

20. For details concerning fieldwork in these surveys, and a report of findings see Barnes, Kaase, et al., op. cit., pp. 22-23 and 589-91.

21. See Alan Marsh, "The 'Silent Revolution,' Value Priorities," op. cit., In this critique of the value-change hypothesis, Marsh argues that the Post-Materialists' endorsement of social change is a shallow lip-service to currently-fashionable goals, and unrelated to their personal values--which are event more acquisitive than those of the Materialists: they seek "liberty and equality for the society, and income and security for themselves." More recently, Marsh tests this hypothesis by measuring the personal values, as well as the societal goals of a sample of the British public. He finds a correlation of +.22 between personal Post-Materialism and societal Post-Materialism. Though he describes the correlation as "only" .22, the crucial fact is that it is positive, not negative as had been hypothesized. See Marsh, Protest and Political Consciousness (Beverly Hills: Sage, 1977), pp. 177-92. The strong relationship between Post-Materialism and the Protest Potential Scale (which Marsh played a leading role in devel-

oping) provides powerful additional evidence that more than lip service is involved.

22. See Inglehart, "Political Action," in Barnes, Kaase, et al., _op_. _cit_.

23. Data from survey cited in footnote 10.

24. For examples, see Ford Foundation Energy Policy Project, A Time to Choose: America's Energy Future (Cambridge, Mass.: Ballinger, 1974), "Advisory Board Comments;" and National Academy of Sciences, _Energy in Transition_, 1985-2010 (San Francisco: Freeman, 1980).

Social Change and the Political Culture of Problem-Posing in Advanced Industrial Societies: The Case of Canada

David V. J. Bell

ABSTRACT

In order to identify forms of social change politically relevant to advanced industrial societies, this paper redefines social change as "problem posing". It then discusses the relevance of political culture to the recognition and "management" of perceived problems by political elites, academics and the general public. The paper concludes with a brief outline of six problems facing contemporary Canada: national integration, the North, identity and cultural survival, ethnic diversity and conflict, economic inequality, and political participation. These problems are the subject of a series of analytical volumes authored by several scholars under the general editorship of David V. J. Bell and Edgar J. Dosman.

INTRODUCTION

Governments are management systems par excellence. Faced with complex demands and expectations arising both in the environment of the political system and increasingly from within the growing bureaucracy of government itself, governmental institutions engage in classic management behaviors: identifying priorities; devising programs and policies that allocate and re-allocate scarce monetary, material, and human resources; and assessing the effectiveness of these programs in light of policy priorities.[1]

Of course governments do more than merely "manage" the tensions and conflicts arising in society. Governments must attend to the need to "legitimize" their actions, and as a result frequently engage in symbol manipulation that has little connection with the objective situation to which it purportedly is addressed.[2] Yet even this activity can be regarded as a form of political management, different only in degree from the kind of public relations efforts mounted by private corporations. Indeed the management metaphor is peculiarly appropriate to the concerns of this paper, which attempts to investigate how both social change and value change affect the pattern of political demands and expections, thereby in turn affecting the way in which governments "manage" the problems of advanced industrial societies. The paper modifies the concepts of social change and political culture to adapt them to these concerns, and concludes with an overview of a range of social problems that currently challenge the management capabilities of the Canadian political system.

THE CONCEPT OF SOCIAL CHANGE IN POLITICAL SCIENCE[3]

Political scientists have found the concept of social change very difficult to define. In a review of the literature on "Violence and Social Change" published in 1968, Henry Bienen confesses at the outset that

> Every modifier of change except 'worldwide' creates difficulties for me because I admit to being uncertain about what constitutes rapid, fundamental change; thus obviously I am in some difficulty over what change means, lacking criteria for specifying degrees of change. It is one thing to be able to differentiate between an avalanche and a snowball and another to be able to distinguish in the realm of social change without committing a host of fallacies ... (Bienen, 1968: 2-3).

Faced with so challenging a task of conceptual clarification, Bienen chooses to drop the concept entirely, and substitute in its place the term modernization. Other political scientists have adopted a similar strategy. Holt and Turner (1970: 151) find the concept a useful common ground for students of political development who otherwise disagree. Despite terminological disputes on other matters, according to Holt and Turner "[students of development] all deal ... explicitly or implicitly... with the phenomenon of social change." Similarly Apter (1970: 153) insists that "modernization is a form of social change." But neither Apter, nor Holt and Turner, bother to define what the generic term social change actually means.

Equating social change with modernization yields unsatisfactory results, particularly for our purposes, because it leads to the curious conclusion that fully modernized societies cease to experience social change. This point can be illustrated with reference to Karl Deutsch's brilliant work on social mobilization. Focussing on the transitional processes that break down traditional loyalties, values, etc., and permit or encourage adoption of "modern" outlooks, Deutsch (1961) defines social mobilization as a complex of sub-processes including urbanization, literacy, education, exposure to modern mass media, economic development and growth, and secularization. Political consequences of social mobilization involve a widening of the "politically relevant stratum" of the population and an expansion of the scope and effectiveness of governmental activities. The concept of social mobilization, therefore, offers an analytic breakdown into component parts of "the forces of modernization." It shares the nine attributes of modernization identified by Huntington (1971: 288-290): The process as a whole is "revolutionary" (i.e. it involves "radical and total change"), "complex," "systemic," "global," "lengthy," "phased," "homogenizing," "irreversible," and "progressive." To the extent that the dichotomy between tradition and modernity is valid,[4] the concept of social mobilization provides a useful lens through which to study how the transition takes place. Deutsch even describes for each of the subprocesses thresholds of "significance" and of "criticality".

But how can one conceptualize social change in societies that have long since passed Deutxch's critical thresholds?[5] How relevant is the concept of social mobilization for analyzing social change in an advanced industrial society? After modernization, what? Precisely this kind of question led to the appearance of what Huntington calls "modernization revisionism," best exemplified in the work of Daniel Bell and other theorists of Post Industrial Society.

SOCIAL CHANGE AS PROBLEM-POSING

For a society like Canada which passed the critical thresholds of social mobilization half a century ago, concepts of social change that emerge from the literature on modernization have very limited relevance. The processes described by these concepts may have ceased entirely (e.g., increases in the rate of literacy), assumed less significance (e.g., urbanization) or been eclipsed by other novel processes. Efforts to understand these "post modern" changes - and the kind of society they produce - include works as diverse as the economist John Kenneth Galbraith's "New Industrial State", philosopher Herbert Marcuse's "one dimensional society", political scientist Zbigniev Brzezinski's "technetronic age", and sociologist Daniel Bell's "post industrial society". We can recognize the partial validity of all of their concepts in the Canadian context. And yet the concepts fail to capture the uniqueness of recent Canadian history. Canada is an advanced industrial society to be sure, with its "technostructure", disturbing elements of "one dimensionality", abundant evidence of the "new social patterns" characteristic of the "technetronic age", and plenty of indications that our economy, occupational distribution, and decision-making processes typify those found in other "post industrial societies". All of these tendencies have emerged and gained strength in the past three decades. But many other important social changes have occurred as well.

One way to get an intellectual handle on this wider range of issues is to borrow from Daniel Bell an approach to social change as problem-posing. Bell tells us that "changes in social structure [which he defines as "the structure of roles designed to coordinate the actions of individuals to achieve specific ends"] pose 'management' problems for the political system Bell, 1973: 13). This approach allows us to pick out politically important patterns of social change from the swirling confusion of universal Heraclitean flux, provided that we develop an acceptable methodology for identifying political "problems".

Unfortunately, Daniel Bell offers little theoretical or operational clarificaton of his concept of problem posing. A parallel approach that is more thoroughly explained appears in Sidney Verba's discussion of "Sequences and Development". Verba (1971) begins by characterizing government decision making in terms of five "problem area": penetration, participation, legitimacy, distribution, and identity. Each of these problem areas can become "problematic" if people in society "do not accept the way things are done in relation to that aspect of decision-making" (p. 300) and therefore, make it a political "issue or an arena of conflict".[6] Occasionally issues become so intense that extraordinary responses are necessary. The political elites find that they are unable to respond adequately to the issue through the existing political institutions and processes. Instead, some new institution must be set up. At that point the problem area has generated a "crisis", which Verba defines as

> a situation where a problem arises in one of the problem areas (that is, members of the society are discontented with one of the five aspects of the decision process), and some new institutionalized means of handling problems of that sort is required to satisfy the discontent. (p. 302).

Verba's approach leads to an emphasis on patterns of institutionalization and institutional innovation, thereby linking it to the Parsonian emphasis on structural differentiation as the hallmark of social change. The focus on institutionalization also makes it easier to identify the "salience of any particular problem at some point in time" because the appearance of the new institution constitutes an important "historical trace". But can we relate institutional change to social change? Do crises, in other words, arise as a result of underlying social change? The answer must be equivocal. Verba acknowledges that many crises originate "within the governing elite" (p. 302) itself, as a result of "redefinition of political goals on the part of political elites" (p. 305) or in response to "government performance in other areas". (p.304) These intra-governmental crises may or may not result from social change. A third category of crisis is, however, a direct consequence of social change that "increases the relevant population for political activity." (p. 304). In elaborating this point, Verba betrays a bias in favour of the modernization approach, for he illustrates his argument with reference to "processes of social mobilization", which, (as pointed out above) long ago ceased in advanced industrial societies.

This brief critique of Verba's work brings us back full circle. We still require a technique for operationalizing the notion that politically relevant forms of social change pose management problems for the political system. This task involves the following steps.

1. Devising a theoretical and an operational definition of "problem".

2. Examining origins of problems with special emphasis on their relationship to various kinds of social change.

3. Assessing the way in which the political system responds to problems.

DEFINING PROBLEMS: INSIGHTS FROM SOCIOLOGY

Although the term problem (in the sense I am using it) is relatively new to political scientists, it has been a concern of sociologists at least since the founding of the Society for the Study of Social Problems and publication of its journal Social Problems in the early 1940's. Proof that the founding of a journal does not guarantee scientific breakthrough is the widely shared judgement that "A comprehensive theory of social problems does not yet exist...." (Merton and Nisbet 1961:vii; 1966:v; 1971:v. Quoted approvingly by Kitsuse and Spector, 1973:407). Kitsuse and Spector go so far as to claim that the major theoretical approaches to social problems fail either to provide a suitable definition "amenable to empirical investigation" or to justify the addition of the concept of social problem "by distinguishing its content from that of other previous or related categories". (p. 408) They fault Merton's approach because it gives the final say in determining what constitutes a social problem to the sociologist rather than to the member of society. (For a contrary view of Merton see Manis, 1974). The following table outlines Merton's approach.

Table 1: MERTON'S APPROACH TO THE DEFINITION OF SOCIAL PROBLEMS[7]

		SOCIOLOGIST'S DEFINITION	
		Social Problem	No Social Problem
MEMBER'S DEFINITION	Social Problem	(1) "Manifest" Social Problem	(2) "Spurious" Social Problem
	No Social Problem	(3) "Latent" Social Problem	(4) "Normal" Social Condition

Although Kitsuse and Spector find the approach of Fuller and Myers preferalbe to Merton's because it stresses "both the objective conditions and the subjective awareness of social problems", (p. 412) they think it too gives too little weight to public perceptions and awareness.

The question of whether to accept public definitions of social problems or insist on verification of their existence by sociologists, has been extensively debated in the literature. Manis (1974) argues against accepting "vox populi" (the voice of the people) because he feels the people are often wrong, misled, or misinformed. The most useful approach in my view is one that follows Kitsuse and Spector's (1973: 415) suggestion that "the explanation of the 'subjective element' or social problems - the process by which members of groups or societies define a putative condition as a problem - is the distinctive subject matter of the sociology of social problems". But this emphasis on the subjective element should be placed in a wider context which I call the political culture of problem posing; and the "groups" examined should include a cross-section of relevant political actors including the mass media, political elites, professionals, and academics. As political scientists, we are particularly interested in social problems that become political issues and subsequently "pose management problems for the political system". We can carry analysis of[8] these problems forward to study their impact on the political system; and backward to trace their origins in either social change (i.e. changes in the social structure); cultural change (changes in attitudes, values and beliefs); or both. We might diagram the relationship among these variable as follows.

Figure 1: A MODEL OF THE RELATIONSHIP BETWEEN SOCIAL PROBLEMS, SOCIAL STRUCTURE, CULTURE AND THE POLITICAL SYSTEM.

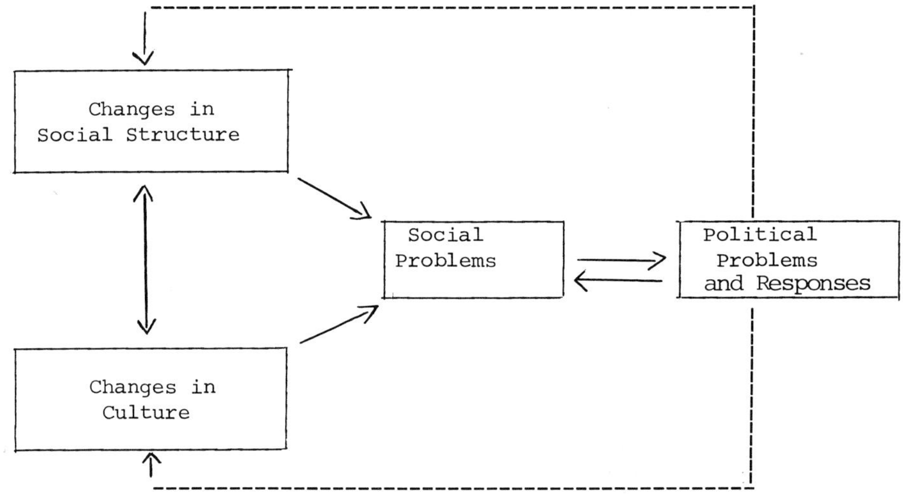

Not all social problems do become politicized. Nor do social problems necessarily result from cultural or social <u>change</u>. Activities of the political system may cause social problems to arise. (See in this regard Cairns, 1977). For our present interests, the above model has the advantage of

1) providing a general technique for identifying politically relevant social (and cultural) change.

2) pointing toward investigation of political culture in terms of its relationship to particular problems.

The latter point requires some elaboration.

THE POLITICAL CULTURE OF PROBLEM POSING

Credit for introducing the concept of political culture to political scientists properly goes to Gabriel Almond. Without reiterating my account of the intellectual history of the concept (Bell and Tepperman, 1979, Ch. 1), it must be noted that the conceptualization of political culture that came to dominate work in the field (Almond and Verba, 1963) was oriented to a particular problem whose importance was highlighted by the cold war struggle between the United States and the Soviet Union. The opening sentences of The Civic Culture read as follows:

> This is a study of the political culture of democracy and of the social structures and processes that sustain it. The faith of the Enlightenment in the inevitable triumph of human reason and liberty has been twice shaken in recent decades. The development of Fascism and Communism after World War I...[and] events since World War II have raised questions of the future of democracy on a world scale. [Emphasis added]
>
> (Almond and Verba, 1963:3)

Despite the anachronism inherent in extending Almond and Verba's approach to other societies at other historical phases of evolution, many scholars have continued to use their approach or to reject the general concept of political culture on the mistaken assumption that their approach is the only one possible. On the contrary, we should feel no compunction about modifying the conceptualization of political culture to relate it to the particular problems we wish to investigate. For political culture has a pervasive significance for the study of problem posing. Political culture constitutes a cognitive and evaluative filter that shapes our perception of problems: how we understand or interpret them; how we assign importance to them; and how we perceive solutions to them. This remark applies to everyone: members of the mass public, political elites, and even academics. Definitions of what constitutes a problem presuppose an implicit or explicit image of "normality". In other words, perception of a social problem implies a discrepancy between what is viewed as "reality" and some sort of "ideal". (Ross and Staines, 1974: 19). To the extent that ideals are ideologically based, i.e., rooted in a fairly coherent system of values, beliefs and attitudes, perceptions of social problems will vary with ideological orientations.

Indeed, one can view competing ideologies as offering, among other things, a different "picture" of the problems facing a society. This picture is necessarily selective: it characteristically portrays some problems as crucial, others as less important, and still others as non-existent. An ideology also links problems to solutions counselling a particular set of policies or structural reforms to deal with each. Liberalism, especially in its early formulations, saw private property, the market economy, and the destruction of feudal institutions as the salvation of society. Liberalism's heroes became socialism's villains. Entrepreneurs were defined as parasitical capitalists preying on the surplus labour of the proletariat, the salt of the earth. Only public ownership of the means of production could overcome the ills engendered by liberal society. The radically different portraits of presumably identical societies or situations emanating from people in competing ideological camps profoundly illustrates the extent to which an ideology constitutes a weltanshaung or world-view.[9]

Even without plunging into the ideological aspects of problem perception, important work can be done comparing problem perceptions of different groups in society. For purposes of illustration, let us consider how one might study problem perceptions of three groups - the academic community, the general public, and governmental elites - using both direct and indirect (less obtrusive) measures of problem perception and problem orientation. (See Table 2 on following page)

A number of interesting implications follow from these alternative approaches to problem diagnosing. It would be fascinating to compare the three groups' perceptions; and to relate the direct findings with indirect measures of problem attention. Such comparisons give insight into the following questions:

(a) How well can the elites "read" public opinion and discern what problems the public feels should be given most attention?

(b) How well can academics anticipate future problems and develop problem orientations independent from government priorities?

(c) How adequately do existing interest groups express widespread dissatisfaction?

(d) How effectively do elites translate their perception of problems into attempted solutions?

(e) To what extent does academic research appear socially relevant?

The approach would not necessarily answer the causal questions unearthed by Herbert McCloskey's study of "issue convergence" in the views of elite and mass with respect to particular election issues. Indeed it is interesting that the concept of problems does not overlap very much with the idea of issues and elections. In a given election, problems may be ignored by all members of the political elite because they are unable to formulate approaches to the problem that will be politically viable in different regions in the country; or because it is in the interests of elite members to ignore or remain silent about fundamental problems that challenge the position of their class or group as a society.

Having suggested various approaches to identifying or diagnosing problems, it is equally important to develop an appropriate methodology for actually analysing the problems and relating them to the underlying patterns of social and cultural change. Obviously, each problem area would require

Table 2: Approaches to the Study of Problem Perception

TARGET GROUP[10]	MEASUREMENT Direct	METHOD Indirect
1. Academic community	- convene a conference or study group to decide collectively what constitutes the important political problems - interview academics for the same purpose	- observe the pattern of research over time to discover what problems have received most attention from social scientists and other academics
2. Public at large	- survey research (as in the I.B.R. quality of life study) which asks respondents to identify what they perceive to be the most significant problems affecting their society. (See paper by Stevenson and Ornstein)	- study conflict areas and conflict arenas to identify those problems which generate the most heated conflict in society - study those vocal groups who try to dramatise their problems through various techniques
3. Governmental elites	- interview elite members and ask them to rank political problems - convene a conference in which members of the governmental elite are asked collectively to prioritize problems	- do an inventory of task forces, royal commissions and other special agencies set up to report on problems in white papers, etc. - assess legislation and/or political debates to determine which problems receive most attention - study other responses, e.g. major policy programs or structural innovations such as the Anti-Inflation Board (AIB) - analyse shifting expenditure patterns over time

individualized research methods to attack it. The only general point to make is that the problem should be examined longitudinally (over time) with a focus on the particular types of social and political cultural change most closely associated with it. It would further be important to develop indicators that would allow use of quantitative data wherever possible. With regard to social change, some of the social mobilization indicators could still be used, but we also require indicators of social changes found in advanced industrial societies but absent or insignificant in societies at an earlier stage of development. With regard to value change, the work of Inglehart and others interested in post-materialism present both a suitable methodology for measuring value change and a set of findings relevant to our inquiry. Such criticisms of Inglehart as are offered in this volume by Stevenson and Ornstein question the interpretation rather than the validity of Inglehart's findings. It would also be interesting to relate the analysis of problems to the time period at which (a) academic recognition of the problem occurs; (b) public outcry is expressed; (c) governmental attention or action follows.

The same techniques that allow us to observe how various groups identify problems let us look as well at how they perceive the problem, explain its occurrence, and indicate alternative solutions to it. And thus we can study the political culture of problem perception and problem resolution amongst the various groups in society, noting contrasting cultural configurations and assessing cultural change over time. Survey research provides a useful primary method for studying the public at large and a supplementary technique for studying elite and academic perceptions. Frequently, however, surverys fail to probe beyond problem perception to inquire about problem diagnosis and views concerning problem resolution. It is the latter aspect of (particularly elite) political culture which most greatly affect policy. Understanding these aspects requires in depth interviews and careful content analysis of speeches, reports, articles, etc. We should obviously try to relate cultural change to social change, and both to governmental response and policy innovation.

To complete our methodology, we need to develop techniques for analysing the response to problems in terms of their effectiveness and their efficiency. We can distinguish policy change from structural change, and attempt the very difficult task of assessing the short range and long range consequences of each.

The following list provides a partial inventory of problems that have arisen in Canada as a consequence of recent social change. Before proceeding to outline these problems, I must explain which of the above methods I have used in selecting them. The problems outlined below are deemed important by a small group of scholars interested in the study of recent social and political change in Canada. Together we are authoring a number of volumes in a series entitled "Canada in Transition: Crises in Development" published by McClelland and Stewart under the general editorship of Edgar Dosman and myself.

With one or two exceptions, each of the following problems is the subject of one or more volumes published or in preparation for the series. My sketchy outlines summarize a great deal of conceptual and empirical work carried out by the series authors.

a) Problem of National Integration

The problem has two main manifestations:

(i) the demands arising out of Quebec as a consequence of the social, economic and political changes associated with the "quiet (and not-so-quiet) revolution, culminating in the election in 1976 of the Parti Quebecois. (See McRoberts 1976, and 1980).

(ii) the demands and discontent arising in the West partly as a result of a substantial shift of economic power to the province which own gas and oil resources whose commercial value more than tripled in less than a decade. (See Richards and Pratt, 1979.)

Fundamental differences in political culture complicate this problem. Canadians, in both the elite and general public, hold sharply different images of Canada. To some, the federal government must be the instrument for a strongly centralized nation from sea to sea. To others, Confederation was an agreement of autonomous units to grant only limited power to the federal government. For them the provincial governments are the foci of what is and must remain a loosely knit decentralized state. At the extreme, the Parti Quebecois has urged that Quebec gain political sovereignty in the context of an economic association with the rest of Canada. Thus different images of Canada have been accompanied by specific proposals for restructuring Canadian federalism.

Some observers have argued that the Canadian political system, with its single member constituency, party discipline and concentration of power in the Cabinet, provides no adequate mechanism for the expression of regional discontent. A number of groups and individuals have recommended replacing the Senate with a body better able to represent the various regions. A few have even recommended borrowing or imitating such American features as the abandonment of party discipline in the House of Commons to permit regional interests to vote together or engage in logrolling on legislation affecting their areas. Such adaptations as have been made, including more provincial autonomy, expanded mechanisms for federal-provincial bargaining and negotiation, etc., have proved ineffective responses to Western alienation (See Darling, 1980) and Quebecois nationalism. Understandably, the problem has assumed nearly crisis proportions in the course of the current efforts to patriate and reform the British North American Act. Differences in political culture are exacerbated by the pattern of social change and the exigencies of constitutional change.

b) Problem of the North

Despite John Diefenbaker's stirring, rhetorical appeal in the late fifties to pursue and fulfill our "northern destiny," Canadian interest in the Arctic remained minimal until the discovery of gas and oil reserves and the demonstrated possibility of arctic ocean navigation (a result of technological breakthroughs in ship construction created a threefold set of problems for which virtually no policy guidelines existed. How should the North be developed, and by whom? How should Canadian sovereignty in this area be asserted and defended? How should government respond to the new militance of various native groups, vigorously pushing, with the assistance of environmentalists and other interests, for recognition of their aboriginal rights? (Dosman, 1975, 1976).

Just as images of Canada affect the problem of national integration, so too different conceptualizations of the North complicate responses to this challenge. Is the North a kind of colony of Ottawa or should it become an independent province? (or should the boundaries of the present provinces be extended north to encompass this territory?) Political culture and communications clearly interact with each other. The advent of modern media has transformed the social topography of the North, and has led to qualitative changes in the life patterns and value orientations of its sparse population. (Valaskakis, 1979). As in other settings, the Indian and Inuit peoples have experienced a startling increase in cultural awareness that involves both greater awareness of "alien" groups and increased interaction with members of their "own" group. (Connor, 1972: 329) Indeed, change has reverberated throughout the entire native community, resulting in heightened political consciousness, new forms of organization, and a cultural renascence in art, music, poetry, handicrafts and letters.

c) Problem of Identity and Cultural Survival

It is not only native people in Canada who have experienced identity problems. English Canadians in particular have had to face an identity crisis involving several dimensions. For the first century of its existence, Canada retained "national symbols", including flag and anthem, that were British or colonial in origin. Throughout this period, Canada has experienced high rates of immigration and population turnover, and extensive penetration of its economic and cultural institutions by the U.S. Hence, at a cultural level, Canadians (particularly anglophones) have had to redefine their identity replacing British with indigenous Canadian symbols; articulate a Canadian cultural consciousness in fiction, drama, popular culture, music and art to offset the powerful influence of the United States; and create or support institutions (in many instances publicly owned) for the dissemination of this culture and introduce regulations on Canadian context in the mass media. These efforts have met only partial success: the problem of identity will persist for the forseeable future. (See Bell and Tepperman, 1979).

d) Problem of Ethnic Diversity and Conflict

Closely intertwined in Canadian identity are two rather contradictory cultural themes. On the one hand Canadians have congratulated themselves for displaying tolerance of minority groups all of which contribute to a colorful or ethnic "mosaic." On the other hand, Canadians have at times attempted to assimilate ethnic minorities by introducing policies modeled on the American "melting pot", or even exclude certain groups from immigration to Canada thereby assuring that all the faces in the mosaic would remain white. For some the slogan "true north strong and free" has been interpreted to give license to very overt forms of racism. Recent shifts in the pattern of immigration have brought to Canada what the 1974 Federal Green Paper called "colorful and unusual" ethnic groups from places like South Asia, the Far East, Africa and the West Indies. (See Hawkins, 1972: Tables 10-12 and passim for relevant data.) Although it is difficult to gauge the level and significance of consequent rises in racism (a fact that did not deter the New York Times from publishing a story on Toronto's "severe racial problems")[12] the situation undoubtedly constitutes a problem that will become more severe in the decades ahead. (Again, see Bell and Tepperman, 1979).

e) Problem of Economic Inequality

Economic inequality is omnipresent in societies. For Canada, the most problematic inequalities are those related to class, region and gender. In all cases both absolute deprivation (poverty) and relative deprivation must be considered. And each form of inequality must be related to the conceptual framework within which it is perceived and interpreted. For there exists a variety of different conceptions of the causes of inequality and the degree of responsibility of governments to alleviate it. Canada has fairly strong cultural commitments to the use of government to redistribute wealth in terms of both class and region. We have had schemes for unemployment insurance for over four decades; various programs for redistrubuting wealth to "have not" provinces in line with what Herschel Hardin (1974) calls our "ethic of redistribution". But recent countertrends in attitudes are much in evidence, in part because of the influence of American-style neo-conservatism. How these contradictory cultural tensions will be worked out, remains to be seen. Two things appear certain: not only have class differences in income (not to mention wealth) increased in recent years (see Manzer, 1974:55) but the number of people living below the "poverty line" appears also to have increased (Manzer, 1974: Tables 2-21 to 2-23). Considered alongside recent economic performance indicators which show that unemployment has gone up while inflation has continued at high rates, increased labour unrest seems eminently understandable. (See, inter alia Strikes and Lockouts an annual compilation published by Labour Canada.)

Inequality has other dimensions as well. As women have experienced a revolutionary change in self-image and aspirations, leading to among other things, a more active role in the work force, the question of equality between the sexes has taken on unprecedented significance. (See Manzer, 1974: Figure 5: 4.) Inspired in part by cultural and political developments in the United States, the women's movement represents a potent force in Canadian society. It will have important political, social and economic ramifications.

f) Problem of Participation and Alienation

Most of our normative theories about political participation--and the practices that follow from them--were formulated in the nineteenth century when political and social conditions were quite different than today. The scope of government was more limited, the number of individuuals and politically relevant groups smaller, and the bureaucracy almost non-existent. Communications were slower and mass media consisted almost entirely of newspapers. Most recent textbook discussions of political participation would aptly fit nineteenth-century society. One might never guess that the government's scope has expanded astronomically, the proportion of the population eligible to vote is ten or twenty times larger, the bureaucracy is enormous, communications are possible at the speed of light, and telephone, radio and television have all appeared, along with Xerox and other technetronic miracles. The concept of participation stands badly in need of modernization, not to mention post-modernization. Revised theories might take account of such (unofficial) practical innovations as "hot line" shows in which politicians and bureaucrats respond directly to citizen inquiries; popular opinion polls as a form of referendum; Xerox as an instrument for informing the public (consider the Pentagon Papers); tape recorders, privacy and surveillance; television and politics as instant replay; and the revolutionary development of two-way electronic communication such as Canada's Telidon System.

Despite the anachronistic treatment given in most texts, political participation is qualitatively different now than twenty-five years ago, and it will continue to change in response to both technological and conceptual innovation, including freedom of information, worker participation and industrial democracy. Canada's variation on this common theme concerns the growth of what is almost a "fourth level" of government--federal-provincial "executive federalism"-- for which there exists no adequate mechanism for public participation beyond live television coverage of a tiny fraction of what transpires.

CONCLUSION

The six problems outlined above illustrate the way in which social change and shifting value configurations interact to challenge the management capabilities of the political system. To understand how and why the political system responds to such problems requires attention to the subjective aspect of problem perception and interpretation as well as to the objective changes in the social structure. Hence, the political culture of problem posing contributes to the study of public policy in advanced industrial societies.

REFERENCES

Almond, Gabriel and Sidney Verba. The Civic Culture. Princeton: Princeton University Press, 1963.

Apter, David. "Political Systems and Developmental Change" in Holt and Turner, 1970.

Bell, Daniel. The Coming of Post-Industrial Society. New York: Basic Books, Inc., 1973.

Bell, David V.J. "Methodological Problems in the study of Canadian Political Culture." Canadian Political Science Association Annual Meeting, Toronto, June 1974.

Bell, David V.J. Power, Influence and Authority: An Essay in Political Linguistics. New York: Oxford University Press, 1975.

Bell, David V.J., and Lorne Tepperman. The Roots of Disunity. Toronto: McClelland and Stewart, 1979.

Bienen, Henry. Violence and Social Change: A Review of Current Literature. Chicago: University of Chicago Press, 1968.

Binder, Leonard et al. Crises and Sequences in Political Development. Princeton: Princeton University Press, 1971.

Brzezinski, Zbigniev. Between Two Ages: America's Role in the Technetronic Era. New York: The Viking Press, 1970.

Connor, Walker. "Nation-Building or Nation-Destroying?" World Politics XXV No. 3, 1972.

Darling, Howard. The Politics of Freight Rates. Toronto: McClelland and Stewart, 1980

Deutsch, Karl W. "Social Mobilizaton and Political Development." American Political Science Review, LV No. 3, 1961.

Dosman, Edgar J. The National Interest. Toronto: McClellant & Stewart, 1975.

Dosman, Edgar J., ed. Arctic Sovereignty. Toronto: Oxford University Press, 1976.

Galbraith, John Kenneth. New Industrial State. Boston: Houghton Mifflin, 1967.

Hawkins, Freda. Canada and Immigration: Public Policy and Public Concern. Montreal: McGill-Queens University Press, 1972.

Holt, Robert T. and John E. Turner. The Methodology of Comparative Research. New York: Free Press, 1970.

Horowitz, Gad. "Toward the Democratic Class Struggle" in Trevor Lloyd and Jack McLeod, editors Agenda 70. Toronto: University of Toronto Press, 1968.

Huntington, Samuel P. "The Change to Change." Comparative Politics, 1971.

Kitsuse, John and Malcolm Spector. "Toward a Sociology of Social Problems." Social Problems, 1973.

Lauer, Robert H. Perspectives on Social Change. Boston: Allyn and Bacon, Inc., 1973.

Mallory, J.R. "Five Faces of Canadian Federalism" in P.A. Crepean and C.B. Macpherson, eds. The Future of Canadian Federalism. Toronto: University of Toronto Press, 1965.

Manis, Jerome. "The Concept of Social Problems: Vox Populi and Sociological Analysis." Social Problesm, 1974.

Manzer, Ronald. Canada: A Socio-Political Report. Toronto: McGraw-Hill Ryerson, 1972.

Marcuse, Herbert. One Dimensional Man. Boston: Beacon Press, 1961.

MacRae, Kenneth (ed.) Consociational Democracy: Political Accomodation in Segmented Societies. Toronto: McClelland & Stewart, 1974.

McRoberts, Kenneth and Dale Posgate. Quebec: Social Change and Political Crisis. Toronto: McClelland & Stewart, 1976. 2nd edition, 1980.

Merton, R.K. and R.A. Nisbet (eds.) Contemporary Social Problems. New York: Horcourt, Brace, 1961; 1966.

Parsons, Talcott and Edward A. Shils et al. Toward a General Theory of Action. Theoretical Foundations for the Social Sciences. New York: Harper & Row, 1957.

Parsons, Talcott and Edwards A. Shils et al. The Social System. New York: The Free Press, 1957.

Pye, Lucian. Aspects of Political Development. Boston: Little, Brown, 1966.

Resch, Charles. The Greening of America. New York: Bantam Books, 1971.

Richards, John and Larry Pratt. Prairie Capitalism: Power and Influence in the New West. Toronto: McClelland & Stewart, 1979.

Ross, Robert and Graham Staines. "The Politics of Analyzing Social Problems." Social Problems, 1973.

Torrance, Judith. "Cultural Factors and the Response of Governments to Violence: The Case of Canada." Ph.D. Dissertation, York University, 1975.

Valaskakis, Gail. "A Communicational Analysis of Interaction Patterns: Southern Baffin, Eastern Arctic." Unpublished Ph.D. Thesis, McGill University, 1979.

Verba, Sidney. "Sequences in Political Development" in Binder et al., 1971.

NOTES

1. I recognize that this image of governmental action imputes far more "rationality" to the process than it deserves, but for our purposes it highlights the management aspects of the governmental process.

2. M. Edelman Political Language: Words that Succeed and Policies that Fail. New York: Academic Press, 1977.

3. I am here confining my attention to main-stream ("bourgeois") political science, and ignoring the use of the concept by Marxists, who generally define social change in terms of socialist "human emancipation." Such scholars speak of "meaningful social change" with the implicit assumption that non-meaningful social change is either self-contradictory or irrelevant. Cf. Bentley Le Baron, "Marx on Human Emancipation" reprinted in Shugarman, 1974. Cf. also Horowitz's (1968: 243) definition of "programs of social change, i.e.,...policies which will reallocate social values in the interest of the underprivileged."

4. Actually, trenchant criticisms have greatly undermined its validity. For a summary, see Huntington, 1971: 293-298.

5. The case of Canada provides an obvious example. Although national aggregate data mask some important regional variations, Canada as a whole has been socially mobilized for at least half a century. The percentage of the population living in urban areas surpassed 50 by 1921. The literacy rate (age 5 and over) hit 90% in the same year. (The lowest provincial rate was New Brunswick's 86.57).

6. This concept of issue resemble C. Wright Mills' distinction between (private) "troubles" and (public) "issues".

7. From Kitsuse and Spector, 1973: 411. The authors characterize Merton as emphasizing the primacy of "objective" over "subjective" factors in defining social problems. I disagree. In my view Merton merely stresses the sociologist's subjective views, and treats them as a surrogate for objective conditions.

8. See in this regard Ross and Staines, 1973, who discuss the "shift from private problem to public issue" with special attention to the role of the media, "officialdom", and "private interest groups." My Figure 1 and the discussion that follow it focus on the origin of social problems in the environment of the political system. To extend the model, the category of "political problems" should be elaborated to include political identification of the problem, efforts to diagnose it, and policy responses to it. The latter can be ranged along a continuum from policy change to structural change.

9. For this reason, it would be interesting to correlate data on problem perception by individuals with data on their ideological preference or self-definition. To the extent that materialism and post-materialism constitute ideologies, one would expect materialists to perceive problems differently than post-materialists. Indeed, such differences are

implicit in the survey operationalization of the concepts: respondents are asked to rank order societel goals. See Inglehart's essay in this volume.

10. One could, of course, examine other target groups such as business elites, interest group leaders, journalists, etc.

11. Obviously a number of these problems have a much longer historical tradition, but they have been intensified by changes that have taken place since World War II. Note that several of these problems parallel the five "problem areas" Verba (p. 299) discusses, which include:

    a) penetration problem--"how much effective control the central government has"
    b) participation problem--"who has some influence over the making of governmental decisions"
    c) legitimacy problem--"basis on which and the degree to which the decisions of government are accepted by the populace"
    d) distribution problem--"extent to which the decisions of government are used to distribute and redistribute material benefits"
    e) identity problem--who belongs "within the domain of the government?"

12. A story appeared in the New York Times, February 27, 1977 under the headline "Upsurge of Racism in Toronto Afflicts South Asian Immigrants." It reports South Asian immigrants' difficulties finding housing and avoiding conflict in Toronto; widespread use of terms of opprobrium such as "paki"; a survey that confirmed that in interviews conducted in eight Toronto and two Ottawa schools for the Human Rights Division of the Federal Secretary of State, a majority of 225 youngsters aged 12 to 15 years displayed overt "racism" to a degree that "demands emergency action". Reference was made to numerous incidents on subways of harrassment and assault; it was further reported that "27 of 30 real estate agencies and 11 of 15 private employment services reached in a telephone check made a practice of screening out non-whites if clients requested it." Some groups in Toronto reacted vigorously to the New York Times story, claiming that it distorted and exaggerated the extent of the problem in Toronto.

Changing Values and the Politics of the Quality of Life

H. M. Stevenson and M. D. Ornstein

ABSTRACT

The orthodox political sociology of the liberal capitalist state, entrenched between the second world war and the late 1960's, has in recent years been subject to major revision. In the face of an impressive resurgence of Marxist political economy in the West, there has at the same time been a vigorous attempt to reconstitute a non-Marxist political sociology of late capitalism. The central theme that informs an otherwise diverse body of work is that the latest stages of development of the advanced capitalist countries have generated a quantitative and qualitative transformation in the expression of demands by individual citizens, and that these changes are rooted in cultural and psychological influences rather than in the class forces and class struggle which are central to the Marxist dialectic. This paper attempts to situate a major development in empirical political sociology--the systematic measurement of perceptions of the quality of life--in this theoretical enterprise. We then examine the implicit argument (surprisingly unexamined to date) that psychological and value changes are associated with structurally unpredictable differences in perceptions of the quality of life, and that these perceptions stimulate new patterns of political demand and action. The research reported here is part of the project on "Social Change in Canada" directed by Tom Atkinson, Bernard Blishen and the authors at the Institute for Behavioural Research at York University. The project has been generously supported by the Social Sciences and Humanities Research Council of Canada (grant #S75-0332).

INTRODUCTION

Orthodox political sociology until quite recent times described the "welfare states" of advanced capitalist countries in terms of the attenuation of class cleavages; the end of ideology and destabilizing political conflict; the organization of political participation and legitimacy in a flexible equilibrium of competition amongst plural social groups and parties, and the effective management of the public welfare by the pluralist state. Crucial to this argument were a series of social-psychological postulates explaining the necessary protection of a system of elite bargaining from mass mobilization and ideological conflict. The most important of these postulates were: (a) the high degree of public consensus and satisfaction concerning the goals and achievements of society (Lipset, 1960); (b) the role played by the family in the intergenerational transmission of political party identification, which formed a bulwark of stable partisanship against the ideological manipulation of free floating voters (Campbell, et. al., 1960); (c) membership in voluntary associations which gave meaningful scope to social and political life, restraining the alienation which might otherwise motivate radical political behaviour (Kornhauser, 1959), and (d) the formation within primary and secondary associations of values and relations of authority complementary to those characteristic of the system of government (Eckstein, 1961; Eckstein and Gurr, 1975; Easton and Dennis, 1969). Within these limits, the active citizenry was composed of the most psychologically secure and satisfied individuals (Lane, 1959). Any concerted mobilization of the inactive was seen as injurious to the health and stability of democratic society, bringing to the surface the irrational grievances and dissatisfactions of those psychologically unable to cope with a "rational" order of things (Kariel, 1970).

Against this happy confidence in the health and stability of capitalist society, the year 1968 represented a startling confrontation. The impact of the political revolt of youth, and the intimations of new radical coalitions outside of the conventional framework of party politics in that year, prompted a re-examination of the theory and practice of the welfare state. The street warfare in Chicago and Paris; the treason of the clerks and students; the ideological ferment of anarchism, Trotskyism, Maoism and the "green" movements for ecology and peace; the militant irredentism of ethnic groups, all combined to question the psychological foundations of the orthodox sociology of the capitalist welfare state. The restraint upon political participation and ideological manipulation through the satisfaction of needs by economic growth and the inculcation of political trust and loyalty through webs of group interaction seemed to have failed in the face of a rising tide of political activism and ideological conflict. The politics of happiness had given way to the politics of disorder.

While the political fervour of 1968 quickly abated, the economic recession of the 1970's produced new discomforts for orthodox political sociology. If there was little intellectual and political vitality to the "counter culture" of the 1960's, the end of the end of ideology was nevertheless apparent in the growing conflict between the established "liberal" defence of the capitalist welfare state and the neo-conservative attack on its possibility and desirability. These ideological developments accompanied growing evidence of a fiscal crisis requiring government austerity and cutbacks against social programmes, with no relief from taxation and inflation. With the ideological and economic basis of the welfare state now in question, there was further growing evidence of political disaffection and instability. Deflationary policy reduced confidence in the capacity of the state to respond to demands, intensifying corporate fragmentation and competition for the allocation of state revenues and for exemption from the impact of deflationary policy. Escalating public alienation from government was reflected in the disintegration of traditional political party constituencies, and in the fragility of government based upon unstable minority or coalition support (cf. Bell, 1977).

These historical pressures have forced a major effort at reconstituting a political sociology of late capitalism that will counter the increasingly sophisticated understanding of these problems in Western Marxism. A central theme in this reconstitution of non-Marxist political sociology is that the very advance of capitalism has generated new cultural and psychological forces which undermine the capacity of the political system to generate public satisfaction both in conditions of economic growth and of recession. We move to an examination of the theoretical arguments developed around this theme, before proceeding to an empirical examination of a key hypothesis contained in them.

CHANGING VALUES AND THE POLITICS OF THE QUALITY OF LIFE

The unifying theme in contemporary non-Marxist political sociology is that the sources of ideological conflict and political disorder lie not in the class structure of the capitalist state but in the frustration of cultural expectations or value-orientations which the political system cannot or does not adequately satisfy. There are two relatively distinct strands of theory here, both of which suggest an increase in public dissatisfaction with the quality of life, and an increasing link between such dissatisfaction and political activity.

The first such theoretical perspective on the political problems of modern capitalism locates the causes of politicized dissatisfaction in the stimulation of want, and demands for the public satisfaction of private wants, without any corresponding stimulation of a cultural or ideological restraint upon the expression of want or need. A stimulating philosophical introduction to this position is contained in Leiss, 1976, where the argument turns on the effects of a mass-consumption, high-intensity market society. These it is argued make inherently ambiguous the relationship between want and need, inherently problematic the rational satisfaction of human need in a finite environment, and increase rather than decrease the limits to human satisfaction.

A more explicitly political theory that tends towards the same underlying argument about the unregulated and unsatisfiable stimulation of demands is contained in the work of Lowi, 1971; 1979. Here it is argued that the pluralist model of liberal capitalist democracy contains essentially correct descriptions of the origin and character of differentiated sources of power, but that these have been given an exaggerated and dangerous twist in an ideology of process rather than substance. The absence within the theory and practice of pluralist politics of a coherent public philosophy, as opposed to the glorification of group and individual self-interest, limits the technocratic competence of the state to produce justice and welfare. It makes social planning impossible and reduces welfare planning to the indemnification of damages rather than the righting of wrongs. As opposed to evaluating the substance of public demands and formulating public policy to address them, the pluralist state seeks to recognize or create the formal, organizational requirements for group participation in the bargaining of demands. The fundamental contradiction in this institutionalization of pluralism is, however, that against the formal promise of participatory democracy the realities of the distribution of power in capitalist society result in the institutionalization of privilege through regulatory policy which delegates state power to established interests, and through redistributive policy which protects the powerful by subsidies and guarantees in a system of "permanent receivership." Expectations, therefore, of the just reconciliation of demands in society are simultaneously raised by the legitimation of group entry to the pluralist system, and frustrated by the failure of the state to authorize a public interest that would give substance to its promise of justice and welfare.

Finally, this theme of the stimulation of expectation and demand without corresponding restraints in the value system is given very explicit form in the work of Daniel Bell, 1976; 1977. Bell argues that there has developed a growing disjunction between a capitalist order based upon ideals of efficiency and self-denial, originating in the puritanism and protestant ethic of the pre-modern period, and a culture of self-gratification and self-indulgence, spawned by the rise of mass production and mass consumption in the modern era. Furthermore, aggravating this first contradiction, there has developed a growing disjunction between the glorification of plenty and individual self-gratification and the growth of the "public household" in which more and more collective goods and services are controlled in the public sector, requiring more and more regulation of economic growth and social consumption to satisfy public as opposed to private needs.

The success of the welfare state in expanding the public household has stimulated a "revolution of rising entitlements," the satisfaction of which through the provision of social, cultural and welfare services cannot be balanced against the requirements of state investments in production and accumulation. In the absence of an effective ideological restraint upon demands for self-gratification, the governments of advanced capitalist states are faced with a "double bind" in which demand outpaces supply.

> The emerging system of state capitalism lacks the kind of philosophical legitimation that liberalism has provided. . . The democratization of demands . . .is subject to few constraints or fewer than those represented by the limited credit available to individuals or firms that at some point would have to pay their debt rather than "postpone" them by increasing the public debt. (Bell, 1977 p. 118).

The endemic problems of inflation so produced, and the resulting pressures towards deflationary policy exacerbate the corporate fragmentation of society, and reduce confidence in the capacity of the state to respond to demands. Even where social expenditures are maintained, there is dissatisfaction with the quality of service and with the disproportional administrative and bureaucratic costs of government programmes. The "double bind of democracy wreaks its contradictory havoc in the simultaneous desire for more spending (for one's own projects) and lower taxes and less interference in one's life" (Bell, 1977, p. 135).

The arguments so far summarized stress the absence of values which might restrain the quantitative escalation of insatiable demands, and give order and stability to an otherwise incoherent and unstable fragmentation of society. Political disorder in this perspective is due to the unrestrained stimulation of competition for scarce resources, and the resulting frustration and dissatisfaction. The second theoretical perspective in contemporary non-Marxist political sociology, however, emphasizes the emergence of new values which produce qualitatively not quantitatively different patterns of demand.

The most extensive effort at formulating this position is contained in Inglehart's The Silent Revolution (1977). This revolution consists of the replacement of concerns for material consumption and scarcity with post-material concerns for the quality of life, and the replacement of class cleavages as the source of ideological differences by psychological and generational cleavages. The dynamics of the shift in value priorities are related to the prosperity experienced by Western nations following World War II, and the absence of war within their national boundaries during that period: "people are safe and they have enough to eat." These conditions are presumed, following Maslow's theory of motivation to shift the motives of human behaviour upward in a hierarchy of needs from physiological and safety needs to needs for belongingness, esteem and self-actualization. The clamour of 1968 is reduced in these terms to a silent revolution in which Marxism and mysticism remain marginal alternatives to the central debate over materialism and post-materialism--a debate which does not challenge the survival of the capitalist welfare state, but shifts its direction from growth and consumption to stability, conservation, participation and the inner fulfillment of human needs.

Apart from an attempt to develop a single index of post-material values, Inglehart devotes the greater part of his empirical justification of this argument to a consideration of subjective indicators of the quality of life. He accepts therefore the general argument underlying the growing body of empirical research dealing with subjective indicators of the quality of life: that the "objective" prosperity of advanced capitalist countries, far from producing a concomitant sense of well-being, has resulted in the stimulation of subjective criticism of aspects of the "quality of life." This criticism is voiced even, or especially, by those most materially advantaged in these societies. The close connection between the theoretical logic of Inglehart's work and the empirical research focused upon subjective indicators of the quality of life is evident in the first major discussion of the latter research:

> People in policy-making positions cannot ignore protests of inequity coming from aggrieved portions of their constituency, particularly if these protests are supported by substantial evidence. They are accustomed to dealing with grievances which derive from monetary need; they are finding themselves increasingly concerned with needs which are primarily psychological. Assuring dignified treatment of minorities, providing fulfilling experiences for old people, protecting natural beauty for defenders of the environment, providing a sense of physical security to people living in the inner cities...Data which demonstrate that the psychological rewards of life are seen by one self-conscious component of society to be inferior to those of another have obvious implications, especially in a nation in which a substantial part of the population is no longer disturbed about food and housing but is very much concerned with its "higher order" needs. (Campbell, et. al. 1976, p. 392).

Summary

There are major differences amongst the various theoretical perspectives we have discussed, but they all suggest the core hypotheses reflected in this quotation: vis., that politically significant demands, grievances or dissatisfaction in late capitalist society are increasingly divorced from traditional lines of economic cleavage and inequality; that they are increasingly a product of psychological or cultural change; that they increasingly reflect the highly subjective evaluation of the quality of life rather than more "objective" concerns with material growth and the share of income, and that they prompt a far reaching requirement for change in traditional definitions of welfare and of public policy.

THE POLITICAL RESPONSE TO THE QUALITY OF LIFE

In this section we attempt a very simple empirical investigation of the link between subjective perceptions of the quality of life and political attitudes, using data from a survey of the Canadian population. It is surprisingly the case that despite the clear invocation of such a link in recent theory, no systematic empirical investigation of its form has, to our knowledge, been undertaken. There was much earlier, however, a considerable development of theory and measurement to account for problems of activism on the radical right or left that has a direct relevance to this problem in contemporary theory. We have in mind the elaboration of frustration-aggression theory in application to politics (cf. references in Stevenson, 1977), and the associated development of measures of personal aspiration and achievement, and of more straightforward measures of satisfaction/dissatisfaction with aspects of personal life experience. These measures are in fact the direct antecedents of most measures of perceptions of the quality of life.

As applied to radical political behaviour, however, this research has been of dubious explanatory value. The likelihood of such behaviour, generically conceptualized in terms of approval of modes of unconventional protest and violence, is increased both for those who experience positive aspiration achievement and for those who experience aspiration deprivation (Grofman and Muller, 1973). There is only very weak evidence that lower levels of job and life satisfaction are associated with left-wing political ideology amongst workers (Blackburn and Mann, 1975), and it is argued that individuals take leftist positions only if they blame the government and political system for their own and more general economic difficulties (Portes, 1971; Stevenson, 1977). The latter qualification amounts to saying, however, that those individuals have leftist orientations in the first place, making the argument circular or tautological.

The interest in any further examination of such links between value satisfaction or gratification and political responses is, nevertheless, stimulated by the new directions in non-Marxist political sociology that we have discussed. Here the problem is no longer to account for minority or deviant forms of political action, but supposedly for a mass phenomenon, encompassing a much more varied repertoire of political interests and demands than is contained within the left/right ideological continuum.

It seems reasonable as a minimal strategy in this connection, therefore, to examine the extent to which various measures of dissatisfaction with the quality of life have direct or unique effects on measures of various orientations towards politics. We examine, that is, the extent to which these effects dominate those of traditional demographic or structural cleavages in the population, as the theory suggests. Secondly, however, we examine a variety of non-linear forms of the political response to the quality of life, particularly interactions involving age (a key factor in Inglehart's argument) and personal or political alienation (frequently, if ambiguously, conceptualized as constraining or exacerbating the politicization of private concerns).

Analytic Strategy and Data

Measures of a variety of political attitudes are regressed on two groups of variables: one measuring the subjective quality of life; and one measuring individuals' socio-demographic attributes, including age, marital status, education, income, etc. The question is whether the quality of life measures have any impact on political attitudes, holding constant the socio-demographic variables. In selecting the variables, we have attempted to ensure broad coverage while using variables whose validity and reliability can be established from previous research of our own or others. The exact item wordings are given in Appendix A, so we only briefly describe them here.

The quality of life variables are obtained by summing two or more items. Each includes measures of each respondent's satisfaction with his or her "life as a whole," "financial situation," and marriage (or "romantic relationships" for those not married). Job satisfaction was not included because only one half the sampled respondents were in the labour force and no reasonable surrogate for the variable among non-workers was available. A personal disaffection score, derived from a series of semantic differential items, was also included as a more effective alternative to the general life satisfaction measure of the quality of life as a whole.

Two additional variables were added to the life satisfaction measures to test the proposition that the impact of life satisfaction on political attitudes might be conditioned by levels of personal efficacy and interpersonal trust. We reasoned that the translation of individual differences in life satisfaction had two prerequisites: the belief that personal misfortunes are not entirely due to one's own inability to carry through his or her plans; and some level of trust in other people; without this trust the sort of collective interest that most forms of political activity presuppose cannot solidify. Both the main effects of efficacy and trust and their multiplicative interactions with the four other quality of life measures are considered in the analysis. To investigate the possibility of non-linear effects of the six quality of life measures, six quadratic terms, constructed by taking their squares, are also formed.

The demographic variables employed as controls in this analysis include measures of gender, age, marital status. educational attainment, occupation, and income. They are described in detail in Appendix A.

The thirteen dependent variables measuring political orientations have been (a bit arbitrarily) divided into three groups according to whether they measure general orientations towards political issues on which there is cleavage between right and left (labelled "left-right issues" henceforth), views related to government and associated institutions ("government related issues"), or federal political party identification (measured by three dummy variables). The first group includes measures of support for social welfare measures, and minority rights, agreement that the law should be changed to make it illegal for management to hire strikebreakers in labour disputes, support for more redistributive taxation, and agreement with a statement that there is "too much difference between rich and poor." The government-related issues include measures of satisfaction with government, political efficacy, disagreement with government priorities, support for the use of extra-parliamentary forms of protest to influence government, and of attention to the news media (labelled "political salience"). Appendix A gives the items used to form these measures.

This analysis is based on a survey of approximately 3300 Canadians that was conducted by the Survey Research Centre of York University in May, June and July 1977. The target population included all non-institutionalized Canadians of age eighteen or more living outside the very sparsely populated area of northern Canada.

Table 1 contains the analyses of variance and Tables 2, 3, 4 the regression coefficients for the measures, respectively, of left-right issues, government related issues, and federal political party identification. For each dependent variable there are three columns of figures. The first contains the regression coefficient for the regression of the dependent variable on each independent variable alone (except for marital status and occupation where the other dummy variables are held constant). For the quality of life measures, the second column contains the regression coefficient for each variable when it and all the socio-economic variables (but <u>none</u> of the five other quality of life measures) are used as independent variables; for the socio-economic variables, the second column contains the regression coefficients obtained when all the socio-economic variables (but none of the quality of life measures) are in the regression. The third column for each dependent variable contains the regression coefficients for the equation obtained when all the quality of life measures and socio-economic variables are entered. All the variables are standardized, except for the dummy variables which measure gender, marital status, occupation, "income unknown", and party support.

Results

First, excluding the effects of personal efficacy and interpersonal trust, the variances reported in the two leftmost columns of Table 1 show that there is no strong relationship between individuals' perceptions of the quality of life and their political views. The four quality of life measures explain less than 2.5 per cent of the variance in all but two of the political attitude measures; when the socio-demographic variables are held constant, the explained variances are considerably smaller. That almost all the variances are significantly different from zero testifies more to the large sample size than to the large magnitudes of the effects. The very large reduction in the impact of the quality of life measures produced by the introduction of controls for the conventional demographic variables would suggest a very great caution in accepting the new political sociology's emphasis upon perceptual--psychological factors as explanations of contemporary political phenomena. The large impact of life satisfaction on satisfaction with government suggests either a similarity in making judgements of satisfaction in diverse areas--certainly a complex process involving both perceptions and levels of expectation--or the existence of a methodological artifact. In either case, it does not modify the caution expressed above.

From the third and fourth columns of Table 1, it is apparent that the addition of interpersonal trust and personal efficacy to the four quality of life measures considerably raises the magnitudes of the observed variances, even when the socio-demographic variables are held constant. The rightmost column of Table 1 shows the additional variance explained when the quadratic effects of the quality of life and the alienation measures, and the eight multiplicative interaction terms that are significant at the .05 level (net of the main effects of both quality of life and socio-demographic variables), are entered in the regression. They generally make rather unimpressive contributions to the total explained variance. We now examine the directions and magnitudes of the effects of the quality of life variables on the three groups of dependent variables in turn. While, for completeness, measures of the

TABLE 1 ANALYSIS OF VARIANCE FOR REGRESSIONS OF POLITICAL ATTITUDES ON QUALITY OF LIFE MEASURES AND SOCIO-DEMOGRAPHIC VARIABLES

	Proportion of Variance Explained (adjusted for degrees of freedom)							
	Quality of life measures exc. trust and efficacy		Quality of life measures inc. trust and efficacy		Socio-demographic variables			
Dependent Variable	Zero-Order	Unique	Zero-Order	Unique	Zero-Order	Unique	Total	Additional variance due to curvilinear effects and interaction*
Left-Right Issues								
Support for social welfare	.020	.011	.073	.046	.057	.030	.103	.016
Support for minorities	.007	.003	.009	.008	.035	.035	.044	.008
Outlaw strikebreaking	.004	.001	.017	.005	.046	.042	.061	.003
Too much inequality	.022	.007	.043	.018	.047	.022	.065	.015
More redistributive taxation	.034	.015	.060	.026	.073	.038	.098	.007
Government Related Issues								
Political salience	.013	.001	.032	.005	.144	.116	.150	.006
Legitimation of protest	.012	.005	.018	.009	.095	.086	.105	.005
Satisfaction with government	.068	.070	.069	.073	.021	.026	.095	.013
Disagreement with government priorities	.018	.012	.081	.064	.024	.008	.089	.028
Political efficacy	.021	.004	.089	.040	.104	.065	.144	.008
Federal Political Party Identification								
Liberal	.006	.003	.006	.003	.013	.010	.016	.006
Conservative	.002	.001	.021	.017	.020	.016	.037	.000
New Democratic Party	.006	.005	.008	.006	.018	.016	.024	.003

*including all terms with coefficients significant at .05, net of main effects

impact of the socio-demographic variables that are employed as controls are presented in the Tables in full detail, no attempt is made to treat the socio-demographic differences systematically in the discussion below.

a. Left-Right Issues

Comparing the regression coefficients of the six attitudual measures (in the top six rows on Table 2), interpersonal trust has the most consistent and strongest effects on the five left-right issues. Its effects survive statistical controls for the socio-demographic variables (comparing the coefficients in columns (1) and (2) for each dependent variable) and for the five other quality of life measures (comparing columns (2) and (3)). The negative values of its regression coefficients (Table 2, row 5) show that higher levels of interpersonal trust are associated with more conservative political opinions, especially as regards "support for social welfare," and agreement that "there is too much difference between rich and poor," and support for more redistributive taxation. Individuals who believe they live in a social environment that is predictable, and which is therefore subject to properly directed efforts to change it, are less likely to support government efforts to equalize opportunity and standards of living.

Similarly, higher levels of financial satisfaction are consistently associated with more conservative positions, except on the issue of outlawing the use of strikebreakers, where it has no effect once the socio-demographic variables are held constant. It is significant that financial satisfaction affects political attitudes net of the three variables measuring the linear and quadratic effects of income and whether it was reported. This finding is, of course, consistent with the observed negative relationship between income and support for liberal positions on these left-right issues (see the regression coefficients in the third to last line of Table 2). It is not consistent with the suggestion in Inglehart's work that those most materially satisfied are less conservative, although it is clear that these issues do not directly tap "post-materialist" dimensions of political interest. As evidenced by the negative coefficients of the square of income, individuals at the top and bottom of the income spectrum are further to the right than would be expected from its linear effect on three of the issues. Individuals who did not know or would not disclose their family income levels are also significantly to the right of people in the median income category on three of the issues.

General life satisfaction has very weak effects on these political attitudes. With the socio-demographic variables held constant, it is negatively related to support for more

TABLE 2 REGRESSION OF LEFT-RIGHT ISSUES ON QUALITY OF LIFE MEASURES AND POLITICAL ATTITUDES

	Dependent Variable														
	Support for social welfare			Support for minorities			Outlaw strikebreaking			Too much inequality			More redistributive taxation		
Independent Variable	1	2	3	1	2	3	1	2	3	1	2	3	1	2	3
Quality of Life Measures															
General life satisfaction	.00	.04†	.08*	.02	.03	.04	-.02	.02	-.01	-.06*	-.03	.03	-.07*	-.04†	.06†
Personal alienation	.05*	.01	.03	-.02	-.03	.02	-.02	-.04†	-.04†	.08*	.05*	.04†	.11*	.07*	.07*
Financial satisfaction	-.11*	-.04†	-.07*	-.04†	-.03	-.05*	-.05*	.01	.00	-.13*	-.08*	-.08*	-.15*	-.10*	-.10*
Satisfaction with marriage	.05*	.09*	.08*	.01	.05†	.03	.03	.04	.03	.01	.02	.03	-.03	-.02	.00
Interpersonal trust	-.24*	-.20*	-.19	-.07*	-.07*	-.08*	-.12*	-.07*	-.07*	-.16*	-.11*	-.11*	-.18*	-.13*	-.13*
Personal efficacy	-.09*	-.04†	-.03	-.04†	-.03	-.03	-.04†	.00	.00	-.11*	-.05*	-.03	-.11*	-.06*	.02
Socio-Demographic Variables															
Gender (0 for men, 1 for women)	.13*	.10*	.14*	.21*	.23*	.24*	-.04	-.06	-.04	.10*	.09†	.11*	-.04	-.07	-.04
Age	-.07*	-.11*	-.07*	-.14*	-.10*	-.09*	-.07*	-.07*	-.06*	.00	-.02	-.00	.10*	.06†	.07*
Square of age	-.02	-.03	-.05†	-.06	-.01	-.01	-.07*	-.06†	-.07*	.00	-.02	-.02	.08*	-.01	.00
Marital status (compared to married)															
Never married	.12	.08	.16	.18*	.11†	.15*	-.03	-.03	.02	.02	.08	.09	-.02	.08	.05
Separated or divorced	.11	-.01	-.04	.04	-.02	.00	.01	-.07	-.03	.14	.06	.05	.16	.09	.04
Widowed	.09	.07	.19	-.14	-.02	.04	-.15	-.02	.02	-.09	-.20†	-.17	.25*	.04	.03
Education	-.14*	-.11*	-.07*	.04	.03	.05†	-.12*	-.09*	-.08*	-.17	-.13*	-.11	-.20*	-.11*	-.08*
Square of education	-.01	.04†	.03	-.03	.02	.02	-.06	-.02	.02	-.02	.00	-.01	-.05	-.05*	-.06*
Occupation (compared to persons outside the labour force)															
Professional, manager	-.35*	-.09	-.01	-.01	.04	.09	-.16†	-.06	-.04	-.34*	-.08	-.01	-.45*	-.10	-.01
Skilled non-manual	-.14†	-.01	.03	.13†	.16†	.17†	.05	.04	.04	-.22*	-.14†	.09	-.34*	-.19*	-.13†
Semi & unskilled non-manual	.00	.05	.05	.17*	.17†	.17†	.19*	.14†	.13†	-.02	.00	.01	-.12	-.04	-.04
Skilled manual	.00	.09	.07	.06	.16†	.15†	.23*	.13†	.12	-.11	-.10	-.09	-.09	-.05	-.03
Semi & unskilled manual	.15*	.16†	.14†	.14†	.22*	.21*	.37*	.25*	.24*	.12†	.08	.07	.01	.01	.01
Farmer	-.37*	-.28*	-.25*	-.26*	-.07	-.07	-.33*	-.38*	-.37*	-.07	.01	-.03	-.01	-.02	.04
Family income, logarithm	-.13*	-.12*	-.08*	.00	-.04*	-.02	-.06*	-.09*	-.08*	-.13*	-.10*	-.07*	-.21*	-.18*	-.13*
Square of log income	-.01	-.03	.02	-.03	-.03	-.03	-.06*	-.06*	-.06*	-.03	-.06*	-.06*	-.01	-.07*	-.06*
Income Unknown (dummy variable)	-.02	-.02	-.04	-.04	-.07	-.07	-.15*	-.16*	-.17*	-.02	-.10	-.12†	-.05	-.14†	-.13†

† significant at .05
* significant at .01

Column 1: simple correlation between the dependent and independent variable
2: for quality of life measures: regression coefficient with all socio-demographic variables held constant
for socio-demographic variables: regression coefficient when all socio-demographic variables are entered
3: regression coefficient when all independent variables are entered

N.B. All variables are standardized <u>except</u> the dummy variables for sex, marital status, occupation, and income unknown

redistributive taxation (b=-.04, in Table 2, row 1) and to the belief that there is too much difference between rich and poor (b=.04). When the other quality of life measures are also controlled, the effect becomes positive yielding a beta of .06. This change of sign could be due to the existence of a methodologically inflated correlation between general life and financial satisfaction (due to component items' similarity). On the other hand, general life satisfaction is positively related (not quite significant at .05) to support for social welfare and for minorities, with only the socio-demographic variables held constant. The correlation of general life and financial satisfaction is .52 and work by McKennell, Atkinson and Andrews (1978) suggest that the true correlation, corrected for method but not for reliability, would be about .55, so the methodological effect is not that large. This uncertainty is due more to the weakness of the relationships than to the methodological difficulties present here, which could be resolved by employing unmeasured variables to allow the method effects to be explicitly represented (see Joreskog and Sorbom, 1977).

Higher levels of personal alienation and of personal efficacy are both positively related to support for more redistributive taxation and for the statement that there is too much difference between rich and poor. Satisfaction with marriage has a positive significant effect on support for social welfare and for minorities. The relevant regression coefficients are so weak that we make no further comment here.

These results can be summarized as follows: interpersonal trust has strong and consistent effects on left-right issues. Individuals with higher levels of trust are more conservative. Similarly, higher levels of financial satisfaction are associated with conservative attitudes. There is, apparently a weak tendency for higher levels of general life satisfaction to be associated with more liberal stands, but the evidence is not strong and the magnitude of the effect is certainly very small.

b. Government Related Issues

The five items gathered under this category bear on quite different aspects of political orientation, so we proceed by dealing with them individually. The measure of attention to the news media labelled "political salience" is strongly, positively related to education and age. With the socio-demographic variables held constant, none of the quality of life measures has a standardized regression coefficient over .07. Statistically significant results are obtained to show that politics is more important to individuals with higher levels of general life satisfaction and trust. With the socio-demographic variables held constant, support for extra-

TABLE 3 REGRESSION OF GOVERNMENT RELATED ISSUES ON QUALITY

Independent Variable	Dependent Variable: Political Salience 1	2	3	Legitimation of Protest 1	2	3	Satisfaction with Government 1	2	3	Disagreement with Gov't Priorities 1	2	3	Political Efficacy 1	2	3
Quality of Life Measures															
General life satisfaction	.07*	.04+	.05	-.10*	-.08*	-.09*	.22*	.24*	.17*	-.01	.01	.06+	.07*	.05*	-.01
Personal alienation	-.04+	.01	.04	.02	.03	.00	-.09*	-.11*	.00	.06*	.04+	.05*	-.09*	-.05*	-.02
Financial satisfaction	.12*	.03	.01	-.07	-.05+	-.02	.20*	.24*	.15*	-.08*	-.04+	-.05+	.12*	.06*	.00
Satisfaction with marriage	.04	.01	-.01	-.08*	-.04	.00	.07*	.10*	-.03	.06*	.09*	.09*	-.01	.00	-.03
Interpersonal trust	.15*	.07*	.07*	.06*	.05*	.06*	.06*	.06*	.04+	-.26*	-.23*	-.23*	.23*	.16*	.14*
Personal efficacy	.09*	.01	.00	.01	.00	.03	.12*	.15*	.05*	-.10*	-.06*	-.05*	.22*	.15*	.14*
Socio-demographic Variables															
Gender (0 for men, 1 for women)	-.12*	-.11*	-.13	.01	.00	.01	.15*	.16*	.10*	.06	.03	.07	-.14*	-.12	-.13*
Age	.14*	.32*	.31*	-.28*	-.27	-.27	.12*	.08*	.07*	.03	.02	.06+	-.09*	-.02	-.04
Square of age	-.05*	-.12*	-.12*	.08*	.03	.04	.05*	.01	-.02	-.03	-.08*	-.10*	-.06*	-.01	-.01
Marital Status (compared to married)															
Never married	-.25	.01	.01	.42*	.08	.05	-.12*	.03	.10	-.08	-.01	.07	.13	.03	.03
Separated or divorced	-.32	-.18+	-.17+	.15	.07	.05	.00	.01	.12	.08	.00	.06	-.19	-.12	-.09
Widowed	-.01	.05	.04	-.21	.04	.01	.32*	.18+	.21*	.06	.01	.13	-.09	.15	.12
Education	.23*	.25*	.24*	.17	.08*	.07*	-.08*	-.06+	-.07*	-.12*	-.07*	-.02	.29*	.20	.16*
Square of education	-.04	-.09*	-.09*	.02	.06*	.07*	.04+	.03	.03	.01	.02	.01	.04	.02	.03
Occupation (compared to persons outside the labour force)															
Professional, manager	.45*	.00	-.03	.05	-.08	-.08	.01	.15+	.03	-.24*	-.14	-.05	.56*	-.18+	.10
Skilled non-manual	.24*	.00	-.01	-.06	-.11	-.10	.09	.20*	.12	-.12	-.08	-.03	.24*	.09	.05
Semi & unskilled non-manual	.08	-.03	-.03	.00	-.07	-.06	.02	.12	.11	.05	.08	.07	.01	-.07	-.06
Skilled manual	.07	-.08	-.08	-.13+	-.11	-.08	.01	.14+	.07	.03	.03	.01	.00	-.05	-.04
Semi & unskilled manual	-.11	-.10	-.10	-.07	-.07	-.06	.05	.15+	.16+	.11	.08	.05	-.17*	-.15+	-.10
Farmer	-.17	-.30*	-.34*	-.51*	-.34*	-.33*	.07	.12	.03	-.18*	-.21	-.15	-.05	.09	.04
Family income, logarithm	.18	.12*	.10*	.06	-.01	.00	-.04	.01	-.07*	-.09	-.07*	-.03	.18*	.10*	.06*
Square of log income	-.06	-.02	-.02	.00	-.01	.00	.03	.02	.00	.01	-.00	.01	.02	.04+	.03
Income Unknown (dummy variable)	-.03	.04	.04	-.02	-.02	-.01	-.12+	-.14+	-.16*	-.01	-.01	-.02	-.02	.04	.04

† significant at .05
* significant at .01

Column 1: simple correlation between the dependent and independent variable
2: for quality of life measures: regression coefficient with all socio-demographic variables held constant
for socio-demographic variables: regression coefficient when all socio-demographic variables are entered
3: regression coefficient when all independent variables are entered

N.B. All variables are standardized <u>except</u> the dummy variables for sex, marital status, occupation, and income unknown

parliamentary forms of political protest is negatively related to general life satisfaction and positively to interpersonal trust.

There are strong quality of life effects on the measure of satisfaction with government which is composed by summing evaluations of the three levels of government. To eliminate partisan considerations, all the regression coefficients (in columns 7, 8, and 9) are values obtained with federal and provincial party identification held constant. Whether or not there are controls for the socio-demographic variables and the other quality of life measures, general life satisfaction and financial satisfaction are moderately strongly, positively associated with satisfaction with government. With all other variables controlled the two regression coefficients are .17 and .15, respectively. Personal efficacy and trust also have weaker, positive effects. It is worth noting that satisfaction with marriage, though it is known to be an important component of general life satisfaction has almost no relationship to satisfaction with government. This lead us to discount the argument that the effects of general life and financial satisfaction are purely methodological in character--since satisfaction with marriage also uses items of similar format.

Disagreement with government priorities is associated strongly, negatively with interpersonal trust; weakly, positively with general life satisfaction, satisfaction with marriage, and personal alienation; and weakly, negatively with financial satisfaction. The implication is that the divergence with government priorities expressed by individuals with high levels of overall life satisfaction occur within the context of a general acceptance of government and of conventional modes of political expression. The strongest effect, however, is that of interpersonal trust: individuals who have a generally trusting view of human nature tend to support the political status quo. Individuals who believe that "most people can be trusted," are not "just looking out for themselves," and would not "try to take advantage of you" seem to have the same confidence in government.

Political efficacy is a measure of the extent to which the government and legislators are seen as understandable and responsible to the citizenry. With the socio-demographic variables but none of the other quality of life measures held constant, political efficacy is strongly associated with interpersonal trust (b=.16) and personal efficacy (b=.15) and weakly associated with general life satisfaction (b=.06), financial satisfaction (b=.05) and personal alienation (b=-.05). But, when they are simultaneously entered in the regression only the first two effects survive, as is shown in the rightmost column of Table 3. It seems sensible that people who trust those around them and feel able to successfully plan their own lives should have higher levels of confidence in their ability to understand and influence government. Beyond this there are no visible effects of the quality of life on political efficacy.

c. Political Party Identification

A glance at the explained variances in the three bottom rows of Table 1 provides convincing evidence that neither socio-economic variables, nor measures of the quality of life provide the basis for very good predictions of which party a person will support. Since the three dummy variables for support of the Liberals, Conservatives and New Democrats are not standardized in the analysis, the regression coefficients in Table 4 read simply as percentage differences in party support It should be noted that not everyone is classified as a supporter of one of these three parties; we have not presented regressions showing support for the Social Credit Party or the correlates of calling oneself an independent, or saying one has no preference.

With the socio-demographic variables (but not the other quality of life measures) held constant, higher levels of general life satisfaction are positively associated with support for the Liberals and negatively with New Democratic Party support. The same pattern holds for financial satisfaction and also for personal efficacy--indeed all three variables have effects of very nearly the same magnitudes. For each increase in general life satisfaction of one standard deviation, the probability of voting Liberal increases by 2.5%, of voting Conservative increases by 1.0% (n.s. at .05), and of voting NDP declines by 2.0%! It is important to note that this is not simply a restatement of the previous finding about satisfaction with government (which has found to be positively related to general life and financial satisfaction), since that analysis included a statistical control for partisanship. With only these data, it is unfortunately impossible to distinguish the possibility that higher levels of life satisfaction lead to support for the party in power from the hypothesis that they lead to support for the policy positions of the Liberal Party, presently in power. A new survey, conducted after a change in government, would tell us the answer.

Except for the additional finding that interpersonal trust is positively associated with Conservative Party support, no other results emerge from this analysis. Indeed, when all the variables are entered in the regressions (in the 3rd, 6th, and 9th columns of Table 4), the multicolinearity renders statistically insignificant many of the effects described above.

TABLE 4 REGRESSIONS OF THE DUMMY VARIABLES MEASURING FEDERAL POLITICAL PARTY IDENTIFICATION

	Dependent Variable								
	Liberal Party Support			Conservative Party Support			New Democratic Party Support		
Independent Variable	1	2	3	1	2	3	1	2	3
Quality of Life Measures									
General life satisfaction	.024*	.022*	.007	.016	.009	.011	-.019*	-.017*	-.005
Personal alienation	-.013	-.009	.004	-.012	-.010	-.005	.006	.006	-.004
Financial satisfaction	.041*	.030*	.023†	.012	.001	-.005	-.023*	-.021*	-.013†
Satisfaction with marriage	.010	.019*	.010	-.005	-.013	-.025	-.013	-.017*	-.010
Interpersonal trust	.007	.000	-.005	.058*	.054*	.053*	-.004	.000	.003
Personal efficacy	.027*	.018†	.009	.011	.008	.002	-.022*	-.021*	-.015†
Socio-Demographic Variables									
Gender (0 for men, 1 for women)	-.023	-.019	-.021	.021	.037†	.025	-.001	.001	.001
Age	-.013	-.001	-.003	.033*	.040*	.034*	-.003	-.005	-.003
Square of age	-.003	.002	-.002	.006	.000	.001	-.007	.000	.005
Marital status (compared to married)									
Never married	.054†	.054	.072†	-.053	-.004	-.019	-.036*	-.047*	-.063*
Separated or divorced	-.057	-.041	-.014	.025	.061	.047	.068*	.062	.039
Widowed	.030	.061	.076	.038	.039	.017	-.025	-.013	-.026
Education	.024*	-.011	-.010	.002	.019†	.008	.003	.015†	.016†
Square of education	.005	-.002	-.002	-.003	.007	-.004	-.011	-.010	-.010
Occupation (compared to persons outside the labour force)									
Professional, manager	.109*	.095*	.083†	.024	-.003	-.019	.019	.004	.013
Skilled non-manual	.046	.044	.035	.046	.034	.026	-.005	-.017	-.011
Semi & unskilled non-manual	.028	.025	.024	.028	.031	.032	.050†	.041	.042†
Skilled manual	.019	.020	.012	.020	.028	.032	.032	.022	.026
Semi & unskilled manual	-.010	-.012	-.012	.018	.040	.046	.068*	.067*	.064*
Farmer	-.074	-.081	-.087	.192*	.200*	.181*	-.037	-.033	-.029
Family income, logarithm	.039*	.041*	.032*	.018*	.027*	.022	-.008	-.010	-.004
Square of log income	.014	.024*	.023†	-.009	-.004	-.005	.007	.006	.007
Income Unknown (dummy variable)	-.016	.003	.001	.008	.002	.003	-.072*	-.056*	-.053*

† significant at .05
* significant at .01

Column 1: simple correlation between the dependent and independent variable
2: for quality of life measures: regression coefficient with all socio-demographic variables held constant
for socio-demographic variables: regression coefficient when all socio-demographic variables are entered
3: regression coefficient when all independent variables are entered

N.B. All variables are standardized <u>except</u> the dummy variables for sex, marital status, occupation, and income unknown and the dependent variables for federal political party identification.

d. Quadratic Effects and Multiplicative Interactions

The rightmost column of Table 1 shows that the addition of the six quadratic effects and eight multiplicative interaction terms does little to raise the total explained variances. However, the listing of which terms are statistically significant, in Table 5, is of interest. Since there are a total of thirteen regressions, there is a better than fifty-fifty chance that each term will be significant for at least one of the dependent variables. So we focus on the terms which have effects in three or more of the regressions.

By this criterion, the quadratic term for general life satisfaction, which reaches statistical significance in five of the thirteen regressions, is worth considering. In three of these four cases, the regression coefficients have the same positive signs as the linear term. So, at the extremes of general life satisfaction, levels of support for social welfare, satisfaction with government, and disagreement with government, priorities are higher than would be predicted from the linear term alone. A more detailed analysis should examine the tails of the distribution of general life satisfaction.

Rather similar results are obtained for the measure of personal alienation, but the quadratic terms for financial satisfaction, satisfaction with marriage, trust and efficacy do not seem of much interest. In no case are they statistically significant (at .05) in more than two of the thirteen regressions.

In defining the interaction terms of interest, we hypothesized that differences in the quality of life might affect political attitudes only if they coexisted with sufficiently high levels of interpersonal trust or personal efficacy to make the individual confident of his or her ability to effectively influence the political process. So, eight multiplicative interaction terms were formed and those that were statistically significant at .05, net of all the main effects, were entered in the regressions. These terms and the values of their standardized regression coefficients are shown in Table 5. At a glance it can be seen that our hypothesis is not confirmed. Few of the interaction terms reach statistical significance and the mixed signs of their regression coefficients make it difficult to hazard any generalization as to the nature of their effects.

Finally, following Inglehart's argument that younger cohorts socialized in the post second world war period are more susceptible to the psychological influences motivating post-materialist values, we examined the interaction between age and measures of satisfaction with the quality of life. The relevant evidence in Table 5 is weak, but it does, in the case of the interaction of age with financial satisfaction, give

TABLE 5 SQUARE AND MULTIPLICATIVE INTERACTION TERMS SIGNIFICANT AT THE .05 LEVEL WHEN ENTERED STEPWISE, NET OF ALL MAIN EFFECTS. TABLE ENTRIES ARE THE NAMES OF DEPENDENT VARIABLES FOR WHICH A GIVEN TERM IS SIGNIFICANT; THE CORRESPONDING STANDARDIZED REGRESSION COEFFICIENT FOLLOWS

Dependent Variable	Square terms		Multiplicative interaction interpersonal trust		Multiplicative interaction with personal efficacy		Multiplicative interaction with age	
	Name of dependent variable	Beta	Name of dependent variable	Beta	Name of dependent variable	Beta	Name of dependent variable	Beta
General life satisfaction	support for social welfare	.07	support for social welfare	-.07	legitimation of protest	-.04	political salience	.06
	satisfaction with government	.07	disagreement with government priorities	-.05	political salience	-.06		
	disagreement with government priorities	.11						
	Liberal Party identification	-.05						
	New Democratic Party identification	-.05						
Personal alienation	support for social welfare	.05	outlaw strike breaking	-.03	too much inequality	-.06	political efficacy	.04
	satisfaction with government	.07	satisfaction with government	-.07	political efficacy	.04	outlaw strike breaking	.05
	disagreement with government priorities	.09	New Democratic Party identification	-.04			legitimation of protest	.05
Financial satisfaction	support for social welfare	.04	support for social welfare	.06	support for minorities	-.06	support for social welfare	-.06
			support for minorities	.06			outlaw strike breaking	-.05
			too much inequality	.04			too much inequality	-.09
			legitimation of protest	-.04			more redistributive taxation	-.05
			satisfaction with government	.05			disagreement with government priorities	-.05
Satisfaction with marriage	satisfaction with government	-.07	support for minorities	-.06	support for social welfare	-.06	more redistributive taxation	-.04
	disagreement with government priorities	.09	more redistributive taxation	-.04	too much inequality	.06	legitimation of protest	-.05
			satisfaction with government	.05	disagreement with government priorities	-.04		
			political efficiacy	.04				
			Liberal Party identification	.04				
Interpersonal trust	no significant terms		no such term		no such term		more redistributive taxation	-.04
							support for minorities	.04
Personal efficacy	too much inequality	.07	no such term		no such term		Liberal Party identification	-.08
	political efficacy	-.09						

tentative support to Ingelhart's prediction. Whereas, (as indicated earlier), higher levels of financial satisfaction are associated with more conservative political orientations, there is a consistent pattern of interaction shown here which indicates a muting or reversal of the relationship amongst younger Canadians. Whether this is evidence of a persisting effect of differential socialization as Ingelhart suggests, or whether there is a maturation process in which aging is associated with increasing conservatism cannot, however, be determined from these results.

Conclusions

The results reported here suggest the need for a very critical and skeptical appraisal of recent theoretical development in non-Marxist political sociology. There is no support in our results for the notion that traditional structural cleavages are displaced by psychological motivations as explanations of political orientation in the mass public. Public political attitudes in this analysis are largely eccentric and disorganized, poorly rooted in the structure of society or of the individual personality. Nevertheless, our analysis suggests that structural factors remain important to such coherent political activity as there may be--as important as any independent variation in socialization and personality development. This suggests that there are good reasons for interest in contemporary Marxist alternatives to bourgeois political sociology--alternatives which argue that politics is rooted in the structural arrangement of classes in a capitalist social formation, in the mediation of class interests through political organization, and in the representation and integration of class forces in state action. Theories of political change which fail to link ideological changes to these underlying social and political roots cannot make sense of concrete political struggles or of the objective momentum of political change. Sophisticated analysis of these dynamics would, of course, be concerned with ideological articulation, but that articulation cannot be seen as a mechanical response to a changing economic structure, which thereafter takes on an independent and decisive role in producing a new political order. Crude economism is characteristic of the theoretical arguments we have reviewed here, although the economism is submerged in the idealist and voluntarist logic of the main argument for the decisive significance of new patterns of value and motivation.

We have looked at the argument that political demands and protest in late capitalist societies reflect dissatisfaction with the quality of life, whether that dissatisfaction be assumed to arise from the frustration of new values or from the unregulated stimulation of expectations about the satisfaction of individual and group interests. There is very little evidence in our results to support such argument. Dissatisfaction with the quality of life in general terms is associated with dissatisfaction with governments and with a lower propensity to support the ruling party in the national government, but it is associated also with support for, rather than opposition to, existing public policy priorities. Financial dissatisfaction is associated with dissatisfaction with governments, with lower support for the ruling party, with opposition to public policy priorities, but with support for social welfare programmes and principles. In this latter connection, there is no evidence either of a dissatisfied "backlash" against the capacities and costs of the "welfare state", or of a general tendency for conservative political orientations to be associated with the frustration of material as opposed to non-material values. There is some evidence, however, that younger and older cohorts in the population respond differently to material satisfaction -- younger people being inclined to less rather than more conservative political orientations in response to high levels of financial satisfaction.

While these results, therefore, indicate some connection between political demands or protest and dissatisfaction with the quality of life, the connections are statistically weak and substantively inconsistent with arguments for a weakening of the traditional supports of the capitalist welfare state or for a redirection of politics from cleavages based on material inequalities to those based on post-material values. Furthermore, the influence of psychological factors on politics is, in our results, much more strongly evident in relation to feelings of inter-personal trust and competence than to feelings of dissatisfaction with the quality of life. That is, feelings of political efficacy and, by interpolation from well established findings, actual political participation are much more motivated by a sense of interpersonal trust and competence than by frustration with the quality of life. Support for the political status quo is correspondingly motivated more by a sense of interpersonal trust and competence than by satisfaction with the quality of life. This suggests that psychological support for the capitalist political order is relatively securely based in the greater political activism and conservatism of those for whom privelege in this kind of society has not prevented the erosion of a sense of trust and competence in interpersonal relations that is typically brought about by the stress on competition and consumption as standards of personal worth. Until there is compelling evidence of a significant change in these latter values, there will be little reason to anticipate any significant process of political change or disorder along the lines outlined in the recent political sociology discussed here.

Appendix A

I. Measures of the Quality of Life

1. General life satisfaction: This variable is measured by summing the standardized scores of items, that read as follows:

a. All things considered, how satisfied are you with your life as a whole? Which number comes closest to how you feel? (responses are chosen from a card showing an eleven point scale in which the value 1 is labelled "completely dissatisfied," the value 11 is labelled "completely satisfied," and the value 6 is labelled "neutral.")

b. Here is a picture of a ladder. At the top of the ladder is the best life you can imagine--the ideal life. At the bottom of the ladder is the worst life you can imagine. Where on the ladder would you place your present life? (the ladder runs from the bottom value 0, labelled "the worst you can imagine," to a top value of 10, labelled "the best you can imagine.")

c. We want to learn how Canadians feel about different parts of the lives they lead--for example, how they feel about where they live or where they work. We would like you to give a grade to a number of parts of your life, just as teachers give grades to students. Please give each of the following parts of your life a grade which best expresses your judgement of it. What grade would you give your life as a whole? (responses were scored from 1, for a grade A, to 10, for a grade of F).

d. A repetition of a. above, later in the instrument.

2. Personal disaffection: Six semantic differential ratings of "your present life" are summed to yield this measure. The continua are labelled at the ends (of a seven point scale) with the adjective pairs: boring--interesting; lonely--not lonely; meaningless-meaningful; useless-useful; disappointing--rewarding; disgusting--enjoyable.

3. Financial satisfaction: This variable is created by summing standardized scores for ratings of "your financial situation" obtained by three items with the form of the measures of general life satisfaction, 1a, 1b, and 1c, above.

4. Satisfaction with marriage or romantic relationships: This variable is obtained by summing ratings of "your marriage" (for married persons) or "your romantic

relations" (for the unmarried) of the form of 1a and 1b, above.

5. Interpersonal trust: The three item scale developed for the SRC election studies from Rosenberg's "faith in people" scale is used here. See Robinson and Shaver (1969: 615-7).

II. Measures of Socio-Demographic Variables

Only three of these variables are not defined in a self-explanatory way. Educational attainment in years is estimated from the mid-points of ten response categories. Family income takes on one of eighteen values equal to the mean of the logarithms of the bottom and top values of the categories of income chosen by the respondent. Respondents who refused to state their family income or did not know it, were given the modal value. To insure the adequacy of this treatment of missing values, a dummy variable, labelled "income unknown," with the value one for persons with income missing and zero otherwise, was also included in the regression. The occupation variable describes the occupation of the respondent when he or she was employed and that of his or her spouse when the respondent was not in the labour force. The retired were assigned their previous occupations. Jobs were divided into six categories on the basis of differences in levels of skill and the manual-non-manual division. These six categories are formed by collapsing the sixteen "unit groups" established for Canadian census occupational titles by Pineo, Porter, and McRoberts (1977). Our skilled non-manual category includes supervisors, semi-professionals, and skilled clerical and sales workers; the skilled manual category contains technicians, supervisors and skilled craft workers; the unskilled non-manual category includes semi-skilled and unskilled clerical and sales workers; and the unskilled manual category includes semi-skilled and unskilled craft workers and farm labourers. A seventh occupational category contains individuals who neither work nor reside with a working spouse. Six dummy variables measure the difference between this residual category and the six occupational groups described above.

III. Measures of Political Attitudes

A. Left-Right Issues.

1. Support for Social Welfare: Ratings of the amount of effort to be devoted by government to health and medical care, providing assistance to the unemployed, creating more jobs, helping the poor, building public housing, education, helping retired people, and workman's compensation were summed. The responses presented on a

card ranged from "much less effort" (scored 1), through "less effort " (2), "about the same effort" (3) and "more effort" (4), to "much more effort" (5).

2. Support for minorities: Four ratings from the question about government effort described above were summed to obtain this measure. They dealt with protecting the rights of native people, eliminating discrimination against women, protecting the environment, and providing daycare.

3. Outlaw strikebreaking

4. Too much inequality

5. More redistributive taxation.

Each of these measures is a single item response to a statement read. The responses, presented on a card, were scored as follows: strongly disagree--1, disagree--2, neither agree nor disagree--3, agree--4, strongly agree--5. The statements read this way: (3) During a strike, management should be prohibited by law from hiring workers to take the place of strikebreakers. (4) There is too much of a difference between rich and poor in this country. (5) People with high incomes should pay a greater share of the total taxes than they do now.

B. Government Related Issues

1. Political Salience: This measure of attention paid the news media is obtained by summing the four items listed below (with weights, respectively of 7, 11, 7, 11 to compensate for their unequal variances). The scores assigned the responses are in parentheses.

   a. How often do you read a daily newspaper, everyday (4), several times a week (3), about once a week (2), or less often (1)?

   b. Do you read the newspaper editorials frequently (3), sometimes (2), or never (1)?

   c. How often do you watch the news on television, everyday (5), several times a week (4), about once a week (3), or less often (2)? Never watch scored (1).

   d. How much attention do you usually pay to news and current events, a great deal of attention (4), some attention (3), very little attention (2), or none at all (1)?

2. Legitimation of protest: A four part question was used to construct this scale, by simply adding the responses. It reads:

We would like to know how you feel about different kinds of protest which might be used to get the government to change its policies. What about strikes, do you think they can often be justified (scored 3), that they can sometimes be justified (scored 2), or that strikes are never justified (scored 1) to change government policy? What about...

...boycotts?
...legal and peaceful demonstrations, like marches, rallies, and picketing?
...illegal but peaceful demonstrations, like sit-ins? (emphasis in original)

3. Satisfaction with government: This measure is obtained by summing the three responses to this question:

We would like to know how you feel about the actions and programs of different levels of government. How satisfied or dissatisfied are you with:

a. the federal government in Ottawa?
b. the government of this province?
c. the government of this city (town/county)?

(the eleven point satisfaction scale described in IIa, above is used for responses).

4. Disagreement with government priorities: Respondents were asked how much effort they felt that "government should put into a number of activities" ranging from social welfare issues (like "health and medical care" and "helping the poor") to economic priorities (like "cutting inflation") to priorities in other areas (including "eliminating pornography," "foreign aid," and "protecting the environment"). In each area, he or she could give one of the five responses to indicate that "much more," "about the same effort," "less effort," or "much less effort" should be devoted to each one. This variable measures the overall extent to which the respondent departs from a position of absolute support for the status quo in which he or she would call for "about the same effort" in each of the twenty-one areas. Two points are added to the score for each response calling for "much more" or "much less" effort, and one point for those calling for "more" or "less" effort.

5. Political efficacy: This measure is formed by summing responses to four statements, as developed in the Michigan U.S. National Election Studies. The "strongly agree" response, is scored 1, "disagree" is scored 2, "agree" is scored 3, and "strongly disagree" is scored 4. The statements read:

Now, I would like to talk to you about some opinions that you hear different people giving. As I read each one, I would just like you to tell me offhand whether you strongly agree or strongly disagree:

a. Generally, those elected to Parliament soon lose touch with the people.

b. I don't think that the government cares much what people like me think.

c. Sometimes politics and government seem so complicated that a person like me can't really understand what's going on.

d. People like me don't have any say about what the government does.

BIBLIOGRAPHY

Atkinson, T. (1977), Is Satisfaction a Good Measure of the Quality of Life? Paper presented to the Meetings of the American Statistical Association, Washington, D. C.

Bell, D. (1976), The Cultural Contradictions of Capitalism, New York: Basic Books

Bell, D. (1977), The Future World Disorder: The Structural Context of Crisis. In: Foreign Policy 27: 109-135

Blackburn, R. M. and M. Mann. (1975), Ideology in the Non-Skilled Working Class. In: M. Bulmer (Ed.) Working Class Images of Society, London: Routledge and Kegan Paul

Campbell, A., P. Converse, W. Miller and D. Stokes. (1960), The American Voter, New York: Wiley

Campbell, A., P. Converse and W. L. Rodgers. (1976), The Quality of American Life, New York: Russell Sage

Easton, D., and J. Dennis. (1969), Children in the Political System: Origins of Political Legitimacy, New York: McGraw-Hill

Eckstein, H. (1961), A Theory of Stable Democracy, Princeton, N. J.: Center of International Studies

Eckstein, H. and T. Gurr. (1975), Patterns of Authority: A Structural Basis for Political Inquiry, New York: Wiley

Grofman, B. N. and E. N. Muller. (1973), The Strange Case of Relative Gratification and Potential for Political Violence: The V-Curve Hypothesis. In: American Political Science Review, LXVII: 514-39

Inglehart, R. (1979), The Silent Revolution, Princeton: Princeton University Press

Johnston, W. and M. Ornstein. (1979), Social Class and Political Ideology in Canada. Paper presented to Annual Meetings of the American Sociological Association, Boston

Joreskog, K. G. and D. Sorbom. (1976), LISREL III. Estimation of Linear Structural Equation Systems by Maximum Likelihood Methods, Chicago: National Educational Resources Inc.

Kariel, H. S. (Ed.) (1970), Frontiers of Democratic Theory, New York Random House

Lane, R. (1959), Political Life, New York: The Free Press

Leiss, W. (1976), The Limits to Satisfaction, Toronto: University of Toronto Press

Lipset, S. M. (1960), Political Man, Garden City: Doubleday

Lowi, T. J. (1971), The Politics of Disorder, New York: Norton

Lowi, T. J. (1979), The End of Liberalism: The Second Republic of the United States, New York: Norton

Mann, M. (1970), The Social Cohesion of Liberal Democracy. In: American Sociological Review, 35: 423-39

McKennell, A., T. Atkinson and F. Andrews. (1978), Structural Constancies in Surveys of Perceived Well-Being. Paper presented at Ninth World Congress of Sociology, Uppsala

Pineo, P. C., J. Porter and H. A. McRoberts. (1977), The 1971 Census and the Socio-Economic Classification of Occupations. In: Canadian Review of Sociology and Anthropology, 14: 91-102

Portes, A. (1971), On the Logic of Post Factum Explanations: The Hypothesis of Lower Class Frustration as the Cause of Leftist Radicalism. In: Social Forces, 50: 26-44

Stevenson, P. (1977), Frustration, Structural Blame and Leftwing Radicalism. In: Canadian Journal of Sociology, 2: 355-72

Social Value Change and Economic Development: Idiosyncrasies and Non-Linearities

Jesse Goldstaub

ABSTRACT

Management, in an international context, tends to interpret uncertainty and instability as risk. The dynamics of economic development, with its concommitant value change, are replete with idiosyncracies and non-linear patterns of evolution. The interactions and interdependencies of industrial, newly industrializing, and less developed countries heighten the potential vulnerabilities of all parties to the political manifestations emanating from the attempt to use managerial, administrative, and planning techniques as well as infuse technological hardware into systems which do not have the social value structure or institutional framework to absorb them.

A scant thirty years has elapsed since the world has consciously broken with the classical dogma of an invisible hand maintaining irrevocable control over the equilibrium of the economic system and not merely perceived the potentiality of calculated and intentional interference in the status quo, but morally mandated such action relative to less developed countries (LDC's). During this time, the term "development" has been commonly understood to mean growth of production, economic diversification and viability, equitable distribution of income, enhancement of wellbeing (whatever that is) and advances toward full employment. It has also signified national dignity and prestige, political integrity, internal and external security.

Development implies change from the present state to a preferred state. It signifies movement over time towards an objective and it involves setting of goals. Since these goals represent something positive, approximation of them can be conceived of as "progress", the definition of which depends upon social values and a consensus of opinion. In effect, it is directed, sustained, social change and this change is manifested as an interaction of social units in relationships which are generally atypical vis-a-vis previous or current norms. This type of dynamics obviously goes far beyond the sheer economic and encompasses the distribution of interests among significant ethnic, regional, occupational, class, caste, and other organized groups and the perception and articulation of these interests.

One of the principal fixations in industrial nations is that of setting high store on development-oriented attitudes. An attitude is a way of looking at things which is preconditioned by values, generally or individually held.[1] It is said that certain values, hence certain attitudes, are proper for development and others are inimical to development. This is said because our somewhat unique experience as developed systems had taken a particular and peculiar course. Any pronounced deviation therefrom is both suspect and doomed. That is our attitude. We very definitely view with favor an attitude which fosters innovation. The capacity to innovate is tantamount to being deified in our eyes.

Of particular concern in development orientation are the attitudes of individuals towards such values as change, work, acquisitiveness, learning, mobility, and status improvement, and the availability and effectiveness of various incentives and sanctions to achieve individual and social behavior consistent with a national effort. It follows, logically, that the structure of authority and the composition, coherence and values of the governing elites are of importance, as well as the elements of their doctrine, their lines of communication, their relationship to counter-elites and other influential groups within and without that society, and the instruments through which authority is exercised.

Using the context of a system/sub-system or inter-system frame of reference, it is appropriate to speak about the international system in terms of the accommodative capacity. This accommodative capacity is a major part of development, whose criterion and measure might be stated as the ability to sustain successfully and continuously new types of goals and demands and create new types of organizations. Ultimately, therefore, the system evolves the potential for responding efficiently and more or less autonomously to some new range of problems and, in so doing, retains the capacity to cope with different relationships, both internal and external, without totally disrupting the structure of the system or its functioning.

A direct implication of the stress on capacity is the fact that all systems have some outer limit to their capabilities. Systems can be overloaded by demands which are too formidable as such or which constitute simply too many at any one time. Hence, the acquisition of new capability as a measure of success, progress or development is better portrayed as a specialized role structure and differentiated (rather than monolithically rigid) orientation, which together give the system a responsiveness to problems, i.e., capability. Since differentiation alone can mean a dilution of capability, it is necessary to have, at one and the same time, a balancing play of integrative forces to provide cohesiveness and rational direction.

It is generally held that, when change occurs in any part of a social system, it sets in motion a series of compensatory adjustments in other parts of the system until a new dynamic equilibrium is effected by such mutual adjustment. There has also been a consistent view that the development process is uni-directional, i.e., always upward. Yet, empirical experience shows the governments of Ethiopia, Uganda, Tanzania, Zaire, Burma, and other countries have followed policies directed at restricting or prohibiting private investment of foreign capital at various times in their "development" programs and have thereby engendered rapid and blatant regressions in large sectors of their economies, some proceeding so far as to cause a reversion to subsistence production. Moreover, countries frequently change their positions over time; compare the situations of Japan and/or Germany with England (i.e., Great Britain). Countries can and do cross that nebulous dividing line between underdeveloped and developed, and in both directions as well, it should be emphasized.

It has also been assumed in the usual aggregate national planning methodology that projected plan targets can be treated as if they are the end result of uniform growth rates and posited as the effect of a compound interest formula, despite the reality of the development process being "lumpy" and discontinuous operationally. The resources allocation approach to macro planning implies implementation. However, good sectoral data are invariably either lacking completely or highly inadequate. Not only is there a paucity of supporting data for effective macro planning but program and project planning are usually sorely neglected and ill-articulated with one another and within the overall macro framework. The same may be said of macro and micro planning efforts. The result is badly coordinated linkages and gestation periods for development activities, with minimal action elements included in the planning schedule.

Reluctantly, the new witchdoctors of the international technocratic Establishment have had to admit that systems, even (and perhaps especially) technological systems, can and do deteriorate, disintegrate, and perish. Not merely is there no guarantee that development is the natural order of things--as industrial society has been gratified to believe since well before the debacle of the U.N. Development Decade--but the concept of homeostatis loses its applicability when large hybrid social structures are concerned, particularly when they are made up of an amalgam of social forms and technological linkages or accouterments.

Technology and Development

The development process implies economic growth, social modernization and political integration as simultaneous phenomena. The entire social system--defined as the totality of human forces at work which comprise the nation--is being transformed, especially by the assimilation of the substance and attitudes associated with science and technology. The tendency is to forget in our enthusiasm for the marvels of technology that machines will not serve society unless they are serviced, and it is thus that the structure of human organization has had to adjust to its equipment. (No more salient illustration can be provided than to recall one's last humiliating encounter with a computer, even if nothing was folded, spindled, or mutilated.) While an ever increasing amount of intellectual effort is committed to evolving more improved, refined and sophisticated tools, more exotic and esoteric administrative and management systems, little thought has been given to the ends which should be served. Change, rapid and unrelenting change, is welcomed as progressive and desirable, although there is a tremendous and tragic difference between allowing change to occur under the impact of technological revolution and consciously selecting the type of change we want to bring about <u>through</u> technology.

Advances of science and technology which have made possible the amelioration of so many economic hardships in the currently developed portion of the world may also lead to the negation of civilization. It is very difficult, under these circumstances, to retain a childlike faith in the ability of modern science to work unfailingly beneficient miracles. It is now becoming apparent as well that as technology has created material surpluses, it has also accentuated scarcities. It has even necessitated the organization of distributive mechanisms which maintain or reinforce inequities. In economically advanced nations, this contrast between redundancy and scarcity has become pronounced. Their prosperity has made critical the orderly and disciplined management and conservation of urban and rural land, energy resources and a host of natural resources. Moreover, a rise in living standards has increased the need for public services, as larger numbers of individuals with low incomes are enabled to obtain both a wider range of consumer goods and fuller access to health, sanitation, transportation, recreation and cultural services and facilities, and a spectrum of administrative services.

There is, it seems, still minimal cognizance of the fact that by applying technological innovations to economics man has become enmeshed in new relationships which have created an ever more concentrated, integrated, sophisticated and mutually interdependent system structure among people and nations engaged in material production, distribution of goods and services, and communication. Given the capability of the smallest unstable component of a system to destabilize a relatively stable, complex system, the potentialities for disaster are manifest, in that shocks or pressures sufficiently large to change the system state may be of sufficient magnitude not only to result in outcomes which are counterintuitive and undesirable but which irrevocably alter the system structure and thereby the very essence of the total system.

The major question concerning our reliance on technology and our capacity to control and direct it is bound up with the character of technological society, which is oriented toward the principle of rationalization or "efficiency", as it is often construed. Invariably, the scale of social institutions is large--the larger the better, it had been believed, so as to obviate the duplication of functions and redundancy of economic, social or political strucures.

In the golden ghetto in which the world's affluent live, technology is extremely complex, and a bureaucratic mode of organization links huge sub-systems together. Moreover, in the larger scale, highly complex, technological organizations comprising the systems components of a global network, dependency on remote decision making is normative. Moreover, the "high-technology" which has evolved from several generations of technological hardware and software development is one which is built around the concept of fail-safe dependability. Even if this were perceived as part of our modern mythology, the joining of error-prone humanity and potentially error-free technology would still make for a terrifyingly disasterous combination.

The human being is an organic system, and, as such, can be assumed to have a predilection for homeostasis. But technological systems are not organic systems, they are made up of linkages of hardware, software, and administrative and managerial technique, which have been developed at different times and, in many cases, for different objectives. Such systems do not have the interdependent integrity of organic systems, only the interdependence. Recurrently, managerial systems have been put together as a matter of convenience, simply because the components have been available in industrial societies at a particular point in time, easily detachable from other systems combinations which had been conjured up for other purposes, but which could be reshuffled in new permutations and combinations to give new results and innovative capabilities.

If the systems themselves are vulnerable because their combination with humans in some way, shape, or form renders them so--and not because they are indeed vulnerable by their nature as unnatural, non-integral systems--then complex systems are all the more vulnerable because the highly-trained people who are required to interact with, manage, and service the techno-managerial systems which have been spawned are simply not available in sufficient numbers even in the most advanced industrialized countries, much less in the remainder of the world.

Nevertheless, bureaucratization of social, economic, and political structures is proceeding apace (Professor Parkinson would be vindicated if only half as much were accomplished), despite the fact that the excessive compartmentalization which results tends to reinforce resistance to the change which must permeate through institutional structures before the mutually supportive cycles of technological and bureaucratic expansion can be broken into and rendered responsive--for want of a better term to depict compliance with objectives and procedures mandated by a concensus arrived at through broad-based participation.

The industrial mentality has rather persistently regarded five years as a time frame for long-range planning, when social processes--even in a Tofflerian age--still take perhaps two to four times that long to play themselves out in such countries, and substantially longer in those societies where the institutional infrastructure of industrial systems is still being built. Nevertheless, as socio-economic problems mount, interdependencies intensify and the efforts to bring planning in line with the notion of efficiency which has become normative in the technocratic enclave will force such activity to the level of the global system, where these operational biases will engender a more pronounced predisposition towards dysfunctionality, while more and more of the decision-making mandate is removed from the purview and control of its ultimate constituency.

Interdependence and NIEO

The inescapable reality of interdependence has called forth an array of responses representing the evolution of a tentative and detectable framework of international policy-setting mechanisms, such as the negotiations on non-proliferation of nuclear weapons, the U.N. Law of the Sea Conference, the so-called North-South Dialogue, the Code of Conduct for Transnational Corporations negotiations, and a multiplicity of summit conferences by various actors in the system. Quite unmistakably, the perception the less developed and developing countries now have of the extent to which industrial countries themselves, or the multinational corporations headquartered in them, are dependent on their resources increases their potential bargaining position. Not only does the vulnerability of the industrial nations represent a new stage in world relations, but this altered state of affairs is underscored by the realization that the industrial powers are reticent to use massive military intervention to guarantee their needs with the same precipitousness that characterized the era before Vietnam. In addition, the multinationals have fewer options open to them in finding substitute sources for materials than the resource rich nations have in exploiting those resources. The traditional conception of the industrialized world as a monolithic bloc has been severely eroded, despite the attempts of various industrial nations to continue to project this image. As a consequence, the developing societies have the added advantage of using the heightened economic competition among industrial nations for leverage in pricing and trade arrangements.

Clearly, fundamental structural changes are taking place in global economic and political relationships. What is not clear, however, is whether the more fortunate of the less developed countries are capable of mustering and mobilizing the the requisite skills and incorruptable leadership to ensure that the potential new wealth flows will be distributed in a manner which will ameliorate mass poverty.[2]

The basic assumption behind development is that the structures and processes which can be regarded as sub-systems move the system, by their own dynamics, in preferred directions and that the stages of development can be identified by combinations or clusters of evolving processes and structures. Full development would be represented by the ideal stages of the process which a particular society entertains as being its optimal goal, whether that means pre-eminence in terms of mass affluence, political and/or military power, scientific achievement, etc.

Reasoned observation of the phenomena will confirm that economic growth and economic development are not one and the same thing, although the tendency has been to use the terms as virtually synonomous and essentially interchangeable since their conceptual institutionalization in the early 1950's. Growth, in material terms, has brought appreciable benefits to the world's population in the aggregate, and to the more affluent peoples of the globe in particular. The demonstration effect has proven as effective a means of provocation and incentive to effort in the more developed countries of the world as it has in the lesser developed, and the notion of self-sustained growth as a universal objective for mankind is as pervasive in the former as in the latter. The growth that has been experienced previously has incited a level of demand for even greater distribution which simply has not been met in toto since the raising of world consciousness, is not being provided for at present--as witness the vociferousness of the demands for a New International Economic Order--nor can it be satiated by potential levels or rates of future growth.[3] It is this failure which could have exacerbated the inflationary pressures which were being built into the structure of the world economy after the Second World War and reinforced as a part of an already highly integrated and interdependent international economic mechanism in the mid-1960's.

The dynamics of development are, indeed, replete with paradoxes, not the least of which is the fact that an improvement in the economic conditions of an underdeveloped country may expand the purported gap between itself and the advanced economies, because the impact of better medical care and better nutrition reduces infant mortality, increases the life expectancy of the poorest elements of the population base, and, in consequence, substantially reduces the conventional per capita GNP figure.[4]

Comparing national systems by employing GNP or per capita GNP figures is a specious exercise to begin with, for a number of salient reasons of a technical nature.[5] These considerations aside, it would seem vastly inappropriate to consider the less developed world as a monolithic and homogeneous entity. Rather, it is absolutely necessary to recognize its diversity. There exist wider differentials in income levels within the Third World, as it is referred to, than within the industrialized world and, in fact, there is a greater disparity in growth rates in the so-called Third World category than in the industrialized segment. Rapidly expanding economies in Brazil, Venezuela, Columbia, Mexico, South Korea, Taiwan, Hong Kong and Malaysia have outpaced the growth rates of Canada, Britain, and the United States within the time frame of the last two decades. The incremental, almost exponential, growth rates of the Middle Eastern oil countries certainly puts the lie to any conception of the Third World as a cohesive stereotype of consistently low average incomes, living conditions, and growth rates. It may be more accurate to view these states as the Third World of OPEC countries, the Fourth World of non-OPEC newly industrializing countries (NIC's), and a Fifth World of states whose present lack of absorptive capacity and potential invokes visions of triage on a national scale.

What is particularly dismaying is a simultaneous surrender to the temptation to view all the "emergent nations" as free from the unabashed economic materialism and desire for power manifested in the developed countries, in the face of their demands for steel plants, even if there is a paucity or absence of raw materials, or international airlines, even if there is no currently or potentially profitable market area. The fact is that they clamor for automobiles (with 150 miles of paved all-weather roads intact, betimes leading nowhere), hi-fi equipment (in villages where there is no electricity) and all the goodies and gadgets which the demonstration effect has induced them to believe are intrinsic concomitants of our current, precarious, quasi-utopian condition. The inevitable result of this dual standard has been the exposure of the insidious nature of the demonstration effect; at least as it is increasingly perceived by societies whose historical experience and belief systems are very different from those of the industrialized Western and Eastern Bloc countries.

Our myopic cultural superiority (read arrogance) may contribute to our undoing. It is neither a pretence that is laudable nor is it affordable at this stage of a very dangerous game. The costs of vainly expending greater and greater effort in postulating the usual linear solutions to problems in the more economically advanced societies and filtering them through the perception of a huge interlocking organizational network are simply too high. Past failures can only be duplicated, with a vengeance, by intensifying the pursuit of methods which do not work even in industrial societies (but are conventional and broadly acceptable) and attempting to apply them in less economically developed countries with vastly disparate institutional structures. It must be recognized that all systems do not respond in a similar manner to a given environment or situation, because they select different responses to their perceived situations or problems on the basis of their own particular goal structure and internal logic. These differences in logic and goals depend on the system's inherent and learned disparities, which could be characteristic of an entire group of systems or be unique from system to system, sub-system to sub-system, or country to country.

The Dynamics of Development Administration

The virtually unanimous demand for development compels one to ask whether there are mechanisms whereby such things are accomplished or whether the approach is more like Johanny Appleseed: Just scatter a few billion dollars along the way and let Nature take its course. There is, it seems, a middleman who must utter the proper incantations. These new national and international witchdoctors are called development administrators and, while there is no essential difference in terms of apparent official function between public administration and development administration, there is a definite difference insofar as the kind of activities engaged in. The movement of people, the reconciliation of interests, the coping with and evolution of new relationships, the creation of new procedures, the special undertakings known as development programs and projects, are a vast departure from the normal, ingrained, and established civil service administrative patterns.

The term "civil service" is not quite accurate to describe the features of administrative patterns common to less developed systems (or even more developed systems) and the use of "public service" even more a misnomer, for the attitude towards the public of public servants is one of superiority and the pervading motivation has been self-serving. The style and procedures have been legalistic, formalistic, inelastic and authoritarian, with almost unassailable status arrangements. In most of these countries, employment requirements tend to be rigid, at times little more than resurfaced vestiges of the colonial regime. Patronage is based on kinship and corruption is pervasive; there is no orientation towards goal setting and individual initiative is strangled. Functions are restricted to control and regulation plus a few limited services, with a marked bias in the direction of over-centralization. There is what amounts to a continuous administrative crisis.

This administrative crisis is not rooted in the conventional hue and cry over the shortage of technical personnel. On the contrary, it has its base in the essential deficiency of relevantly trained administrators and the lack of adequate and relevant organization. A number of uncomfortable questions have to be asked about the proper incentives to encourage people in less developed countries to become top technical and professional types. In professionalizing personnel and changing to an innovation-supportive environment, how can professionalism be prevented from becoming self-serving? In the effort to foster greater professionalism, do bureaucrats need protection? If they have to be provided with autonomy, how much autonomy?

More questions pose themselves. Is it best to work with or within old agencies, inside or outside of the civil service, or from within a newly created structure? With the evident bent towards centralization, how can control and review be insured if decentralization is opted for? If there is a lack of experience with local autonomy, is it possible to coordinate, at the local level, community development programs (urban or rural) in the context of responsiveness to national goals? Is reducing demands a feasible alternative or can other instruments be used to ease the burden on administration and management? Is it possible to rely on political organizations, interest groups and associational groups in the activation mix? Where in all this should the decision-making apparatus be located?

Administrative friction is a cost and a very high one, not only socio-politically but economically. The absorptive capacity for efficient and effective use of foreign aid in less developed systems is directly contingent on the administrative and managerial sub-system capacity, the amount of systems overload it will bear, and the degree of differentiation and integration of functions. While economically developed and underdeveloped systems seem to have similar kinds of administrative and managerial problems, there is far less of a range of effective options available to the latter when solutions are sought and when institutions are created and built.

Development practitioners have enshrined as unadulterated wisdom the view that one of the most important institutions that has to be built, and usually one of the most sensitive points in inter-systems relations, is the planning function. The allusion, ideally, is to a viable, dynamic entity, participating fully in the reappraisal, reevaluation, and recasting of development strategy as an ongoing process at all levels of decision-making, with the capacity to formulate and assess programs and projects and assure their proper implementation. What has been manifested thus far has in the main been the establishment of planning offices which churn out paper plans on demand, although relatively few countries have gotten that far in accumulating technical expertise, even now.

When the establishment of a national planning office is forced, a disaster at times ensues in which it is skillfully turned into a mechanism for the power elite neutralizing potentially obstreperous individuals by naming them to these sub-ministerial circuses, which also incapacitates the talents of some fine young professional staff for several years, before the organization becomes known as the largest leper colony in the land and is rendered defunct. The rationale in many cases for creation of such an organization (and its abortive institutionalization) is to have an acceptable funnel for foreign aid and technical assistance, which have usually gone into a host country and out of it as well, _in toto_. There has been little distinction between hardware and software in the hard sell. The double bed, for all of its purported maximization of opportunity, has probably ruined more marriages than are admitted to in public or private; and in the case of the marriages of convenience that developed countries have entered into with less developed nations, not to mention the sordid affairs through the years, there is more reason to believe that twin beds, with financial/material aid in one and technical assistance in the other would be a far more effective strategy than the "all or nothing at all" approach.

Since human systems do at least tend to optimize a given organization vis-a-vis a specific _set_ of variables, the ideas of mission, objective, goal and purpose become starkly significant. However, even in the case of economic development, the behavior of governments and the process of technological growth would make the presumption of a rational purpose _a priori_ a seemingly premature exercise, if not completely open to question. National priorities are subject to recurrent change as both the course of external (international) events and internal pressures impact national sub-systems. This is only to be expected. Still, keen perspective is necessary at this very critical juncture in world history and the disconcerting rapidity of social value change cannot be allowed to obscure reality with illusion. The concern with technology, human or natural resources, or energy _per se_ has beclouded the true issues of the next two decades. The level of urbanization in more developed countries has led to fiscal breakdown and physical decay. In North American, particularly the United States, a devastating process of urban triage is going on. But in less developed countries, already suffering from systems overload, the real period of rapid urbanization is yet to come, when agricultural productivity will impel the displacement to urban areas of rural populations which still comprise an average of sixty per cent of total population in less developed countries as an aggregate.[6] Unless effective mechanisms are quickly put into place for coping with the potential technological unemployment of half of the world's labor force, and its concommitant inundation of cities unprepared to plan and manage efficiently, the results will, quite literally, shake the earth.

Employment and Education: A Modern Morass

While there are blatant and tangible forces which may impinge upon the international system in decidedly deleterious ways, there are also those which can insidiously militate toward functionally negative resolutions of the devleopment process. In 1946, the United States committed itself to a policy of "full employment", without at that time making a sensitive and totally systematic analysis of either the range of implications or choices. The nebulous American domestic unemployment target was originally estimated at 3 per cent and is now being debated at about 5½ per cent, give or take a further indeterminate margin of tolerance. In Britain, France, Italy, and West Germany, the targets and levels of tolerance have been substantially different, both from one another and from the political determination made in the United States and in Canada. The Scandanavian countries and Japan set benchmarks for employment and unemployment according to their own specific historical experience and social priorities.

Whatever the arithmetic variation within the industrial world, it is not as important as the fact that institutionalized foreign aid efforts have exported the advanced economies' perception of full employment as a development objective. Labor force sample survey technique for assessment of unemployment, conducted in establishments as standard full time measure, leads to monsterous distortions when attempted in less developed societies. (This is not to say that household survey census data obtained in non-industrialized nations leaves much less to be desired.) However, the brutal reality of existence in LDC's is that of rampant underemployment, particularly in the continually growing segment of non-rural population no longer engaged in subsistence agriculture and unabsorbable in small industrial sectors established with capital-intensive technology.

Along with its labor force manifestations, the philosophy of full employment, which is now embedded as a primal demand in the NIEO Declaration, has an inherent education component. It internalizes the stance that the experimental, problem-solving attitude is a psychological set which, it is believed, can be conditioned into people through education. Impelled by this notion (and aid money), the overseas trained planning elite have repeatedly directed that elementary schools and schools of every description be built broadcast, with little evidence of physical, locational, or logistical feasibility. The result has been more semi-literate youngsters thronging the urban concentrations of LDC's with a school leaving certificate but without absorbable labor market skills. They and a tidal wave of potential secondary school entrants, with not a ghost of a chance of being accommodated by facilities or especially by qualified teachers, constitute political and social dynamite.

International Threat Analysis

Historically, the advantage enjoyed by the expatriot enterprise--nationally owned or privately held--operating in a less developed country has been knowledge. Indeed, the balance of power in any competitive bargaining relationship derives from the possession of skills, techniques, and information. The capacity to assess how much the opposing party needs what the party making a proposal has to offer is critical. Management uses its knowledge to make decisions. Knowledge concerns experiences gained in the past, while decision-making is inherently about a future time frame. And the most important characteristic of the future is its essential uncertainty. It is not a total and absolute uncertainty, however--that would engender utter chaos. It is uncertainty in a substantially relative sense and the predilection of management-type humans is to equate uncertainty with threat and assess it as risk.

There is also the tendency to rely on deterministic models, hedged in by neat and consoling parameters, to linearly project the past into the future, in the expectation that it will be largely accurate "all other things being equal". In an equilibrium system, the odds are in your favor when postulating more of the same. However, as has been pointed out, the international system, especially post 1973-74, is not an equilibrium system; it has very unstable parameters (to put it politely) and, in addition, the power and intensity of random, external and indigenous, elements in quite pronounced. If you blythly project such instability into the future, it is almost like playing Russian roulette with an automatic pistol: there is the iron-clad certainty that you are going to blow your brains out on the very first round, courage and panache not withstanding. Yet these exotic exercises in mental masturbation have become commonplace; and, all too unfortunately, almost all planning, public or private, has such dangerous delusionary properties. The "solution" too often posed for this "technical problem" is to build more complex models to compensate for the higher levels of what is construed as uncertainty.

In addition to the foregoing considerations, it is believed

that Man is--in the natural order of things--one of the superior mammals and, as such, he is not mono-value maximizing. His values come in sets rather than being singular, and his behavior is more complex than the lower mammals and other creatures, in that it is not uni-directional. A plurality of values does not lend itself to the reduction of behavior according to the criterion of economic efficiency which underlies model making.

When dealing with social values, it is imperative to understand that the component elements and parameters of relevance have been altered in a dramatic and revolutionary manner by the pervasive impact of twentieth century technology on both our physical world and on our conceptual frameworks. Power is deployable throughout the international system and the interdependent and vulnerable network of international finance and trade encompasses the vital interests of all nation states. At the very same time, international boundaries are transcended by mutually shared concerns over pressure on finite food supplies, and the cumulative degradation of the global ecology.

The most significant aspect of the now mythological notion of national sovereignty[7] lies in the fact that it is ultimately incapable of deterring the transmission of ideas, wants, and what is alluded to of late as "life styles". Not merely resources can be construed as wasting assets, but isolation, anonymity, privacy, and values--individually or collectively held--are the subject of preservation and conservation in resistance to impinging exogenous concepts which threaten to radically affect the manner in which any society perceives itself and holds certain truths to be self-evident as a fundamental legitimation of its functional viability and structural integrity. Yet, in our world system, the traditional distinction between international and domestic issues becomes increasingly irrelevant because problems are transmitted from one sub-system to another with the ease and rapidity of an epidemic. Supposedly internal concerns almost always have international ramifications and few international events do not translate themselves into matters which have to be addressed or conditions which must be accepted and/or adjusted to domestically.

Threats to operational continuity which organizations from industrial nations have increasingly encountered in their environment are not invariably political in character or motivation, nor do they derive, of necessity, from disparities between heightened expectations of economic development and perceived realities.[8] However, events have rather consistently shown a consonance of political instability and such cognitive dissonance,[9] which involves macro- or micro-economic risk.

It is at the middle stages of socio-economic development that aspirations and expectations are most likely to have been elevated by promises of change and also frustrated in great measure by the constant problems of national development plan, program, and project implementation. It is in transitional societies that dissatisfaction (dysfunctional politico-economic tension) peaks in intensity as a result of the manifest inability to resolve the conflict of unmet demands through available institutional structures such as political parties and election procedures. For it has become manifest, if "more developed" systems would only learn from what are alluded to as "less developed" systems, that the inability to gain access to, attain membership and participate in, and formulate the goals of, institutional forms which are available in an organized society results in those members of a social system, so disenfranchised, using methods outside institutionalized means to make their demands heard and have their needs met--violently, if necessary.

The potential for conflict to increase risk is a function of the nature of the threat, the conditions under which it occurs, and the response capabilities of the institutions or organizations affected. Threats range from debt repudiation, nationalization, expropriation, curtailment and/or disruption of raw material supply, deterioration or interdiction of marketing distribution networks, labor unrest, kidnap and ransom of expatriot executive personnel, urban guerrilla activities, terrorism and insurgency, civil war, revolution, military invasion and regional conflict to superpower confrontation employing geo-economic strategies for geo-political objectives or vice versa.

The identification of particular types of threats through the use of indicator formats, and the determination that these threats entail palpable risks, requires that risks be further delineated as region, country, industry, firm, or even project specific. Threat (the clear awareness of exposure and its nature) and risk(qualifiable and quantifiable constraints on, or costs of, actual or potential operations) vary by sector of activity and the extent to which that sector is perceived as being critical to a foreign country's "national interests".

The structure and style of individual firms differ and their sensitivity to and perception of events in the external social, economic, and political environment varies as well. In larger corporations which are highly decentralized, regionally or by product, multiple centers of environmental analysis may exist independently of one another. The dangers posed by the potential of widely conflicting analyses are exacerbated by the predilection to construct quantitative indices and rank country operations by alleged risk. Such assessments are internalized in corporate planning because they are expressed as simple quantities (even out to several decimal places), regardless of the reliability of the evidence upon which they may be based. This, despite Aristotle's admonition in the First

Book of Nicomachean Ethics that it is the mark of a wise man not to require a greater degree of precision than the subject matter admits to.

Hence, questions have to be formulated concerning the probability of conceivable or even implausible politico-economic events occurring and the conditions under which they occur affecting the firm. Since decision-makers, in actuality, often attribute precision to information that is inherently subjective and, by default, tend to focus on small-scale concerns rather than on the larger picture, the meaningful issues for a domestic or transnational enterprise need to be selected and the factors influencing these issues defined before policy and strategy options deriving from an analysis can be explored.

In other words, "What makes YOU afraid?"

NOTES

1. See Jesse Goldstaub, Communications: Purposes, Processes, and Potentials. Toronto: Ryerson, 1980, pp. 7-2 to 7-4.

2. It should be noted that the development which Brazil has experienced has benefited only the top 10% of the population, while the bottom 40% saw their share of gross income decline from 10.6% to 8.1% during the U. N. First Development Decade. In fact, during the 1960's, Brazil's richest 5% increased their share of the national pie from 27.8% to 36.8%; a pattern approximated repeatedly the world over. For additional perspective on Brazil as a case in point, refer to Jesse Goldstaub, "Living With Inflation: The Brazilian Experience", Proceedings of the 49th Annual Couchiching Conference-1980, tape, Couchiching Institute on Public Affairs (formerly the Canadian Institute on Public Affairs), Toronto, Canada.

3. There are as substantial and inherent frustrations in "have" societies as in "have not" societies because the wants generated by the pursuit of the growth ethic are more oriented towards those goods which are not subject to the tricks of modern technology. These "positional goods", as they are often referred to, cannot be mass produced, with unit costs being lowered by enlarging output schedules. Their attraction in fact derives from their very scarcity or uniqueness.

4. The extended family system, still the prevalent form of social organization in LDC's, provides all its members with intra-family services of some sort, which are valuable --often life-sustaining--but do not enter into the national accounts statistics.

5. The work of Robert Summers and his University of Pennsylvania group for the United Nations International Comparison Project is a prodigious effort designed to solve some of these procedural constraints and conceptual shortcomings.

6. The possibility of marked technological changes in the food growing process, including the use of hydroponic methods, will have even more of an impact on production than the "green revolution" at its much vaunted apogee of success. What is required, however, is not merely improved yields but the concommitant infrastructure (food storage, transport, and distribution) programs which will decrease the consistent 35%-45% wastage and spoilage loss from current output and get the vast preponderance of agricultural produce in less developed nations to people and not rats.

7. Cf. Jesse Goldstaub, "The Development Game", copyright 1977 (reprints 1978, University of Calgary, and 1980, University of Toronto), pp. 22-23.

8. See James C. Davies, "Toward A Theory of Revolution", *American Sociological Review*, February 1962, p. 6, for his exposition of the "J-curve of revolution"; and Chalmers Johnson, *Revolutionary Change*. Boston: Little, Brown, 1966 as well as his *Revolution and the Social System*. Stanford, Conn.: The Hoover Institution on War, Revolution, and Peace, 1964, for an identification of the four sources of pressures for social change that produce violence, i.e. exogenous (foreign) value changing, endogenous (domestic) value changing, exogenous environment changing, and endogenous environment changing. Included in the environmental changes are the introduction of increasingly advanced technology into developing societies, stimulation of the economic development process by production for external markets, and the alteration in domestic skill and knowledge profiles which drastically affect labor force absorbability and relative scales of remuneration. There may very well be a stimulative effect on political instability simply in the perceived incompatability of norms and values deriving from pressures to change and the countervailing desire to maintain and protect valued resources, relationships, or positions.

9. Among the more pertinent references on this subject are I.K. Feierabend, R. L. Feierabend, and B. A. Nesvold, "Social Change and Political Violence" *in* H. D. Graham and T. R. Gurr, eds., *Violence in America: Historical and Comparative Perspectives*, Vol. II. Washington, D.C.: U.S. Government Printing Office, 1969; Ted R. Gurr. *Why Men Rebel*. Princeton: Princeton University Press, 1971; and Douglas Hibbs, Jr. *Mass Political Violence: A Cross Causal Analysis*. New York: Wiley, 1973.

Part III
Values, External Exchange Processes and the Employment Relationship

A. Value Systems and External Exchange Processes

Relationships Between Social Values, the Education System and the Structure and Performance of Labour Markets

Klaus Weiermair

ABSTRACT

The paper makes an attempt to show how design changes and reforms in education affect the behaviour of labour markets and the nature of the employment relationship. Of particular relevance in this context are aspects of socialization and qualitative uncertainties associated with educational output which are shown to heavily influence the structure and performance of labour markets. Changes in the system of education are in turn identified as the results of deeper and more fundamental changes in the system of social values of a given society. Consequently, labour market behaviour is postulated to be in large measure a function of social values and social value changes contrary to orthodox views in economics which postulates a strict process of economic technological determinancy.

I

In the past, a fair amount of literature in a number of social science disciplines have postulated and analyzed relationships between employment, education and social values under either explicit or implicit assumptions of a strict economic/technological determinancy and supremacy. It is e.g. the orthodox view in economics that economic development, or in the case of industrialized countries, economic growth, ultimately determine size and composition of labour force and, hence, the system of education. While usually a host of qualifications are made and while potential imperfections in this linkage from growth to labour market and education system are recognized the causality is nevertheless assumed to strictly run from economic forces created in product markets to labour and education as the derived inputs of the economic system. Neoclassical explanations regarding the economics of human capital formation (Becker 1964), the nature of the employment relationship (Alchian & Demsetz 1972) and/or the extent of division of labour in organization-external and -internal labour markets (Stigler 1951, Kilbridge & Wester 1966) typically share this assumption and methodology. A somewhat similar causality of economic forces ultimately determining the production and utilization of skills, can be found in marxian analyses of labour and education although market forces now are replaced by the economic interest, power and control of capital owners who thereby also control the process of education and training (Bowles and Gintis 1975). A functional view of education is also entertained in much of sociological analysis where it is viewed as either a linkage between the social standings of different generations or as a source of social stratification among members of society at given points in time. Long-run social trends (equilibria) are in turn postulated to establish status consistencies which suggests a convergence of such status consistencies across countries at similar levels of economic development/growth (Archer and Giner 71). Given education's role in social stratification, sociologists have understandably turned much of their attention to studying access to education rather than analyzing social forces underlying and leading to changes in systems of education beyond those traditionally spelled-out by economists.[1]

If we were to accept such reasoning and the implied conceptualization with respect to the interrelationship between social values, education and labour, we should also be able to find a convergence in structures and systems of education, the employment relationship and the structure and behaviour of labour markets at least across those countries which are at similar levels of economic development. Similarly, we should expect great similarities in the pattern of allocation of work and workers within comparable organizations across equally industrialized countries. None of the numerous micro and macro comparisons in the fields of labour and education undertaken throughout the industrialized part of the world but notably in Europe, Japan and the United States, have been able to rigorously and clearly confirm such a convergence.[2] Rather, we seem to find large and persisting differences across industrialized countries with respect to the nature of the employment relationship, the division of labour, the pattern of work organization and the type and amount of schooling and training held by workers. This paper attempts to explain divergencies of this kind focusing on social values and social value changes as the primary explanatory variables. The paper is organized as follows: part II will provide a discussion of economic factors linking education and employment or the production and utilization of skills, part III will demonstrate the strategic importance of social values in the design of the education system and, finally, part IV will briefly discuss implications of social value differences with respect to the structure and performance of organization-external and -internal labour markets.

II

We shall start our discussion of linkages between education and labour or the education- and employment-system by first analyzing economic properties of qualifications which in the main are produced through the system of education. Subsequently, we will describe typical adjustments and adaptations of firms and individuals to the availability of alternate forms and levels of human capital.

Qualifications obtainable within a given social system of education (learning and training) are linked to the system of employment and, hence, to the internal allocation of labour within employing organizations, through three distinct elements or characteristics. These are: 1) cognitive and noncognitive skills produced through education and training and destined for ultimate utilization in employment, 2) information about skill levels and skill proficiencies and its availability to both the potential employer and the skill holder, and finally, 3) social qualifications acquired as joint products of schooling or training through various forms of socialization processes, which yield alternative attitudes and values with respect to work and work organization. In short, we can distinguish skill-, information- and social-dimensions in the process of human capital formation, all of which have economic value to the individual and to society and all of which effect the performance of labour markets. As will be shown later, variations in the forementioned dimensions of human capital formation are mainly determined by the way in which we design systems of education. Before probing much further in this direction, we have to develop more fully as to what these skill dimensions precisely entail and how they are acquired.

The formation of cognitive and vocational skills are the more obvious and important aspect of education, a view which has been emphasized particularly by those economists who maintain a functional interpretation of education and educational processes. For purposes of economic analysis, it is useful to distinguish between general-, occupation-, and job-or-firm-specific skills.[3] General skills are defined as those skills which can be applied in employment universally and throughout all firms, industries or sectors. Most prominent among these skills are general communication skills, interpersonal relation skills, organization and problem-solving capabilities, etc. Many of these skills are acquired in formal schools but they can be equally learnt in the home environment, parts could be taught in vocational training, probably a very small part is learnt through work experience. Occupational and/or vocational skills can be defined as skills which enable a person to execute a given cluster of tasks, traditionally constituting an occupation. For the most part, vocational and professional schools provide avenues to acquire such skills, with on-the-job-learning and -training acting both as a substitute and complement to schooling. Home-environment typically provides less opportunity for developing these skills. Finally, job- and firm-specific skills are acquired in the context of a specific job in a given organization and essentially entail familiarity with the physical and human environment of the work place and its productive use. These skills are foremost learnt through on-the-job experience and -training. Schools and training programmes which specialize in occupational-, or professional education sometimes include firm-specific aspects in their curricula. Neither general schooling nor home environment contain noticeable elements of firm-specific training. Intertemporal and/or cross-country comparisons of education systems show large variations both in the composition and overall pattern of this skill production process. E.g., we can discern jurisdictions or cultures which emphasize the production of general type skills compared to countries which spent a higher share of resources on the formation of occupation- and firm-specific skills; similarly, great variances can be observed with respect to the origins of human capital formation in that some countries rely more heavily on private sector involvement (employer-sponsored forms of training and education) while others may have delegated all forms of human capital formation to the institutionalized sector of education.

The second dimension of skill formation is concerned with the labeling of skills and associated variances in the pattern of production and consumption of such labels or "signals".[4] Skills and qualifications can in principle be documented informally or formally through certification. The latter can either be very detailed spelling out every functional area of cognitive, affective and sensomotoric qualification or very general certifying in the extreme case merely areas of competence or maturity. Systems of training and education can vary appreciably with respect to the type and completeness of certification. E.g. many vocational skills acquired through training in the home environment or on-the-job rarely are certified and information pertaining to these skills, therefore rest with the individual skill holder and the employer. Behavioural qualifications also are rarely documented to any great detail in school reports particularly at higher levels of education, unless character development has remained an integral part of the education system.[5] But even the certification of cognitive skills can produce substantial informational uncertainties to both skill holder and skill user, such as is e.g. true for an education systems which heavily differentiates with respect to schooling quality- and testing-(certification-) procedures.

Our last dimension in education relevant to subsequent discussions on linkages between education and employment deals with what we referred to earlier as social capital formation. Among the socialization processes at work and in school, we concern ourselves merely with those social values and skills relevant to the employment sector. Among the most important ones are values towards work, perceptions and aspirations with respect to individual development and values underlying competitive or cooperative behaviour. Again, we find variations both across countries and over time as to a) which sectors perform most of the socialization, and b) which values are to prevail. E.g. for some specific categories of workers, a large amount of socialization with respect to the forementioned values may take place at work; this is particularly true when training occurs at an early age and is performed by the employer such as can be found in many European apprenticeship training programmes. Alternatively, socialization to work values may be contained in curricula of formal schooling or it may be left out of school curricula and instead be delegated to third institutions such as the family, the church, the media or other specialized agencies such as occupational counselling, etc. For the employer and/or the employment system, it is obviously not irrelevant as to who performs most of the socializing nor is its content. An internalized value system which stresses and reproduces loyalty, trust, restraint, subordination, acceptance of group norms, cooperation and consensus formation provides a very different economic environment for the production and utilization of skills than one which stresses evolutionary individualism, self interest, opportunism, competition, contract and litigated resolution, no matter whether these values have been generated through family, school or work experience. Having briefly explained the meaning of skill-, information-, and social properties in the human capital formation process, we turn our attention now to the underlying economic interests among labour market participants in the production and utilization of the forementioned skill categories. In so doing, we assume that individuals want to maximize expected lifetime earnings and firms attempt to capture and maximize worker productivities net of wage payments over their expected period of tenure, subject to given constraints such as e.g. the institutional make-up of the education system, labour market information uncertainties, level of risk aversion, etc. When choosing between investments in general-, occupation-, job- or firm-specific skills workers must be foremost concerned with their long-term career mobility and option-returns contained in either human investment alternative[6] for given distributions of native ability. The worker's choice between skills and qualifications of differing portability (marketability) consequently, consists of weighing costs of restraining future career choice through extensive skill specialization and costs of potential immobilization through firm-specific human investments[7] against the benefits of higher productivity and earnings associated with specialization. Although the literature has produced a rich account of the many implications of skill specialization within the firm vis-a-vis the employment relationship,[8] main-stream economics was quick to conclude that underlying economies dictate workers to undertake relatively more general-type training and to secure their returns particularly those of firm-specific training through increased actual or potential mobility (Becker 1964, Parsons

1972, Pencavel 1972). High mobility would in turn push competitive firms to reduce human investments to a bare minimum of induction-, health- and safety- and supervisory training, all varieties of firm-specific human investment; on the other hand, general-type training would in this environment be entirely delegated to the educational sector. Since presently, North-American labour markets portrait this scenario the neoclassical paradigm was said to perform well: our perspectives change, however, very quickly if we were to apply human capital theory to other jurisdictions where organization-external mobilities are very low such as is e.g. the case with some European countries or Japan. The latter not only illustrates the limitations of "methodological individualism" but also show the necessity for an interdisciplinary approach in order to provide satisfactory or "universally valid" explanations for the process of human capital formation which would hold across countries and over time.

For as Fox and others (Fox 1974) have argued convincingly, mobility behaviour itself can be socially predetermined. To the extent that individual workers keep themselves closely attached to organization-external labour markets in order to preserve their maximum perceived personal worth (maximum opportunity) instead of specializing and investing in firm-, job- and task-specific skills within the employing organization, such action may simply reflect low faith and trust in an otherwise socially more diffuse long-term employment relationship where workers may perceive little control over the gains from organization-specific human investments in particular or cooperation in general.[9] The latter reasoning reflects, however, a very specific and probably culturally determined view of the employment-relationship e.g. one, which interprets it as a pure economic exchange, which ideally is to be contractually secured on account of high levels of mistrust among the partners to the exchange. At the other extreme, we might postulate an employment exchange which takes place in an atmosphere of high trust and empathy providing a low cost/risk environment for employer sponsored forms of schooling and training, general- as well as firm-specific. Attempts to "ex post" rationalize varying environments for the formation of human capital in terms of their inherent economic characteristics, such as differences in transaction costs for human resources (Bodenhoefer 1967), levels of opportunism (Williamson, Wachter & Harris 1975, Williamson 1976) or potential for employee shirking (Alchian and Demsetz 1972) fail to recognize the paramount importance which has to be attached to social values and their changes over time and across borders as ultimate determinants. To the extent that values such as trust, loyalty, restraint or alternatively contract and litigated resolution, independence and mistrust enter as inputs into the educational process they have to be reckoned as independent factors determining both the system of education and the structure and behaviour of labour markets.

If individual endeavours to remain mobile and acquire relatively more general-type schooling and training or at the other extreme, to strive for longer-term attachments to jobs and employers and acquire more occupation- and firm-specific training become ends in themselves, one might query welfare implications of such alternate skill distributions under either value system. The following tentative generalizations can be offered in this context: if economic growth and technological change require ever increasing shares of general skills as opposed to occupation-, job- and firm-specific skills no welfare losses should arise from high mobility and biases towards general-type schooling; contrary in this case technological change is well matched to social change, thereby, reducing both transaction costs of human resource development and facilitating adjustments in the educational sector to manpower requirements signalled in the labour market. If technological and economic changes require relatively less general-type training and schooling either the education sector, the employment sector or both will have to adjust. With high mobility of manpower resources and competitive markets prevailing throughout major changes are likely to take place in the educational sector, which will respond with the provision of new facilities and programmes for the formation of occupation specific skills.[10] If labour markets are less than perfect and/or if prevailing social values prevent changes of education, major adjustments are likely to occur in the system of employment through restructuring of jobs and organization-internal labour markets together with changes in the recruitment-, training- and promotion-policies of firms. As to how precisely the enterprise sector will adjust both in terms of manpower policies and the structuring of its labour force depends in addition critically on the quality (accuracy) of information about skills produced along with the formation of human capital. The economics of production and utilization of skills is, therefore, intrinsically tied to the dimension of skill labeling and its informational value in both organization-external and -internal labour markets, a focus to which we will turn next. Formal or informal certification of skills has economic value both to the individual skill holder and to the user of skills e.g. the employer. Complete and accurate information on individual qualifications through documentation in educational certificates is of economic significance to the employer in the sense that it lowers costs of hiring (choosing appropriate potential employees for the organization) and costs of placement/assignment (matching the candidate to a specific job or task in the organization). The more specific and accurate the testing and formal certification of cognitive, affective and sensomotoric skills in education the higher its informational value in organizational-external labour markets and, consequently, the lower will be the human resource costs to the employer. Selection and screening of potential employees invariably requires real resources. This poses the question as to who is likely to perform this function, the education system or the employment system, who is to shoulder the cost and which sector could perform this function more efficiently in terms of social cost. The latter derive in the main from possible mismatches of skills to jobs and are heightened when only a small range of substitute skills are available e.g. an education system which only offers very few schooling alternatives at either secondary or tertiary levels could be such a case in point. The costs of screening and sorting human resources will similarly be higher the greater the variance of educational standards for specific education and skill levels with respect to entrance tests, curricula or final exams.[11] Faced with increases in informational uncertainty with respect to qualifications employers have essentially the choice to invest more resources to effectively screen and evaluate new employees, they can themselves undertake human investments in order to obtain information on individuals as a by-product of on-the-job training and experience or they can hedge against quality uncertainty by hiring a higher level of qualification than what is actually required for a given job/task. As will be shown later, the option chosen depends largely on the degree of competition in labour markets and the structuring of the education system.

With respect to the skill holder's (worker's economic interests in revealing true ability (qualification potential) through screening,[12] Stiglitz has shown this to be conditioned by the skewness in the distribution of ability among all workers, the extent to which individuals are informed about their own abilities, the degree of their risk aversion and the structuring of the education system.[13] If some form of majority voting on matters of education exists and if the distribution of abilities is such that the mode lies below the mean, less than the social optimum amount of hierarchical screening will occur.[14] Also, individuals who are uninformed about their own abilities will have less incentives to undergo screening, a tendency which is further strengthened by the existence of risk aversion. Finally, worker incentives for self-selection and screening are heightened with increases in penalties or rewards associated with incorrect/correct sorting of skills and workers. Variations in the latter are to a large measure determined by the density and range of skill qualifications in the education system and the coarseness or fineness of screening. The greater hierarchical distances between different levels of skill formation offered by the education system and the finer the screen the higher will be the pay-offs or potential losses to individuals for correct/incorrect screening. High returns from screening associated with the forementioned configurations of the education system will act in a competitive market like high returns to schooling; individual students/workers will attempt to buy more screening or more similar-type market "signals" pertaining to particular skills or more accurately their informational value.[15]

Whether this in turn will lead to proliferation of signals through new labeling of skills, curricular- and schooling developments or whether the original polarization of skills will continue cannot be predicted unambiguously. Much will depend on the relative costs of acquiring such signals, on whether employers consider entry barriers appropriate screening devices in terms of the relative costs of skill acquisition and on the degree of control exercised by skill holders over future production and employment of such skills and skill substitutes. Historically, monopolistic practices were easier or at least more successful in such professions as law and medicine than e.g. in management or accounting which in turn were probably more successful than other professions such as economics or sociology.[16] Where new layers of skills (qualification) were developed such as was e.g. true for many paraprofessional and technical programmes, employers were shown to be slow to adjust to such new signals or labels.[17] At the other extreme, too much vertical and horizontal gradations of skills can create also quality uncertainty and, hence, the question of skill ladders and certification becomes one of appropriate aggregation in both the production and labeling of skills.[18] Similar economic arguments can be advanced with respect to the social dimensions of human capital except that here, we find that much less testing and certification on social skills is done in either the education or the employment system.

Following our discussion on some of the major economic-theoretical underpinnings of education in terms of the production and consumption of human capital we now proceed to formulate hypotheses as to how rational firms will adjust their personnel policies when faced with specific structural changes in education which have occurred in a number of industrialized countries. Among these are the secular rise in the provision of general-type schooling relative to job-, occupation- and firm-specific schooling and training and, secondly, the increase in quality uncertainty due to a combination of larger differentiation in school programmes or curricula, greater heterogeneities of social skills embedded in the labour force and a secular decline in the amount of screening performed by the educational sector. With respect to the former, the firm can choose to either standardize skills particularly at the lower end of the spectrum and impose heavier managerial controls e.g. change the nature of the work organization, supplement the lack of job/work oriented training provided in the institutionalized sector through various forms of employer sponsored training or where feasible engage in educational upgrading of specific jobs which prior may have required only little vocational or firm-specific preparation. In competitive markets with high levels of organization-external labour mobility and short-run attachment of workers to jobs and to firms, changes in work organization and educational upgrading will dominate. Hence, the secular trend to reduce occupation- and job-specific skills (e.g. in the form of vocational programmes such as apprenticeship) are apt to create a greater polarization of skills in the organization-external labour market, which is further reinforced by the employer, who is now faced with wider distances between job ladders and skill levels. Hence, he would incur higher costs and risks of training and, consequently, is likely to reduce training within the firm and redesign work organization in order to minimize cost.[19] Only where extensive job- and task ideosyncracies exist on account of specific technologies and/or where long-run attachments of workers to the firm prevail will it be in the interest of the enterprise to internalize training and create long and thin job ladders with ample promotional flexibility. Incidentally, the latter is likely to also provide better economies for the establishment of autonomous groups, teams or more generally alternate forms of higher worker participation.

III

In the past, many economists no doubt were in full support of the idea to expand universal education and to increase general schooling for everybody. This was particularly true during the early years of the human capital revolution, when it was believed that increases in the level of general-type schooling and training were the panacea to economic growth and would essentially alleviate all labour market problems (Denison 67, Coleman 66). The great push towards more proliferation, less screening and more university-type (less vocational-type) preparation in education though came from other social science disciplines, notably education, political science and sociology and/or reflected in the main deep-seated philosophical perspectives and social value perceptions on education. With respect to the latter, we can find much evidence in the heated debates over comprehensive education and over educational reforms which in West-Germany took place over the past two decades[20] and which are about to start now in Japan.[21] In this context, education is always viewed as the great equalizer facilitating social change such as e.g. freeing workers politically, advancing the quality of working life and/or equalizing opportunities for everybody. Many of the proposed and executed reforms in education throughout the industrialized world have, apart from confusing demands for a greater equalization of educational opportunities with demands to equalize educational outcomes led directly into institutional growthmanship of education with all its consequences.[22] Although by 1980, it was clear that educational reforms and changes have nowhere achieved the economic targets hoped for originally,[23] there are no clear signs of changes in educational policies in the foreseeable future. From that we can conjecture that design changes in the system of education whether they were early school reforms in the U.S.A. or

recent educational reforms in Europe and Japan, have never been overly concerned with their labour market implications but rather with the implementation of existing or changing social values. Hence, drives for the realization of a more individualistic society based on the notion of "evolutionary individualism" and an acceptance of pluralistic values must necessarily lead to the establishment of an educational system which can be built around individual differences rather than group averages or group norms, one which is concerned with maximizing individual development rather than the development of distinct groups or classes and one which will minimize indoctrination of specific values or character traits in order to promote pluralism. The latter is reinforced through increases in the heterogeneity of the population facilitated through liberal immigration policies. This in turn leads to the creation of an education system in which each school can set its own standards with respect to curriculum, entrance or final exams and which aims at preparing everybody for continued education in universities in order to maximize career mobility potential. The consequences will be a reduction in the hierarchical structuring of education and increases in the lateral differentiation of skills and qualifications thereby increasing polarization of skills and quality uncertainty in the labour market.
At the other extreme, we can still find education systems which have a rich vertical structure and which show little lateral differentiation by virtue of complete standardization of curriculum and performance tests across given levels of education (skill formation). In this system, individuals are tightly sorted and screened according to their educational qualifications, thereby, reducing such costs in the open labour market. While correlations exist between economic development/growth and the general pattern of education, the above discussed specific design parameters of education and their variation across time and jurisdictional borders (with all its labour market implications) are shown to be attributable to fundamental social values and social value differences.

With the exception of behavioural qualifications[24] increases in quality uncertainty of qualifications create general patterns of organizational response. In highly competitive labour markets, firms are not likely to engage in more screening to discriminate between good or bad certificates or to sort good from bad workers since on account of externalities, they will not be able to reap the returns from such general-type screening. The more probable adjustment mechanism will be for firms to segment organization-internal labour markets e.g. to standardize lower level qualifications/skills around the lowest possible common denominator and to upgrade managerial qualifications in terms of educational requirements in order to hedge against quality uncertainty with respect to supervisory skills.[25] If organization-external labour mobilities are low or there is long-run attachment of workers to the firm, the employer will find it profitable to invest in screeening, thereby, increasing the number of organization-internal mobility and the flexibility of internal manpower allocation.

Although the question of labour market performance will be taken up in a latter part of the paper, we may note at this point that increases in the amount of organization-internal labour market segmentation should increase social human resource costs on three counts:

1. There will be less than the social optimum of job-, occupation- and firm-specific schooling, training and screening for the reasons just mentioned.

2. There will be an overinvestment in general-type schooling due to an unnecessary amount of educational upgrading of jobs.[26]

3. There will be less than optimal upward mobility between jobs and occupations at the cost of extensive lateral inter-firm mobility imposing heavy transaction costs on society in terms of extensive job search, frictional unemployment and inflation.

IV

On concluding on the interrelationships between social value system, education and labour markets, we now briefly discuss the performance characteristics of labour markets encountered under the extreme regimes of either modernistic values or traditional values. We refer in this context heavily to the work of Fox and Hirsch (Fox 1974, Hirsch 1976) with respect to the development of modernistic values and to a number of experts on the Japanese education and employment system concerning traditional values (Abbagglen 1973, Okuchi, Karsh and Levine 1974, Yoshino 1968, Rohlen 1976).

Following Hirsch and Fox, we characterize advanced industrialized countries and societies by a high level of individualization and ever increasing tendencies to commercialize relationships of our human existence. Both trends have resulted in the transformation of socially diffuse relations, such as has been also true traditionally for the employment relationship, into very specific, narrowly defined economic exchanges with all of its implications of carefully calculated and jealously guarded reciprocation and its contractual securement. In addition to these evolutionary dynamics of bad faith and distrust, high levels of differentiation and functional specialization, have forced personnel/manpower functions of the firm into the organization-external labour market from where these functions have to be repurchased by the employer albeit at much higher social costs. We are referring here in the main to the screening, training and sorting of workers which in the modernistic system is performed by the organization-external labour market. The net results of these developments yield an organizational environment of low human investment, low attachment of workers to the firm and distinct external reference points for manpower to the organization-external labour market. In the aggregate, this has translated into high and costly job search, frictional unemployment and high levels of inflation on account of opportunistic behaviour of labour market participants and inherent wage drift. Conversely, we can still find traditional yet industrialized societies such as e.g. Japan where traditional social institutions and -social norms have remained an integral part of life and where this has created a set of implicit social exchange relations which are found gratifying for the parties involved. An atmosphere of rich social reciprocal exchange facilitated through personal ties and ample opportunities and economies for human investment, participation and flexible deployment and adjustment of manpower is here created, typified further by a high level of intrinsic values towards work. In the aggregate, this has translated into high productivity, low interfirm mobility and unemployment and low levels of inflation initiated elsewhere through collective bargaining and inflationary wage settlements.

If we leave the big question of convergence versus divergence aside and for others to discuss at this conference, it is interesting to not in finishing that the constant and ever penetrating desire and drive to increase efficiencies so typical of modern societies appear to have stripped most industrialized countries of all their social context which we now seem to have to reintroduce albeit at much higher social costs and, probably, in much less effective ways. Hirsch's and Millendorfer's[27] contentions about the paradox of the efficiency drive may probably after all be true: by searching and insisting on efficiencies everywhere and in every human relationship we may end up in the long-run with less instead of more efficiency since we will all be caught up in a compulsive distributional battle with no consensus and little incentives to increase what we want to distribute.

BIBLIOGRAPHY

Abbagglen, J. (1958), The Japanese Factory: Aspects of Its Social Organization, Free Press

Alchian, A. and Demsetz, H. (1972), Production, Information Costs and Economic Organization, AER 62: 777-795

Archer, M. and Giner, S. (1978), Contemporary Europe: Social Structures and Cultural Patterns, London: Rutledge and Paul

Becker, G. (1964), Human Capital: A Theoretical and Empirical Analysis with Special Reference to Education, NBER: New York

Bowles, S. and Gintis, H. (1975), The Problem With Human Capital Theory: A Marxian Critique. In: American Economic Review: papers and proceedings, No. 65: 68-78

Coleman, J.R. (Ed.) (1966), The Changing American Economy, Basic Books

Denison, E. (1967), Why Growth Rates Differ, Washington: The Brookings Institute

Fox, A. (1974), Beyond Contract: Work, Power and Trust Relations, London: Faber and Faber

Gaspari, Ch. and Millendorfer, H. (1978), Konturen einer Wende Strategien fuer die Zukunft Styria, Graz

Gintis, H. (1976), The Nature of Labor Exchange and the Theory of Capitalist Production. In: The Review of Radical Political Economics 8: No. 2

Hirsch, F. (1976), Social Limits to Growth, Cambridge: Harvard University Press

Hirschman, A.O. (1970), Exit, Voice and Loyalty, Cambridge, Massachusetts

Kilbridge, M. and Wester, L. (1966), An Economic Model for the Division of Labour. In: Management Science 12: B255-269

Okuchi, K., Karsch, B. and Levine, S. (Ed.) (1974), Workers and Employers in Japan: The Japanese Employment Relations System, Princeton and Tokyo University Press

Parsons, D. (1972), Specific Human Capital: An Application to Quit Rates and Lay-off Rates. In: Journal of Political Economy 80: 1120-1143

Pencavel, J. (1977), Wages, Specific Training and Labour Turnover in U.S. Manufacturing Industries. In: International Economic Review 13: 53-64

Rohlen, B. and Frager, R. (1976), The Future of a Tradition, Japanese Spirit in the 1980s, in: Lewis, A. (Ed.), Japan: The Paradox of Progress, New Haven: Yale University Press, 255-278

Stigler, G. (1951), The Division of Labour is Limited by the Extent of the Market. In: The Journal of Political Economy LIX: No. 3

Wachter, M.L. and Williamson, O. (1979), Obligational Markets and the Mechanics of Inflation. In: The Bell Journal of Economics 10: 549-571

Williamson, O., Wachter, M. and Harris, J. (1975), Understanding the Employment Relation: The Analysis of Idiosyncratic Exchange. In: The Bell Journal of Economics 6: 250-278

Yoshino, M. (1968), The Japanese Managerial System, Cambridge: MIT Press

FOOTNOTES

1. For a discussion, see: Randall, C. (1971), Functional and Conflict Theories of Educational Stratification, American Sociological Review 36: 1002-1019

2. See e.g. Dore, R. (1973), British Factory-Japanese Factory: The Origins of National Diversity in Industrial Relations, University of California Press

   Lutz, B. (1976), Bildungssystem und Beschaeftigungsstruktur in Deutschland und Frankreich, in: Mendius, H.G. (Ed.), Betrieb Arbeitsmarkt, Qualifikation, Vol. 1, Frankfurt

   OECD (1970), Occupational and Educational Structures of the Labour Force and Levels of Economic Development, Paris

   OECD (1969), Statistics of the Occupational and Educational Labour Force in 53 Countries, Paris

3. This is an extended version of Becker's classification of general and firm-specific skills and training, for reference see: Becker, G. (1964), Human Capital, in: National Bureau of Economic Research, New York

4. For the definition of this term and its usage, see: Spence (1973), Job Market Signaling. In: The Quarterly Journal of Economics 87: 355-374

5. For a discussion of comparative patterns of socialization at school: see e.g., Moehlman, A.E. and Roucek, J.S. (Ed.) (1951), Comparative Education, New York

   Ringer, F.K. (1979), Education and Society in Modern Europe, Indiana University Press

6. The concept of option returns in education is discussed: Weisbrod, B.A. (1964), External Benefits to Public Education: An Economic Analysis, Princeton University Press

7. For the development of the economic argument, see: Donalson, D. and Eaton, B. (1976), Firm Specific Human Capital: A Shared Investment or Optimal Entrapment. In: Canadian Journal of Economics IX: No. 3 462-472

8. For a comparison of competing paradigms, see: Alchian, A. and Demsetz, H. (1972), Production, Information, Costs and Economic Organization, AER 62: 777-795

   Williamson, O., Wachter, M.L. and Harris, J. (1975), Understanding the Employment Relation: The Analysis of Idiosyncratic Exchange. In: The Bell Journal of Economics 6: No. 1, 250-278

Edwards, R. (1975), Individual Traits and Organizational Incentives: What makes a "good" worker?. In: The Journal of Human Resources II: 51-68

Goldberg, V., Bridges Over Contested Terrain: Exploring the Radical Account of the Employment Relationship. In: The Journal of Economic Behaviour and Organization (forthcoming)

Nutzinger, H. (1976), The Firm as a Social Institution: The Failure of the Contractarian Viewpoint. In: The Economic Analysis 10: No. 3-4, 217-337

9. For a general discussion on the economics of cooperation, see: FitzRoy, F.F. and Mueller, D. (1977), Contract and the Economics of Organization, West-Berlin: International Institute of Management, Discussion paper No. 25

10. Externalities in the provision of general-type training and schooling will dictate its location in the institutionalized sector

11. For a fuller discussion on the market mechanism and the social and private costs of screening, see: Akerlof, G.A. (1976), The Economics of Caste and of the Rat Race and Other Woeful Tales. In: The Quarterly Journal of Economics 89: 600-617

Akerlof, G.A. (1970), The Market for "Lemons": Quality Uncertainty and the Market Mechanism. In: The Quarterly Journal of Economics 84: No. 3, 489-500

Riley, J. (1976), Information, Screening and Human Capital. In: The American Economic Review 66: No. 2, 254-260

Miyazaki, H. (1977), The Rat Race and Internal Labour Markets. In: The Bell Journal of Economics 8: 394-418

Salop, J.K. and Salop, S.C. (1976), Self Selection and Turnover in the Labour Market. In: The Quarterly Journal of Economics 90: No. 4, 619-627

Arrow, K.J. (1973), Higher Education as a Filter. In: The Journal of Public Economics 2: 193-216

Stiglitz, J. (1975), The Theory of "Screening", Education and the Distribution of Income. In: The American Economic Review 65: No. 3, 283-300

12. This would include both institutionalized screening and self-screening in self selection processes.

13. Stiglitz, Ibid., p. 289ff

14. This in turn may give rise to the establishment of private and non-comprehensive schools facilitating self-selection and screening.

15. For a discussion of the market mechanism, see: Spence, D. (1973), Job Market Signaling. In: The Quarterly Journal of Economics 3: 355-374

16. For an economic analysis of licencing, professional earnings and conduct and barriers to entry, see also: Scitovsky, T. (1966), An International Comparison of the Trend of Professional Earnings. In: The American Economic Review 54: 24-42

    Kessel, R. (1958), Price Discrimination in Medicine. In: The Journal of Law and Economics 5: 20-53

    Illich, I. (1970), Deschooling Society, New York

17. For a Canadian empirical study related to the development of community colleges, see e.g.: Skolnik, M.L. and McMullen, W.F. (1970), An Inquiry into Substitution Between Engineers and Technologists. Report submitted to the Committee of the Presidents of the Universities of Ontario, No. 70-2

18. A detailed discussion on optimal levels of aggregation can be found in: Schweikert, K. and Grieger, D. (1975), Die Steuerungsfunktion von Zertifikaten und formalisierten Ausbildungsgaengen fuer das Beschaeftigungssystem, Goettingen

20. For some empirical proof, the reader is referred to the work of LEST (laboratoire de l'economie et sociologie du travail) in Aix-en-Provence, who have collected comparable data on French English and German firms and tested hypotheses regarding differences in work organization on the basis of observed differences in the education system. For an english version, see: Krais, B. (1977), Relationship Between Education and Employment and Their Impact on the Education and Labour Market Policy, West-Berlin: European Center for the Promotion of Vocational Training

20. See e.g. Offe, C. (1975), Berufsausbildungsreform: Eine Fallstudie ueber Reformpolitik, Muenchen: Max Plank Institut

21. Cummings, W. (1976), The Problems and Prospects for Japanese Higher Education in: Japan: The Paradox of Progress, Yale University

22. A situation where essentially only educationists decide as to what is good for mankind and where all budgetary controls rest within the education system. For a discussion, see: Dore, R. (1976), The Diploma Disease, Education, Qualifications and Development, London. For a general discussion, see also Illich, I. (1970), Deschooling Society, New York.

23. These were stimulation of economic growth, more equal distribution of income and an improvement in the functioning of the labour market.

24. Screening and training for behavioural qualifications can be considered a more firm-specific human investment and as such are more insulated from competitive pressures in the labour market.

25. Note that in our explanation, the development of organization-internal labour market segmentation is essentially the result of changes in the system of education.

26. See also Freeman, R. (1976), The Overeducated American, New York

27. Millendorfer, H. and Gaspari, Ch. (1978), Konturen einer Wende Strategien fur die Zukunft, Wien

Social Organization and Changing Consumer Values

Robert N. Mayer and Francesco M. Nicosia

ABSTRACT

The purpose of this paper is to expand the way cultural values are related to consumer behavior. The paper argues that cultural values must first be connected to social institutions and only then to consumer behavior. Viewed from this perspective, some commonly-cited changes in cultural values can be interpreted in new ways, with quite surprising managerial implications.

INTRODUCTION

The topic of this paper is changing consumer values. These values are presumed to be a source of motivation for consumers and thereby a concern of managers in the private and public sectors. Much speculative writing as well as some empirical research has been devoted to the topic of consumer values. One reads, for instance, that there is a swing from the traditional Protestant value of delayed gratification to the hedonistic value of immediate gratification (White, 1980). Or one reads about a small but growing trend toward "voluntary simplicity," where less and simple is preferred to more and complex (Elgin and Mitchell, 1977).

We will return to these intriguing ideas later, for we want to devote the first part of our remarks to some definitional and conceptual issues. Put in somewhat dramatic form, we want to assert that:

(1) there are no consumer values, only cultural values and consumer norms,
(2) the consumer norms that do exist are not very strong influences on consumer behavior,
(3) much of what we think of as change in cultural values is really a shift in the kind of activity in which these values are expressed.

The purpose of the first part of the paper is to clarify these statements.

CULTURAL VALUES OR CONSUMER VALUES?

The question of whether we are discussing <u>cultural</u> values or <u>consumer</u> values is much more than a question of semantics. It bears on central issues in the study of values, such as: (1) the extent to which behavior reflects values, (2) the ways in which values are learned, and (3) the ways in which values change. From a managerial point of view, the distinction elucidates the influence of values on consumer behavior pertaining to energy conservation or the use of credit. We intend to show that thinking in terms of cultural values rather than consumer values highlights the processes that connect values and consumer behavior.

There are many lists of values that supposedly characterize American culture. There is also a great deal of variation in the words, names, and labels used to identify these cultural values. Robin Williams' (1960) oft-cited list of American values contains expressions like "active mastery," "open world view," "rationalism," "orderliness," "universalism," and "individual personality." Philip Kotler's (1972) list of changing values uses completely different words to describe American values: "self-reliance," "hard work," "religious convictions," "husband-dominated home," "respect for individual," "postponed gratification," "sexual chastity," and "independence." There are many other lists of words describing cultural values but the key research questions are: (1) is there any consensus as to what constitutes a cultural value, and (2) is there any consensus on the specific values that characterize American culture?

While most authors are not explicit about what constitutes a cultural value, there does seem to be a minimal, implicit consensus that cultural values are widely held "beliefs" that affirm what is desirable and strongly direct action. Beyond this, however, there is little agreement concerning the number and specific content of American values.

The definition of cultural values given above is useful in conceptualizing change in cultural values. Change may occur either (a) in the degree to which values are widely held or (b) in the extent to which values do guide action. The eventual result may be the disappearance of old values and the appearance of new ones.

Consider the traditional American value of "self-reliance." It is probably safe to say that in 1880 this value was widely shared and guided behavior. Today, one hundred years later, the value is still widely shared, but it may no longer be a strong guide to action. For a variety of reasons, Americans increasingly allow and even expect public and private organizations to define and meet such needs as safe products, generous wage settlements, and quality health care. One can imagine that if people continue to rely on government and other organizations rather than on themselves, the value placed on individual self-reliance will gradually disappear, perhaps to be replaced by a new cultural value.

Sometimes a population's beliefs change, but change in everyday behavior comes more slowly. For example, American beliefs regarding the equality of women have changed dramatically in the last twenty years, but it will probably be at least another twenty years before the general population consistently acts on the basis of these new beliefs.

The point of these examples is that change in cultural values may be defined as a shift in the proportion of people who adhere to a particular belief and/or the extent to which a belief influences action. Both are part of the process by which cultural values change, but only one may be observable at a given point in time.

What are the specific cultural values that exist in the United States today and which may be subject to change in the future? We noted previously that there are many lists but very little consensus regarding the number and content of American cultural values. Since there have been no systematic research efforts to collect these lists and derive a taxonomy of cultural values, we have looked at a number of popular lists (Inglehart, 1977; Mitchell and Baird, 1969; Rokeach, 1973; Williams, 1960; Wilson, 1970; Yankelovitch, 1974) and have done an "intuitive" analysis of the labels in these lists. We have extracted seven possible classes or types of cultural values.

The first three types refer to the means of action and the next four to the ends or goals of action. The means of action can refer to the internal capabilities of the actor or to the external tools available to the actor. Cultural values also prescribe or proscribe certain means of pursuing goals. The three type of cultural values referring to the means of action are summarized below along with examples:

(1) the actor's capabilities -- e.g., "self-reliance," "active mastery"
(2) the tools in the actor's environment -- e.g., "technological optimism," "progress," "scientific rationality"
(3) prescribed or proscribed means -- e.g., "honesty," "fairness"

The remaining four types, as mentioned, refer to the goals themselves. In summary form, they are:

(1) the intended beneficiary -- e.g., "individualism," "collectivism," "humanitarianism," "patriotism," "success ethic"
(2) the overall distribution of benefits -- e.g., "egalitarianism," "elitism"
(3) the kinds of benefits sought -- e.g., "materialism," "personal growth," "voluntary simplicity," "self-realization"
(4) the timing of rewards -- e.g., "delayed gratification," "immediate gratification"

The point of our analysis of the items commonly found in lists of cultural values is that the dimensions contained in these lists are at a level of abstraction that transcends particular types of activities like work, politics, education, religion, or consumption. In other words, cultural values are very general guides to behavior. A cultural value can influence a specific type of behavior or action only when the value has been translated to the level of a norm. It is the role of what we call "social institutions" to create these activity-specific norms. Let us look at these institutions more closely.

INSTITUTIONS AND CONSUMPTION

The term institution has many meanings in the social science literature. We use it here to refer to a regularized pattern of interaction among people, through time and space. Thus, factories, schools, clubs, armies, churches, labor unions, department stores, and restaurants are all examples of institutions. To emphasize the variability of institutions, the following table lists two institutional forms for each of six types of activities.

Table 1:
Examples of Social Institutions

Activity	Alternative Institutional Forms
production	factory guild
religion	cult church
procreation	monogamy polygamy
education	school tutorial
politics	totalitarian democracy
recreation	professional team club

The primary purpose of an institution is to direct the activities necessary to attain the goals of its members--for instance, to help provide food and shelter, to defend the population from invasion, or to transmit knowledge. And the generation and enforcement of norms is the primary mechanism by which institutions function. Norms are rules for the activities within the institution.

The norms that characterize a particular institution are related to a society's cultural values in one of two ways. First, institutional norms are bounded by cultural values. To illustrate, the cultural value "freedom of choice" prevents a private firm from specifying where its employees will live. Second, some norms interpret cultural values into clearer criteria for the performance of specific activities in an institution. For example, in an American business firm, the cultural value "achieve personal success" is interpreted by norms such as "work hard," "be punctual," and "take reasonable risks." The same cultural value may be translated into different norms in another society. Thus, in a French firm, being successful entails retention of one's own property and the minimization of risk. In a Japanese or Russian firm, being successful may be interpreted by still other norms.

The view of society which we are proposing is shown in Figure 1. Institutions intervene between cultural values and human activity via the generation and enforcement of norms. Hence, instead of asking which consumer values influence consumer behavior, we reformulate the question as follows: <u>which institutions create which norms bearing on which consumption activities?</u>

Figure 1: Interrelationships Among
Cultural Values, Institutions, and Activities*

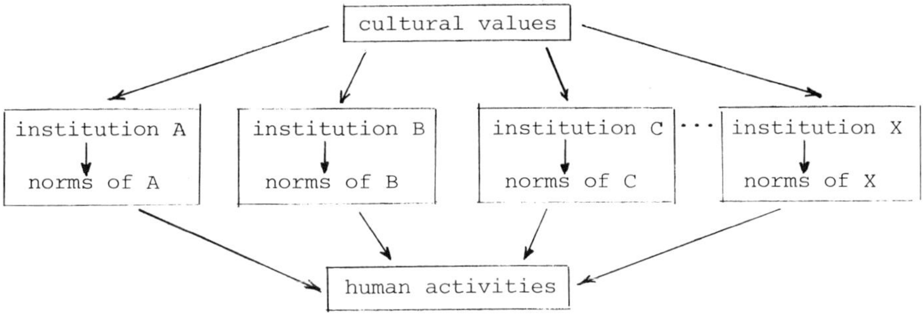

* Of course, a variety of feedback loops are possible (see Nicosia and Mayer, 1976).

In searching for norms bearing on consumption activities, it should be remembered that not only institutions that primarily encompass consumption activities (e.g., laundromats, restaurants, buying clubs) are capable of generating and enforcing consumption norms. Institutions that mainly encompass non-consumption activities (e.g., factories, universities, political parties) may do so as well. For example, people learn consumption norms from their parents and spouse, but also from their co-workers, fellow students, and co-religionists.

Drawing a comprehensive picture of the institutions which influence consumption activities via the generation of consumption norms lies far beyond the scope of this paper. For managerial purposes, it is often sufficient to develop such pictures at the level of one product class or one market segment. Nevertheless, we will try to make some general remarks about consumption institutions in affluent societies. In traditional societies, a variety of different types of activities (work, religion, education, politics) take place within one institution--the family. In modern, affluent societies, however, different types of activities take place in their "own" institution outside the home. Work takes places in factories and offices, education in schools, religion in churches, medical care in hospitals, socialization in day care centers.

Consumption activities also seem to have moved out of the family, but in a different fashion. Rather than consistently shopping, eating, or vacationing in the same place and with the same non-family members, consumption activities occur within a diverse and shifting array of institutions. This has important consequences for consumption norms. First, to the extent that consumption activities take place in a large number of institutions, norms are less likely to be consistent. Second, to the extent that consumption activities are performed alongside a changing array of other consumers, consumption norms are less likely to be communicated and enforced via group pressure. Given this institutional arrangement for many consumption activities, it is not surprising that the main norms operating in modern consumption institutions are "the customer is always right" (i.e., the customer need not follow any norms) and "pretend that other consumers don't exist" (e.g., don't report shoplifters or discuss your purchase decisions with other customers).

In short, a reasonable generalization about the nature of consumption norms in modern, affluent societies is that consumers experience either a lack of norms, or perhaps several competing but weakly enforced norms (e.g., the child who eats dinner at home one night, with friends the next, with the babysitter the next, and with his family at a restaurant the next). Sociologists have a term for such a state of normlessness, "anomie," and this state is not considered a very positive state either for the individual or the society! From a manager's point of view, anomie makes consumer behavior difficult to predict and influence.

APPARENT CHANGE IN CULTURAL VALUES

Suppose one accepts our conceptualization of cultural values as extremely general evaluative standards and of institutions as the major intervening mechanisms by which cultural values are translated into norms guiding particular types of activities in particular settings. It is then possible to interpret apparently changing cultural values as unchanging values which have been filtered through new institutions.

One often hears that Americans are becoming more materialistic. Yet, one can interpret this change in behavior in two ways. One is that this reflects a basic value change toward greater importance being placed on material goods as a goal. The other interpretation is that Americans are really enacting the traditional cultural values of "achievement" and "success" in a new institutional sphere--consumption rather than work (for elaboration, see Nicosia and Mayer, 1976).

Other social observers have noted a shift toward simpler lifestyles emphasizing harmony with nature (Kanter, 1978). Generally this is interpreted as the emergence of a new cultural value, reverence for nature. It is also possible to regard these new lifestyles as an expression of the unchanging American value of "humanitarianism" or "concern for others." This cultural value was traditionally expressed through behavior in political institutions. Given decreasing faith in the efficacy of government and the increasing militancy of "have-not" groups, some people have chosen to express their humanitarianism by treating the natural environment (i.e., future generations and non-human organisms) with increased respect (Mayer, 1976).

In sum, cultural values may be more resistent to change than one might at first think. If institutional change provides an alternative avenue for the expression and interpretation of a cultural value, then the value may remain intact. But cultural values do sometimes change. Why? As we are about to see, institutions may encourage as well as forestall changes in cultural values.

ACTUAL CHANGE IN CULTURAL VALUES

Every theory of change in cultural values posits that cultural values change in response to other changes in society. The agent of change may be technology, population, the natural environment (e.g., drought), or institutional change. When cultural values change in response to non-institutional factors like technology, population, or the natural environment, institutions may set limits on the behavioral impacts of these changes. For example, American values concerning natural resources seem to be changing in response to their reduced availability (at prices people consider reasonable). Yet, conservation behavior seems to be lagging behind this change in values. A major reason is that the institutional arrangements of our work, recreation, and residential activities have not yet changed. Consequently, programs designed to change energy awareness and attitudes may have little impact on energy consumption until institutional change occurs.

Institutional change may also serve as a catalyst for change in cultural values. Recall that the translation of cultural values into activity-specific norms is rarely the primary function of an institution. (Perhaps it is in the case of religious institutions.) Rather, the primary purpose of an institution is usually to solve an everyday problem of human existence. Thus, as institutions change to more effectively achieve their main objectives, change in cultural values may take place. For instance, as work institutions strive to save time in the production of goods, the cultural value regarding the pace of activity may be altered. The "time is precious" norm that pervades the workplace may eventually effect the cultural value regarding the use of time and eventually influence the norms governing non-work activities. Our own research shows, in fact, that today's affluent consumer is more concerned about the time it takes to repair broken appliances than about the money it costs. What we may be observing is a change in cultural values resulting from change in work institutions.

REVIEW OF MANAGERIAL IMPLICATIONS

We have tried to stress both states and processes in our discussion of changing cultural values. We have indicated the importance of studying institutional change in addition to cultural change, and we have shown the various ways in which the two interact. Let us summarize the key points for managers of private and public organizations in understanding shifts in American cultural values.

First, change in cultural values may be more apparent than real. What may actually be occurring is a shift in the institutional arena in which a cultural value is translated into an activity-specific norm. For instance, some observers have taken the soaring popularity of jogging and other physical fitness activities as evidence of a shift toward more hedonistic and selfish values. We suggest that these self-improvement activities reflect the traditional American value of achievement shifted from the production and political spheres to the consumption sphere.

The same type of process explains the supposed shift from a high value being placed on work to a high value being placed on leisure and material goods. An alternative explanation is that the growing preoccupation with leisure and consumer goods is an attempt to enact the traditional value of personal achievement. This value was originally relevant to occupational activities. Given certain institutional shifts (e.g., blue-collar wage increases are a function of seniority rather than individual productivity), however, it may be difficult to achieve personal success and individual distinction on the job. As a result, consumption may become the new arena for the enactment of the traditional value of individual achievement.

Taken together, these examples alert managers to what may be a fundamental social process in modern, affluent societies. This process entails the enactment of cultural values through consumption activities that traditionally have been enacted through work, political, religious, or other types of activities. Hence, the challenge for managers is to monitor change in institutions and norms as closely as change in cultural values.

The second major process we have discussed is change in cultural values that result from institutional change. Here, institutional change promotes behavior that is inconsistent with cultural values, and cultural values gradually adjust to reduce the "cognitive dissonance" that ensues. An example is the oft-observed shift in the time orientation of American consumers, from the future to the present, from delayed to immediate gratification. This shift is a rational adaptation to inflation and to institutional changes which reduce personal risk (e.g., more lenient bankruptcy laws). In this instance, it is useful to know that cultural values are changing, but the analysis of institutions provides an explanation for the cultural change and helps gauge its likely consequences.

A third major process involving the interaction of cultural values and institutions occurs when a change in cultural values brought about by non-institutional factors (e.g., technology, population, natural environment) fails to influence behavior because of institutional resistance. This seems to be the case with values concerning natural resources and the environment. The traditional view of the environment as something to be conquered and exploited appears to be changing. Yet, the expectation that this value transformation will lead to more environmentally compatible consumption patterns has not, to date, been borne out. There are so many institutional factors that promote the use of resources (e.g., utility rate structures, foreign competition, the location of work sites) that appeals to conserve on the basis of a new cultural value have been largely ineffective.

But what about the trend toward "voluntary simplicity" and "small is beautiful" lifestyles? Doesn't this represent a new value that has broken through the resistance of existing institutions? If such a new cultural value is in the making, we should ask whether consumers really want "less" or whether they want more of some other things that they are not currently getting.

We believe, without any hard data to support us, that the trend toward simpler lifestyles is not primarily a function of new cultural values. Rather, it is part of the long-standing attempt by consumers to achieve prestige through individuality. In a society characterized by spreading affluence, it becomes difficult to achieve distinction through the consumption of more, better quality, or even different goods than ones neighbors. Instead of conspicuous consumption, first we observe the trend toward nonconspicuous consumption, followed by conspicuous <u>under</u>consumption, as the refuge of the status-seeking consumer. Note that the strategy of conspicuous under consumption predates the environmental movement and the energy crisis, for VW's began appearing in the driveways of upper-income families in the early sixties.

It makes quite a difference whether one views simpler lifestyles as the reflection of new vs. traditional cultural values. If new values are at work, a strategy of "demarketing" would be appropriate. This would involve discouraging consumer demand (or encouraging the demand for less.) If voluntary simplicity really reflects the traditional American value of achieving prestige through individuality, then a strategy of "remarketing" is called for (Nicosia and Wind, 1978). Remarketing recognizes that consumers are a bundle of energy, constantly searching for ways to fulfill their desires. Hence, the goal of management is not to squelch demand but rather to redirect it in new directions (e.g., less energy consumptive lifestyles, but not less enjoyment).

There is another difference in the two interpretations of the trend toward simpler lifestyles. If a new cultural value is fueling the trend, then the trend is likely to grow in strength. If the traditional value of individuality lies at the heart of the trend, the trend is inherently self-defeating. For as more and more people try to conspicuously underconsume, it no longer aids in achieving individuality. Hence the next step in achieving individual distinction might be resurrecting the old status symbol, the Cadillac!

CONCLUSION

Cultural values are properties of societies or collectivities. Of course, individuals "carry" and transmit cultural values, but cultural values transcend particular individuals. Because cultural values are properties of a society, they can be related (as cause or effect) to other societal-level properties. Foremost among these are institutions.

In this paper, we have shown the importance of studying cultural values in relation to institutional arrangements. If this is done carefully, managers will be able to distinguish real from apparent change in cultural values and determine pathways by which cultural values ultimately influence consumer behavior.

Finally, the speculations contained in this paper - however persuasive and intriguing - must be translated into concrete hypotheses and then empirically tested. This will not be easy, for neither cultural values or institutional arrangements can be measured with the individual-level techniques with which marketing researchers have become so adept. Yet, these measurement challenges must be met if marketers are to provide top management (private or public) with comprehensive and accurate data for policy making.

REFERENCES

Elgin, D. and Mitchell, A. (1977), Voluntary Simplicity: Life-Style of the Future? In: The Futurist 11: 200-209, 254-261.

Inglehart, R. (1977), The Silent Revolution, Princeton, New Jersey: Princeton University Press.

Kanter, D. (1978), The Europeanizing of America: A Study in Changing Values. In: H. Hunt (ed.), Advances in Consumer Research, Vol. 5, Ann Arbor: Association for Consumer Research.

Kotler, P. (1972), Marketing Management: Analysis, Planning, and Control (2nd edition), Englewood Cliffs, N.J.: Prentice-Hall, Inc.

Mayer, R. (1976), The Socially Conscious Consumer--Another Look at the Data. In: Journal of Consumer Research 3: 113-115.

Mitchell, A. and M. Baird (1969), American Values, Menlow Park, California: Stanford Research Institute, Report No. 378.

Nicosia, F. and Mayer, R. (1976), Toward a Sociology of Consumption. In: Journal of Consumer Research 3: 65-75.

Nicosia, F. and Wind J. (1978), Sociology of Consumption and Trade-Off Models in Consumer Public Policy. In: W. Denney and Lund (eds.) Research for Consumer Policy, Cambridge, Massachusetts: Center for Policy Alternatives.

Rokeach, M. (1973), The Nature of Human Values, New York: The Free Press.

Williams, R., Jr. (1960), American Society: A Sociological Interpretation (2nd edition), New York: Knopf.

White, A. (1980), Remarks to the American Marketing Association's 63rd Annual Conferences as reported in: Marketing News (July 11): 3.

Wilson, I. (1970), How Our Values Are Changing. In: The Futurist 4 (February). Yankelovitch, Daniel (1974), The New Morality, New York: NcGraw Hill.

Possibilities and Limits of Influencing Consumer Behavior

Gerhard Reber

ABSTRACT

The possibilities and limits of influencing consumer behavior are discussed with reference to fundamental theoretical positions. The example of differing opinions about trans-situational consistencies in behavior is used for a critical discussion of both the behavioral and the cognitive approaches. A "contingency approach" is suggested as an alternative, which in contrast to the prevailing cognitive school takes motivational and situational variables into account. In addition to the plea for this change in emphasis in the area of the objects of research methodological implications are discussed briefly.

I. INTRODUCTION

No question about it: it is possible to influence the behavior of consumers. Anyone with a trace of sensitivity for the "reasons" shaping his own behavior and that of others whom he knows well, knows intuitively that such influence is possible. Research results include myriads of examples of novel changes in attitude or behavior, brought about by the strangest kind of rewards: Zimbardo (1969, p. 265), for example, summarizes the results of an experiment in dissonance as follows:

> Subjects whose initial attitude toward eating Japanese grasshoppers was one of strong dislike reported liking them more and approved of more strongly worded personal endorsement for them after having eaten some at the request of a disliked, negatively evaluated communicator, as compared to the attitude change of Eaters responding to the inducement of a positive communicator and of Controls not given the experimental treatment. There was a trend for this result to be strongest with no monetary incentive for eating the grasshoppers and weakest when a 50-cent incentive was added.

Equally surprising results have been published in such quantity that we could easily fill a whole book with the summaries, which would make entertaining reading indeed.

Such a collection of "anecdotes", however, would not provide a coherent theory enabling us to explain and predict the possibilities and limits of influence. The literature includes not only experiments of the kind I have cited, but also theories of varying scope and more or less thoroughly researched. However, no integration of these theoretical approaches has taken place as yet, so that any decision to adopt one of these "partial" theories shapes a researcher's overall opinion of the limits of influence. If he decides to follow the traditional behavioristic line, for example, he will allow much acreage within the boundaries; if he tends toward classical motivation theory, he draws much narrower limits, since he will agree with Ernest Dichter that behavior roots in relatively stable motives and attitudes (Dichter, 1964, p. 396):

> No successful advertising can ignore the stable, enduring attitudes of the consumer public. Since attitudes affect the way a product is seen, affect the very perception of facts, facts alone cannot combat hostile attitudes.

Under the influence of the"cognitive revolution" in psychology (McGuire, 1976, p. 314), modern psychology seems to tend more strongly toward a rejuvenation of the behavioristic approach. This is a surprising development, because the cognitivists were originally opponents of behaviorism.

Because an evaluation of the traditional theoretical approaches is central to our topic, we will first focus on basic viewpoints, especially on the question of transituational consistencies in behavior. Simply raising this latter question is a criticism of the cognitive approach: it pays too little attention to situational contexts. A second flaw is the neglect of "classical" motivational aspects of behavior. An "integrative approach" is suggested as a solution, i. e. an approach which takes motivational and cognitive variables into account as well as the situational context. This effort results in a program that we could, if forced to give it a name, call "a contingency approach to consumer behavior". I shall try to clarify this approach further and provide a number of examples.

II. THE PROBLEM OF TRANSITUATIONAL CONSISTENCIES

1) Deconstruction of the Dispositional Position in Psychology

In exploring the transituational consistencies in the behavior of a person we are simultaneously looking for the limits of influence. "Influence" is the effect of environmental stimuli. To the extent that the subject shows consistent behavior in various different environments, i. e. situations we can assume that the effects of the environmental stimuli are tempered by his personality; the degree of consistency reflects the limits of the possibility of influencing his behavior.

The assumption that behavior shows transituational consistencies dates from ancient times, as Allport (1937, p. 57) shows. In our own century the behavioristic attack on the traditions of introspective, mentalistic psychology includes strong criticism of the concepts which had been used to explain such consistencies. This created an important dispute that continues to stir up wave after wave of discussion and research: the situational versus dispositional dichotomy.

> According to the situational view, changes in a person's behavior over time as well as differences among individuals are seen as resulting from environmental or situational influences. The second approach, the dispositional one, has been guided by the belief that, while it is true that there may be general principles of behavior that apply to most people, it is no less true that people differ among each other in a variety of ways. In order to properly account for the diversity of behavior, according to this view, it is necessary to provide some systematic framework for understanding individual differences. For the most part, this has involved the development of constructs encompassing some relatively stable predispositional attitudes of the individual such as his abilities, personality traits, beliefs, attitudes, or motives, and the construction of measures of these attributes. (Blass, 1977, p. 1) The dispositions are not directly observed but are inferred from behavior signs (trait indicators), either directly or indirectly (Mischel, 1973, p. 253).

The field of psychology today, and especially its applied areas, seems to have a split personality: on the one hand, the situational approach seems to dominate. On the other, trait assumptions regarding structure are seen in the existence of hundreds of test designed to infer dispositions and almost none to measure situations. "The same belief in global traits that manifest themselves pervasively is perhaps best seen in the projective test assumption that responses to vague or minimal stimuli will reveal individual differences in fundamental, generalized dispositions." (Mischel, 1973, p. 253).

The latest turn in the discussion of the situational vs. dispositional dichotomy was - according to Bem/Allen (1974, p. 507) -, initiated by Walter Mischel. His meticulous study of the validity of the dispositional approach leads him to the following conclusion (Mischel, 1968, p. 177):

> Response patterns even in highly similar situations often fail to be strongly related. Individuals show far less cross-situational consistency in their behavior than has been assumed by trait-state theories. The more dissimilar the evoking situations, the less likely they are to produce

> similar or consistent responses from the same individual. Even seemingly trivial situational differences may reduce correlations to zero. Response consistency tends to be greatest within the same response medium, within self-reports to paper-and-pencil tests, for example, or within directly observed nonverbal behavior. Intraindividual consistency is reduced drastically when dissimilar response modes are employed. Activities that are substantially associated with aspects of intelligence and with problem-solving behavior - like achievement behaviors, cognitive styles, response speed - tend to be most consistent.

Even those who adhere to the dispositional position must admit that "the failure of many personality measures to predict behavior reliably has been a major problem in the systematic study of individual differences ... the poor performance of many measures is indisputable, ..." (Blass, 1977, p. 8).

This tendency toward a strengthening of the situational position is further reinforced by current developments in cognitive theory. As mentioned earlier, these theories initially contradicted the behavioristic approach. Today more and more cognitive psychologists tend to draw closer to behavioralism. Nisbett/Valins, for example, who are attribution theorists, agree with Bem's behavioristic proposition that "... we often survey our behavior toward an entity and then infer that our attitudes toward the entity are consistent with our behavior toward it." (Nisbett/Valins, 1971, p. 1, Bem, 1967). This proposition is an alternative to the explanation of the relationship between attitudes and behavior from a dispositional point of view. The latter is based on the assumption that identifying (stable) attitudes enables us to predict behavior. However, as Fishbein demonstrates, this assumption has led to some difficulty (Fishbein, 1966, p. 199):

> It is my contention that we psychologists have been rather naive in our attempts to understand and to investigate the relationship between attitudes and behavior. More often than not, we have attempted to predict some behavior from some measure of attitude and found little or no relationship between these variables. Rather than utilizing our failures in a constructive way, we have, to a large extent, gone blindly ahead only to further confuse ourselves and compound our problems. Indeed, rather than question our basic assumption that there is a strong relationship between attitude and behavior, we have tended to blame our failures on our measuring instruments, on our definition of attitude, or both.

The difficulty of explaining the relationship between attitudes and behavior has led some authors to try their luck with a curious solution: they use one theoretical system to connect attitudes and attitude change, but need an additional theory to connect behavior and behavior change. Zimbardo/Ebbesen, for example, use this dichotomous approach (Zimbardo/

Ebbesen, 1969, p. 85):

> Research relevant to this topic has unfortunately indicated that such a conclusion is false ... Changes in attitude are not necessarily accompanied by changes in behavior. Furthermore, when changes in behavior do occur, they are rarely, if ever, general or enduring. ... Can dissonance theory help? Unfortunately, it cannot. The theory does suggest methods which will produce attitude change following behavior change, but it does not suggest how to produce or maintain the changes in behavior. All is not lost. Another approach (called social learning) does suggest techniques for producing and maintaining behavior change and for producing change in what we have been conceptualizing as attitudes.

Surprisingly enough Zimbardo published a book[1] in the same year, in which he states with justified pride that dissonance theory can be applied not only to subjective variables(such as attitudes) but also to:

> "behavioral: amount of food requested and water consumed; reaction time; task persistence; setting a task level of difficulty; recall of negative attributes; recall in incidental learning; amount of verbal and eyelid conditioning; frequency and duration of shocks given to another person.
>
> physiological: release of free fatty acid in response to hunger and stress; galvanic skin response to electric shock, and basal skin resistance to situational demands." (Zimbardo, 1969, pp. 267, 268).

Another approach, which applies the theoretical constructs of attribution theory to divergent perceptions of the causes of behavior by the actor and observer, stresses the "nonprofessional simplification" which all of us use in our observations and which - unjustly - reinforce a certain prejudice in favor of the dispositional position. On the basis of reviewed data Jones/Nisbett (1971, p. 2) theorized that "there is a pervasive tendency for actors to attribute their actions to situational requirements, whereas observers tend to attribute the same actions to stable personal dispositions". Mischel (1973, p. 264) draws the following conclusion: "It seems as if traits may be the consistent attributes that other people have. When describing other people, we seem to act more like trait theorists, but when we attempt to understand ourselves we function more like social behaviorists." Mistaken views about the causes of behavior on the part of the observer come about - according to Jones/Nisbett - because of an "informational bias, an information-processing bias and linguistic distortions".

These research results arising out of various different approaches seem to discredt the dispositional position. We would have to conclude, in effect,that there is "... little evidence that traits exist anywhere but in the cognitive structure of the observers (Jones/Nisbett, 1971, p. 10), that transituational consistencies appear only in connection with "... aspects of intelligence and with problem-solving behavior" (Mischel, op. cit.) and that in general the limits of influence on behavior are very broadly drawn. The total deconstruction of the dispositional position works so strongly against my intuition, that I must seek alternative explanations for the cited results, even though I realize that this "intuition" might be interpreted by others as the observer's tendency toward simplification. I tend to agree with Bem/Allen (1974, p. 510), whose neobehavioristic leanings lead them to the following conclusion:

> We are not here denying the well-documented biases and illusions which plague our intuitions, ... But in terms of the underlying logic and fidelity to reality, we believe that our intuitions are right; the research, wrong."

2) A Contingency Approach to the Understanding of the Limits and Possibilities of Influencing Behavior

Our contingency approach begins with a reconstruction of some aspects of the dispositional position. The first step is in line with Allport's suggestion to replace the "nomothetic" by an "idiographic" approach. This suggestion of Allport's is not novel; he has used it again and again to defend his dispositional position against seemingly disconfirming empirical results. The next step is an attempt to show that stable motives, that is, "motivational and emotional arousal", are more strongly relevant for behavior than the behavioristic and the modern cognitive schools assume. The final step in developing the contingency approach is to consider the role of the situational, i. e. the environmental components.

a) Reconstruction of some aspects of the dispositional position

aa) In 1928 Hartshorne/May tried to prove the existence of stable personality traits, using school children as subjects. The results discredited the dispositional position strongly, Allport, however, defends his position with the theory that the results of these experiments came about because of their "nomothetic" character. According to Allport, "nomothetic" thinking must be replaced by "idiographic" thinking:

> Hartshorne/May assumed that an honesty-dishonesty dimension could be used to characterize all the pupils in the sample and that the differences among the children could be specified in terms of their degree of honesty. In contrast, Allport's idiographic view emphasized that individuals differ not only in the way in which traits are related to one another in each person, but that they differ also in terms of which traits are even relevant. Thus in commenting upon the fact that Hartshorne/May found lying and cheating to be essentially uncorrelated, Allport noted that one child may lie because he is afraid of hurting the feelings of the teacher, whereas another may steal pennies in order to buy social acceptance from his peers. For neither of these two children do the behaviors of lying and cheating constitute items on a scale called "honesty", a concept which exists in the head of the investigator, not in the behavior of the children. Accordingly, the low correlations "prove only that children are not consistent in the same way, not that they are inconsistent with themselves." (Allport, 1937, p. 250). To put the same objection in slightly different terms, the research will yield the conclusion that a sample of individuals is inconsistent to the degree that their behaviors do not sort into the equivalence class which the investigator imposes by his choice of behaviors and situations to sample. (Bem/Allen, 1974, p. 509).

The need for an idiographic view is especially obvious in the light of the abovementioned differences in perception and information processing between observer and actor. Tests, surveys and experiments are in permanent danger of being structured nomothetically: the underlying concepts, classifications, relationships, connections and situative assumptions often seem clear and relevant merely to the experimenter, the tester or the interviewer. Yet the results are more likely to be - erroneously - attributed to the condition of the subjects than to the character of the tests, questions, experimental designs, etc. or to the subjective interpretation of the investigators.

No one seems to question the existence of the "nomothetic trap", and yet Allport's insight has rarely been translated into research programs based upon explicit and systematic avoidance of these dangers. A systematic idiographic approach is recognizable in Kelley's (1955) psychology of personal constructs and its associated assessment procedure, the Role Repertory Test. His namesake's Harold Kelley's attribution theory (1967, 1971, 1972) also contains numerous references to the psychology of the subjects. For instance, the concept of a "causal schema" is stipulated as "... a general conception the person has about how certain kinds of causes interact to produce a specific kind of effect. Each schema can be described in terms of a hypothetical matrix of data that summarizes the attributor's beliefs and assumptions about the distribution of the effect over various combinations of the causal factors". (Kelley, 1972, p. 1).

Modern, or shall we say, fashionable action research tries to be methodically innovative along the lines of the idiographic perspective. The objective is clearly to put the subject in focus and remove the observer to where he belongs, into the background, to make the observer as "invisible" as possible. It remains to be seen how well action research can accomplish this. Up to now this school seems to have produced plans and programs rather than results.

ab) Various disputes within general cognitive theory have led to more widespread consideration of motivational dispositions. I am thinking, for example, of Festinger's theory of cognitive dissonance (Festinger, 1957; Brehm/Cohen 1962) and in particular of a certain experimental paradigma called "inadequate justification", "counterattitudinal advocacy", forced compliance" or "insufficient reward" (Festinger/Carlsmith, 1959; Cohen, 1962; Rosenberg, 1965; Aronson, 1966; Nuttin, 1975). The disagreement concerning this paradigma focuses on two decisive points. They are: (a) Do persons have a relatively stable drive to keep their cognitive systems in a dissonance-free, "consonant" condition? (b) What effect does "commitment", i. e. "volition" have, and what conditions give rise to it? Thus cognitive processes (perception, information processing, memory systems, etc.) were suddenly not as important a topic within cognitive theory as the motivational processes functioning as releasers for the cognitive ones.

As far as the drive toward consonance is concerned, there is no agreement as to its exact definition. Pepitone's description is typical for the thinking surrounding this concept. He speaks of a "... need to maintain the validity of the cognitive structure, a need for meaning and 'cognitive clarity'. The cognitive structure is essentially a mirror of reality. When information threatens to crack or shatter the mirror, forces are created that tend either to prevent damage or to refocus the mirror." (Pepitone, 1966, p. 273). Most investigators assume further that the drive to reduce dissonance is one of the "social", i. e., "learned" motives (see, for example, Zimbardo, 1969, p. 280):

> By increasing the predictability of behavior (on an actuarial basis), consistency oils the machinery of social interaction and facilitates the management of behavior. Moreover, behavior that is not under the spurious control of interpersonal predictability appears as a danger to others, and they will take steps either to increase its predictability (i. e., make it consistent with rationally perceived causes, with past behavior, or with their own behavior), or to reject or even isolate the inconsistent offender from the society.

Any effort to reduce dissonance can come up against motivationally opposing forces - for example, the curiosity drive (Berlyne, 1960) - and lose its impact as a result of this encounter. Because of such motivational conflicts the drive to achieve consonance never leads to a "... static paradise, in which balanced cognitions languish in blissful harmony" (Zimbardo, 1969, p. 282). Singer (1966, p. 63) assumes "... that a small amount of inconsistency is preferred to total consistency, but that a large amount of inconsistency is motivating".

Such assumptions are in line with activation theory, which holds that a drive to reduce dissonance is aroused only by activation above an optimal level (Berlyne, 1968). Nuttin (1975) has pointed out the importance of a high degree of perturbation or arousal for dissonance-reducing effects of the kind described above in a quotation from Zimbardo.On the basis of a meticulously planned series of experiments he developed a totally new interpretation of the results of experiments with "forced compliance". He shows, for example, that attitude change was highly probable only when embarrassing, strange, novel or unusual stimuli (in the experiments: a trivial remuneration, relative deprivation, priceless illegitimate exam points, unexpected severe blame, and hot-pants) caused a high degree of perturbation (arousal).

Besides unspecific arousal and a specific drive concept dissonance theory incorporates an additional motivational force: that of commitment. Prerequisites for the occurrence of commitment are subjectively experienced freedom of choice (which may be,objectively seen, an illusion) and the conclusion of a decision-making process by such a choice. Commitment is especially strong when the choice is made public and when the chosen alternative or course of action involves the risk of being wrong, of self-exposure, of potential loss (Zimbardo, 1969, p. 279).

> Commitment invariably leads to dissonance when it becomes inextricably linked with one's self-definition. When one perceives that his choice places him on the same evaluative continuum as the object of his choice, then he becomes involved with the experimental function of his response in defining his personal worth, intelligence, sentitivity,etc. Commitment forces one to articulate his position, thereby increasing the chance of a definitive test of its validity and of being proven wrong (Zimbardo, ibid).

We can summarize as follows: within the theory of cognitive dissonance the attempt to find the reasons for the existence and the reduction of dissonant cognitions has led to a reconstruction of the theories and concepts surrounding "motivation". This reconstruction comes close to opinions typical for proponents of the dispositional position. Especially noteworthy is the fact that going back to motivational constructs became necessary in order to explain the phenomenon of high degrees of arousal (dissonance, conflict, perturbation, risk of losing the self-concept, etc.). This seems to reinforce the theory recently forwarded by the Nestor of German motivation research, Hans Thomae (Thomae, 1979, p.281):

> Theories which consider motivation and behavior a function of cognitions, are built on the grounds of observation in relatively relaxed situations, i. e. in situations in which the individual's competency can achieve its full effect. ... The old question, whether "open", unspecialized, basic needs influence behavior more strongly than strongly specialized needs, or vice versa, can thus be answered by identifying the determinants of the "degree of specialization". A high degree of tension in the siutation temporarily "specializes" all motivational and cognitive processes and puts them into the service of tension reduction. A low degree of tension, i. e., a low degree of arousal, gives basic motives such as the drive to self-actualization, a chance to come into effect. In relaxed situations all those processes have a chance, which aim at understanding reality. There is a kind of openness,a receptiveness for the "meaning", the content of the situation, which are overridden in less relaxed situations by acute needs.
>
> Obviously a research approach is needed that comes closer in its assumptions to social reality than many purely motivational (for example, historically oriented) or purely cognitive (for example, attribution theory) approaches, if we wish to come closer to an understanding of the complex interaction of the processes we have called "motivational" and "cognitive".

b) The person/environment-relationship

A pure "person only" condition exists neither in real life nor in research. Behavior always takes place in an environment, in a situation that is either natural or - in an experiment - artificially determined. Lewin's teaching has made this clear enough, and yet research projects in which the person/environment interaction is carefully handled are exceptions rather than the rule.[2] <u>The problem is essentially one of identifying</u>

situations in which intrapersonal ("dispositional") characteristics have more influence on behavior than environmental factors, or vice versa, i. e. of finding persons whose behavior tends more toward stability in changing environmental situations. In order to accomplish this it is necessary to conceptualize personalities and situations. Since up to now theories and constructs have been developed mainly to apply to persons, not to situations, there is a theoretical deficit which needs to be filled in with a "theory of situations". Tajfel/Turner as well as Milgram and Blass stress this point:

> Ultimately, social psychology would like to have a compelling theory of situations which will, first, present a language in terms of which situations can be defined; proceed to a typology of situations; and then point to the manner in which definable properties of situations are transformed into psychological forces in the individual (Milgram, 1965, p. 74).

> One approach to refining situational predictions is the recognition of the possibilities that a particular variation in the situational input may have different effects on individuals with different personality, or other stable characteristics. Analogously, the weak empirical evidence for consistency of personality should not hamper efforts at refining concepts and measures of personality to make them more meaningful and useful in the prediction of behavior. An important step in accomplishing this goal is a conceptualization of personality dispositions that recognizes that only a limited number of situations may arouse a particular disposition, and that a behavior must be logically linked to the personality disposition in order for a measure of that disposition to be a predictor of that behavior(Blass, 1977, p. 13).

The following will essentially be in line with Milgram's suggestions. First, however, we must come back to the identification of persons whose behavior tends to be more or less stable, and consider the aspect that behavior consistency may itself be an individual difference characteristic. Bem/Allen (1974, p. 512 ff) conducted an experiment in which they showed that individuals who identify themselves as consistent on a particular trait dimension will in fact be more consistent cross-situationally than those who identify themselves as highly variable. (The self-reports were controlled by means of mother's, father's und peer's reports, group discussions and evaluation of spontaneous friendliness.) In their discussion of the results Bem/Allen mention a hypothesis of Mischel's, according to which higher cross-situational variability may well be the work of highly refined discriminative competencies (Mischel, 1973, p. 267), which enable the person to respond appropriately to subtle changes in situational contingencies. Such an individual may be precisely the person who is most predictable from a knowledge of the situation. "In short, if some of the people can be predicted some of the time from personality traits, then some of the people can be predicted some of the time from situational variables" (Bem/

Allen, 1974, p. 517).

Mischel himself underpins his "cognitive" thesis by showing (a) that according to his results "mental abilities" seem to have much better temporal and cross-situational stability and influence than most of the social traits and motivations traditionally favored in personality research (Mischel, 1968) and (b) that the pervasive and substantial "first factor" found on tests such as the MMPI (Butcher, 1971) often labeled with terms connoting "adjustment" at the positive and "maladaption" character structure at the negative end, reflects to a considerable degree the individual's level of cognitive-social competence and achievement. "The individual who knows how to be assertive with waiters, for example, or who knows how to solve certain kinds of interpersonal problems competently, or who excels in singing, is capable of such performances enduringly" (Mischel, 1973, p. 267).

Bem/Allen's and especially Mischel's viewpoints are perhaps concentrated too much on cognitive processes. Such processes are no doubt important for those interested in consumer behavior. One has only to think of the "informational overload" the consumers are faced with: information about products, prices, amounts, packages, product features, etc. must be processed, and differences in "mental abilities" no doubt cause differences in the outcome of this process. However, motivational processes are at least as, if not more important in the study of consumer behavior as cognitive processes. They must not be neglected, even though their study has proven to be a more difficult project than expected. Using a cognitive theory - dissonance theory -, we have tried to show that cognitive processes cannot be explained without using motivational constructs such as arousal (Nuttin), (learned) drive (Pepitone, Brehm/Cohen), and volition/commitment (Brehm/Cohen, Zimbardo).

One way of introducing the motivational component into a person/situation-analysis was shown in the above quotation from Thomae. He hypothesizes that persons who have reached a state of intrapersonal tension arising out of extremely strong needs or the perception of strong normative demands in the environment lose their - potentially stronger or weaker - ability to respond appropriately to subtle attributes of the environmental stimuli. They concentrate their cognitive potential on simplifying the situation in order to reduce tension. This means that for the purpose of predicting behavior it is important not only to know how subtle the differences in the situations are, but also to identify their arousal-producing potential.

We are now ready to continue the development of the "theory of situations" Milgram suggested: in the language of "cognitive" and "motivational" terms we can proceed to design a simple typology of situations. As far as the person is concerned, we will adhere to the classical differentiation between motivational forces and cognitive-intellectual abilities (competencies). As far as the environment is concerned, we will differentiate situations according to the degree of structuredness (analogous to the cognitive dimension of the person) and their normative character (analogous to the motivational dimension of the person).

All of these four person/environment aspects are continuously interacting. Research by activation theorists shows, for example, that ill-structured environments are arousal-producing. In analysing the structuredness of the situation, we pay special attention to the novelty, surprisingness, complexity and ambiguity of the stimuli in the environment (Berlyne, 1968). The research in the realms of activation theory and of attribution theory shows that this classification is useful for theory construction. Attribution research shows, for example, that when stimuli are ambiguous and the subject holds an attitude with little confidence, he continues testing his attitude with behavior that reflects the opposite attitude rather than the one he holds.[3] In other words, it has been shown that subjects show a constant behavior against their attitudes when there are not enough stimuli in the environment which clearly and adequately confirm these attitudes. An example: the stronger a buyer's wish to possess a certain product, the more he advocates "counterattitudinal arguments" in his conversation with the salesman, in order to evoke as many good reasons as possible speaking for the product and confirming his wish to buy it.

This kind of attitude-testing behavior seems to take place, however, only when the situation is relatively relaxed. Relaxation is made difficult when the environment mobilises normative potential (for example, when a salesman tries to hardsell the customer and exerts strong pressure). Research results arising out of dissonance theory are especially relevant here: the higher the degree of arousal, the higher the degree of "contagion" (Nuttin, 1975, p. 194), which results in an attitude change. Brehm, a proponent of reactance theory, a branch of dissonance theory, states that if the buyer in a hardsell situation experiences the salesman's behavior as an impingement on his, the buyer's, freedom of choice, then a change of attitude is likely: the buyer reverses his positive attitude toward the product and decides to buy another or to consult another salesman (Brehm, 1966, 1972). The same reaction is likely to occur if the buyer suddenly realizes that it is not the salesman, but himself who is providing the positive arguments.

Other experimental results of dissonance and of attribution theory show that the consequences of arousal depend partially on whether the subject perceives the arousal to originate within himself ("internally caused") or whether he perceives it to be "externally caused". In attribution theory, for example, it has been shown that achievement-oriented persons tend to attribute failure to external rather than to internal causes and continue their achievement-oriented behavior, whereas persons oriented toward the avoidance of failure tend to attribute failure to internal causes (Weiner et al., 1971). In dissonance theory it has been shown that the higher the commitment, the less "neutral" and "objective" the cognitive processes with which the environment is explored and classified. This does not change the basic quality of relatively constant cognitive/intellectual competencies unless the degree of activation becomes so high that the person can no longer cope with it at all. It does result, however, in a strong tendency to use cognitive processes to defend the chosen alternative and to discount the rejected ones. The quality of the cognitive competencies is reflected in the degree of sophistication with which the person goes about the process of dissonance reduction, keeping his personal value scheme intact.

A summary of the criteria discussed so far results in the following classification: the environment is classified according to its <u>structuredness</u> and its <u>normative character</u>, the person according to his <u>motivational</u> and <u>cognitive</u> charactetistics. If we dichotomize each of these criteria, we arrive at the following sixteen types of situations:

		Person							
		M strong	C high	M weak	C low	M strong	C low	M weak	C high
Environment	ST well NC intense	1		2		3		4	
	ST ill NC mild	5		6		7		8	
	ST well NC mild	9		10		11		12	
	ST ill NC intense	13		14		15		16	

M = motivational forces: strong, weak
C = cognitive abilities: high, low
ST = structuredness: well, ill
NC = normative character: intense, mild

This relatively simple classification scheme shows that seemingly contradictory research results can nevertheless be regarded as valid, since each experimenter has worked with different types of situations, so that his results apply to certain situations and not to others. A contradiction arises only when results gleaned from one type of situation are tested against another. An example: the perspective represented by attribution theory (human behavior is guided by cognitive exploration of the environment; Kelley, 1971) can be considered useful for explaining behavior in relatively relaxed situations (mild normative character of the environment and weak intrapersonal motivational forces, i. e. situations 6, 8, 10, 12); whereas the perspective respresented by dissonance theory (human behavior tends to work toward a consistent, not toward an objective image of the world) is useful in situations in which the motivational forces are strong (5, 7, 9, 11).

III. CONSEQUENCES FOR EXPLAINING AND INFLUENCING CONSUMER BEHAVIOR

The basic principles described above lead to two consequences for explaining and influencing consumer behavior: the first concerns the object of study, the second the methods.Research and practical work in the realm of influencing consumer behavior should:

1) focus more strongly on the person/environment interaction and
2) be more idiographically oriented.

1) Consequences in the Realm of the Person/Environment Relationship

The basic consequence is summarized by Mischel in general terms as follows:

> Rather than talk about "behavior", it may be more useful to conceptualize behavior-contingency units that link specific patterns of behavior to the condition in which they may be expected. Accurate descriptions require specifying as precisely as possible the response mode of the behavior as well as the contingencies in which it is expected to be of high or low frequency. ... Thus rather than describe a person as "aggressive", it would be necessary to qualify the mode of aggressive behavior (e. g. verbal insult but not physical attacks) and the specific contingencies (e. g. when criticized for poor athletic performance on playground but not in class). (Mischel, 1973, p. 278).

This means that in order to explain and influence buying behavior it is necessary to define as explicitly as possible the environment in which the behavior is to take place. Is the consumer to be influenced while sitting in front of the television set in the relaxed atmosphere of his home? during a shopping trip to the supermarket? in a crowded football stadium? in a small specialized store or at a political rally? The number of variables to be considered and the complexity of their interrelationships tend to become most formidable, so that simplifications will be unavoidable. These will do the least harm if care is taken to consider the most essential characteristics of the "behavior-contingency units" being studied. The classification scheme presented above offers a guideline for the identification of the essential characteristics. The scheme is of a very simple basic structure and contains very few categories which have not already been explored by one or several of the various schools of behavioral science. This enables us to find existing theories and research results relevant for the person/environment unit we have defined as our object of interest, and to use them as guidelines in the attempt to explain and/or influence consumer behavior.

Every description of a type of situation should contain details regarding:

a) the structuredness of the stimuli in the environment
b) the normative character of the stimuli in the environment
c) the cognitive competencies of the consumers to be influenced
d) the motivational characteristics of the consumers to be influenced.

a) The structuredness of the stimuli in the environment is given on the one hand by the sheer volume of information the consumer has to perceive, process in his working memory and store in his long-term memory, and on the other by the characteristics of the stimuli, i. e. their degree of novelty, surprisingness, complexity and ambiguity.

Informational overload created by numerous and not easily differentiated stimuli (for example, by a huge array of products being offered for sale, with many differences in price, amount, packaging and quality) can exceed the consumer's capacity for perceiving and thinking and cause him to shop very uncritically, even though he may act in the illusion of freedom of choice. In such ill-structured situations individual differences can determine behavior most strongly. These interindividual differences are of no interest to the supermarket owner, as long as the overload leads to the purchase of some of the products being offered. For a particular manufacturer this situation is less desirable, since the chances of his product's being purchased are no better than those of the others. To the degree that the situation is ambigously structured (as, for example,in projective testing), the subject will expect that virtually any response from him is equally appropriate, variances due to individual differences will be greatest and the direct influence of the environmenal stimuli will be weak.

The motivational consequences of ill-structured stimuli depend on the subject's arousal level; if it is low, then stimuli which are novel, exciting, incomplete, conflicting and not trivial are received well, for example, a novel advertisement is welcomed as relief from boredom. If the arousal level of the subject is high, that is, higher than "optimal" as defined by activation theory, then ambiguous stimuli tend to be blocked out, the subject tends to prefer well-structured information which helps him to resolve conflict and dissonance and reduce arousal. Messages intended to be received in relaxed situations (for example, at home in the living room) must thus be different from those intended to be received in situations characterized by high arousal (for example, buying an important, infrequently purchased product or choosing between people in public or private life).

Considering cognition in general,it seems safe to say that effective and direct influence is possible to the extent that stimuli are offered which make the subject certain about how to categorize them, and provide the learning conditions required for successful construction of the expected "appropriate" behavior. "When subjects expect that only one response will be right ... and all subjects are motivated and capable of making the appropriate response, then individual differences will be minimal and the situational effects prepotent." (Mischel, 1973, p. 276)

b) The normative character of the stimuli in the environment is not a new concept in psychology (the term superego is applicable here), but neither in general psychology nor in its younger branch of social psychology (Tajfel/Turner, in press; Stroebe, 1977) has it been thoroughly researched. Here modern "sociology of consumption" (Nicosia/Mayer, 1976) enters the picture. In some social settings the rules and prescriptions for enacting specific role behaviors impose narrow limits on the range of possible behaviors (i. e. in church, at school, in a theatre, at a conference, at a semi-automated production line,soldiers or glamour girls in a parade, passengers at the airport and in the plane), while in others the range of possible behaviors is broad and often the individual can select, structure and reorganize situations with minimal macrosocial constraint.

> Raush (1965) found that in a sample of American boys, friendly acts led to unfriendly responses in 31 % of the instances in game situations but only 4 % of the time at mealtime.
>
> Fairweather (1967) showed that accurate predictions of posthospital adjustment for mental patients hinges on knowledge of the environment in which the ex-patient will be living in the community, such as the availability of jobs and family support, rather than on any measured person variables or in-hospital behavior.
>
> It has been an observed characteristic of macrosocial processes in recent times, that income distribution has not followed changes in education distribution as closely as expected (e. g. Wright, 1978). This can be explained in the following way: jobs differ widely in the responsibility, authority and skill they are perceived to involve. Pay rates differ in proportion to their perceived responsibility, etc. Individuals from certain groups, such as women, blacks and working class are selected into low responsibility jobs; this practice is supported by customs, traditions and widely-held societal values and beliefs. That is, women, blacks and workers will tend to have lower incomes than men, whites and managers because they tend to be given jobs lower in the scale of responsibility, etc. Education cannot alter this tendency because education in itself cannot alter sex, race or class (Meadows, in press).

Tajfel/Turner suggest conceptualizing the influence of macrosocial norms with the help of a continuum between two extremes, called interpersonal behavior and intergroup behavior:

> At one extreme (which most probably cannot be found in its "pure" form in "real life"), is the interaction between two or more individuals which is fully determined by their interpersonal relationships and individual characteristics,

> and not at all affected by various social groups or categories to which they respectively belong. The other extreme consists of interactions between two or more individuals (or groups of individuals) which are fully determined by their respective memberships of various social groups or categories, and not at all affected by the interindividual personal relationships between the people involved ... Examples nearing the interpersonal extreme would be the relations between wife and husband or between old friends. Examples near the intergroup extreme are provided by the behavior of soldiers from opposing armies during a battle; or by the behavior at a negotiating table of members representing two parties in an intense intergroup conflict." (Tajfel/Turner, p. 3)

In order to identify the conditions determining the adoption of forms of social behavior nearing one or the other extreme by the consumer we must, according to Nicosia/Mayer, study the prevalent cultural values as well as the existing institutions and the norms, sanctions and rewards they administer. For all the important stages in the consumption process - purchase, use, maintenance, repair, disposal -, they give impressive examples showing the value of a careful study of the normative character of the environment before an attempt is made to explain or influence consumer behavior, especially if an attempt is being made to alter consumer public policy (Nicosia/Mayer, 1976;Nicosia/Wind, 1978).

An essential point for the influencer to understand is the fact that not only the person being influenced, but also he himself has a certain position in the field of social forces. Surely this is a truism, but a person wishing to detect the "true nature" of another he wants to influence easily forgets that that person is already influenced by the mere fact that he is being approached with interest. Changes in behavior tend to be followed by reciprocal changes in the behavior of others (Gouldner, 1959). It may be difficult to influence a consumer to buy a Ford compact car, if all persons who are suicidal risks were advised to drive a Pinto with Firestone tires - unless, of course, the consumer is one of those desperate persons.

The assessment of (c), the cognitive competencies and (d), the motivational characteristics of the consumers are of course objects of research for general psychology as well as for its applied area of consumer behavior. (Nicosia, 1966; Britt, 1966, 1970; Engel et al., 1969, 1973; Howard/Sheth, 1969; Kroeber-Riel, 1975, 1980, etc.) Only at first glance do the arguments speaking for a stronger concentration on situational factors in consumer behavior seem to push approaches centering on the individual into the background. Further work on motivational and cognitive processes and their interaction within the individual will always be at the core of our efforts to improve our ability to explain and influence consumer behavior. The "objective environment" as a whole is irrelevant, relevant are only those parts of it which influence the behavior in which we are interested, and which parts these are, is determined by the physical and physiological attributes of the consumer. We must remember also that these attributes are not passive, but rather open and capable of constructing individual environments.

> It has become plain that rather than mimicking observed responses or returning memory traces from undisturbed storage vaults, the observer selectively constructs (generates) his renditions of "reality". Indeed, research on modeling effects has long recognized that the products of observational learning involve a novel, highly organized synthesis of information rather than a photocopy of specific observed responses (Mischel, 1973, p. 266).

These considerations need not lead to a dispute between a "psychology of consumption" and a "sociology of consumption" (Reber, 1978), but instead guide us toward an integrated theory such as the one conceptualized by Lewin. The idea has been worked out, but its rigorous application has been neglected.

The core of Lewin's integrated theory is the psychological part, the "model of consumer behavior". Its contents are prerequisite knowledge for any private or public marketer. Specific applications are always applications in specific environments, which must be scrutinized carefully, i. e. more carefully than has been the case up to now. Beyond that it is necessary, especially if influence is to be exerted and changes are to be effected, to take into account the "change rate" of behavior, which is determined by the motivational and cognitive structure of the person.

c) Idiographic Consequences

Reflections on one's own viewpoint seem to be a basic requisite for an idiographic approach. Preceding any attempt to define, explain and influence someone else's behavior it is necessary, as a "preliminary exercise", to attempt a self-documentation, a description of one's own position in a given environment. A designer of skis told me that skiing today is very much different from ten or fifteen years ago, because most skiers are now relatively skilled, use slopes prepared in a certain way and must have an appropriate ski. Ten or fifteen years ago he himself was still a beginner and also had more time. Because he is now an expert and spends what little time he has on the harder runs, he never "sees" the many beginners tumbling their way down on the easier runs, and has no knowledge of their experience with slopes that are objectively different (different physically and perhaps in the way they are prepared) from the ones he uses. In other words, he has literally lost sight of at least one important target group and has no source of inspiration for designing for this group.

The basic goal for the study of the "actors" in which the "observer" is interested (see the above reference to the divergent perceptions of the causes of behavior, Jones/Nisbett, 1971), is to come as close as possible to the "personal constructs" (Kelley, 1955) of the actor, which reflect his evaluation of his environment and himself. On order to accomplish this it seems necessary to listen, as often as possible, to the actor himself, in the situation of interest:

> ... a conflict does arise if an investigator refuses to relinquish the power to decide which behaviors of which people are to be studied in which situations; the logic of idiographic assessment requires that the individual himself must be given this power, whereas the particular concerns of the investigator may require these decisions to be fixed parameters. (Bem/Allen, 1973, p. 511)

Modern action research tries to give as much of this as possible to the actor. Surely it is possible to cultivate "self-reports", to improve the methods used for eliciting and interpreting these. The self-reports may be supplemented by observer reports, which should pay special attention to the interpretation of situational stimuli, since differences in these interpretations can be of particular interest. Another method attempts to partially neutralize the differences between actor and observer by having the observer put himself "in the shoes of the actor", assuming his role even to the point of obeying the norms and rules of the groups which are relevant for the actor (Goffman, 1961).

However, these methods may introduce actor bias, especially when "social desirability" is high and the actor's "ego" accepts it. Here we must take recourse to traditional "paper-and-pencil" tests, projective testing and psychophysiological (psychobiological) methods.

Paper-and-pencil tests have their disadvantages: the questions are rarely of the "open" type; often it is quite unclear what the tests are measuring ("intelligence is what intelligence tests measure"), and environmental differences are neglected. These disadvantages do the least harm when aspects of intelligence and problem solving are being investigated, since these characteristics are among the most transituationally stable (Mischel, 1968, p. 177). Much more difficult to handle are motivational states and processes, at the same time, these are extremely important variables in consumer behavior. In assessing motivational dispositions projective tests based on Freud's and Murray's work are used, which reveal interindividual differences with the help of ill-structured stimuli. The actor's responses must, however, be interpreted by a trained and capable observer, and even a strong protagonist of this method, David McClelland, is forced to admit that even the most sophisticated tests of this kind (for example, the TAT), are not sufficiently reliable:

> Projective ... measures of human motivation have difficulty satisfying the reliablility criterion. ...If college students are tested a week apart, their motive score will correlate only in the .15-.30 range, meaning that a person whose score is high the first time is almost as likely to score low the second time. (McClelland, 1971, p. 14)

Fenz (1964) emphasizes even more strongly that projective tests are problematic, especially in situations characterized by high arousal. He demonstrated that in TAT stories constructed on the day of their jump, novice parachutists denied any fear of jumping. This effect, however, was limited to a highly relevant stimulus picture of a man about to parachute. That they were in fact made anxious by the impending jump was evidenced by their increasingly steep GSR[4] gradient produced only to parachute-relevant words with increasing proximity to jump time.

The last remaining bastion for producing "hard facts" are psychobiological measures. They have the disadvantage that the instruments necessary for their application detract from the real-life character of the situation. Also, the conclusions that may be drawn from the results are relatively undifferentiated. At most these measures can show the degree of emotional arousal and whether it is of positive or of negative quality for the actor. Nevertheless, Kroeber-Riel (1979) was able to show how these disadvantages can be partially overcome and how useful this method can be in the area of consumer behavior. Without doubt it is an important development when the basic arousing qualities of stimuli in the environment can be experimentally demonstrated. The instrument can then be used, for example, to discover which advertising appeals and picture material, copy etc. is most attention-getting, which colours are most arresting, which product- or package design is more appealing, which political slogans are best, etc.

Psychobiological measures are not yet sophisticated enough for content-specifying differentiation in the realm of motivation, such as would be necessary, for example, as a guideline for decisions having to do with product assortments. In these cases we fall back on long series of systematic and therefore time-consuming experiments, which are always in danger of being dominated "nomothetically" by the experiments and the experimental design. Thomae uses the alternative of observing and analysing long behavior sequences ("Tages- und Lebensläufe", i. e., daily records and life histories, Thomae, 1968) and of conflict processes (Thomae, 1974). He assumes that personal characteristics come out most clearly in conflict situations.

The above brief and admittedly superficial description of the weaknesses of existing methods for arriving at idiographic results shows that both theorists and practicioners must approach the problem of the limits and possibilities of influencing consumer behavior with much patience. In practice this means that each potential influencer must not only make an effort to continue developing the theory of consumer behavior on the psychological and sociological level, but also that he must - for the present - make the best he can of inaccurate and time-consuming methods for testing his theories about behavior in general and the possibilities of influencing consumer behavior in particular.

BIBLIOGRAPHY

Abelson, R. P. et al. (Eds.) (1968), Theories of Cognitive Consistency: A Sourcebook, Chicago: Rand McNally

Allport, G. W. (1937), Personality: A Psychological Interpretation, New York: Holt

Aronson, E. (1966), The Psychology of Insufficient Justification, in: Feldman, S. (Ed.) (1966), 115 - 133

Berlyne, D. E. (1960), Conflict, Arousal and Curiosity, New York: McGraw-Hill

Berlyne, D. E. (1968), The Motivational Significance of Collative Variables and Conflict. In: Abelson et al. (Eds.)(1968) 257 - 266

Bem, D. J. (1967), Self-Perception: An Alternative Interpretation of Cognitive Dissonance Phenomena. In: Psychological Review 74: 183 - 200

Bem, D. J., Allen, A. (1974), On Predicting Some of the People Some of the Time: The Search for Cross-Situational Consistencies in Behavior. In: Psychological Review 81: 508-520

Blass, T. (1977), On Personality Variables, Situations, and Social Behavior. In: Blass, T. (Ed.), 1977, 1 - 23

Blass, T. (Ed.) (1977), Personality Variables in Social Behavior, New York: Wiley

Brehm, J. W.(1966), A Theory of Psychological Reactance, New York: Academic Press

Brehm, J. W. (1972), Responses to Loss of Freedom: A Theory of Psychological Reactance, Morriston: General Learnig Press

Brehm, J. W., Cohen, A. R. (1962), Explorations in Cognitive Dissonance, New York: Wiley

Britt, S. H. (1966) (2nd ed. 1970), Consumer Behavior and the Behavioral Sciences: Theories and Application, New York: Wiley

Butcher, J. N. (1971), Objective Personality Assessment, New York: General Learning Press

Cohen, A. R. (1962), An Experiment on Small Rewards for Discrepant Compliance and Attitude Change. In: Brehm/Cohen, 1962, 73 - 78

Dichter, E. (1964) Consumer Motivations, New York:McGraw-Hill

Engel, J. F., Kollat, D. T., Blackwell, R. D. (1969) (2nd ed. 1973), Consumer Behavior, New York: Holt, Rinehart and Winston

Fairweather, G. W. (1967), Methods in Experimental Social Innovation, New York: Wiley

Feldman, S. (Ed.) (1966), Cognitive Consistency:Motivational Antecedents and Behavioral Consequents, New York: Academic Press

Fenz, W. D. (1964), Conflict and Stress as Related to Physiological Activation and Sensory, Perceptual, and Cognitive Functioning, Psychological Monographs 78, Whole No. 585

Festinger, L. (1957), A Theory of Cognitive Dissonance, Evanston, Ill.: Row, Peterson

Festinger, L., Carlsmith, J. M. (1959), Cognitive Consequences of Forced Compliance, In: Journal of Abnormal and Social Psychology 58:203 - 210

Fishbein, M. (1966), The Relationships between Beliefs, Attitudes, and Behavior, In: Feldman, S. (Ed.), (1966), 199-223

Goffman, E. (1961), Asylums, Garden City: Doubleday

Gouldner, A. W. (1959), Reciprocity and Autonomy in Functional Theory, in: Gross, L. (Ed.), Symposium on Sociological Theory, Evanston, Ill.: Row, Peterson, 241 - 270

Hartshorne, H., May, M. A. (1928), Studies in the Nature of Character, Vol. 1: Studies in Deceit. New York: Macmillan; quoted from: Bem/Allen (1974), 509, 519

Howard, J. A., Sheth, J. (1969), The Theory of Buyer Behavior, New York: Wiley

Jones, E. E., Nisbett, R. E. (1971), The Actor and the Observer: Divergent Perceptions of the Causes of Behavior, New York: General Learning Press

Kelley, G. A. (1955), The Psychology of Personal Constructs, New York: Norton, 2 vols.

Kelley, H. H. (1967), Attribution Theory in Social Psychology, in: Levine, D. (Ed.), Nebraska Symposium on Motivation: 1967. Lincoln: University of Nebraska Press, 1967, 192-238

Kelley, H. H. (1971), Attribution in Social Interaction, Morristown: General Learning Press

Kelley, H. H. (1972), Causal Schemata and the Attribution Process, Morristown: General Learning Press

Kroeber-Riel, W. (1975) (2nd ed. 1980), Konsumentenverhalten, München: Vahlen

Kroeber-Riel, W. (1979), Activation Research; Psychobiological Approaches in Consumer Research. In: Journal of Consumer Research 3: 240 - 250

McClelland, D. (1971), Assessing Human Motivation, New York: General Learning Press

McGuire, W. J. (1976), Some Internal Psychological Factors Influencing Consumer Choice. In: Journal of Consumer Research 2: 302 - 319

Meadows, I. (in press), Quality of Working Life: Progress, Problems and Prospects, Manuscript to be published in: Die Betriebswirtschaft, 1981

Milgram, S. (1965), Some Conditions of Obedience and Disobedience to Authority. In: Human Relations 18: 57 - 76

Mischel, W. (1968), Personality and Assessment, New York:Wiley

Mischel, W. (1973), Toward a Cognitive Social Learning Reconceptualization of Personality. In: Psychological Review 80; 252 - 283

Nicosia, F. M. (1966), Consumer Decision Processes: Marketing and Advertising Implications, Englewood Cliffs, N. J.: Prentice-Hall

Nicosia, F. M., Mayer, R. N. (1976), Toward a Sociology of Consumption. In: Journal of Consumer Research 3: 65 - 75

Nicosia, F. M., Wind, Y. (1978), Sociology of Consumption and Trade-Off Models in Consumer Public Policy, Institute of Business and Economic Research, University of California, Berkeley, Reprint No. 126

Nisbett, R. E., Valins, S. (1971), Perceiving the Causes of One's Own Behavior, New York: General Learning Press

Nuttin, M. (1975), The Illusion of Attitude Change. Towards a Response Contagion Theory of Persuasion, London: Academic Press

Pepitone, A. (1966), Some Conceptual and Empirical Problems of Consistency Models. In: Feldman, S. (Ed.) (1966), 257 - 297

Raush, H. L. (1965), Interaction Sequences. In: Journal of Personality and Social Psychology 2: 487 - 499

Reber, G. (1978), Individuum, Individuum über alles ... In: Die Betriebswirtschaft 38: 83 - 102

Rosenberg, M. J. (1965), When Dissonance Fails: On Eliminating Evaluation Apprehension from Attitude Measurement. In: Journal of Personality and Social Psychology 1: 28 - 42

Sarason, I. G., Smith, R. E., Diener, E. (1975), Personality Research: Components of Variance Attributable to the Person and the Situation. In: Journal of Personality and Social Psychology 32: 199 - 204

Singer, J. E. (1966), Motivation for Consistency. In: Feldman, S. (Ed.) (1966), 47 - 73

Stroebe, W. (1977), The Level of Social Psychology Analysis: Towards a Solution of Our Crisis, Paper given at the Carleton University Social Psychology Conference, Ottawa, May 8 - 14

Tajfel, H., Turner, J. (in press), An Integrative Theory of Intergroup Conflict. In: Austin, W. G., Worchel, S. (Eds.), The Social Psychology of Intergroup Relations, Monterey: Brooks/Cole

Thomae, H. (1968), Das Individuum und seine Welt, Göttingen: Verlag für Psychologie

Thomae, H. (1974), Konflikt, Entscheidung, Verantwortung, Stuttgart: Kohlhammer

Thomae, H. (1979), Zur Motivation sozialen Verhaltens. In: Heigl-Evers, A. (Ed.), Psychologie des 20. Jahrhunderts, Vol. 8, Zürich: Kindler, 276 - 282

Weiner, B., Freize, I., Kukla, A., Reed, L., Rest, S., Rosenbaum, R. M. (1971), Perceiving the Causes of Success and Failure, New York: General Learning Press

Wright, E. O. (1978), Race, Class and Income Equality. In: American Journal of Sociology 83: 1368 - 1397

Zimbardo, P. G. (1965), The Cognitive Control of Motivation, Glenview: Scott/Foresman

Zimbardo, P., Ebbesen, E. B. (1969), Influencing Attitudes and Changing Behavior, Reading: Addison/Wesley

Zimbardo, P. G., Weisenberg, M., Firestone, I., Levy, B. (1969), Changing Appetites for Eating Fried Grasshoppers with Cognitive Dissonance. In: Zimbardo, P. G. (1969), 44 - 54

NOTES

1. The book summarizes five years of research, that is, sixteen systematically planned experiments in which the motivational components of cognitive dissonance theory are explored.

2. Sarason et al. (1975) examined 102 studies involving 138 analyses of variance which appeared in the 1972 issues of the Journal of Personality and Social Psychology and the Journal of Personality and in the 1971 und 1972 issues of the Journal of Counselling and Clinical Psychology. They found that the average percentage of variance accounted for by either personality of situational variables alone was relatively small (8.7 and 10.3% respectively), but that the average percentage of variance due to personality/situation-interactions was even smaller - only 4.6%.

3. It is quite possible that if the attitude of the low confidence subject is confirmed by his behavioral test then he might subsequently express attitudes equal in strenght to those of the subjects who initially held the attitude with much confidence. If the behavior validation attempt disconfirms the hypothesis, then the most paradoxical pattern of all would result: subjects who are most likely to display the behavior would be least likely to express attitudes in line with the behavior. An important task facing investigators in this area is to determine those conditions where hypothesis-testing behavior will occur and to differentiate such behavior from behavior that expresses attitudes that are more firmly held. (Nisbett/Valins, 1971, p. 13)

4. When visual stimuli are too weak to elicit correct verbal identification because they are presented below visual threshold, autonomic (GSR) responses may still reflect both the nature of the stimuli and/or the nature of the mistaken identification.

B. Industrial Relations

Theoretical Dilemmas and Value Analysis in Comparative Industrial Relations

Michael Shalev

ABSTRACT

This paper is concerned to suggest some limits and possibilities of value analysis in elucidating the causes of cross-national variation in industrial relations. Theories of comparative industrial relations are discussed with respect to a number of choice-points on which scholars are in dispute, and are illustrated with reference to a particular substantive area, that of strike behavior. Subsequently, several major contributions to the field are reviewed with an eye to the role of values in their analysis. Several critical issues are taken up - in particular the autonomy of values from structural features of the industrial relations environment. We conclude that more explicit and sophisticated theorizing of values is needed if they are to have explanatory power in comparative industrial relations.

INTRODUCTION

This paper is essentially a literature review designed to acquaint non-specialists with theories of the causes of national diversity in industrial relations (IR). While drawing heavily on an earlier study with similar terms of reference (Shalev, 1980), it differs from that study in two major respects. Firstly, in the present paper we attempt to illuminate general problems and tendencies in comparative IR by explicitly organizing the discussion of examples around a number of predefined strategic choices which we believe are germane to theorizing in this field. Secondly, in view of the overriding concern of the present volume with the value dimension of social and economic life, we devote particular attention to the contributions and limitations of values in causal theories of comparative IR.

It should be added that "values" have here been interpreted loosely and without any attempt at definitional rigor. This is nothing to be proud of, but in an exploratory attempt to ask questions which have generally been ignored in the discipline under study, it is perhaps understandable. Nevertheless, some of the complexities of the concept of values may be briefly noted at this early juncture. When IR theorists and other theorists too speak of values they may be referring to at least three different things: social/cultural "norms", subjective perceptions ("consciousness"), or ideologies (world views). Correspondingly, they may also have in mind three different sorts of causation: values as defined by social definitions of good behavior, values as defined by the interaction between social structure and individual or collective human agency, and values as defined by strategic choices designed to serve concrete ends. Finally, they may utilize values with respect to several different units of analysis - such as whole societies, classes, or workplaces. Generally speaking, the theorists whose work we shall be reviewing relate to values as "norms", that is as beliefs and meaning-systems prevalent in whole societies. And in focusing on values they wish in general to emphasize the integrating as opposed to the dividing forces in social life, and the subjective as opposed to the objective realm of social determination.

Turning now to the state of comparative IR, we may note that while Dunlop - still the most influential theoretician in the field of IR - insisted long ago that to acquire theoretical wisdom in this field would necessitate the adoption of a comparative approach, and despite attempts initiated by the International Institute of Labor Studies to reorient the field along these lines, comparative analysis continues to play a relatively insignificant role in the discipline. Furthermore, from the earliest to the most recent forays into comparative IR, the bulk of the literature has been descriptive in content and comparative only by implication (e.g., Marquand et al., 1939; Dunlop & Galenson, 1978). Rather like the Victorian gentleman on his "grand tour," the reader is presented with a diverse selection of exotic ports of call and left to draw his own conclusions about their relevance to each other and to the traveller himself.

It would therefore be fair to say that the limited body of "comparative" work which has been produced in IR is rarely if ever self-consciously theoretical in either purpose or method. "Theorizing" is here construed to mean either that scholars would use comparative analysis as a means of verifying a priori hypotheses, or that they would seek to produce abstract generalizations derived from research findings in a variety of national contexts. Whether deductively or inductively, such theorizing would address itself to identifying the causes of similarities and differences in the development, structure and dynamics of salient characteristics of IR systems. I have in mind here characteristics such as the following: Why has a mass working class party failed to emerge in the United States? (See, for example, Kassalow, 1969). Similarly, how is one to account for the traditionally greater ideological radicalism of Norwegian socialism compared with the Social-Democratic movements of Sweden and Denmark? (Galenson, 1952). What is the relationship between labor market conditions and the emergence of collective bargaining as a mechanism of job regulation? (Sturmthal and Scoville, 1969). Under what political conditions do governments receive the cooperation of union movements in programmes of wage restraint? (Headey, 1970; Edelman & Fleming, 1965). By comparison between more and less "advanced" national cases, what predictions can be generated as to future patterns of IR? (Kerr et al., 1960; Dore, 1973). Finally - and this is an issue which will shortly occupy us in the present paper - how can we explain the differential rates and forms of strike activity characteristic of different countries?

THE FOUR QUESTIONS

In short, comparative analysis raises substantively interesting and important questions and offers a natural and fruitful avenue for the advance of theory in the discipline as a whole. Nevertheless, comparative IR is the chosen concern of only a small and perhaps diminishing group of specialists, and it has been studied in a largely non-theoretical manner and with little conscious effort to integrate past and present scholarship. Despite this lack of integration, which extends even to the disparate strands of contemporary research, it is possible to discern a number of important theoretical choice-points on which scholars are in dispute. For simplicity of argument and presentation, the choices concerned are presented as stark dichotomies. Obviously, in practice the issues which they raise and responses to these issues are more subtle and complex than this implies. It should be added that the first three of these four issues arise in all industrial relations theorizing.

1. What is the generic, tendential character - if any - of IR? Both at the level of collective bargaining and that of whole societies, theorists are divided over whether there is an evolutionary tendency in these relations towards the containment of conflict, or whether they are inherently unstable. The former school inclines to define symptoms of consensus - regulatory frameworks and institutional arrangements - as the key dependent variables for students of IR, while the latter prefers to focus on phenomena which express conflict and contradictions, most obviously the strike.

2. To what extent may industrial relations be explained in their own terms, without recourse to the wider environment? The debates between Ross and Dunlop over union wage policy in the late 1940s, and their strongly contrasting forays into comparative industrial relations a decade later, are indicative of what is involved here (Dunlop, 1944, 1958; Ross, 1948; Ross & Hartman, 1960). Ross argued for explanations centered on the nature of unions as institutions, while Dunlop saw the institutional content of IR as little more than window-dressing: dissimilar institutions were inclined to behave similarly when operating in a common environmental context.

3. Which aspects of the environment impinge most closely on IR? Theorists who see the political economy as consisting of two institutionally isolated spheres tend to view IR as a "subsystem" of the economic sphere and the polity as being a purely exogenous force. The opposing view is that IR comprise part of the totality of class relations, and that the employment nexus and the political nexus of these relations are intimately connected analytically despite wide variations in the empirical form which this connection takes. A related issue is whether the environmental determination of IR is a one-way street, or whether the actors in IR must also be seen as acting upon and influencing their environment. Regarding the polity and public policy as given in the analysis of IR implies that the participation of workers and employers in the political process is not a proper subject for study.

4. To what extent is national diversity in IR bound up with the character

of the wider political economy, and to what extent is it a feature of idiosyncratic factors like "values" or "historical accidents"? Convergence theorists have argued that all advanced industrial societies, by virtue of their common needs and material infrastructures, tend to produce similar social structures and similar behavior patterns in institutional realms such as the IR System. Such variation as can be discerned in these institutions is traced to factors which predate or are otherwise independent of the modern economy. The opposing view holds that among the Western nations, IR must be expected to reflect national peculiarities in the development and form of the capitalist economy and the way this has shaped the political context.

This paper will provide concrete illustrations of the significance of the choices outlined above for theorizing in comparative IR in two ways. First, by examining several contrasting approaches to a particular substantive question, namely why strike rates and patterns differ among the Western nations. Secondly, by comparing two extreme approaches to a particular analytical question, namely the role of values as an explanatory tool for comparative studies of IR in general.

CONTRASTING APPROACHES TO THE STRIKE

The inevitable starting point for any discussion of international comparisons of industrial conflict is Ross & Hartman's seminal work. This work is most often remembered for the rather extreme position taken by the authors on the first of the theoretical issues which we have raised - namely, the fate of industrial conflict in the longue durée. Ross & Hartman (1960: esp. Chapter 5) argued that in the postwar world, economic affluence, employer benevolence and the interventionist state had facilitated the workings of natural maturational tendencies in unions and collective bargaining. The results were more accommodative labor-management relations and union abandonment of strikes in favor of the more efficient and "respectable" path of political action. The roots of Ross & Hartman lay in Ross' underlying conception of union behavior as a product of the union's quest for survival as an organization, and of its leaders' instinct to survive at the helm of this organization. In a comparative analysis of industrial conflict with an earlier collaborator, Ross argued that the strike had "maintained a vigorous existence" in the United States, because union officials felt "impelled to utilize it to solve their own political problems and facilitate the survival and growth of the organizations they lead" (Ross & Irwin, 1951:339). In the low-strike nations of Britain and Sweden, on the other hand, unions and their leaders were relatively free of the pressures of employer resistance, internal disunity (jurisdictional and factional), and decentralized competitive bargaining.

Here we find exemplified the classic institutionalist approach to IR, which locates the sources of cross-national diversity squarely within the IR System proper: the organizational maturity and internal politics of unions, employer acceptance of unionism, and bargaining structure are the key explanatory variables. More recently, Clegg (1976) and Kassalow (1977) have reaffirmed the continuing attraction of these institutional variables to IR specialists dealing with the strike phenomenon. Furthermore, institutional variables are viewed by these analysts as possessing causal status, rather than as symptoms of more fundamental features of societies which constitute the deeper sources of IR behavior. Ironically, it was Kassalow who earlier put forward the dissenting view in holding that "it is misleading to attribute ... independent institutional status" to IR systems; that instead "a study of the social, economic and political substructure is far more critical for an understanding of unionism and labor relations" (1959:172).

A similar concern with the environmental context of industrial conflict is evident in the work of a number of contemporary scholars - by no coincidence from outside the field of IR proper - who have constructed critical alternatives to the Ross-Hartman approach. Taking as his starting point the fourth of the theoretical dilemmas we have pinpointed, Ingham has made the case that in order to explain variations in both institutional structures and levels of conflict institutionalization, it is necessary to focus on "features of a society's economic and technological system which shape the organization of, and the social relationships between, those groups engaged in the process of production" (1974:8). This approach is contrasted with mainstream "convergence" theory (Kerr _et.al._, 1960), which can deal with institutional differences only by resorting to "_cultural_ and _historical_ factors which are not intrinsic to capitalism as such but are features of the pre-industrial social order" (1974:9).

For Ingham, both the distribution of power and the superstructure of regulatory mechanisms which condition the behavior of the contending parties in industrial relations (workers, employers and the state) should be located in a society's economic "infrastructure". Ingham selects industrial concentration, technical and organizational complexity, and product differentiation and specialization as the infrastructural characteristics most salient to the development of IR Systems. To further simplify the argument, he focuses primarily on the manner in which infrastructural variables influence the structure and strategies of employer organizations, paying only secondary attention to the corresponding features of union movements, and (by his own admission) virtually ignoring the role of labor political parties and the state. Thus the question posed is, under what conditions "centralised institutions for the regulation of conflict" will develop - it being accepted that these are the proximate cause of low strike levels - and essentially, the answer is that such institutions will be found in societies where each sector of the economy is dominated by a small number of large-scale employers.

Given the "low level of competition within and between the sectors" in such an economy, employers will be encouraged to join together in "a dominant, solidary and powerful" association (1974:42). By rendering the power relationships and potential points of conflict between labor and capital more "visible", and also by making it possible for employers "to _impose_ normative regulation" on industrial relations, the existence of a strong employers' association favors the institutional supression of overt conflict. In addition, the same conditions which bring about high levels of concentration - limited domestic markets and late industrialization - also favor greater product specialization and less complex production systems

(Ingham's other infrastructural variables). The result is a less differentiated and fragmented trade union structure, which reinforces the existing potential for centralization and institutionalization of industrial relations.

While Ingham's analysis is obviously inspired by Marx, it belongs within that stream of the Marxist tradition which is determinist in flavor, emphasizing structure rather than process as the major conditioning influence on class relations. The alternative process-oriented view is represented in the recent work of a number of political sociologists who argue that industrial conflict should be seen as one of two major working class strategies - political action is the other - in the acting out of class conflict in capitalist societies (Shorter & Tilly, 1974; Korpi, 1977; Hibbs, 1978). By insisting that the strike is much more than an incident of the collective bargaining process - that it is instead a species of class conflict, the status of which is tied to the fortunes of the major classes in the political arena - these theorists take a clear stand on the third of the theoretical issues raised above: the polity is crucial, and endogenous, to IR.

In terms of the substantive predictions of the theories concerned - although not their rationale - there is actually a clear precedent to be found in a strand of Ross & Hartman's analysis mentioned earlier. They argued, on empirical grounds, that under conditions in which the state plays a major role in the political economy generally, and IR (collective bargaining and the determination of employment conditions) specifically, the relevance of the employer as a target for union demands is diminished. (See also Knowles, 1952 and Blumer, 1954). In the post-Keynsian era, unions were recognizing that "the state can influence the workers' economic welfare more powerfully through tax policy, public spending, economic planning, and social welfare legislation than the unions can affect it through collective bargaining" (Ross & Hartman, 1960:58). Political action was a particularly effective and desirable alternative to the strike in countries with "a labor party with close trade union affiliations" (1960:68). Labor parties, especially when in power, become the target for demands which would otherwise be directed against employers, and in addition, union leaders are reluctant to sanction industrial action which would endanger "their" party.

Similar arguments can be discerned in Hibbs' (1978) 12-nation comparison between strike levels and the political power of the working class (operationalized in terms of "left" party control over the executive branch). In Hibbs' view the reason why strikes tend to wither away under leftist governments is that in pursuing interventionist economic and social policies, such governments move the "locus of class conflict" out of the labor market and into the political process. Pizzorno's (1978) conceptualization of the relationship between unions and the state as one of "political exchange" takes this kind of argument a step further by pointing to certain prerequisites of the political bargains which underlie trade union willingness to sanction industrial peace. Some of these prerequisites are institutional - for example that unions have sufficient membership coverage and organizational control to guarantee that their members will go along with the dictates of restraint. Others are political - for example labor parties must have sufficiently great and durable leverage over public policy to make the political route a rewarding one for the unions. Still others are economic - there must be sufficient growth for workers' real incomes to rise, but continued prosperity must be intimately enough linked with pressures to hold down labor costs (e.g. due to export dependence) that a cooperative strategy appears both beneficial and desirable to labor leaders.

AN INTEGRATED PERSPECTIVE

In several recent papers (Korpi and Shalev, 1979 and 1980) Walter Korpi and I have also argued the case for a political interpretation of industrial peace. This interpretation was formulated with the four theoretical choice-points outlined earlier very much in mind, and can be conveniently summarized in terms of each one of them.

1. We reject the hypothesis of a universal evolutionary trend towards diminishing overt conflict in employment relations. Since the sources of this conflict lie in generic features of IR in capitalist societies - such as the dependence of sellers of labor power on those who buy it and their insecure status under a market system of labor allocation, the factual as well as legal subordination of labor to capital in work, and the opposing interests of wage-earners and profit-makers in income distribution - it must be regarded as a systemic feature of these societies. Nevertheless, while in all capitalist societies power resources - the ability of social actors to reward and punish other actors - are unequally distributed between capital and labor to the disadvantage of the latter, in practice the degree of inequality of power between them varies over time and between societies. In particular, through combination and collective action - principally in trade unions and political parties - the sellers of labor can considerably enhance their power resources relative to capital.

   The "power difference" model of social conflict (Korpi, 1974) predicts that variations in the inequality of power resources between contending collectivities are associated with variations in the conflict strategies open to them, and hence in the likelihood that they will have recourse to overt forms of conflict on the tactical level. We argue that in application to industrial conflict in democratic capitalist societies, this model suggests that under conditions where wage-earners succeed in building strong collectivities, they discover advantages in pursuing their conflicts with capital via the political rather than industrial arena, and that as a consequence the strike loses its attractiveness as a tactical instrument.

   Specifically, where the working class is highly mobilized in a unified and centralized union movement with strong ties to a labor-based party, which succeeds in acquiring stable control over the legislative and executive branches of government, the polity constitutes a more effective arena than collective bargaining for the pursuit of long-term working class goals in respect of the aforementioned problems of insecurity, subordination and income inequality. The immediate conflicts of interest inherent in the employment relationship do not disappear, but for the most part they are played out without recourse to work stoppages. The strike becomes a fetter on labor governments concerned to achieve social stability, economic growth and the assent of capital to their continued domination of the polity. However, in return for their restraint union members reap the benefits of state action to produce higher levels of employment, more redistributive tax and expenditure policies, and legislative enhancements of workers' control rights in the workplace (Korpi & Shalev, 1980:326; Hibbs, 1977; Stephens & Stephens, 1979).

2. The status of institutions in the theory sketched above is that of symptoms rather than causes. Collective bargaining and dispute-settlement arrangements are largely reflections of the distribution of power and the outcomes of conflicts between labor movements (unions and parties), employers and the state at the time these arrangements came into being. The institutional framework of IR should therefore be viewed as a residual outcome of past conflicts, reflecting attempts by the actors to routinize exchange relations and to economize on power resources. Its existence indicates that the parties have 'accepted' the terms and forms in which conflicts of interest between them can be resolved. However, in view of the persistence of fundamental inequalities of power and advantage, this acceptance is typically conditional and pragmatic in nature, and may be in part engineered by the stronger party (Fox,1973). The forms and functions of IR institutions, therefore, basically depend on the underlying difference in power resources between the parties. Insofar as, once in existence, such institutions acquire a degree of "functional autonomy," they should still be regarded principally as having the status of intervening variables in comparative theories, the task of causal explanation being reserved for factors in the social, political and economic environment.

3. It will be evident that the IR system is analytically undetachable from the polity in our theory. Far from ascribing to the thesis that the economic and political spheres of action become institutionally isolated in modern societies (Dahrendorf, 1959), we argue that it is precisely the strength and character of working class mobilization in the political arena which is the chief determinant of the behavior of labor organizations in the industrial arena of class conflict.

4. While the structural cleavages endemic in capitalist methods of labor allocation, production and income distribution are universal, their concrete consequences for working class collective action are mediated by variations in both the context in which capitalism develops and the characteristics of its development in different nations. On the one hand, it must be recognized that although relationships to the means of production in the long run give rise to the most important conflict groups or classes in capitalist societies, a multitude of other cleavages can and often do provide competing bases for conflict. The most important of these cleavages - which, by "cross-cutting" the wage-earners, hinder their propensity to act collectively and on a unified basis - appear along the lines of occupation, religion, race, ethnicity, language

and region. On the other hand, it is evident that differences in the timing and speed of industrialization are responsible for significant cross-national variations in class structure - for example the relative significance of the manual industrial workforce compared with white-collar workers, peasants, and the petit-bourgeoisie - which set upper bounds on recruitment to labor movement organizations. In addition, certain developmental tendencies of the capitalist economy - such as ownership concentration or skilled worker "proletarianization" - which are sometimes regarded as universal, in practice exhibit considerable cross-national variation, which in turn has important implications for working class mobilization. For example, greater centralization of capital may enhance the organizational centralization of IR institutions (as Ingham has argued); and a more vigorous craft stage of industrialization may strengthen occupation at the expense of industry and therefore class as a basis for unionization.

The structural character of the factors so far pointed to as conditioning working class mobilization - whether they derive from national peculiarities of capitalist development or from cleavages with pre-capitalist roots - carries with it a danger of falling prey to determinist explanations. In real life social actors <u>choose</u> from a range of strategic choices when confronting structurally-based dilemmas. This is evident in the varying ways in which the labor parties of different nations have defined their constituencies in pursuit of the goal of achieving majority support under conditions in which the manual working class constitutes only a minority of the electorate (Przeworski & Sprague, 1977). It is also evident in the differing manner and degree to which these parties have pursued the class interests of their core constituents in making policy choices - choices which in turn exert a powerful influence on their ability to mobilize the working class electorate (Martin, 1973; Korpi, 1978; Castles, 1978). Thus, explanations of national diversity in IR must be pursued at a variety of levels: at the level of the context of capitalist development as well as the peculiar form which capitalism takes in different nations; and at the level of process and collective choice as well as that of structurally imposed constraints on social action.

DUNLOP VS LIPSET ON VALUES

Thus far we have sought to raise a number of fundamental issues facing IR theorists at the comparative level of analysis, by referring to studies which are united by a concern with a particular <u>dependent</u> variable, namely industrial/class conflict. At this point the focus of the presentation of contrasting views will shift to the <u>independent</u> variable of "values". We shall begin by summarizing the views of two theorists, Dunlop & Lipset, whose respective positions on the explanatory status of values in comparative IR are sharply opposed. Dunlop's approach, inspired by Parsonian sociology, treats what he calls "ideology" as an essential component of an IR system and implies that variations in the <u>content</u> of ideologies are epiphenomenal to the universal stabilizing <u>function</u> which they perform. Lipset, on the other hand, regards social values as the taproot of critical differences in trade union behavior between different nations. We shall argue that both of these approaches are unsatisfactory, and that greater insight can be gained by treating values analytically as lying midway between social structure and behavior, and potentially moderating the relationship between the two.

As is well known, Dunlop (1958) formalized the IR System as one in which the chief actors in the employment sphere (unions, employers, the state) engage in the production of a "web of rules," under constraints imposed by the contexts (market, technological, and power) in which they operate. In terms of the four dilemmas which we have repeatedly emphasized, Dunlop occupies a distinctive theoretical position and one which is in several respects opposed to our own. We both agree that institutions should play a subordinate role to environmental conditions in IR theories. However, Dunlop insisted that conflict is a peripheral and gradually diminishing force in IR, and that the study of IR should therefore focus upon manifestations of consensus ("rules"). He also viewed the polity as exogenous to the IRS and of limited significance to it, and held closely to the convergence view that both the economic infrastructures and the institutional superstructures of the advanced societies are evolving in similar directions. Variations in the IR System proper (as opposed to its outputs) - such as differences in the organizational strength and conflict strategies of labor movements - were seen by Dunlop as originating in unsystematic and largely uninteresting historical and political forces, and were of far less significance for IR behavior than impersonal forces like markets and machines. (For some recent, impressive examples of comparative research in this tradition, see Elbaum & Wilkinson, 1979; Streeck et. al., 1978).

For present purposes, what is of most interest about Dunlop's theory is its treatment of the value sphere. According to Dunlop, in addition to the "actors" and "contexts" of IR, "A further element is required to complete the analytical system: an ideology or a set of ideas and beliefs commonly held by the actors that helps to bind or to integrate the system together as an entity" (1958:16). It was made clear (1958:17) that consensus between the participants on "an acceptable role for each actor" is a necessary feature of the IR System. Nevertheless, elsewhere (on the same page) Dunlop seemingly qualified this axiom by limiting it only to stable systems. Given the functionalist starting-point of Dunlop's theory there is actually no contradiction here, since equilibrium is assumed to be an inherent characteristic of social systems in general and the IRS in particular. This assumption receives concrete expression in the notion that the output of the IR System (the dependent variable in the study of industrial relations) is the web of rules, and conflict is merely a temporary surface phenomenon (1958:27, 380). It is interesting, however, that in the following passage, Dunlop himself recognized ideological conflict and combative labor-management relations as logical possibilities.

> Thus, in a community in which the managers hold a highly paternalistic view toward workers and the workers hold there is no function for managers, there would be no common ideology in which each actor provided a legitimate role for the other; the relationships within such a work community would be regarded as volatile, and no stability would likely be achieved in the industrial-relations system (1958:17).

The empirical resemblance of the above description to, say, French IR could surely not have escaped a seasoned observer like Dunlop. But his materialistic theoretical bias, explicitly seeking in "technological and market forces" rather than "political and ideological considerations" the key to national diversity in industrial relations, precluded any meaningful utilization of ideology as an independent variable (1958:iv). That Dunlop's concept of ideology is virtually redundant for explanatory purposes will be apparent to even the superficial reader of his text. Thus, in the elaborately detailed cross national examination of the rules produced by IR Systems in the coal and construction industries, not a single mention is made of ideological differences. Even more interesting is Dunlop's treatment of the Yugoslav national system, which begins with the surprising admission that "The ideological content of workers' councils is an independent factor in the creation and growth of workers' councils" (1958:283). Nevertheless, workers' self-management is interpreted primarily as a specific institutional device for coping with compelling universal problems posed for the managers of industrial relations by the process of economic development, particularly the necessity of creating a disciplined work force. While the ideologically-generated distinctiveness of Yugoslav industrial relations is indicative of the scope for variation in the preferences of the elites who construct the IR Systems of countries at early stages of economic development, the forces of modernization bring about increasing convergence between systems. In the mature industrial society, ideologically-motivated constraints on the operation of technological and market forces give way to a "greater pragmatic emphasis" (1958:283). As was spelled out more explicitly in Dunlop's subsequent collaborative work in the framework of the famous Interuniversity Study (Kerr et al., 1960), this means that within the universe of advanced capitalist (and even communist) societies, ideology turns into a theoretical non sequitur.

In marked contrast Lipset (1961-2), while accepting most of the core assumptions of the convergence theorists yet reacting perhaps against their excesses, attempted to bring the concept of a "dominant value system" to the forefront in explaining national IR peculiarities among countries explicitly recognized as sharing similar economic as well as political and cultural characteristics. Why, Lipset asked, were American unions more conservative, less class-conscious, more militant, more bureaucratized and more narrowly based than labor movements in Northern Europe - i.e., the other "predominantly Protestant, relatively affluent, industrialized nations ... [with] relatively stable democratic political systems" (1961: 81, 75)? The answer lay in the two core values of American society: "Achievement," the belief that individuals should strive "to be a 'success'," and "equality," the notion that success should be open to and striven for by all. With their stress on the primacy of individual action and the individual's responsibility for his fate, these American values negate the legitimacy of class-based organizations and ideologies. By placing few limits on workers' aspirations and legitimizing the notion that the realization of these aspirations justifies recourse to any available means, the same primal values make those unions which do take root instrumental, self-interested, and ruthless (hence their exceptional propensity to strike and to engage in corrupt practices).

The validity of this type of argument depends on whether one is willing to accept, with Lipset, that social structures can be characterized in normative terms and that social action is normatively-based. A case can be made for the opposite view: that dominant value systems are symptomatic of more truly structural features of societies (such as inequalities of power and advantage); that they serve largely to rationalize the superior achievements of the advantaged and tend to be at least passively negated by the disadvantaged; and that while it can illuminate the "vocabularies of motive" utilized by or imposed upon social actors, recourse to social values fails to explain the deeper origins of the behavior of classes in conflict. To put it another way, observed correlations between dominant values and the behavior of the subordinate class are spurious if both are in fact the product of the social (class) structure and the way in which class relations have evolved within this structure.

The failure of American labor to consciously and permanently embrace socialist values (and strategies, tactics, and organizational forms) can hardly be explained by pointing out that American workers ascribe to non-socialist values. This reasoning is evidently tautological. We also need to know why a particular set of values comes to dominate in a particular society. On this point Lipset offers very little guidance. He refers vaguely to the historical origins of value differences, but the only historical hypothesis which is concretely specified is that industrialization under an aristocratic elite (Europe) favors ascriptive values, whereas achievement values are succored where the commercial classes were dominant (America).

KENDALL'S ANGLO-AMERICAN EXCEPTIONALISM

Many other students of comparative IR have also argued that "American exceptionalism" (the weakness of socialist consciousness and politics in the United States) is a result of the favorable conditions for widespread acceptance of capitalist values of competitive individualism, conditions created by the absence of a feudalistic social and political structure prior to industrialization (e.g. Sturmthal, 1951; Lorwin, 1957). Kendall (1975: Chapters 1 and 12) has pointed to the role of capitalist ideological hegemony in forcing the structure and strategy of the American labor movement (and, he argues, British labor as well) into a different mold to that which is characteristic of the nations of continental Europe. He hypothesizes that economic interests and cleavages emerged in much purer form in the Anglo-Saxon countries because industrialization occurred in a context relatively free of "the trammels of a pre-capitalist past." On the one hand, the role of pre-capitalist institutions (the church and the monarchy) was no longer an issue in national life by the time of industrialization; while on the other, a greater "sense of homogeneity of the national labour force" developed than in Europe, where feudalism (later, peasant proprietorship), family-based enterprises, and regional and linguistic cleavages fostered local rather than diffuse loyalties.

In addition, in contrast to authors (Lipset for instance) who seek to explain the character of social movements which arose in reaction to capitalism, without making reference to the characteristics of capitalism itself, Kendall also focuses on the vigor of entrepreneurial capitalism in Britain and the U.S. as an important source of Anglo-American exceptionalism. Citing a variety of geopolitical and historical causes, he argues that industrialization came earlier in these nations than in Europe and was based on superior technology and markets. Together with more open recruitment into the entrepreneurial class and easier access to investment funds, these conditions favored the growth of a laissez-faire economy. As a result, the role of the state and politics in economic life was more limited, and mass support for the competitive market system was greater in Britain and America than on the continent. Thus incorporating both capitalist and pre-capitalist social and economic formations into his explanatory universe, Kendall arrives at the conclusion that the British-American and European contexts are sharply differentiated at the level of values - specifically in the degree to which "the prevailing modes of human economic behaviour are characterized by rules of abstract economic rationality" (1975:310). And he goes on to argue that this value difference is responsible for some of the contrasts which can be observed at the level of IR - specifically, the economism and internal unity of the British and American union movements, compared with politicization and religious/ideological divisions in Europe.

Just how crucial the value element is in Kendall's argument is open to debate. The choices of strategy and organization made by the different labor movements could equally well be interpreted as more or less rational responses to the objective contexts in which working class mobilization took place in different societies. Primary among these objective conditions in the United States are those which historically have awarded capital a privileged position in class conflict - such as its leverage over political institutions including parties and the courts, its ability to exploit immigration and ethnic diversity in attacking unionization and other forms of working class solidarity, and the powerful weapons (such as rapid technological change and oligopolistic product markets) at its disposal in class struggles at the point of production (Shalev and Korpi, 1980). The hegemony of capitalist values appears from this perspective mainly as a reflection of the underlying difference in power resources between labor and capital, although the material payoffs which the mobilized sector of the American working class has enjoyed under relatively unbridled capitalism must have contributed as well to the latter's legitimacy (e.g. Lorwin, 1957: 33; cf. Przeworski, 1980). Kendall's analysis may also be criticized for ignoring the substantial differences in both context and behavior that exist within his two comparison groups, especially the obvious contrasts between Britain and the U.S. in terms of class composition and consciousness, the level and forms of worker mobilization, etc. Nevertheless, he does provide a useful illustration of how value analysis can be used to link structure to behavior in explaining variations between national IR Systems.

MAURICE AND SELLIER ON GERMANY VS FRANCE

Our two remaining examples of the part played by values in comparative IR theories differ from Kendall's work in two important respects. Firstly, the comparisons being performed are much more focused, in each case involving only two countries. Secondly, in both studies there is an attempt to operate simultaneously at both the macro and micro levels of analysis:

differences of behavior within the enterprise are of equal interest to IR behavior at the national level,yet the explanation of these differences rests on societal as well as enterprise-level variables.

The first study to be reviewed is a comparison of France and Germany recently reported by Maurice & Sellier (1979). According to these authors, among the characteristics of French IR which cry out for explanation when comparisons are drawn with Germany, are the "charismatic" rather than "bureaucratic" character of French unions and their inclusive coverage of white-collar as well as manual workers; the slower growth and lesser legitimacy of collective bargaining in France; and the more militant and politicized handling of shopfloor issues. Their argument proceeds at two distinct levels. On the first, already familiar macro level, it is suggested that differences in the timing and pattern of industrialization, the organization of capital, and the formative demographic, economic and political contexts of class formation and mobilization have conditioned the differing character of class organization and conflict in the two societies. For example, among the factors which favored the emergence of a more unified and organizationally disciplined union movement in Germany was the more rapid creation and homogenous composition of the manual working class, lending it a more solidaristic and bounded character; and the high degree of cartelization of capital, which encouraged strong and centralized organization on the employer side.

The second level of Maurice & Sellier's analysis takes off from certain differences which they have observed at the micro level of IR in contemporary France and Germany. These differences center on the contrasting treatment of occupational skills in the management of enterprises and the operation of labor markets. German society and state policy have been characterized by educational values which give priority to vocational over theoretical training and which see responsibility for such training as lying with employers, rather than (as in France) with the state. As a result of this peculiarity of "the relationship between the enterprise and society," the status and rewards of workers in German industry are closely linked to their occupational qualifications, whereas in France these are most dependent on their mobility within internal enterprise labor markets and hence on criteria such as seniority and job evaluation. These characteristics are complemented and reinforced by the ideas which guided employers in the design of systems of enterprise management. In line with the respect of German employers for craft values, Maurice & Sellier argue that the management of the production process is much less centralized and hierarchically structured than in France.

But as Reynaud (1979) has argued, the origins of the differences in value orientations on which Maurice & Sellier focus are obscure, and their assumption that behavior originates in values is sociologically unsound. Yet their analysis is nevertheless something more than a curious combination of the normally competing structural and normative modes of analysis. In some respects it also offers a fruitful interaction between the two modes. The authors' discussion of the differing conflict strategies of French and German unionism is instructive here. In France the unions rely heavily on strikes in resolving plant-level disputes and anchor such conflicts in an ideological critique of the entire system of social relations, whereas in

Germany they have been willing to accept severe restrictions on the use of militant tactics at factory level while aggressively pursuing concessions on codetermination in the political arena. This contrast is explained by Maurice & Sellier in terms of the greater "legitimacy" of the enterprise in Germany, itself a consequence of: (1) The high social prestige which industry has enjoyed as a result of its "technical performance and dynamism;" (2) The fact that at an early stage in the evolution of modern class relations the state and the army imposed on employers the duty of recognizing workers' rights to participation in management; (3) The valued status of the enterprise in the workers' eyes due to its role in providing vocational training; and (4) The fact that in a decentralized structure of control, workplace conflicts are less likely to escalate and become politicized, while in this same structure codetermination has a payoff for workers in the form of the leverage exercized by works councils over such vital issues as recruitment, promotion and job assignment.

In the end, the authors argue that values - in the form of legitimacy in Germany and its denial in France - guide the behavior of the actors in IR with respect to three key variables: the position of the enterprise in society; worker respect for managerial functions and its counterpart, employer recognition of unions; and the status of workers in the enterprise. It is useful to have these ideological differences clarified, since they provide an obvious link between the objective environmental features which shape IR behavior, and behavior itself. However, Maurice and Sellier are most convincing in their use of values when they are able to pursuasively attribute these values to structural and contextual features which would perhaps just as easily stand on their own. The degree to which "legitimacy" can stand on its own, or is rather a foregone conclusion in the light of more tangible socio-economic data, is ambiguous in their analysis. As an exercize in verstehen, their contribution is unquestionably substantial - far more so than our capsule summary would suggest. But they do not appear to offer a theoretical framework capable of explicitly integrating values into the analysis of comparative IR.

DORE ON VALUES AND "JAPANESE EXCEPTIONALISM"

The final work to be reviewed here, Dore's British Factory - Japanese Factory (1973), is somewhat more successful in this respect. Ironically, however, in Dore's case there is no attempt to elevate values to the pinnacle of the analysis; the object is rather to directly confront their actually rather limited theoretical utility in explaining one of the great unsolved puzzles of comparative IR, Japan. As Dore points out, Japanese IR are typically viewed either as the product of cultural uniqueness (the importation of Japanese family patterns, respect for the aged, etc., into the work setting), or else the consequence of a cultural lag (the "normal" social consequences of economic development having not yet neutralized Japan's anachronistic labor market and IR characteristics). Dore proposes a novel alternative to those of the proponents and opponents of the convergence thesis: he hypothesizes that Japan's "late development" has telescoped its employment system into becoming the image of the West's future.

The explanation which Dore provides for "Japanese exceptionalism" proceeds on several different levels. Firstly, he points out that the modern large-enterprise system of permanent employment emerged in a specific context - that of a destroyed economy and state. Under these circumstances, both the workers' drive for security and organization, and management's interest in restoring the supply of skilled labor, were rationally served by enterprise-based employment. Secondly, however, Dore shows that there are demonstrable historical precedents for the modern system, although he adds that such precedents have a variety of different origins. Some were an unconscious carryover from feudal times and some were consciously adapted from traditional practices, while others were borrowed from abroad.

Thirdly, and most importantly, it is argued that the special circumstances under which the capitalist economy and class structure came into being in Japan have had decisive consequences for the subsequent character of class relations. For example, the relative weakness of class consciousness in Japan compared with Britain is linked to the fact that the feudal period of cultural homogeneity more closely preceded industrialization and also that the educational system was from the first much more universalistic in curriculum and structure. In other words, in contrast to the impetus which European-style feudalism is generally said to have given to class conflict, Japan's "pre-capitalist trappings" worked to the benefit of class collaboration.

In any event, the contextual features of industrialization which Dore is most concerned to stress are those which he believes are common to all second-generation industrializers, and which he hypothesizes are responsible for similarities in their IR systems (dualism, enterprise unionism, job security, seniority-based promotion, highly developed welfare and training schemes, etc.). Some examples of contextual factors consequent upon late development are: The absence of an indigenous technological evolution and its characteristic craft stage favor the enterprise rather than the market or public provision as the primary arena of occupational training. The development of an educational system prior to industrialization renders an intra-enterprise career system appropriate to both workers' and employers' needs. The fact that other countries have already experienced the union challenge and developed "social technologies" for neutralizing it encourages employers to promote non-market mechanisms of worker commitment to employment. And so does the fact that egalitarian values have already overtaken the <u>laissez-faire</u> ideology of early capitalism.

Dore thus concludes that while specifically Japanese attributes - both cultural and historical - provided a congenial environment for the growth of a paternalistic capitalist strategy, the critical factor is that such a strategy appeared economically rational to Japanese but not British employers because industrial relations in Japan were institutionalized more than half a century later than in Britain. A more concrete illustration of his emphasis on rational choice may be helpful here. In discussing managerial policies of recruitment, training and promotion, Dore states that:

> The Japanese employer had reasons for recruiting young school-leavers and training them that the British employer hadn't - their easy

> availability, their cheapness, their disciplined willingness to learn, and the fact that, because of the technological leap and the faster rate of growth, the market could not provide for his needs so that he would have to do his own training anyway. His experience of steadier growth made him more optimistic about the future: he could calculate that if he invested in training and devised schemes to keep his workers in order to recoup his investment, market conditions would be likely to <u>allow</u> him to keep them fully occupied. Seniority scales and other long-term incentives followed naturally - and were that much easier to afford since the young workers, competing for entry into the firms which offered good prospects, were hirable at such low initial wages (1973:413).

Whither values in this analysis? Dore is not an extremist. He concedes, for example, that commonality between the emergent working and capitalist classes in industrializing Japan as a result of a common heritage of culture, education and family life "may have been one of the facilitating factors which made Japan's employment system possible" (1973:284). Furthermore, he argues that in addition to the critical factor of <u>timing</u>, the choices made by Japanese industrialists were also shaped by <u>ideology</u>: their Confucian world-view gave them confidence in the efficiency of benevolence, and their moral code - reinforced by a desire to raise their social status relative to the bureaucracy and the military - also encouraged them to adopt a more benevolent stance than industrialists in most other societies. The attitudes and values of Japanese workers were similarly congenial to a paternalist mode of IR.

Yet values are derived not only from national character and culture, but also from what Dore calls "situational differences." Japan's moral code had relevance for the shaping of its employment system because of the nature of the options open to the actors in the late development context. Graduate employee managers whose labor force consisted of primary school graduates, who had never experienced a truly <u>laissez-faire</u> economy, and who were forewarned of the implications of <u>capitalist industrialization</u> for class relations, had every reason to sponsor innovations in the security, control and remuneration of labor, especially when they judged that despite their inconsistency with the competitive individualist values underlying Western capitalist enterprise, these innovations were likely to have <u>profitable</u> results. Values, in other words, link, mediate, facilitate, and may even moderate the impact of historically specific structures on institutions and practices of IR. But they do not directly cause, and they cannot stand alone in our theories.

<u>CONCLUSIONS</u>

Firstly, some concluding comments on the comparative IR field <u>per se</u>. It has been argued that scholars with a theoretical interest in this field face four dilemmas. Simplistically, these may be defined as choices between conflictual and consensual objects of study, between factors, external or internal, to IR Systems as explanatory loci, between treating environmental (especially political) factors as endogenous or exogenous to IR processes, and between emphasizing systemic rather than accidental antecedents of national peculiarities in the IR environment. These by no means represent all of the issues which confront the field, but we have found them particularly pertinent in our own work on industrial conflict. In this connection we have argued for a perspective which in relation to each of the dilemmas chooses the first of the two options indicated.

The notion of choices is however intended to be didactic rather than definitive. For example, while it is tempting to view the divisions between theorists as revolving around competition between paradigms and ideologies, especially along a "critical-Marxist" versus "functionalist-reformist" axis, they are in practice somewhat more subtle than this (cf. Cox, 1978). As we have seen, even scholars closely identified with the liberal-pluralist/convergence view are divided among themselves on important issues like the choice between conflict and consensus as dependent variables or between institutions and their environment as causal variables. At the same time, theorists whose inspiration is Marxist differ in the aspects of Marx's thought to which they assign predominance - particularly in whether they regard the parameters of social conflict as being predetermined by the organization of production, or rather emphasize the way in which classes moulded by the productive system shape their own destinies by collective action within a context defined by both economic and extra-economic forces.

Posing the choices in terms of grand-theoretical questions sharpens some important issues - most notably the relationship between the political and economic spheres of social action. Furthermore, when consciousness of these larger questions is absent, comparative IR sometimes falls victim to a rather unsystematic and analytically unrewarding eclecticism. Nevertheless, what the field needs most urgently at this juncture are theoretically aware attempts to construct integrated models without falling victim to a different kind of trap - that of being so blinkered by partisan considerations of discipline and weltanschaung that theory becomes narrow and mechanistic. The possibility, for example, of a fruitful interchange between political sociologists and IR institutionalists - one which stands to the benefit from a close reading of the IR classics - deserves fuller attention.

A second direction which comparative industrial relationists might profitably pursue is that of more systematic and focused comparison. On the one hand, we have studies like that of Maurice and Sellier or Dore, which on the basis of detailed study of one or two cases generate sophisticated and plausible hypotheses. But the validity of these hypotheses can only be fully explored by arraying the cases already examined against other critical cases. For example, by contrasting Germany and Japan to France we could construct a fascinating test of the relevance of late development, education/training, and the internalization of labor markets for national diversity in IR. At the other extreme, comparisons which are pitched at a high level of generality, such as the ubiquitous Europe-America contrasts, stand to benefit from greater disaggregation. For instance, the immense differences between France and Germany which Maurice and Sellier have observed pose a powerful challenge to the generalized notion of the European experience suggested in studies such as Kendall's. Comparative analysis is most successful when carried out on the basis of intimate familiarity with the peculiar characteristics of national systems and their historical roots. At the same time, national peculiarities only acquire meaning in a comparative perspective. In view of this paradox, analysts must attempt to operate simultaneously in both the national and cross-national frameworks - meaning that the all too popular Victorian traveller's approach to "comparison" is woefully inadequate.

Our attempt to analyze some comparative theories of IR in terms of their use of values has revealed a number of pitfalls which deserve to be noted. From a functionalist perspective (Dunlop), values are treated as analytically undifferentiated across national systems, and therefore a dead end as far as comparative explanation is concerned. This is also true of studies (Kendall, to some extent) which identify values so closely with particular structural configurations that from an explanatory viewpoint they (values) are effectively made redundant. An alternative approach (Lipset) is to treat values in effect as a residual category necessary to account for national deviations from allegedly universal tendencies. The problem with this approach is that it lays far too great a strain on values for explanatory purposes, in particular failing to recognize the extent to which values _are_ "functional" in the sense of serving interests rooted in structural characteristics of socio-economic systems.

Between extreme structural-functionalist and subjectivist approaches lie a number of possibilities. One of these is to treat values simply as one of a multiplicity of "strategic factors" which determine national IR characteristics (e.g. Walker, 1969). This of course simply sidesteps the difficult issue of how it is that values are interconnected in origin and impact with other strategic factors. It seems to us that Marx was right in conceptualizing this interconnection as dialectical - consciousness having the power to shape history and yet itself being irrevocably shaped by objective historical forces. The objective defines, yet is itself redefined by the subjective. Thus, social actors are frequently confronted by an existential need to make strategic choices between objectively possible courses of action. In several different senses values play a role in this process of choice: as perceptions of interests, as ideologies, and as cultural inheritance. Strategic choices, once acted upon, redefine future constellations of values and future existential choices. These, it seems to us, are the theoretical insights reflected in the more successful attempts in the IR field to use values comparatively - Dore's, with its emphasis on how managerial strategies in Japan were both normatively coherent and rational; and Maurice and Sellier's, showing how strategic behavior is both consistent with and reinforces the ideologies of French unions and employers.

It is therefore suggested that the conflict strategies of labor and capital ought to be treated as the variable of central interest in comparisons (whether cross-national or over time) of IR (Commons, 1932); and that doing so opens up promising avenues for exploring interactions between objective structures of power and opportunity and the understandings of the real people who make history.

BIBLIOGRAPHY

Blumer, Herbert. (1954), Social Structure and Power Conflict. In: Arthur Kornhauser et al. (eds.), Industrial Conflict, New York: McGraw-Hill, 232-9

Castles, Francis G. (1978), The Social Democratic Image of Society, London: Routledge

Clegg, Hugh (1976), Trade Unionism under Industrial Relations: A Theory Based on Comparisons of Six Countries, Oxford: Blackwell

Commons, John R. (1932), Labor Movement. In: Encyclopedia of the Social Sciences, 8, New York: Macmillan, 682-96

Dahrendorf, Ralf (1959), Class and Class Conflict in Industrial Society, London: Routledge

Dore, Ronald (1973), British Factory - Japanese Factory: The Origins of National Diversity in Industrial Relations, University of California Press

Dunlop, John T. (1950)(1944), Wage Determination Under Trade Unions, London: Blackwell

Dunlop, John T. (1958), Industrial Relations Systems, New York: Holt

Dunlop, John T.& Walter Galenson (eds.) (1978), Labor in the Twentieth Century, New York: Academic Press

Edelman, Murray & R.W. Fleming (1965), The Politics of Wage-Price Decisions: A Four-Country Analysis, Urbana: University of Illinois Press

Elbaum, Bernard & Frank Wilkinson (1979), Industrial Relations and Uneven Development: A Comparative Study of the American and British Steel Industries. In: Cambridge Journal of Economics, 3(3), September, 275-303

Fox, Alan (1973), Industrial Relations: A Social Critique of Pluralist Ideology. In: John Child (Ed.), Man and Organization, London: Allen & Unwin, 185-233

Galenson, Walter (ed.) (1952), Comparative Labor Movements, New York: Prentice-Hall (Pages 104-172 contain Galenson's own chapter on Scandinavia)

Headey, Bruce W. (1970), Trade Unions and National Wage Policies. In: Journal of Politics, 32(2), 407-439

Hibbs, Douglas A. Jr. (1977), Political Parties and Macroeconomic Policy, In: American Political Science Review, 71(4), 1467-87

Hibbs, Douglas A. Jr. (1978), On the Political Economy of Long-Run Trends in Strike Activity. In: British Journal of Political Science, 8(2), 153-75

Ingham, Geoffrey K. (1974), Strikes and Industrial Conflict, London: Macmillan

Kassalow, Everett M. (1959), Discussion of Arthur Ross' Paper. In: Proceedings of Twelfth Annual Meeting of Industrial Relations Research Association, 170-173

Kassalow, Everett M. (1969), Trade Unions and Industrial Relations: An International Comparison, New York: Random House

Kassalow, Everett M. (December 1977), Industrial Conflict and Consensus in the United States and Western Europe: A Comparative Analysis, Unpublished paper. Partially published in: Proceedings of the Thirtieth Annual Meeting of the IRRA

Kendall, Walter, (1975), The Labour Movement in Europe, London: Allen Lane

Kerr, Clark et al. (1960), Industrialism and Industrial Man: The Problems of Labor & Management in Economic Growth, Harvard University Press

Knowles, K.G.J.C. (1952), Strikes - A Study in Industrial Conflict, Oxford: Blackwell

Korpi, Walter (December 1974), Conflict, Power and Relative Deprivation. In: American Political Science Review, 68(4), 1569-78

Korpi, Walter (December 1977), Strikes, Industrial Relations and Class Conflict: The Case of Sweden, Paper presented to the Conference on Contemporary International Labor Problems, Madison

Korpi, Walter (1978), The Working Class in Welfare Capitalism: Work, Unions & Politics in Sweden, London: Routledge

Korpi, Walter & Michael Shalev (1980), Strikes, Power, and Politics in the Western Nations, 1900-1976. In: Political Power and Social Theory, Vol. 1, 301-34

Lipset, Seymour Martin (1961 and 1962), Trade Unions and Social Structure. In: Industrial Relations,1(1), 75-89 and 1(2), 89-110

Lorwin, Val R. (1957), Reflections on the History of the French and American Labor Movements. In: Journal of Economic History, 17(1), 25-44

Lorwin, Val R. (1963), Labor Organizations and Politics in Belgium & France. In: Kassalow (Ed.), National Labor Movements in the Postwar World, Northwestern University Press, 150-70

Marquand, H.A. et al. (1939), Organized Labour in Four Continents, London: Longmans, Green & Co

Martin, Andrew (1973), The Politics of Economic Policy in the United States; A Tentative View from a Comparative Perspective, Beverly Hills & London; Sage

Maurice, Marc & Francois Sellier (November 1979), Societal Analysis of Industrial Relations: A Comparison Between France & Germany. In: British Journal of Industrial Relations, 17(3), 322-36

Perlman, Selig (1966) (Reprint of 1928 edition), A Theory of the Labor Movement, New York: Augustus M. Kelley

Pizzorno, Allessandro (1978), Political Exchange & Collective Identity in Industrial Conflict. In: Crouch & Pizzorno (Eds.), The Resurgence of Class Conflict in Western Europe since 1968, London: Macmillan

Przeworski, Adam (1980), Material Bases of Consent: Economics and Politics in a Hegemonic System. In: Political Power and Social Theory, Vol.1, 21-66

Przeworski, Adam & John Sprague (September 1977), A History of Western European Socialism, Paper presented at the Annual Meetings of the American Political Science Association, Washington D.C.

Reynaud, J.D. (November 1979), Conflict and Social Regulation: A Sketch of a Theory of Joint Regulation. In: British Journal of Industrial Relations, 17(3), 314-21

Ross, Arthur (1948), Trade Union Wage Policy, Berkeley: University of California Press

Ross, Arthur M. & Donald Irwin (1951), Strike Experience in Five Countries, 1927-1947: An Interpretation. In: Industrial and Labor Relations Review, 4(2), 323-42

Shalev, Michael (March 1980), Industrial Relations Theory and the Comparative Study of Industrial Relations and Industrial Conflict. In: British Journal of Industrial Relations, 18(1), 26-43

Shalev, Michael and Walter Korpi (February 1980), Working Class Mobilization and American Exceptionalism. In: Economic and Industrial Democracy, 1(1), 31-62.

Shorter, Edward and Charles Tilly (1974), Strikes in France 1830-1968, Cambridge University Press

Stephens, Evelyn Huber and John (1979), The Labor Movement, Political Power and Workers' Participation in Western Europe, pre-publication manuscript

Streeck, Wolfgang, Peter Seglow and Pat Bayley (October 1978), Railway Unions in Britain & West Germany: Structural Sources of Cross-National Differences & Similarities. In: International Institute of Management (Berlin) Discussion Paper No. 78-80.

Sturmthal, Adolph and James G. Scoville (eds.) (1973), The International Labor Movement in Transition, Urbana: University of Illinois Press

Walker, Kenneth F. (June 1969), Strategic Factors in Industrial Relations Systems - A Programme of International Comparative Studies. In: IILS Bulletin, No. 6, 187-209

Price, Power, Social Justice and Other Union Values

Jack Barbash

ABSTRACT

When the details of the collective bargaining agreement are distilled for their vital essences we conclude that what unions want fundamentally are price and power. Because unions everywhere are infused with a revolutionary or reform spirit price and power are likely to carry with them a strain of social justice as well.

DEFINITIONS

American unions are best understood in the context of collective bargaining. Collective bargaining in the United States is a process in which unions, as designated representatives of employees in specified units, and the appropriate employer(s) negotiate terms of employment at various stages of the process, and engage in such other supporting activities as the parties find necessary to enhance their effectiveness.

The terms of employment set down in the collective agreement are very detailed. It is not uncommon for agreements to run more than 100 pages, and this does not include health and welfare provisions and grievance interpretations. But when the details of the contract are distilled for their vital essences we conclude that what unions want fundamentally are price and power. Because unions everywhere are infused with a reform or revolutionary spirit, price and power are likely to carry with them a strain of social justice as well.

Price, power and, to a somewhat lesser degree, social justice represent the main rubrics for the values which unions seek to advance through their collective and political bargaining. Value, as I use it here, is a principle which people feel

---

* Bascom Professor of Economics and Industrial Relations, University of Wisconsin-Madison. Prepared for International Conference: Management Under Differing Value Systems, Toronto, October 16, 1980.

committed to so strongly that they are willing to incur risks or sacrifices in its behalf. Price, power, social justice and their attendant values is what this paper is about.

Collective bargaining is very much a game in which the counters are price and power. Mostly the union and management play the game as if one side's advantage comes at the expense of the other's. In other words, collective bargaining is a distributive game in which the object is "to resolve pure conflicts of interests,"[1] modified by a minimum ground of common interest. The common interest consists of maximizing the fund from which both parties draw their respective factor returns; the distribution of the fund as between wages and non-wages becomes the prime subject of negotiation.

PRICE

The price of labor has evolved from a simple wage rate to an intricate compensation structure. The compensation structure specifies performance standards, effort measurement, the terms of tenure, transfer and advancement, the composition of compensation, and the adjustment of the structure to change. The price of labor is special among the factor prices in that it requires specification of the terms of utilization and accountability by management to be operative. For example, a salary of $1000 without further specification has no meaning unless accompanied by detailed specifications relating to effort and tenure etc.

The union interest in the price of labor goes beyond a simple "more." In actuality, the price of labor monetizes strongly held values of what the price represents. We call these values: (1) equity, (2) the living wage and (3) income security. Equity means the maintenance of an acceptable relationship among the diverse jobs and their wages. "Compar[isons] are important to the workers. They establish the dividing line between a raw deal and a square deal."[2] The equity principle is institutionalized in a job-wage structure.

The living wage, we learn from one of the Webb's unionists, is one in which workingmen "will secure a sufficiency of food and some degree of personal and home comfort, . . .not a miserable allowance to start on."[3] Or, in the words of two American trade union economists at the time: The living wage represents "the needs of the workers and their families to maintain at least a minimum standard of living according to general economic conditions of the time."[4] The French go even further: "Wages are not the price of merchandise . . . but a minimum income for a 'predefined way of life.'"[5]

Income security is represented in the provisions which protect job tenure, or which guarantee minimum weekly, annual or, in a few cases, lifetime pay; and after that a pension. The object of income security is to shift the risks of uncertainty and waiting from the employee to the employer, to convert wages from a variable to a fixed cost which will (in the words of a union statement) "immunize . . . income and the security of their families for a period of time against effects flowing from fluctuations in the volume of business." Income security reflects a contra-market bias in the sense that the union's strategy is to deflect the risks of the market away from its constituents for as long as it can without driving the employer out of business.

The collectively bargained social security system is the latter-day application of income security. Commonly known as health and welfare, this aspect of income security consists of income supports to offset wage loss due to illness and its expenses, old age, unemployment and death. The principle itself is not new. Unions in the west were "benevolent" or "friendly" societies before they were bargaining associations. What is new is that the benefits are part of the employer's compensation structure and that dependents as well as active workers are covered.

POWER

Union power figures in two contexts in collective bargaining. First, there is the power which is necessary to bring the employer to the bargaining table to negotiate an agreement. Absent union power to withhold the labor of employees and, occasionally, the power to withhold consumption of the emloyer's product, the employer will not voluntarily share his price and power prerogatives with a union--which is what collective bargaining is about. Second, there is the power given up by the employer in rendering himself accountable to the union, as the labor bargain necessarily requires. If the union can't shut down the employer by withholding labor and market demand, and the employer continues to operate the plant with "strikebreakers," violence and obstruction may result.

The labor bargain has generated social turmoil over two centuries precisely because it does raise critical questions about the allocation of power among unions, workers and employers, and ultimately about capitalist power. The labor bargain which involves a union carries with it an additional challenge. The employer is confronted with an active institutional presence on his premises, as well as in the economy at large, to check and balance the exercise of power which had previously been exercised unilaterally.

The employer fully understands that he has to negotiate price bargains for the factors of production since price bargains are the name of the business game. But no factor bargain other than the bargain for labor carries with it essential constraints on subsequent utilization. Collective bargaining constantly challenges the employer's freedom and flexibility of action--the qualities about his work which we know he prizes most. To sharpen the trauma even more, the union represents a constituency from a "lower" social class with, like as not, an "alien" ideology.

Western employers have been able to come to terms with their bargaining antagonists through the professionalization of their industrial relations functions. But we know now in the United States that coming to terms does not necessarily mean permanent acceptance. All it means is that the employer is simply trying to cut the costs of bargaining but waiting for the day, if it comes, when it will be expedient to shed the essentially onerous restraints on his power.

The not uncommon threat of an employer to close the plant rather than bargain with a union, or the employer who resists the union at a cost which seems disproportionate to the loss which he would suffer if the union came in, is not all that psychologically "irrational." In effect, the employer is saying that he puts a higher value on power than on price.

Management ideology, however, tends to exaggerate the impairment of its power under collective bargaining. Collective bargaining or, for that matter, any other method of joint dealing still leaves the initiative with management--whether the management is capitalist, socialist or whatever. At most, the management, by the nature of the process, is subject to checks for only a small minority of decisions.

The loss of some power which predisposes the employer against collective bargaining predisposes the worker in favor of it. What brings workers to unions, to begin with, are perceived power disparities in bargaining without a union. In fact, it is very likely that it is power, more than "more," which the worker sees in the union.

Bargaining enables the union and its members to stand on a footing of proximate equality with management. What matters to the unionists "is not so much that the employer owns the means of production but that he possesses a high degree of advantage over them."[7] Unlike "participative management"--human relations, job enrichment, management by objectives, etc.--only bargaining is based on the workers' own collective power to withhold their labor, and only the bargaining relationship based on the union's withholding ability imposes, for the moment, a measure of equality between the parties.

Bargaining establishes the terms of employment as a matter of right. "The full attainment of dignity and self respect . . .

cannot rest on favor or good will alone. It must in some way be warranted by the institutional order and available as the basis of a claim of right."

It is precisely working conditions as rights which distinguishes collective bargaining from the employer's unilateral administration of employment. The rights are both procedural and substantive. The procedural rights are represented in the due process of the grievance-arbitration mechanism.

Substantive due process is seen, for example, in the principle of discharge for "just cause" which holds management to account for the reasonableness of its acts. Another substantive right is seniority which establishes an objective rule based on length of service for layoffs, promotions, transfers, shift and vacation choices, depending on the terms of the specific contract.

Collective bargaining of substantive rights, by way of further example, seems to have established the principle that an employee has an equitable interest--what the Webbs called a "vested interest"[9]--in his tenure on the job; in the event of material impairment of that vested interest due to technological change, merger or liquidation, the employee has a valid claim on his employer for compensation to offset the resulting losses. Severance pay, advance notice, relocation, retraining and early retirement represent the common remedies for displacement.

BARGAINING POWER

The union is, at its core, an organization to enhance the effectiveness of its bargaining power. Maintenance of the union as a bargaining-effective organization means the ability to command support from rank and file, including striking when necessary, and the ability to "command respect"[10] from the employer, which means getting him to take union strike threats seriously. This argument for the bargaining essence of the union rests on three propositions amply supported by history:

1. The maintenance of the union as a bargaining organization will prevail in any clash with other goals.

2. The maintenance of the union as a bargaining organization has proved to be historically the fundamental working principle on which its structure and governance rests.

3. Unions left to their own devices (as Lenin instructed us) tend to choose the bargaining option over the revolutionary option.

NEGOTIATIONS

Collective bargaining, especially the negotiation part of it, is a game played for its own sake as well as for the price and power values it is supposed to advance. Bargaining functions according to well understood rules and roles which are disregarded at the peril of unsettling the players.

The setting for the negotiation game is a rectangular table (never a round table or no table) with the antagonists physically confronting one another. It is always de rigeur for for the parties to demand (or to reject outright). Always demand, never request, ask, urge or implore--to do so violates the toughness rule. Each side must, at first, always demand much more than it expects to get and the other side must, at first, concede nothing or concede much less than it is likely to later. If one side makes a concession the other must make a concession in return.

Because the parties are not fools, they have developed ways of communicating their more realistic expectations. But this relatively straightforward communication has to take place away from the public bargaining table, either through a mediator, or when the principal negotiators from each side retreat to another venue to carry on the "real negotiations."

The reason why the real negotiations are carried on away from the goldfish bowl can be traced to the macho spirit which dominates the public face of the negotiations. Under the macho code no player may cast doubt on the resolve of his side to pursue its objectives at any cost, concede weaknesses in its positions or acknowledge strengths in the position of the antagonist.

The theatrical behavior of the union representatives at the table is not aimed only at their antagonists; it is directed to the rank and file who have to be continually reassured that they are not being "sold out" to the employer. The management side, being a different kind of political organization--more of a hierarchy, that is--is not under the same pressure. Nevertheless, management cannot afford to show signs of premature tender-mindedness for fear of creating false expectations, or for fear of creating the impression among its stockholders and the business community that it is "giving the company away."

The gamesmanship of the negotiations is only one part of a larger adversary mold into which the bargaining relationship is cast. To begin with, it is the essential character of bargaining--not only of negotiations--to accentuate the adversary nature of the relationship more than is warranted by the need to prevail.

THE ADVERSARY RELATIONSHIP

Ideology sharpens adversarialism. Trade unionism is, historically, a product of social movements which, in turn, put high symbolic value on adversary attitudes and postures, which are equated with revolutionary militancy. For this reason, foreign visitors of socialist persuasions find it hard to understand how the "class enemies," that is the union and the management, can shake hands after agreement has been consummated.

On the whole, the parties seem to favor the adversarial mode. The union's "main job is to challenge and protest managerial actions";[11] management's main job is to resist.

The American parties stop short of pursuing an overriding class struggle by coming to periodic agreement over the main terms of the relationship. They have even normalized their adversarial relationship through due process methods like grievance-arbitration. From time to time unions and managements in various industries have given expression to visions of an even more constructive, integrative, problem-solving and trusting relationship, but invariably these experiments are forced to revert to adversarial type.

Management prefers the adversary relationship because it fears that union collaboration would dilute management power and thereby impair efficiency. The union prefers the adversary relationship because it is most compatible with the union's bargaining effectivensss. The less the union is responsible for making joint decisions with management to begin with, the more credibly it can "grieve" over the decisions later.

The adversary principle, it is argued, in a variation on Adam Smith's invisible hand also best serves the public or general interest. Far from being pathological or aberrant, the tension generated by the adversary principle is normal and, if kept in bounds, even helpful. The assumption is that the parties can be kept "honest," so to speak, only by the countervailing checks and balances which the tension produces.

(Tension is probably a better word than conflict to describe the nature of the employer-employee interaction. Conflict implies one side winning over the other; tension implies equilibrium or a balance of forces--which is what collective bargaining and industrial relations are more nearly about.)

SOCIAL JUSTICE

Social justice as a union value is difficult to define analytically. It is part rhetoric evocative of its reform-revolutionary-socialist-cultural antecedents. Social justice as doctrine is conveyed in such words as solidarity, redistribution, labor movement, industrial democracy, etc.

In common parlance, social justice is meant to apply to unions which rise above their own group egotism. Social justice applies also to movements of the disadvantaged which aspire to bring themselves out of deprivation. For the disadvantaged low-wage worker--say, Chavez' Chicano farm workers--the achievement of unionism, even business unionism, is a movement for social justice.

For unions of better-off workers, social justice is collective bargaining that favors low-paid workers. Unions which pursue antidiscrimination policies are engaged in a social justice objective. In general, industrial unions have stronger social justice impulses than do craft unions because industrial unions speak for a broader constituency and are more closely identified with the struggles for full employment, civil rights and social welfare. But industrial unions do not carry the revolutionary association they once did. Unions affected with a strong social justice motivation are likely to incorporate health and welfare terms sooner.

Unions of low-wage ethnic workers are also social justice institutions when they undertake programs in education, upgrading, housing, health, counseling and multilingual publication. "Uplift unionism"[12] was Robert Hoxie's term for it more than a half-century ago, but without the pejorative meaning which goes with the term today.

CHANGES

There is a conviction abroad in the land that retarding influences in the larger world economy are forcing American unionism into retreat. The long cycle of union growth, not only in membership but in the improved working conditions, is at an end. The union posture as challenger for most of the near half-century since the New Deal is giving way to a reactive posture. From a strategy of offense, the unions are turning to a strategy of retrenchment. Not all of the forces at work in this turn-around have emerged suddenly. Many have been boiling for a long time but have only now surfaced.

The coming era of retrenchment is necessarily causing a rethinking of price and power precepts in union circles. On the price side, wage-price inflation is forcing a recognition of social responsibility. That is, the price of labor cannot be negotiated solely to serve the interests of the bilateral parties.

SOCIAL RESPONSIBILITY

Social responsibility, if it has meaning, means (1) self-restraint, but with the threat of external intervention never too far away, (2) a longer term horizon, (3) more inclusive solidarity with community, society and economywide concerns. Social responsibility says, in effect, forego self-interest now in order to benefit later. Social responsibility appeals to rational self-interest, but an implicit altruism is involved in getting the parties to forego the relative certainty of the present for the uncertainty of the future.

The National Accord represents a limited social-contract type of problem-solving undertaking between the American labor movement and the American government. The labor movement commits itself to wage moderation in return for commitments from the government to maintain real income and refrain from forcing mass unemployment as an anti-inflation device. (As this is written the election of a Republican administration puts the status of the accord in considerable doubt.)

Collective bargaining, we have said, is an adversary game but with a common interest sufficient to sustain the common fund which finances wages and profits. This seemed to work well enough when the United States occupied an unchallenged position in the world economy. Now that the U.S. has come down in the world, the question is being seriously asked in many quarters, including union quarters, whether the inhibitions which stand in the way of enlarging common interest need to be reexamined. The question has become more insistent in the light of the consensus view that the Japanese economic "miracle" is precisely a product of the more collaborative spirit which permeates Japanese industrial relations. The assumption that more collaboration will enhance efficiency is far from proved, but it has many believers.

The auto and steel industries--unions and management both--are among those who are engaged in experiments to broaden common interests in the quality of working life and, in the case of autos, through a variation on codetermination. To be sure, the parties' willingness to reexamine old adversarial ways can be explained as a crisis reaction which will go away if and when the economy returns to better times. It is far too early to draw conclusions. What it is possible to say provisionally is that unions and managements with a long history of adversarial struggles are willing to take some risks in the search for more affirmative relationships.

MULTILATERAL BARGAINING

Power relationships are being altered to include more claimants than the traditional two parties. Each of the newer parties--the state in behalf of wage-price stability, civil rights activists (including the state) in behalf of black workers' interests--demands recognition to secure more effective representation of their central objectives. Only an activist third party with a primary focus on economic stability or civil rights, it is argued, can protect these positions with the necessary determination.

The government bargains with sanctions which range from "hard" to "soft," from persuasion to legal compulsion. The wage-price restraints which the government is after partake more of politics than of economics; the main problems are how to get acceptance and enforcement, not how to model the correct wage-price-employment relationship.

The civil rights interests--whether represented by the activists or by some branch of the state, or both--perceive themselves as bargainers and, for the most part, use bargaining to gain their ends. The bargaining objectives are more jobs and job rights for minorities, indemnification for past discrimination, and an active black presence in the unions. To make their objectives credible the civil rights interests curtail or threaten to curtail established union and management power. The state, also asserting civil rights interests, threatens civil and criminal penalties and the withholding of federal procurement.

VALUE CONCEPTS

What we think we have done here is some preliminary spadework in the compilation of a vocabulary of values which figure significantly and even vitally in unionism and industrial relations. Price, power and some measure of social justice provide the rubrics for the catalogue of the particular value concepts that follows.

- accountability
- adversarialism
- bargaining
- business unionism
- craft unionism
- civil rights
- class
- codetermination
- common interest
- conflict
- constructive, affirmative, problem-solving, trust, mutual survival
- demands
- dignity
- just cause
- labor movement
- living wage
- long run/short run
- machoism
- management rights
- market/anti-market
- militancy
- "more"
- normalization
- participative management
- power
- price
- protest
- reasonableness

due process
efficiency
effort
equity
fairness
gamesmanship
grieving and grievance
group egotism
human relations
ideology
industrial democracy
industrial unionism
reform
revolution
rights
security and insecurity
seniority
social contract
social justice
social partners
social responsibility
solidarity
tension
violence

FOOTNOTES

1. Richard Walton and Robert McKersie, A Behavioral Theory of Labor Negotiations (New York: McGraw-Hill, 1965), p. 4.

2. Arthur M. Ross, Trade Union Wage Policy (Berkeley: Univ. of Calif. Press, 1948), p. 51.

3. Beatrice and Sidney Webb, Industrial Democracy (London: Longmans, Green, 1879, Vol. 2), p. 587.

4. Nathaniel Goldfinger and Everett Kassalow, "Trade Union Behavior in Wage Bargaining" in New Concepts in Wage Determination, ed. by George W. Taylor and Frank Pierson (New York: McGraw-Hill, 1957), p. 9.

5. Jean Marchal, "Wage Theory and Social Groups" in The Theory of Wage Determination, ed. by John T. Dunlop (New York: St. Martin's Press, 1957), p. 149.

6. United Auto Workers, Special Convention, 1967, Collective Bargaining Resolution, pp. 18-19.

7. Selig Perlman, A History of Trade Unionism (New York: Macmillan, 1929), p. 67.

8. Philip Selznick, Law, Society and Industrial Justice (New York: Russell Sage, 1969), p. 117.

9. Webb Industrial Democracy, pp. 562-64.

10. John R. Commons, Industrial Goodwill, (New York: McGraw-Hill, 1919), p. 15.

11. Fred Harbison and John Coleman, Goals and Strategy in Collective Bargaining (New York: Harper, 1951), p. 20.

A Theory of Employer Attitudes and Behaviour Towards Trade Unions in Western Europe and North America

Roy J. Adams

ABSTRACT

Employer attitudes and behaviour towards trade unions differ significantly between Europe and North America. In Europe employers are typically organized into strong associations and federations which cooperate with labour and government in pursuit of consensus solutions to national problems. European employers, in general, fully accept unions as the legitimate representatives of worker interests. North American employers, in contrast, have not formed strong associations, do not accept the right of unions to represent worker interest generally, and do not cooperate with unions in search of solutions to public issues. The theory holds that these differences may be traced to the initial strategy of the labour movement (political vs. economic) and the resultant intervention of government in the industrial relations system.

Anyone familiar with modern industrial relations systems cannot help but notice that the behavior of employers in North America and Europe is quite different. In Europe employers generally accept trade unions as legitimate and necessary institutions in democratic society. Rarely do they overtly attempt to dissuade employees from becoming union members. European employers have formed industrial associations and national federations which are recognized by society, government and organized labour as the authoritative representatives of industry in regard to social and labour management affairs. Through either formal or informal mechanisms employer organizations commonly seek to reach national consensus with labour and government over major issues of common concern.

The North American situation is quite different. Employers typically pursue independent and uncoordinated objectives in the social and labour arena. Although there are many national employers' organizations (e.g., The Chambers of Commerce, The Canadian Manufacturers' Association, The U.S. Business Roundtable, and the Canadian Business Council on National Issues) there are none with the membership density or authoratative stature in regard to social and labour issues comparable to their European counterparts. By and large North American employers grudgingly tolerate unions because they are a fact of life rather than because of any formal recognition that unions have a positive social role to play. Many North American employers hold that unions are unnecessary where management "does right willingly." It is quite common for employers to attempt to avoid unionization. It is taken for granted that non-union employers will continually attempt to discourage employees from becoming union members and establishing collective bargaining. Because they have overtly hostile attitudes towards unions and because their organizations are weak employers rarely join with unions and governments to reach national concensus over critical issues. Instead labour and management typically lobby hard for their own preferred policies which are often considered unacceptable and detrimental to the other side.

These observed differences might lead the casual observer to conclude that the basic attitudes or value systems of European and North American employers are fundamentally divergent. The thesis of this paper is that the basic attitudes and values of employers on both sides of the Atlantic are essentially the same. The variance in observed behaviour is the result, not of underlying attitudes, but rather of critical historical events and resultant differences in industrial relations systems.

Early Response of Employers to Unions

The commonality of employer attitudes in regard to trade unions is indicated by their initial reaction to the emergence of the labour movement. Everywhere the first response of employers was to destroy or contain the unions. In both Europe and North America one may find examples of some combination of the following tactics being put to use against union organization:

1. Victimization: the dismissal of workers suspected of union sentiments.

2. Yellow dog contracts: requiring workers to sign individual contracts stating that they were not trade unionists and would not become trade unionists.

3. Company or yellow unions: encouraging pacific employee organizations designed to reduce the attraction of "free" unions.

4. Blacklists: the distribution of the names of workers suspected to be union organizers and the subsequent refusal of employers to hire people on the list.

5. Refusal to negotiate with worker representatives.

6. The use of strikebreakers, lockouts and strike insurance to counteract strikes, the primary basis of union power.

To the continental employer, according to Landes, "a union was a conspiracy against public order and morals; a strike an act of ingratitude; the effort of labour to raise wages the indiscipline of an impatient son. All of this was evil. And there is no negotiating with evil."[1]

In Germany typical practices of early employers were "the blacklisting of strikers and the supplying of strikebreakers, the operation of employment offices, propaganda on behalf of the employer viewpoint during labor disputes, and the promotion of legislation favorable to the employer." Employers also encouraged the development of "yellow" or company unions which by World War I had a large membership.[2]

Common devices used in France were "Blacklists, firing of unionists, lockouts, agents provacateurs, and spies." Company unions were also prominent in the first decade of the twentieth century.[3]

In Britain an employers' association in the engineering industry agreed, in the 1850's, to the following rules:

- No member would employ a trade unionist

- No member would "receive" a "deputation of workman or unions".

- All members would require each of their employees to sign a document stating that the employee "was not and would not become a union member."[4]

Students of Swedish labour often claim that most employers were not intent on destroying unions. Nevertheless, as a result of a strike in 1899 employers at Sundsvall declared that they "would not hire a single union man, and that every man who hoped to keep his job must sign a non-union contract."[5] Until the 1930's Swedish employers made very frequent use of lockouts to keep unions weak.

All of the tactics noted above were in common use in the U.S. and Canada. In the infamous "Mohawk Valley Formula" employers consciously combined the entire range of anti-union tactics to fight the surge of unionism.[6]

If scholars had addressed the questions of employer attitudes and behavior towards trade unions in 1880 they would not have found much difference between Europe and North America. At about that point in time, however, the industrial relations systems began to evolve in different directions.

The European Pattern

From about 1880 European unions expanded their base of membership from skilled to unskilled and the mainstream embraced a philosophy which called for the uplift of the entire class of working people. The capitalist system was condemned as inherently exploitative and the long term objective became the replacement of capitalism with socialism. In several countries links were established between unions and labour or socialist parties.

Despite employer opposition union membership, strikes and the support for labour/socialist political parties all grew substantially. (See tables 1, 2, 3). In response to increasing union membership strength, militancy and political power governments began to pursue a more conciliatory policy towards labour. Laws forbidding union organization as conspiracies in restraint of trade were repealed. Strikes were made legal. Instead of backing employers in disputes governments began to act as mediators attempting to bring labour and management together. Labour's grievances became major political issues.

Table 1

Union Membership
1890 - 1920
(000's)

	1890	1900	1910	1920/21
France	404	492	977	2,000
Germany	278	680	2,017	7,568
G.B.	1,100	1,200	1,662	6,418
Belgium		45	118	800
Denmark		77	102	279
Sweden		44	85	280
Netherlands			59	467

Source: Kendall, Walter (1975), The Labour Movement in Europe, London: Allen Lane. Some of the figures are rough estimates.

Table 2

Electoral Support
of Socialist and Communist Parties
1900 - 1920

	Socialist	Communist
1900-5	4,807,000	NA
1909-12	6,529,000	NA
1918-20	12,853,000	620,000

Source: Kendall, 1975. Combined total votes from France, Germany, Italy, Britain, Belgium, Netherlands and Denmark.

Table 3

Number of Industrial
Disputes (5-year averages)

Year	Number
1896-1900	2504
1901-5	3545
1906-10	6148
1911-15	5102
1916-20	5034

Source: Kendall, 1975. Combined total from France, Germany, Italy, Britain and Belgium.

In such an environment employers began to realize that the tactics of overt beligerance were likely to be counterproductive. Instead of containing unions, active opposition was more likely to produce increased government intervention. Moreover, given the political objectives of labour employers had good reason to fear for the survival of the capitalist system itself. The idealistic political strategy of labour in Europe produced a threat not merely to individual employers but rather to employers as a class. Given the nature of this threat employers began to unite for, in the words of one contemporary observer, "sheer self-preservation."[7]

As a result of either direct government intervention or the threat of government intervention employer associations expanded in size and scope and recognized unions as the legitimate representatives of the working class. Several examples may be cited. During the 1890's labor political power increased in Sweden. The Swedish Employers' Federation was founded in 1902 as the direct consequence of a national three day strike. In 1906 the unions were recognized broadly by the association as the spokesmen of the working class and as the bargaining agents for workers generally.

In Germany, after the removal of the anti-socialist laws in 1890, union membership and support for the socialist party grew rapidly. German employers began to associate more thoroughly in response and the German Employers' Federation was founded in 1913. At the end of World War I a socialist government rose to power. Pressure was applied to employers to recognize the trade unions as the bargaining agents for labour and that was done in 1918. Although many employers considered it to be an effront to their "personal liberty" collective bargaining spread.[8] The Employers' Federation expanded from 61 associations representing 500 enterprises in 1913 to 200 associations representing 100,000 enterprises in 1920.[9]

In Britain the Engineering Employers' Federation was founded in 1896. The 1915 to 1920 period was one of considerable worker military, increasing radicalization of labour organizations, and growth in the support for the Labour Party. In response to these forces the government applied pressure on employers to associate more extensively and to recognize and negotiate with the unions. Collective bargaining expanded dramatically. Membership in the Federation increased from 816 firms employing about 200,000 manual workers in 1910 to 2,440 companies employing about 700,000 workers in 1920.[10]

French employers began to organize in the 1890's "in response to the growth of unions, the increase in strikes, and fears of increasing intervention by the State."[11] In 1899 the socialist Alexandre Millerand became a cabinet minister and issued decrees regulating wages, working conditions and hours, and creating a network of Regional Labour Councils. The formation of the Metalworking Employers' Association was the direct result.[12] In the troubled period following World War I the General Confederation of French Production came into existence. Collective bargaining expanded but fell into disuse as the result of a depression in the early 1920's. The Confederation was able to attract only a minority of individualistic french employers into membership until the late 1930's when the Popular Front Government led by Socialist Leon Blum came to power. There were massive sit down strikes. The Blum government pressured the employers to recognize and negotiate with the unions. As a result of the Matignon Accord the employers federation expanded greatly and took on new functions.[13]

A similar developmental pattern occurred in other countries: The political power of labour increased, government responded by applying pressure on business to recognize and negotiate with unions, employer associations expanded in number, size and scope and established on-going relationships with the unions.

The achievement of national recognition meant that unions acquired a moral legitimacy which they had not previously enjoyed. It soon became socially and politically unacceptable for European employers to interfere with the right of association or to refuse to negotiate with unions. Recognition meant that unions became the bargaining agents not merely for their own members but rather for the entire class of relevant workers. But for the unions there was a price to pay. By accepting recognition and by entering into regular patterns of interaction with employers they gave up, in practice if not in theory, the credibility of their goal of revolutionary societal transformation.

In return for union recognition employers received de facto acceptance of the legitimacy of capitalist enterprize. France and Italy were exceptions. In those countries the mainstream of the labour movements clung to their radical objectives. Because they have done so, the efforts of government to bring about stable labour-management relations have been less than successful. Employers continue to complain that they cannot deal matter-of-factly with organizations whose avowed public goal is the destruction of capitalism.[14]

To European employers generally recognition did not mean that they were prepared to fully share the power to manage. For the most part employers, through their associations, insisted that negotiations should take place on an area or industry rather than on a plant by plant basis. Some of the older craft unions opposed this bargaining structure but the wider-based unions generally approved it. By agreeing to multi-employer bargaining over basic terms and conditions of employment employers intended to maintain control over most managerial decisions. They continued to vigorously oppose any union presence in the enterprize. In some countries the associations compelled the unions to explicitly recognize management's right to manage. For example, in the December Compromise of 1906 the Swedish unions accepted the right of employers "to hire and dismiss workers, direct and allot work and employ any workers they chose."[15] In 1898 the Engineering Employers' Federation in Britain required unions to sign an agreement containing the following statement:

> "The Federated Employers, while disavowing any intention of interfering with the proper functions of trade unions, will admit no interference with the management of the business..."

Twenty-four years later a new agreement stated:

"The Employers have the right to manage their establishments and the trade unions have the right to exercise their functions."[16]

Despite such statements British employers were not very successful in excluding union representatives from the enterprize. During World War I and again in the World War II and post war era strong shop stewards movements emerged. These informal organizations which were often separate from the union establishment did place serious constraints on managerial prerogatives. They often hindered the implementation of new techniques and insisted that long established customs and practices be respected. Their demands were supported by the use or threat of "wildcat," "unconstitutional" or "unofficial" strikes. It is no coincidence that British employers have been more prone to fight unionization on a plant by plant basis than other European employers.

In several countries where management was more successful in excluding unions from the enterprize the void in worker representation at the shop level was politically unacceptable. Works councils, established either through legislation or collective bargaining, were the usual compromise. To employers the councils were more acceptable than shop floor unions because they were composed of company employees rather than outsiders. In most cases the councils were provided with a productionist rather than a consumptionist mandate. They were also forbidden to negotiate collective agreements - a function which the unions insisted that they exclusively retain. Nor were the councils permitted to strike. Employers did not willingly accept the councils. In many cases they fought vigorously against them. However, by holding out for no employee representation they achieved a compromise which was more acceptable than the alternative of union organization in the plant. From an employer's perspective the strategy was quite successful. For several decades the councils were to have very little influence on the power to manage.[17]

With the establishment of multi-employer bargaining several countries passed extention of agreements legislation. These provisions allowed negotiated terms to be extended to employers who were not party to the negotiations. They protected associated employers from low wage competition and provided the unions with a means of providing more universal benefits. Since non-associated employers could be compelled to implement terms over which they had no control extension provisions encouraged the growth of employer associations. In North America where extension provisions are all but non-existant most employer associations consist of small and weak firms. In Europe, however, large employers who may influence association policy are more highly associated than are small firms.[18]

After World War II new social issues came to the fore: reconstruction, inflation, wage and price controls, unemployment, active manpower planning, the quality of worklife, and new demands for workers participation in management. Labour, management and the state all had strong interests in these issues and each party had organizations though which their interests could be pursued. Either formally or informally national decision-making in regard to employment related issues became tripartite.

Regardless of their level of membership density trade union federations came to be regarded by the state and by society as the national voice of the working class. The National Employers' Federations filled the same role in regard to the interests of capital. A tradition was established of seeking concensus. Society came to expect labour and management to take the public interest into account in their dealings with each other and with the state. It also came to expect the state to seriously attempt to reach consensus before proceeding with legislation. Collective bargaining in the broadest sense of the term became a multi-level process. National labour and social standards were often produced by agreements between some combination of the three principal actors.

National negotiations were accompanied by union-association bargaining at the industry level over wage and benefit movements. Any breakdown in these high level bargaining processes could produce much immediate public discomfort. Conflict could also exacerbate inflation and recession. Thus,the public held the parties accountable for their actions and bargaining rounds were widely discussed by society. Social recognition meant the acceptance of social responsibilities. Wage and benefit bargaining became more technical and less power based.

To effectively participate in these processes employers' associations expanded staff, took on new functions and acquired new members. Today the associations are dominant institutions in European Industrial Relations Systems. In several countries association membership density exceeds that of the unions. It has been estimated that between 60 and 90% of employers belong to associations engaged in labour relations activities.[19] This unity is not, however, a negation of individualism. Strong employer associations are a mechanism designed to defend the ability of managers to make decision as they see fit.

The North American Pattern

North American developments were quite different and as a result employers developed a distinctive strategy. In 1880's the mainstream of the labor movement decided to limit itself to craft organization and emphasized economic action against employers over political action. Socialism was firmly rejected. Nor was there to be any alliance with a political party. As a result there was no serious political threat to capitalism. Employers did not have to seek public and union acceptance of capitalist enterprise. It was granted freely. Union leaders continually reaffirmed their acceptance of the capitalist system. Trade unionism did represent a challenge to management's power to manage but it was manifest as a threat to specific employers in specific industries at specific times and places rather than as a general threat to employers as a class.

One might intuitively expect that employers would be more receptive to unions which pledged allegiance to the system but quite the contrary occurred. The moderation of the labor movement led employers to believe that the unions could be destroyed or at least contained.

Where unions were able to compel companies to recognize and negotiate with them as a result of their market power they were also able to compel employers to sign collective agreements which over time became elaborated and made serious inroads into the rights of management. For example, unions imposed seniority provisions regarding layoffs and promotions, manning schedules and crew sizes, job descriptions and classifications, restrictions on the implementation of new technology or restrictions on the manpower consequences of technological change. There were mandatory union membership provisions and requirements that companies must use union labour. There were restrictions and requirements regarding training and overtime and the sub-contracting of work. The ability of management to impose discipline was constrained by grievance procedures and by the threat of strikes.

To protect against such incursions companies often required unions to sign collective agreements which contained "managements rights" clauses similar to the general provisions noted above in regard to Sweden and Britain. Moreover union leaders often went on record stating that it was not their intention to usurp the role or responsibility of management. Nevertheless when workers experienced job-related problems because of management decisions unions sought to restrict those decisions. Mine worker unions negotiated the price of the product; clothing worker unions participated in the establishment of production standards; construction and printing unions specified who the employer would hire and the level of skill to be attained by workers. As one observer noted "at some time or place unions have negotiated on subjects embracing every area of management."[20]

Despite the strength of unions in organized companies the employer strategy of plant by plant opposition had considerable success. By the 1930's less than 15% of the relevant labour force in Canada and the U.S. was unionized.[21] In that decade, however, union militancy increased and unions began to expand into the mass production industries. By broadening their base of membership unions became a more considerable political factor. On the other hand the political and social influence of business was at a low level because of the collapse of the economy in 1929. Government policy shifted to support for labour. By that point an embryonic collective bargaining system had taken shape. Modest attempts had been made by the Wilson Administration after World War I and by the Roosevelt Administration in the early 1930's to encourage labour and management to reach a national accomodation. But the will to achieve such an accomodation was not strong on either side. By the 1930's unions had a vested interest in the existing system. For the most part they thought of themselves as representatives of their own members and sought to represent all employees in their separate jurisdictions. They did not vigorously seek general recognition from employers as the societal representatives of the entire working class. Instead they sought legislation which would allow them to extend decentralized collective bargaining to new sectors of the economy. The Wagner Act, passed in 1935, reflected these concerns. A Labour Relations Board was established which had the power to determine employee units appropriate for collective bargaining. To become the bargaining agent for employees in each such unit unions had to convince a majority to vote in favor of unionization and collective bargaining. Most of the weapons used by employers to oppose unionization - the blacklist, the yellow-dog contract, discharge for union activity, spies, company unions and other "threats of reprisal or promises of benefit" - were made illegal. At first the Labour Relations Board forbade employers to make any statements regarding unionization since negative statements from employers would almost certainly have an intimidating effect on employees. However, employers argued that this policy infringed their "right of free speech." As the result of a court case they quickly recovered their right to resist union organization provided that they did not engage in blatantly coercive behaviour. The Taft-Hartley Act of 1947 enbedded the right in law and public policy. Soon after the American initiative an almost identical policy was adopted throughout Canada.

THE CONTRASTS

In both Europe and North America governments have pursued policies designed to expand union recognition and orderly collective bargaining. However, the policies chosen created quite different expectations of employer behavior. In Europe governments said to employers: "You must recognize the unions as the bargaining agents for workers generally. You must take the initiative and work out an appropriate accomodation." In effect North American governments said to employers: "You do not have to recognize unions; you do not have to reach an acceptable accomodation with organized labour. You may continue to fight unionization; you may attempt to convince employees not to join unions, not to establish collective bargaining. Your only social and legal responsibility is to refrain from overt coercion. If you are unsuccessful in your attempts to convince employees to remain non-union then you must bargain 'in good faith' with the agent they choose to represent them."

This approach provided employers with an ethical mandate to continue with their beligerant behaviour towards unions. Today North American employers fight strongly against unionization in part because of this ethical mandate and in part because of the success achieved by North American unions in limiting employer discretion. In the overwhelming preponderence of union organizing cases employers attempt to persuade their employees to reject unionization. Typically employers argue that unions are outsiders who are more concerned with collecting dues and accumulating power than in the interests of employees. They argue that unions cause strikes and that strikes mean lost wages and perhaps lost jobs. They claim that unions cannot be counted on to bring about job improvements and that present benefits might even be lost. In short where employers do not outrightly infringe the law implicit threats replace explicit threats.

This behaviour is generally tolerated by North American societies because unlike Europe trade unions have never been widely accepted as an idealistic force for democracy. At its core union philosophy in North America is pragmatic and while pragmatism may have provided the union movement with strength in the difficult formative period it has also become a long term source of weakness. In practice "business" unionization appears to the public to be self-interested and self-serving and thus the notion of unions as instruments of democracy seems incongruous. Most North Americans would probably subscribe to the proposition that unions are unnecessary where management "does right willingly." It is common for unionization to be considered the consequence of management failure.[22]

Because of the prevalence of these attitudes government did not prevail upon employers to recognize unions as the general representatives of working class interests. Moreover because unions have never posed a credible threat to employers as a class employers have seen no reason to unite for their defense. These attitudes also explain the widespread indifference in North America to the absense of collective representation in many parts of the economy.

Given this milieu it is also understandable why employers see no advantage in cooperating with unions in search of consensus solutions to national problems. To do so might suggest that unions have a legitimate claim to be recognized as the societal spokesmen for workers generally. Were this perception to become widely accepted it might be increasingly difficult for non-union employers to maintain active opposition to unions and for employers generally to defend their present domain of discretion against further incursions by labour, by the state or by both.

The situation in the U.S. and Canada is not precisely the same. Since the 1960's a unified labour movement in Canada has supported the socially idealistic New Democratic Party. Moreover, many well-known Canadian trade unionists are publicly avowed socialists. In Canada socialism has fewer negative connotations than in the U.S. In short the Canadian labour movement may be considered more apparently idealistic than the U.S. labour movement.

In the mid-1970's the CLC made a bid for national recognition as the representative of working class interests. It published a "Manifesto" in which it agreed to cooperate with employers and government in the public interest. In return it wanted real power. No concrete change in formal decision-making mechanisms resulted from the gesture. Moreover, many unionists opposed the move believing that Congress would be coopted by government and business. Nevertheless since the mid 1970's there has been more consultation between labour, government and business organizations than during previous periods. Moreover, the CLC has concluded agreements with business organizations concerning the appropriate direction of policy in regard to a few public issues. Whether these developments are an indication of fundamental changes to come or merely abberations around the norm is yet to be seen.

The Theory

Many of the observations reported in this essay are well known. In the past, however, the "facts" have usually been assessed from a worker or union perspective. Employer behaviour has typically been accepted as a given rather than as a phenomenon to be explained. However, the variation in the behaviour of European and North American employers requires explanation in its own right. The theory developed in this essay is summarized in schematic form below

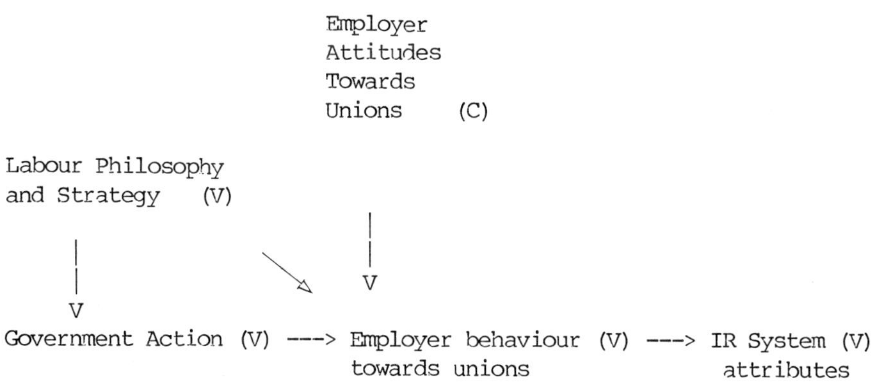

V = Variable
C = Constant

The theory holds that the attitudes of employers towards trade unions in both Europe and North America are fundamentally the same. Employers place a very high value on the power to manage free from restriction and unions are a prime threat to that objective. Stemming from this value orientation the initial behaviour of employers towards unions in both Europe and North America was essentially the same. In defense of their power to manage employers sought to either destroy or contain the emerging unions. Today employer behaviour towards unions varies considerably. In Europe employers recognize unions as the legitimate representatives of the working class; in North America they do not. In Europe employers have formed strong organizations to deal with social and labour matters; in North America they have not. In Europe employers frequently interact with labour and the state in search of consensus solutions to pressing national issues; in North America they do not.

The theory suggests that these differences are primarily the result of government action. In Europe governments demanded that employers recognize unions as the legitimate representatives of workers generally or face state intervention toward that end. North American governments never made such demands on employers.

Union behaviour has had both a direct influence on employers and an indirect influence through the medium of the state. In Europe the mainstream of the labour movement, faced with intransigent employers, rejected the capitalist system and organized broadly to achieve social change through political action. This strategy influenced both the government action and the change in employer behaviour noted above.

North American unions, faced with similar employer intransigence, adopted a very different strategy. Pragmatic craft unionism, accepting of capitalism, became the mainstream.[23] Pressure for comprehensive recognition was neither exerted nor granted. Moreover, the embracing of pragmatism, although it resulted in strength and survival in specific enterprize and industrial situations, produced political and social weakness. The philosophy of "more, more, more" appeared to lack an idealistic base and thus was incapable of arousing widespread social and political support. Employer belligerence came to be accepted as a reasonable stance towards union self-centredness.

This variation in employer behaviour has had major consequences for the operation of present day industrial relations systems. Individualistic belligerence in North America contributes significantly to the high level of overt conflict and to the restriction of the extent of employee participation in management by right. However, employers caught in the web of strong unions in spite of their belligerence have seen their rights to manage dissipated to a greater extent than their European counterparts. In Europe collective acceptance of unions has produced a low level of industrial conflict and wide spread establishment of employee participation mechanisms. Most employees work in establishments where some form of participative structure has been established. Until recently, however, employers through their associations have been able to restrict the depth of participation. While recognizing the legitimacy of collective employee representation at the national level and at the industrial level and at the peak level within corporate hierarchies they have been able to maintain a great deal of control over managerial functions. In short, workers' participation in enterprise management in Europe is extensive but shallow; in North America it is restricted but relatively deep. This pattern has, however, been changing in recent years and workers in Europe have, through political means, been acquiring more influence on managerial decisions.[24]

The theory presented here is very general. Admittedly Europe and North America are not invariant entities. Thus Britain in many ways stands between continental Europe and North America on several of the factors discussed. In turn Canada stands between Britain and the United States. France and Italy are exceptional because of the continuing ideological militancy of their unions. The general theory requires refinement to take account of such variations. Nevertheless, we believe that the dominant patterns and relationships have been identified.

Notes

1. Quoted in Kendall, Walter (1975), The Labour Movement in Europe, London: Allen Lane, p. 7.

2. Taft, Philip (1952), Germany. In: Galenson, Walter (ed.), Comparative Labor Movements, N. Y.: Russell & Russell.

3. Lorwin, Val (1954), The French Labor Movement, Cambridge: Harvard University Press.

4. Wigham, Eric (1973), The Power to Manage, London, Macmillan.

5. Robbins, James J. (1942), The Government of Labor Relations in Sweden, Chapel Hill: University of North Carolina Press.

6. See Bonnett, Clarence E. (1922), Employers' Associations in the United States, N. Y.: Macmillan; McCaffree, Kenneth M. (1966), A Theory of the Origin and Development of Employer Associations, Proceedings of the fifteenth annual meeting of the Industrial Relations Research Association; Dulles, Foster Rhea (1966) Labor in America, N. Y.: Crowell.

7. The comment is attributed to the first managing director of the Swedish Employers' Federation in 1907. See Johnston, T. L. (1962), Collective Bargaining in Sweden, Cambridge: Harvard University Press, p. 70.

8. Malles, Paul (1973), The Institutions of Industrial Relations in Continental Europe, Ottawa: Labour Canada.

9. Bunn, Ronald F. (1965), Employers' Associations and Collective Bargaining in the German Federal Republic. In: The Southwestern

Social Science Quarterly, Vol. 46, No. 2.

10. Wigham, 1973.

11. Lorwin, 1954.

12. The Role of the UIMM Among Employers (1976), Paris: Union des Industries Metallurgiques et Minieres.

13. Ehrmann, H. W. (1957), Organized Business in France, Princeton University Press.

14. The Role of the UIMM Among Employers, 1976.

15. Forseback Lennart (1976), Industrial Relations & Employment in Sweden, Stockholm: The Swedish Institute.

16. Wigham, 1973.

17. Sturmthal, Adolf (1964), Workers' Councils, Cambridge: Harvard University Press.

18. Structure, Scope and Activities of National Central Employer Organisations (1970), London: International Organisation of Employers. This observation is contrary to the argument put forth by Ingham that centralization of power and authority in employers' associations is related positively to the level of industrial concentration. See, Ingham, G. K. (1974), Strikes and Industrial Conflict, London: Macmillan and Jackson, Peter and Keith Sisson (1976), Employers' Confederations in Sweden and the U. K. and the Significance of Industrial Infrastructure. In: British Journal of Industrial Relations, Vol. XIV, No. 3.

19. Structure, Scope and Activities of National Central Employer Organisations, 1970.

20. Chamberlain, Neil (1948), The Union Challenge to Management Control, New York: Harper & Row.

21. Derber, Milton (1970), The American Idea of Industrial Democracy, Urbana: University of Illinois Press.

22. The AFL-CIO has supported numerous legislative initiatives in the general interest of workers. Nenvertheless, in the public mind these statements and activities are eclipsed by the self-serving image which emerges from decentralized collective bargaining.

23. The explanation for this union strategy, generally held in North

America, is that the union movement had no real choice because conditions unique to America precluded the success of the more idealistic, communitarian approach dominant in Europe. The validity of this explanation is not directly relevant to the argument of this paper. Our purpose is to demonstrate the effects of the choice irregardless of the reasons for it. See Perlman, Selig (1970), The Theory of the Labor Movement, N. Y.: Augustus Kelley and Galenson, Walter (1961) Why the American Labor Movement is not Socialist. In: American Review, Winter.

24. Roberts, B. C. (ed.) (1979), Towards Industrial Democracy, London, Croom Helm.

The Nonwage Impact of Unions

Joseph B. Rose

ABSTRACT

The purpose of this paper is to discuss the nonwage impact of unions on management in North America. This is clearly a broad topic and therefore I wish to limit my comments to four areas. First, I will briefly consider the philosophy of North American trade unionism and the centrality of collective bargaining in the indusrial relations system. In the second part of the paper, consideration will be given to recent research findings on the nonwage impact of unions on management. Third, if the union impact has been positive, as some studies suggest, how do we account for employer resistance to trade unions? Finally, I wish to discuss an issue of great importance in the province of Ontario at the moment, namely how to deal with the plant shutdowns, technological change and layoffs. Particular emphasis will be placed on examining the impact of collective bargaining on job security.

UNION PHILOSOPHY

Two facets of trade union philosophy in North America are "business unionism" and "job consciousness". Business unionism denotes the pragmatic nature of labour organizations to seek short-run improvements in the economic and social well-being of their members. This perspective has been a dominant theme with organized labour, dating back to Samuel Gompers, the first president of the American Federation of Labor (AFL). Gompers eschewed commitments to any long-run political or social ideology, preferring instead to concentrate on short-term gains through collective bargaining (Kochan, 1980). A primary concern of organized labour then, as well as today, has been the development of job consciousness as distinct from class consciousness. By emphasizing the primacy of the individual employment relationship as opposed to being more reformist minded, the labour movement became pragmatic, conservative and preoccupied with securing job-related goals through collective bargaining. This is not meant to suggest that North American unions are totally uncommitted to social change. As Crispo notes: "Acceptance of this approach need not entail the total absence of any commitment to reform of the overall socio-economic-political system, but any such reform instincts are limited to relatively modest changes and not to revolution or transformation" (Crispo, 1978).

Notwithstanding the strong historical influence of American-based unions in Canada, organized labour in this country has developed a somewhat broader view of social responsibility and political ideology (Kovacs, 1971 and Williams 1971). I do not wish to convey the impression that Canadian unions are not preoccupied with the pursuit of bread-and-butter issues, but simply to point out some departures from the American model. For one thing, Canadian labour would appear to have a deeper commitment to the ideal of social justice. The Canadian Labour Congress (CLC) is far less conservative than the AFL-CIO and has established close ties with the New Democratic Party at both the federal and provincial levels. In addition, organized labour has not been reluctant to engage in political action to secure bargaining goals which have been difficult to achieve at the bargaining table. The successful campaign to obtain mandatory dues checkoff in collective agreements in Ontario represents a recent example of political action. In addition the frequency with which provincial labour laws are amended and the proclivity for reform and experimentation in labour policy in Canada contrasts sharply with the American system (Weiler, 1980 and Morris, 1978).

While it is important to note these distinctions, the fact remains that trade union philosophy in both countries is reinforced by a trade union structure characterized by the principles of exclusive jurisdiction, loose federations of autonomous unions and local union control over collective bargaining. Consequently, collective bargaining is highly decentralized with most collective agreements negotiated at the level of the individual company or plant (Christy, 1975). In contrast with Western Europe, there are relatively few examples of industry-wide or broad regional negotiations. To a large extent decentralized bargaining structures reflect the representational interests of management and labour. In a recent study of several fragmented Canadian industries, e.g., air transportation and grain handling, several parties expressed a desire to maintain the status quo and opposed the notion of wider-based bargaining (Bairstow, 1978). In the construction industry, there has been widespread labour-management conflict following the consolidation of bargaining structures (Rose, 1980A). Whether organized labour will develop a more "cosmopolitan" outlook remains problematical. One commentator on Canadian labour laments: "the role and function assigned to the national and international trade unions is too narrow and the emphasis on self-centred-self-help is too great" (Williams, 1971).

It seems reasonable to inquire why this philosophy persists and to consider whether it is capable of coping with future challenges. It has been argued that three factors underlie the American labour movement's pursuit of narrow bread-and-butter issues in collective bargaining. These are: (1) job-consciousness and conservatism among rank-and-file union members; (2) environmental and employer pressures to limit union attention to narrow economic goals and avoid political goals; and (3) the preferences of top union leaders. It has also been said that: "Over time the success of unions in pursuing these narrow goals in collective bargaining, and the failures of broader reform movements reinforced the position of those advocating a narrow bread-and-butter strategy and helped to perpetuate this perspective" (Kochan, 1980).

Using data from the 1977 Quality of Employment Survey, Kochan sought to determine the priorities and goals of American workers and the extent to which their expectations were being met (Kochan, 1980). On the first issue, the results indicate that a majority of union members would like to expand the range of union goals. While workers expect their unions to give a higher priority to traditional economic issues, between 60 and 75 percent desired efforts to improve the quality of working life (e.g., a greater say on job and more interesting jobs). A comparison of member priorities and union performance indicates that unions are performing most effectively on the members' highest priorities and that gaps exist between expectations and performance on quality of working life issues. In conclusion, it seems unlikely that the central importance of economic issues in collective bargaining will be altered in the near future and, even if unions are successful in expanding the domain of bargaining to non-traditional issues, these gains will not be at the expense of reducing union influence over bread-and-butter issues.

THE NONWAGE IMPACT OF UNIONS

We can distinguish two types of union impact on management; one involves collective bargaining and the other is based on political action. Collective bargaining has a direct impact consisting of the terms and conditions of employment contained in collective agreements as well as a spillover effect from the union to the nonunion sector (e.g., wages or an acceptance of seniority). The political impact may result from organized labour's support for specific labour-management relations legislation, e.g., mandatory dues checkoff, or support for economic and social policies which do not exclusively benefit union members. My primary emphasis here will be on the direct impact of collective bargaining on management in unionized firms. Brief reference will be made to the use of political action to supplement collective bargaining.

Space limitations preclude an exhaustive treatment of the range of union impacts or even lengthy treatment of a sample of issues. Accordingly, several key issues have been selected for discussion and the empirical evidence of union impact is summarized. We begin by examining the union impact on economic efficiency. According to the monopoly view of unionism, unions have a negative impact because: they raise wages above the competitive level leading to low labour/capital ratios in unionized firms, impose inefficient work rules and lower output through strikes. Conversely, the collective voice/institutional response view of unionism argues that unions have positive effect on productivity by reducing quit rates and by inducing management to adopt more efficient management policies. Let us examine the evidence with respect to employee turnover and productivity (Freeman and Medoff, 1979).

Turnover

It has been argued that unions reduce quit rates because (1) workers believe they have an effective voice in achieving desirable working conditions and (2) because seniority provisions play a greater role in promotions and provide additional protection against layoff. Since union workers can achieve desired working conditions by "sticking around" they are less prone to resort to exit and entry mechanisms to achieve these ends. The organization will benefit from unionism by lowering hiring and training costs, stabilizing work groups, and, in the process, raising organizational efficiency (Freeman and Medoff, 1979).

Recent studies show that unions reduce quit rates.

> Our own research using newly available information on the job changes and employment status of thousands of individuals and industry-level turnover rates, shows that with diverse factors (including wages) held constant, unionized workers do have significantly lower quit rates than nonunion workers who are comparable in other respects .... Moreover, consistent with the claim that unions provide better representation for workers with greater seniority, the evidence suggests a larger reduction in exit and a larger increase in job tenure for older male workers than for younger male workers. (Freeman and Medoff, 1979).[1]

For older men (48-62 in 1969), the estimated reduction in quit rates attributable to unionism was 107 percent (tenure increased 38 percent); for younger workers (17-27) in 1969) quit rates dropped 11 percent (tenure increased 15 percent). Another study reported that stronger seniority provisions reduce employee turnover in manufacturing (Block, 1979).

While Freeman and Medoff believe the "voice" aspect of collective bargaining accounts for the lower turnover of union members, Kochan's analysis of the Quality of Employment survey data suggests that the main effect of unions is to reduce the "ease of leaving". In other words unions provide their members with a better package of benefits than is available to them in the external market (Kochan, 1980). Regardless of which explanation is accepted, there is strong evidence that unions reduce turnover.

Productivity

Freeman and Medoff have challenged the view that unionism is a major deterrent to productivity gains. Indeed, they argue unionism leads to higher productivity in some sectors not only because of greater capital intensity and higher labour quality, but by what has been called "institutional-response" factors. In other words, management adjusts to unions by instituting changes designed to improve the efficiency of the firm. After controlling for capital intensity and skill, they found that productivity was substantially higher (20 to 25 percent) in the unionized sector of the manufacturing industry and represented "an amount that could roughly offset the increase in total costs attributable to higher union rates" (Freeman and Medoff, 1979). However, not all of the evidence was positive. A negative productivity effect was reported in bituminous coal, an industry plagued by labour relations problems.

What proportion of the productivity gain is related to reduced turnover and "institutional-response" factors? A recent study of the cement industry indicates that about one-fifth of the positive productivity gain is associated with lower quit rates. The remainder appears to be the result of changes in management personnel and policies following unionization.

> Interestingly the enterprise typically changed plant management, suggesting that the union drive was an important signal to top management of ineffective lower-level managerial personnel. The drive thus provided valuable information or shock of a distinctive kind. Perhaps most importantly, the discussions with union and management officials in the cement industry indicated that firms often adopted more efficiency-oriented and less paternalistic personnel policies in response to unionism in order to raise productivity and meet higher wage demands (Freeman and Medoff, 1979).

Furthermore, there was little evidence indicating that strikes had a significant overall impact on society in terms of lost goods and services. While this conclusion probably holds for Canada as well, the proportion of time lost due to work stoppages rose significantly in the seventies in Canada, and in some years the proportion of total time lost was double that of the U.S. Also, given inter-industry variations in strike activity, the general rule may be less applicable to certain sectors. For example, it is noteworthy that the union impact on the U.S. bituminous coal industry in the mid-sixties was positive; however, considerable political instability within the United Mine Workers Union, a rash of wildcat strikes, and a steady deterioration of labour-management relations produced a negative productivity effect in the mid-seventies (estimated at 20 to 25 percent). Thus, while there is some strong evidence of a positive union impact on productivity, it would be unwise and premature to generalize these results across all sectors.

> Ultimately, the effects of collective bargaining on productivity depend on the ability of the union and the employer to develop an effective working relationship and upon the absence of constraints on the ability of management to adjust to higher labor costs by modifying its personnel practices, adapting new technological innovations, and upgrading the quality of its labor force (Kochan, 1980).

Management rights and union participation

Perhaps the most significant nonwage impact of unions is found in the application of grievance and arbitration procedures. In all but one Canadian jurisdiction, public policy requires all collective agreements to provide for binding arbitration as the final step in the grievance procedure. The impact of grievance arbitration has been particularly strong in the areas of discipline and discharge and the application of seniority. Such provisions have afforded union members security from arbitrary, discriminatory and capricious employer behaviour and required employers to prove their disciplinary decisions were for "just cause". Such blanket protection does not exist for most nonunion workers, although it is noteworthy that the Canada Labour Code entitles some nonunion workers to arbitration in unjust dismissal cases. With respect to the application of arbitration to seniority, union members are able to protect their right to certain benefit provisions, e.g., pensions, as well as protect their employment status, e.g., in promotion and layoff decisions. Although seniority enjoys some support in the nonunion sector, its coverage is generally narrower.

Thus, collective bargaining has become an important mechanism for defining and protecting unionists' property in work and imposing limits on managerial discretion. Notwithstanding this outcome, management control has not been as severely circumscribed as some critics would suggest. For example, we might consider the positive impact of grievance and arbitration procedures on management. These include: (1) certain assurances of uninterrupted production during the life of an agreement, (2) the imposition of a union responsibility to screen frivolous grievances which may take up management time, and (3) the formal grievance procedure functions "as part of a business organization's information system, and the data it generates can be used for diagnostic, evaluative and corrective (i.e., for management) purposes" (Lewin, 1978). In addition, since the union impact is largely confined to bread-and-butter issues, management is able to retain substantial control over issues affecting productive efficiency As I shall demonstrate below, management has successfully retained control over decisions affecting plant shutdowns, technological change and layoffs.

A potential threat to managerial autonomy can be envisaged if there is a narrowing of workers' "zones of acceptance", i.e., a reduction in the scope of managerial discretion or decision-making. The 1977 Quality of Employment survey found evidence that workers desire and expect to participate in a variety of job-related decisions.

> ...almost all the respondents agreed that workers should have at least some say over safety equipment and practices and over how work is done. Ninety percent believe workers should have at least some say over wages and salaries, just under 80 percent hold this for the days and hours people work, and 60 percent have this view regarding hiring and lay-off decisions (Kochan, 1980).

The desire for increased participation was found to be greatest among union members, younger workers and those earning higher hourly wages. As with other nonwage outcomes, "the desire for participation appears to increase in direct proportion to the extent to which the union has been successful in achieving higher wage goals" (Kochan, 1980). Whether the desire for increased participation will eventually prompt unions to seek improvements in the quality of work life is uncertain. To date, most efforts to humanize work in North America have occurred in the nonunion sector and there is little support for the worker participation schemes found in Western Europe.

Finally, what is known about the relative impact of collective bargaining and political action? Lewin evaluated the impact of American unions on business accountability. He concluded that the most tangible evidence is that collective bargaining, the collective agreement and the grievance procedure "are the leading mechanisms through which this accountability is achieved". Nevertheless, Lewin felt that the direct union impact has been modest, limited to relatively few issues, and its indirect impacts through political action may be more substantial than its direct impacts through collective bargaining. In particular, union political activity supporting social and economic legislation (as distinct from legal reforms of collective bargaining) in the areas such as civil rights, employment and training, and pension reform, have significantly affected union and nonunion businesses (Lewin, 1978). The applicability of these findings to Canada is unclear, given the political orientation of Canadian labour and provincial control over labour-related policy issues. Moreover, since numerous provincial labour laws provide for labour-management advisory committees to study labour problems and propose legislative remedies, organized labour has probably had a greater impact on collective bargaining legislation in this country. For example, the construction industry advisory committee was instrumental in bringing province-wide bargaining to Ontario in 1978.

MANAGEMENT'S RESPONSE TO UNIONISM

Considering some of the positive nonwage impacts of collective bargaining, it seems reasonable to inquire why employers strongly resist unions and collective bargaining. Freeman and Medoff suggest four possible explanations. First, managers see the benefits of unionism accruing directly to their subordinates and imposing costs on them in terms of diminished power, reduced flexibility, and a need to work harder. Second, although unions may have a positive effect on productivity, wages also tend to be higher, the return on capital may be lower and strikes may curtail production. Consequently, unionization involves a risk as to whether the firm can rationalize its operations, have a harmonious relationship with the union and remain profitable. Since the costs and benefits of unionism can vary among sectors and the prediliction of management is to avoid risks, opposition is to be expected. Third, unionism poses a serious threat to managerial personnel and operations, particularly in its initial stages. Following union certification it is not uncommon for firms to institute changes in organizational policies, structure and personnel. Finally, "unions are seen as both a source and an effect of managerial failure" (Freeman and Medoff, 1979). To begin with, unions are perceived as organizations which impede management's ability to operate efficiently. Furthermore, the formation of unions is largely a response to managements' mistakes and thus an indicator of past performances.

The intensity of management opposition to unions has been described in a recent Conference Board survey (Kochan, 1980). Management opposition to new union organizing was described as a top labour relations priority in firms with no, or a relatively low proportion of organized employees and a middle-range priority among firms with some unionization. There was also less strong opposition to unionization in new plants among highly-organized firms in highly-organized industries where the economic and labour relations experience is relatively favourable. An example of a favourable relationship is the automobile industry, where in 1979 GM agreed to automatically recognize the UAW and extend the national agreement to any new auto plants it opens in the U.S. On the other side of the ledger, strikes, escalating wages and low productivity have significantly contributed to management opposition to new union organizing in the construction and coal mining industries. Finally, there appears to be widespread management opposition to white-collar unionization, regardless of the experience with blue-collar unions. There may be two additional and important factors which contribute to the intensity of management opposition, but which are difficult to measure. The first involves the views of top corporate management, not only with respect to the costs and benefits of unionism, but their personal attitudes towards unions. Second, the current socio-political milieu may play an important (yet intangible) role in determining the intensity of management response to unions.

Opposition to unions is also a matter of how management perceives union impact. A recent study of hospital managers' perceptions of the nonwage impact of unions in the U.S. found that: (1) management decision- and policy-making became more standardized and formalized; (2) the quality of supervision and management improved, but supervisory jobs were more difficult and the overall ability of management to run a hospital effectively had diminished; (3) nonsupervisory employees found the hospital a more desirable place to work but their performance and commitment to the organization declined; and (4) organizational performance as measured by the quality of patient care was negatively affected (Maxey, 1980). In an effort to determine the basis for these perceptions a model was constructed and tested. The principle finding was that managers' assessments of the "union impact on organizational performance were strongly tied to their views of union effects on their own roles and, projectively on the motivations and actions of unionized workers" (Maxey, 1980).

Thus we need to bear in mind that management values play a large role in assessing union impact and determining the intensity of management response. The management goal of achieving organizational efficiency constitutes an important element in management opposition to unions. In the unionized context, the goal remains the same, but is limited by the union's ability to satisfy its members expectations. When scarce resources exist, the world of management rights may collide with the world of job conscious unionism.

PLANT SHUTDOWNS, TECHNOLOGICAL CHANGE AND LAYOFFS

While seniority has provided job security for long-service employees, the evidence suggests that union members are extremely vulnerable to plant shutdowns and technological change. In the U.S., it has been observed that:

> A minority of unions have been successful in negotiating income-security provisions that supplement the unemployment compensation system during short, temporary layoffs. A smaller minority of unions have negotiated provisions protecting the income and job security of employees affected by permanent job loss due to technological change or plant shutdowns (Kochan, 1980).

For example, fewer than 10 pecent of the major agreements provide for advance notice of technological change or plant shutdown, 11 percent provide for relocation allowances and less than one third provide for interplant transfers (Kochan, 1980).

This finding partially reflects the values which labour and managment bring to the bargaining table. For one thing, the preoccupation of unions with achieving short-run economic goals is a limiting factor. In addition, unions appear to be unable (due to management resistance) or unwilling (due to its low priority during periods of prosperity) to negotiate comprehensive measures to promote long-term employment or income security. Consequently, they have been forced to respond to crises such as plant shutdowns on a case-by-case basis. Under these circumstances, most unions lack sufficient bargaining power to save jobs and are put in the position of attempting to trade off their members' property in work for economic compensation to soften the impact of job loss, e.g., severance pay. This tendency is reinforced by the general conservatism of rank-and-file members and employer pressures to restrict union bargaining to a narrow range of economic issues.

Not only do we need to recognize that unions make this type of tradeoff, but we need to explain managements' response to union demands for greater employment and income security. On the whole, management seeks to maintain the status quo in nonwage bargaining. This goal is particularly relevant in areas which are perceived as impinging on management rights and imposing substantial costs. One study concluded: "This pattern of responses suggests that private-sector management bargains hardest on those issues that affect its flexibility and efficient utilization of the work force, (i.e., the nonwage factors most directly affecting productivity)" (Kochan, 1980). Over 90 percent of the managers surveyed indicated their nonwage goal was to tighten existing procedures or to maintain the status quo on issues such as subcontracting, layoff and recall prcedures, flexibility in employee assignments and income security (e.g., severance pay). Their goal achievement in these four areas ranged from 76 to 94 percent (Kochan, 1980).

What has been the Canadian experience? A recent study indicates there is a general attitude of mistrust between labour and management which makes it difficult to resolve problems such as redundancies and layoffs through the collective bargaining process. When these limitations were contrasted with the broad legislative protection found in Western Europe, the Commission called for legislative action (Carrothers, 1979). As I have commented elsewhere, the recommendations fell into three areas.

> With respect to <u>processes</u>, it recommends the enactment of legislation which recognizes redundancy management as a shared responsibilty. It also endorses joint consultation as the mechanism for commenting on managementdecisions to change operations and for determining if redundancy is avoidable or determining what steps can be taken to minimize or cushion the effects of layoffs. In the area of <u>avoiding and limiting layoffs</u>, the report stresses the importance of re-employment through such devices as relocation, retraining, placement assistance and the use of severance pay to regulate layoff schedules. As for <u>mitigating the effects of layoffs</u>, the

> Commission urges that public training and resources be available to assist displaced workers and that early retirement schemes and pension portability be expanded and upgraded. The study further recognizes the necessity of extending protection to unorganized employees (Rose, 1980B).

The limited coverage of collective bargaining in this area can be illustrated in two ways. First, we can examine collective agreement provisions in several Canadian jurisdictions. In Table 1, data is presented on a number of issues associated with technological change (there was no published data on plant shutdowns in these jurisdictions). The general pattern is that a majority of unionized employees do not have contracts which either preserve their jobs or cushion the economic impact of job loss.[2] While there are some interprovincial differences (probably reflecting legislative requirements and union strength), two generalizations can be made. There is some evidence unionized employees are afforded a degree of protection in the areas of advance notice of technological change, consultation and opportunities for either training or retraining. There is also evidence (outside of British Columbia) that union members receive little protection in terms of advance notice of layoff, relocation allowances, transfer arrangements, severance pay and arbitration of disputes over technological change. In several instances, over 90 percent of the employees have no contract provision to protect them. Moreover, many of the contracts contained relatively weak provisions for protecting union members.

The limited protection afforded by collective bargaining has also been illustrated by the national attention several recent plant shutdowns have received. In Ontario, for example, workers engaged in plant sit-ins at both Houdaille Industries and Wagner Brake and Lighting to dramatize their demands for improved severance pay and pension benefits. The simultaneous shutdown of the Winnipeg Tribune and the Ottawa Journal highlighted another issue of employer accountability. One newspaper chain has attempted to relocate displaced workers, whereas the other initially expressed the view that it had no responsibility to assist its former employees find new jobs.

These developments suggest that plant closings are becoming a major social and political issue. Not only are the contractual obligations of employers limited, but existing legislation in Ontario has been sharply criticized by organized labour. The Employment Standards Act only provides for advance notice when employment is terminated. Accordingly, the UAW is now backing legislation which would require corporations to justify plant shutdowns to a public tribunal, provide six months notice and guarantee that workers and communities would be compensated for the social costs of a shutdown (Donner, 1980). While it is difficult to predict how the government will respond to this package, business will undoubtedly resist any attempt to require public disclosures. But, as the recession deepens, we can expect organized labour to increase pressure on the government to broaden the

Table 1

Collective Agreement Provisions and Technological Change
(Percentage of Employees Covered)

Issue	Ontario[1]	Alberta[2]	British Columbia[3]	Canada[4]
1. Technological Change-Advance Notice				
no provision	40%	83%	38%	68%
some provision	60%	17%	62%	32%* (*Also includes consultation)
2. Technological Change-Advance Notice of Layoffs				
no provision	90%	97%	56%*	91%
some provision	10%	3%	44% (*90% have no special provision regarding permanent layoff)	9%
3. Technological Change-Consultation				
no provision	48%	95%	61%	(see * above)
some provision	52%	5%	39%	
4. Technological Change-Training/Retraining				
no provision	65%	84%	58%	73%
some provision	35%	16%	42%	27%
5. Technological Change-Relocation Allowance				
no provision	96%	99.9%	—	91%
some provision	4%	.1%		9%

Issues	Ontario[1]	Alberta[2]	British Columbia[3]	Canada[4]
6. Technological Change-Transfer Arrangement				
no provision	70%	87%	--	--
some provision	30%	13%		
7. Technological Change-Severance Pay				
no provision	92%	91%	60%	77%*
some provision	8%	9%	40%	23% (*refers to a wage or employment guarantee)
8. Technological Change-Arbitration of Dispute				
no provision	95%	99.7%	80%	--
some provision	5%	.3%	20%	

Sources: 1. Ontario Ministry of Labour provided data over the phone on 2,350 contracts covering 878,532 employees. These include private sector agreements covering 200 or more employees and public sector agreements for the current year.

2. Alberta Labour, Negotiated Working Conditions in Alberta Collective Agreements, 1979-80 Edition. Data covers 731 agreements in the private and public sector for all sizes of bargaining units.

3. British Columbia Department of Labour, Negotiated Working Condition 1980. Data covers 379 contracts and 314,077 employees (67 percent of the 1979 unionized workforce), in all sizes of bargaining units.

4. Labour Canada, Canadian Industrial Relations Perspectives. Data based on agreements covering 500 or more employees for the year 1977.

scope of business accountability.

Finally, I am skeptical that organized labour will abandon its philosophy of business and job conscious unionism in favour of Western European models of industrial democracy. The future will witness a continuation of the strong emphasis on collective bargaining for achieving economic goals. The pursuit of certain goals through political action will continue, but largely as a supplement to collective bargaining and as a response to short-run conditions. In my opinion, the values organized labour holds dear are unlikely to experience a renaissance.

BIBLIOGRAPHY

Bairstow, F. (1978), Report of the Commission on Wider-Based Collective Bargaining, Ottawa: Labour Canada

Block, R. (1978), The Impact of Seniority Provisions on the Manufacturing Quit Rate. In: Industrial and Labor Relations Review 31: 474-481

Carrothers, A.W.R. (1979), Report of the Commission of Inquiry into Redundancies and Lay-offs, Ottawa: •Labour Canada

Christy, R. (1975), The Structure of Collective Bargaining in Hameed, S.M.A. (ed.), Canadian Industrial Relations, Toronto: Butterworths

Crispo, J. (1978), Industrial Democracy in Western Europe: A North America Perspective, Toronto: McGraw-Hill Ryerson Limited

Donner, A. (1980), Plant Closings are Becoming a Social Issue. In: Globe and Mail (Toronto), September 8, B5

Freeman, R. (1976), Individual Mobility and Union Voice in the Labor Market. In: American Economic Review 66: 361-368

Freeman, R. and Medoff J. (1979), The Two Faces of Unionism. In: The Public Interest 57: 69-93

Kochan T. (1980), Collective Bargaining and Industrial Relations, Homewood: Irwin-Dorsey Limited

Kovacs, A. (1971), The Philosophy of the Canadian Labour Movement in Miller R. and Isbester F. (eds.), Canadian Labour in Transition, Peterborough: Prentice-Hall

Lewin, D. (1978), The Impact of Unionism on American Business: Evidence For An Assessment. In: Columbia Journal of World Business 13: 89-103

Maxey, C. (1980), Organizational Consequences of Collective Bargaining: A Study of Some Noneconomic Dimensions of Union Impact. In IRRA Proceedings 33: 94-102

Morris, C. (1978), A Comparison of Developments on Both Sides of the Border in Bairstow, F. (ed.), The Direction of Labour Policy in Canada, Montreal: Industrial Relations Centre, McGill University

Rose, J. (1980A), Public Policy, Bargaining Structure and the Construction Industry, Toronto: Butterworths

Rose, J. (1980B), Redundancies and Layoffs: A Broader Analysis and Stronger Recommendations Needed. In: CAUT Bulletin 28: 3

Weiler, P. (1980), Reconciable Differences: New Directions in Canadian Labour Law, Toronto: The Carswell Company Limited

Williams, C.B. (1971), Trade Union Structure and Philosophy: Need For A Reappraisal in Miller R. and Isbester, F. (eds.), Canadian Labour in Transition, Peterborough: Prentice-Hall

NOTES

1. See also Freeman, 1976

2. It should be noted that in some jurisdictions, e.g., the federal and British Columbia, public policy limits the introduction of technological change by requiring advance notice.

The German Model of Codetermination: Programmatic Perspectives, Confrontative Issues and Prospective Developments

Franz-Jürgen Säcker

Table of Contents

A. WORKER PARTICIPATION IN CORPORATE MANAGEMENT - A HISTORICAL SURVEY

According to experience gained over the last 100 years the stability of the Western democratic industrial societies in Europe seems to be substantially dependent on the structure of social relationships within enterprises. The demand for industrial democracy is, of course, of much more recent date than the demand for political democracy.[1] Since the end of the First World War, however, in addition to demands for socialization of the economy raised by socialist and communist groups, the demand for industrial democracy has been at the center of political arguments in the majority of Western European states, at least. As you know, co-determination acts became effective in Sweden in 1977[2], and in the Federal Republic of Germany in 1978.[3] At the supranational level the demand is being made within the European Communities for a co-determination statute roughly oriented to the German model to apply to transnational companies.[4]

In Italy,[5] France,[6] and England[7], the situation is so far still relatively quiet. The reason for this lies in the fact that the socialist and communist parties and trade unions consider co-determination in its German form to be a betrayal of the working class because it "de-radicalizes" the trade unions and integrates them into the capitalist system.[8] The supporters of free enterprises and of a liberal market economy, on the other hand, reject co-determination because they fear that co-determination means "cold" socialization and is the first step towards communism.[9] The German trade unions and political parties on the other hand are in principle unanimous in their view that co-determination of capital and labor within a company provides a third course between capitalism and communism, in other words, a final stage of development.[10] The German Federal Chancellor even likes to talk about the "German Model" in his lectures on co-determination. Co-determination in a company is thus in these terms neither transitory nor provisional; on the contrary, it has complete validity. What does this model look like? How does it compare with the alternative system of collective bargaining?[11] How are we to judge the political stability of this system? And what about the economic efficiency of companies under the conditions laid down by co-determination on a parity basis?

In order to give satisfactory answers to all these questions we first have to consider how important co-determination is in the German system of collective labor legislation. Asking about the meaning of, and the necessity for, industrial co-determination for workers is a typical product of modern industrial society with its division of labor as it has developed since the end of the 18th century. The man who lives in isolation on an island like Robinson Crusoe, or who is a craftsman or in a one-man firm, such a man is his own master. He has the legal right to make his own decisions and not to have them made for him by others. There are no instructions to dictate his rhythm of work; he has no superior to reprimand him; he cannot be dismissed; he can, of course, starve if his work is poor, but modern social legislation protects him from this risk, too. For the independent worker the demand for co-determination would indeed be pointless. The man who enjoys self-determination needs no collective protective institution to shield him, or to safeguard his personal dignity and freedom. It is not until the worker is integrated into and subordinated to factory work with its division of labor and functions that the question of worker participation in factory and company management arises. The liberalism of the 19th century ("Manchester liberalism") - in Europe we like to talk about paleo-liberalism - had not yet recognized these problems. In those days the belief was that recognition of general, individual civil rights would of itself lead to a just and fair system - the quasi-automatic result, as it were, of the process of the self-interested self-realization of all citizens. The belief in legal freedom and equality for all, which had only just been attained as a result of the enlightenment and the French revolution, was not allowed to become confused by the reality of economic constraint and inequality of a large number, at least, of the working class. It was only after a long and bitter struggle that the workers, now gradually organizing themselves, were able to wrest from the state the right to lay down unalterably in collective agreements, uniform, general minimum working conditions for their members, and to strike for better working conditions without having to fear the imposition of penal sanctions.[12]

The possibility of improving general working conditions and especially wages, holidays, and working hours by concluding collective agreements proved, however, to be insufficient from the workers' point of view. Despite collective settlements, the individual worker on the job was, to a large extent, still not self-determined. As in the past the worker remained subject to the employer's authority to issue directives both concerning his job and the place of work; as in the past he had no influence on the organization of working conditions or his place of work (i.e. in the concrete 3-dimensional place of production or administration in which he had to work).[13] Similarly no collective agreement could cover entrepreneurial planning, organizational, and management competencies (i.e. decisions on investments, diversification, production, location, prices, and marketing).[14] Out of this situation, in which the individual worker remained as before dependent on the employer, there arose at the end of the 19th century the demand for workers to exert an influence on the organization of the social, personal, and economic affairs of the place of work, and the company as a whole.

B. LEVELS OF CO-DETERMINATION: PLANT AND ENTERPRISE

In the First World War a start was made to meet this demand with the Hilfsdienstgesetz - roughly translated Auxiliary Service Act - of 1916 and then, more comprehensively, in 1920 with the Works Councils Act (Betriebsrätegesetz). During the National Socialist era this worker participation was superseded by fascist working regulations with commitment to a Führer model. It was not until the end of the Second World War, that the development which had begun in the Weimar Republic could be resumed in the individual federal states. Laws on works councils were passed in the federal states, and in 1952 were superseded by the "Betriebsverfassungsgesetz" (Works Constitution Act) which applied throughout the Federal Republic.

In 1972 the Betriebsverfassungsgesetz was fundamentally amended and given its current form. Just as in the preceding version of 1952, this act gives jobholders the right to participate in social and personal matters and to demand financial compensation (social plans) when factories are closed down and work is cut back.[15]

The board of management has to give the works councils comprehensive information concerning the economic affairs of the company (§ 106 Shop Constitution Act) and has to report in full and in good time about the following entrepreneurial measures and shall produce the necessary records therefore in so far as the same shall not jeopardize operational and business secrets,

- manpower requirement planning (§ 92),
- planning for technical plants, working process, and operations (§ 91),
- planning for alterations and dismissals of more than thirty jobholders (§ 111 of the Shop Constitution Act in conjunction with § 17 of the Act To Provide Protection Against Unwarranted Dismissal.[16] Articles 111 to 113 of the Shop Constitution Act oblige the employer to consult the works councils for the intended steps, to aim at an agreement with the works councils upon financial compensations when factories are closed down in order to cushion any socially detrimental effects. Such agreements exceed those provided for by the council directive of the European Communities to avoid in particular transfers of enterprises, plants, or parts of business being detrimental for the workers.[17]

But all these are only information rights of the works councils, not co-determination rights. Therefore employees in the coal, iron, and steel industries were given in 1951, with the encouragement of the occupation powers, additional co-determination rights on the enterprise level. Jobholders in the other joint stock companies were given in 1952 the additional right to a third of the seats on the company body which elects and dismisses the members of the management board. In Germany this body, which formerly consisted solely of shareholders, is known as the "Aufsichtsrat" (supervisory board). The Co-determination Act of 1976 extends the scope of co-determination by giving the employees of joint stock companies and companies with limited liability half the seats on the supervisory board. The members who have been elected by the share-holders can be removed from office by a three-quarters majority of the votes cast at a shareholders' meeting (§ 103 German Stock Corporation Act). On the labor side are representatives from the trade unions, from the blue-collar workers, from the white-collar workers, from the white-collar employees, and one representative from the executive employees with managerial responsibility.

Fig. 1 Model of parity co-determination in the coal and steel industries

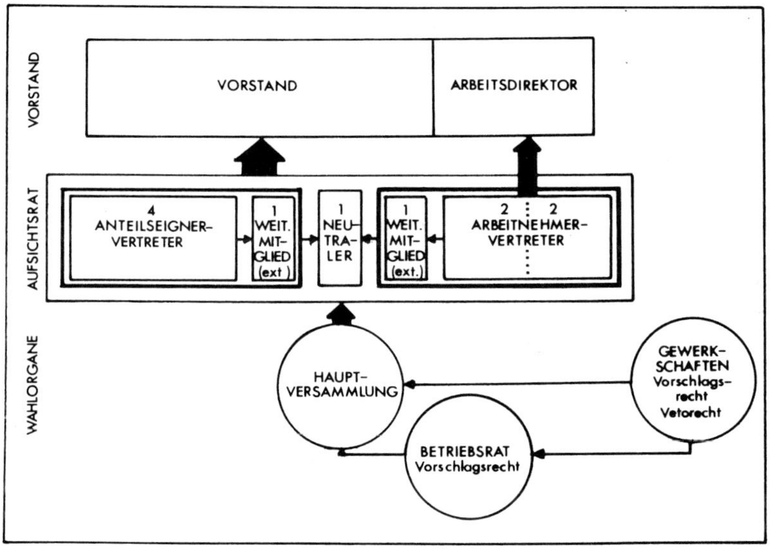

Fig. 2 Model of the Labor Management Act 1952/72

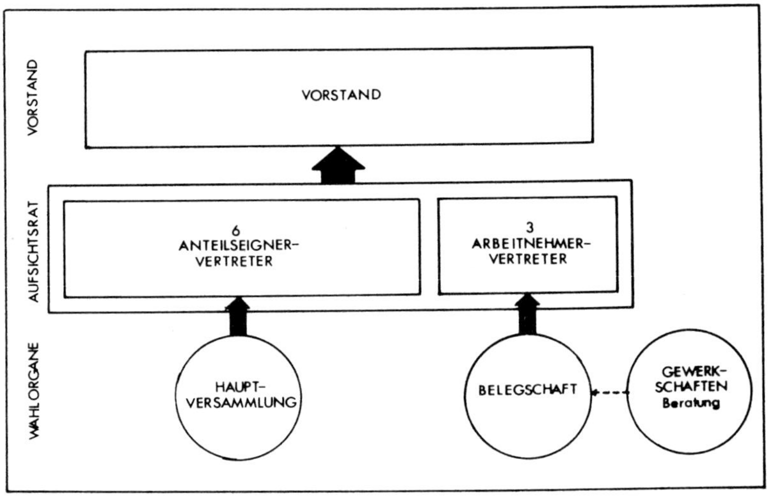

Notes to Fig. 1 and 2

Vorstand	= Board of Management
Arbeitsdirektor	= Labor Director
Aufsichtsrat	= Supervisory Board or Council
Anteilseignervertreter	= Representatives of Sharehoulders
Weitere Mitglieder	= Additional Members
Neutrales Mitglied	= Neutral Member
Arbeitnehmervertreter	= Representatives of Workers
Hauptversammlung	= Shareholders Meeting
Betriebsrat	= Works Council
Gewerkschaften	= Unions
Belegschaft	= Workers
Wahlorgane	= Electoral Colleges

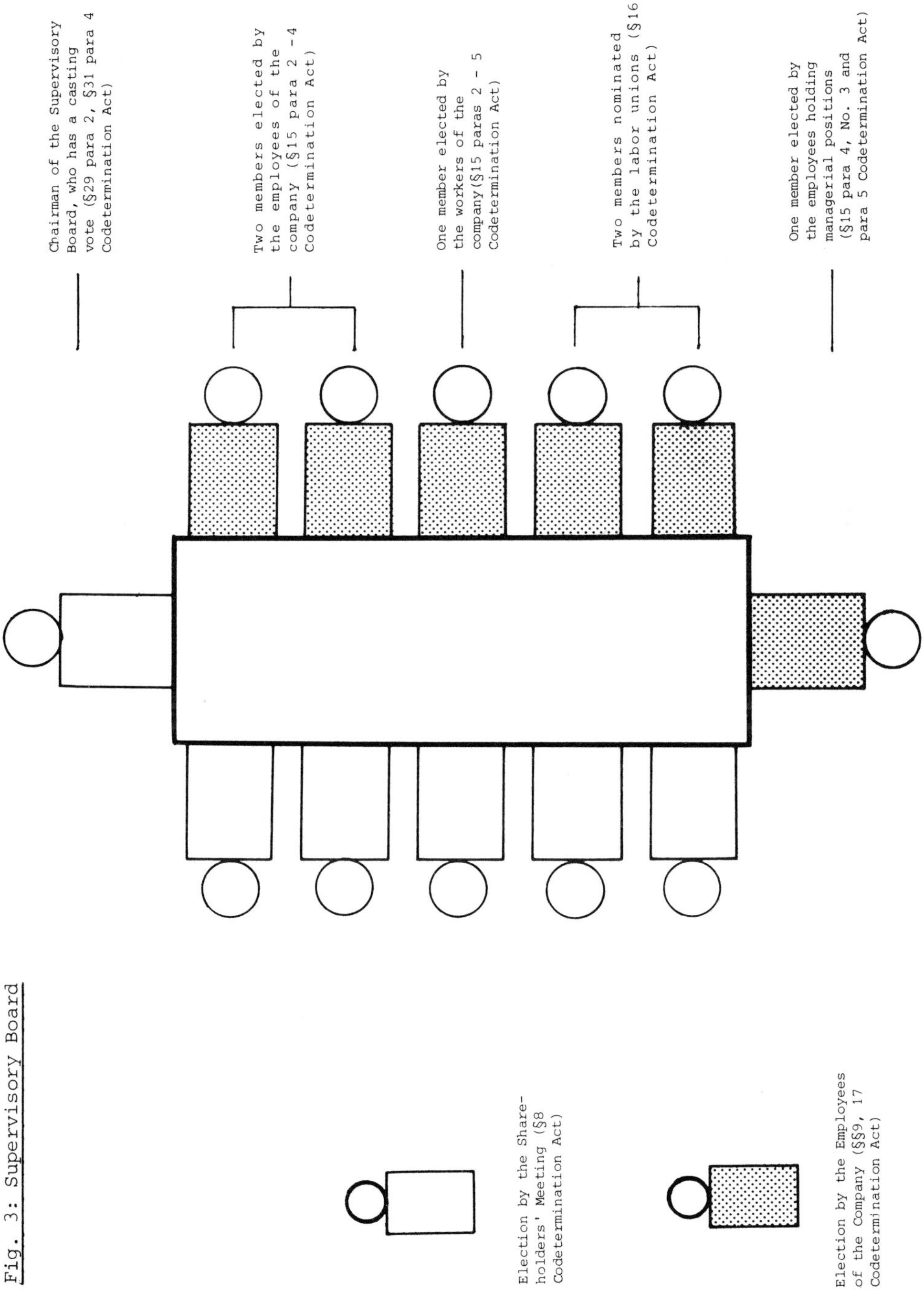

Fig. 3: Supervisory Board

Chart 1 is the list of the present member unions of the Federation of German Trade Unions (DGB), which has 7,500,000 members.

CHART 1

1.	Construction (IG Bau, Steine, Erden)	518,000
2.	Mining and Energy (IG Bergbau und Energie)	362,000
3.	Railroads (Gewerkschaft der Eisenbahner Deutschlands)	414,000
4.	Teachers and Scientists (Gewerkschaft Erziehung und Wissenschaft, GEW)	159,000
5.	Horticulture, Agriculture, and Forestry (Gewerkschaft Gartenbau, Land- und Forstwirtschaft)	41,000
6.	Trade, Banking, and Insurance (Gewerkschaft Handel, Banken und Versicherungen)	314,000
7.	Wood and Synthetic Materials (Gewerkschaft Holz und Kunststoff)	145,000
8.	Fine Arts (Gewerkschaft Kunst)	42,000
9.	Leather (Gewerkschaft Leder)	55,000
10.	Metal Industries (IG Metall)	2,681,000
11.	Food, Drink, Tobacco, and Restaurants (Gewerkschaft Nahrung, Genuß, Gaststätten)	252,000
12.	Public Service, Transport, and Communications (Gewerkschaft Öffentliche Dienste, Transport und Verkehr, ÖTV)	1,099,000
13.	Postal Services (Deutsche Postgewerkschaft)	429,000
14.	Textiles, Clothing (Gewerkschaft Textil, Bekleidung)	290,000
15.	Police (Gewerkschaft der Polizeibeamten Deutschlands, GdP)	152,000
16.	Chemicals, Paper, and Ceramics (IG Chemie, Papier, Keramik)	651,000
17.	Printing and Paper (IG Druck und Papier)	146,000

(December 31, 1978)

The largest single union within the DGB is the IG Metall with 2,681,000 members. These unions have nearly a monopoly on representation for workers. Only in the organization of employees has a rival to the DGB arisen in the Union of German Employees (DAG) with 500,000 members.

German unions see themselves as unitary unions (Einheitsgewerkschaften) rather than as ideologically oriented unions (Richtungsgewerkschaften). Their ideological and political mentality is laid down in their statutes. Doubts may be expressed whether this mentality is in fact always conformed to in view of the historic alliance between social democracy and the union movement. As important as the idea of the unitary union is the principle of the industrial union (Industrieverbandsprinzip). The unions have organized themselves not as craft unions, i.e. as an association, but as industrial unions, i.e. as associations of workers and employees in a particular industry. The individual union therefore represents all persons employed in an industry regardless of their occupation and regardless of whether they are workers, or employees. Collective bargaining takes place between one union and one employers' organization (industry-wide agreement - Verbandstarifvertrag) or between one union and a particular employer (Firmentarifvertrag). This usually ensures labor-peace for the duration of the collective bargaining agreement, and any strike is illegal which during the collective agreement aims at changing matters already regulated by the agreement. Strike, or lockout measures between work councils and employers are forbidden. Chart 2 shows the strike and lockout statistics:

CHART 2

Year	Number of workers involved	Days lost
1950	79000	380,000
1951	174000	1,593,000
1952	85000	443,000
1953	51000	1,488,000
1954	116000	1,586,000
1955	597000	847,000
1956	25000	264,000
1957	45000	2,386,000
1958	202000	780,000
1959	22000	62,000
1960	17000	38,000
1961	21000	65,000
1962	79000	451,000
1963	317000	1,846,000
1964	6000	17,000
1965	6000	49,000
1966	196000	27,000
1967	60000	389,000
1968	25000	25,000
1969	90000	249,000
1970	184000	93,000
1971	536000	4,484,000
1972	23000	66,000
1973	185000	563,000
1974	250000	1,051,000
1975	36000	69,000
1976	169000	534,000
1977	34000	24,000
1978	488000	4,290,000
1979	77000	483,000

Functions of Trade Unions

I. Right to enter into collective agreements and right to strike (Article 9, para 3 Basic Law of the Federal Republic of Germany)

II. Rights of participation according to shop constitution law and the co-determination laws

III. Participation in the enactment of laws

1. Associations autonomously create law in collective bargaining agreements (Tarifvertragsgesetz)
2. Associations are entitled to participate in the law creating acts of trade cooperative associations (industrial safety regulations)
3. Associations participate in arbitration boards
4. Co-determination in making collective bargaining agreements generally binding (see § 5, paras 1 - 5 Tarifvertragsgesetz)
5. Co-determination in the establishment of working conditions (§§ 2, 5, 6 of the Gesetz über die Festsetzung von Mindestarbeitsbedingungen)
6. Right to be consulted through membership in advisory councils of individual ministries
7. Legal rights to be heard and to advise (see e.g. § 11 of the Tarifvertragsgesetz, § 94 of the Bundesbeamten-Gesetz, BBG)

IV. Participation in administrative functions

1. The right to propose members for the organs of social security (Selbstverwaltungsgesetz of August 23, 1967)
2. Membership in committees and workshops concerned with social policy
3. Rights of participation according to the Law of Vocational Training (Berufsbildungsgesetz)
4. Rights of proposal for chambers of workers (Arbeitskammern) in Bremen; and rights to send representatives to economic chambers (Wirtschaftskammern) in Bremen and Rheinland-Pfalz
5. Participation in other institutions concerned with economic policy (Rationalisierungskuratorium der Deutschen Wirtschaft, Verband für Arbeitsstudien, Deutscher Normenausschuß, Landwirtschaftliche Marktverbände)

6. The right to make largely binding proposals to committees concerned with the welfare of youths (Jugendwohlfahrtsausschüsse), charitable institutions (Versorgungsanstalt) of the Federation and the Länder, administrative boards of the post office, the railways, the Kreditanstalt für Wiederaufbau, and the Deutsche Landwirtschaftliche Rentenbank
7. The right to make largely binding proposals to organs of the Federal Employment Office (Bundesanstalt für Arbeit), and for the committees for the protection of employees against unlawful dismissal at the employment offices of the Länder
8. The right to make proposals to the administrative board of the import and supply offices (Einfuhr- und Vorratsstellen)
9. Membership of trade unions in many advisory committees of governmental offices
10. The right to make proposals to radio and television councils (or the respective advisory councils of programming in Nordrhein-Westfalen); to the voluntary control office of the film industry; and for the supervisory boards of the Max-Planck-Gesellschaft

V. Participation in jurisdictional tasks

1. Labor jurisdiction: right to propose court associates (Beisitzer), rights to advise in matters of organization, participation in the nomination of the chief judges (see § 20; § 37, para 2; § 43, paras 3, 15, 34, 36 of the Arbeitsgerichtsgesetz)

   Representation of association members through statutory representatives in trials before the labor courts (§ 11 of the Arbeitsgerichtsgesetz)

   Federal disciplinary courts: right to make proposals

C. PHILOSOPHY OF PARTICIPATION

The demand for the introduction of co-determination has been justified in the Biedenkopf Report and the Bullock Report basically with three arguments:

1. "Industrial and economic changes"[18]

The idea of worker participation in economic decisions is intended to serve as a safeguard for the employees' human dignity and to offer them a better chance for exercising their basic right to professional freedom in large industrial enterprises. The employee who works in a dependent position has lost the individual position to which his personal dignity gives him the right and is now merely "a cog in the wheel". His position in the company is that of an object deprived of self-determination. Only if employees could influence all company policy from the early planning stage would their interests be effectively represented. Only then would there be a chance of freeing them from their position as objects and of solving, in the long term, conflicts between unions, works councils, and management. In this way co-determination shall improve effective supervision of economic power of large companies. The economic power wielded by large firms, which is beyond the commodities and labor market, and is of overall economic importance, must be supervised. The integration in the company management of groups with an interest in the firm leads to a distribution of economic power. Thus, co-determination is the expression of the principle of power-distribution in free societies, which, in principle, distinguishes such societies from socialist economies with their centralized administration. By preventing an excessive concentration of power, co-determination supplements the now valid antitrust law. Worker participation thus offers a guarantee against every abuse of economic power, abuse which could not be prevented by using external control mechanisms alone such as are offered by the law against restrictions on competition. Thus, co-determination neutralizes the political power of large firms which is so detrimental to the functioning of the free and social constitutional state ("freiheitlicher, sozialer Rechtsstaat") and the functioning of a free private-law system.

2. "Social changes" (industrial democracy)

The second argument in favor of organizing co-determination points to the need to democratize the economy. The earliest use of the term "industrial democracy" which I could find was by Sidney and Beatrice Webb in 1897 as the title of their book on the structure and functions of trade unions. The democratic principle should be respected not only when organizing state decision-making, but also when organizing large enterprises. Every free social system can demand inalienably that both the state-political and the socio-economic exercise of power must have democratic legitimation. The modern large firm as a social structure of socio-political relevance and immense power should be subject to the principles of this free system. If the special features of the company are taken into account, this demand can be achieved by having the management of the company, where position, dismissal, and supervision are concerned, authorized by all the groups affected by company policy, in other words, by the employees, too. In this way the "fourth class" would be integrated into the state and the company, and this is the only way to achieve longterm political stability in states which consider the principles of free enterprise to be the best way of organizing the economy.

3. "Trade union and legislative developments"[20]

The intention is that co-determination should lead to equal rights for capital and labor in a social market economy. Capital and labor, disregarding the functional difference between them, make the same contribution towards achieving successful production (in work-intensive companies more, in capital-intensive companies less) which means that, to generalize, one is justified in speaking of the equal importance in all companies of the production factors "capital" and "labor." Each factor is dependent on the other and both are equally indispensable to the company. The legal system must take this fact into account on principle by giving capital and labor equality within a company in the form of a dualistic rather than capital-monistic company structure, thus reducing the class conflict between the owners of the means of production and the employees themselves. It is not merely the owner, it is also the employee who bears the risks involved in entrepreneurial decisions. The risk borne by the employee, namely of losing his job, is equal to the risk involved in capital input. In many cases the former is even greater, for in limited companies the owner is only liable to the extent of the capital he has put in. The loss of this capital obviously has far less effect on his living standards than has the loss of his job on the employee. In the positive ruling of the Federal Constitutional Court from the March 1, 1978 concerning the compatibility of the Co-determination Act with the constitution, this aspect was emphasized in order to deny any infringement of the constitutional guarantee of private property.[21]

4. Special character of the contract of work[22]

In Germany the Biedenkopf Commission, which was set up by the government to investigate the problems associated with co-determination, added another argument. This commission justified co-determination on the basis of the special legal, economic, and social character of the working relationship as it is structured by the contract of work, the organizational integration of the employee into the working process, the utilization of the employee's labor, and the terms of authority associated with this, which are inherent in the working relationship. The fact that the employee belongs to the "social association" known as the company is used to construct a claim to participation in entrepreneurial planning for the achievement of the company's aims.

D. SCOPE AND GENERAL PRINCIPLES OF THE CO-DETERMINATION ACT OF 1976

1. The two-tier management structure of German Company Law

All these political and ideological demands quoted in justification of co-determination say nothing at all about the practical organization of co-determination in a company. In Germany there was from the outset unanimous agreement on the point that direct employee participation in the decision-making body could not be considered for the following two reasons:

a) The delegates elected by the labor side have too little expert knowledge,

b) the board of management must lead the company homogenously in the eyes of the world; the board can therefore not be a heterogenous mixture of "them" and "us" managers.

Co-determination could therefore only be implemented by including the labor side in the process of selecting the board of management, that is, in authorizing and supervising it. For this reason the demand for co-determination concentrated from the outset on the supervisory board, which according to German corporation law functions as the elector and supervisor of a company's board of management.

The German Stock Corporation Act (Aktiengesetz) prescribes a two-tier system of administration for the "Aktiengesellschaft". The basic principle is the separation of the control function from that of management. The supervisory council cannot be charged with management functions (§ 111, para 4 German Stock Corporation Act). It is no part of the supervisory board's duty to participate in organizing day-to-day-business. A member of the board of management may not simultaneously be a member of the supervisory board (§ 105 German Stock Corporation Act). The supervisory council may only require that specified types of important, risky business receive the prior consent of the supervisory council (§ 111, para 4, sentence 2 German Stock Corporation Act). If in such a case the supervisory board refuses to approve a business matter, the shareholders' meeting can, however, overrule the supervisory board in every case with a three-quarters majority.

The legal division of function and responsibility is clear and establishes that the board of management directs and is responsible for the operations of the company (§ 76 German Stock Corporation Act), while the supervisory council controls the board of management. The board of management has specific and detailed obligations as regards reporting on the company's affairs to the supervisory council (§ 90 German Stock Corporation Act, § 25 Co-determination Act). The law requires a continuous flow of information to be transmitted by the management to the supervisory council on the state of the enterprise and on envisaged management policy. Moreover, the supervisory board may at any time request a report from the board of management on the affairs to the company and on its legal and business relations to connected (dominating or dependent) enterprises (§ 90, para 3 German Stock Corporation Act). The board of management has to submit the report if possible in time to enable the supervisory board to make its position clear before the transactions are entered into (§ 90, para 2, No. 4 German Stock Corporation Act).[24] Because the management of the dependent company is often not informed in time or not competent, according to the French Sudreau Commission, it is necessary to make sure within groups of companies that the personnel representation can talk with the real holder of management power.[25] Therefore, foreign multinational groups should be obliged to appoint a representative for each of their subsidiaries to be answerable for the group's overall policy.

In conclusion:

The board of management of the dependent company is obligated to inform the work councils and the supervisory board on a timely and thorough basis and must provide supporting documentation regarding all important planning matters and business events intended by the controlling company, which may have substantial influence upon the situation of the dependent enterprise (§ 90, para 4 German Stock Corporation Act, §§ 90, 92, 106, 111 Shop Constitution Act). Therefore, directives of the dominating company which require that the management of the dependent company inform the work council or the supervisory board later than the law commands are not valid. This is a difficult situation for the board of management in the controlling and in the dependent enterprise. Both want to follow the law which has validity in the country of the dependent company because multinational companies do not stand outside, but inside the rational legal system of the countries in which they live.[26] But both must see that the economic operations of the combine are successful, that in a free market system, in which the enterprises operate, not only information but also secrets and confidential statements are elements on which an enterprise depends in the interest of its survival.[27]

Furthermore, the supervisory council has the right to investigate the company's affairs, and in so doing it may inspect the company's books and records (§ 111, para 2 German Stock Corporation Act). A managing director can receive a prison sentence or a fine (§ 400 German Stock Corporation Act; § 82, No. 3 Limited Liabilities Company Act) if he knowingly makes an untrue or obscuring statement of the financial situation of the company to the public. The members of the board of management of a stock corporation who fail to comply with §§ 90, 111, para 2 German Stock Corporation Act shall be required to do so by the court of register by assessment of administrative penalties (§ 407 German Stock Corporation Act).

A feature of German and most other European joint stock company laws is that it provides for a strict division of powers analogous to the division of political power. The electorate in general political elections have their counterpart in the shareholders who assemble for general meetings. The supervisory board corresponds to parliament, which elects and supervises the government. The board of the company corresponds to the executive council, and the chairman of the board to the president or chancellor of the republic. In this system the shareholders have only one function, namely, to make basic decisions (§ 119 Joint Stock Company Law). They make decisions on the articles of association, the object of the company, capital increases and reductions, and on utilization of the profits made. They may only decide questions of management if the board of management so requests (§ 119, para 2 German Stock Corporation Act). But this never happens in reality.

Otherwise their powers are restricted to the electing of the members of the supervisory board from the shareholders' side, who, together with the representatives elected by the labor side, form the "parliament" known as the supervisory board. The supervisory board is there to select the most suitable top management for the company and to dismiss it if it fails (§ 31 Co-determination Act) and to keep a check on the orderly conduct of business (§ 111 Joint Stock Companies Law, § 25 Co-determination Act). The supervisory board is legally bound not to betray any of the company secrets imparted to it. The management board of the joint stock company has to manage the company independently and on its own responsibility. Members of the supervisory board and the board of management should be guided solely by the best interest of the company.[28] They make themselves liable for damages and must be dismissed if they allow themselves to be guided by special interests which are not connected with their own company. However, as it is very difficult concerning decisions on long-term forecasts to determine what is, on concrete terms, in the company's interest, it is very often possible in fact to use the company's interest as a cover for following up special interests without running the risk in business practice of claims for damages or of loss of mandate. After working for years on German supervisory boards, a famous man stated with resignation that it was easier to get a grip on a slippery eel than it was to make a supervisory board member liable. Since the supervisory board consists of an equal number of representatives from both the shareholders' side and the labor side, legislation provides for the protection of property by granting the chairman of the supervisory board, who is appointed by the shareholders, a conflict-resolving casting vote when a stalemate has been reached. Under these circumstances the Co-determination Act now valid in Germany cannot be described as co-determination on a parity basis. The Federal Constitutional Court has explicitly stated in its decision on the Co-determination Act that the chairman of the supervisory board can use his casting vote whenever a vote is taken and has thus consciously refrained from commenting on the question of whether unrestricted co-determination on a parity basis is compatible with the constitution.[29]

2. Important exceptions for limited liability companies

In a limited company (GmbH) the shareholders' meeting has more far-reaching competencies than in a joint stock corporation (AG), as the Federal Constitutional Court has confirmed.[30] In the limited company the shareholders establish the annual statement of accounts (§ 46, No. 1 Act Concerning Companies with Limited Liabilities). The supervisory board has no right to decide on the determination of the financial statements (§ 25, para 1, No. 2 Co-determination Act; § 171 German Stock Corporation Act; § 47 No. 2 Act Concerning Companies with Limited Liabilities). The shareholders can draw up directives for policy on the conduct of the business, they can issue general instructions (§ 37 Limited Liability Companies Act) and decide on measures applicable to the examination of the management (§ 46, No. 6 Limited Liability Companies Act). The supervisory board cannot prevent this, but it can object to unlawful instructions which are not in the company's best interests.[31]

3. Special problems for multi-national groups of companies

This right of the supervisory board is very important for groups of companies.

A "controlling (dominating) company" is a company which being the last instance accumulates the leading power in the sense of concern-law, regardless whether and to what extent this power is exercised by the top management of another concern-company ("Teilkonzernspitze"). As a general principle the act actually tends to work on the assumption of the unity of the concern. The "Teilkonzernspitzen" closest to the dominating company are only considered as being the controlling company in the definitely regularized case in which the controlling company of the concern does not fall within the rules of the act (§ 5, para 3 Co-determination Act). "Concern-companies", the employees of which are considered to be employees of the controlling company, are only those domiciled in the Federal Republic of Germany. Employees of concern-companies domiciled abroad are not reckoned to belong to the controlling company, this is also the case in so far as these employees are occupied in works situated in the Federal Republic of Germany.[32]

If no contract of dominating exists, then a controlling enterprise may not use its influence to cause a dependent enterprise to take disadvantageous legal transactions or to take or omit measures to its disadvantage (§ 131 German Stock Corporation Act). The board of management of the dependent corporation is not obliged by law to follow the directives of the controlling enterprise. The board must even refuse to follow a directive, if an orderly and conscientious manager of an independent enterprise would not have taken the legal transaction or would have taken or omitted the measure. Otherwise the members of the board of management are jointly and severally liable (§§ 93, 317, para 2 German Stock Corporation Act). For example, a service agreement between the dominating and dependent enterprise is disadvantageous and forbidden, if there are no adequate compensations for the recurring consideration in money, which the dependent company pays to the dominating company.[33] Inadmissible are prices and conditions in contracts between connected enterprises which an orderly and conscientious manager of an independent enterprise would not have accepted. Inadmissable are directives of the dominating company which forbid the board of the dependent company to serve only the interests of its company.

It is the function of the supervisory board to control this legal obligation of the management. Each member of the supervisory board is entitled to take a motion to court in order to declare a directive inadmissable which violates the interests of the company.[34]

E. RIGHTS AND FUNCTIONS OF THE SUPERVISORY BOARD AND OF THE INDIVIDUAL MEMBER - DETAILS

The functions of the supervisory board in the whole and the rights of its single members you can see in the following charts. The charts show the rights of the supervisory board in the whole. Chart 3 shows you the rights which may not be referred to a committee. Chart 4 shows you the rights of the supervisory board which can be referred to a committee. Chart 5 shows you the rights of the individual members of the supervisory board. These rights are very important. They can be used alone by the jobholders' supervisory board members. In chart 5 a) all the rights are enumerated which each member of the supervisory board has within the supervisory board. 5 b) gives two members of the supervisory board the right to request a report on the affairs of the enterprise and its relations to connected enterprises from the board of management. 5 c) enumerates the rights of each member of the supervisory board as concerns the shareholders' meeting. Charts 6 and 7 enumerate additional rights and claims of the single members against the enterprise.

CHART 3

RIGHTS OF THE SUPERVISORY BOARD WHICH MAY NOT BE REFERRED TO A COMMITTEE FOR THE PASSING OF A RESOLUTION IN LIEU OF THE SUPERVISORY BOARD (§ 25, PARA 1 CO-DETERMINATION ACT, § 107, PARA 3 AktG)

1. Appointment of the members of the board of management, especially the appointment of the labor director (§§ 31, 33 Co-determination Act)
2. Removal of the members of the board of management for an important reason (§ 31 Co-determination Act; § 84, para 3 AktG)
3. Nomination of a member as chairman (and as deputy chairman of the board of management (§ 31 Co-determination Act; § 84, para 2 AktG)
4. Revocation of the nomination of the chairman of the board of management for a good reason (§ 31 Co-determination Act; § 84, para 3 AktG)
5. General supervision of the management (§ 25, para 1 Co-determination Act, § 111, para 1 AktG)
6. Resolutions to the effect that certain kinds of transactions may only be entered into with the consent of the supervisory board (§ 25, para 1 Co-determination Act; § 11, para 4, sentence 2 AktG)
7. Right to request conscientious and faithful reports from the board of management on the affairs of the association and its legal and business relations to connected enterprises which may have substantial influence upon the situation of the association (§ 25, para 1 Co-determination Act; § 90, para 3 and 4 AktG)
8. Examination of the annual financial statement, of the report of the management, of the proposal for the appropriation of the accumulated earnings and of the examination report by the auditors (§ 7 German Law on the Accounting by Major Enterprises; § 25, para 1 Co-determination Act; §§ 171, 314, para 2, 331, para 3, sentence 3 AktG)
9. Calling of the shareholders' meeting if the welfare of the enterprise requires it (§ 25, para 1 Co-determination Act; § 111, para 3 AktG)
10. Issuance of standing orders ("rules of business") for the supervisory board and - in the case of stock corporations - for the board of management (§ 77, para 2 AktG)

CHART 4

RIGHTS OF THE SUPERVISORY BOARD, WHICH ARE REFERRED TO COMMITTEES

1. Conclusion and cancellation of the contracts of employment with the members of the board of management (§ 25, para 1 Co-determination Act; § 112 AktG)[36]
2. Contracts with members of the supervisory board (§ 25, para 1 Co-determination Act; §§ 114, 115 AktG)
3. Single measures of supervision, inspection and examination of the books and records of the enterprise (§ 25, para 1 Co-determination Act; § 111, para 2 AktG)

CHART 5

THE RIGHTS OF THE INDIVIDUAL MEMBERS OF THE SUPERVISORY BOARD[37]

a) The rights of each member of the supervisory board within the supervisory board

1. Participation in the meetings of the supervisory board (§ 25, para 1 Co-determination Act; § 109, para 1 AktG)
2. Invitation to the meetings with the agenda and the preparatory documents for this meeting
3. The right to propose motions to the supervisory board
4. The right of two members to call the supervisory board (§ 25, para 1 Co-determination Act; § 110, para 2 AktG)
5. Adjournment of passing resolutions if the standing orders give this right
6. Motion for a renewed ballot on the same issue, if the first ballot has finished in a tie and the standing orders give this right to each member of the supervisory board
7. Participation of members of the supervisory board not belonging to the committees in the meetings of the committees if the chairman does not decide differently in the individual case (§ 25, para 1 Co-determination Act; § 109, para 2 AktG)
8. Distribution of the records of the meetings of the supervisory board (§ 25, para 1 Co-determination Act; § 107, para 2, sentence 3 AktG)

9. Distribution, at least acknowledgement of the reports of the board of management (§ 25, para 1, Co-determination Act; § 90, para 5 AktG)
10. Distribution, at least acknowledgement of the annual financial statement and of the examination report by the auditors (§ 170, para 3 AktG; § 7, German Law on the Accounting by Major Enterprises)

b) The right of two members of the supervisory board to request a report on the affairs of the enterprise and its relations to connected enterprises from the board of management (§ 25, para 1 Co-determination Act; § 90, para 3, sentence 2 AktG)

c) The rights of each member of the supervisory board as concerns the shareholders' meeting

1. Participation in the shareholders' meeting (§ 25, para 1 Co-determination Act; § 118, para 2 AktG)
2. Sending out of the preparatory documents concerning issues to be decided on by the shareholders' meeting (§ 25, para 1 Co-determination Act; § 125, para 3 AktG)
3. Sending out of the resolutions passed at the shareholders' meeting (§ 25, para 4 AktG)

CHART 6

ADDITIONAL RIGHTS OF THE INDIVIDUAL MEMBERS OF THE SUPERVISORY BOARD TO APPEAL TO A COURT IN THE FOLLOWING CASES:

1. Action for invalidation and for voidability of resolutions of the shareholders' meeting (§ 245, No. 5 AktG, applicable also to the company with limited liability)[40]
2. Action for invalidation of resolutions of the supervisory board[41]
3. Action for a judicial decision of the legal composition of the supervisory board (§ 6, para 2 Co-determination Act; § 98 para 2 No. 2 AktG)
4. Action for the appointment of an absent member of the supervisory board (§ 6, para 2 Co-determination Act; § 104 AktG)
5. Action for the appointment of an absent, but required member of the board of management (§ 31 Co-determination Act)

CHART 7

CLAIMS OF THE INDIVIDUAL MEMBERS OF THE SUPERVISORY BOARD AGAINST THE ENTERPRISE

1. Granting of compensation (emoluments) for the services (§ 25, para 1 Co-determination Act; §§ 113, 114 AktG)
2. Reimbursement of expenses (§§ 675, 670 BGB)[42]
3. Right to report to the voters[43]

For the appointment and removal of the members of the management board, the act lays down a multi-step procedure with declining majority requirements (§ 31 Co-determination Act). The supervisory board shall appoint the members of the board of management by a majority of at least two-thirds of the votes of its members on the first ballot. The chairman of the supervisory board can use his second vote after the second ballot only if it has resulted in a tie. But there is an additional intermediate step between the first and the second ballot. This involves the setting up of a special conference committee consisting of the chairman of the supervisory board, one member each of the board representing the employees (Figure 4). This committee, which must be constituted for every company after the election of the chairman of the supervisory board and his deputy, has to recommend to the supervisory board a candidate for appointment within a month from the first unsuccessful ballot. The appointment of a member of the board of management may be revoked by the supervisory council for an important reason. In particular a gross violation of duties, incapability of proper management or withdrawal of confidence by the shareholders constitutes such a reason (§ 84, para 3 German Stock Corporation Act).

Fig. 4 Committee of the supervisory board for the preparation of the appointment and removal of the board of management (§§ 27 para 3, 31 para 3 Co-determination Act)

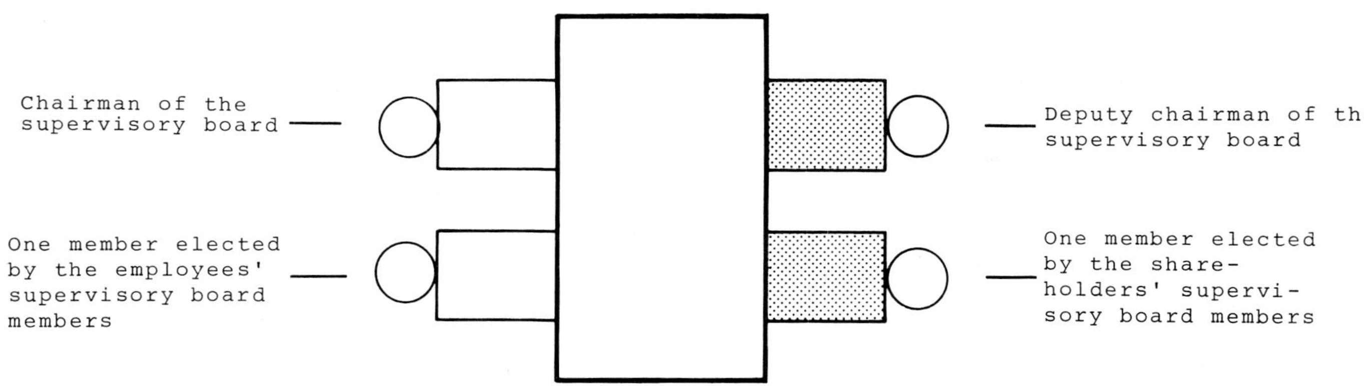

F. CONCLUSION: WORKER PARTICIPATION, WORKABILITY OF THE ENTERPRISES AND EFFICIENCY OF THE ECONOMY

The ideological and socio-political justifications of co-determination have been countered chiefly with the following six objections:[44]

1. The members of the board of management and those who shall become members in the future and their subordinate executives will, as regards their personal career, in future become dependent on the representatives from the labor side on the supervisory board because, in order to avoid becoming the focal point of conflicts, they will attach importance to unanimous re-election. For this reason aspects of efficiency and performance will, under certain circumstances, be neglected if these lead to conflicts with the representatives from the labor side.[45]
2. There is the danger that the obligation to show greater consideration towards the representatives from the labor side will weaken the negotiating position of employers during collective bargaining. The negotiators from the employers' side, in as far as they come from companies falling under the Co-determination Act, will perhaps offer less resistance to excessive demands in the belief that the company's competitiveness is adequately safeguarded - at least up to their own retirement. The members of the board of management like in principle to think about the future as long as that future covers the period of their own election and re-election, but not always further ahead than that. The representatives from the labor side on the other hand, especially those with Marxist training, think in substantially longer terms; for they want to create paradise on earth.
3. Innovation and rationalization investments, which are job-destructive and which cannot be combined with expansion investments in expanding departments, will probably become more difficult to implement; safeguarding jobs will become the dominating company objective in companies falling under the Co-determination Act, as long as the existence of the company as a whole is not endangered.[46] But the competitiveness of companies falling under the Co-determination Act will not only be adversely affected by the fact that it will be more difficult to adapt the number of employees at any drop in demand for their products.
4. Owing to these difficulties with which company managements are well acquainted - and this is the fourth objection - companies will not readily react to increased demand for their products by appointing more labor but will prefer to put up with longer delivery dates when production cannot meet increased demand despite overtime and shift work.

The unemployed and newcomers to the labor market will thus have less chance of finding a job. Parity co-determination can therefore be associated with the danger not only that technological structural change is impeded due to a lack of willingness to assume risks in R & D investments, but that adaption to changes in economic trend will not be carried out in time. Co-determination thus can reduce the dynamism of competitive market processes.[47]

5. There is at the same time the danger that companies falling under the Co-determination Act will screen themselves off from external market control[48], owing to the possibilities of collusion between capital and labor which are concentrated in such companies, and will, by exerting pressure on political channels, try to slip past the state's law on competition.[49]

6. It will be typical for the behavior of the representatives from the labor side on the supervisory board not to follow a policy which is differentiated according to the risk involved, but rather one of suitable return on equity. The definition of "suitable" will indicate a return roughly equal to the interest on borrowings. This policy will lead to less willingness on the part of investors to take greater risks in the form of pioneer investments, because the particularly high risk of losses in this field is not counterbalanced by correspondingly high profits. The state will then be compelled to an ever increasing extent to step in as a pioneer investor indirectly via research investments;[50] and in this way the market economy will increasingly be undermined.

Above all, trans-national companies with German subsidiaries will in future have greater difficulty in transferring if they themselves would wish those profits made to the amount of the risk taken in making the investment. If the profits made are higher than the average profit rates of German industry, the employees will object to a distribution of the profits unless they themselves are given an adequate share including higher fringe benefits. Representatives from the labor side never oppose the making of high profits; experience has shown that they motivate management to use market dominating positions at the consumers' expense if only to allow them to present their electors with higher remuneration and fringe benefits. They will therefore never oppose high profits but will oppose the distribution of those profits.[51]

These are the most frequent misgivings expressed by critics of co-determination on a parity basis. Whether these misgivings will prove to be correct in the future cannot be assessed with certainty at the present time. In the long term, I am afraid, the boards of companies will consist less of impatient, enterprising pioneer businessmen, and more of patient, friendly administrators who are keen on compromise, avoid making decisions involving high risks, and who are trained in political bureaucratic day-to-day business. Thus in the Federal Republic of Germany, the seats on the boards of large public companies and public banks are now often being occupied by civil servants and politicians instead of men with industrial backgrounds. The only hope thus remaining is that the technostructure below board level is adequately motivated in the long term and excellently trained, so that the company can be run well despite the deficiencies at board level.

To me it also seems probable that the boards of management in companies which are not effectively supervised by the shareholders will increasingly tend toward the labor side because they have to work together constantly within the company. Many shareholders, especially foreign shareholders, are far removed from the production line and are scarecely in any position to check the accuracy of many of the arguments put to them by the German management or by the representatives of the job-holders. They fear the risks of a "Germanization" of the supervisory board if they elect one, two, or three Germans as shareholders' representatives in the supervisory board. But even if it is not necessary, most multinational companies think that it is better to do so in order to reprehend and, if the occasion arises, to refuse arguments of the jobholders' representatives.

Looking at some of the prospects that could evolve from co-determination the best advice to give to shareholders is to develop a consistent strategy of clear entrepreneurial objectives towards the management of multinational groups of companies. Such management would pursue economic goals in recognition of the particular legal and social conditions prevailing at different company locations, whereas national management of local subsidiaries should have the autonomy to pursue the company's best interests as it sees fit.

Supervision would rest with the shareholders, and management must be aware that, regardless of the constraints imposed by more employee co-determination, shareholder interests will be respected. Failing this, multinationals are almost certain to follow the lead of large public corporations and a majority of large joint and open stock companies in West Germany, becoming institutions for the conservation of jobs, and showing a margin of profit only large enough to allow for some shareholder accruals to the loans and capital risk market.

NOTES

1. See v. Teuteberg, Geschichte der industriellen Mitbestimmung in Deutschland, 1961; Horn-Kocka, Law and the Formation of the Big Enterprises in the 19th and Early 20th Centuries. Studies in the History of the Industrialization in Germany, France, Great Britain, and the United States, 1979; Gamillscheg, Die Mitbestimmung der Arbeitnehmer. Eine Skizze der Anfänge, in: Liber Amicorum A.F. Schnitzler, 1979, pp. 101 et seq.

2. Act on the Joint Regulation in Working Life; see F. Schmidt, Die Reform des kollektiven Arbeitsrechts in Schweden, 1978, pp. 84 et seq.; Hanau, Gesetzliche und kollektivvertragliche Mitbestimmung in der Privatwirtschaft nach schwedischem Recht, in: Gamillscheg; Blanc; Jouvan; Davies; Hanau; Runggaldier; Summers, Mitbestimmung der Arbeitnehmer in Frankreich, Großbritannien, Schweden, Italien, den USA und der Bundesrepublik Deutschland, 1978, pp. 89 et seq.; Gärtner, Neue Formen der Mitbestimmung, in: (1978) Personal, pp. 71 et seq.; Birk, Die Reform des kollektiven Arbeitsrechts in Schweden, in: (1979) Arbeit und Recht, pp. 65 et seq.; Lind, Employee participation in Sweden, Employee relations, Vol. 1 No. 1 (1979), pp. 11 et seq.; Goldberg-Wolff, Verhandelte oder kodifizierte Mitbestimmung, DBW 40 (1980, pp. 205 et seq.; Asard, Employee participation in Sweden 1971-1979: The Issue of Economic Democracy, in: Economic and Industrial Democracy, Vol. 1 (1980), pp. 371-393; Victorin, Co-Determination in Sweden: The Union Way, in: Journal of Comparative Corporate Law and Securities Regulation 2 (1979), pp. 11-140; Myrdal, The Swedish Model - Will It Survive?, in: British Journal of Industrial Relations, Vol. XVIII (1980), pp. 57 et seq.

3. Act concerning Co-determination of Job-holders of May 4, 1976 (§ 41: "This act shall come into effect on July 1, 1976"). See Fitting; Wlotzke; Wissmann, Mitbestimmungsgesetz, 2nd ed., 1978; Fabricius, Gemeinschaftskommentar zum Mitbestimmungsgesetz, 1976; Hoffmann; Lehmann; Weinmann, Mitbestimmungsgesetz, 1978; Lux, Mitbestimmungsgesetz, 1977; Kittner; Fuchs; Zachert, Arbeitnehmervertreter im Aufsichtsrat, 1977; Bense, Mitbestimmungsgesetz 1976, 1978; Schneider-Kingsman, The German Co-determination Act, 1976; Furlong, Labor in the Boardroom, 1977, pp. 137 et seq.

4. Proposal for a "Statute for the European Company." Supplement to Bull. EC 4/75; Commission of the European Communities, Employee Participation and Company Structure in the European Community, Supplement to Bull. EC 8/75; see Kolvenbach, Employee Councils in European Companies, 1978,

pp. 37 et seq.; Ficker, Die europäische Entwicklung zu einem Aufsichtsratssystem für Großgesellschaften, in: Festschrift für J. Bärmann, 1975, pp. 299 et seq.; G. Schnoor, Arbeits- und sozialrechtliche Fragen der europäischen Integration, 1964, pp. 42 et seq.; H. Hofmann, Mitbestimmung der Arbeitnehmer in Gesellschaftsorganen und grenzüberschreitende Unternehmenszusammenschlüsse in der Europäischen Gemeinschaft, Diss. Bonn 1976; Pipkorn, Integrationswirkungen einer transnationalen Regelung der wirtschaftlichen Mitbestimmung im Statut für Europäische Aktiengesellschaften, in: (1977) Schweizerische Aktiengesellschaft, pp. 37 et seq.; Pipkorn, The Legal Framework of Employee Participation Methods at National and International Level and Particularly within the European Community, in: Economic and Industrial Democracy, Vol. 1 (1980), pp. 99-123; Constas, The Developing European Community Law.

5. See Runggaldier; Säcker; Wachter, Das italienische Arbeitnehmerstatut, 1978, Zeitschrift für Arbeitsrecht, pp. 387 et seq.; Runggaldier, Fragen der betrieblichen Arbeitnehmervertretung in Italien, in: Gamillscheg; Blanc; Jouvan; Davies; Hanau; Runggaldier; Summers, Mitbestimmung der Arbeitnehmer in Frankreich, Großbritannien, Schweden, Italien, den USA und der Bundesrepublik Deutschland, 1978, pp. 123 et seq.; Freni-Guigni, Lo statuto dei lavoratori, 1971, pp. 81 et seq.

6. See Leistner, Die französische Aktiengesellschaft mit Beteiligung der Arbeitnehmer - ein soziales Experiment, in: (1976) Die Aktiengesellschaft, pp. 122 et seq.; Blanc-Jouvan, La participation des travailleurs à la gestion des entreprises en droit français, in: Gamillscheg; Blanc; Jouvan; Davies; Hanau; Runggaldier; Summers, Mitbestimmung der Arbeitnehmer in Frankreich, Großbritannien, Schweden, Italien, den USA und der Bundesrepublik Deutschland, 1978, pp. 33 et seq.; Leminsky, Entwicklung und Formen der Mitbestimmung in einigen westeuropäischen Ländern, in: Vom Sozialistengesetz zur Mitbestimmung, Zum 100. Geburtstag von Hans Böckler, 1975, pp. 427, 441 et seq.; Simon-Wieczorek, Die Stellung des Arbeitnehmers in der Unternehmensreform in Frankreich, in: Recht der Internationalen Wirtschaft, 1975, pp. 409 et seq.

7. Lecher, Gewerkschaftsvertreter und -politik in Großbritannien, in: (1977) WSI-Mitteilungen, pp. 443 et seq.; Davies, Co-determination by Workers of Decisions at Plant and Enterprise Level in the U.K., in: Gamillscheg; Blanc; Jouvan; Davies; Hanau; Runggaldier; Summers, Mitbestimmung der Arbeitnehmer in Frankreich, Großbritannien, Schweden, Italien, den USA und der Bundesrepublik Deutschland, 1978, pp. 61 et seq.; Kahn-Freund, Industrial Democracy, in: (1977) The Industrial Law Journal, pp. 65 et seq.; Kuda,

Arbeitnehmerkontrolle in Großbritannien. Theorie und Praxis, 1970, pp. 156 et seq.; Batstone; Boraston; Frenkel, Shop Stewards in Action, 1977; Ward-Fraser, Workers and Employers - Documents on Trade Unions and Industrial Relations in Britain Since the Eighteen Century, London 1980; Sorge-Warner, Manpower Training, Manufacturing Organisation and Workplace Relations in Great Britain and West Germany, in: British Journal of Industrial Relations, Vol. XVIII, 1980, pp. 318 et seq.; Reilly, Participation, Democracy and Control Forms of Employee Involvement, in: Management Survey Report No. 45, British Institute of Management Foundation; Hay-Morris, Industrial Economics, Theory and Evidence, Oxford 1979; Loveridge, What is Participation? A Review of the Literature and Some Methodological Problems, in: British Journal of Industrial Relations, Vol. XVIII, 1980, pp. 297 et seq.; Davies, The Bullock Report and Employee Participation in Corporate Planning in the U.K.; in: Journal of Comparative Corporate Law and Securities Regulation (1978), pp. 245-272; Thomson, Trade Unions and the Corporate State in Britain, in: Industrial and Labor Relations Review, Vol. 33, No. 1, pp. 36 et seq.; Roberts, Towards Industrial Democracy: Europe, Japan and the United States, London 1979.

8. See Summers, Worker Participation in the United States and the Federal Republic: A comparative Study from an American Perspective, in: (1979) Recht der Arbeit, pp. 257 et seq.

9. See for instance Institut für Marxistische Studien und Forschung, Mitbestimmung als Kampfaufgabe, 1971, pp. 91, 304 et seq.; Gugelberger, Kritik bürgerlicher Mitbestimmungskonzeptionen, in: (1974) Sozialistische Politik, pp. 2 et seq.; Dötz-Premssler, Zur Funktion und Praxis sogenannter Mitbestimmungsmodelle in der BRD, in: (1974) Neue Justiz, pp. 492 et seq.; Deppe; Jung; Schäfer, Welche Ziele verfolgen die Empfehlungen der "Biedenkopf-Kommission"?, Informationsbericht Nr. 4/1970.

10. See Triesch-Stahn, Mitbestimmung in der Diskussion, Vol. III, 1969; F. Böhm, Mitbestimmung als Gleichberechtigung von Kapital und Arbeit oder als Vertragsanspruch der Arbeitnehmer aus dem Arbeitsverhältnis, in: Böhm-Briefs, Mitbestimmung - Ordnungselement oder politischer Kompromiß, 1971, pp. 206 et seq.; Werner, Unternehmensverfassung in einer marktwirtschaftlichen Ordnung, in: (1975) Wirtschaft und Wettbewerb, pp. 179 et seq.

11. See Deutscher Gewerkschaftsbund, Mitbestimmung - eine Forderung unserer Zeit, 1971, p. 11; H.O. Vetter, Gewerkschaften und Mitbestimmung in der sozialstaatlichen Demokratie, in: (1975) Das Mitbestimmungsgespräch, pp. 145 et seq.;

O. Brenner, Perspektiven der deutschen Mitbestimmung, Arbeitsheft 226 der Industriegewerkschaft Metall, 1972; Gewerkschaften und Mitbestimmung. Ein Referentenleitfaden aus dem Curriculum-Projekt "Mitbestimmung und politische Bildung" des DGB mit Vorwort von Vetter, 1977, pp. 280 et seq.

12. See to this problem Biedenkopf, Auswirkungen der Unternehmensverfassung auf die Grenzen der Tarifautonomie, in: Festgabe für Kronstein, 1967, pp. 79 et seq.; Hanau, Eigentum und Tarifautonomie in den Gutachten zu den Verfassungsklagen gegen das Mitbestimmungsgesetz 1976, in: (1978) Betriebs-Berater, pp. 1593 et seq.; Zöllner-Seiter, Paritätische Mitbestimmung und Art. 9 Abs. 3 Grundgesetz, 1970, pp. 22 et seq.; Säcker, Die Institutions- und Betätigungsgarantie der Koalitionen im Rahmen der Grundrechtsordnung, in: Das Arbeitsrecht der Gegenwart, ed. G. Müller, Vol. 12 (1975), pp. 17, 46 et seq.; Badura; Rittner; Rüthers, Mitbestimmungsgesetz 1976 und Grundgesetz, 1977, pp. 154 et seq.; Kübler; Simitis; Schmidt, Mitbestimmung als gesetzgebungspolitische Aufgabe, 1978, pp. 209 et seq.

13. See Krause, Der deutschrechtliche Anteil an der heutigen Privatrechtsordnung, in: (1970) Juristische Schulung, pp. 318 et seq.; Säcker, Gruppenautonomie und Übermachtkontrolle im Arbeitsrecht, 1972, pp. 7 et seq.; Scheuner, Staatliche Verbandsbildung und Verbandsaufsicht in Deutschland im 19. Jahrhundert, 1978, Der Staat, Beiheft 2, pp. 97 et seq.; E.R. Huber, Deutsche Verfassungsgeschichte, Vol. V, 1978, pp. 768 et seq.; F. Neumann, Koalitionsfreiheit und Reichsverfassung, 1932, pp. 3 et seq.; Brütt, Das Koalitionsrecht der Arbeiter in Deutschland und seine Reformbedürftigkeit, 1903, pp. 262 et seq.

14. See Säcker-Joost, Betriebszugehörigkeit als Rechtsproblem im Betriebsverfassungs- und Mitbestimmungsrecht, 1979.

15. See Hueck; Nipperdey; Säcker, Lehrbuch des Arbeitsrechts, Vol. II/2, 7th ed., 1970, pp. 1066, 1485 et seq.

16. See Fitting-Auffarth, Betriebsverfassungsgesetz, 12th ed., 1977; Dietz-Richardi, Betriebsverfassungsgesetz, 5th ed., 1973; Galperin-Löwisch, Betriebsverfassungsgesetz, 5th ed., 1975/76; Kammann; Hess; Schlochauer, Betriebsverfassungsgesetz, 3rd ed., 1978; Weiss, Betriebsverfassungsgesetz, 1978; Sahmer, Betriebsverfassungsgesetz, 1978; Brecht, Betriebsverfassungsgesetz, 1972; Peltzer-Boer, Betriebsverfassungsgesetz, Labor Management Relations Act, 2nd ed., 1977; The rights of co-determination in social matters are enumerated in § 87 of the Betriebsverfassungsgesetz (see for instance Wiese, Das Initiativrecht nach dem Betriebsverfassungsgesetz, 1977). The rights in personnel matters are enumerated in §§ 92-104 of the Betriebsver-

fassungsgesetz (see Rummel, Wirkungstendenzen der Mitbestimmung des Betriebsrats bei personellen Entscheidungen, Diss. Mannheim 1977). The rights in economic matters are enumerated in §§ 106-113 of the Betriebsverfassungsgesetz (see Gege, Die Funktion des Wirtschaftsausschusses im Rahmen der wirtschaftlichen Mitbestimmung, 1977; Fritsch, Die Ausgestaltung von Sozialplänen, eine rechtstatsächliche Untersuchung, Diss. Bochum 1976; Ohl, Der Sozialplan. Recht und Praxis kompensatorischer Leistungen für den Verlust des Arbeitsplatzes, 1977; Fuchs; Der Sozialplan nach dem Betriebsverfassungsgesetz 1972, 1977; Kaven, Das Recht des Sozialplans, 1977). The individual jobholders' rights of participation and complaint are enumerated in §§ 75, 81-86 of the Betriebsverfassungsgesetz (see Niederalt, Die Individualrechte des Arbeitnehmers nach dem Betriebsverfassungsgesetz 1976).

17. See Federal Labor Court, Kassel, ruling of May 22, 1979, in: (1980) Neue Juristische Wochenschrift, pp. 83 et seq.

18. See Council Directive of February 14, 1977, 77/187/EEC.

19. Report of the Committee of Inquiry on Industrial Democracy (Bullock Report) London 1977, pp. 20 et seq. (For a critique see Prentice, Employee Participation in Corporate Government, in: (1978) The Canadian Bar Review, pp. 277 et seq.); Bericht der Sachverständigenkommission zur Auswertung der bisherigen Erfahrungen bei der Mitbestimmung (Biedenkopf-Bericht), 1970, pp. 34 et seq.

20. Bullock Report, pp. 22; Biedenkopf-Bericht, pp. 32 et seq.

21. Bullock Report, pp. 27; Biedenkopf-Bericht, pp. 29 et seq.

22. See (1979) Der Betrieb, pp. 593 et seq.

23. Biedenkopf-Bericht, pp. 99 et seq.

24. See for instance O. Kunze, Mitbestimmung in der Wirtschaft und Eigentumsordnung, in: (1972) Recht der Arbeit, pp. 257, 265 et seq., and Wirtschaftliche Mitbestimmung als Legitimationsproblem, 1970, pp. 18 et seq.; Farthmann, Mitbestimmung und Systemänderung, in: (1974) Merkur, pp.969 et seq.

25. See Lutter, Information und Vertraulichkeit im Aufsichtsrat, 1979, pp. 55 et seq.

26. Rapport du comité d'étude pour la reform de l'entreprise (Rapport Sudreau), Paris 1975, pp. 106 et seq.

27. See International Labour Organisation, Tripartite Declaration of Principles Concerning Multinational Enterprises and Social Policy, 1977, pp. 11 et seq.; Organisation for Economic Co-operation and Development. Committee of Experts on Restrictive Business Practices of Multinational Enterprises, Paris 1977, pp. 66 et seq.; Kukat, Verhaltenscodices für multinationale Unternehmen, in: (1979) Recht der Internationalen Wirtschaft, pp. 293 et seq.

28. See to this point Druey, Geheimsphäre des Unternehmens, 1977; Säcker, Informationsrechte der Betriebs- und Aufsichtsratsmitglieder und Geheimsphäre des Unternehmens, 1979, p. 14.

29. See Raiser, Unternehmensinteresse, in: (1976) Festschrift für R. Schmidt, pp. 101 et seq.; Raisch, Unternehmensinteressen, in: (1976) Festschrift Hefermehl, pp. 347 et seq.; R. Hoffmann, Das Unternehmenswohl bei den mitbestimmten Unternehmen und die angemessene Berücksichtigung der Belange des Betriebs und der Arbeitnehmer im Betriebsverfassungsgesetz, in: G. Müller, Das Arbeitsrecht der Gegenwart, Vol. 15 (1978), pp. 38 et seq.; Mertens, Zuständigkeiten des mitbestimmten Aufsichtsrates, in: (1977) Zeitschrift für Unternehmens- und Gesellschaftsrecht, pp. 270, 275 et seq.; Junge, Das Unternehmensinteresse, in: (1978) Festschrift E.v. Caemmerer, pp. 547 et seq.; Kittner, Unternehmensverfassung und Information, in: (1972) Zeitschrift für Handels- und Wirtschaftsrecht, pp. 208, 226 et seq.

30. (1979) Der Betrieb, pp. 593, 594, 595, 597, 600. The Federal Constitutional Court has confirmed the prevailing opinion with its decision; see Säcker, Anpassung von Satzungen und Geschäftsordnungen an das Mitbestimmungsgesetz 1976, 1977, pp. 73 et seq.

31. (1979) Der Betrieb, pp. 593, 598; Säcker, Anpassung von Satzungen und Geschäftsordnungen an das Mitbestimmungsgesetz 1976, 1977, pp. 30 et seq.; Mertens, Allgemeine Grundsätze zur Anwendbarkeit des Mitbestimmungsgesetzes, in: (1976) Die Aktiengesellschaft, pp. 113, 119; Hommelhoff, Unternehmensführung in der mitbestimmten GmbH, in: (1978) Zeitschrift für Unternehmens- und Gesellschaftsrecht, pp. 119 et seq.; Wiedemann, Aufgaben und Grenzen der unternehmerischen Mitbestimmung der Arbeitnehmer, in: (1978), Betriebs-Berater, pp. 5 et seq.; Baumann, GmbH und Mitbestimmung, in: (1978) 142, Zeitschrift für Handels- und Wirtschaftsrecht, pp. 537, 565 et seq.

For the opposite view see Reuter-Körnig, Mitbestimmung und gesellschaftsrechtliche Gestaltungsfreiheit, in: (1976) Zeitschrift für Handels- und Wirtschaftsrecht, pp. 494 et seq.; Vollmer, Die mitbestimmte GmbH - gesetzliches Normalstatut, mitbestimmungsrechtliche Satzungsgestaltung und gesellschaftsrechtlicher Minderheitenschutz, in: (1979) Zeitschrift für Unternehmens- und Gesellschaftsrecht, pp. 135, 143 et seq.; Naendrup, Mitbestimmungsgesetz und Organisationsfreiheit, in: (1977) Arbeit und Recht, pp. 225, 268, 271 et seq.; Reich-Lewerenz, Das neue Mitbestimmungsgesetz, in: (1976) Arbeit und Recht, pp. 261, 272 et seq.

32. See note 29. The best interests of the company are not necessarily those of the shareholders'; see Federal Constitutional Court, in: (1979) Der Betrieb, pp. 593, 602.

33. See Säcker, Die Wahlordnungen zum Mitbestimmungsgesetz, 1978, pp. 44 et seq.

34. Bundesgerichtshof, in: (1976) Juristenzeitung, p. 408; Ihde, Der faktische GmbH-Konzern, 1974, pp. 58 et seq.; Martens, Die Auswirkungen der erweiterten Mitbestimmung auf die Konzernpraxis, in: Der GmbH-Konzern, 1976, pp. 108, 118 et seq.; Wiedemann, Die Bedeutung der ITT-Entscheidung, in: (1976) Juristenzeitung, pp. 392 et seq.; Langen, Zur Haftung eines herrschenden Unternehmens aus erteilter Weisung, in: (1977) Der Betrieb, pp. 151 et seq.; Emmerich-Sonnenschein, Konzernrecht, 2nd ed., 1977, pp. 203 et seq.; Scholz-Emmerich, Kommentar zum GmbH-Gesetz, 6th ed., 1978 Appendix II, notes 95 et seq.; E. Rehbinder, Konzernaußenrecht und allgemeines Privatrecht, 1969, pp. 384, 449 et seq.; K. Müller, Die Haftung der Muttergesellschaft für die Verbindlichkeiten der Tochtergesellschaft im Aktienrecht, in: (1977) Zeitschrift für Unternehmens- und Gesellschaftsrecht, pp. 1, 24 et seq.; Stahl, Das Verbot der Benachteiligung abhängiger Aktiengesellschaften, Diss. Freiburg, 1972, pp. 38 et seq.

35. See Säcker, Die Rechte des einzelnen Aufsichtsratsmitglieds, in: (1979) Neue Juristische Wochenschrift, pp. 1521 et seq.

36. See Martens, Paritätische Mitbestimmung und Aufsichtsratssystem, in: (1973) Betriebs-Berater, pp. 118, 1132; Hölters, Die zustimmungspflichtigen Geschäftsführungsmaßnahmen im Spannungsfeld zwischen Satzungs- und Aufsichtsratsautonomie, in: (1978) Betriebs-Berater, pp. 640 et seq.; Mertens, Zuständigkeiten des mitbestimmten Aufsichtsrates, in: (1977) Zeitschrift für Unternehmens- und Gesellschaftsrecht, pp. 270, 280 et seq.; Säcker, Anpassung von Satzungen und Geschäftsordnungen an das Mitbestimmungsgesetz 1976, 1977, pp. 38 et seq.

37. See Säcker, Anpassung von Satzungen und Geschäftsordnungen an das Mitbestimmungsgesetz 1976, 1977, pp. 34 et seq. For the opposite view concerning limited liability companies see Rittner, Die Anstellungsverträge der GmbH-Geschäftsführer nach dem Mitbestimmungsgesetz, in: (1979) Der Betrieb, pp. 973 et seq.; Werner, Anstellung von GmbH-Geschäftsführern nach dem Mitbestimmungsgesetz, in: Festschrift R. Fischer, 1979, pp. 822 et seq.

38. See Säcker, Die Rechte des einzelnen Aufsichtsratsmitgliedes, in: (1979) Neue Juristische Wochenschrift, pp. 1521 et seq.

39. See note 38.

40. See note 38; Lewerenz, Leistungsklagen zwischen Organen und Organmitgliedern der Aktiengesellschaft, 1977; K. Schmidt, Insichprozesse durch Leistungsklagen in der Aktiengesellschaft, in: (1979) Zeitschrift für Zivilprozeßrecht, pp. 212 et seq.

41. See Reichsgericht (166) RGZ, pp. 129, 131; Bundesgerichtshof (11) BGHZ 231; Immenga, Die Problematik der Anfechtungsklage im GmbH-Recht, in: (1973) GmbH-Rundschau, pp. 5 et seq.

42. See Naendrup, in: Gemeinschaftskommentar zum Mitbestimmungsgesetz, § 25, pp. 81 et seq.

43. See Säcker, Vorkehrungen zum Schutz der gesetzlichen Verschwiegenheitspflicht und gesellschaftsrechtliche Treuepflicht der Aufsichtsratsmitglieder, in: (1979) Festschrift R. Fischer, pp. 635 et seq.

44. See Säcker, Informationsrechte der Betriebs- und Aufsichtsratsmitglieder, 1979, pp. 58 et seq.

45. See Prosi, Volkswirtschaftliche Auswirkungen des Mitbestimmungsgesetzes 1976, 1978; Ortlieb, Mitbestimmung in unserer arbeitsteiligen Leistungsgesellschaft, in: Meves-Ortlieb, Macht Gleichheit glücklich?, 1978, pp. 63 et seq.; Büschges, Wirtschaftliche Mitbestimmung der Arbeitnehmer im Unternehmen und soziale Marktwirtschaft, in: Festschrift R. König, 1973, pp. 515 et seq.; Werth, Mitbestimmung - Deutsche Reformpolitik auf falschen Wegen, 1973, pp. 76 et seq.

For the opposite view see Hensch, Die Bedeutung von Mitbestimmung und Selbstbestimmung am Arbeitsplatz für die Willensbildung im Unternehmen, in: Die Bedeutung gesellschaftlicher Veränderungen für die Willensbildung im Unternehmen, Schriften des Vereins für Sozialpolitik 1976, pp. 411 et seq.; Küller, Mitbestimmung und Betriebswirtschaftslehre, in: (1975) BFuP pp. 26 et seq.; Hax, Mitbestimmung der Arbeitnehmer, in: Festschrift für C. Schmid,

1972, pp. 212, 223 et seq.; M. Schneider, Unternehmer und soziale Demokratie, in: (1973) Archiv für Sozialgeschichte, pp. 243 et seq.; Hemmer-Borsdorf, "Gewerkschaftsstaat" - Zur Vorgeschichte eines aktuellen Schlagworts, in: (1974) Gewerkschaftliche Monatshefte, pp. 640 et seq.

46. See note 45 and Poole, Industrial Democracy and Managers. An Explanatory and Critical Perspective, in: The Journal of Industrial Relations 22 (1980): 54 et seq.

47. See note 45 and Inhoffen, Die Entlassung von Arbeitnehmern in der mitbestimmten Unternehmung (1979), pp. 136 et seq.

48. See Gäbler, Participation and the Working of the Price Mechanism in a Market Economy, in: Heathfield, The Economics of Co-determination, pp. 46 et seq.; Albach, Steigende Verschuldung und sinkende Eigenkapitalrentabilität deutscher Unternehmen - Das Investitionsklima in der Bundesrepublik Deutschland, in: (1979) Die Aktiengesellschaft, pp. 121 et seq.

49. See Watrin, The principles of the social market economy - its origins and early history, in: (1979), ZgO, pp. 405 et seq.; Guest-Knight, Putting Participation into Practice (1979), pp. 309 et seq.

50. See Brockhoff, Zur Entwicklung der realen Forschungs- und Entwicklungsaufwendungen der industriellen Unternehmen, in: (1977) Der Betrieb, pp. 2280 et seq.

51. See Prosi, Volkswirtschaftliche Auswirkungen des Mitbestimmungsgesetzes, 1976, pp. 33 et seq.

For the opposite view see Krell, Mitbestimmung und Marktwirtschaftsordnung, in: Mitbestimmungs- und Wirtschaftspolitik, ed. Nemetz-Becker, 1967, pp. 119 et seq.

C. Industrial Democracy and Quality of Worklife

The Co-Determination and Quality of Work Life Movements Compared

Donald V. Nightingale

Co-determination and quality of work life have emerged as the two predominant strategies in the industrialized western nations for addressing the human problems faced by the modern work organization. This paper explores these two movements and shows how each arose from its political and cultural context. In particular, the role of ideology and trade unions in shaping the goals and strategies of the two movements is examined.

The decade of the 1970's witnessed the emergence of two significant initiatives in Western industrialized nations which will have profound effects on the lives of working people. The two initiatives -- co-determination and quality of work life -- are similar in many respects, but each is uniquely tailored to the political, economic and cultural environments from which it arose. Although both co-determination and quality of work life have enjoyed remarkable success and widespread support in a rather short period of time, considerable controversy rages over the capability of each to address the problems of the modern work organization.

The terms "co-determination" and "quality of work life" are general labels which subsume a variety of forms. Academics, politicians, employers, trade unionists, and journalists have used these terms to cover a wide variety of specific organizational forms. These forms differ in ideological depth, and they have been advanced by groups with differing political and economic interests.

Co-determination is a uniquely European phenomenon; quality of work life has its theoretical and empirical origins in Europe (England and Norway), but, nevertheless, it has been embraced by North Americans as their strategy for meeting the challenges posed by the modern work organization.

There are social, cultural, political and economic conditions which have shaped the co-determination movement in Europe and the quality of work life initiatives in North America. This paper will examine co-determination and quality of work life as products of their respective environments and will, in the process, analyze the similarities, dissimilarities and prospects of each.

CO-DETERMINATION

The term, "co-determination" has assumed a great variety of meanings. Co-determination is called "medbestammuncke" in Sweden, "mitbestimmung" in Germany, and "cogestion" in France. In general, it refers to a form of industrial democracy in which worker representatives serve on the senior management boards of industrial companies. Some, but not all forms of co-determination allow full voting rights of worker representatives on the Boards. Some forms of co-determination allow parity (or near parity) representation of shareholder and employee interests.

By and large, co-determination has been supported by left-of-centre political interests; nevertheless, the proponents of co-determination have argued from a wide diversity of perspectives. Among these perspectives are the following:

(a) co-determination is the first step in the direction of ultimate worker control of the enterprise;

(b) co-determination is a means of extending democratic practices found in the society's political institutions to the workplace;

(c) co-determination will improve the quality of corporate decisions by involving a wide set of interests and perspectives in the decision making process;

(d) co-determination will improve labour-management communications and remove sources of misunderstanding.

Some form of co-determination is found in the Federal Republic of Germany, Sweden, Denmark, Norway, Austria, and the Netherlands. Co-determination is not found in England, France, Italy, or Belgium. In England, the Bullock Committee Report recommended a program of co-determination but the report was tabled because of employer and trade union opposition.[1] In France, the Sudreau Report recommended a form of co-determination but it too was opposed by labour and employer interests.

While the legislation governing co-determination in most western European countries carefully delimits the sectors and the size of companies in which co-determination is mandatory, the following regulations apply:

Austria - a 1973 statute requires that 1/3 of Board represent employees;

Denmark - a 1973 statute requires two employee representatives on the Board;

Netherlands - a 1973 law made Supervisory Boards mandatory; members were to be "co-opted" by the Board from a list of nominees to represent shareholders and employees;

Norway - a 1971 law requires that 1/3 of Board members (a minimum of two members) are to represent worker interests; a "company assembly" with 1/3 worker representatives must approve major employment decisions;

Sweden - statutes in 1972 and 1976 require two worker representatives on the Board;

Federal Republic of Germany - statutes in 1947, 1951 and 1976 require parity representation of employee and shareholder interests on Boards;

Luxembourg - 1/3 of the members of a council of administration represent employees.

The Common Market Fifth Directive of 1972 recommended (but did not mandate) that the two-tier board structure be introduced in member countries and that worker representatives participate on the supervisory boards.

An interesting historical curiosity is the manner in which co-determination was first introduced in Europe. The co-determination model was imposed on Germany by the British occupational forces. The purpose was to prevent the re-emergence of concentrations of power in the hands of industrialists. Although co-determination has worked well in Germany and although Germany has enjoyed a remarkably stable and positive labour-management relationship in the post-war era, England has not accepted this model and does not appear likely to do so in the near future.

QUALITY OF WORK LIFE

The term "quality of work life" was first used by Albert Cherns at the Arden House Conference in 1972. Cherns viewed the term as a metaphor, a neutral label in place of the more evocative term, "industrial democracy." The strategy was brilliantly successful. While the labels, "industrial democracy", "power sharing", "humanization of work", "self-management" and "co-determination" were acceptable to neither management nor labour in North America, the term, "quality of work life" touched a responsive chord and gained immediate popularity.

North American management looked with disbelief upon the spread of democratic decision-making structures in large European organizations. From the pluralist and libertarian perspective of North America, the innovations in democratic practices emerging in Europe in the 1970's were regarded as dangerous intrusions into the domain of management and shareholder rights.

Furthermore, North American trade unionists (unlike their European counterparts) cannot support co-determination. Each generation of trade union leaders remembers the struggles and hardships of the past. Cooperation and joint problem solving at the board level is entirely alien to North American trade unionists. They fear co-optation by management and suspect that union representatives on boards of directors would be outnumbered and overwhelmed by management and shareholder interests.

Trade unions in North America are not so powerful or secure as their counterparts in Europe. In the face of stagnant or declining membership and fierce management opposition to relatively mild reforms (such as the Labor Reform Act of 1979), many trade unionists in North America are suspicious of sweeping legislative initiatives which may jeopardize the trade union movement. For them, the protection and enhancement of their member's interests are best secured through an adversarial, not a collaborative relationship with management.

In this environment, the modest, ad hoc, and particularistic reforms proposed by quality of work life advocates are more palatable than the sweeping statutory reforms favoured in Western Europe.

For their part, North American managers strongly oppose the principle of involving unions or workers directly on Boards of Directors. Even the appointment of Douglas Fraser to the Board of Directors of the Chrysler Corporation has received near universal condemnation in the American business press. We are a long way in North America from accepting the parity co-determination programs of Western Europe.

The North American system of collective bargaining is irretrievably adversarial. This system is believed by most North American trade unionists to be the most effective means of protecting the interests of their members. The changes to this system that are envisioned include only relatively modest adjustments designed to strengthen the hand of one side or the other. Trade unionists in Canada and the United States are unwilling to embark upon a program of substantial change in the distribution of power which might significantly weaken their ability to protect their members' interests.

The popularity of quality of work life is the result of the confluence of several events; the seminal theoretical work of Trist and Emery; the inspired and creative experimentation of Thorsrud and Walton; and pressing labour relations and human resource problems at the workplace which have provided fertile ground for the new initiatives. However, while innovations and experiments continue at an accelerating pace, it appears that the QWL movement in North America is theoretically and intellectually running down. We may very soon see that practice begins to drive theory rather than the reverse, as we have seen over the past decade.

CO-DETERMINATION AND QUALITY OF WORK LIFE COMPARED

Both co-determination and quality of work life are forms of "industrial democracy". Both co-determination and quality of work life are endeavours designed to address the new and increasingly intractable problems created by an educated and demanding work force. Both endeavours are designed to reform the workplace and its methods of management and work. Both strategies are fundamentally conservative -- that is, they are designed to preserve the present system by introducing incremental adjustments which will ultimately have the effect of diffusing demands for more substantial change.

While the notion that co-determination is designed to preserve existing institutional arrangements may sound strange to most North Americans, the evidence suggests that co-determination has had a stabilizing influence in those countries which have adopted it. Two of the countries in Europe with no provision for co-determination and little or no current interest in "industrial democracy" -- France and Italy -- have the strongest communist parties in Europe. England, which is hopelessly mired in bitter class and labour-management confrontations, faces an uncertain economic future. The most buoyant economies of Western Europe -- West Germany, Sweden and Holland -- have the strongest co-determination laws.

Co-determination and quality of work life differ in many fundamental and important respects. In fact, the difference between the two initiatives is great and neither can substitute for or replace the other.

Ideology

Perhaps the most fundamental difference between the two centres on ideological underpinnings. The co-determination movement in Europe is the product of left-of-centre political interests and is regarded (although not universally) as an evolutionary step toward eventual worker control. Co-determination has been the product of social democratic political parties; but it has also (to a large extent) been union inspired, and unions have been the main beneficiaries of co-determination laws.

The quality of work life movement in North America is widely regarded as a means of diffusing labour militancy and of deflecting demands for more substantial changes in the way organizations are managed.

Co-determination is a politically-based initiative to change the system of governance of work organizations. Quality of work life is not a matter of political doctrine; it is a matter of organizational policy.

The philosophical rationale underlying co-determination is not inconsistent with prevailing notions of distributive justice, and removal of elites and concentrations of power. Quality of work life, on the other hand, finds its theoretical rationale in socio-technical design. Quality of work life is justified not as a plank in a broad political platform, but as a cost-effective approach to labour peace and higher productivity.

Co-determination has become a matter of political doctrine in Europe. The government is an important party in the promulgation of co-determination laws. In North America, on the other hand, quality of work life has been largely independent of government initiatives. It remains exclusively an issue of management strategy (e.g., the Dana Corporation, General Motors, Proctor & Gamble). Consequently, quality of work life has been ad hoc and particularistic, there are few uniform practices -- even within companies which have adopted quality of work life as a matter of organizational policy. For example, within Proctor & Gamble, plants differ from one another -- improvements are constantly made and each new plant endeavours to improve upon the innovations introduced in the most recent plant.

Why have European workers and trade unionists looked to the political and governmental spheres to improve their lot while North American workers have not? The reason centres on the class consciousness of European workers and the social caste system of European management. In Europe there is a centuries-old conviction among the working class that the only recourse of the underprivileged is the government (parliament, duke, or king) and that social justice and social improvements come through government edict and not through the efforts of individuals or of trade unions.

The differences between co-determination and quality of work life are deeply embedded in political and cultural differences between Europe and North America. In North America (especially in the United States) we celebrate the values of individualism, personal liberty, and individual responsibility. The doctrines of classical liberalism dominate our thinking about the workplace and our political institutions. The individual is viewed as the singular unit of society, and society's institutions are designed to enhance and protect personal freedoms. This ethic pervades society and shapes the perceptions and actions of all its institutions, including work organizations. North Americans are resentful of government intrusion in their lives (again, this statement applies more to Americans than to Canadians). In this cultural environment, changes, when they must be made, tend to be more pragmatic, individualistic, and incremental.

Role of Trade Unions

Co-determination reinforces and strengthens trade unions. Although trade unions can be and have been involved in many quality of work life initiatives in North America, most quality of work life initiatives have been designed to weaken the appeal of trade unions or to reduce the threat of unionization. Quality of work life can be used to weaken unions while it can also provide opportunities for improvements in work life that cannot be attained through collective bargaining; North American trade unionists are consequently placed in a difficult position. They cannot easily oppose initiatives which would improve the conditions of work of their members; nevertheless, many know that the trade union movement and their unions in particular may be weakened by widespread adoption of quality of work life initiatives. Trade unionists in North America are currently seeking ways in which they can be effective partners with management and thereby take some of the credit for the new initiatives.

Many North American trade unionists now recognize that quality of work life initiatives -- in one form or another -- will gain in popularity. Trade unions cannot continue to oppose quality of work life without jeopardizing the appeal of trade unionism to working people. Trade unionists must search for an effective role without compromising their ideals and without jeopardizing their members' interests. The extent to which quality of work life initiatives will gain the support of Canadian and American trade unionists is difficult to predict. American trade unionists, who have always taken a "more bread and butter" approach to collective bargaining than their Canadian counterparts, seem more willing to embrace the principles of quality of work life and to risk the dangers that this strategy entails.

The concentrations of economic and political power which have emerged from the co-determination movement in Europe has frightened many trade unionists in North America. In Canada and the United States, the autonomy of the union local is carefully protected. Local trade union leaders jealously guard their power and protect their jurisdictions from interference by the national or international officials. Collective agreements and labour policy in North America are made, by and large, at tens of thousands of bargaining tables; the prospect of the introduction of centralized bargaining is not particularly appealing to North American trade unionists.

Co-determination is consistent with the "social unionism" of European trade unions. The quality of work life movement in North America is more consistent with the "job unionism" of Canadian and American unions. In North America there is a deep commitment to collective bargaining between "equals" and adversarial relations are deeply embedded in the North American system.

Source of Change

As mentioned earlier, co-determination has been initiated by labour in Europe; co-determination has been accepted reluctantly by management as a price for labour peace and cooperation.[2]

Quality of work life is generally management-initiated. Although neither co-determination strategy comes closer to redefining the relationship between capital and labour than does the quality of work life strategy. Under quality of work life, management's right to manage is not questioned. The traditional relationship between labour and capital is not altered. In fact, corporation law in both Canada and the United States discourages labour representatives on boards of directors. Members of boards are obligated by law to represent shareholder interests.

Co-determination is tailored to the European two-tier board system. In North America the single board system is universal; and it is not easily altered. Under these circumstances, co-determination is incompatible with prevailing North American practices.

Worker representation on boards of directors in Europe is mandatory, covered by statute, and enforced by the courts. Quality of work life, on the other hand, is voluntary, not covered by statute and is tailored to the expectations and experiences of individual firms. Many joint labour-management quality of work life initiatives contain "bail-out" clauses by which either party can terminate the experiment if it feels that its interests are jeopardized. Quality of work life initiatives in North America tend, therefore, to be more ad hoc and conducted on a trial-and-error basis.

Co-determination focuses on the entire organization and its system of governance. It is concerned with major policy decisions and it involves the most powerful members of the organization. The focus of quality of work life, on the other hand, is the worker and his job. Quality of work life initiatives focus on the production system on the shop floor. The focus is the individual, his self-worth, dignity, and opportunities for growth.

Co-determination involves worker representatives interacting with senior executives. The voice and counsel of employee representatives is heard at the highest organizational levels. Quality of work life, on the other hand, is more personal and face-to-face. Workers are directly involved and arrangements tend to be more informal. Quality of work life initiatives impact directly on first line supervision, and have little effect on senior executives. This may explain the enthusiasm of senior managers in North America for QWL concept, while supervisors remain skeptical about its merits.

In Europe, change has been initiated largely by senior members of the trade union confederations and their political allies in social democratic political parties. In North America, the quality of work life movement has been initiated and supported largely by managers and academics -- particularly by those in business schools. In both Europe and the United States, the rank and file worker has remained largely a spectator to these changes.

CONCLUSION

This paper has shown that co-determination differs from quality of work life in philosophy, form, and intent. Co-determination is mandatory, politically-motivated and universally applicable; quality of work life is voluntary, apolitical, and designed to meet individual expectations and needs.

The two initiatives will continue on the trajectory of recent years. Co-determination will remain largely a European phenomenon; it is very unlikely to appear to any extent in North America in the immediate future. Where it is justified, it will be justified on the basis of employee ownership, and not on the basis that labour has a right to share in policy-making decisions with shareholders. North American quality of work life has its intellectual roots in European theory and practice (Tavistock, and Norway's Work Research Institute) and is readily transferrable to Europe. In fact, Europe is pioneered in many quality of work life initiatives which involve "green field" sites and redesign of large production systems.

It is unclear at this writing which of the two strategies -- co-determination or quality of work life -- have ultimately benefited the working person more. Quality of work life holds more promise than co-determination for improving the job satisfaction and involvement of the average shop floor worker. However, it is becoming increasingly clear that without access to policy related information and without access to decision-making opportunities at the policy level, workers in North America will continue to suffer when faced with technological change and plant closures. Perhaps the brightest future lies with countries such as Sweden, which have significant initiatives in both co-determination and quality of work life areas.

FOOTNOTES

1. In fact, co-determination in England has had a very uneven record. British Steel began an experiment of worker directors in 1968 which continues to this day. However, a labour government experiment in the post office in 1978 has been discontinued. Seven trade unionists were put on the post office's 19-member board of directors. Absence of union and manager (especially supervisor) support resulted in failure of this initiative.

2. Parity representation has been opposed by management and shareholder interests in Germany. In the "Montan" (mostly mining and steel) industries, companies were structured to circumvent the law. A challenge of the 1976 co-determination law was brought by employees before the constitutional court. In 1979, the court upheld the law and argued that it was not an infringement on property rights and did not abrogate free collective bargaining.

Management and Quality of Worklife: A Clash of Values?

Todd D. Jick

ABSTRACT

A critical role in the successful implementation of improved quality of working life (QWL) is that of the manager. This paper examines the degree of compatibility between managerial values and QWL principles. Evidence is presented, drawn to a large extent from part-time MBA students, which suggests that while managers may relate positively to QWL values, commensurate actions and changes are not immediately forthcoming. Given these findings, prospects for the future of work reform are considered.

INTRODUCTION

"This course will examine research and various viewpoints on individual well-being at work. The underlying assumption is that the well-being of people at work is a worthwhile organizational objective."

(Excerpt from description of MBA course entitled, "Quality of Organizational Life")

"What about organizational outcomes, I mean, productivity?"

(Reaction of MBA student.)

The above exchange reflects the central focus of this paper, namely, the degree of compatibility between managerial values and the quality of worklife (QWL) "movement." Whereas business effectiveness is typically measured on the basis of bottom line profits and efficiency, work reformers have advocated the use of multiple criteria (e.g. social cost accounting) and have acknowledged multiple stakeholders (including employee and societal interests). In comparing these two perspectives in their purest forms, the premises are indeed completely different.

However, there are indications that these extreme value positions are blurring today. One can point to QWL projects which have adapted to the realities of business survival and, conversly, one finds young managers weaned on 1960's values of corporate responsibility and individual growth opportunities who are questioning the monolithic profit motive. In short, the values embedded in both perspectives seem to be changing.

Thus, it is the purpose of this article to look more closely at the changing landscape of managerial values as challenged and tested by radically new approaches to organization design based on a QWL philosophy. As the influence and decision-making power of today's younger managers grow, their values are expected to play a central role in the shaping of organizational policies in the 1980's.

The next section will discuss the contrasting value positions that organizations face today and indicate the nature of their choices and dilemmas. Following this, a set of independent observations and data will be presented which suggest how managers feel about, and react to, QWL values. The pattern and implications of this speculative evidence will be considered in the concluding section.

VALUES AT THE CROSSROADS

One aspect of the turbulent environment faced by organizations in the 1970's and 1980's is the QWL issue. The QWL movement has captured a lot of attention in the last decade in many parts of the world, particularly in Europe and North America. It symbolizes efforts to redesign organizations to be more responsive to human well-being. The main components, defined by Walton (1973), are as follows:

> (1) adequate and fair compensation, (2) safe and healthy working conditions, (3) opportunities to use and develop human capacities, (4) future opportunity for continued growth and security, (5) social integration and (6) constitutionalism in the work organization, (7) balance of work and total life space, and (8) a socially relevant worklife.

How these criteria are related to productivity and profitability (i.e. traditional business outcomes) has been a muddy issue for many QWL advocates. Some claim the relationship between QWL and productivity (e.g. turnover, absenteeism, grievance rate) is curvilinear (Walton, 1973), although the particular slopes of the curve would clearly vary between settings. Other proponents claim more broadly that productivity is positively affected but that bottom-line results are not the primary goal. As Guest (1979:85) concluded from the GM Tarrytown experiment, "Getting the process of worker involvement going was a primary goal with its own intrinsic rewards. The organizational benefits followed." Yet there is also evidence from numerous studies that satisfaction and productivity are inconsistently related (Berg, Freedman and Freeman, 1978). Moreover, numerous QWL case studies which do show positive results may not be representative of the universe of cases since "failures" are rarely reported in the literature. Thus, it is difficult to be confident about a consistent relationship between so-called economic and human ends.

As a result, QWL remains typically identified as an approach distinctly different from the traditional pursuit of business goals. Both means and ends appear to be different. Trist (1978:16) contrasted the features of the "new organizational paradigm," fostering high QWL for all concerned, with that of the "old organizational paradigm," which constrains employees to a poor QWL. Table 1 summarizes the respective features of the old and new paradigms. The new paradigm is described by

TABLE 1

OLD PARADIGM	NEW PARADIGM
The technological imperative	Joint optimization
Man as an extension of the machine	Man as complementary to the machine
An expendable spare part	A resource to be developed
Maximum task breakdown, single, narrow skills	Optimum task grouping, multiple, broad skills
External controls (supervisors, specialist staffs, procedures)	Internal controls (self-regulating subsystems)
Tall organization chart, autocratic style	Flat organization chart, participative style
Competition, gamesmanship	Collaboration, collegiality
Organization's purposes only	Members' and society's purposes also
Alienation	Commitment
Low risk taking	Innovation

(adapted from Trist, 1978:16)

Trist (1978) as "emergent," the working out of a new organizational philosophy involving radically different values and assumptions. Technocratic and bureaucratic principles are to be replaced by a new respect for human resources and participation. Moreover, organizations are to serve ends other than those of their shareholders. Trist (1978) concluded that organizations are presently in a transition state between the old paradigm and the new, and that adaptation to the new paradigm is necessary and inevitable in order to regain a steady organizational state.

Hackman and Oldham (1980) suggest a parallel set of choices to those detailed by Trist (1978). They argue that organizations are currently at a "fork in the road" with two routes facing them. The first route, called "Route One," involves redesigning jobs to fit people and is consistent with enriched work, personal growth, and Trist's new paradigm. "Route Two," conversely, emphasizes fitting people to jobs and attempts to maximize technological and engineering efficiency (Hackman and Oldham, 1980:260) as found in Trist's old paradigm. This approach is steeped in the traditional economic model of organizational efficiency.

Notably, Hackman and Oldham (1980:268), unlike Trist (1978), conclude that Route Two (i.e. the old paradigm) is likely to be favoured in the 1980's. They believe that Route Two is more consistent with the behaviral styles and values of both employees and managers in contemporary organizations. Route One would be contrary to too many well accepted practices such as top down management, secure management control of employee behaviour, and the measurement of organizational effectiveness exclusively in terms of economic efficiency. Although the trend is not presented as irreversible, managers are described to be ultimately more comfortable with Route Two.

Before evaluating these contradictory prognoses, Trist's forecast of the new paradigm vs. Hackman and Oldham's Route Two, consider that there are parallel value dilemmas faced by managers and organizations in the post-Watergate era. Hennessey (1980) lists numerous value dilemmas, each of which appears to be an impossible choice. These include: ends vs. means, individual vs. organizational goals, freedom vs. control, justice vs. order, conscience vs. rules, individual integrity vs. group loyalty, and risk vs. security. (Some of these choices are more abstract representations of the old vs. new paradigm dilemma). These dramatic, albeit somewhat overstated, predicaments can be moral in nature. Donaldson and Waller (1980:34) noted that managerial acts of omission or commission can indeed bring heavy costs to others in terms of income, health, well-being, or even life itself. Thus, they conclude, that managers often face choices between ethical behaviour, on the one hand, and a single-minded determination to pursue the interests of their employer (which can involve questionable ethics.)

Another way of capturing the predicament faced by young managers was suggested by Banks (1977). He observed that youthful executives are demanding accommodations between conventional business values and individual values. That is, he argues that the strongest trend at work today is a kind of popular individualism in which personal values will interact and influence organizational values. Thus, young executives proclaim entitlement to interesting and useful work as a legitimate right as well as the right to participate in decisions which affect their work lives such as geographic relocation.

To summarize the discussion thus far, it appears that organizations are currently at a crossroads, a period of transition, or what might more accurately be described as a state of limbo. In simple terms, the alternative competing principles before the young generation of managers and MBA's are being posed as follows: the old paradigm vs. the new (Route Two vs. Route One), organizations ruled by economic expediency vs. organizations ruled by moral, ethical, and individualistic values - in short, a choice between traditional organizational values and a normative vision of organizations as they ought to be designed and organized. Trist (1978) observes that this transitional state is an uncomfortable place to be and that a steady state choice will ultimately emerge.

But how these predicaments will be reconciled and which choice will likely rise to the top is a serious matter of contention. As already indicated, the prophetic predictions of Trist (1978) and Hackman and Oldham (1980) are indeed divergent. The remainder of this paper will consider some recent "signals" on the soul-searching state of managerial values in resolving the perceived trade-off between the old and new paradigms.

SIGNS OF THE TIMES

This section presents three diverse pieces of evidence which shed light on managerial responses to QWL type perspectives. The "data" are intended to be suggestive and should be no means be seen to reflect an exhaustive presentation of the literature or a rigorous research study. However, the strength of evidence derives from its diversity in scope, focus, and methodology: an experimental exercise in values clarification, a literature review and archival analysis of the role of managers in work reform, and observations of MBA students reacting to the QWL concept. Each of these will be discussed below.

(1) An Exercise in Values Clarification

Values clarification has become a popular technique in recent years and has been adapted in many organizational behaviour courses and training programs. One such exercise, "Values in Business," has been utilized to reveal underlying principles upon which organizational decisions might be based (Lau, 1979). Morris (1980) modified the exercise and summarized the average results for MBA students. These results will be instructive for understanding whether and how managerial values are changing today.

The first phase of the exercise asks subjects to rank-order a list of "values in business items" according to their personal beliefs. Subjects were asked to consider themselves as the director of a hypothetical corporation. The values or principles ranked were as follows:

1. Career growth and development of personnel
2. Concern for personnel as people
3. Efficiency
4. Ethics (morality)
5. Managerial and organizational effectiveness
6. Political responsibility
7. Profits
8. Providing goods and services for society
9. Quality of goods and services
10. Social responsibility

Typically, no more than one-third of student subjects ranked "Profits" as their top priority value. These results are consistent with the new paradigm values which consider the organization's scope to include interests other than profits.

In the next phase, students were asked to rank-order the same items but this time "according to the priorities that they believe are actually assigned to the values in the business world." Interestingly, the results were quite different. About 90% of the subjects assigned "Profits" to be their first choice. That is, they believed that in reality businesses run first and foremost with profit margins as their focus. Thus, in their eyes, the new paradigm has not replaced the old although they seem to prefer otherwise.

In order to force the issue a bit further, the third phase of the exercise randomly assigned subjects to groups of three to six members for the purpose of arriving at consensual rankings. These small group settings may approximate organizational reality to a greater extent than solo individual actions. The group was told to act as if it was the top decision-making team in a large corporation but that the basis for its rankings should be the personal sentiments and values of group members and <u>not</u> their perceptions of how businesses actually operate.

Despite these instructions, Morris (1980) indicated that the results of this phase tended to be much closer to Phase II than Phase I, that is, most small groups ranked "Profits" as the first priority in the business world.

These experimental results suggest that while expressed values may be congruent with the new paradigm, "actions" (as indicated by collective decisions) do not yet follow. How managers would like to behave and how they actually will behave appear to be at odds with each other. The new paradigm "lip-service" may be nullified by the harsh realities of organizational survival or by group decisions which reflect organizational norms, pressures, and constraints. However, it should also be noted that Morris (1980) reported that there were also persuasive attempts in the group decision-making stage on behalf of values such as "Ethics" and "Quality of goods and services." Inevitably, however, "Profits" seems to win out. In terms of a "figure-ground" image, the old paradigm remains the dominant figure in the foreground, while the new paradigm provides the background shadows!

Similarly, a large survey of Harvard Business Review readers regarding business ethics produced parallel results (Brenner and Molander, 1977). While most respondents favored ethical codes and embraced the concept of social responsibility, they also reported that ethical codes would not substantially improve business conduct. Again, the operationalization of values into action was impeded by organizational factors. Brenner and Molander (1977:62) suggested two key factors: a) ethical conduct is frequently not rewarded by the organization and b) competitive pressures from outside the organization often push ethical considerations into the background. Again, values may be of the "new paradigm" but behavior stems from the old.

(2) Managerial Reactions to Work Reform

Other evidence of the responsiveness of managers to work reform efforts is suggested in a provocative recent book entitled, Managers and Work Reform: A Limited Engagement (Berg, Freedman, and Freeman, 1978). As the title suggests, their main conclusion is that managerial involvement in the work reform movement is, at best, limited. While the new paradigm may emerge from other forces, they argue that managers will remain largely uninterested, ambivalent, or powerless to deal with worker discontents.

Here is their argument in more detail. In assessing many of the classic QWL experiments monitored by Walton (1979), Berg, Freedman, and Freeman (1978:165) point to some serious contradictions between the humane objectives of reformers and the actions of managers involved, including:

(1) The lapses of managers who failed to follow through on efforts which had heightened the expectations of workers.
(2) Managers who were simply unwilling to reduce supervision.
(3) Managers who could not 'contend' with the expansion of work to be performed by the relevant work unit or by the larger plant.
(4) Managers who required more predictability and control than the experiment could offer.

According to Berg, et.al., (1978), the reactions of managers was more than a matter of resistance to change, a typical supervisory response to many new situations. Instead, they argue that managers 'as managers' rather than as managers of change could not tolerate the disruptions fostered by QWL and the threat to their authority. Thus the authors concluded that managers do not "fit" the perspective of those who urge work reform because it requires a complete revolution in managerial thinking.

Berg, et. al. (1978) contend, furthermore, that managers are really rather unconcerned with worker discontent. Despite the efforts of work reformers through workshops, journals, and the media, Berg et. al. (1978) conclude that line managers are minimally exposed to the key concepts of QWL. Those who are opposed to these ideas, moreover, are especially mindful of the costs and skeptical of the rewards QWL claims to offer their firms. They often believe that improved morale may not be the key to corporate success. Moreover, productivity in the long run may not be as critical as immediate concerns for personal career and succession opportunities, short-term profits and cost-cutting. As such, the "engagement" of managers in QWL ranges from disinterested to limited, Berg et.al. (1978) argue. There is neither deep commitment nor great concern from most managers.

To take their argument one step further, managers should surely not be expected to be in the vanguard of the work reform movement.[1] While this is in part a function of the difference in managerial values, Berg et.al. (1978) also seem to suggest that organizational constraints play a significant role as well. That is, even when new paradigm values emerge, they are torpedoed by old paradigm reward systems. If managers continue to be rewarded for rigidly defined organizational goals and motivated by traditional career paths, then the enthusiasm for QWL will, as Berg et.al. (1978) argued, continue to be modest. Thus, they would conclude that Route Two remains most familiar, most rewarded, most convenient, and most likely to be continued.

(3) <u>Part-Time MBA Students' Reactions to the QWL Concept</u>

The last piece of impressionistic evidence pertains to my personal experiences teaching an untypical course for part-time MBA students which was entitled, "Quality of Organizational Life." The business school curriculum is typically dominated by courses which offer technical skills and expertise. Courses in marketing, accounting, finance, and management science usually adopt this skills-orientation. Basically, such courses prepare students for organizations "as they are", largely to fit students to organizations. It assumes congruence between the values of students and those of organizations whereby personal success and organizational success (e.g. profits, growth) neatly converge.

In contrast, the course I taught on QWL heralded a "VIVE LA DIFFERENCE" approach. It attempted to unravel the underlying assumptions and values of contemporary organizations and assess the utility of the QWL approach. There was less emphasis on skills and more emphasis on "skills to what end?", less emphasis on organizational needs and more emphasis on individual needs, in short, more emphasis on issues of the relationship between individuals and their workplace. It asked the questions, "Should organizations be changed? Can they be changed? How? And who's going to change them?" It was concerned with costs, however, not only traditional bottom-line issues, but also the costs to individuals and society of career success, profit motive obsession, and job-related stress.

Specifically, the course dealt with (a) the QWL concept and movement, (b) the dynamics of the QWL process, (c) the QWL of MBA's in their work, and (d) the question of who's accountable and who's interested in QWL. The course was intended to help MBA's improve their own QWL, as well as that of their subordinates, to clarify value assumptions and biases, and to raise consciousness about issues of human resource management.

From the course content and class discussion emerged a series of value issues discussed in this article: For example, are QWL and capitalism (e.g. profitability) compatible? Can one initiate and manage humanistic reforms without jeopardizing personal career advancement? Do QWL changes grow more out of structural change or attitude change? How does one evaluate organizational effectiveness and QWL effectiveness in ways other than through "hard" data? Value premises were challenged and tested as students grappled with these questions.

In essence, students were confronted with one recurrent dilemma - the tension between the normative vision of the QWL designers and dreamers, on the one hand, and the harsh realities of organizations as they are, and as they were seen through the personal experiences of the part-time students.

Students thus were smack in the middle between the manifestations of the old and new paradigms, between Route One and Route Two! The intriguing question was how they would respond and in which direction they were headed.

On the one hand, it seemed that the course did provoke growing acceptance of new paradigm values and concepts. A sample of their final evaluation comments suggests how values may have been changed in the course:

Student A: "Made me aware of some issues I never knew existed."

B: "Modified my views on work and organizations."

C: "In spite of my relatively conservative outlook and reactionary nature, I find myself aware that this approach has some merit and deserves further consideration."

D: "It helps me to be more aware and more sensitive to the people around me."

E: "Although our opinions regarding corporate moral responsibility differ somewhat, I value your point of view and plan to work towards implementing some of the concepts discussed and thereby do my part to improve the general quality of worklife for all employees. I also found that your perspectives caused me to do some personal soul-searching to the point that, in the future, I will be far less the hard-nosed businessman than when I first entered your course." (Personal correspondence)

Despite the comments from these students (especially Student E), it was not clear that commensurate actions would necessiarily follow however. Class discussions suggested that, even with the best intentions towards work reform, and an acceptance of some new values, the barriers in organizations appeared formidable to students. They often expressed a somewhat pessimistic outlook to the question "Whither QWL?", by reminding each other of the very real constraints they faced. Many expressed feelings of powerlessness that they could make a difference. Moreover, they seemed unprepared to sacrifice what they considered their own self-interest. Finally, they were often unable to envision a successful change effort in their own organizations where the QWL values faced the litmus test for viability. While some personal attitudes and behavior may have changed in the direction of the new paradigm, the prospect for structural change thus was less likely. Interestingly, then, while these managers who were "indoctrinated" by QWL had apparently begun to adapt the new paradigm values, they remained unclear as to how and when QWL changes would realistically occur.

DIRECTIONS FOR THE FUTURE

From the impressionistic evidence presented above, it appears that managerial values and actions are loosely coupled and poorly correlated. Although values may be increasingly consonant with the new paradigm, real changes in organizations and managerial behaviors do not appear to be immediately forthcoming. In this sense, the prognoses of Trist (1978) and Hackman and Oldham (1980) may be both right and wrong. We may be headed in the direction of Route One, new paradigm values as Trist (1979) predicted, but firmly entrenched in the old paradigm (Route Two) organizational structure and design. A state of ferment and tension may exist for a lengthy period until some external forces (e.g. inflation rates, changing demographic of the workforce) shift the balance (Berg etal 1978)

An alternate interpretation is that change is inevitably a slow process, incremental in form, and will slowly follow shifts in managerial values (and values throughout the organization). This suggests that work reform, as embodied in QWL, will take decades to evolve and emerge.

What we may begin to see, in the meantime, is an interesting amalgam of the old and new paradigms, if not a distinct synthesis of the two. That is, we may neither find ourselves unable to budge from Route Two nor able to make the radical transition to the new paradigm. And instead of an uncomfortable limbo state, we may create a third viable alternative. This is one implication of Walton's (1979) recent conclusion that in successful QWL innovations, managers behaved as if both economic and human values count. Too much emphasis on one at the exclusion of the other inevitably contributed to ineffectiveness. As Walton (1979) reported:

> "A commitment to dual outcomes is congruent with the values increasingly held by knowledgeable people, but also it has proved to be the most practical approach to making significant advances toward either end...in most work structures there is an abundance of opportunities to make change that will advance both objectives." (p. 94-95)

This third route proposal needs to be considered seriously. As suggested above, it could be portrayed as a synthetic product of the two choices typically put before us.

But, it also could be the middle stage of a three-stage schema, parallel to that suggested by Sethi (1979) regarding corporate responsibility (Table 2). According to Sethi (1979) corporate responsibility evolves in three stages. Stage One (as the old paradigm and Route Two) is minimalistic, reactive, and based on traditional economic and legal criteria. Stage Three, at

Table 2.
A Three-Stage Schema for Classifying Corporate Behavior

Dimensions of Behavior	Stage One: Social Obligation Proscriptive	Stage Two: Social Responsibility Prescriptive	Stage Three: Social Responsiveness Anticipatory and Preventive
Search for legitimacy	Confines legitimacy to legal and economic criteria only; does not violate laws; equates profitable operations with fulfilling social expectations.	Accepts the reality of limited relevance of legal and market criteria of legitimacy in actual practice. Willing to consider and accept broader — extra legal and extra market — criteria for measuring corporate performance and social role.	Accepts its role as defined by the social system and therefore subject to change; recognizes importance of profitable operations but includes other criteria.
Ethical norms	Considers business value - managers expected to behave according to their own ethical standards.	Defines norms in community related terms, i.e., good corporate citizen. Avoids taking moral stand on issues which may harm its economic interests or go against prevailing social norms (majority views).	Takes definite stand on issues of public concern; advocates institutional ethical norms even though they may seem detrimental to its immediate economic interest or prevailing social norms.
Social accountability for corporate actions	Construes narrowly as limited to stockholders; jealously guards its prerogatives against outsiders.	Individual managers responsible not only for their own ethical standards but also for the collectivity of corporation. Construes narrowly for legal purposes, but broadened to include groups affected by its actions; management more outward looking.	Willing to account for its actions to other groups, even those not directly affected by its actions.
Operating strategy	Exploitative and defensive adaptation. Maximum externalization of costs.	Reactive adaptation. Where identifiable, internalize previously external costs. Maintain current standards of physical and social environment. Compensate victims of pollution and other corporate-related activities even in the absence of clearly established legal grounds. Develop industry-wide standards.	Proactive adaptation. Takes lead in developing and adapting new technology for environmental protectors. Evaluates side effects of corporate actions and eliminates them prior to the action being taken. Anticipates future social changes and develops internal structures to cope with them.
Quality of Worklife	Old Paradigm Route Two	Transitional State? Synthesis?	New Paradigm Route One

Adapted from Sethi, S. Prakash, <u>Academy of Management Review</u> 1979, Vol. 4, 1, p. 67.

the other extreme, and most similar to the new paradigm and Route One, involves anticipatory and preventive social responsiveness, that is, it portrays organizations as recognizing the importance of profitable operations but includes other criteria. It operates according to what Sethi (1979) calls "proactive adaptation." Stage Two, is one in which social responsibility brings corporate behavior "up to a level where it is in congruence with currently prevailing social norms, values, and performance expectations." (p. 66) It is not a radical departure from traditional patterns of corporate behavior but the organization is one step ahead of the legal codification of societal expectations. Individual managers are responsible for their own ethical standards and that of the corporate collectivity.

Applying Sethi's (1979) 3-stage schema to corporate QWL, managerial values seem to be converging on Stage Two. New expectations and values may then be reflected in small organizational adaptations but radical departures remain unlikely. In this sense, managers remain sensitive to prevailing and changing social norms (e.g. perceived "entitlements" at work such as a safe and non-excessively stressful environment) prior to legal codification of new regulations but not at the vanguard of substantial change. It is expected then that the winds of change in organizations will be more wispy than tumultuous as managerial values accomodate to organizational constraints and as economic and human values accomodate to each other.

REFERENCES

Banks, Louis, "Here Come the Individualists," Harvard Business Review , 1977, 6 pp.

Berg, Ivan, M. Freedman, and M. Freeman, Managers and Work Reform: A Limited Engagement, New York: The Free Press, 1978.

Brenner, Steven N. and E. Molander, "Is the Ethics of Business Changing," Harvard Business Review, January-February 1977, pp. 57-71.

Donaldson, John, and M. Waller, "Ethics and Organization," Journal of Management Studies, Vol. 17, No. 1, 1980, pp. 34-55.

Guest, Robert, "Quality of Worklife - Learning from Tarrytown," Harvard Business Review, July-August, 1979, pp. 76-87.

Hackman, Richard and G. Oldham, Work Redesign. Reading, Mass.: Addison Wesley, 1980.

Hennessey, John Jr. "The Place of Values in Teaching Organizational Behavior," Exchange, Vol. 5, No. 1, Winter 1980, pp. 3-4.

Lau, James B. Behavior in Organizations: An Experiential Approach, Homewood, Illinois: Richard Irwin, 1979.

Morris, Michael, "Modifying the 'Values in Business' Exercise to Examine Holier-than-Thou Attitudes toward Profits," Exchange, Vol. 5, No. 2, 1980, pp. 34-36.

Sethi, S. Prakash, "A Conceptual Framework for Environmental Analysis of Social Issues and Evaluation of Business Response Patterns," Academy of Management Review, Vol. 4, No. 1, January 1979, pp. 63-74.

Trist, Eric, "Adapting to a Changing World," in Adapting to a Changing World, George Sanderson (ed.), Labour Canada, 1978, pp. 10-20.

Walton, Richard, "Quality of Working Life: What Is It?" Sloan Management Review, Fall 1973, pp. 11-21.

_______________, "Work Innovations in the United States" Harvard Business Review, July-August 1979, pp. 88-98.

NOTES

1. In fact, Berg et.al. (1978) don't believe that the problem is within manager's power to resolve anyway. Instead, the problem in the workplace is in the structure of the institutionalized roles in which managers are incumbents (p. 173). That is, they suggest that work reforms specific to a workplace will yield trivial results compared with macro social influences that determine social advantages, job security, prestige, income, etc.

D. Social and Economic Rationale of Organization-Internal Labour Markets

Bridges Over Contested Terrain: Exploring the Radical Account of the Employment Relationship

Victor P. Goldberg

INTRODUCTION

In standard microeconomic analysis the nature of the employment relationship and the manner in which work is organized are ignored. Firms are presumed to buy labor services in impersonal factor markets and to combine labor with other factors according to fixed recipes (summarized by production functions) to attain output. While a useful simplification for many purposes, this stylization obscures many interesting questions. In recent years the economics profession has shown renewed interest in going beyond this simple picture and achieving a deeper understanding of the employment relationship.[1]

Radical economists have been particularly active contributors to the new literature.[2] However, their work has developed in isolation from their more conventional brethren. There is little recognition in the radical literature that non-radicals are exploring the nature of the employment relationship; and the non-radicals, aside from Williamson (1980), have generally ignored the radicals' efforts.

It is easy to understand why those who are not true believers have been put off by the radicals' work. There are too many distractions—Marxist jargon, ideologically colored language, and an unabashed rooting interest in the workers.[3] However, if one can overcome these impedimenta, there is much of value. This essay is a first pass at integrating the radical analysis into the growing literature on the employment relationship. I will concentrate on one work from the radical camp, Richard Edwards' Contested Terrain (1979). While it is representative of the genre, I should point out that it differs in some significant details from other radical efforts--radicals, like everyone else, differentiate their product. I will try to purge the discussion of most of the aforementioned distractions. While this might well distort the message Edwards was attempting to convey, it will, I believe, facilitate the integration of significant elements of his analysis into conventional economics.

Edwards' work is a useful vehicle for promoting integration. His analysis is much less vulnerable to Williamson's (1980) criticism that the radicals naively overstate the feasibility of non-hierarchical modes of organization. Further, he explicitly recognizes that organizational form will reflect profitability considerations. Thus, compare Edwards and Williamson:

> It is well known that most industries confront a variety of possible techniques, and that the relative costs of required inputs will influence which is chosen....
>
> What is less well known is that there is also an important social element in the development and choice of technique. Firms confront a range of techniques that differ not only with respect to required inputs, but also in the possibilities for control over their workforces. A superior technology may be one that facilitates the transformation of the firm's labor power into useful labor, even if that technology entails a larger bill for other inputs or even a larger wage bill per hour of operation.
>
> While it remains true that capitalists undoubtedly seek those technologies that are most profitable, we now must admit that there are several considerations that enter into the calculation of profitability. One is technical efficiency, the ratio of physical outputs to the physical inputs; another is the cost of the various inputs and the value of outputs; yet a third is the extent to which any technology provides managers with leverage in transforming purchased labor power into labor actually done. (Edwards, 1979, p. 111-12)

> ...the neoclassical firm is characterized as a production function. Economizing thus takes the form of efficient choice of factor proportions, while issues relating to the organization of work mainly involve economizing on transaction costs. The latter rarely surface, much less are prominently featured, under the production function approach.
>
> Economizing on transaction costs involves choice among alternative modes of organization. A comparative institutional assessment of the properties of alternative modes thus supplants the conventional calculus of cost minimization. (Williamson, 1980, p. 6)

Much of the work force in large twentieth century firms is employed in "internal labor markets" which are shielded to some degree from external market forces.[4] The workers have considerable job security, and layoff procedures will depend upon seniority rules. Internal promotion ladders and elaborate governance mechanisms (including grievance procedures and detailed job descriptions) are typical features. It is not entirely obvious why this particular arrangement would prove to be efficient. (By "efficient" I mean that it would survive in competition with other organizational alternatives.) Most attempts by non-radical economists have had as their central element the existence of job- or firm-specific human capital. Wachter and Williamson (1978, p. 556) make the point succinctly:

> Devising obligational labor contracts has advantages wherever laborers provide services for which specific training or learning by doing is important....Where workers acquire imperfectly transferable skills, the firm and the worker have an interest in

> devising a governance structure to assure a continuing, cooperative relation between them. Such a relation is much less important (indeed, is unimportant) where fungible skills are involved. While there is a positive correlation between the degree of job skill and the degree of idiosyncracy involved in an assignment, the correlation is not perfect. Idiosyncratic jobs of all kinds, whether highly skilled or otherwise, are what concern us. (Emphasis added.)

However, I would like to develop another line of explanation indirectly suggested by Edwards' analysis which does not require the existence of idiosyncratic tasks.

That will be developed in Section IV. I will begin, however, in Section II by discussing Marx's distinction between labor and labor power, which provides the starting point for Edwards and the other radicals.[5] The distinction, I will argue, is a central element in the non-radical analyses as well. The names are different, but they deal with the same phenomena. The investigators do, however, emphasize different aspects, their choice of emphasis being dictated at least in part by their ideological priors.

The general contours of Edwards' argument will be laid out in Section III. It will not be subjected to critical analysis. Instead, in the following Section, I will present four general propositions which are at least roughly consistent with the historical record presented by Edwards. This expositional strategy will, I hope, provide the reader with the flavor of Edwards' argument without getting him unnecessarily bogged down in its details. It also frees me to explore some matters that go beyond Edwards' concerns. I suggest first that the growth of large corporations beginning in the latter part of the nineteenth century resulted in strong pressures to develop processes that avoided reliance on specialized workers with unique skills and in a shift of the locus of technical knowledge from the workers to the firm's management (Section IV A). Second, even if the paperwork costs associated with labor turnover were trivial and workers had no firm- or job-specific skills, there would still be cause for a firm to establish an elaborate governance structure for employees and for employees to achieve considerable de facto job security (Section IV B). Third, rapid growth facilitated the successful operation of non-union industrial relations systems of many large firms; their continued success will be jeopardized by low or declining growth rates (Section IV C). Fourth, the organization of work will be influenced by considerations of power (Section IV D).

If workers do receive substantial de facto job security, it would seem that there would be little opposition to converting de facto protection to de jure. That has not, however, been the case. In Section V, I argue that without collective action it is unlikely that American workers would have succeeded in attaining formal recognition of job security, and I explore some possible explanations. Concluding remarks follow.

LABOR POWER AND LABOR

Labor power, which the employer buys, is the worker's capacity to do work, while labor is the actual physical effort of the employees. Edwards (1979, p. 12) notes: "Workers must provide labor power in order to receive their wages, that is, they must show up for work; but they need not necessarily provide labor, much less the amount of labor that the capitalist desires to extract from the labor power they have sold.... There is a discrepancy between what the capitalist can buy in the market and what he needs for production."[6]

The employment relationship is not, as the radicals suggest, unique in this regard.[7] Most exchange relationships will entail, in varying degrees, the type of gap between promise and execution implicit in the labor-labor power distinction. The appearance of uniqueness arises from the fact that the assumptions of conventional microeconomic analysis preclude the existence of such a gap. The simplifying assumptions of that analysis obscure four basic facts which are of considerable importance in shedding light on the nature of exchange in general and the employment relation in particular. First, people are not omniscient; their information is imperfect and improving it can be costly. Second, not all people are saints all of the time; economic actors can be expected to behave opportunistically. They will on occasion take advantage of the vulnerability of others, engage in strategic behavior or follow their own short-term interests at the expense of the long-term interests of other parties. Third, the parties cannot necessarily rely on outsiders to enforce their agreements cheaply and accurately. Finally, exchange relations are not ahistorical; they take place within a specific social context.[8]

Parties cannot always count on getting precisely what they bargained for, be they employer-employee, franchisor-franchisee, steel producer-fabricator, or even husband-wife. Indeed, it always pays for a party not to perform its part of an agreement if that nonperformance does not decrease the probability that the other parties will fulfill their obligations and if it suffers no loss (penalties, foregone future earnings, or loss of "goodwill") as a consequence of nonperformance. (In such a world there would be not be exchange, only unilateral, unrelated acts.) However, people's willingness to enter into a relationship and what they are willing to pay (or do) generally will depend upon their expectations regarding the other parties' future performance. Moreover, these expectations depend in part on the terms of the relationship itself. If, for example, a firm were to pay a transient worker $5000 today for work to be performed over the following year, the probability that the work actually would be performed is extremely low; by better coordinating the payment stream with the worker's performance (weekly wages, piece rates, etc.) that probability could be increased. The options are many. Thus, if a firm were worried about the continued supply of input X, it could require the supplier to post a bond, write contracts which include large penalties if a supplier failed to comply, carry greater inventories of X, utilize a production technology which allowed the firm to substitute Y for X, choose a technology utilizing a more standardized input, devise payment schemes which discouraged breach, and so forth. In general, by intelligently structuring the terms of their subsequent interaction, parties can attain some of the benefits of cooperation while containing the costs which might arise from opportunistic behavior.[9]

A general theory of the employment relationship would explain why the structure varies over time, place, industry, and so forth. It would also develop the relationship between these structures and outcomes (which might range from predictions of quit rates to propositions about job satisfaction or demands for codetermination). Neither Edwards nor any of the non-radicals have presented such a theory. Nor will I do so here. Rather, the various analytical forays have concentrated on only certain aspects of the structuring problem. The narrow focus—necessary if the subject matter is to remain manageable—has obscured their many common features.

Summarizing this new and rapidly growing literature is beyond the scope of the present essay. It is useful, however, to note briefly some of the more important recent contributions. Alchian and Demsetz (1972) concentrate on the workers' "shirking" and the benefits arising from policing this behavior. Formal models of the "principal-agent problem" are in this spirit.[10] One particular aspect of this problem--the incentive effects of fixed hourly wages versus piece rates—has been investigated by Pencavel (1977). Simon (1951) starts with the proposition that the parties are ignorant about the future and that there are gains to be had by postponing decisions until more information becomes available; by accepting the authority relationship—by agreeing today to obey the employer's orders tomorrow--employees can improve their lot. Freeman and Medoff have primarily been concerned with the role of unions in facilitating employee "voice" as a substitute for "exit."[11] Human capital theorists have focused on the problem of assuring compensation for relation-specific expenditures; if firms are to provide on-the-job training or workers are to acquire firm-specific skills, then they will require some devices which would enable them to capture some of the rewards from such efforts.[12] Williamson (1980) analyzes the comparative merits of authority and other lesser forms of hierarchical organization in coping with various "transaction cost" problems.[13]

Edwards concentrates on control, "the ability of capitalists and/or managers to obtain desired work behavior from workers" (p. 17). The three elements of control are:

> 1. Direction, or a mechanism or method by which the employer directs work tasks, specifying what needs to be done, in what order, with what degree of precision or accuracy, and in what period of time.
>
> 2. Evaluation, or a procedure whereby the employer supervises and evaluates to correct mistakes or other failures in production, to assess each worker's performance, and to identify individual workers or groups of workers who are not performing work tasks adequately.
>
> 3. Discipline, or an apparatus that the employer uses to discipline and reward workers, in order to elicit cooperation and enforce compliance with the capitalist's direction of the labor process (Edwards, 1979, p. 18).

He then traces the changes in the systems of control that have emerged in the last century. That argument will be summarized in the following section.

CONTESTED TERRAIN: THE EVOLUTION OF THE EMPLOYMENT RELATIONSHIP ACCORDING TO EDWARDS

In the mid-nineteenth century most industrial firms were small operations with few employees. The owner-entrepreneur frequently worked in close contact with his employees. His first-hand knowledge of the production process simplified supervision as did his personal ties to and knowledge of the employees. For such firms, the task of worker control (and motivation) was handled in an informal and unstructured manner. This Edwards designates "simple control." Simple control continues to exist today in the numerous small firms inhabiting what Averitt (1968) has suggestively called the periphery.[14]

In the last quarter of the nineteenth century, however, economic forces favored the growth of considerably larger firms with labor forces well beyond the size that could be supervised by a single owner or a handful of trusted subordinates.[15] These large firms found it necessary to search for new devices for directing, evaluating, and disciplining their employees. The devices were many, ranging from simple compensation schemes like piece rates, through subsidized housing, to the modern complex system Edwards designates "bureaucratic control."

The simplest approach, delegating authority to foremen, entailed a number of difficulties. The foremen's knowledge of the work process was often not adequate to permit proper evaluation. Also, the foremen's goals were not completely coincident with those of the owners; foremen themselves required supervision lest they pursue their own interests at the expense of the firm. Moreover, the foremen's power to fire workers and to mete out discipline without review by higher authorities within the firm created additional problems. The firm had to absorb the costs arising from worker displeasure with what was perceived as arbitrary treatment (for example, strikes, sabotage, and high turnover).

Edwards discusses three early responses to the problems arising from the loss of control--scientific management (or Taylorism), welfare capitalism, and employee representation in the form of company unions. These he regards as experiments in control which essentially failed, although elements of each of them have survived.[16] Scientific management provided management with improved knowledge of the production process enabling firms to reorganize production tasks. This reorganization also resulted in individual jobs that were easier to analyze and facilitated the setting of standards of performance against which workers could be evaluated. Large bonuses for performance exceeding high production standards were a prominent element of Taylor's system. Despite great publicity, few large firms adopted much of Taylor's apparatus. One reason was that it was very management intensive, substituting for skilled (but not well-controlled) workers a combination of expensive managers and less-skilled workers. A second reason, which Edwards emphasizes, is worker resistance. Skilled workers at some firms were sufficiently well-organized (or indeed, were spurred to organize by the appearance of the time-and-motion men) to defeat the attempts.[17]

Welfare capitalism entailed providing workers with a number of non-wage benefits--recreational facilities, medical care, pensions, saving plans, company-owned housing, and so forth. By quitting or by behaving in a manner that increased the risk of being fired, an employee would sacrifice the future non-wage benefits. From the owner's viewpoint, welfare capitalism could decrease the costs arising from high labor turnover, make workers more subject to discipline, and aid in the fight against unionization (those with union sympathies could be fired). Moreover, by emphasizing the carrot rather than the stick, it was hoped that welfare capitalism would help legitimize the firm's authority in the worker's eyes. However, it did not succeed. Most of the programs failed to survive the Depression. Welfarism's failure, Edwards states, occurred "because it did not deal with the fundamental issue of power within the firm."[18]

Employee representation through the company union appeared to offer employers a number of advantages. Formal grievance mechanisms and procedures for appealing disciplinary actions provided channels for reducing costs arising from worker discontent. It also served as a convenient check on arbitrariness on the part of foremen and other lower level supervisors. (In effect, establishing channels for feedback from the employees permitted closer supervision of the intermediate supervisors.) The company union had the added virtue, of course, of being a substitute for the less attractive (from the company's viewpoint) alternative, the independent union. Like welfarism, however, company unions foundered in the Depression.

Edwards argues that the strategy that ultimately proved successful (even though that success would be impermanent) was to embed the control process in the structure of the work. The structural strategy had two variants. In "technical control" the control was embedded in the physical structure of the job—machine pacing, for example, made it more difficult for workers to alter their pace. In "bureaucratic control" the firm establishes elaborate rules and procedures for directing, evaluating, disciplining, and rewarding workers; the carrot of future promotions awaits those whose behavior benefits the firm. Let us consider each of these in turn.

A firm's choice of a production technique will depend in part on the effects of that technique on management's ability to control the labor force. <u>Ceteris paribus</u>, if a technique improved the ability to elicit work from employees, that technique would be favored. The assembly line (or, in meatpacking, the disassembly line) provided such an advantage. Moreover, technological changes in the latter part of the nineteenth century and in the twentieth have tended to favor continuous-flow technology (as opposed to single-unit or small-batch production).

With the assembly line, the individual worker had less freedom to vary his work pace. If he slowed down, work would pile up at his station—a rather clear signal of lagging performance. The worker's ability to vary his level of output (or the pace of his input) was drastically attenuated. He could possibly vary the <u>quality</u> of his output, although the firm had the incentive to make this option unattractive to the worker. With the assembly line the foreman's role is altered; he does less policing of work pace, but possibly more evaluation of product quality.

The assembly line's skill requirements were not, in general, great. Edwards attributes this to the need to maintain a credible sanction of dismissal. If the reserve army of the unemployed were to pose a threat to job holders, it was necessary that the reserve army could actually perform the work. Interchangeable workers with limited job-specific knowledge were ideal in this regard. Ford, the epitome of assembly-line production, counted on the availability of those with limited skills. Its extensive recruitment in the black and physically handicapped populations was a manifestation of this approach.

While with technical control the individual had relatively little to say in determining work's pace or pattern, this was not true for the plant's workers as a whole. The conflict was, in Edwards' (1979, p. 127) felicitious phrase, displaced, not eliminated. The workers had a common interest in determining work pace and in policing the firm's efforts to redefine the employment agreement by increasing that pace. The homogeneity of the labor force and its low skills made it easy for the firm to substitute for individual workers in the short run or for a large portion of the work force in the long run. However, the interconnectedness of the line made the firm extremely vulnerable to short-term disruptions—quickie sitdowns, wildcat strikes, sabotage, and slowdowns—even if only a small portion of the work force were involved. Technical control provided an attractive environment for building industrial unions.

By the end of the 1930's it had become clear to many large firms that they would have to live with independent industrial unions. More elaborate rules for governing the employment relationship were required. Formal procedures for reviewing grievances were supplemented by providing detailed job descriptions which served as the basis for evaluating performance. Wage rates established through collective bargaining were keyed to job descriptions rather than to individual performance. With the sanction of firing circumscribed by the increased job security that normally accompanied unionization, the firm required more finely tuned sanctions, for example, fines or suspensions, for motivating or disciplining employees. These Edwards identifies as elements of a policy of bureaucratic control.

The bulk of Edwards' discussion of bureaucratic control, however, is not concerned with those instances in which that form of control was introduced as a modification or an extension of technical control. Newer firms with non-union labor forces (IBM and Polaroid are recurring examples) and non-production jobs (middle management) are the primary foci of his attention. The rewards are designed to pay off to people who stay with the corporation for long periods. Job ladders provide considerable opportunities for workers to improve their lot over time. Polaroid, for example, has seven pay steps (with five percent increments) associated with each job, and there are opportunities for moving to a higher level job. Its policy is to fill job openings by promotion from within. Jobs are advertised on company bulletin boards and employees apply; promotion takes seniority into account. In addition, the firm offers a bonus to employees who have been with the firm for five years.

Bureaucratic control is not without problems. The job ladder holds out few additional rewards to those who have gone as far as they could reasonably expect to go. (Designing job ladders to keep the carrots forever dangling before all employees can be a prohibitively expensive proposition.) Motivation of senior workers can be a difficult task. Not surprisingly, studies find that, other things equal, older workers receive higher pay and lower ratings by their supervisors than do their less senior peers.[19]

The centrality of job security in the bureaucratic control system obviously complicates the task of adjusting the size of the work force to changes in the business cycle or to longer term changes in product demand or supply conditions. To some extent the corporation can mitigate its costs of providing protection for its tenured workers by rapid growth; or it can attempt to shift the burden of adjustment to others. These include probationary workers, employees of firms in the periphery which do business with the corporation (for example, subcontractors and franchisees), and employees of subsidiaries located in foreign countries in which employees do not have job security ("guest workers" would be a variant on this). If, in fact, cutbacks are required, the firm is placed in a most awkward position. Workers with seniority bump those with less. High-price labor replaces low-price labor. The average price and productivity of a firm's work force could easily move in the opposite direction if the firm is forced to cut back.

A third problem with bureaucratic control also stems from the strong presumption of permanence of the employment relation. Workers are not likely to remain "term takers" forever. Where "exit" plays so minor a role, it is natural to expect workers to turn to "voice."[20] The voice can be raised within the employment relationship in the form of increased participation (industrial democracy or codetermination). Or workers can turn to the political arena to impose external constraints on the employer.

Edwards goes on to relate his analysis of control to the theory of segmented labor markets, which plays a prominent role in radical analysis. While some of that discussion is quite provocative, consideration of it would take us somewhat far afield. I will, therefore, not pursue this line of inquiry here.

INTERNAL LABOR MARKETS

The radicals, especially Braverman, argue that the twentieth century has seen a deskilling of the industrial labor force. Whether the evidence is adequate to support this proposition is unclear, especially since measurement of so amorphous a concept as labor force skill levels is problematic.[21] We can, however, put forth with greater confidence a more modest proposition regarding labor force skills. The growth of large corporations beginning in the latter part of the nineteenth century resulted in strong pressures to develop processes that avoided reliance on specialized craftsmen with unique skills and in a shift of the locus of technical knowledge from the workers to the firm's management. This, in essence, is how Chandler (1977, p. 493) characterizes the employment relationship in the modern corporation:[22]

> The craft unions....made little effort to unionize those industries where administrative coordination paid off. Workers in the mass production industries, where the large modern industrial enterprises clustered, were primarily semiskilled and unskilled workers. Those industries employed few skilled craftsmen. With the coming of the modern factory, the plant manager and his staff took over from the foreman the decisions concerning hiring, firing, and promotion, as well as those on wages, hours, and conditions of work. As the

> enterprise grew, such decisions were placed in the hands of middle management. Policy matters were determined by executives in new personnel departments housed in the central office.

Further, it is probably true that for significant portions of the labor force, notably members of industrial unions and lower level white collar workers, we would find that the amount of job-specific and firm-specific knowledge required is small. Henry Ford noted, for example, that most automobile assembly line jobs could be mastered within a week.[23] To the extent that such jobs are characterized by job security, elaborate governance structures and other accoutrements of internal labor markets, the explanation must lie elsewhere.

In this Section I will first develop the argument regarding the change in skills; I will then propose an explanation for the development of internal labor markets with de facto job security that does not require the existence of firm-or job-specific skills. The effects of a decline in a firm's growth rate on the efficacy of the bureaucratic control strategy will then be explored. Finally, I will touch briefly on questions regarding power.

A. Change in Skills. As a general proposition, a firm is reluctant to rely on specialist providers of key inputs, including labor. It faces the threat that the owner of the key input will act opportunistically, taking advantage of its position as a bottleneck. Moreover, as firm size increases, the firm is even more vulnerable to this threat. The supplier has a greater incentive to cheat since the size of the appropriable quasi-rents is apt to increase with firm size; the rewards to mitigating the threat increase. By reducing its dependence on that particular factor, the firm can partially mitigate that threat. Standardized parts can be substituted for custom-made ones, patent-protected inputs can be avoided, and so forth.

In the employment context, workers with unique skills or trade secrets fill the bottleneck role. In the pre-1880 world of very small firms and local markets, the rewards to a one-shot exploitation of that position were not likely to be great (especially if the owner were intimately involved in production and shared some of the special skills and knowledge). The costs in terms of damage to the worker's future reputation added an additional damper to the incentive to cheat.[24] The growth of large firms in the post-1880 period dramatically altered this situation. The potential rewards to exploiting the position as bottleneck escalated as firm size increased. The relative attractiveness (and survivability) of production processes not relying on unique skills or trade secrets not controlled by the firm was enhanced.[25]

The firm is not only vulnerable to the opportunism of the single worker with special skills. Workers acting in concert could also play the role of bottleneck whether skilled or not. The existence of a union could be expected to influence the nature of the job. Reduced skill requirements make it easier for firms to substitute for their labor force en masse by moving to nonunion states or abroad (or by hiring scabs). So long as these options appear feasible, reducing skill requirements has attractive features for the firm. If, however, the firm comes to perceive those options as effectively foreclosed, then pursuit of this low-skill strategy will lose some of its attractiveness.

The firm's ability to monitor the work process decreases as firm size increases. The costs arising from this control loss could be (and were) at least partially contained by changes in the organization of work.[26] Production processes which limited the ability of workers to alter their effort (technical control) were favored as were those amenable to systematic analysis and in which techniques could easily be described, communicated, and evaluated. Skilled workers with unique talents presented problems, their performance being difficult to monitor simply because it was less well understood. Generally, this meant that processes employing craftsmen with special skills were less attractive. The rise of scientific management and the bitter conflict between its practitioners and the craftsmen seems unsurprising in this light. Nor is the concentration of job knowledge in the firm, rather than the work force, unexpected.[27]

If workers cannot be easily replaced, disciplining them might be a difficult task. In the nineteenth century, skilled workers were in this position; they were generally able to control the pace of their work by taking unscheduled breaks and by frequent absences.[28] This was not a serious problem at a time when an erratic transportation system made it desirable for manufacturers to carry large working inventories. But as production rates increased in the late nineteenth century, the costs to the firm arising from these casual work habits rose disproportionately. Thus, the firm's increased need for discipline of the work force also tilted the balance in favor of technologies not requiring highly skilled labor.

B. <u>Deferred Compensation and De Facto Security</u>. Suppose that none of the work performed for a large firm required firm- or job-specific skills. Further, assume that all the paperwork costs associated with labor turnover were inconsequential. Even in these extreme circumstances there would still be good reason for the large firm to establish an elaborate governance structure for employees and for the employees to achieve considerable <u>de facto</u> job security.

To direct workers to perform certain tasks and to discourage behavior that impairs performance, the firm requires devices which impose costs on the worker for non-compliance. The ability to impose costs is enhanced by making quitting expensive for the worker. If the worker could simply walk away without cost, any particular punishment (say a suspension or fine) could be ignored; if, however, quitting imposed a substantial loss on the worker, he would be vulnerable to the threat of punishment--the deterrents become credible. Further, a high exit cost can be a powerful deterrent in its own right. The firm can use the threat of termination to influence the worker's behavior.

The firm has available a number of devices with which to penalize exit, or what amounts to the same thing, reward continuation.[29] One device is to pay a premium wage (like Ford's five dollar day), the sacrifice of that premium being a cost of leaving borne by the worker.[30] Note that the premium is not paid "up front;" it is deferred so that the payment is contingent upon the worker's continued satisfactory (from the employer's viewpoint) performance. Deferral enables the firm to enforce the agreement without recourse to the expensive judicial system; if legal enforcement were free, up front payment would suffice. Nonwage compensation (in the form of pensions, health insurance, company-provided housing, and so forth)[31] and internal promotion ladders are more complex variations on this. Firms (and employees) will not be indifferent between the forms the compensation takes. The penalty or reward structure can be fine-tuned to achieve specific purposes. For example, a pension which can be collected only if the worker remained with the firm makes for a very high penalty in the employee's final years on the job. Termination of pensions or leases on company-owned housing in the event that the employee goes on strike raises the cost to the worker of this particular form of exit.[32]

It should be clear that the larger the deferred payment, the greater is the employer's incentive to cheat. If worker distrust were sufficiently high at the formation stage, the contingent reward would be heavily discounted; the strategy would not be viable. Assuming that that hurdle has been surmounted, the effect of such opportunistic termination on a firm's good will — the reaction of its other employees and its future employees — would be a significant deterrent. Ceteris paribus, the firm's credibility would be a declining function of the gap between the deferred compensation and the expected future output of the worker (or group of workers); for example, if a firm alleged that a worker had been careless or performed a bit too slowly, other workers would have cause to be dubious if by firing that worker the firm avoided paying a large pension. Turning this around, to maintain a given level of good will, the firm would have to offset the increased gap by meeting a higher standard of proof in justifying a termination.[33] If termination were the firm's only sanction, then, paradoxically, raising the penalty could reduce its ability to discipline the work force.[34] This suggests that a natural extension of deferred compensation arrangements in large firms is a system of lesser penalties (fines, suspensions, bad evaluations) to discipline lesser transgressions and a fact-finding procedure which workers might reasonably perceive as fair for identifying violations.

We have derived the essential elements of the employment relationship without invoking either paperwork costs associated with turnover or specific human capital. Allowing for the former does not give rise to any new difficulties; it simply makes continuation of the relationship more attractive for the parties. The existence of specific capital does raise new questions, but this is not the place to explore them. Three observations will suffice. First, it is not necessary to presume that some specific capital is involved when studying such labor market phenomena as turnover rates. (For example, in Mortensen's "Specific Capital and Labor Turnover" (1978) the analysis goes through even if there exists no specific capital at all — exit costs arising from any source are sufficient.) Second, specific capital might in some instances be a device for achieving control. Thus, if the firm were to encourage the worker to make investments in firm-specific capital, the possible sacrifice of the stream of returns to this non-transferable asset would serve as an exit barrier for the worker.[35] Third, it is quite possible that a firm adopting a strategy relying heavily on deferred compensation would take advantage of the situation and choose technologies which are relatively more idiosyncratic-skill intensive. Note the reversal in causality. Deferred compensation would not be the result of idiosyncratic skills; rather its existence would cause their coming into being.

C. Bureaucratic Control and the Firm's Rate of Growth. The successful innovators of the bureaucratic control strategy for nonunion workers were firms like IBM and Polaroid which were situated in rapidly growing markets. It is not necessarily true that bureaucratic control contributed to the success of these firms; rapid growth might simply have provided a favorable environment with the firm prospering in spite of the strategy. Even if it did contribute, the transfer of this "organizational technology" to slow-growth environments need not succeed. There are two lines of argument suggesting that a high growth rate facilitates bureaucratic control, and that low or declining rates can cause some serious difficulties.

First, workers in an internal labor market are isolated to some degree from the external market. If the firm were growing rapidly, it would be recruiting regularly in the external market and would have to adjust the employment package offered to new recruits to reflect their opportunity cost. This information can then be used to guide revision of the terms of employment of the previous employees.[36] Thus, rapid growth provides as a side benefit low-cost information on external labor market conditions and reduces the need for "voice" mechanisms (for example, unions) or exit. Moreover, a rapidly growing firm would have a greater incentive to maintain its reputation in the labor market and would, consequently, be less likely to behave opportunistically than would a slowly growing, or declining, firm. Ceteris paribus, lowering the growth rate would increase the probability of unionization, increase the cost imposed on workers by the barriers to exit they face under the bureaucratic control system, and impair the firm's ability to adjust the employment agreement to take into account external market conditions.

This argument could be extended to provide one possible reason for downward rigidity of wages. In the upswing a larger number of firms are recruiting new employees than in a slump. In a slump, fewer firms would feel compelled to search the external market, and therefore, the likelihood that current market information will be incorporated into the internal wage structure declines. Moreover, if the terms offered new recruits in a slump are less attractive than those paid current employees, the firm is under less pressure to bring the pay structures into line than if the reverse were true.[37]

Second, because of the reliance on deferred payments, current compensation for new workers is "too low" and for old workers "too high." With rapid growth, the addition of new workers keeps overall costs down. Reducing the growth rate increases the ratio of dead wood to new blood. If the firm accurately anticipated its future growth path, it could devise an optimal deferred compensation scheme to fit that pattern. My conjecture is that for reasonable assumptions, the lower the growth rate, the lower would be the share of deferred compensation in the total wage package. A more promising line of inquiry, I believe, would take seriously the possibility that the firms adopting the bureaucratic control strategy in the last three decades have systematically underestimated the difficulties associated with both low growth and a declining growth rate. Since the high growth rates experienced by many firms in the 1950's and 1960's are not sustainable and since the demographics of the post baby-boom era will reduce the supply of new workers, it seems quite plausible that the system of bureaucratic control with non-union work forces will come under considerable pressure for change in the next decade. More generally, this sort of "non-rational expectations" story can generate interesting patterns of rapid adoption of an innovation followed by great disenchantment and induced search. If the innovation is difficult to undo ("irreversability" is a bit too strong a word), then mistakes of this sort can have a significant impact on the path along which the employment relationship evolves.[38]

D. Power and Efficiency. Williamson (1980, pp. 35-36) states: The organization of work is, predominantly, a transaction cost issue....(W)hether hierarchy has redeeming efficiency properties or is mainly to be understood in power terms can scarcely be assessed except as transaction cost issues are confronted." This formulation is somewhat misleading. Efficiency is not, as Williamson has properly emphasized,[39] simply a technical matter. An efficient institution is one that survives in a particular context. The efficacy of a particular arrangement will depend upon the ability of the parties to exert legal or extra-legal power. Thus, it might well have been profitable for a firm to expend resources in opposing unionization of its labor force in 1920, while a similar strategy in 1940 — even with the nature of the job unchanged — would have been irrational because of the worker's increased ability to impose costs on the firm at the later date.[40] Attempts to explain the existence and behavior of unions on "efficiency" grounds which ignore this are apt to misfire.[41]

His formulation also leads Williamson to downplay the fact that contracting parties can have the ability to exercise their power within the relationship and that the design of the employment relationship will take this factor into account. As a consequence, the picture he paints of the modern employment relationship tends to ignore the manner in which employees restrict the employer's power.[42] His argument can be interpreted as demonstrating that, for organizing work, the pure authority relationship circa 1920 was superior in many respects to its predecessors — inside contracting, putting out, etc. It cannot, however, help explain why the pure authority relationship failed to survive in many industries, but was superceded by arrangements in which the employer's power was attenuated by a system of "checks and balances." Nor does it permit evaluation of the numerous varieties of the modified authority relationship, ranging from procedural due process to codetermination, that have evolved or which constitute much of the feasible range of future prospects.

Conflict and struggle are, of course, fundamental elements of the radical's world view, and it is, therefore, quite natural for issues of power to surface in their analyses. Williamson is undoubtedly correct in arguing that in many instances their treatment of the issue has been naive at best. But I do not want to get bogged down in a discussion of the merits of the various radical treatments of matters of power. Instead, I merely want to point out that an important, perhaps the most important, lesson the non-radicals should draw from the radical account is to take issues of power seriously.[43] This lesson will, I suspect, meet with great resistance.

COLLECTIVE ACTION AND JOB SECURITY

While firms generally want to encourage the presumption that a job is to be a long-term affair, they have historically been opposed to granting the workers formal job security. The typical employment agreement of fifty years ago could easily be terminated by the firm. Notice requirements were short, employees received little or no compensation for their reliance, and the employer was not required to show cause. If the law had initially given potential employees the right to tenure, they would have voluntarily "sold" it to the employer as a condition for entering into the agreement (or else they would have remained potential employees). The benefits to the employees afforded by job security —protection of "investments" made outside the employment relationship but in reliance on its continuity (for example, in a home, a neighborhood, or in establishing roots), protection from arbitrary dismissal, protection of the surplus of their deferred compensation over their expected future value to the firm, protection of job-specific human capital, and so forth--were not, in general, sufficiently attractive to outweigh what employers would offer them to accept a contract without protection of job security.

That is a rather bold generalization, but I believe that it is in accord with the facts for the period preceding passage of the Wagner Act. Experience in a closely related area, franchising, tends to confirm this. As argued above, a system relying heavily on the carrot of deferred compensation will result in considerable de facto job security. Procedures for appealing disciplinary actions, including outright terminations, are natural accompaniments of such systems. The costs to the firm of converting the de facto protection to de jure are likely to decline as deferred compensation becomes a more prominent element in the total package. Nevertheless, the experience of franchisees suggests that although the cost to the firm of formal recognition declines, it is still considerable. Even though the franchisee's considerable relation-specific investment would appear to make de jure protection more valuable than in the labor context, minimal protection has remained the norm. Without collective action by franchisees the de jure protection would not, in general, have been forthcoming.[44] The similarities between the franchise and employment relationship suggest that similar forces were at work. Why then have workers—and franchisees—pursued the goal of increased security through collective action (collective bargaining or political action) when they did not find it sufficiently valuable in one-on-one contracts? The answer is by no means clear, but some plausible conjectures can be put forth.

Collective action—whether through collective bargaining, political action, or extra-legal channels (including the threat of violence)—can plausibly influence the level of job security achieved in a number of different ways. With individual choice of contract terms, the nature of the contract will be determined by the marginal man—the earnings/security combination will be chosen so that the last employee is indifferent between his contract and the next best alternative. With collective action, the interests of the average existing employee are the relevant concern. If the differences between the marginal and average employee are systematic, the resultant contracts will differ. In the employment context (and no doubt others) such divergences are likely. Average existing employees are likely to be older, have higher moving costs (for example, uprooting a family), and have more deferred compensation to lose than the marginal employee. All these influences would lead to a greater demand for security when the employees act collectively.[45]

If by collective action employees can attain a larger compensation package, then, so long as job security is not an inferior good, we should expect them to get more of it. That is, collective action causes the individual's budget constraint to shift outward. While plausible, I doubt the explanatory power. Casual empiricism suggests that there is little relationship between income and formal security for workers or franchisees in the absence of collective action. Of course, if collective action yields future rewards to members of an organization (deferred compensation contingent upon continued membership) then the individuals will want to increase the likelihood that they will be able to capture these rewards. Termination protection can be a means for achieving the rewards of collective action as well as an end in itself.

Collective action can, in effect, lower the "relative price" of formal security. In the absence of a union or specific legislation, individual workers would find the opportunity cost of de jure job protection excessive. It would, in effect, grant them a "hunting license" — the right to sue in court for damages or reinstatement. Given the penurious nature of contract remedies (including the general rule that the plaintiff bear his own legal expenses), the hunting license is of little value. Collective action alters this. For one thing, it facilitates pooling of these costs since the union, not the individual would bear them.[46] Also, by providing a governance structure which supplants the rules of the common law, the union can lower the costs of pursuing redress.[47] Moreover, as a general rule, linking a relationship to other similar ones reduces the costs of extra-judicial enforcement. Thus, while the individual worker acting alone is in no position to impose significant costs upon the employer, the collective ability to impose costs — for example, with the strike or boycott threat —could be used to protect the individual's security.[48]

To the "shift of the budget constraint" and "change in relative prices" it is natural to add the remaining element of the textbook diagrams — altered preferences. The great efforts to raise or otherwise alter workers' consciousness have undoubtedly had an impact. Indeed, much of the flamboyant rhetoric of Edwards and the other radicals is directed at altering workers' perceptions. My failure to pursue this line of inquiry further here is not based on a conviction that such pursuit would be fruitless; it simply means that I have little to contribute. I will, however, suggest one plausible conjecture. It is quite likely that unions would be induced to err systematically by providing "too much" job security.[49] Collective action is facilitated by framing issues in an "us versus them" manner and by building worker solidarity — my brother, right or wrong. The lower the level of trust (or the greater the benefits to the union of maintaining distrust) the more likely it is that the union would support a worker with a dubious case in a termination dispute. The survivability of the union would be enhanced by backing the worker. Extension of this protection imposes real costs on workers; decreased ability to discipline the labor force results in decreased productivity which would be reflected in compensation packages. Nevertheless, the misperception might still enhance the probability that the union survives (and thrives).[50]

CONCLUDING REMARKS

The differences between the radical accounts of the employment relationship and those of non-radical economists should not be dismissed in a false spirit of ecumenicalism. Serious disagreements regarding which questions are important and the criteria for evaluation will almost certainly remain even if consensus on many points were to emerge. Nevertheless, it is important to recognize that there is a meaningful, albeit difficult-to-define area over which the two perspectives are not so far apart, and moreover, that communications across the ideological boundaries are likely to be mutually beneficial.

In this essay I have presented a summary of a contribution of one of the radicals. I have also demonstrated that the radical vision of the employment relationship in large modern corporations can, at least in its broad outlines, be derived using the same essential theoretical framework that has implicitly characterized most of the non-radical contributions; the difference is, in large part, a matter of emphasis. In addition, a number of general arguments regarding the employment relationship have been presented. With suitable reworking these might be transformed into formal propositions or testable hypotheses. The present essay is, of course, highly preliminary. The argument has, I hope, been sufficiently suggestive to encourage further exploration along these lines.

FOOTNOTES

*The author would like to acknowledge helpful comments from Zvi Adar, Andrzej Brzeski, James Buchanan, Richard Nelson, Douglass North, Alan Olmstead, Sam Rosenberg, John Roemer, Warren Samuels, Steven Sheffrin, Roger Sparks, Katherine Swartz, David Teece, and the participants at the Conference on the Evolution of The Right to Property, Port Ludlow, Washington, June 1980. The usual disclaimers apply.

1. For earlier contributions, see Coase (1937) and Simon (1951). The employment relationship was, of course, of central interest to the institutionalists; see especially Commons' (1909) study of the evolution of shoemaking. Neoclassical economists in the beginning of the century gave considerable attention to the nature of the employment relationship; see the detailed discussions in Marshall (1920, pp. 365-94) and Pigou (1962, pp. 411-641).

2. See, for example, Marglin (1974), Braverman (1974), Stone (1974), Gintis (1976), and Edwards (1979).

3. The radicals undoubtedly would find much of the language of the non-radicals ideologically loaded and/or offensive.

4. For a description of internal labor markets, see Doeringer and Piore (1971).

5. A number of readers of a previous draft have questioned whether this use of the labor-labor power distinction is a proper reading of Marx. That appears to be a reasonable question for students of Marx to mull over. I will pass; for my purposes what Marx said or meant is not of great moment. It is enough that the present-day followers have utilized the labor-labor power distinction in the manner described in the text.

6. See also Gintis (1976, pp. 36-37) and Braverman (1974, pp. 54-58).

7. Edwards (1979, p. 12); see also Gintis (1976, pp. 36-37, 41).

8. I have developed some of the implications of explicitly recognizing these facts elsewhere. See Goldberg (1976a, 1976b, 1977, 1979a, 1979b, 1980). See also Macneil (1974), Williamson (1975, 1979, 1980), and Klein, Crawford, Alchian (1978).

9. It is not necessary that both parties actively engage in the design activity. At this level of generality it does not matter whether one party puts out standard contracts on a take-it-or-leave-it basis, the bulk of the terms are supplied by the legal system, or the agreement is the outcome of lengthy negotiating sessions.

10. Alchian and Demsetz ignore the fact that breaking the employment relationship (quitting or firing) can impose substantial costs on one of the parties. Alchian does take this into account in subsequent work (although that work is not directly concerned with the employment contract; see

Klein, Crawford, and Alchian (1978)). For examples of analysis of principal-agent problems, see Harris and Raviv (1978), Shavell (1979), and Holmstrom (1979).

11. The exit-voice terminology is Hirschman's (1970). See Freeman (1976, 1979), Freeman and Medoff (1979), and Medoff and Abraham (1978, 1979).

12. See Becker (1962) and Parsons (1977).

13. See also Wachter and Williamson (1978) and Williamson, Wachter, and Harris (1975). The latter provides a useful discussion of some of the alternative analyses (including Alchian-Demsetz and Simon).

14. Averitt (1968) distinguishes between the firms at the core and the peripheral firms. The former are the large, integrated, managerially decentralized firms which account for the bulk of output in the American Economy. While the firms on the periphery are small, there are lots of them --Edwards suggests that about eleven million of the twelve million firms in the country should be put in the peripheral category.

15. For an excellent analysis of the factors leading to the rise of the large managerial corporations, see Chandler (1977); both Edwards and Braverman cite earlier work by Chandler extensively. However, Edwards is at best vague as to what the sources of the growth of firm size were; see Edwards (1979, p. 27).

16. Taylorism plays a much more central role in Braverman's analysis; see Braverman (1974, pp. 85-138).

17. I have seen no discussion of whether employers attempted to compensate the skilled workers for the decreased value of their skills that would result from adopting Taylor's programs.

18. Edwards (1979, p. 97). It is not clear that this means anything more than "it failed because it didn't succeed." Edwards is more convincing in documenting the failure than in explaining it. For a more complete discussion of the demise of welfare capitalism, see Brody (1968).

19. Edwards (1979, p. 152) does not cite the evidence supporting this assertion. For recent studies arriving at this conclusion, see Medoff and Abraham (1978, 1979).

20. See Hirschman (1970).

21. Braverman (1974, pp. 214-23) summarizes a study by James Bright (1958) which does provide a rough measure of skill content and which suggests that skill content declines with automation.

22. See also Rodgers (1978, pp. 24-26); Walker and Guest (1952), Feller (1973, pp. 730-31, 760-71), and Fox (1974). See especially Fox's discussion of "low-discretion" jobs (1974, pp. 25-30).

23. Ford (1922, p. 111) estimated that in his plants circa 1920 43 percent of the jobs require one day or less of training, 36 percent from one day to a week, 6 percent from one to two weeks, 14 percent from one month to a year and 1 percent from one to six years.

24. The discussion in the text ignores the legal restrictions on the worker's ability to exit. If the employer can call upon the state to aid in enforcement that could considerably alter the situation. Commons' (1968, p. 285) remarks on the legal enforceability of employment contracts in twentieth century America are apposite:

> What he sells when he sells his labor is his willingness to use his faculties according to a purpose that has been pointed out to him. He sells his promise to obey commands. He sells his goodwill.
>
> But even this promise has no exchange-value. When the business man sells his goodwill he promises to stay away and not compete. His goodwill is a separable asset attached to his going business and transferred to another. Likewise, when the laborer sells his physical product he sells his promise to stay away and not exercise his will upon the product. But when he sells his labor he sells his promise to stay on the job with it. This is usually a valueless promise, not because he will not stay on the job, but because the law, in recent times, refuses to compel him to stay. The indentured servant, the former contract laborer or apprentice, the peon, even perhaps the slave, had sold his promise to work, and the law enforced the promise by punishing him for the crime of running away, or permitted the purchaser to punish him for disobedience. The laborer's promise was an enforceable contract, a legal duty to work. But the Thirteenth Amendment to the Constitution forbids involuntary servitude of every kind except as punishment for crime of which the person must duly have been convicted in a court of law. Hence the laborer can lawfully change his mind without penalty inflicted upon his body. And, to change his mind is to violate his promise.
>
> But if his body can no longer be offered as security for the fulfillment of his promise to work, his separable assets, his tools, houses, furniture, animals, are security that may be levied upon in damages. Yet even these, by statute during the past eighty years, have been so liberally exempted from execution that a suit to recover damages for breach of contract by laborers is, in fact, an empty remedy. (Emphasis in original.)

25. In some contexts the unique employee is very hard to avoid — sports, entertainment, and top management are the primary examples. Even there, substitution away from superstars is possible. The relative success of such

"no name" teams as the Miami Dolphins, Seattle Supersonics, Atlanta Hawks, and Baltimore Orioles and the continuing high ratings of "Charlie's Angels" despite the turnover of angels provide examples.

26. The close parallel between the changes in the organization of work and the organization of management around the turn of the century should be noted. As firms grew, the hierarchical form of organization became more unwieldy; firms introduced a number of changes to offset the control loss arising from this source. The most significant was the development in the 1920's of the decentralized (or M-form) firm. See Chandler (1977) and Williamson (1970).

27. Specialized craftsmen might suffer if new techniques were implemented, and they would have incentives to suppress such new techniques when they control the technology. The weakening of the craftsmen's control of technical knowledge meant that the relevant decision maker (the firm's management) would be in a position to reap rewards from introducing a technology that relied less on highly skilled labor. Thus, indirectly the growth of technologies less reliant on skilled labor was encouraged.

28. For a discussion of the casual work rhythms of earlier days and of observation of the holiday for "Saint Monday," see Thompson (1967, pp. 70-79).

29. See Goldberg (1979b, pp. 101-103) for an indication of the variety of devices available.

30. Klein and Leffler (1980) emphasize the importance of the threat of losing a premium as an aid to assuring enforcement of contracts.

31. There are other reasons why firms might find in-kind compensation more desirable than cash payments (deferred or otherwise). Progressive income taxes would be a factor today, although they are irrelevant for the pre-Depression period in which welfare capitalism thrived. A second reason is that some of the expenditures (on health, accident prevention, and improved working conditions, for example) had a positive impact on the worker's productivity. In addition, by packaging a group of customers for health insurance or other services the firm might attain economies otherwise unavailable (or at least avoid adverse selection problems); since unions also attempted to provide such group services, provision by the firm might also have lowered the probability that its workers would be organized.

32. For examples of such terminations, see Edwards (1979, pp. 92-93).

33. This presumes that the level of "trust" or "loyalty" is fixed. Two extensions of the discussion in the text are immediately apparent. First, <u>ceteris paribus</u>, we can anticipate that trust would decline as the size of the organization grows. This factor provides further support for the non-idiosyncratic skill explanation for the emergence of internal labor markets. Second, neither trust nor loyalty are beyond the influence of the firm. It has an incentive to invest in enhancing both. Edwards places considerable emphasis on the efforts of capitalist firms to create a sense of loyalty to

the firm. It was, he suggests, one element in the strategy of welfare capitalism (p. 91). It plays a more important role in his discussion of bureaucratic control:

> Working-class orientations and patterns of interacting yield to more bureaucratic, so-called middle-class ways. The notion of family ("the IBM family") that includes both management and workers resurrects a concept not relevant since the entrepreneurial firm. The workers begin to use the first person plural differently; "we" now means "we the firm," not "we the workers." The workers' ability to create a workday culture begins to fade, just as, on a grander level, the working class loses its ability to make its own class culture. (p. 148)

He suggests that in the upper level (salaried) jobs, the reward system promotes organizational loyalty; at lower levels job evaluations are more likely to emphasize rules, orientation and dependability (pp. 149-51). For an elaborate analysis of trust and the employment relationship, see Fox (1974). By relegating this discussion to a footnote, I do not mean to belittle its importance. Surely, a serious analysis of the Japanese lifetime employment arrangement — a puzzle which theories of the employment relationship will have to confront — will have to take into consideration matters of trust and loyalty.

34. It is generally true that penalties that are widely perceived as being wholly disproportionate to the alleged misdeed, will be difficult to enforce. I am adding to this an additional complication — the belief by relevant observers that the enforcer benefits directly from enforcing the penalty.

35. Note that the exit barrier inherent in firm-specific skills can be utilized by the firm to enable it to capture some of the rewards from providing broadly marketable skills to the worker. Rather than just providing general training the firm can offer a "tied package" thereby increasing the probability that the worker would choose not to leave.

36. The pressures toward internal equity are strong, but they are not inexorable. It is possible for existing employees to lag behind the new hires. Such divergences would, however, cause difficulties and lead to an increased demand for the "voice" mechanisms alluded to in the text. The firm must balance the expected benefits from selectively rewarding new hires against the anticipated costs (including morale problems and the increased probability of unionization). The argument in the text assumes that firms would generally resolve this problem by opting for internal equity.

37. Elsewhere (Goldberg, 1980, p. 347) I present another argument for downward rigidity:

> Suppose....that the firm alleges that demand has declined and that the labor force should receive less compensation. If it could reduce the wage and lay off no one, it gets the same labor force as before, but at

> a lower wage. While the firm might well be telling the truth, the incentive to dissemble should not go unnoticed by the union. A policy of wage rigidity combined with layoffs, however, will mean that the firm can lower its wage bill only by decreasing the size of its labor force — the rewards to misrepresentation are reduced.

For similar arguments, see Wachter and Williamson (1978, p. 555) and Klein, Crawford, Alchian (1978, p. 317). Since in a slump there would be little search of external market conditions and therefore little objective evidence of those conditions, workers would be even less willing to accept the firm's representations. This further enhances the attractiveness of the wage rigidity cum layoff strategy.

38. This line of argument can be extended to shed light on mergers and the market for corporate control. Suppose that managers are given the implicit promise tht they will not be dismissed in their last years with the firm even though their earnings at that time might exceed their worth to the firm. This sort of promise is easy to honor if the firm is growing rapidly. With slow growth, meeting these obligations can be more difficult. If an outsider is less bound by the promise, then the existing firm is vulnerable to a takeover. Takeovers provide an opportunity to renege on the implicit promise. The newcomer is not as constrained as the initial owners by reputational effects; indeed, such behavior might enhance its reputation with the relevant population (including its own employees whose opportunities are improved by the acquisition of new jobs to append to its internal labor market).

Further pursuit of this argument is beyond the scope of this essay. Yet it is enough to raise disquieting questions. If some of the "economies" arising from a merger are simply transfers to the newcomers resulting from "confiscating" the deferred compensation of the old management, then it is easy to refrain from enthusiasm. Moreover, if current managers learn from the mistakes of past managers, compensation packages will be redesigned to reduce their vulnerability (either by taking less deferred compensation or by taking it in a form less subject to an opportunistic taking).

39. See the quotation of page 2, <u>supra</u>. Williamson (1980, p. 33) suggests that proposals for reforming the employment relationship should reflect "a decent respect for human nature as we know it."

40. Passage of the Wagner Act was a significant factor. But the increased extra-legal power of workers also mattered. In England collective bargaining contracts were not legally enforceable until the 1970's, but that had little impact on their actual enforceability. Ironically, the Supreme Court's justification for finding the Wagner Act constitutional was that extra-legal labor violence had an adverse effect on interstate commerce:

> ....the fact remains that the stoppage of those manufacturing operations by industrial strife would have a

> most serious effect upon interstate commerce. In view of respondent's far-flung activities, it is idle to say that the effect would be indirect or remote. It is obvious that it would be immediate and might be catastrophic. We are asked to shut our eyes to the plainest facts of our national life and to deal with the question of direct and indirect effects in an intellectual vacuum. Because there may be but indirect and remote effects upon interstate commerce in connection with a host of local enterprises throughout the country, it does not follow that other industrial activities do not have such a close and intimate relation to interstate commerce as to make the presence of industrial strife a matter of the most urgent national concern. When industries organize themselves on a national scale....how can it be maintained that their industrial labor relations constitute a forbidden field into which Congress may not enter when it is necessary to protect interstate commerce from the paralyzing consequences of industrial war?

(National Labor Relations Board v. Jones & Laughlin Steel Corp. 301 U.S. 1,41 (1937)).

41. See, for example, Mayers and Thaler (1979, p. 573).

42. Williamson states (1980, p. 21): "The Authority Relationship posits at the outset that a superior-subordinate relation will govern in both operating and strategic respects. To be sure, the zone of acceptance of the employment relation, within which workers will accept orders without resistance, is limited by formal and informal agreement. But a command hierarchy is a prominent feature of the Authority Relation."

43. The point is well established amongst non-economists. Feller (1973, p. 465), for example, states:

> Because of the necessity of consent, managements have over a period of 200 years developed changed ideologies to justify their authority and to create thereby the necessary ethic of work performance. The establishment of rules in a collective agreement can serve as a substitute for such ideologies. And the process of collective bargaining, including periodic conflicts over the content of the rules, can serve to channel the natural desire of employees to exercise strategies of independence into acceptable forms and to legitimize the result.

44. For a discussion of the eighteen-year battle preceding the passage of the Automobile Dealer's Day in Court Act see Macaulay (1966). Courts have extended protection to dealers by broad interpretation of the antitrust statutes and by extending contract law doctrines such as unconscionability to protect dealers; see Goldberg (1979b) and Jordan (1978).

45. See Freeman (1978) for development and testing of this hypothesis.

46. It is possible that other institutions might emerge to perform the function of insuring against the cost of litigation arising from allegedly improper terminations. Since such insurance is subject to severe moral hazard problems, it would not be surprising to find that provision would be feasible only if it were part of a package tied to the other services performed by a union.

47. Summers (1969, p. 538) argues that the common law treatment of the employment relationship is totally inconsistent with the actual law that has emerged under collective bargaining.

It should be noted that vigorous protection of workers from termination could result in higher production costs, some part of which the workers would ultimately have to bear; the crucial point, however, is that the collective action would reduce the relative price of increased security.

48. The linkage to other relationships can be accomplished indirectly. The effects of a particular termination on a firm's reputation are communicated by informal channels, for example, by utilizing the informal communication channels of reputation and good will. Formal collective action can make this mechanism more effective and less costly for the workers.

"Formal" does not necessarily mean "legal." As noted above (note 40) collective bargaining agreements in England were not legally recognized as binding contracts until the 1970's, yet they were effectively binding for decades prior to that date.

49. For a different argument that unions will push too many grievances of little merit, see Feller (1973, p. 753).

50. This argument might plausibly have a life-cycle variation similar to that alleged to characterize regulated industries; see Bernstein (1955).

BIBLIOGRAPHY

Alchian, A. and H. Demsetz, 1972, Production, Information Costs, and Economic Organization, American Economic Review 62, December, 777-95.

Averitt, R. T., 1968, The Dual Economy (Norton, New York).

Becker, G. S., 1964, Human Capital (Columbia University Press, New York).

Bernstein, M. H., 1955, Regulating Business by Independent Commission (Princeton University Press, Princeton).

Braverman, H., 1974, Labor and Monopoly Capital (Monthly Review Press, New York).

Bright, J. R., 1958, Automation and Management (Boston).

Brody, D., 1968, The Rise and Decline of Welfare Capitalism, in J. Braeman, et. al. (ed.), Change and Continuity in Twentieth-Century America: the 1920's (Ohio State University Press, Columbus).

Chandler, A. D. Jr., 1977, The Visible Hand (Harvard University Press, Cambridge).

Coase, R. H., 1937, The Nature of the Firm, Economica ns 4, 386-405.

Commons, J. R., 1909, The American Shoemakers, Quarterly Journal of Economics 24, 39-84.

Commons, J. R., 1968, The Legal Foundations of Capitalism (University of Wisconsin Press, Madison).

Doeringer, P. and M. Piore, 1971, Internal Labor Markets and Manpower Analysis (Heath, Boston).

Edwards, R. C., 1979, Contested Terrain (Basic Books, New York).

Feller, D. E., 1973, A General Theory of the Collective Bargaining Agreement, California Law Review 61, May, 663-856.

Ford, H., 1923, My Life and Work (Doubleday, Garden City, NY).

Fox, A., 1974, Beyond Contract: Work, Power, and Trust Relations (Faber and Faber, London).

Freeman, R. B., 1978, The Exit-Voice Tradeoff in the Labor Market; Unionism, Job Tenure, Quits, and Separations, manuscript.

Freeman, R. B., 1979, Why Do Unions Increase Job Tenure? Harvard Institute of Economic Research Discussion Paper #723, October.

Freeman, R. B. and J. L. Medoff, 1979, The Two Faces of Unionism, Public Interest 57, Fall, 69-93.

Gintis, H., 1976, The Nature of Labor Exchange and the Theory of Capitalist Production, Review of Radical Political Economy, 36-54.

Goldberg, V. P., 1976a, Regulation and Administered Contracts, Bell Journal of Economics 7, Autumn, 426-48.

Goldberg, V. P., 1976b, Toward an Expanded Economic Theory of Contract, Journal of Economic Issues 10, March, 45-61.

Goldberg, V. P., 1977, Competitive Bidding and the Production of Precontract Information, Bell Journal of Economics 8, Spring, 250-61.

Goldberg, V. P., 1979a, Protecting the Right to be Served by Public Utilities, Research in Law and Economics 1, 145-56.

Goldberg, V. P., 1979b, The Law and Economics of Vertical Restrictions: A Relational Perspective, Texas Law Review 58, December, 91-129.

Goldberg, V. P., 1980, Relational Exchange: Economics and Complex Contracts, American Behavioral Scientist 23, January/February, 337-52.

Harris, M. and A. Raviv, 1978, Some Results on Incentive Contracts with Applications to Education and Employment, Health Insurance, and Law Enforcement, American Economic Review 68, March, 20-30.

Hirschman, A. O., 1970, Exit, Voice, and Loyalty (Harvard University Press, Cambridge).

Holmstrom, B., 1979, Moral Hazard and Observability, Bell Journal of Economics 10, Spring 74-91.

Jordan, E., 1978, Unconscionability at the Gas Station, Minnesota Law Review 62, June, 813-56.

Klein, B., R. G. Crawford and A. A. Alchian, 1978, Vertical Integration, Appropriable Rents and the Competitive Contracting Process, Journal of Law and Economics 21, October, 297-326.

Klein, B. and K. Leffler, 1980, Non-Governmental Enforcement of Contracts: The Role of Market Forces in Assuring Quality, manuscript.

Mayers, D. and R. Thaler, 1979, Sticky Wages and Implicit Contracts: A Transactional Approach, Economic Inquiry 17, October, 55-74.

Macaulay, S., 1966, Law and the Balance of Power (Russell Sage, New York).

Macneil, I. R., 1974, The Many Futures of Contract, Southern California Law Review 47, May, 691-816.

Marglin, S. A., 1974, What Do Bosses Do? Review of Radical Political Economy 6, Summer, 33-60.

Marshall, A., 1920, Industry and Trade (Macmillan, London).

Medoff, J. L. and K. G. Abraham, 1978, Experience, Performance, and Earnings, manuscript.

Medoff, J. L. and K. G. Abraham, 1979, Can Productive Capacity Differentials Really Explain the Earnings Differentials Associated with Demographic Characteristics? The Case of Experience, Harvard Institute of Economic Research Discussion Paper #705, May.

Mortensen, D. T., 1978, Specific Capital and Labor Turnover, Bell Journal of Economics 9, Autumn, 572-86.

Parsons, D., 1977, Models of Labor Market Turnover: A Theoretical and Empirical Survey, in R. Ehrenberg (ed.) Research in Labor Economics, Volume 1 (JAI Press, Greenwich).

Pencavel, J. H., Work Effort, On-the-Job Screening, and Alternative Methods of Remuneration, in R. G. Ehrenberg (ed.) Research in Labor Economics, Volume 1 (JAI Press, Greenwich).

Pigou, A. C., 1962, The Economics of Welfare (fourth edition) (Macmillan, London).

Rodgers, D. T., 1978, The Work Ethic in Industrial America 1850-1920 (University of Chicago Press, Chicago).

Schumpeter, J. A., 1950, Capitalism, Socialism and Democracy (third edition) (Harper and Row, New York).

Shavell, S., 1979, Risk Sharing and Incentives in the Principal and Agent Relationship, Bell Journal of Economics 10, Spring, 55-73.

Simon, H. A., 1951, A Formal Theory of the Employment Relationship, Econometrica 19, July, 293-305.

Stone, K., The Origins of Job Structure in the Steel Industry, Review of Radical Political Economy, Summer, 61-97.

Summers, C. W., 1969, Collective Agreements and the Law of Contracts, Yale Law Journal 78, March, 525-75.

Thompson, E. P., 1967, Time, Work-Discipline, and Industrial Capitalism, Past and Present 38, December, 56-97.

Wachter, M. L. and O. E. Williamson, 1978, Obligational Markets and the Mechanics of Inflation, Bell Journal of Economics 9, Autumn, 549-71.

Walker, C. R. and R. H. Guest, 1952, The Man on the Assembly Line (Harvard University Press, Cambridge).

Williamson, O. E., 1970, Corporate Control and Business Behavior (Prentice-Hall, Englewood Cliffs, NJ).

Williamson, O. E., 1975, Markets and Hierarchies (The Free Press, New York).

Williamson, O. E., 1979, Transaction-Cost Economics: The Governance of Contractual Relations, Journal of Law and Economics 22, October, 233-61.

Williamson, O. E., 1980, The Organization of Work: A Comparative Institutional Assessment, Journal of Economic Behavior and Organization 1, 39-60.

Williamson, O. E., M. L. Wachter, and J. E. Harris, 1975, Understanding the Employment Relation: The Analysis of Idiosyncratic Exchange, Bell Journal of Economics 6, Spring, 250-78.

The Employment Relationship as a Form of Socio-Economic Exchange

Tom Keenoy

ABSTRACT

The objective of this paper is to provide an outline framework for the analysis of the work-employment relationship within the conceptually broader context of industrial relations. Primary theoretical emphasis is placed on the role of social power as the central analytical variable and, to this end, most of the paper is concerned with delineating the 'power-dependence paradigm' as the most apposite conceptual apparatus for the analysis. The final section of the paper provides an account of some of the operational considerations in using the framework. Regarding social values, the epistemological issue addressed in this paper, albeit somewhat obliquely and inconclusively, concerns the status of sociological analysis: to what extent is it possible to develop a conceptual framework for the analysis of industrial relations which is ideologically uncontaminated by either employer or employee interests? This paper attempts to capture some of this elusive ground.

INTRODUCTION

The basic premise upon which this paper is built is that the role of social power, as a pervasive feature of socio-economic relations, has been accorded only minimal significance in the explication of industrial relations. This weakness in the available conceptional apparatus has been increasingly recognised in recent years. The work of Alan Fox (1973, 1974) in analysing the apparently mystifying functions of pluralist ideology is perhaps the most celebrated, though there numerous other examples. Hill (1974, p. 232), in an incisive discussion of workgroup behaviour, points out that the "question of power and legitimacy are central to an analysis of industrial relations, particularly those between men and management", and Hyman and Fryer (1975, p. 160), who operate within the Marxian paradigm, are similarly adamant: "the notions of power, control and dependence are essential for any proper understanding of trade unionism".

This neglect is, in part, a reflection of the historical demarcation of the economic from the social dimension of the employment relationship: a split embodied in the emergence of labour economics and the more traditional industrial sociology(1) as academic sub-disciplines. The former still continues to place considerable reliance on the marginal productivity paradigm (Mulvey, 1978) despite long-recognised inadequacies (Dunlop, 1964) while it is only in the last twenty years that the latter has extended beyond group dynamics. (Smith, 1961). The net effect was that social power, as an explanatory variable, virtually disappeared.

The approach adopted in this paper involves a rejection of explanations based on conventional market theory and an abandonment of the industrial relations systems perspective (Dunlop, 1958; Wood et al 1975). Both of these approaches to the employment relationship suffer from a fundamental antipathy to the role of social power as a significant determinant of the bargaining context and bargaining outcomes (2). For 'market theorists' (3) these come in the form of wage-prices and for conventional systems thinking they are usually construed as the 'rules' in industrial relations. The weaknesses of both can be illustrated with a brief critical comment on the work of John Dunlop.

In any attempt to reach an understanding of Dunlop's elaboration of his industrial relations systems concept it is important to recognise the extent to which it was informed by his major preoccupation, labour economics. In confronting the central issues in labour economics he was certainly no stranger to arguments about the role of social power in explaining behaviour in the employment relation. His somewhat vitriolic debate with Arthur Ross in the 1940's concerned the priority which should be accorded to the relative merits of economic and political factors as determinants of trade union wage policies. (See Dunlop, 1944, 1964, and Ross, 1948). He was also an active participant in the still unresolved issue concerning the role of 'economic' and power' forces as the determinants of the level of wages. (Dunlop, 1964). In the earlier exposition, in 1944, he developed two concepts of bargaining power but concluded that such a notion was only useful insofar as it reflected market forces since, in the long run, these are dominant. This confirms that Dunlop held to the 'traditional' economistic view of power which had been vividly described by one of his contemporaries, Charles Lindblom; he points to the theoretical ambiguity which follows from drawing a distinction between market forces and 'human' (social) forces in the establishment of the price of labour: in the model of perfect competition, power is absent and, therefore, the "supposition that bargaining power is an alternative to the power of competition in wages and price determination is invalid" (ibid., p. 399) for wages and prices are set by human beings within the context of competitive forces.

Lindblom, of course, is referring to what is probably the most central and deeply-rooted 'paradigm assumption' of traditional market theory and, needless to say, this 'power-vacuum' also informed Dunlop's economic thinking. The ideological significance of this for his approach in Industrial Relations Systems is perhaps best expressed by Rothschild who states that "the basic model of perfect competition was both an abstract analysis of a decisive economic force and a Utopian formulation of a society in which power is so widely and thinly distributed that its influence can be neglected". (Rothschild, 1971, p. 9, emphasis added). With regard to Dunlop's system, it is this model of society, seemingly endemic to the tradition of economics within which he has consistantly operated, which underscores his account of the significant contextual variables. Just as power is theoretically an aberration in the economic sphere so too in the social sphere of rule-determination in industrial relations. Thus, Dunlop does not ignore the role of power out of negligence or closed minded conservatism: he has studiously relegated it to the parameters of his schema because it is not considered to be theoretically important; insofar as it is an 'effective' variable it is subsumed by imperfections in the operation of market forces.

Unfortunately, by burying power in the sea of market imperfections Dunlop has effectively excluded the role of human agency in actively manipulating the contextual variables. Within the competitive model there is, logically, no room for any significance to be attached to human agency but, insofar as a theory of rule-determination within industrial relations is a useful enterprise, even economists have conceded that social values, mediated through social action, have a determinate influence on the rules. The point is that the last thing the rules in industrial relations reflect is long term economic forces: actors, within the constraints imposed by social consciousness and social structure, can be viewed as seeking to control economic forces in their attempts to protect and advance perceived interests. In what is an ironic paradox, the rules 'produced' through the Dunlopian system are a measure - albeit, in cases of redundancy, a rather sobering measure - of the extent to which human agency can actively subvert the operation of market forces.

The very act of regulation within the labour-capital relationship, conducted by rule-makers who legitimate each others' activity, is antithetical to the presumed 'autonomic regulation' by market forces, one of the paradigm assumptions which informs Dunlop's model. Having set up his technical, market and political contexts as independent variables he then reduces them to theoretical impotence by ignoring both the processes used to articulate their significance and the fact that the 'rules' in industrial relations are intrinsically a reflection of short-term market imperfections. The three contextual variables can only become theoretically determinate by recognising that they constitute power resources which, in the competitive process of rule-making, may or may not be available to some or all of the actors. To treat them simply as mute 'system properties' almost vicariously controlling the output of actors' interactions is to miss the point that their significance lies in the extent to which they are actively 'organised' and utilized by the actors. Power is a residual category in Dunlop's system because it has virtually no place at all in the economic theorising that informed his deliberations in 1958.

Power and Social Values

Not least among the reasons for the failure to give adequate prominence to the role of social power is the conceptual and methodological quagmire which must be traversed in order to arrive at a satisfactory grasp of the concept. The issue is compounded by the central and pervasive role of social power in sociological analysis for any general definition is invariably - and inevitably - couched in fairly abstract forms while any attempt to operationalise the concept is - necessarily - situationally specific. Predictably, the subtleties of abstraction are often crushed in the mechanism of empirical measure.

Initially, the difficulties stem from the amount of 'work' the concept is expected to do: it is employed at all levels of inquiry from two-person interactions to the analysis of societal structures. It can be construed as a generalised property of 'social systems' or as a specific capacity mobilized by institutions and actors in the process of interaction: hence conceptual confusion can arise from the tendancy to treat power as either a property of structure or as a property of action. In any adequate theorisation, both properties must be accommodated for social action always takes place in a structural context. This indicates, as Giddens (1979) has suggested, that there may be good grounds for operating with two concepts, one referring to power-in-action, one reflecting the structure of constraints. Indeed this dual characterisation underlies several of the recent contributions to the debate about power. Lukes (1974), in his advocacy of a three-dimensional model, while providing a succinct account of the epistemological problems germane to any discussion of power, has, fundamentally, gone little beyond asserting the priority of 'power-as-structure'. Similarly, Fox (1974), in his critique of pluralist ideology, insists that the most accurate means of evaluating the social contribution of collective bargaining is to assess its impact on the redistribution of rewards at societal levels: in such a context, it is clear, pluralist ideology stands revealed as a series of hollow promises. In essence, what Fox points out is that for all the apparent socio-economic disturbance resulting from trade union action, little more than marginal change occurs in the structure of institutionalised inequality: structured power relations are seen to have an overarching determinate impact on the exercise of situational power; the latter being viewed as a mere epiphenomenon.

In the second place, as this last example suggests, the debate about power has become firmly located in the realm of values and ideology. Lukes insists that power must be regarded as an "essentially contested" concept by which he means that "any given interpretation or conception of (power) is inextricably tied to further background assumptions which are methodological and empistemological, but also moral and political assumptions, which themselves partly govern which reasons count in favour of one conception rather than another". (ibid., 1979, p. 262). While this clearly endorses the contemporary rejection of the idea that social science can be 'value-free', Lukes selection of 'power' for such singular treatment seems disingenuous for what he is arguing would seem to apply equally to all the concepts of social scientists. In this respect, his criticism constitutes a statement about the endemic limitations of the social scientific enterprise and, as such, is a clear specification of the epistamological parameters within which we must operate. Thus, by a curious irony, while Lukes' argument can be construed as a refutation of Weber's claims to 'value-freedom' it also constitutes a partial endorsement of Weber's position with regard to the status of sociological analysis. There are two particular aspects of Weber's approach which are usually taken as distinctive. Firstly, his emphasis upon 'social action' and secondly, his use of 'ideal types'. Sociology is defined as an enterprise - he calls it a 'science' - "which attempts the interpretive understanding of social action in order thereby to arrive at a causal explanation of its course and effects". Social action is limited to the "subjective meanings" of the individuals or groups displaying social behaviour or engaging in social interaction. The 'scientific' or methodological procedure through which the "interpretive understanding" of "subjective meanings" may be attained is ideal-typical analysis. In this respect it should be noted that an ideal-typical conception in no case refers "to an objectively 'correct' meaning or one which is 'true' in some metaphysical sense" - thus the sociological enterprise, which is an 'empirical science', is distinguished from such 'dogmatic disciplines' as jurisprudence and social philosophy. (Weber, 1964, p. 88 ff). Whether Weber succeeded in separating the 'empirical' from the 'dogmatic' is still, of course, a matter of considerable dispute (Giddens, 1974; Runciman, 1972) and, fortunately, a debate which lies outside the scope of the present endeavour. It seems reasonable to suggest that, whatever the definitive conclusions regarding Weber's epistemology may be, that he attempted to create a framework whereby sociology could be conducted as a 'disciplined' enterprise: this could be achieved by explicitly recognising the abstract or ideal character of the typifications that the observer utilizes to make sense of social reality. Having recognised this limitation the observer can guard against the intrusion of his own values in any substantive analysis since the rational constructs he uses as a basis for generalisation remain his creations and are in no sense part of 'social reality'. In this respect the concepts of sociology are heuristic devices and sociological knowledge is always relative. For Weber, the actual process of describing and interpreting social reality always reduces that reality to salient, abstractions; salient, that is, to the observers' sociological purposes and social values.

The formulation of power offered in the following pages should be regarded as an attempt to abide by the spirit of Weberian methodology. Indeed, the power-dependence paradigm, to which we now turn, is grounded in Weber's consideration of the forms of social domination.

THE POWER-DEPENDENCE PARADIGM

The power-dependence paradigm(4) is best regarded as a methodological device designed to create some 'sociological space' within which the inherently tendentious concept of power can be contained if not defused. It should not be confused with 'ideal-type' since it does not represent a one-sided accentuation of social reality: it consists of a series of logically related propositions which, fundamentally, are informed by a conflict model of society. The most that a generous critic might concede is that it approximates to an average-type model of the 'mechanics' of power-relations. There are ten basic propositions:

(i) power is a property of all social relationships;

(ii) social structures are thus, by definition, power structures;

(iii) power relationships are characterised by mutual dependence;

(iv) power-dependence relationships are typically associated with the allocation and distribution of scarce resources;

(v) dependence is potentially, if not characteristically, conflictual;

(vi) social order is (thus) socially constructed and, fundamentally, a negotiated order;

(vii) this negotiated order may be said to constitute a 'structurally legitimate' normative framework since it is (fundamentally) sustained by the prevailing power structure, and will, typically reflect the extant distribution of power;

(viii) authority is an ephemeral and essentially problematic property of the social norms regulating the behaviour of actors in power-dependence relationships;

(ix) social norms may be said to be 'socially legitimate' when they are endowed by the actors with authority;

(x) the role of social values and ideologies is critical to an understanding of negotiated order - they may be viewed as the intervening variable between structural and social legitimacy.

These propositions - their rationale is elaborated below - constitute the basic conceptual elements for the analysis of the employment relationship within the context of industrial relations. They do not constitute a theory of industrial relations although, clearly, they can be used to generate specific hypotheses and could be utilized, heuristically, as a basis for such a theory. At this stage the point should also be made that it is still an incomplete conceptual framework since it only provides a basis for the analysis of the 'mechanics' of power relations - it contains no specific propositions relating to the exercise of power, or to the bases of power, or to the dynamics of power-relationships. The latter are all crucial to an understanding of power relationships and to the analysis of behaviour in industrial relations.

In its present form the framework can only be utilized to illuminate the basic structure of industrial relations - it says nothing about the existing distribution of power in industrial relations; it provides only minimal indication of the causal factors in social change; and it provides no significant clues as to why industrial relations 'systems' take different institutional forms (i.e. it is a-historical). Its primary methodological function is to ensure that the theoretical centrality of power in any analysis of the social ordering of industrial relations remains unquestioned.

One of the seemingly gratuitous consequences of limiting the framework in this manner is that it facilitates the avoidance of some of the more intractable epistemological problems noted above. There has been a tendency, particularly in more recent accounts of power (Fox, 1973; Lukes, 1974; Clegg, 1979) to treat it as an insidious property of social structures and, in some instances, there is even the implication that power (or more accurately, the unequal distribution of power) is almost exclusively a feature of capitalism: power has become the deus ex machina which contains the revolution. (c.f. Lane, 1974). The consequence of this has been that the identification and analysis of social power has become even more confused for there has been a shift in emphasis from explaining what power is and how it works to a condemnation of its existence. At the root of this - seemingly increasing - confusion lies a failure to draw an adequate distinction between the sociological analysis of social power and the social mechanisms and processes whereby it is 'legitimated' and the socio-philosophical evaluation of particular modes of social organisation. The use of differing social ideologies to legitimise power structures undoubtedly creates different forms of organisation (c.f. Weber, 1964) and certainly may produce and legitimise a differential structure of rewards, prestige and privilege (Urry and Wakeford, 1973). However, primary emphasis upon the role of legitimatory ideologies - at the expense of the 'fact' of power which, in terms of the present perspective, is viewed as a defining characteristic of all forms of social organisation - engenders both sociological and philosophical impotence since it merely leads to the truism that all forms of ideology are manipulative legitimations.

The framework outlined above represents an attempt to demarcate - but not divorce - the analysis of the sociological mechanics of power from moral evaluations of the use of social power on 'the human condition'. This is not to suggest that it is possible to have an articulate 'science of society' devoid of social philosophical contamination, but merely an attempt to draw certain distinctions in order to pre-empt unnecessary confusions.

POWER, DEPENDENCE AND CONFLICT

Despite Bierstedt's pessimism, the 'definition' offered above - 'power is a property of all social relationships' - can hardly be seen as problematic. This is so because, as it stands, it is singularly indiscriminate if not entirely inoffensive: it merely refers to a defining characteristic of sociation. Nevertheless, it does seem to constitute a useful starting point since it identifies power as a ubiquitous feature of social relations and emphasises that, fundamentally, any discussion of social power must be located within the context of a social relationship: in this respect it is power which is the scaffold of social structure. Sociologically, power is never a property of individuals though it is always social actors who exercise power; the exercise of power always takes place within the constraints - which may be both ideological and structural - of particular social relationships. The 'definition' only becomes sociologically significant when related to the conceptually contingent properties of dependence and conflict which distinguish power from other generalised properties of social relationships.

With the possible exception of random social encounters, all purposive social relationships involve mutual dependence. Relationships such as mother-child, husband-wife, student-teacher and worker-employer can clearly be viewed as social interactions in which both actors contribute to the satisfaction or 'wants' of the other actor. The dependence of one actor upon another is a function of the extent to which each actor continues to want or 'need' what the other supplies to the relationship and the extent to which each has alternative supplies of what the other provides. Such a characterisation (c.f. Emerson, 1962) means that 'power' will not necessarily be observable in any specific social relationship though its potential use always exists. This implies that either actor may be in a position to impose sanctions on the other. The limiting cases are those situations where the weaker actor withdraws completely from the relationship because he no longer derives any perceived benefits from it and where the stronger actor decides to dispense with the services of the other actor. (In principle both these cases are identical in that they involve the termination of the relationship).

Although social relationships are characterised as involving mutual dependence it is obvious that, in many instances, one actor is more dependent than the other - and the same is true of social relationships involving collectivities. In other words, one actor may be said to be more powerful than - or less dependent on - the other actor. "In short, power resides implicitly in the other's dependency". (Emerson, 1962, p. 32). It is important to point out that this does not mean that social relationships are either balanced relations (i.e. where there is mutual dependence as in a situation of bi-lateral monopoly) or, given differential dependence, imbalanced to the extent that one actor can totally dominate the other. (i.e. one actor exercises all the power). The analyses of both Dahrendorf and Blau seem to be constrained by this 'either - or' conceptualisation. Blau appears to be working with a dichotomous notion of dependence for he discusses exchange in terms of either unilateral or mutual exchange (1964, p. 321); and Dahrendorf appears similarly constricted for his basic argument is that in all imperatively co-ordinated associations there is one group or aggregate which 'participates in the exercise of authority' and one which is 'excluded from the exercise of authority' (1958, p. 172). It seems both more realistic and conceptually more accurate to view social relationships as involving variable, differential dependence. This emphasis on the differential nature of dependence - which means that both actors may be seen as having some power over each other - is crucial and intrudes at all points in the analysis of

always the possibility that the achievement of one set of interests will be inimical to the attainment of the other set of interests. This is not to suggest that all social relationships - or all power-dependency relationships - are fundamentally calculative in character, for this implies that social man is amoral in his dealings with others and incapable of any activity other than the single-minded pursuit of self-interest. What it does mean is that social man is not self-sufficient and hence his social interaction is guided (in some instances determined) by his physical, material, social and spiritual 'needs'. Since, in many instances, these require the acquisition of 'scarce resources' there is always the potential for social conflict. Given such a characterisation, the single-minded pursuit of self-interest becomes a theoretical impossibility since it presupposes total independence of other men.

In the context of industrial relations, it seems almost otiose to painstakingly elaborate why - in the absence of legitimatory ideologies - they are inherently conflictual. The most commonplace explanation rests upon the differential interests inherent in the structure of market economies though, from the foregoing, it should be clear that differential economic interests are only one basis of dependence relationships. While the economic dimension is clearly crucial to industrial relations it should not be allowed to overshadow other very important sources of conflict - such as the competition for control not only between employer and employee but also within managerial structures and between workers and/or trade unions and trade unionists. It is true that many of these substantive conflicts could be contained within - or reduced to - the economic dimension. However, as Weber (1949) has pointed out, such a process is not without its costs, for it may mean that "the definition of 'economic' is stretched beyond recognition so that all human interests which are related in any way whatsoever to the use of material means are included in the 'definition'. Further, it may lead to the specious reduction of "political, religious, climatic and countless other non-economic determinants" to "historically accidental conditions". (ibid., p. 70). And it is important to remember that this is not simply a Weberian attack on Marx, for he adds that "the one-sideness and the unreality of the purely economic interpretation of history is in general only a special case of a principle which is generally valid for the scientific knowledge of cultural reality". (ibid., p. 71).

The important point for our present purpose is that the focus upon the basic economic conflict between employer and employee, may, in some instances, lead to a failure to recognise the significance of other sources of industrial conflict which may, in particular contexts, have much more far-reaching consequences for the conduct and pattern of industrial

industrial relations.

Thus, for example, it has long been recognised that collective bargaining is an institutional process which permits the temporary resolution of the conflicting interests within the employment relationship: the actors are seen to engage in defining and re-defining the terms of their mutual interdependence. (Stevens, 1963; Walton and McKersie, 1965). This is not to suggest that there is, in any sense, an equality of power between salient actors, but that, whatever the distribution of power, there is a sense in which, as Emerson puts it, "it might be meaningful to talk about the parties being controlled by the relationship itself". (1962, p. 34, emphasis added). Thus, even if the actors themselves define their behaviour as 'free collective bargaining', they may still be viewed as co-operating out of expediency. Further, and related to this, the rationale for characterising collective bargaining as a 'mixed' relationship involving both co-operation and competition (Stevens, 1963; Anthony, 1977) between the actors becomes self-evident: their dependence on each other induces them to co-operate for mutual benefit while their conflicting interests ensures continued competition in order to extract greater benefits from each other. Such a characterisation does not, of course, exclude the possibility of what Walton and McKersie (1965) refer to as 'integrative bargaining' which, at one level, can be viewed as an overt recognition of mutual dependence by the parties - nor, alternatively, does it exclude the possibility that one actor may destroy the relationship rather than compromise or concede on a particular issue. Blau seems to substantiate this characterisation, for although "both partners gain advantages from a stable exchange relationship" it is best described as "a situation that resembles a mixed game with some common and some conflicting interests". (ibid., pp. 98-9). Differential dependence means that the actors are constrained to co-operate with each other and, in the context of industrial relations, this results in "temporary accommodations" which reflect the extant dependence of the various actors.

This 'mixed-game' feature also provides the conceptual link with conflict and the theoretical foundation for the assumption that power-dependence relations are characterised by permanent, but not necessarily permanently visible, conflict. In the absence of 'pure altruism'(5), social actors can be seen to 'associate' in order to create mutual satisfactions which could not have been obtained independently of that relationship. There is a sense in which the actors 'need' each other to supply an otherwise unobtainable 'good' - whether this be esteem, affection, wages, profit or even social power. Hence the actors, by definition, have vested interests, and where there are vested interests there is an endemic source of conflict since, potentially, there is

relations. For example, to mention only three, differences in managerial ideology (Bendix, 1963; Child, 1964), in occupational culture (Salaman, 1974), and racial conflicts (Rimmer, 1972), are all, potentially, more significant than 'simple' economic conflict.

There is, of course, a quite voluminous literature on the causes, consequences, functions and control of social and industrial conflict which, fortunately, it seems unnecessary to review. The situation is perhaps best summarised by Fox (1971): "From Marx to Mayo thus takes us from a point at which conflict is the dynamic of all constructive social change to a point at which it figures as the destruction of social hope". (ibid., p. 145). Given the structural basis of the endemic conflict of interests, industrial conflict in all its manifest and latent forms (Hyman, 1972) is, predictably, viewed as a normal phenomenon. And, given the mutuality of dependence, it follows that attempts by the salient actors to resolve their differences through some form or more or less institutionalised process of social negotiation is also predictable.

Evidence of the usefulness of the power-dependence paradigm is widespread in the literature of industrial relations. As Emerson has perceptively suggested: "We conventionally fall back upon simple exchange propositions without explicitly acknowledging them". (1972, p. 40).

As early as 1776 Adam Smith wrote: "In the long run the workman may be as necessary to his master as his master is to him; but the necessity is not so immediate". (Quoted in Phelps-Brown, 1962, p. 160). Hyman and Fryer (1975, p. 161) make the same point in a less euphemistic fashion: "Put simply, the employer can normally survive without labour for longer than the worker can survive without employment". This emphasis upon the centrality of the economic dimension of power-dependence is a recurrent underlying theme. It finds its most coherent expression in the Marxist and pro-Marxist perspective though, with small effort, it can also be found in the work of those who may be considered less radical and even among those who fall into the more 'conservative' category.

One of the more incisive statements of the Marxist position is to be found in Vic Allen's (1966) analysis of exchange in the labour market which rests on the now commonplace assertion that there is an inherent tension - and endemic conflict - in the employer-employee relationship since wages are a 'cost' to the employer and a 'profit' to the employee. Rationally, the employer can be expected to minimize costs while the employee attempts to maximise his profits. "Because of these two conflicting pressures there can never be a permanent agreement over price". (ibid., p. 21). The outcome of these transactions will predominantly be governed by the degree of competition between employees for jobs (c.f. Perlman, 1928) and the degree of competition for labour between employers. Thus, Allen argues that trade unionism arises out of the structural conditions generated within market economics; and collective organisation by employees to alter the "unevenly distributed freedom" of the market may be viewed as an attempt to ensure that neither party will contract out of the exchange since every market transaction involves some element of duress. (Hence, just as the rules arrived at through collective bargaining constitute 'temporary accommodations', so the strike or the lock-out constitute 'temporary withdrawals' of work). Hyman is more succinct, if less incisive: "For while the powers of the employer are enormous, he is at the same time dependent on his labour force". (1975, p. 25). However, it is important to note that such conclusions about the character of capitalist economies are not confined to Marxists. Blumer (1947, p. 273) has argued that: "Fundamentally, workers and management in our economy are necessarily in conflict with each other. I don't say this in a Marxian sense. I refer merely to the fact that workers...are seeking to secure benefits...and management is seeking opportunities for business profit. As our economy is organised, these respective interests enter normally in opposition".

Of those writing in a less radical vein, Fox (1971) explicitly utilizes what he calls "power-dependence _theory_" (_ibid_., p. 54) as a central plank in his analysis of power and, while the emphasis on power-dependence as such is less evident in Dahrendorf's (1959) analysis, it is equally significant since he explicitly links it to Marx: "Industrial enterprise, being an imperatively co-ordinated association, has in it two quasi-groups which we may designate, following Marx, as those of capital...and of wage labor..." both of which are "united by certain latent interests which, being contradictory, place them on the opposite sides of conflict relation". (_ibid_., p. 242). However, one of the more interesting of the 'less radical' commitments to power-dependence can be seen in the work of Chamberlain and Kuhn (1965) whose approach is fundamentally informed by liberal-democratic values. They see power-dependence as a _consequence_ of the emergence of collective bargaining in Western society where, they claim, the "most characteristic aspect of contract" is its voluntary nature. While such freedom exists for an individual the same is not true, they argue, for collectives - and here their argument becomes somewhat contingent - since it is simply not feasible for a large body of employees to leave _en masse_ to seek employment elsewhere. Similarly, management have little chance of completely replacing a workforce overnight. Hence, so long as the institution of collective bargaining is preserved "it requires that some agreement be reached between the parties. Thus neither party is _independent_ under collective bargaining". Furthermore, "for each, the achievement of its own function is dependent upon a working relationship with the other" and "This fact of mutual dependence cannot be overstressed, for it is perhaps the most fundamental aspect of modern industrial society". (*ibid.*, pp. 424-5). Union-management dependency is thus viewed as a 'functional necessity', illustrating that power-dependence analysis can, technically, be accommodated within systems theory.

The use of power-dependence analysis can also be discerned in the more 'conservative' approaches to industrial relations. This can be illustrated by reference to the work of Frank Tannenbaum (1964). His socio-psychological account of the emergence and function of trade unionism can be identified as an historical account of the transformation in the character of dependence between employer and employee which resulted from the 'industrial revolution'. The tightly-knit structure of traditional values characteristic of feudal social organisation provided the 'worker' with a coherent conception of his 'place in society': there could be no mistaking his ranking in the status hierarchy. With industrialisation this rigid structure of power-dependence relationships (c.f. Hicks, 1969) was destroyed and man was "made free in a way he had never been free before": he was cast out into the sea of anarchic and anomic market forces which dislocated him from 'society': Tannenbaum views modern trade unionism as an attempt by the workers to re-create the security of the 'old order' of power-dependence structures.

Finally, in this section, in order to avoid any unnecessary confusions, it seems useful to clarify the theoretical status of the basic framework and indicate how it is demarcated from the propositions of more conventional exchange theory.

Firstly, if it is not already apparent, it should be clear that the power-dependence paradigm is tautological in character.(6) It constitutes no more - and no less - than a set of related heuristic axioms which provide the core assumptions informing any analysis of industrial relations. In the analysis of any specific structure of power-dependence relations the 'interpretative understanding' of the actors' social action (or inaction) must be conducted with reference to the basis of dependency, the power resources available to actors, the way in which actors choose to utilize that power and the social values and ideologies which inform their behaviour. (See below).

Secondly, the perspective of socio-economic exchange which has been outlined above, means that the voluntaristic emphasis in conventional exchange theory cannot be sustained. Heath (1976, p. 19) points out that for all the major theorists "an exchange will take place only if *both* participants believe that the exchange provides them with *more* utility than does any other option currently open to them". In effect, this presupposes that participants will be better off than if the

the exchange did not take place and it implies that the actors have a considerable degree of choice. Both the supposition and the implication are clearly inappropriate to industrial relations. Exchanges involving wage-cuts, lay-offs,or redundancy, the introduction of a closed shop or a reduction in profits, may be, and often are, perceived by the actors in such exchange relations as involving a loss or a cost as well as being experienced as coercive. "Puzzingly, most exchange theorists ignore or omit these coerced exchanges". (*ibid.*, p. 20).

The conceptual logic which generates such seemingly gross omissions stems from the assumption (c.f. Blau, 1964; Emerson, 1972) that any fruitful discussion of exchange may *start* with the working assumption of 'equal power' or 'equal dependence'. As indicated earlier, it is more appropriate to view the process of socio-economic exchange as, at a minimum, taking place within the constraints of the prevailing distribution of power for, as noted by Human and Fryer (1975, p. 60), most analyses of exchange tend to "presuppose the *prior* existence of rules, rates and currency of exchange, and the determination of this prior framework is itself typically the outcome of power relations". At a more basic level of analysis, as Weber has cogently argued, "even on the utopian assumption that all competition were completely eliminated, conditions would still lead to a latent process of selection". Even if social conflict were reduced to 'mere' social selection differential dependence would still emerge since "in principle a process of biological selection remains". (1964, p. 132ff). This clearly implies that the "free-market analogy" (Hill, 1974) utilized by exchange theorists, certainly insofar as industrial relations is concerned, must be abondoned.

And thirdly, this raises considerable doubts about the validity of the general implication that exchanges create, sustain or restore balance in the relationship. This is, in part, a product of the 'free-market analogy' but is also derived from the specious assumption that the use of power by an actor *necessarily* leads to a proportionate decrease in his power. (An actor may, as Blau suggests, 'expend his social capital' by demanding the return of 'obligations' but this seems to be of only marginal relevance to his available power resources or on his capacity to enforce others to comply with his wishes. • Blau is emphasising the normative overlay of social exchange at the expense of the structural foundation which may, in any case, have determined at least some elements of the normative guides). Emerson (1972) is more equivocal on this issue but still insists that "exchange relations tend to change toward balance" (*ibid.*, p. 66). Conceptually, the notion of 'balance' - which is sometimes but not always associated with 'equilibrium' - is a methodological minefield for to suggest that a relationship is 'balanced' implies criteria for making such a judgement and the likelihood is that covert use will be made of the '_status quo_' as a basis for deriving such criteria. Similarly, this tendency to treat the _status quo_ as the 'measure' of balance preempts considerations of the possibility that the actors in industrial relations may, in the pursuit of perceived interests, utilize tactics and strategies designed either to deliberately _create_ conflict and 'imbalance' or to _maintain_ the 'system' in 'disequilibrium'. Given differential interests, actors may be viewed as acting rationally when attempting to maintain or increase their control or their power over other actors. Such a perspective would seem to be inimical to the current thrust of exchange theory. Just as the assumption of 'equal power' must be rejected as misleading so too the assumption of exchanges leading to balance must be abandoned.

One of the more obvious consequences of these latter assumptions is that in the analysis of unequal exchange the role of power is likely to be translated into the 'norm of reciprocity'.(7) This troublesome, multi-purpose concept is invariably associated with notions of 'fairness', shared meanings and shared values. It is true, for example, that an actor may perceive a _particular_ exchange as 'fair' but such a definition will always be situation-specific and may obscure the fact that the same actor perceives all other aspects of that exchange relationship as grossly 'unfair'. Indeed, the actor's definition of 'fairness' may be conditioned by his conception of what is fair _given_ the constraints of the relationship. Mann (1973), for example, refers to the "pragmatic acceptance" by workers of the constraints under which they operate. The 'norm of reciprocity' seems similarly misleading: mutual agreements or temporary accommodations may be based on social expediency and little else. Emerson (1972) doubts the distinctive usefulness of the norm of reciprocity, arguing that it is, by definition, an attribute of social exchange and that "what Gouldner calls the 'norm' of reciprocity may be little more than a widespread human recognition of the contingencies intrinsic to all social exchange". (_ibid_., p. 61). And Hill offers support: "interaction can and does become habitual and can be stable over time without either party attaching moral value to it or treating it as legitimate in terms of social values". (1974, p. 230). In addition, as Weber has pointed out, a social relationship depends upon "mutual orientation" - no more and no less; 'reciprocity' would be an additional characteristic dependent upon the actor's subjective definitions. (1964, pp. 118-120).

More specifically, what all this suggests is that the notions of 'fairness' and the 'norm of reciprocity' are best excluded as _general_ analytical constructs since their specific appropriateness is singularly dependent on the actors' subjective definitions in the context of prevailing ideologies: as such they refer to part of that which has to be explained and cannot be treated as given, a priori, general social values or orientations. Legitimation of the prevailing power -dependence structures is always, in this scheme of things, problematic.

In part as a result of the foregoing reservations concerning the general propositions of exchange theory, the distinctiveness of the present formulation can be ensured by characterising industrial relations as those structures of socio-economic (rather than merely 'social') exchange deriving from the employment relationship. The initial advantage of this is that it ensures a continuing 'semantic reminder' that it is necessary to theorise the social and economic dimensions of industrial relations in conjunction with each other. Secondly, and more importantly, it places emphasis on the social nature and socially constructed character of work and production relations. There has been a tendency for the latter, especially within the purview of economic analysis, to be construed as fundamentally, if not solely, economic in character since the demand for and supply of the labour resource involves systematic exchange of wage prices and costs.

However, some of the industrial relations which may have a significant impact on the wage-cost, wage-price exchange relationship, such as inter-managerial, intra-union and, even in some instances, inter-personal relations, are not necessarily primarily economic in character. (More generally, of course, governmental intervention may seriously interfere with so-called market forces). And, as has been consistently emphasised, conceptually, it must be recognised that economic exchange never takes place in a social, political or cultural vacuum. Social power, both as a structural property and as a resource which is differentially available to actors within industrial relations, is the medium through which abstract market relations are transformed into concrete, socially constructed, employment relations. Power, dependence and conflict take precedence over the invisible hand of marginal unit costing.

POWER-DEPENDENCE AND NEGOTIATED ORDER

The characteristic features of socio-economic exchange structures clearly indicate that one of the central theoretical issues in industrial relations is the explication of social order. In any analysis of the character and functioning of the employment relationship - which is arguably the major socio-economic relationship in industrial society - it is necessary to examine whether this relationship is best regarded as one based on free contract or one which is fundamentally coercive and exploitative in character. This issue is not merely central to the Marxist critique of industrial relations, but is also reflected in the traditional concern of the social reformist perspective with the identification and establishment of the most 'effective' institutional machinery; in the theoretical convergence on the 'rules' in industrial relations; and in the labour economists' concern to resolve the indeterminancy of the bargaining problem in wage theory. (Indeed, it is also one of the central themes which informs managerial thinking and theorising - especially that, from Hawthorne onwards, which focusses on 'good management practice').

This section will be directed toward explaining the extent to which, within the framework of the power-dependence paradigm, the social order of employment relations can be regarded as a socially constructed negotiated order.

The power-dependence property of the employment relationship indicates that actors are impelled to co-operate in order to accommodate their mutual dependence; this 'constrained co-operation' is conducted within the existing differential distribution of power through a variety of more or less institutionalised social processes - which may generically be termed processes of job regulation and control. Thus it may be argued that the 'rules' in industrial relations are the institutionalised outcome - they are not necessarily compromises - of power relationships. They regulate - but do not necessarily determine - the behaviour of the parties to those relationships. The various rule-making processes are therefore conceived as social mechanisms whereby the endemic conflict that characterises these structures is _temporarily_ resolved. It follows that the rules enjoy an unstable, shifting status being subject to the vicissitudes of the relative dependence (and power) of the actors. Hence, conformity with a rule or norm does not endow it with 'legitimacy': it is merely a behavioural indication of its 'authoritativeness'. The rules may be said to constitute a _de facto_ normative structure since - in the absence of a legitimatory ideology - they only continue to govern behaviour so long as they are enforced. The decision to transgress such rules typically results in sanctions becoming operative, a 're-emergence' of the endemic conflict, and a resumption of the prevailing (socio-political) negotiation processes. Logically, this would seem to indicate that the 'rules' governing employment relationships and work behaviour together with the rules established for the administration and enforcement of the latter constitute an imposed and fundamentally coercive social order.

Such a conclusion, however, in that we are concerned with a sociological account of the employment relationship, is both conceptually and empirically an oversimplification. Conceptually, it depends upon a view of power in which the dominant actor is assumed to have the capacity to determine _all_ the 'regulations' which govern the actions of the subordinate actor. It is a view which entails stretching the meaning of coercion beyond its etymological limits.

Empirically, there are noteable examples of the supply of labour being actively controlled by cohesive labour organisation. On occasion, such as in printing (Child, 1967) and dock-work (Hill, 1976, Bell, 1967), employers are sometimes forced to employ labour which would normally be considered surplus to their requirements. While such worker control over the 'demand for labour' is unusual, there is considerable evidence which demonstrates the extent to which organised workpeople can subvert the operation of wage-payment systems, control the production process, and determine productivity levels. (Such a power is, of course, exercised within the context of a relationship in which they remain subordinate in terms of the overall distribution of control, prestige and rewards). In addition, there are many instances where the extant rules are a product, not only of the conflicting interests which characterise the wage-work employment relationship, but also of active co-operation, such as Gouldner's (1965) celebrated 'safety rules'. More generally, with regard to what are normally taken to be the 'core' rules of industrial relations: the substantive rules are more obviously the product of the endemic conflicting interests, while the procedural reules - since both parties may be seen to have pragmatic interests in stabilizing the conflict process - may be viewed as the product of mutual interests. This is not to imply that they are not the outcome of a power conflict but that, typically, they may be invested with 'greater legitimacy'. (In these examples the legitimacy of the rules is dependent on the <u>perceived</u> interests of the relevant actors).

More importantly, the conclusion that the rules constitute a coerced social order reflects a failure to appreciate the underlying character of the relationships within the power-structure. It ignores the impact of the differential dependence experienced by the actors: with the possible exception of such cases as forced labour in prison camps(8), the employment relationship is never one in which one actor is in a structural position to totally dominate the other actor(s). It may, on occasion, come close to this but it would be mistaken to conclude, for example, that such situations are widely prevalent in industrial societies. The power-relationships of industrial relations are invariably characterised by bargaining and negotiation which, in itself, is an indication of <u>some</u> differential distribution of power, however unbalanced. In this respect it seems reasonable to conclude that the vast majority of the 'rules' in industrial relations enjoy <u>de facto</u> recognition from the actors who are subject to them. Actors regulate their relationship by reaching accommodations and 'working relationships' even though their "normative aspirations" (Fox, 1971) may remain unachieved. The latter are, perhaps perpetually, constrained by the rules that have been recognised and 'agreed upon' as 'authoritative'. These extant rules may be viewed 'as the best we could get in the circumstances', and thus the legitimacy of such rules remains problematic.

Since the rules are recognised as *de facto* authoritative prescriptions they will be referred to as the '*structurally legitimate*' framework of rules regulating behaviour within industrial relations. 'Closed shop' provisions exemplify why such a concept is both necessary and appropriate. A person who seeks employment may consider the rule that he must join a trade union before being employed to be 'unjust', 'inequitable' and nonlegitimate. Those who enforce the rule (which may include the employer) may argue that they have all discussed the matter and agreed - either unanimously or through some form of voting procedure - that the rule is a 'just', 'equitable' and legitimate rule. The prospective employee, despite his refusal to legitimate this condition of employment, may well concede the matter of principle on grounds of expediency: by doing so he gives *de facto* recognition to the rule and it thus becomes an 'authoritative' norm governing his behaviour. Significantly, there are no *sociological* criteria to resolve this question of legitimacy. An observer - sociological or otherwise - might reasonably conclude that the rule *is* legitimate because it is supported by the majority definition of reality. However, this conclusion only holds given a particular set of values for, fundamentally, the issue is about the sanctity of individual and collective rights - which are ultimately irreconcilible - not about majorities and minorities. The person who was reluctant to follow the rule and join the union may - in behavioural terms - have been 'proved wrong' but it cannot be said that his perception was 'mistaken', merely, perhaps, ill-informed in terms of a *rational* model of socio-economic behaviour.

Thus the suggestion that the rules and norms established through the various rule-making processes may be characterised as being 'structurally legitimate' simply because their existence is supported by the prevailing power-structure. They are 'authoritative' to the extent that they are recognised as governing behaviour by those who are subject to them. And they retain this 'authoritativeness' so long as they are enforced either unilaterally, 'jointly', by the State or collectively through self-regulation. In the absence of an acceptable legitimation, actors conform to the rules because to do otherwise would invoke sanctions and, in certain instances, generate overt conflict. In this respect the rules prescribe the normative criteria of acceptable behaviour within a given structure of power-relationships.

Actors may be prepared to endure certain sanctions and forego certain benefits in their attempt to either revise or maintain the existing rule or in order to create a new rule. Hence workers may accept the loss of wages resulting from a 'work-to-rule', an overtime ban or a strike. Management may accept the production losses incurred through refusing to agree to a rule-revision proposed by workpeople. And political parties (or governments) may be prepared to forego the support of a particular group of citizens or endure social protest in order to retain an existing rule or resist the introduction of a new one. Thus there are two important characteristic features of the decision to transgress or refuse to recognise a structurally legitimate rule. Firstly, sanctions become operative. (The severity of their impact will obviously be dependent on the distribution of power between the dependent actors involved in the relationship). Secondly, it will typically result in an overt conflict which will typically be processed through a socially institutionalised form of conflict-resolution. (Such a process may well include the 'structurally legitimate' use of strikes). It is important to remember that there are covert forms of conflict-resolution and, also, that these are not always clearly recognisable as 'socially institutionalised'. For example, an actor may choose to resolve the conflict he perceives in the relationship by withdrawing from that relationship - it has become commonplace to refer to certain kinds of turnover and absenteeism as being symptomatic of industrial conflict. (Hyman, 1972). And there are some forms which are only 'institutionalised' by <u>one</u> actor, for example, employees may actively engage in subversion of certain rules by participating in the establishment and enforcement of 'informal work norms' which supersede those arrived at through a more recognisable form of conflict-resolution such as unilateral imposition or collective-bargaining. (Lupton, 1963; Roy, 1969). The 'structurally legitimate' framework may be subverted through other processes such as direct sabotage or deliberate poor work. (Ridley, 1971; Brown, G., 1977). The other important aspect of conflict-resolution is that the conflict is rarely, if ever, completely resolved: given the conceptualisation of power-dependence, conflict is an enduring, even if somnolent, social property of the relationships. This again emphasises the appropriateness of seeing the structurally legitimate framework as a normative framework of "temporary accommodations" (Anthony, 1977) which endure only so long as those in a position to transgress the rules refrain from doing so.

Thus far in the elaboration, if you are still with me perceptive reader, it is possible to detect a considered degree of sociological utilitarianism. Power-dependence and the regulative processes which characterise socio-economic exchange have been treated as substantively calculative in character. While there are indeed substantial grounds for arguing that the nature and content of work in contemporary industrial society offers the prospective employee little other than instrumental return - see Fox's (1974) insightful if pessimistic account of the dynamics of low-trust relations or even Braverman's (1974) more radical account of the same phenomena which was appropriately sub-titled 'the degradation of work in the twentieth century' - it would be mistaken to conclude that social action within the context of the employment relationship is informed solely by instrumental-economic values. (If only in terms of 'subjective meaning' there remain considerable sectors of employment - particularly in service organisations - where active commitment to stated organisational 'goals' is a pre-requisite to performance). And, more generally, although economic dependence is invariably seen as most significant in the ordering of social relations, it also seems clear that the cash-nexus alone is no more than a fragile component of social order. Weber (1964, p. 324 ff), for example, points out that dependence relations based on purely material interests are inherently unstable. "Normally, other elements, affectual and ideal, supplement such interests" - though even these may be insufficient to ensure stability. In addition what is necessary "is the belief in legitimacy". Economic power, of itself, is not seen to constitute 'authority' even though (subordinate) actors comply: the fact that they do so "is referable only to the formal obligation, without regard to the actor's own attitude to the value or lack of value of the content of the command as such".

In more mundane terminology, this suggests two things. Firstly, that while power may be 'effective' - in the sense that it can 'get things done' - it only becomes 'efficient' when it is tied to some form of legitimatory ideology: the creation of social legitimacy permits a much greater economy in the use of power. And, secondly, that social values can be seen to operate as a transformative medium which has the effect of ameliorating if not resolving conflict. (In a Marxist framework, 'bourgeois ideology' is sometimes viewed as a social tranquilizer to which the social actors become addicted). Thus, if an employer can rely upon a workforce which believes, or has been persuaded to believe, in the 'rights of private property' or 'the dictatorship of the proletariat', then their compliance can be viewed as willing rather than coerced or constrained. Equally, of course, social values, insofar as they orientate social action, can have the opposite effect: thus 'ideology' can be seen to operate <u>both</u> as a keystone of social order and as a stimulus to social change. Although this distinction is not one which has always been made sufficiently clear in the industrial relations literature - despite an increasing concern with ideology in recent years - there are some parallels which can be drawn in the analyses of power. Duverger (1972), for example, in his analysis of the relationship between power and social interaction, concludes that power is best viewed as 'two-faced' since it has both integrative and divisive consequences. The fact that ideology can be viewed in a similar way only serves to highlight the intimacy between the two concepts. The pervasiveness of power in social relations, and, in particular, the exercise of power, is invariably associated with some attempt to legitimise that power.

Furthermore, these divisive and integrative aspects of power and ideology find reflection in the 'dual' character of power-dependence which emphasises the mutual as well as the conflictual aspect of socio-economic exchange. Mutual interest necessarily coexists with mutual antagonism. And it is this 'dualism' which has been a central source of obfuscation in discussions of the problematic status of the 'rules' in industrial relations. For example, Fox, who has examined this problem in depth, while clearly recognising the difficulties, does not appear to see a way through them: "It is not possible to draw a sharp dividing line between imposing a normative system by power and negotiating one by consent... Negotiated agreements must therefore be expected to have varying degrees of legitimacy _for either party_ depending on the extent to which they feel conscious of having been pressured into accepting its terms against their will". (1971, p. 160, emphasis added).

The concept of legitimacy is invariably associated with the, now unfashionable, concept of authority. The latter is usually construed as the polar opposite of power and this leads to the implicit (if not explicit) assumption that a social relationship is _either_ one of power _or_ one of authority. However, given power-dependence and Fox's formulation, which clearly indicates that the rules enjoy differential legitimacy 'for either party', it is possible for a social relationship to be _both_ a power-reflationship and an authority-relationship _at the same time_. By extension, it is arguable that the _central problem_ Fox has highlighted can be clarified by having _two_ concepts of legitimacy: one characteristic of power-relations - structural legitimacy - and one characteristic of authority relations - social legitimacy.

Social legitimacy refers to a property conferred upon a rule or norm by those who are _subject_ to that rule or norm. More precisely, actors are seen to _subject themselves_ to the rule or norm. Social legitimacy rests entirely in the actors' perception of the 'rightness' of a particular rule or norm: like beauty, it resides in the 'eye of the beholder'. Alternatively, if an individual actor - despite his power to disregard a rule if he so chooses - perceives any challenge to that rule as being 'unethical' (i.e. as an anti-social act) then that particular rule can be said to enjoy social legitimacy. We are concerned in this context with a specific characteristic of the actors' orientation to the rules. It is the actor's definition of the situation. which determines whether a rule enjoys social as well as structural legitimacy. Barnard's (1956) highly original analysis of authority can be used to illustrate the distinction. For Barnard authority (i.e. 'social legitimacy' in our terms) is endowed upon an order (rule) by the person who is required to obey the instruction. It does not become an authoritative order until the recipient recognises the order as being legitimate for him. Authority is thus delegated upwards in the sense that the source of the instruction is 'granted permission' to give the orders by the recipients. It must be stressed that conformity with the norm occurs regardless of the strength of the underlying structural legitimacy. Consequencly, the withdrawal of social legitimacy is extremely difficult - if not impossible - to sanction. As Blau (1964, p. 201) puts it: "compliance can be enforced with sufficient power, but approval cannot be forced regardless of how great the power". Nor does it necessarily involve the emergence of overt conflict for, in many instances there may be no immediate or perceived change in behaviour - while the actor may have divested a rule of social legitimacy it remains structurally legitimate so long as he does not transgress it - he may, of course, not have the capacity to transgress it. What this emphasises is that structural legitimacy is an enduring characteristic of the rules whereas social legitimacy is ephemeral in character.

There are a number of important points requiring elaboration which emerge out of this brief summary. Firstly, structural legitimacy - although it rests upon mutual dependence - does not depend upon consensus over means or ends (which is not to say that such consensus is necessarily absent). In all instances actors are constrained by the relationship itself since the exchange that takes place is considered - by at least one of the actors - as being more beneficial to no exchange at all. In the context of industrial relations, what this means is that 'social order' and stability may be maintained through a normative structure which, while it may not be overtly perceived as coercive, is regarded by the subordinate actors as non-legitimate. (The existence of various forms of employee 'counter-cultures', which have been repeatedly documented since Roethlisberger and Dickson (1939) is circumstantial evidence, if not definitive proof, of such perceptions).

Secondly, social legitimacy is an additional but unstable characteristic of the rules since it depends upon consensus over both means and ends. For this reason it is both the more problematic and the more interesting feature of any analysis of rules. Given the characterisation of power-dependence, the 'existence' of social legitimacy is clearly intimately bound up with the role of social values and ideology. Since, at this point in the argument, we are only concerned with perceived interests - as opposed to 'real' interests, whatever they might be - there is no contradiction in asserting that there can be consensus over means and ends in the context of what is, theoretically, a relationship characterised by endemic conflict. Notwithstanding Berger and Luckmann's (1967) memorable observation that "power in society includes the power to produce reality", it also seems possible that social actors can, at least, make choices from the range of socially available values. In so doing, they can be seen to actively endorse one form of social order rather than another. This is recognised even by those operating within a more radical framework of analysis: Mann, for example, has identified what he calls a "profound dualism in the worker's situation and his consciousness". (1973, p. 68). He suggests that periodic outbursts of militancy are symptomatic of the tension created by this dualism - the worker's unmistakable experiences of conscious deprivation generates antagonism while his satisfaction with economic returns facilitates "a factual, if not a normative" consensus within the relationship. Similarly, Parkin, in his analysis of class inequalities, distinguishes three 'meaning systems' which are available to social actors: the dominant, the subordinate and the radical value systems. Of these, the dominant value system is seen to constitute "a moral framework which promotes the endorsement of existing inequality". (1971, p. 81).

It should be clear, thirdly, that this analytical distinction between social and structural legitimacy constitutes only a skeletal framework for any empirical analysis of rules. Empirically, one would expect to find a complex mosaic of 'legitimacy' dependent upon a systematic delineation of interests, issues, procedures and orientations. (Rules are, as noted above, only the <u>outcome</u> of power-conflicts). Within the context of the prevailing distribution of power industrial relations are best characterised as 'mixed' situations where there is some consensus some of the time with regard to means and/or ends. For example, both employer and employees might be united in the belief that some form of 'joint regulation' would be in their mutual interests, though this would not pre-empt the possibility of considerable conflict over the precise form that such a mechanism should take. Similarly, workers and management might be at one in believing that a weekly wage is the 'best method' of transacting their exchange yet this may well be associated with considerable conflict over the values placed on their respective contributions to that exchange.

Finally, on 'legitimacy' there is one further point that merits elaboration. It was noted above that conformity with a socially legitimate norm is independent of the strength of the underlying structural legitimacy. There are numerous work situations where structural legitimacy - although enduring - is inadequate to ensure an <u>acceptable</u> level of performance on the part of employees. For example, it seems reasonable to suggest that the laws which carefully regulate the right to strike in the electricity and gas supply industries are invested with social legitimacy by the employees of those industries: unregulated strike action could result in very serious danger to human life and, consequently, such action is viewed as 'unethical'. One might consider policemen and firemen to hold similar views - though strike action on the part of such employees is not unknown. And what has been referred to as the "increasing fragmentation of normative regulation" (Flanders and Fox, 1969, p. 161) has, in recent years, become manifest in previously unprecedented work-spheres in Great Britain - doctors, nurses, ambulance drivers and other personnel directly or indirectly involved in health care have turned to methods, such as working-to-rule and striking, which are normally confined to the industrial sphere. In situations where such occupational groups as these choose to divest the rules of social legitimacy it is significant that there is very little that 'society' can do - the possible social costs are enormous - except make appeals to conscience (or grant the wage-increase) for, despite the possible illegal nature of strike action, it is hardly practical to prosecute, imprison or sack such workers. What is of significance in several of these work contexts is that structural legitimacy alone appears to be insufficient to ensure a socially acceptable level of work-performance.

The power (and potential power) of such employees is rarely given sufficient emphasis - the one exception being the 'professions' (Johnson, 1972) - in the argument about the basis of social order in industrial relations. It seems clear that the extent to which social legitimacy is a pre-requisite for the rules governing such actors constitutes an important weakness in the argument that social order is fundamentally an imposed order. It might be argued that such a conclusion ignores the potentially 'mystifying' role of ideology and, in one sense, this is correct. However, all contemporary industrial societies, whether they be 'plan-rational' or 'market rational' types of society (Dahrendorf, 1967), employ such workers and in both types of society, regardless of political and cultural ideologies, the same analysis seems appropriate: what we have described as 'social legitimacy' seems crucial to their effective operation. This is not to minimise the differences between such societies nor to deny that 'society' does have sanctions which can be applied, but to illustrate the theoretical significance of social and structural legitimacy.

The underlying logic of the proposition that social order in industrial relations is 'socially constructed' and, fundamentally, a 'negotiated' order should now be fairly clear for the nature of socio-economic exchange relations is such that a central 'core' of common values is sociologically naive while unadulterated social coercion is inadequate. The regularities in social arrangements - whether these be conceived of as organisational structures, norms or rules - are created and maintained through interactive bargaining processes which operate to temporarily resolve the conflict between the mutual interests and antagonisms of the actors. These processes, it must be emphasised, can only be understood in the context of the extant distribution of power, the power resources available to actors and the social values which inform the actors' orientations.

THE ANALYSIS OF SOCIO-ECONOMIC EXCHANGE

In this final section an attempt will be made to demonstrate how the imperatives which inform the power-dependence paradigm would be reflected in an operational context. Since, almost by definition, any analysis of socio-economic exchange will be situation-specific all that will be attempted is a preliminary specification of the salient elements of any such analysis together with some brief illustrations from the existing literature.

The power-dependence paradigm indicates that there are three basic requirements to any analysis of socio-economic exchanges: they may be distinguished as the structural, the behavioural and the ideational elements: while analytically distinct they are, clearly, empirically interactive and interdependent.

(i) The structural elements

The identification of the structure of a particular complex of socio-economic exchange involves:

(a) the identification of the salient actors;

(b) the identification of the power bases and resources available to the salient actors.

While Dunlop's (1958) long-established three-fold classification of the 'actors' - unions, management and government - is an obvious starting point the actual number of different interest groups in any empirical analysis will vary - partly according to the complexity of the situation and partly according to the level and scope of analysis. Fox (1971) has suggested that in any full examination, the number of "stake-holders" may be considerable. In general, the 'higher' the level and the narrower the scope of analysis the fewer the number of salient actors. It seems possible to specify different actors in terms of their 'primary' and 'secondary' significance but such a procedure is over-bureaucratic and would not add much to analytical clarity since any given actors' significance will be a matter for empirical inquiry and will, in any ase, depend upon the level of analysis.

The identification of the basis of dependency has already been discussed - it is seen to be primarily, though by no means exclusively, economic in character. However, the *a priori* specification of the actors' power bases and power resources is much more problematic. That elusive 'object which corresponds to power' seems best conceived in terms of a series of contingent variables. In an analytical framework they can only be described in general terms since their empirical salience will be variable and their relative significance will be difficult to determine since the 'power base' of any one actor will be made up of a cluster of contingent elements. However, given the present level of theoretical and methodological development, it seems reasonable to argue that precise measurement is less important than analytical clarity.

Insofar as the general analytic framework is concerned, it is fruitful to regard the degree of access to political power as the *primary* power resource available to the actors(9). This is because the nature of the prevailing socio-political institutions (and the associated social ideologies utilized to legitimate them) will determine the *character* of socio-economic exchange in society. First and foremost it will determine whether a society is primarily 'market-rational' or 'plan-rational', - in the latter, to put it bluntly, 'market forces' tend to be viewed as 'ideologically unacceptable' even if their role is not completely subverted. Secondly, it will have a crucial bearing on the tactics and strategies available to the actors. In particular, as recent events in Poland illustrate, it determines which procedural norms and institutions are permitted to operate.

The significance of this variable needs to be emphasised in order to avoid cultural myopia and stress the extent to which the political dimension - which is a *variable* - has tended to become a taken-for-granted parameter. In many instances this is not of particular significance (c.f. Levinson 1966) but in others it has led to what, in retrospect, appears to be naivety. One reason for this seems to lie in the implicit assumption that the 'legal framework' constitutes an almost 'neutral' backcloth to the analysis of industrial relations. It seems more realistic to view the extant 'legal framework' as the institutionalised norms of the values and interests of the State - these may or may not correspond with the values and interests of the two other principal, and perhaps subordinate, actors: employers and employees. Another lies in the inordinate significance that has been attached to collective bargaining as the *prima donna* among methods of job-regulation: an emphasis which has generated the entirely mistaken implication that 'state-intervention' constitutes a temporary abberation in what is, essentially, a bi-lateral process. Historically, the State has always been 'involved' in industrial relations if only by maintaining a policy posture of non-intervention. This is not to suggest that the State is necessarily all-powerful - the outcome of the power-dependence conflict which accompanied the short-lived 1971 Industrial Relations Act is testimony to the power that can be mobilized by British trade unions - but to emphasise the extent to which the State sets the parameters. In addition to its singular influence on procedures it plays an increasingly significant role in the formulation of economic and (sic) incomes policies.

Thus in any general specification of the power bases relevant to socio-economic exchange the actors' degree of access to political power seems fundamental. The important theoretical point to be made is that the dominant emphasis placed upon the role of economic forces as the major determinant of the outcomes of socio-economic exchange is specific to those societies where the economy is primarily or predominantly 'market-rational'.

It follows that, since the degree of freedom permitted to actors in the pursuit of economic power is contingent on the socio-political variable, that access to and control over relevant economic resources must be considered as the second most important power base. Any empirical analysis would undoubtedly reveal a diverse range of complex and inter-related sub-sets of factors which influence and, in some instances, determine the relative economic power (or relative economic dependence) of the various actors.

With respect to their access to and control over economic resources, both employers and employees, together with their respective organisations, are crucially dependent on the extent to which the State decides - or is mandated - to control the economy. In a 'plan-rational' society, the State may be viewed as attempting to pre-empt the other actors from acquiring economic resources though this will rarely be entirely successful (c.f. Granick, 1960). Where actors do manage to build such power bases the objective of the State will be to control or circumvent the independent use of such resources. In 'market-rational' societies - even through such a characterisation may now appear somewhat misleading given the extent to which liberal-democratic governments, to say nothing of the E.E.C., intervene to control 'market-forces' - the objective of the State and its administrative agencies is to influence if not control the use of those economic resources which are ostensibly directed by the other actors. (cf. Winkler, 1975, on the rise of 'corporatism').

While it is tempting to attempt to delineate the sources of

economic power available to each of the other two major actors, such a procedure is fraught with difficulty since most of the 'sub-variables' have differential impact on both actors - this appears to be invariably the case when the analysis is conducted at 'sub-societal' levels.

Apart from the primodial economic resource of capital which is available for deployment and capital assets, such as property - which in any specific analysis constitute part of the extant power-structure - the most important economic sub-variables include the following: the nature and degree of competition in the product market; the degree of product vulnerability; the degree of dispersion of production activities; the degree of competition (between employers) in the labour market; the ratio of factor costs; the degree of competition (between potential employees) in the labour market; the degree of employee (or union) control over the supply of labour; the ease of entry into a skill, trade or profession.

In addition to the latter economic sub-variables there are two others which, while strictly speaking subsumed under 'access to and control over economic resources' usually merit separate consideration in any analysis of industrial relations. These are the nature of the work technology and the nature of the wage payment system. While they will often be very closely related, they can vary independently of each other. (For example, despite the similarity in the work technology which is used in British motor car manufacturing, up until 1971, the character of industrial relations in the various sectors of the industry was crucially influenced by the use of different wage-payment systems).

With regard to the nature of the work technology, the most important aspect for power-dependence analysis is the extent to which actors control and are controlled by the production process and its associated work tasks. The most common-place example cited in this context is the car-assembly line. One of the earlier and more dramatic illustrations of the relevance of this variable is the Trist and Bamforth (1951) study of the move to the 'longwall' production system in the Durham coalmines. It seems reasonable to suggest that a re-analysis of their data in terms of power-dependence would indicate that the dramatic loss of the miners' control over their work activities and over self-determination of their wages were more important factors contributing to the subsequent level of 'inefficiency' than the socio-psychological variables emphasised by Trist and Bamforth (c.f. Blumberg's, 1968, re-analysis of the Hawthorne studies). Although it is an over-simplification, the fundamental change that resulted from the supercedence of the old 'short wall' production system was an inordinate increase in the relative dependence of the miners on the colliery management.

The nature of the wage-payment system can have an equally dramatic impact on the differential dependence of the actors. (And, of course, on relative bargaining power). The wage-payment system will be considered in terms of the extent to which the economic returns it yields are controlled by management or by the employees. (The tactics and strategies employed by the actors in order to increase their relative control over the 'output' of the wage-payment systems are clearly crucial. c.f. Roy, 1969; Lupton, 1972). The key variable seems to be the extent to which the payment of wages or salaries is <u>directly</u> related to a measurable or identifiable output. Generally, it appears that the control of systems which are based on 'simple attendance', i.e. hourly, weekly or monthly rates lies in the hands of the employers, for employees governed by such rates only have a limited range of tactics open to them. They may seek additional payments for special conditions or focus their attention on fringe benefits: although the most likely course of action will be to create overtime work and demand premium payments.

In contrast, once the employer seeks to increase the degree of control over employee behaviour through the use of work-measurement techniques and/or the introduction of wage-payment systems which ostensibly relate rewards to performance, a while new range of potentially negotiable issues are 'added' to the socio-economic exchange. Ultimately, and paradoxically, this may result in the employer ceding control of the wage-payment system to the employees (Brown, W., 1962) since the latter, usually, play a key role in the establishment of the effort-reward ratios characteristic of payments-by-results, piecework and measured daywork systems and since such systems are prone to ossification and degeneration.

This discussion of technological and wage-payment variables should not be taken to imply particular importance to these variables as determinants of economic power within the relationship as a whole - indeed, it perhaps emphasises the very limited area of activity available to particular individuals and groups in employment relationships. They will tend to be seen as the more significant variables in any plant-level analysis of industrial relations since they constitute significant influences on the process of socio-economic exchange for the actors at that level.

The third, and final, general power base is the degree of actor cohesion which, while it will often be critically influenced by access to political and economic power resources - and is clearly subordinate to them - appears to be sufficiently distinct to merit separate consideration. (c.f. the 8-month strike of the miners in 1926: despite an almost complete lack of political power and relatively small economic resources their action was independently sustained through social cohesion. Holton, 1976). In very general terms, the degree of actor cohesion - which presupposes some form of collective organisation - seems to be primarily contingent on ideological consensus over ends if not also over means. Without consensus over ends it is unlikely that a collective organisation can be formed, far less sustained. Dissensus over means and ends will invariably result in failure to effectively mobilize the available political and economic resources and, in certain instances, may be viewed as the primary reason for defeat over a particular issue. (Again, c.f. the lack of social cohesion at national level in the 1926 General Strike). This does not, of course, pre-empt the possibility of actors utilizing the available resources in an incompetent fashion or actors either deliberately choosing not to use their power or simply not being aware of the power resources available.

The degree of actor cohesion among workpeople, while it presupposes a working degree of consensus over ends and means, does not, thereafter, simply depend on the degree of organisation (i.e. as measured in terms of percentage membership) but is also dependent on a range of contingent structural variables. At a national level, the degree of ideological consensus among national trades unions may be highly significant. (c.f. the British T.U.C. with many European trade union movements, some of which are divided between Catholic, Protestant and Communist influences).

More specifically, worker cohesion is influenced by the character of trade union organisation (c.f. Turner, 1969, on 'open' and 'closed' trade unionism); the structure of worker/union organisation at both industry and plant level - multi-unionism, despite shop steward combine committees, still tends to be viewed as a barrier to worker cohesion, though much will depend on the specific issue; the degree of union job-control - the extent of the closed shop will, of course, also reflect the range and effect of sanctions available to 'ensure' cohesion; and the precise geographical location of the industry or plant may facilitate, as a result of socio-cultural isolation, a much greater degree of normative control over 'deviant' behaviour. Similarly, other variables, such as the character and form of the organisational technology and the nature of the wage-payment systems may have a crucial impact on worker cohesion. Finally, there are what might generically be termed the influence of ideational variables: occupational cultures and ideologies may generate cohesion while differential perceptions of status and prestige may militate against the development or maintenance of cohesion. (Lockwood, 1966).

Social cohesion among employers remains a singularly neglected field. This is partly because their collective organisations appear to be more resistant to researchers but probably of greater significance is the fact that their organisations are more diffuse and defused. (And sometimes more or less impenetrable to the outsider, e.g. Masonic organisation).

From what little evidence that is available it appears that employers' associations have a wider range of functions than either trade unions or occupational and/or professional associations. It also appears that the conflicting interests among employers are more likely to dominate their behaviour than do the conflicts which are endemic to employee organisations. (This may be partly because the withdrawal of an individual company is likely to be, relatively, more critical than the withdrawal of a single individual from union membership. c.f. the withdrawal of Esso and Alcan from their respective employers' organisations after the negotiation of productivity agreements. Companies may be large enough - or think themselves self-sufficient - not to belong to an employers' association. They may also, of course, have ideological objections to membership).

(ii) The behavioural elements

The behavioural elements of power-dependence analysis refers to the social processes, tactics and strategies available to and utilized by the actors in socio-economic exchange. In terms of power-dependence it must be assumed that actors will adopt strategies which are designed to reduce their dependence on or increase their power over the other actor(s). While this presupposes rational behaviour it by no means implies maximising behaviour nor does it necessarily imply that actors will be aware of the full consequences of any action they may take. Quite apart from the theoretical impossibility of such 'knowledge', what Weber has referred to as 'substantive rationality' will, it seems, always be interposed between the elegance of formal rationality and the richness of social reality. Despite this, again following Weber, it is appropriate to use the formally rational model as the basic framework for any empirical analysis.

Emerson, in his original formulation of the power-dependence paradigm, suggested that there are "exactly four generic types of balancing operation". (1962, p. 35). An actor may reduce his dependence on another by (i) withdrawing from the relationship and foregoing whatever it was he derived from the relationship; (ii) cultivating an alternative source of supply thus reducing the level of immediate dependence on one actor; (iii) increase the dependence of the other actor by providing him with a reciprocal service or good; and (iv) coercing the other actor to supply the required service or good. Despite the fact that some of the strategies identified simply could not be realistically pursued because of the pre-existing power differentials, Emerson does highlight some of the more important strategies of dependence-reduction.

The most common is the process of coalition-formation for both defensive and offensive purposes: and this is probably the dominant strategy adopted by actors in industrial relations. There is virtually universal agreement that the primary purpose of trade union organisation was to mitigate the inequality of the bargaining relationship between employer and employee. Individual employees may withdraw from the employment relationship but such action will invariably be contingent on his ability to gain employment elsewhere - usually, on not less favourable terms. However, it would be unrealistic to regard this as a major avenue of dependence-reduction: large-scale individual withdrawal from the employment relationship is more likely to be the result of competition between employers.

Similarly, the cultivation of alternative sources of supply does not appear to be a major strategy characteristic of contemporary industrial relations. While historically, both in Britain and the United States, there are numerous instances of employers 'replacing' their labour force with non-union or 'scab' labour, the use of such tactics is now a relative rarity - not least because of the degree of union organisation and cohesion. And, while there is scant evidence to support such an assertion, the practice of 'moon-lighting' in order to reduce dependence on one employer seems an unlikely generalised form of employee behaviour.

However, the underlying principle of 'cultivating alternative sources' applies to those instances where employers (or investors) decide upon a policy of capital intensification which results in labour being displaced by machinery. Similarly, the investor may decide to withdraw his capital from one form of enterprise - thus creating redundancy - and invest it elsewhere.

Emerson's other tactic, reducing dependence by providing a reciprocal service, would seem to have only limited application to industrial relations because, fundamentally, it presupposes more or less equal resources. It would seem to be most relevant to intra-organisational bargaining proceses; in particular, to those which are normally characterised as 'log-rolling' and to the processes associated with internal power-struggles or 'political in-fighting' (c.f. Levinson, 1966; Heath, 1976; but see also Hoxie, 1920, for an account of employer-trade union collusion which could be viewed as a form of dependence-reduction arising from the provision of reciprocal services).

While Emerson provides a useful starting point to the discussion of the behavioural elements of socio-economic exchange he by no means provides an adequate coverage of the range of coercive, persuasive and manipulative social processes which typify industrial relations. Conceptually, the most glaring weakness is his failure to provide any explicit analysis of the various forms of bargaining. It should be unmistakably clear that an analysis of both inter and intra bargaining processes is central to any analysis of industrial relations conducted within the confines of the perspective advanced in this paper.

(iii) The ideational element

In the previous discussion, the dual role of ideology as a keystone of social order and as a stimulus to social change was emphasised. In any specific empirical analysis attention would focus on the competing and contrasting attitudes and values held by participants regarding both their own situation and those of the other salient actors with a view to establishing the way in which these beliefs are utilized by actors to legitimate existing social arrangements and strategies and how they operate to modify such arrangements or generate new ones. In this context we are specifically concerned with the meanings salient actors provide for their social behaviour and to relate these to the prevailing structure of power-dependence relationships. "A sociological explanation will show why people behave in a certain way partly because of the exigencies of their environment and partly because of how in their society they think it is appropriate to behave and how they see the possibilities open to them". This quotation from Dorothy Emmet (1966) neatly summarises the way in which the analysis of power-dependence structures must be related to the prevailing ideologies of the salient actors. It is, predictably, anticipated that the pursuit of intrinsic differential interests will be legitimated by the actors with reference to sets of values which, typically, will be more or less in conflict(10).

NOTES

1. By traditional industrial sociology is meant the perspective offered, for example, by Miller and Form (1963). In fact Miller was among those who actively advocated the split: "our main job in building industrial sociology is to seek out those principles that are exhibited in work groups and in the socialisation of the worker regardless of the economic and political structures of the larger society. For this objective a study of union-management relations occupies an important but secondary position". (ibid., 1948, p. 395).

2. Space does not permit a full elaboration of my critique of the existing approaches to industrial relations. It will be included in a book, Industrial Relations: Power, Dependence and Conflict, currently in preparation.

3. See, for example, Dunlop (1950, 1964), Pen (1959), Cross (1969), Rees (1973), Burkitt (1975), Mulvey (1978), and Burkitt and Bowers (1979).

4. The specific notion of 'power-dependence relations' is most coherently developed in the work of Richard Emerson (1962, 1972), one of the less well-known 'exchange theorists'. In the context of industrial relations, Somers (1969) is perhaps the best-known attempt to utilize an exchange framework.

5. While it is by no means clear what empirical referent one could give for a relationship of 'pure altruism', it is the theoretical limiting case for the application of power-dependence analysis since it means that an actor to a social relationship has <u>totally</u> relinquished his own interests in the relationship while remaining a 'significant other'.

6. Although it is unnecessary to make the point at length, it should be clear that not all tautologies are useless for the purposes of description or explication - they may provide excellent heuristic devices provided their inherent limitations are explicitly recognised. (c.f. the notion of 'utility maximisation' in economic theory).

7. It is not without irony that Blau, in his ostensible attempt to exclude economic exchange, seems to get trapped in an even more restrictive tautological paradigm than that of power-dependence. This is exemplified by the extortionate demands made upon the concept of 'reciprocity'. In his concluding Chapter, Blau (1964) writes that "reciprocity is an equilibrating force, the assumption being that every social action is balanced by some appropriate counteraction" though "reciprocity on one level, however entails imbalances on others. If persons are obligated to accede to another's wishes because he renders essential services to them for which they cannot otherwise compensate him, their compliance reciprocates for the unilateral services they obtain and in this sense restores balance, but it also creates an imbalance of power". (<u>ibid</u>., p. 336). On one page Blau seems to be utilizing 'reciprocity' as a sort of universal euphemism to account for social norms, social change, power, authority, social structure and social conflict. The net result, as the latter part of the above quotation indicates, is a sort of sociological Catch - 22.

8. For examples of the strategies available to subordinate actors in such situations see Etzioni (1975).

9. This is not to ignore the argument about the relationship of economic to political power - it is not of primary importance in the present context since we are not concerned with a theory of society.

10. Finally, two points of emphasis. Firstly, as should be evident from the last paragraph, the problematic status of 'ideology' within the overall scheme has, for reasons of space, been deliberately underdeveloped. Any full presentation would require both a detail examination of the relationship between social values, ideology and

power (c.f. Lukes, 1974) and a consideration of whether 'ideology' can be viewed as a form of power in its own right (c.f. Clegg, 1979). Secondly, and this perhaps needs little explanation, this paper is very much a working document: I would appreciate any comments, criticisms or mild abuse, that you feel might assist in resolving the numerous problems that still remain.

BASIC BIBLIOGRAPHY

Allen, V. L., (1966), Militant Trade Unionism, London: Merlin Press.

Anthony, P. D. A., (1977), The Conduct of Industrial Relations, London: I.P.M.

Anthony, P. D. A. & Crichton, A., (1969), Industrial Relations and Personnel Specialists, Batsford.

Bachrach, P. and Baratz, M. S., (1969), Two Faces of Power, (1962), in Connolly, (Ed.).

Barnard, C. I., (1956), The Functions of the Executive, Cambridge (Mass.): Harvard U.P.

Bell, D., (1961), The End of Ideology, New York: Free Press.

Bendix, R., (1963), Work and Authority in Industry, New York: Harper & Row.

Berger, J., Zelditch, M. & Anderson, B., (1972), Sociological Theories in Progress, Houghton Mifflin.

Berger, P. & Luckmann, T., (1967), The Social Construction of Reality, London: Allen Lane.

Bierstedt, R., (1956), An Analysis of Social Power, A.S.R., Vol. 15.

Blau, P. M., (1964), Exchange and Power in Social Life, New York: Wiley.

Blumberg, P., (1968), Industrial Democracy: The Sociology of Participation, London: Constable.

Blumer, H., (1947), Sociological Theory in Industrial Relations, A.S.R., Vol. 12.

Braverman, H., (1974), Labour and Monopoly Capitalism, New York and London: Monthly Review Press.

Brown, G., (1977), Sabotage, Spokesman Books.

Brown, S. C., (Ed.), (1979), Philosophical Disputes in the Social Sciences, Brighton: Harvester Press.

Brown, W., (1973), Piecework Bargaining, London: Heinemann.

Bulmer, M., (Ed.), (1975), Working-Class Images of Society, London: R.K.P.

Burkitt, B., (1975), Trade Unions and Wages, Bradford U.P.

Burkitt, T. & Bowers, D., (1979), Trade Unions and the Economy, London: Macmillan.

Chamberlain, N. & Kuhn, J. W., (1964), Collective Bargaining, 2nd Edition, New York: McGraw-Hill.

Child, J., (1967), Industrial Relations in the British Printing Industry, London: Allen & Unwin.

Child, J., (Ed.), (1973), Man and Organisation, London: Allen & Unwin.

Clegg, S., (1979), The Theory of Power and Organisation, London: R.K.P.

Coddington, A., (1968), Theories of the Bargaining Process, London: Allen & Unwin.

Connolly, W. E. (Ed.), (1969), The Bias of Pluralism, Atherton Press.

Cross, J. G., (1969), The Economics of Bargaining, Basic Books.

Dahl, R., (1957), The Concept of Power, Behavioural Science, Vol. 2.

Dahl, R., (1961), Who Governs? Democracy and Power in an American City, Yale U.P.

Dahrendorf, R., (1959), Class and Class Conflict in an Industrial Society, London: R.K.P.

Dahrendorf, R., (1967)., Conflict after Class: New Perspectives on the Theory of Social and Political Conflict, London: Longmans Green.

Deutsch, M., (1973), The Resolution of Conflict, Yale U.P.

Dunlop, J. T., (1944), Wage Determination Under Trade Unions, Kelley.

Dunlop, J. T., (1958), Industrial Relations Systems, New York. Holt & Co.

Dunlop, J. T., (Ed.), (1964), The Theory of Wage Determination, London: Macmillan, 1964.

Dunlop, J. T., (1964a), Productivity and the Wage Structure in Perlman, R., (Ed.).

Duverger, M., (1972), The Study of Politics, Nelson & Sons.

Emerson, R. M., (1962), Power-Dependence Relationships, A.S.R., Vol. 27.

Emerson, R. M., (1972), Exchange Theory, Part I: A Psychological Basis for Social Exchange and Exchange Theory, Part II: Exchange Relations and Network Structures, in Berger, Zelditch & Anderson (Eds.).

Emmet, D., (1966), Roles, Rules and Relations, London: Macmillan.

Etzioni, A., (1975), A Comparative Analysis of Complex Organisations, New York: Free Press.

Fox, A., (1971), A Sociology of Work in Industry, London: Collier-Macmillan.

Fox, A., (1973), Industrial Relations: A Social Critique of Pluralist Ideology; in Child (Ed.).

Fox, A., (1974), Beyond Contract: Work, Power and Trust Relations, London: Faber & Faber.

Fox, A. & Flanders, A., (1969), The Reform of Collective Bargaining: From Donovan to Durkheim, British J. of Industrial Relations, Vol. VII.

Giddens, A., (Ed.), (1974), Positivism and Sociology, London: Heinemann.

Goodman, J. F. B., Armstrong, E. G. A., Wagner, A., Davis, J. E. & Wood, S. F., (1975), Rules in Industrial Relations Theory: A Discussion, Industrial Relations Journal (Nottingham), Vol. 6., No. 1.

Gouldner, A., (1965), Patterns of Industrial Bureaucracy, London: R.K.P.

Granick, D., (1960), The Red Executive, New York: Doubleday.

Heath, A., (1971), Review Article: Exchange Theory, B. J. of Polit. Sc. Vol. 1.

Heath, A., (1976), Rational Choice and Social Exchange, Cambridge (England): C.U.P.

Hicks, J. R., (1969), A Theory of Economic History, Oxford: O.U.P.

Hill, S., (1974), Norms, Groups and Power: The Sociology of Workplace Industrial Relations, Brit. J. of Industrial Relations, Vol. XII.

Hill, S., (1976), The Dockers, London: Heinemann.

Holton, Bob, (1976), British Syndicalism 1900-1914, London: Pluto.

Hoxie, R. F., (1920), Trade Unionism in the United States, New York: Appleton-Century.

Hyman, R., (1972), Strikes, London: Fontana.

Hyman, R., (1975), Industrial Relations: A Marxist Introduction, London: Macmillan.

Hyman, R. & Fryer, B., (1975), Trade Unions: Sociology and Political Economy, in McKinley, J. B. (Ed.).

Johnson, T. J., (1972), Professions and Power, London: Macmillan.

Lane, T., (1974), The Union Makes Us Strong, Arrow.

Levinson, H. M. (1966), Determining Forces in Collective Wage Bargaining, New York: Wiley.

Lindblom, C. E., (1948), Bargaining Power in Price and Wage Determination, Q.J. of Econ., Vol. 62.

Lockwood, D., (1966), Sources of Variation in Working Class Images of Society, Soc. Rev. Vol. 14.

Lukes, S., (1974), Power: A Radical View, London: Macmillan.

Lukes, S., (1979), On the Relativity of Power, in Brown, S. C. (Ed.).

Lupton, T., (1963), On the Shop Floor, London: Pergamon.

Lupton, T., (Ed.), (1972), Payment Systems, Harmondsworth: Penguin.

Mann, M., (1973), Consciousness and Action Among the Western Working Class, London: Macmillan.

Marx, K. & Engels, F., (1968), Selected Works, London: Lawrence & Wishart.

McKinley, J. B. (Ed.), (1975), Processing People: Cases in Organisational Behaviour, London: Holt, Rinehart & Winston.

Miller, D. C., (1948), Comment on Moore, Amer. Econ. Rev., Vol. 13.

Miller, D. C. & Form, W. H., (1963), Industrial Sociology, Harper.

Mulvey, C., (1978), The Economic Analysis of Trade Unions, London: Martin Robertson.

Nichols, T. & Armstrong, P., (1976), Workers Divided, London: Fontana.

Parkin, F., (1971), Class Inequality and Political Order, McGibbon & Kee.

Pen, J., (1959), The Wage Rate Under Collective Bargaining, Cambridge (Mass.): Harvard U.P.

Perlman, R. (Ed.), (1964), Wage Determination: Market or Power Forces?. D. C. Heath.

Perlman, S., (1928), A Theory of the Labour Movement, Macmillan.

Rees, A., (1973), The Economics of Work and Pay, New York: Harper & Row.

Ridley, F. F., (1971), Revolutionary Syndicalism in France, Cambridge (England): C.U.P.

Rimmer, M., (1972), Race and Industrial Conflict, London: Heinemann.

Ross, A. M., (1948), Trade Union Wage Policy. Univ. California Press, 1953. (First published 1948).

Roethlislberger, R. J. and Dickson, W. J., (1939), Management and the Worker, Cambridge (Mass.): Harvard U. Press.

Rothschild, K. W. (Ed.), (1971), Power in Economics, Harmonsworth: Penguin.

Roy, D. F., (1969), Restriction of Output Among Unorganised Workers, Southern Illinois U.P.

Runciman, W. G., (1972), A Critique of Max Weber's Philosophy of Social Science, Cambridge (England): Cambridge U.P.

Salaman, G., (1974), Community and Occupation, Cambridge (England), Cambridge U.P.

Somers, C. G. (Ed.), (1969), Essays in Industrial Relations Theory, Iowa State U.P.

Stevens, C. M., (1963), Strategy and Collective Bargaining Negotiation, New York: McGraw-Hill.

Tannenbaum, F., (1964), The True Society, Cape.

Trist, E. L. & Bamforth, K. W., (1951), Some Social and Psychological Consequences of the Longwall Method of Coal-Getting, Hum. Rel., Vol. 4, No. 1.

Turner, H. A., (1969), Trade Union Growth, Structure and Policy, London: Allen & Unwin.

Urry, J. & Wakeford, J., (1973), Power in Britain, London: Heinemann.

Walton, R. E. & McKersie, R. B., (1965), A Behavioural Theory of Labor Negotiations, New York: McGraw-Hill.

Weber, M., (1949), The Methodology of the Social Sciences, New York: Free Press.

Weber, M., (1964), The Theory of Social and Economic Organisation, Ed. by Parsons & Henderson, New York: Free Press.

Winkler, J. T., (1975), Law, State and Economy: The Industry Act 1975 in Context, Brit. J. of Law and Society, Vol. 2., No. 2.

Wood, S. J. et al., (1975), The 'Industrial Relations System' Concept as a Basis for Theory in Industrial Relations, Brit. J. of Industrial Relations, Vol. XIII.

Wooten, B., (1955), The Social Foundations of Wage Policy, London: Allen & Unwin.

Divergence and Convergence in Industrial Organizations: The Japanese Case

Robert M. Marsh and Hiroshi Mannari

ABSTRACT

The theme of this conference, "Management Under Differing Value Systems," raises the question: how much influence does a "value system" have on management style and organizational practices when other variables known to influence management and organization are held constant? If value systems differ cross-societally, and if values determine management style and organizational structure, one would expect divergence in management and organization from one society to another. A famous instance of this argument is the thesis that Japan has a culturally distinctive, Paternalistic-Lifetime Commitment model for its organizations.

This paper criticizes this divergence argument on the basis of a number of theoretical and empirical considerations drawn from the authors' 12 years of collaborative research in a large and diverse number of Japanese manufacturing firms. We consider the lifetime commitment model as ideology, the weakening of the seniority wage system, the small effect of "Japanese" organizational characteristics on performance, the sources of employees' commitment to their firm, the failure of lifetime commitment values to predict subsequent inter-firm mobility, the causes of inter-factory variations in the voluntary quit rate, and the implications of women's liberation in Japan for lifetime commitment.

Our conclusion, supported by other recent studies, is that Japanese organizations are converging toward, not diverging from their counterparts in other societies, and that structural variables are more important than culture in explaining organizational variations.

The Japanese case is strategic in the literature on economic development because Japan is the major, if not the only, non-Western society to have reached high levels of industrialization, and the society with the highest sustained economic growth rate in the post-war world. An even more compelling reason is that, according to a widespread view, Japan's industrial productivity has developed under a pattern of management and organizational structure that is "distinctively Japanese" and divergent from Western patterns.

According to this view, which I shall call the Paternalism-Lifetime Commitment thesis, or, more briefly, the Lifetime Commitment model, Japanese organizations in both the private and public sectors have the following characteristics. (1) A man's [1] employment is in one organization from the time he completes his schooling until he retires from that organization at age 55 ("lifetime commitment"). (2) Lifetime commitment is supported by Japanese beliefs in the "firm as one family," (*kigyō ikka*) and "familistic management" (*keiei kazokushugi*) (Hazama, 1960: 137). (3) The basic link between the employee and the organization is more a matter of loyalty and reciprocal obligation than a rational economic calculus (Abegglen, 1958: 17). (4) There is a seniority system (*nenko joretsu seido*) according to which pay depends more on age and length of service in the firm than on job or performance. Inefficient employees are retained, and recruitment screening pays little attention to skills directly related to work performance. (5) The strength of lifetime commitment derives not only from the present social structure of Japan, but also from its continuity with Japan's traditional, feudal past. This characterization of the model can be found, with varying degrees of emphasis, in Abegglen (1958, 1969), Matsushima and Nakano (1958), Levine (1958), Matsushima (1962), Vogel (1963), Whitehill and Takezawa (1968), and more recently, Dore (1973), and Rohlen (1974). It is pervasive in popular treatments of Japan in the Western mass media.

Two propositions in particular give the Lifetime Commitment thesis its anti-convergence implications. The model is said to be more characteristic of Japan's large, technologically modernized firms than of its small, technologically less advanced firms; and it is argued that it is the combination of advanced technology and lifetime commitment organization that has enabled Japanese firms to overtake their West European and American competitors (*Fortune*, August, 1963: 139-43; August, 1977: 172-77).

LIFETIME COMMITMENT: SOCIAL FACT OR IDEOLOGY?

Proponents of the Lifetime Commitment model treat it as a close approximation of a social fact that describes the actual norms, values and behavior of male employees, both rank and file, white collar and blue collar. However, it can also be seen as an ideology - a mask that serves the interests of particular groups or strata. Abegglen's (1958) data were based on interviews with management. His assertion that "the worker, whether laborer or manager ... is bound, despite potential economic advantage, to remain in the company's employ ... and ... a system of shared obligation takes the place of the economic basis of employment of workers by the firm" (1958: 17) reflects a strong management bias. Cole came closer to the workers' own perspective in his participant-observer study of two Japanese factories in which he was employed as a worker. To workers, the "permanent employment" system meant limitations on the right of management to fire, not on the right of workers to quit (Cole, 1971).

As an ideology, the Lifetime Commitment model exaggerates the degree of employee identification with the company. Cole found that urban, high school educated workers were more independent in their orientation to the company than those with rural backgrounds and less education. "The cynicism and skepticism of the urban high school educated and mobile Tokyo diecast workers, their willingness to exercise civil rights, their willingness to oppose management ... their competitiveness, and their use of giri [feelings of obligation toward another person or persons] in an instrumental fashion for their own self-interest are all characteristics that can hardly be described as traditionalistic. It is precisely these characteristics which are increasingly common" (Cole, 1971: 277).

In sum, it is fundamental to the argument of this paper that the Lifetime Commitment model be understood for what it is: an ideology which, at particular times in this century, has served the interests of owners (managers) or workers. In the period between the two World Wars it aided large modern firms by encouraging skilled workers not to change firms after they had completed their long, costly apprenticeship training in the firm (Taira, 1962). In the mid-1950's Japan's unemployment rate was relatively high. The economy was just beginning to emerge from its postwar period of sluggish growth. At that time, the lifetime commitment ideology was especially beneficial to workers who might otherwise fear being laid off. By the late 1960's, the capital and labor markets were booming. A falling birth rate and higher educational aspirations reduced the number of new workers entering the manufacturing sector, while the demand for labor was increasing; once again, the ideology of lifetime commitment served the interests of owners and managers more than workers.

It will be the burden of the remainder of this paper to show that this lifetime commitment ideology is seriously deficient as a description of social reality.

THE SENIORITY SYSTEM

Pay rises more sharply with an employee's length of service in the firm in Japan than in the United States. National data for men employed in Japanese manufacturing firms in 1967 show that a 55-year old worker typically received from 4.4 to 5.2 times as much pay as those entering the firm as new recruits directly from school (Toyo Keizai, Tokei geppo, 1967). This seniority wage system has also been shown by an economist to be functional for young companies in lowering their labor costs during their early years of growth (Chao, 1968).

Although age is a major determinant of pay in Japan, its effect is becoming weakened by several recent developments. The traditional assumption was that an employee's contribution to the firm increased with seniority. Under conditions of rapid scientific and technological change, older workers' knowledge and skills become obsolescent, and those with less seniority may in fact have the more valuable contributions to make. In response to the demands of younger workers for higher pay, and the rapidly rising market value of their labor, companies have been raising the pay of younger workers at a faster rate than that of older workers (Toyo Keizai, Chingin soran, 1969: 146-200, and Japan Labor Bulletin, 5.9, September, 1966: 7-8). A Ministry of Labor national survey of 65,000 companies in all industries in 1978 found that, for the first time, the age group receiving the highest wages was not those age 50-54, closest to the 55-year old retirement age, but those 45-49 years old (Ministry of Labor, May 20, 1979, quoted in Japan Foundation Newsletter, August-September, 1979: 5). The survey indicates that the seniority-based wage scale, one of the pillars of the Lifetime Commitment model, is breaking down. Our research revealed that in two large, leading firms, employees' preferences are that ability, skill and job classification should be more important determinants of their pay than seniority (Marsh and Mannari, 1976: 147-51).

Thus, the lifetime commitment system contains at least some of the seeds of its own destruction. The more successful a company is in eliciting lifetime commitment from its workers, or the more economic recessions reduce the hiring of young people, the higher the average age and seniority of its personnel will be, and the greater will be the company's direct and indirect wage and welfare costs. Current pressure to extend the retirement age beyond 55 increases the labor costs of older workers unless wages level off or decline after age 55; but if they do, the seniority wage system is undercut. These factors compel a company to modify its seniority basis of payment, which in turn weakens the degree of lifetime commitment. Odaka Kunio has recognized this "general decline in the sense of belonging to the organization where one is employed, and a gradual obsolescence of the practice of 'lifetime commitment'" (Odaka, 1975: 129).

THE EFFECT OF LIFETIME COMMITMENT ON PERFORMANCE

Proponents of the Lifetime Commitment model, in attempting to identify what is most culturally distinctive or unique about Japanese organizations and management, fail to keep what is most important in perspective. The Lifetime Commitment pattern may be distinctive to Japan -

relative to the United States or Britain, for example - but it does not capture the important causes of why some firms perform better than others. Hiroshi Mannari and I studied the performance of individual workers in terms of company goals, labor productivity at the level of intra-factory work units, and performance aggregated at the level of the factory, in two large, leading firms in the electrical appliance and shipbuilding industires (Marsh and Mannari, 1976). We found that the organizational variables most distinctively "Japanese" - paternalism, company housing, participation by workers in company-sponsored recreational activities, company identification and lifetime commitment - have less causal impact on performance than do the more universal factors of the employee's status in the company, gender, job satisfaction and knowledge of organizational work procedures. The highest performance at both the individual and aggregate levels is found among male employees with higher status in the company, greater job satisfaction and more knowledge of procedures. In other words, contrary to the Lifetime Commitment thesis, the more "distinctively Japanese" an organizational variable is, the less it has to do with performance; performance in Japanese firms appears to have the same causal sources as in Western firms (Marsh and Mannari, 1976: chapter 11).

DEMYSTIFYING THE CONCEPT OF LIFETIME COMMITMENT

Two aspects of lifetime commitment must be distinguished. One is overt role behavior, which can be measured by inter-firm labor mobility, separation rates, and the like. The other consists in the norms and values concerning the desirability, correctness, etc. of staying in one firm versus changing firms. Mannari and I attempted to measure these norms and values by an index of lifetime commitment, based on employees' responses to four questionnaire items. An individual with a high score on this index (a high degree of commitment) would be one who intended to remain in the present organization, perceived other male employees in the company as also intending to remain until retirement, believed males should stay in one firm, and regarded with disapproval ("un-Japanese, disloyal, or opportunisitc") an employee who voluntarily changed firms. The mean lifetime commitment score for male employees was 8.5 in "Electric Factory" and 8.7 in "Shipbuilding Factory," which indicates only a moderate level of support for lifetime commitment norms and values, relative to the theoretical range on the index, 4-12 (Marsh and Mannari, 1976: 241).

When we regressed lifetime commitment score on some 13 variables hypothesized as its causes, we found that in both of the factories we studied, the variables that most conduce to high commitment are: being more satisfied with one's job, older, more cohesive with one's fellow employees, and perceiving that few other firms offer as good conditions as one's present firm. The more "distinctively Japanese" factors - living in company housing, paternalism, and participation in company recreational activities - had no significant effect on lifetime commitment, net of the effect of job satisfaction, age, cohesiveness, and perceived relative advantages of firms.

We see the implication of this finding as demystifying the concept of lifetime commitment. Male employees in Japan do not uniformly support lifetime commitment norms and values, even in large, leading firms. Their "commitment" is not an absolute moral value of unconditional loyalty to the firm. Rather, it is more of a contingent, conditional norm: under certain conditions, I shall stay in this firm and give it my loyalty; but under other conditions, I shall quit the firm if given the opportunity. If men do have a high level of support for commitment values, this is because they derive satisfaction from their job, perceive few other firms as offering better working conditions than their present firm, are older, and more cohesive with fellow employees. When these conditions are absent, Japanese employees do not subscribe to lifetime commitment norms and values. The source of lifetime commitment, then, is not some generalized propensity of "Japaneseness," but rather a set of quite specific, yet universal factors that influence inter-firm mobility rates in other societies as well (Price, 1977).

CAN LIFETIME COMMITMENT VALUES PREDICT WHO QUITS?

Proponents of the lifetime commitment model cite the fact that the separation rate (number of personnel who leave a firm, as a proportion of the firm's total number of personnel) for wage and salary employees in the manufacturing sector is consistently lower in Japan than in the United States (Rōdō Shō Rōdō Tōkei Chōsabu, 1969, U.S. Department of Labor, Bureau of Labor Statistics, 1972). They then argue that Japan's lower separation rate is due to the higher level of support for lifetime commitment norms and values in Japan. Even though, as we have seen, men in Japanese firms vary in their degree of support for lifetime commitment, it is still possible that those employees who do subscribe to these norms and values are more likely to remain in one firm, while those less commited are more likely to change firms.

An opportunity to subject lifetime commitment to the acid test of prediction presented itself to Mannari and me in 1973. We had studied "Electric Factory," a manufacturer of small household electrical appliances, in 1969. At that time, the factory had 1,200 employees, 51 percent of whom were women. Although becoming increasingly mechanized and automated, the factory was still based mainly on assembly line, large batch and mass production technology. One of several plants in a company that employed 13,500 employees, the factory was located in a small city with a rural hinterland, northwest of Kobe. We knew each employee's score on our index of lifetime commitment norms and values as of 1969. In 1973, four years after the conclusion of our field work, we obtained from management a complete list of the employees on the payroll in 1969 who had voluntarily left the company during the period from October, 1969 to November, 1973. Of the 1,033 employees for whom we had 1969 lifetime commitment scores, 294, or 28.5 percent, had left. The annual quit rate was about seven percent. Of the 523 women employed in 1969, 45.5 percent had left by 1973, in contrast to only 10.9 percent of the 510 men.

We regressed quitting (employees who stayed in the company between 1969 and 1973 were coded 1, those who left, 2) on 16 independent variables, each characterizing the employee as of 1969. These included the employee's lifetime commitment, gender, status in the organization, performance, number of previous jobs, perceived promotion chances, cohesiveness, knowledge of work procedures, job satisfaction, etc. Among all employees, when the other 15 variables are held constant, gender emerged as the best predicator of staying vs. quitting (beta = -.27). Lifetime commitment in 1969 had no significant effect on quitting (beta = -.02). Thus, knowing an employee is a woman is more useful in predicting quitting than knowing an employee's degree of lifetime commitment. Gender alone yielded virtually as high a multiple R (.31) as did all 16 independent variables acting together (.34) (Marsh and Mannari, 1977: 69-70). The same multiple regression analysis was carried out for only those employees to whom the lifetime commitment model strictly applied, men. When the single best predictor of quitting - gender - was removed, none of the remaining independent variables was of more than marginal importance in predicting quitting. Even among men, the beta for lifetime commitment was only .02. Thus, lifetime commitment norms and values have no causal impact on subsequent quitting or staying in the firm. Insofar as we can explain separation rates at all, they should be a positive function of the proportion of women employed in a firm. A test of this hypothesis requires a multi-organization sample, in which the unit of analysis is the organization, not the individual employee.

CAUSES OF VARIATION IN THE VOLUNTARY QUIT RATE

In 1976, Mannari and I collected data from a sample of 50 manufacturing firms located in a city in southwestern Japan. The universe was defined as all manufacturing plants in the city that currently employed at least 100 persons. The sample contained one or more firms in each of 13 of the 21 two-digit industries classified in Japan's 1972 Establishment Census of Manufacturing, varying from textiles, food and clothing to iron and steel and petrochemicals. The mean number of employees was 687, with a range from 100 to 11,815 per factory. Of the 50 units studied, 26 were the principal unit of their respective company, 15 were head branches, and nine were branch factories. Data on the dependent variable of interest here, the percentage of 1975 employees in each factory who quit voluntarily during the year, and other organizational structure and technological-economic variables were collected in a questionnaire filled out by a key informant (a senior manager or owner) in each factory. Since we did not collect data on or from individual employees, we cannot use lifetime commitment norms and values as an independent variable.

As can be seen from Table 1, a number of factors are significantly related to the voluntary quit rate. The zero-order correlations indicate that the following characteristics increase the quit rate: a larger proportion of women employees; a less mechanized, less automated production technology, with lower fixed assets per employee; lack of differentiation of ownership from management; the factory is an independent unit, or has only a low degree of dependence on a parent organization; a low administrative intensity and high labor costs and labor inputs by production workers; a relatively large number of hierarchic levels; a low degree of functional specialization in administrative and staff tasks; and being an older factory.

Table 1. Causes of the Voluntary Quit Rate in Japanese Factories[a]

Independent variable	Relationship to Quit Rate: r	Relationship to Quit Rate: Beta, controlling for % women employees
% women employees in factory	.60**	
Automaticity of production equipment	-.47**	-.14
Differentiation of ownership from management	-.45**	-.21
Administrative intensity	-.45**	.21
Internal dependence of factory on parent	-.40**	-.10
Formalization	-.38**	-.09
%man-hours worked by direct production workers, as % of all man-hours worked	.38**	.07
Labor costs as % of all factory costs	.37**	.15
Fixed assets/labor ratio	-.34**	-.10
Mechanization of quality evaluation of production	-.33**	-.08
Age of factory	.31*	-.03
Electricity consumption/ employee	-.31*	-.09
Number of hierarchic levels	.29*	.25*
Functional specialization	-.25*	-.17

(a) The number of factories on which the correlations and betas are based varies from 48 to 31, depending on the number of missing observations.

** Correlation (r) is significant at the .01 level; * .05 level.

* Metric regression coefficient is at least twice its standard error.

One interpretation of these findings flows from a distinction between relatively traditional and relatively modern manufacturing organizations. Although there are inter-industry variations, one can say in general that relative to traditional organizations, modern organizations are characterized by:

Greater mechanization and automation of production technology

Higher capital/labor ratio

Differentiation of ownership from management

Greater internal dependence of a factory on its parent organization

Greater administrative intensity, lower relative labor inputs by production workers, lower labor costs as a proportion of all costs

Greater formalization

Greater functional specialization in administrative and staff tasks

Note that these characteristics are precisely the opposite of those that increase the quit rate. Thus, to the extent that a factory becomes modernized in its technological and organizational structures, its quit rate is reduced. This leads to the further inference that, if we assume a secular trend toward modernization of technology and organization in Japan, the quit rate will remain low and even decline, rather than rising.

However, an alternative interpretation also fits the facts. Since we found in our Electric Factory study that at the individual level, being a woman was the single best predictor of quitting, we re-examined each variable in Table 1 for its effect on the quit rate at the level of the factory, holding constant the best predictor, the percent women employees. The results are displayed in column two of Table 1. With only one exception, none of the variables continued to have any significant effect on the quit rate, net of the percent women employees. At the organizational level, as at the individual level, women are the key element in a factory's quit rate. Our multiorganization data suggest that the basic reason a factory has a higher quit rate is not because it is more traditional (less modernized) in its technological and organizational structure, but because it employs relatively more women.

The implications of this for Lifetime Commitment are unclear. Two alternative scenarios for possible future developments can be suggested. First, Japanese women have higher quit rates than men because traditionally they have been socialized to work only for a few years between completing school and marriage or motherhood. Women have had fewer incentives to seek a career in an organization because they were usually excluded from promotion into supervisory and managerial ranks and the like.

To the extent that this system of role socialization and career disincentives continues, gender and the percent women employees will continue to be the dominant cause of quitting and the quit rate.

Alternatively, a trend toward a less sharp distinction in how males and females are socialized, greater career possibilities for women, etc. would be expected to lower the gender-based differences in the quit rate, and to lower the general quit rate. Thus, ironically, behavioral "lifetime commitment" to one firm could become a result of modernization (of women's roles and occupational statuses), rather than a manifestation of "traditionalism," as the proponents of the lifetime commitment model claim. However, the argument and evidence presented here suggest that if lifetime commitment (staying in one firm) increases in the future in Japan (due to role behavior changes and opportunities for women), it is unlikely that this lifetime commitment will reflect norms and values of unconditional loyalty to one's firm. Rather, "lifetime commitment" will have come to mean the same thing for women as for men: a contingent, conditional outcome of certain specific, yet universal factors, such as job satisfaction, promotion opportunities, cohesiveness with fellow employees, and perceiving that few other firms offer better conditions.

CONCLUSION

The theme of this conference, "Management Under Differing Value Systems," raises such questions as: What are value systems? Do they differ cross-nationally? How much influence does a value system have on management style and organizational structure in given nations when other variables known to influence management style and organization are held constant? It is now fashionable to question the Convergence assumptions of the 1950's and 1960's. In the study of Japanese and Western management and organization, this anti-convergence thesis has been championed by proponents of the Paternalism-Lifetime Commitment model of the Japanese firm.

My research with Hiroshi Mannari over the last 12 years, which we have briefly summarized in this paper, leads to the conclusion that the Lifetime Commitment model exaggerates the "traditionalism" and uniqueness of Japanese management and organization and their divergence from Western counterparts. Other recent studies support our pro-convergence viewpoint. Lincoln, Olson and Hanada (1978) attempted to test the divergence thesis that the greater the Japanese cultural presence (i.e., the more Japanese nationals and the more Japanese-American employees) in Japanese multinational corporations operating in various industries in southern California, the more these units' organizational characteristics will approximate the "distinctively Japanese" type on the following standardized Aston variables.[2]

"Japanese-type" organizations, relative to Western-type, will have:

1. Less functional specialization in administrative and staff roles (because Japanese are more attached to a collectivity, e.g., the organization or a department within it, than to a specialized job).

2. More centralization of decision-making in the organization.

3. Less formalization (less reliance on written, more on verbal communication in the organization).

4. More levels in the organizational hierarchy.

However, only one of these four hypotheses was confirmed empirically. Only functional specialization was significantly negatively related to the Japanese cultural presence in these multinational branch organizations. Lincoln, Olson and Hanada acknowledge that most studies to date provide "little evidence for the existence of ... nonadditive cultural effects" (1978: 845). Beyond this, the Lincoln, Olson and Hanada study begs the question of whether even organizations in Japan fit the "Japanese-type" on these four Aston measures. Lincoln, Olson and Hanada assume that they do, but do not provide data on firms in Japan. Azumi (1979) compared firms in Britain, Sweden and Japan, matched for size, products and status of the factory studied in relation to its parent company. Using the same standard Aston measures, Azumi found only negligible differences by nation in centralization, specialization, formalization and number of hierarchic levels. There was more variation among factories within each nation than between nations, which indicates that organization-specific factors rather than national cultural differences or national values are influencing the scores.

Another kind of convergence finding is that even when the mean scores on structural variables in organizations vary cross-nationally, the relationships between variables tend to be uniform in different nations. For example, in all countries,

> The more employees in an organization, the more formalized and specialized the organization is (Hickson, McMillan, Azumi and Horvath, 1979).

Thus, although Japanese organizations on the average may have fewer employees than those in some other countries, larger Japanese organizations are more formalized and more specialized than smaller ones. This structural relationship is independent of culture and value system.

Another carefully controlled study compared 13 Japanese firms which had operating units in the United States with 14 American companies which had operating units in Japan, matched on an industry-by-industry basis (Johnson, 1977). Managers' communications and decision making practices were studied through interviews with 215 managers in 43 operating units in the two countries. Johnson found "relatively few significant differences ... between Japanese firms in Japan and American companies in the U.S." (p. 20). In particular, no difference was observed in the use of consultative type (ringi system) decision making, contrary to the divergence thesis that this is a "distinctively Japanese" managerial style (p. 20).[3] Johnson concludes that "the assertions of wide scale differences based on cultural factors (and regardless of location or ownership) are unjustified. There is no strong evidence in support of the 'cultural divergence' hypothesis; the preponderance of evidence suggests wide areas of commonality (i.e., convergence) between Japanese and American communications and decision making practices" (Johnson, 1977: 21).

The forces making for convergence between Japanese and Western firms are at least as strong as those making for divergence. Management and organizational structure certainly vary across firms. When one tries to explain these variations, it is undesirable to limit oneself to what is, after all, only one type of explanatory factor - differences in value systems. All too often "culture" or "values" are used as explanations when what is needed is better theory (Johnson, 1977: 22). In my view, we should exhaust as much as possible of the variance in dependent variables on the basis of organizational theory. The question we should be asking is: what is the relative importance of such organizational theory variables as size of firm, dependence, technology, goals, internal structural differentiation, rate of change in market demand and product innovation, in relation to the effect of value systems and culture?

Finally, it should be clear that Convergence theory is more than merely "a mask for United States imperialism." Its intellectual substance draws upon core sociological theories of change that are at least a century old. Manfredi (1964) formulated an elegant theoretical argument to demonstrate why, when social units such as societies or organizations increase in size, they increase in complexity, which in turn <u>reduces</u> the number of possible forms that social arrangements may take, and therefore necessarily leads to increasing <u>convergence</u> among these units. It is regrettable that the current attraction of anti-convergence perspectives has led many scholars to become insensitive to this theoretical basis of convergence. To paraphrase Mark Twain, the reported demise of Convergence theory is somewhat premature.

FOOTNOTES

(1) Proponents of the Lifetime Commitment model do not apply it to women employees.

(2) These measures are called "Aston variables" in recognition of their development by a group of researchers at the University of Aston in Birmingham, England, in the 1950's and 1960's, including David J. Hickson, C. R. Hinings, J. H. K. Inkson, D. S. Pugh and Diana Pheysey, among others.

(3) Odaka (1975: 184-85) declares that the <u>ringi</u> system of "bottom-up" decision-making "is today recognized by progressive Japaese executives to be obsolete, and to hinder rational planning and quick decisions, which are prerequisite to modern management effectiveness."

REFERENCES

Abegglen, James G. The Japanese Factory. Glencoe: Free Press. 1958.

__________. "Organizational Change," in Robert J. Ballon, ed., The Japanese Employee. Rutland, Vt., Tuttle. 1969: 99-119.

Azumi, Koya. "The Structure of Japanese Organizations: A Cross-National Comparison." Unpublished paper. 1979.

Chao, Kang. "Labor Institutions in Japan and Her Economic Growth." Journal of Asian Studies, 28 (Nov. 1969): 5-17.

Cole, Robert E. Japanese Blue Collar: The Changing Tradition. University of California Press. 1971.

Dore, Ronald P. British Factory: Japanese Factory - The Origins of National Diversity in Employment Relations. University of California Press. 1973.

Fortune. "The Fortune Directory: The 200 Largest Foreign Industrial Companies." August, 1963.

__________. "The 300 Largest Industrials Outside the U.S." August, 1972.

__________. "The 300 Largest Industrial Corporations Outside the U.S." September, 1973.

Hazama, Hiroshi. "Keiei-kazoku-shugi no ronri to sono keisei-katei" (The Logic of the Enterprise-family Ideal and its Historical Development) Shakaigaku Hyoron, 11. July, 1960: 2-18, 137-38.

Hickson, David J., McMillan, Charles J., Azumi, Koya and Horvath, Dezso. "Grounds for Comparative Organization Theory: Quicksands or Hard Core?" in Cornelis J. Lammers and David J. Hickson, ed., Organizations Alike and Unlike. Boston: Routledge and Kegan Paul, 1979.

Japan Foundation. Japan Foundation Newsletter. August - September. 1979.

Japan Institute of Labor. Japan Labor Bulletin. Tokyo, Japan 5.9, September, 1966: 7-8.

Johnson, Richard T., "Communication and Decision-Making: A Cross Cultural Study of Japanese and American Companies in the United States and Japan." Unpublished paper, Stanford University. May, 1977.

Levine, Solomon B. Industrial Relations in Postwar Japan. Urbana: 1958.

Lincoln, James R., Olson, Jon, and Hanada, Mitsuyo. "Cultural Effects on Organizational Structure: The Case of Japanese Firms in the United States." American Sociological Review 43. December, 1978: 829-47.

Manfredi, John F. "Societal Complexity and Limited Alternatives," Ch. X (pp. 159-64) in E.W. Count and G.T. Bowles, eds., Fact and Theory in Social Science. Syracuse, N.Y. Syracuse University Press, 1964.

Marsh, Robert M. and Mannari, Hiroshi. Modernization and the Japanese Factory. Princeton University Press. 1976.

____________________________, "Organizational Commitment and Turnover: A Prediction Study." Administrative Science Quarterly 22. March, 1977: 57-75.

Matsushima, Shizuo. Rōmukanri no nihonteki tokuishitsu to hensen. Tokyo, Japan. Diamond, 1962.

____________________ and Nakano, Taku. Nihon shakai yoron. Tokyo, Tokyo University Press. 1958.

Odaka, Kunio. Toward Industrial Democracy - Management and Workers in Modern Japan. Harvard East Asian Series, 80, 1975.

Price, James L. The Study of Turnover. Iowa State University Press. 1977.

Rōdō Shō rōdō tōkei chōsa bu. Rōdō tōkei yōran. Tokyo, Okura Sho. 1969.

Rohlen, Thomas P. For Harmony and Strength: Japanese White-Collar Organization in Anthropological Perspective. Berkeley, University of California Press, 1974.

Taira, Koji. "Characteristics of Japanese Labor Markets." Economic Development and Cultural Change, 10. pp. 150-168. 1962.

Tōyō Keizai. (ed.) Chingin Soran. (Glossary of Wages) 1968 ed. Tōyō Keizai Shimposha (Tokyo: 1969) pp. 146-200.

____________. Tōkei geppō. (Statistical Monthly) 27, December, 1967, p. 8. Tokyo: Toyo Keizai Shimposha.

Vogel, Ezra F. Japan's New Middle Class. Berkeley: University of California Press, 1963.

Whitehill, Jr., Arthur M. and Takezawa, Shin-ichi. The Other Worker. The East-West Center Press, Honolulu, 1968.

Changing Values and the Future of the Employment Relationship[1]

Ronald J. Burke

ABSTRACT

This chapter links changes in employee values over the past several decades to directions in which the employment relationship must move to better fit contemporary values. Traditional and new values are described and the nature of changes in them identified. Relevant changes in the demographic characteristics of the work force of the 1980's are also discussed. The employment relationship of the future must emphasize (1) increasing interest in the quality of work life experiences of men and women at work; (2) greater attempts to individualize the work place in line with differing employee needs; and (3) more attention to the integration and balance of work, family and leisure investments.

In 1974 and 1975 The American Management Association conducted a survey (both interviews and questionnaires) of approximately 850 men and women who manage or work in organizations (Tarnowieski, 1976) about the meaning and purpose of work and life in America on the eve of that country's two hundredth birthday. The following vignettes from a section entitled "The Work Ethic" illustrate some individual's viewpoints relating to work values.

The work ethic may not be declining, but radical changes have taken place. These changes have been influence by increased educational levels, the changing composition of the labor force, affluence, the psychology of entitlement, and a much younger, better-informed employee population -- in short, younger, smarter, more vocal individuals protected by endless legal provisions and the media. Workers are concerned with their "rights" today, and their attitudes differ from those of people who were "lucky to have a job" during the 1930s. Leadership responsibilities in business today include making jobs more meaningful--thus making full use of the talents, abilities, interests, and time of all employees. Companies are concerned with the return on investment in human time, and the changing work ethic is now demanding a return on investment for the time invested by the individual in the company. It is perhaps in the area of individual expectations that the greatest change in employee/employer relationships will occur during the remainder of the twentieth century.

Vice President, Personnel,
(50 to 59 years), department
store chain, North Carolina.

Once the "work ethic" meant personal and collective striving for betterment. There was pride in accomplishment and a feeling of success and fulfillment as goals were reached. You got what you earned. Now, everything seems to be owed to everyone--people seem to think they are entitled to everything as if by some divine right. There is a built-in satisfaction with mediocrity--a group running away from responsibility--and at the same time a demand to participate and to have authority without accepting responsibility. This is reflected in lower productivity and poorer quality (the Monday and Friday cars from Detroit!)

Increased productivity alone is not the answer to our economic problems. There must be a reeducation in and reawakening of the principles of "giving" rather than always "taking", of helping others rather than always expecting to be helped (welfare), of individual pride rather than collective guilt. There is nothing inherently evil in participative management and job enrichment, so long as people realize that there is still a boss. We need to reinstill respect for authority in the workplace to achieve order out of chaos.

Corporate Officer (40 to 49),
medical services corporation,
Massachusetts.

In the past, people worked because there was something in it for them or because they believed in what they were doing. Today, employers can't seem to offer either for most employees. When you take into account food stamps, unemployment insurance, worker's compensation, and other welfare programs and contrast these benefits with high income taxes, inflation, transportation problems, etc., there isn't much "in it" anymore. Also, because we have engineered most of the joy out of most jobs, created a demand for useless products, and established a throwaway economy, the worker has begun to question his own value in industry. Challenging workers to create legitimate and quality goods and services must become industry's first priority.

Personnel Director (under 30),
general contracting company,
Maine.

These vignettes indicate that, at least in some individual's observations, work values are changing (or have changed) and these changes have had an impact on commitment and performance in organizations. However, it is possible that these impressions are idiosyncratic and lack generality.

THE OLD AND THE NEW VALUES

Writings in the academic community over the past decade have also touched on changing values. In order to talk about work values and how they may have changed one must identify both old and new values. Yankelovich (1978) has described the old values as follows:

(1) If women could afford to stay home and not work at a paid job, they did so,
(2) As long as a job provided a man with a decent living and some degree of economic security, he would put up with all its drawbacks, because it meant that he could fulfill his economic obligations to his family and confirm his own self-esteem as a breadwinner and good provider.
(3) The incentive system--mainly money and status rewards --was successful in motivating most people.
(4) People were tied to their jobs not only by bonds of commitment to their family, but also by loyalty to their organizations.
(5) Most people defined their identity through their work role, subordinating and suppressing most conflicting personal desires.
(6) For all practical purposes, a job was defined as a paid activity that provided steady full-time work to the male breadwinner with compensation adequate to provide at least the necessities, and, with luck, some luxuries, for an intact nuclear family.

Hall (1971) provided a glimpse of what the new work values being imported into organizations by the "new breed" of employee. These involved:

(1) Being more concerned about basic values, not merely different values.
(2) A stronger emphasis on behaving in accordance with one's values.
(3) Personal integrity, honesty, openness and realness are more important.
(4) Many of the new values are "humanistic" (personal development, intellectual and emotional growth).
(5) A concern for the ultimate social value of one's work.
(6) The definition of legitimate authority is changing.

Hall draws the following implications for organizations and the management of these organizations, arising from the new values. First, the new breed employee demands challenging work, work that is meaningful and ability stretching. Second, these individuals desire a more collaborative relationship with supervisors, a lowering of the authority distance. Third, they want more opportunity to make their own personal choices. Finally, these individuals value more open and flexible organizational climates.

Sinetar (1980) makes a distinction between traditional work values and new age work values.

	TRADITIONAL WORK VALUES		NEW AGE WORK VALUES	
	Basic Needs:	Management Practices/ Attitudes	Basic Needs:	Management Practices/ Attitudes
	Secruity, Approval of Others, Control, Status, Power, and "Agreement" with External World.		Self-Esteem, Relatedness to Others, Self-Definition, Self-Actualization, Personal Power, Utilization of Own Talents, Directives, Responsibility	
MOTIVATING QUESTIONS	Egocentric Frame of Reference	Object Orientation	Synergic Frame of Reference	Human Orientation
	"Whom do I need to impress?" "What's in it for me?" "Who's in charge?" "What do I need to do to make it?"	Worker and self as an object, a number, a means toward an end. Impersonal quality between levels of organization. Communication: one-way, downward. Attitude of "They're dependent on me(us)," I'm	"How can we get all the diverse elements here to contribute to things working out as much as possible for everyone?" "What can I contribute?" "In what ways is this activity useful?"	Worker and self as a human being, respect for others' individuality. Sense of relatedness between all levels of organization. Communication: two-way. Attitude of mutual trust, mutual respect, mutual cooperation.

continued on next page ..

		Object Orientation Continued responsible for everything around here." Fragmented awareness: departments, functions, policies considered in isolation		
MOTIVATING QUESTIONS	Work as A Sources of Power, Safety, Status "How safe is it to do this, to think this, to act this way?" "What will people say ....?" "What does the boss want me to do?" "How can I get 'mine' out of this?" "Who makes decisions around here?"	Power Orientation Accumulation of material symbols to represent satisfaction. Policies and work problems linked to "survival." Relinquishing power, authority, linked to loss of safety.	Work as a Path to Self-Fulfillment "How does this work contribute value and satisfaction to my life?" "What is the quality of well-being I get from being around here? "What is the quality of work life, and how does it affect me?" "Which of my talents am I using?"	Holistic Orientation Health seen as a function of participation with others. Development of the individual will promote the development of organization Cooperative decision-making programs

Sinetar postulates a shift in basic need structure which, in Maslovian terms (Maslow, 1943) represents a movement from lower level needs (physiological, security) to higher level needs (self-actualization, egoistic). Work, then, must serve a different function, moving from being a source of safety, power and status to being a source of self-fulfillment, growth and satisfaction.

Yankleovich (1978) presents some data reflecting the change in work values. Thus: (1) In the late 1960's almost 50% of all employed Americans looked to their work as a source of personal fulfillment. In 1979 that figure had plunged to less than 25%; (2) In the 1960's, 58% of employed Americans believed that "hard work always pays off". In 1979, only 43% held this belief; (3) In 1979, only 13% of all working Americans found their work truly "meaningful" and more important to them than leisure time pursuits; and (4) using Swedish data, presented below, work decreased dramatically as the source of most meaning in life for men, 18-35 years of age, over a roughly 20 year period of time.

What gives your life the most meaning - family, work, leisure?

	1955	1977
Leisure	13%	27%
Work	33%	17%
Family	45%	41%

On the basis of fairly extensive surveys of work attitudes Yankelovich (19) classified contemporary employees into groups for whom traditional incentives work and for whom they do not work.

<u>Group for Whom Old "Incentives" Work Well (56%)</u>

(a) 22% - older and poorer than the median. Blue collar mostly. One third white collar clerical and service workers. Work is just a habit. Want job security.

(b) 19% - positively work oriented. Comes closest to management idea of the dedicated, hard working employee. Money is important but not as important as the work itself. Older. Only one third under 35.

(c) 15% - real "go getters". Young. 70% are under 35. Want money and to get ahead.

<u>Group for Whom Old "Incentives" Do Not Work (44%)</u>

(d) 27% - "Turned-off". The least motivated to work hard, least well educated, lowest earnings, mostly blue collar, 1 of every 4 workers. Work ethic deteriorated.

(e) 17% - Most strategic for the future. Youngest, 3 of 4 under 35. Largest proportion of college educated, white collar middle management. They provide the clearest evidence of the new values.

Yankelovich then concludes that the three most striking features of the new work values are:

(1) The increasing importance of leisure - work and family have grown less important in the quest for self-fulfillment.

(2) The symbolic significance of the paid job (for women) - unpaid housework has suffered a severe drop in status and the "price of admission" to independence in our society has become a paid job.

(3) The insistence that jobs become less depersonalized - the person comes first, employees refuse to subordinate their personalities to the work role - individuality must be recognized - I am more than my work role - I am myself!

Changing Composition of the Work Force

The Canadian work force of 1980 is dramatically different from the work force of the 1940's and 1950's. Let us consider the following demographic characteristics:

In 1941, two-thirds of the work force had a grade 8 level of education or less; but by 1980 a vast improvement had occurred with only one-sixth of the workforce having a grade 8 level of education or less. Considering age, 1961, 44% of the work force was under 35, in 1971, 45% and in 1980, 53%. Also in 1980, over half of the women, 15 years of age and over, in Canada, are in the workforce.

Two Job/Career Couples

Just under half of the Canadian labor force is made up of working couples. In 1950 seventy-five percent of families fit the norm of that time, i.e., male breadwinner - wife a homemaker. Only fifteen percent of families fit this category in 1980.

Bachman and Johnston (1979) in a study of 17,000 High School graduates present some data which may well indicate what future work values might look like. They reported the following responses to a subset of questions related to work values:

	Response
(1) If you were to get enough money to live as comfortably as you'd like for the rest of your life, would you want to work?	80% Yes
(2) I expect work to be a very central part	

		Response
	of my life	75% Yes
(3)	To me, work is nothing more than making a living.	15% Yes
(4)	I would like a type of work I could forget after the workday was over.	55% Yes

Thus, although work values, sometimes referred to as the work ethic, are changing, one concludes that the work ethic is not "dead", as has been decried by some social commentators.

The information that we have presented so far has been speculative, impressionistic and piece-meal. The data that one would need to empirically substantiate these conclusions is lacking.

Flowers and Hughes (1978), and Hughes (1976) have amassed data from over 10,000 American workers using a theory of human values proposed by Clare Graves. Graves, building on the notion of a need hierarchy developed by Maslow (1943), has postulated the existence of seven human value systems. These are: Reactive (System 1), Tribalistic (System 2), Egocentric (System 3), Conformist (System 4), Manipulative (System 5), Sociocentric (System 6), and Existential (System 7). We will only concern ourselves with Systems 2 through 6, since individuals with System 1 values are not found in work settings.

<u>Tribalistic (System 2)</u>

- A strong need for stability and safety
- Seek authority figures
- Believe one should live according to the lifestyle of one's elders and family relations
- Locked into rigid traditions and values they cannot bring themselves to violate
- Feel threatened by change or anything unfamiliar
- A reactor not an initiator
- Prefers easy work, friendly people and above all a benevolent supervisor
- Rejects responsibility. Prefers a boss who tells him exactly what to do
- Generally a low level of education

<u>Egocentric (System 3)</u>

- Self-assertive, rugged, individualistic
- Believes might makes right
- Restless, aggressive, tough, ruthless with little regard for the consequences of his behavior
- Wants good pay. When he's made enough money he may

either quit or take off from work
- Resists strong authoritarian supervision but will not respond to any other kind
- Needs tight control, close supervision, continuous observation and a boss who is able to exercise authority and power

Conformist (System 4)

- Accepts role in life
- Strives for perfection, subordinating his own desires and needs to the dictates of absolute moral laws
- Typical behavior includes denial, deference to authority, modesty, self-sacrifice, hard self-discipline and little self-indulgence
- Respond to authority figures who present rules in black and white, and who invoke virtues of responsibility and penalties of sin to motivate the workers
- Needs a secure job that rewards loyalty, hard work and honesty under a supervisor who calls the shots; rarely changes a decision and sees to it that the rules are applied without favoritism.

Manipulative (System 5)

- Tries to conquer the world by learning its secrets - not by raw force
- Develops an objective, positive, scientific method for achieving his goals (not fate)
- Places a high value on wealth and possessions, which demonstrate his achievements
- Believes in and practices entrepreneuric values involving gamemanship, competitive efficiency, planning and organizing
- Like variety, chance to "wheel and deal"
- Like compensation and promotions based on results
- Tirelessly works to beat the system
- Responds to hard bargaining and respects mastery and power, but a good boss doesn't ask questions if the job gets done
- Motivated by need to achieve, by the comforts success busy and the respect it engenders
- Approaches job like a game. Uses money to keep score

Sociocentric (System 6)

- Concerned about his relationship to others
- Wants to belong and be accepted
- Believes that if he understands himself and others human harmony will be achieved (highly subjective individual)
- Getting along is more important than getting ahead

- Goodwill valued over free enterprise, cooperative over competitive, social approval over individual fame
- Values a sense of community, interpersonal relations, communication committees, sensitivity, majority rule, and individual personality more than things and possessions
- Identifies with peer group and accepts its dictates in order to obtain approval
- Puts people ahead of the organization and ahead of profits. Negative towards power structures, perceiving them as harmful to people or the environment

Existential (System 7)

- Values spontaneity, simplicity and common sense over conformity and social conventions
- Intensely pre-occupied with his personal development (increasing opportunities to work on problems and set goals that give meaning to his life)
- Tries to understand the purpose of life and to live in a manner which satisfies his personal values without interfering with the values of others.
- Needs challenging work, usually of his own choosing, that requires initiative and imagination and which is important to himself and society
- Wants to do the job in his own way
- Motivated by opportunities to learn, grow, explore new territory, and be original and creative
- Requires little supervision; work facilities are unimportant

Many young managers are primarily existential in their views. Seldom is this found in blue collar or lower paying jobs.

Figure 2 indicates the present distribution by value system and some indication of how these value systems appear to be changing. Recent years have seen a significant and growing increase in the ranks of Socio-centrics and Existentialists -- people with values similar to those held by younger managers -- and a corresponding decrease in tribalistic and conformist values. A development which has baffled old-time union leaders as well as old-line managers. People are becoming more inner-directed and at the same time more concerned with other people. They are looking for meaning in their life and work beyond the level of satisfying survival needs. This trend can be very favorable to management, if companies can adapt, can be responsive to the increasingly sophisticated views of their younger hourly, clerical and professional workers.

Figure 2
Estimated Percentage of U.S.
Workforce by Value System

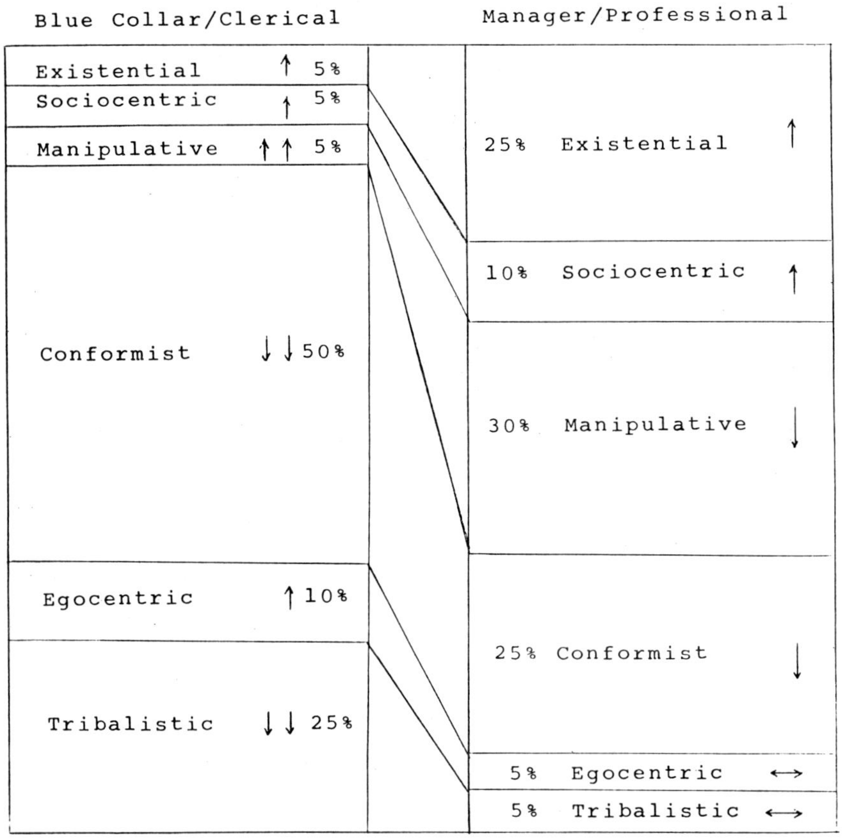

Probable direction of change during next ten years:
↔ No change; ↑ Moderate increase; ↑↑ Significant increase; ↓ Moderate decrease; ↓↓ Significant decrease

Changing Values and the Employment Relationship

Although the empirical evidence is sparse, it is safe to conclude that work values in North America have changed over the past few decades. And there are several factors (education, age, expectations, rising standards of living) that are responsible for their evolution. What are the potential implications of these changes on the future of the employment relationship?

Future of the Employment Relationship

The nature of the employment relationship must change in line with changes in human values. Although one cannot be completely certain about the specific nature of all of these changes in the employment relationship, some directions are beginning to emerge.

First, greater interest in the quality of working life concept will materialize. Trist (1978) has articulated the paradigm shift that has taken place in the role of human resources in work places. North American organizations have shown steadily increasing interest in work place innovations in attempts to bring the work place more in line with contemporary values.

Second, greater individuation, or individuatizing of organizations will take place (Lawler, 1974). Individual differences have been downplayed in the earliest writing in organizational behavior and organizational theory. Only recently has the fact that people differ and may differ widely, in response to common work experiences. Thus greater attempts have been made to develop a fit between individuals and their work places. Individuation will take place in job design and job enrichment, leadership styles and employee participation, hours of work or flex-time, training and development, pay systems with a greater emphasis on cafeteria arrangements and careers and career management. Organizations will continue to be more flexible and responsive to individual differences.

Thirdly, organizations will be more concerned with the facilitation and integration of the work, family and leisure interfaces (Hall & Hall, 1976). This is revealed in the continued interest in dual careers; the movement towards flexible hours of work, the four day work week, and and increasing development of career planning processes in organization.

Flowers and Hughes offer additional suggestions on how organizations might respond to workers with new and different values using Graves' Theory as the backdrop. They proposed that the next decade would see an increase in numbers of employees having value systems at levels 5, 6 and 7. The following chart suggests desirable management responses towards employees with these value systems in terms of Job Design, Growth Opportunities, Leadership Style, and Performance Reviews.

Sinetar (1980) emphasizes the establishment of a network of cooperative communication and mutual support with managerial colleagues and employees to meet new age values. This would rely on (1) increased communication needs and (2) an increasing need to experience work as something that is satisfying on a deep and intrinsic level.

Employee's Value System	Job Design	Growth Opportunities	Leadership Style	Performance Review
System 5 - Manipulative	Do turn work into management-by-objectives game. Don't fail to specify constraints and limits and audit occasionally.	Do let subordinate run the corporate maze and leave rooml for "wheeling and dealing." Don't plan subordinate's career goals or use a structured system.	Do stress rewards and status and relate to subordinate's career goals. Don't force subordinate to follow company policy and procedure.	Do stress personal career advancement opportunities Don't get into win-lose games or tell subordinate what to do.
System 6 - Sociocentric	Do humanize work and promote group interaction. Don't let participation overshadow productivity.	Do provide "helping" opportunities and exposure to more people. Don't create competition or use the "carrot and stick" method.	Do be human, equal, and gain personal acceptance. Don't use power, politics, or manipulation.	Do illustrate how the review process helps people express themselves. Don't overstress individual performance or let the clock control discussions.
System 7 - Existential	Do provide guidelines only and involve subordinates in problem solving. Don't expect blind obedience or fail to get clear commitment.	Do provide movement in any direction. Don't be surprised if subordinate refuses a financial promotion to "do his or her own thing."	Do give subordinate access to information and let him or her make the decisions. Don't tell subordinate what to do or shut off questions.	Do act as a resource and let subordinate participate in the system design. Don't use top management to sell the importance of the review concept.

Individuals who participated in the Tarnowieski survey (1978) also offered some viewpoints on how work and organizations must respond. We would like to conclude, as we started by sharing some of these.

What better proof is there of a decline in the work ethic than the performance level of most workers and the results of their labor? Both are shoddy today and indicate an indifference to the job. This is a direct result of no appreciation for excellence on the part of so many people--both adolescents and adults. Just about everyone today seems to be satisfied with mediocrity. Merely improving productivity is not the solution to this problem. Something within the work environment must change if worker attitudes are to improve. A sense of accomplishment and pride must once again become a part of the work situation. Failing this, the work ethic will continue to deteriorate.

Director of Labor Relations,
(50 to 59), manufacturing
company, Illinois

I believe the big change in employee attitudes toward work is that more people want to be working at what they enjoy. They want to receive personal satisfaction from the work they do rather than just doing what their employer thinks is best. This change is the result of better educational opportunities, and more enlightened management. Employees produce much more in a job situation they like and find the work more challenging and personally rewarding.

Vice President, (50 to 59)
employee and community relations,
credit corporation,
Connecticut

Youth is disillusioned with the world today. Youth takes no pride in doing a job well. This perhaps due to too much mechanization in work methods. Maybe we should revert to the craftsmen system that allowed people to be more creative and imaginative.

Personnel Manager, (40 to 49)
publishing company,
Pennsylvania

Concluding Comment

The thesis we have tried to summarize is as follows. On the one hand, workers in North America over the past three decades have experienced a change in their orientation towards work and their employing organizations. Organizations have adapted, albeit modestly and slowly. Continued adaptation is required for a better fit between the nature of organized work and the needs of employees. We believe that such a fit is important in order to meet the needs of both individuals and organizations. The data that has been presented to support this position has been terribly biased towards experiences in North

America. This results from the fact that I am familiar with this information and could locate it easily. It is not clear whether similar patterns would be found in other countries of the world. We await the findings from other countries in order to answer this question.

In addition, we have focussed on value changes over a fairly short period of time. Readers interested in a more wide ranging treatment of changes in values and the future of employment should consult Toffler (1980) and Ferguson (1980).

BIBLIOGRAPHY

Bachman, J. G., & Johnston, L. D. (1979), The Freshman. In: Psychology Today 13: 78-87

Banks, L. (1977), Here Come the Individualists. In: Harvard Magazine 19, 21-23, 76-78.

Cooper, M. R., Morgan, B. S., Foley, P. M., & Kaplon, L. B. (1979), Changing Employee Values: Deepening Discontent? In: Harvard Business Review 57: 117-125

Ewing, D. W. (1971), Who Wants Employee Rights? In: Harvard Business Review : 22-35, 155-158

Ewing, D. W. (1971), Who Wants Corporate Democracy? In: Harvard Business Review : 12-28, 146-149

Ferguson, M. (1980), The Aquarian Conspiracy, Los Angeles: Cali.

Flowers, V. S., & Hughes, C. L. (1978), Choosing a Leadership Style. In: Organization Dynamics : 48-59.

Graves, C. W. (1970), Levels of Existence: An Open System Theory of Values. In: Journal of Humanitic Psychology 10: 131-155.

Hackman, J. R. (1978), The Design of Work in the 1980's. In: Organizational Dynamics 7: 3-17.

Hall, D. T. (1971), Potential for Career Growth. In: Personnel Administration 34: 18-30.

Hall, D. T., & Hall, F. S. (1976), What's New in Career Management! In: Organizational Dynamics : 17-33

Hughes, C. L. (1976), Managing Without Interference. New York: Advanced Management Research, Inc.

La Berge, R. (1978), Canadians and the Work Ethic. In: G. Sanderson (ed.), Adapting to a Changing World. Ottawa: Labour Canada, 27-33.

Lawler, E. E., III. (1974), The Individualized Organization: Problems and Promise. In: California Management Review 17: 31-38

Lawler, E. E., III. (1976), New Approaches to Pay: Innovations That Work. In: Personnel 53: 42-51.

Lodge, G. C. (1976), The New American Ideology. New York: Alfred Knopf

Lodge, G. C. (1977), Ethics and the New Ideology: Can Business Adjust? In: Management Review : 10-19

Martin, W. F., & Lodge, G. C. (1975), Our Society in 1985 - Business May Not Like It. In: Harvard Business Review 53: 143-152.

Maslow, A. H. (1943), A Theory of Human Motivation. In: Psychological Review 50: 370-396.

Renwick, P. A., & Lawler, E. E. (1978), What You Really Want From Your Job. In: Psychology Today 11: 53-65.

Sheppard, H. L., & Herrick, N. Q. (1972), Where Have All the Robots Gone? New York: Free Press

Sinetar, M. (1980), Management in the New Age: An Exploration of Changing Work Values. In: Personnel Journal 59: 749-755

Tarnowieski, D. (1976), Not of One Mind. New York: Management Association

Toffler, A. (1980), The Third Wave. New York: William Morrow

Trist, E. (1978), Adapting to a Changing World. In: Adapting to a Changing World, G. Sanderson (ed.). Ottawa: Labour Canada

Yankelovich, D. (1978), The New Psychological Contracts at Work. In: Psychology Today 11: 46-521.

Yankelovich, D. (1979), Yankelovich on Today's Workers - We Need New Motivational Tools. In: Industry Week : 61-68

Yankelovich, D. (1974), Changing Youth Values in the 70's. New York: McGraw-Hill.

NOTES

1. I would like to acknowledge the assistance of Steve Pulver in the preparation of the manuscript and Leona Burns in editing and typing the manuscript. Preparation of the paper was supported in part by Imperial Oil Limited and the Social Science and Humanities Research Council.

Part IV
Values and Management Process – Cross-National Comparisons

Sources of Influence on Managers' Value Dimension Structure, Value Dimension Intensity, and Decisions

William Whitely

ABSTRACT

This study introduces a model that distinguishes structural content and degree of integration properties of managers' value dimensions. Separate sources of influence and moderators of influences on these two properties are specified. In addition, the model recognizes managers' values as one of three major influences on their decisions. The multiple sources of influence on decision making and moderators of this influence are also specified. Tests of this model among managers from Australia and India are highly supportive. Implications of the separate findings are discussed throughout.

INTRODUCTION

An examination of the theoretical and research interest in managers' values indicates four questions that have received significant attention. Two of the four questions that have guided much of the research on managers' values follow from the conceptualization of the construct as a dependent variable. In both instances the question addressed revolves around the particular properties of values that are influenced by environmental conditions or experiences. Concurrently, these two thrusts differ in the power, and range of impact, of the sources of influence on values. The first question seeks to examine the fundamental differences in the structure-content of constellations of value dimensions and the integration of values into more parsimonious dimensions that are distinguishable from one group to another. Bem (1970), as an example, reasons that values become more coherent, organized and conceptualized into dimensions as individuals approach adulthood. Differentiation of dimensions results from widespread and powerful group cognitive differences. Differences in value dimensions of managers due to cognitive influences suggest qualitative differences in value reasoning of identifiable groups of managers (England, 1976).

The second conceptual direction, when values are the dependent variable, provides a quite different answer to the question 'what is influenced' and focuses on less powerful sources of influence. This direction is most closely identified with models and research that has examined the influence of demographic, job and organization and career variables on values (Sewell, Haller and Ohlendorf, 1970; Schein, 1971; Edstrom and Galbraith, 1977). What is influenced is the value intensity or degree of internalization rather than the value dimension structure-content. According to this "intensity" approach, individuals act under the influence of basic preferences, in particular the potency (e.g., importance-unimportance) property of these preferences. It is this property of values that is modified by the above mentioned conditions and experiences. Thus, it would seem to be conceptually correct to state that this intensity direction by ignoring structure content differences assumes that certain values are present in all managers, while the structure-content approach makes no such assumption. By removing this assumption the intensity approach is subsumed under the structure-content approach.

The sources of influence in the intensity approach also have limited influence on value dimension intensity. Values seem to vary in their degree of modifiability and change (England, 1968; Lusk and Oliver, 1974). One explanation according to Simon (1947) and Schein (1971) is that values are subject to multiple organization and nonorganization influences on value intensity each of which has a limited scope of influence. Thus, a corallary question is; 'can value dimensions be distinguished in terms of unique sources of influence that modify their intensity, or the intensity of value reasoning?'

Even if these questions regarding the properties of values influenced are answered in the affirmative, they would seem to beg a third general question: 'so what?' Ultimately the relevant question is whether or not these value dimensions, in turn, act as source of influence on important dependent variables such as decisions. For the structure-content approach the critical issue is comparative in nature. If there are contrasting value dimensions that influence decisions on the same problem, comparisons between managerial groups will illuminate the different value reasoning underlying the choices of each. For the intensity approach the issue is the range and nature of decisions affected by the value dimensions which are subject to influences with limited scope. Discussions of values often fail to qualify their arguments in this respect (Edstrom and Galbraith, 1977).

When attention is turned to models and research which conceptualize managers' values as an independent variable there are also two questions which focus on intergroup differences on the one hand, and intragroup differences on the other hand. Intergroup differences have the potential for being tested from decision models that include some combination of intrapersonal, objective and social bases of evaluation and information (Festinger, 1954; Pondy, 1969; Driver and Mock, 1975). However, models and research on managerial decisions that examine intergroup differences in the use of these bases are uncommon when values are the intrapersonal influence (Connor and Becker, 1975).

One source of the intergroup differences are cognitive moderators of relationships between intrapersonal (values), objective and social sources of influence and decisions (Festinger, 1954; Pondy, 1969). Recently these cognitive moderators have been included in psychological models that assign an active role to the individual in providing meaning to, and interpretation of, situations, with subsequent behavioral consequences (Endler and Magnusson, 1976). They state that "the meaning an individual assigns to a situation appears to be the most influential factor affecting his or her behavior," (p. 967). If these cognitive moderators play a prominent role, there is the potential for intergroup differences in the relative weight that value, objective or social bases of influence have on decisions. This possibility has been indicated in prior research (Gross, MacEachern and Mason 1957; Driver and Mock, 1975).

Intragroup variation in sources of influence on decisions can result from differences in problem content. Kluckhohn and Strodtbeck (1961) and Driver and Mock (1975) have documented this relativistic view of the effects of problem content for relationships between personal values and decisions. Thus, the content of the multiple problems confronting managers may alter the relative weight that a particular group places on specific value dimension, objective or social influences, or the relative weight of the major influences in arriving at decisions.

MODEL AND HYPOTHESES

The idea that cognitive functioning influences the structure-content of personality characteristics has recently begun to receive widespread attention. Schema theory (Stotland and Canon, 1973) recognizes that stable and unique interpretations or meanings assigned to stimuli by individuals can have structural consequences. These structural consequences in terms of the integration and differentiation of psychological structure occur even when individuals are presented with the (seemingly) same stimuli (Endler and Magnusson, 1976).

The model in Figure 1 indicates that value orientations and nationality are two cognitive influences on the integration and differentiation of managers' values into unique structural-content dimensions. While prominent in previous research on

Figure 1

MODEL OF THE INFLUENCES ON MANAGERS'
VALUE DIMENSIONS AND ON MANAGERS' DECISIONS

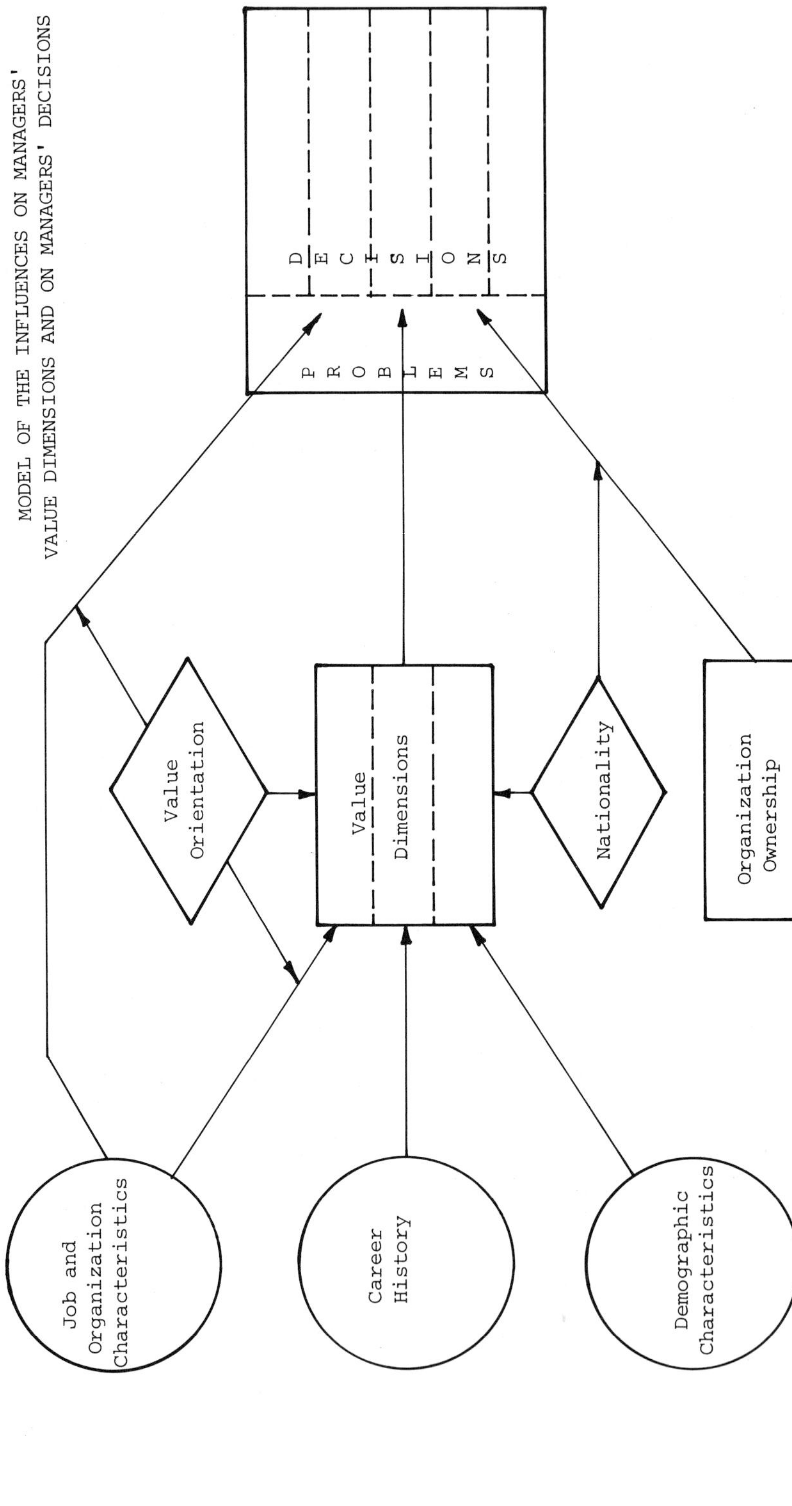

managers values (England, 1976), these cognitive influences have not received much attention in terms of their structural consequences (Whitely and England, 1980). Such structural consequences are important because they suggest wide differences in value reasoning or decision premises (Simon, 1947).

Pragmatism and moralism are the two most prominant and stable value orientations observed among managers regardless of the time period of the study, measure of values used or country in which the study was conducted (Gross, et. al., 1957; England, 1976; Palmer, Veiga and Vora, 1979). These value orientations are also prominent in adolescents (Kohlberg, 1968). The cognitive differences between pragmatist and moralist managers rests on the respective "success-failure" or "right-wrong" meanings they assign to many, though not all, stimuli (England, 1968).

While value orientations represent group cognitive influences on the structure-content of value dimensions of managers (England, 1976), nationality is a more global and diffused source of influence. Conceptualizing nationality as a cognitive construct is common in anthropology and psychology (Goodenough, 1964; Triandis, 1972). Triandis and his colleagues argue that one major source of national cognitive differences are subjective cultures or widely shared patterns of thought and stimulus interpretation unique to a particular country. Hence, nationality includes subjective cultural frameworks that influence the meaning or interpretation assigned stimuli. The consequences of alternative national interpretations would be observed in the form of value dimension differences between managers with the same value orientations, but dissimilar national origins. Value orientation influences should, in turn, be observed through value dimension differences among managers with the same nationality.

H_1: There are structural-content differences in the value dimensions of managers with separate value orientations and with separate nationality.

The model includes three general sources of influence on value dimension intensity. These objective job and organization characteristics, career characteristics and demographic characteristics were chosen for several reasons. First, each category of influence has received considerable previous conceptual and research attention (Porter and Lawler, 1965; Schein, 1971; Berger and Cummings, 1979). Second, as discussed below, there are reasons to believe that managers are not equally affected by these general influences, or by specific influences within each of these general categories. Finally, as previously outlined, each of these three general sources of influence, may impact on the intensity of different value dimensions.

The model indicates that value orientations moderate the relationship between objective job and organization characteristics and value dimension intensity. This view is consistent with the active role of the individual mentioned earlier, and with research that assigns this moderator role to value orientations in perceptual processes and stimulus interpretation (Bruner and Goodman, 1947). In this vein, some research indicates that pragmatist managers assign greater interpretive weight to directly obtained, objective information such as the present job and organization characteristics (Gross, et. al., 1957). In contrast, moralist managers in this study assigned greater interpretive weight to socially mediated information. Search processes also seem to be influenced by the objective or social form of information (Driver and Mock, 1975). Thus, if these differences distinguish value orientations, then the value dimension intensity of pragmatist managers, moreso than the value dimension intensity of moralist managers, should be influenced by objective job and organization characteristics.

> H_2: There is a greater relationship between objective job and organization characteristics and value dimension intensity of pragmatist managers than moralist managers.

The present model follows Schein (1971) in conceptualizing careers in terms of boundary movements. These movements represent distinct combinations of organization staffing practices, individual choice and social processes (Porter, Lawler and Hackman, 1975). Both Schein (1971) and Edstrom and Galbraith (1977) reason that the influence of boundary passages on value dimensions intensity does not occur immediately, but rather is related to the time period since the transition occurred. Boundaries included in this study are organization, position and occupation.

> H_3: There is a relationship between time period since a boundary movement occurred and value dimension intensity.

Demographic characteristics include a broad spectrum of influences on value dimension intensity. In this study the guiding thought was to acknowledge this spectrum, while concurrently restricting the demographic influence to nonorganizational sources; a feat accomplished with one exception. The influences included are age, education, income and similarity of father's occupation. Income has an obvious organization tie. Both education and income are frequent measures of social status, which along with age has previously been found to relate to value intensity in national samples of the United States population (Rokeach, 1973). Age influences on value intensity are commonly attributed to developmental changes (Tyler, 1956) or to cohorts which have been confronted with varying life experiences and conditions (Bengston, 1973). Filley, House and Kerr (1976) summarize several studies indicating educational effects on value intensity.

Culled out for special attention is similarity of father's occupation because it represents such an early family influence, thus suggesting the stability of value dimension intensity over lengthy periods of time. This practice of sons following fathers into the same occupation is widespread and has been recognized for some time (Taussig and Joslyn, 1932). Vocational theories and measures of vocational interests recognize management as an occupation distinct from other occupations in terms of the psychological profile of incumbents (Holland, 1973; Campbell, 1973). Further, research has often found relationships between the father's occupation and son's vocational aspirations (e.g., Sewell, et. al., 1970). If management as an occupation is psychologically distinct, and if sons aspire to and attain the same occupation as their fathers, it suggests that these sons may either internalize certain values to a greater extent than sons whose fathers were not managers. Conversely, in some instances the values of sons following their fathers may indicate less internalization than their counterparts.

H_4: Fathers who were in similar occupations to their managerial sons are likely to have had a greater influence on the degree of internalization of the son's value dimensions than fathers who were in dissimilar occupations.

Recall that the argument was made earlier that the demographic, career and organization sources influence the intensity of different value dimensions. Briefly, the reasoning was based on the varying degree of modifiability of values, which, in turn, suggest that values have both open and closed system properties. The closed system properties have been recognized in terms of the "functional autonomy" of values (Allport, 1950) and would be indicated if some value dimensions relate to the demographic or nonorganization influences, but not organization or career history influences. Further, both Hage and Dewar (1973) and Nightingale and Toulouse (1977) found rather low (r=.20) relationships between dimensions of organization structure and value dimension intensity on change focused and interpersonal value dimensions of general samples of managers. For these reasons the following hypotheses are suggested when accompanied by hypothesis two:

H_{5a}: Demographic and career history variables are related to the intensity of different value dimensions of moralist managers.

H_{5b}: Objective job and organization, demographic and career history variables are related to the intensity of different value dimensions of pragmatist managers.

Three principal bases of influence on decision making are intrapersonal, social and objective factual in nature

(Festinger, 1954; Pondy, 1969; Driver and Mock, 1975). The present model includes all three bases or categories of influence on managers' decisions. Earlier discussion and hypotheses have argued that the structure-content of managers' value dimensions differ as a result of the combined cognitive influence of value orientations and nationality. Dimensional differences suggest that managers are engaging in contrasting value reasoning in decision making. Such differences in value reasoning are conceptually similar to the use of separate decision premises in Simon's (1947) model of administrative man.

> H_6: There are structure-content differences in the value dimensions of managers with separate value orientations and nationalities that relate to their decisions.

Value orientation moderates relationship between objective job and organization characteristics and decisions for the same reasons outlined previously. These value orientations are a cognitive construct that refers to the distinct, stable and consistent meanings or interpretive weights individuals assign to events, contexts and stimuli. Pragmatist managers give greater interpretive weight, and moralist managers less interpretive weight to these objective characteristics.

> H_7: There is a greater relationship between objective job and organization characteristics and decisions for pragmatist than moralist managers.

The present model also recognizes that the problem content can alter the relative weight a manager places on specific influences within each of the intra-personal, social and objective categories, or the relative weight of the three categories in decision making. This property of the model is consistent with the findings of Kluckhohn and Strodtbeck (1961) and Driver and Mock (1975). One explanation advanced for the problem effect is based on the congruence between the specific content of the problem, including the value issues raised, and the specific content of the value dimensions (Hage and Dewar, 1973; Nightingale and Toulouse, 1977). Since specific value dimensions are not identifiable a priori, no hypotheses can be advanced.

Since the problem content can alter the relative weight managers place on particular sources of influence in decision making, corollary hypotheses to the seventh hypothesis are needed to account for pragmatist managers shifting reliance on specific objective job and organization variables. Prior research has established a relationship between organization size and decentralization or specialization (Child, 1973). What is often left unaddressed is what will be delegated. The contention is that pragmatist managers will delegate group maintenance activities, while retaining task allocation and innovation activities. This reasoning is consistent with delegation problems.

Type of ownership of the organization has been found to be a major source of influence on managers' decisions (Pondy, 1969; 1970). With the separation of ownership and management profound changes occur in the social control of organizations. Pondy reasons that when separation occurs managers' decisions become less influenced by ownership interests, and more influenced by personal values or job and organization characteristics assuming satisfactory profits.

Pondy's reasoning partially accounts for the inclusion of nationality as a moderator of relationships between forms of ownership and decisions. The stockholder form of ownership, which represents separation of ownership and management, is much more characteristic of Australian, than Indian organizations (Wheelwright, 1957; Chattapodhyay, 1973). Additional reasoning is supplied by studies that suggest large differences between partnership or proprietorship owned firms in India where there is no separation of ownership and management, and public-limited firms where the separation is found (Chowdhry, 1970; Baumgartel, 1971). These studies, in particular, observe that nonseparation-separation has a large effect on decision and personnel practices in Indian organizations.

Taken collectively, these sources suggest that the type of ownership is a proxy measure of the social system practices, including social or value information and influence practices that affect decisions. Further, national differences are likely due to the more widespread practice of both separation and nonseparation of ownership and management in India than in Australia.

H_8: There is a greater relationship between types of organization ownership and decisions for Indian managers than for Australian managers.

Within the Indian managerial samples, the problem content is also expected to influence the differential contributions by specific ownership types in relationships with decisions. Public limited firms are likely to have lower social stability since they eschew nepotism, are less paternalistic and adopt more impersonal Western management and personnel management practices (Baumgartel, 1971). The opposite conditions are more characteristic of proprietorships and partnership firms. Problem four should elicit these differences.

H_{8a}: Among Indian managers, there is a positive relationship between public limited ownership and selection of a socio-emotional, conflict dampening leader rather than a task-oriented, conflict generating leader.

views of managers handling uncertainty absorbtion and buffering the technical core (March and Simon, 1958; Thompson, 1967). Thus, with increased size pragmatist managers will choose an assistant with high levels of social skill to manage work unit interpersonal activities (see problem four in the appendix).

H_{7a}: Organization size makes a significant contribution to relationships between objective job and organization characteristics and staffing decisions concerned with delegation and specialization of managerial work.

The managers' functional area has been found to influence their decisions due to differences in task goals and interpersonal orientations (Lawrence and Lorsch, 1969). Problem three confronts managers with such task goal and interpersonal issues in a method proposed for funding an R&D project.

H_{7b}: Organization function makes a significant contribution to relationships between objective job and organization characteristics and R&D funding decisions.

The locus decision making varies depending on the nature of the problem (Child and Kieser, 1977). Two of the present problems raise strategic issues, and level of management is likely to make a significant contribution to decisions on both of them. Problem two concerns the termination or retention and retraining of a large number of loyal, but obsolete employees. Problem three concerns a method for financing an R&D project which has implications for organization performance, compensation and employee obsolescence and layoff.

H_{7c}: Organization level makes a significant contribution to relationships between objective job and organization characteristics and strategic decisions.

Two current explanations for span control influences on delegation decisions (problem five) are termed cognitive capacity and social processes (Mackenzie, 1974; Ouchi and Dowling, 1974). The cognitive explanation is that increased spans tax cognitive capacity which leads to increased delegation. The social processes explanation is that increased spans reduce superior-subordinate interaction with corresponding reductions in superiors' knowledge of subordinate performance, commitment and needs, thus reducing delegation. Hence, the cognitive explanation hypothesizes a positive relationship between span of control and delegation, while the social processes explanation hypothesizes a negative relationship. For reasons similar to those for the social process explanation, managers with larger spans would also be more reluctant to make extensive renovations to an employee lunchroom on problem one.

H_{7d}: Span of control will make a significant contribution to relationships between objective job and organization characteristics and decisions on renovation and

This hypothesis follows from the particularly problematic nature of social stability in public limited firms.

> H_{8b}: Among Indian managers, those working in public limited ownership firms are less likely, and those working in proprietorship and partnership firms are more likely to retain and retrain loyal, but obsolete employees at company expense.

This hypothesis follows from the more impersonal practices of public limited firms and more paternalistic practices of partnership and proprietorship firms.

> H_{8c}: Among Indian managers, those working in public limited ownership firms are more likely, and those working in proprietorship and partnership firms are less likely to delegate.

Delegation is a common Western management practice likely to be adopted in public limited firms as a means of developing subordinate expertise. Delegation is not as likely in partnerships or proprietorships since to do so would dilute owner control. Thus, hypothesis 8c indicates a reversal in the signs of the beta weights from those predicted in hypothesis 8b as a result of differing problem contents.

METHOD

Samples and Procedure

Data collection was conducted by experienced members of research institutes in each country to reduce potential cultural biases from contaminating results. National directories of managers in private industry were used to draw random samples stratified by size of firm (number of employees), level of management and function. The source used in India was the Directory of Executives in India, which lists 19,448 managers by top, upper middle or lower middle positions, and by function handled. Size of organization was not given, but the Indian groups are comparable to each other and to their Australian counterparts as shown in Table 1. The Australian sample was drawn from the membership list of the Australian Institute of Management which included 10,000 members listed with complete stratifying information.

The percentage of usable returns in India was 72%, and in Australia 33%. The higher rate in India stems from replacing managers who could not be located for various reasons with another similar in terms of stratifying variables, and to the data collection procedure discussed below. A replacement strategy was not used in Australia. However, overall characteristics of the present Australian sample are very similar to those in the Clark and McCabe (1970) sample, which was five times that of the present one. Final sample sizes are: India, 210 pragmatists and 275 moralists; Australia, 144 pragmatists, 144 moralists. Table 1 presents the sample characteristics for the separate groups of pragmatist and moralist managers in each country.

TABLE 1

SAMPLE CHARACTERISTICS
(Percentages)

Characteristic	Australian Pragmatists (N = 144)	Australian Moralists (N = 144)	Indian Pragmatists (N = 210)	Indian Moralists (N = 275)
Function				
Production/operations	13.2	10.4	9.0	9.5
Sales/distribution	17.3	16.7	19.5	20.7
Engineering	4.9	5.6	3.8	3.3
Finance/accounting	7.0	12.5	7.6	11.6
Personnel/IR	7.0	5.6	9.5	9.5
R & D	2.1	2.8	-	-
General administration	43.1	41.0	45.7	43.6
Other	5.6	6.3	4.8	1.8
Level of Management				
Top Management	58.3	57.0	44.8	45.8
Upper middle	27.8	31.9	44.3	44.0
Lower middle	14.0	11.1	11.1	10.2
Organization Size (employees)				
Small (under 250)	49.0	42.5	40.3	39.9
Medium (251-1999)	29.8	35.5	33.1	34.2
Large (2000 or >)	21.3	21.9	26.6	25.9
Span of Control (direct subordinates)				
0-3	10.4	11.8	10.0	10.6
4-6	18.1	19.6	20.5	19.6
7-10	41.6	39.6	40.9	39.6
11-15	20.2	18.8	19.5	20.0
16 or more	10.0	10.4	10.0	10.6
Ownership Form				
Partnership	9.5	10.4	23.8	22.2
Proprietorship	7.0	5.6	25.2	23.6
Public limited	83.5	84.0	54.3	54.2

TABLE 1
(Continued)

Characteristic	Australian Pragma-tists (N = 144)	Australian Moralists (N = 144)	Indian Pragma-tists (N = 210)	Indian Moral-ists (N = 275)
Age of Manager				
20-29	5.5	2.8	6.2	4.4
30-34	9.2	7.1	16.6	11.6
35-39	13.5	11.3	20.4	21.5
40-44	21.3	17.0	27.5	20.7
45-49	20.6	16.3	12.8	15.6
50-54	12.8	19.1	8.1	12.4
55-59	12.8	13.5	5.7	8.7
60 or more	6.4	12.8	2.4	5.1
Missing	0.0	0.0	0.5	0.0
Education				
Some high school	7.8	8.5	0.9	1.8
High school	14.2	14.2	4.3	7.6
Some college	24.8	38.3	9.5	12.7
Bachelors' degree	36.2	30.5	41.7	32.0
Some postgraduate	10.6	6.4	15.6	15.6
Postgraduate degree	5.0	1.4	0.0	0.0
Missing	1.4	0.7	0.0	0.0
Time in Present Position				
Under 1 year	19.1	14.9	11.4	9.1
2-3 years	26.2	26.2	24.2	22.9
4-5 years	18.4	14.9	19.4	16.4
6-10 years	14.2	17.0	24.4	28.7
11-15 years	8.5	12.1	8.5	12.4
Over 15 years	12.1	13.5	6.6	10.2
Missing	1.4	0.7	0.5	0.4
Total Managerial Experience				
0-1 years	0.7	1.4	3.3	1.1
2-3 years	5.0	3.5	5.2	6.2
4-5 years	4.3	6.4	13.3	8.7
6-10 years	20.6	12.1	40.8	25.1
11-15 years	29.1	23.4	18.5	25.5
16-20 years	14.9	17.0	10.0	16.4
21-30 years	14.2	21.3	5.2	11.6
Over 30 years	10.6	14.2	3.3	5.5
Missing	0.7	0.7	0.5	0.0
Annual Income				
Under $6,000	4.3	11.3	6.6	10.5
$6000-7,999	11.3	17.0	40.8	42.2
$8,000-$9,999	21.3	17.7	28.0	22.9
$10,000-$11,999	14.2	17.0	10.9	10.5
$12,000-$14,999	14.9	12.8	5.7	5.1

Manager's meaning orientations were identified by the dominant meaning assigned to concepts viewed as being highly important. Pragmatists generally assign a successful meaning to high-importance concepts, while moralists generally assign a right meaning to high-importance concepts. Managers who generally assign a pleasant meaning to concepts were not included in this study since they represent only 2-3 percent of the sample in each country.

Once the manager's orientation has been identified, each concept is evaluated according to its likelihood of being translated into behavior. In descending order of likelihood of being translated into behavior are the following combinations using pragmatists as an example: (a) concepts marked successful and highly important are operative values; (b) concepts marked successful and average or low in importance are adopted values; (c) concepts marked right or pleasant and highly important are intended values; and (d) concepts marked right or pleasant and as average or low in importance are weak values. Each concept is then assigned a 4, 3, 2 or 1 numerical value based upon these combinations, respectively. These are the scores that were factored. The operative category for moralist managers are items marked right and high in importance. Hence, values are the product of the attachment of various combinations of unique meanings and unique levels of importance to each of the broad range of concepts.

Independent Variables

The collection of the job and organization, and ownership data utilized the following procedures. Level of responsibility was the number of levels below the chief executive officer. Each manager checked the alternative best describing his functional position. Both organization size and span of control were measured in terms of number of people; the latter being number of direct subordinates. Each manager checked the most appropriate form of ownership category. Career history was measured by having the manager indicate the number of years he had been a manager, length of time with the present organization and length of time in present position. Demographic data was gathered as follows: managers checked the appropriate category for age which was in ten year intervals; the category for highest education certificate or degree attained; annual income in $500 intervals; and father's occupation. Father's occupations were coded in dummy variables for similarity or dissimilarity to that of the son's. Similar occupations included managers or executives, business trade or government official. All other occupations were coded into the dummy category.

TABLE 1
(Continued)

Characteristics	Australian Pragma-tists (N = 144)	Australian Moralists (N = 144)	Indian Pragma-tists (N = 210)	Indian Moral-ists (N = 275)
$15,000-$19,999	22.0	12.8	4.3	2.9
$20,000-$24,999	1.5	5.7	0.9	1.5
$25,000-$34,999	2.8	3.5	0.9	1.8
$35,000-$49,999	2.8	1.4	0.0	0.4
$50,000 or greater	1.8	0.7	1.9	2.2
Father's Occupation				
Government official	17.7	18.4	28.0	34.2
Business trade	32.6	29.1	36.5	26.2
Business executive	17.0	14.9	8.5	8.0
Teaching	1.4	2.8	2.4	5.5
Professional	9.9	10.6	18.0	14.5
Other occupation	19.9	22.7	5.7	11.6
Missing	0.7	1.4	0.9	0.0

A mailed questionnaire procedure was used in Australia and interviews in India. The two data collection procedures can potentially yield noncomparable data due to differences in demand characteristics, which are likely to be greater with the interview than the mailed questionnaire. However, comparison of the present Indian managers data with Thiagarajan's (1968) data on an independent sample of Indian managers using the same values questionnaire and a mailing procedure yielded no statistically significant differences. The similarity of results using different data collection procedures lends some support for the absence of method variance (Campbell and Fiske, 1959) in the measurement of managers values, using the Personal Values Questionnaire (PVQ). Further, other studies using different values measures identify the same orientations and similar value profiles to those found in this study among Indian managers (Palmer, et. al., 1979). Thus, it does not appear that bias in between country comparisons are very great, and in any event, within country comparisons will not be affected.

Value Dimensions and Meaning Orientation

Managers in each country completed a PVQ which consists of 66 concepts concerned with goals of business organizations, personal goals of managers, groups of people, attributes of people and general topics (England, 1968). Measurement of each concept is on a three point importance scale and rank ordering of "successful," "right" and "pleasant" meaning alternatives.

Decision Problems

The five problems used in this study are included in Appendix A. Properties of the problems are discussed here in order to aid later interpretation of results. Managers were asked to indicate their decisions on problems concerned with (]) the renovation of employee cafeteria and rest room facilities; (2) retention and retraining of loyal and good performing, but obsolete engineers; (3) a method of financing a promising R & D project; (4) selection of an assistant; and (5) delegation of a recruiting and selection task. The particular scale properties for each problem are as follows. On problem one high scores indicate more renovation and a greater concern for human relations, while lower scores or less renovation indicate more concern for economic costs. On problem two higher scores or more retention and retraining indicate a greater concern for humanism, loyalty and good prior performance, while lower scores or less retention and retraining indicate a greater concern for economic costs. On problem three, higher scores or willingness indicate more concern for company economic performance, while lower scores or unwillingness indicate human relations, trust, loyalty and compassion. On problem four, the socio-emotional subordinate (John Roberts) is coded 1 with the task-oriented subordinate (Robin Sharp) as the dummy category. Finally, on problem five higher scores indicate progressively greater delegation.

Analysis

Managers were separated into four groups (orientation x country) to examine the structural influence of nationality and meaning orientation. Initial analysis in each of the four groups consisted of principal factor analysis using squared multiple correlations as the communality estimate. Rotation of factors with eigenvalues exceeding 1.0 was by the varimax procedure followed by the generation of standardized factor scores. Paired comparisons of the factors for all groups were made using the coefficient of congruence (Kaiser, Hunka and Bianchini, 1971) to examine the factorial similarity of managers differing in meaning orientation or nationality. This index can be interpreted as a correlation between factors (Kaiser, et al., 1971). The minimal level for an indication of similarity was set at .75 following Scheewind and Cattell's (1971) recommendation.

Separate equations were used in regressing mangers' value dimensions on objective job and organization career history and demographic variables. A similar procedure was used in regressing managers' decisions on value dimension factor scores, the objective job and organization variables and types of ownership. Tests for the significance of the beta weights were conducted when the multiple correlations were significant.

average, 36 percent and 33 percent more variance is accounted for in relationships between these objective characteristics and value dimensions for pragmatist managers than for moralist managers. These results support the second hypothesis.

TABLE 2

AUSTRALIAN PRAGMATIST MANAGERS VALUE DIMENSIONS AND LOADINGS

Value	F1 Groups of Employees	F7 Company Ownership	F11 Antecedents/ Consequences of Subordinate Achievement	F13 Organization Loyalty
Blue-Collar Workers	.78	.10	.14	-0.11
Laborers	.75	.11	.10	-0.17
White-Collar Workers	.72	.12	.03	.03
Technical Workers	.56	.01	.15	.15
Craftsman	.51	.05	.09	.08
Employees	.44	.05	.04	.51
My Co-Workers	.43	.05	.11	.20
Labor Unions	.42	.19	.05	-0.17
Managers	.41	.04	.03	.20
My Subordinates	.40	.07	.52	.00
Owners	.13	.75	.01	-0.01
Stockholders	.26	.65	-0.05	-0.11
My Company	.05	.41	.10	.67
Skill	.09	-0.02	.61	.00
Competition	.16	-0.03	.60	.06
Achievement	.00	-0.04	.43	-0.17
Job Satisfaction	.05	.14	.41	.19
Loyalty	.10	.03	.02	.64
Emotions	.22	.28	.19	.41
Eigenvalue	5.483	1.513	1.302	1.140

Value	F2 Benevolence Stability	F3 Power-Influence	F6 Personal Loyalty	F8 Effective Social Change	F10 Personal Competence Independence
Organization Growth	-0.61	-0.17	-0.08	-0.19	.19
Security	.53		.19	-0.02	-0.19
Dignity	.52	.15	.04	.26	.10
Social Welfare	.50	-0.02	.17	.02	-0.05
Employee Welfare	.43	.03	.21	.08	.14
Prestige	.42	.26	-0.12	.09	.09
Money	-0.01	.66	-0.07	.13	-0.22
Property	-0.10	.59	.09	-0.00	-0.19
Power	-0.11	.47	-0.22	.02	.02

Types of ownership were coded as dummy variables. Following Darlington(1968), tests of the contribution of organization function consisted of running two regressions, once with these variables present and the second time without them, followed by a calculation of the significance of the difference in the proportion of variance.

RESULTS

Hypothesis one proposes that there are differences in the structure-content of the value dimension for the four managerial groups due to value orientation and national influences. This hypothesis requires two kinds of evidence. First, factor solutions must yield dimensions that account for a large enough proportion of the total variance to be theoretically meaningful. Second, coefficient of congruence results must show major differences in the factors structures of the managerial groups. Factor solutions yielded fourteen and thirteen dimensions for Australian moralist and pragmatist managers respectively. Eleven and seven factors were identified for Indian pragmatist and moralist managers respectively. The factor solutions account for between 47 and 56 percent of the total variance among the four groups. Because of the large number of dimensions and number of items, only those factors found to be similar in two or more groups and those correlated with one or more dependent variable are displayed. Further, only values with significant factor loadings ($p>.40$) on one or more dimensions are displayed because they were used in labeling the factors and make the largest contribution to factor score definition (Rummel, 1968). Tables 2 through 5 display the factor loadings and eigenvalues.

Coefficient of congruence results indicate only three instances of factorial similarity among the managerial groups which suggests large value reasoning differences between the four groups. One factor is similar in all groups and is labeled as a Groups of Employees dimension (F1 for both Australian groups and Indian moralists, and F5 for Indian pragmatists). Two additional similarities were found among Indian managers. F1 for the pragmatists and F5 for moralists indicate a similar Paternalism dimension. F4 for both groups indicates similar Organization-Individual integration. Hypotheis one is therefore supported.

Hypothesis two proposes differential relationships between objective job and organization characteristics and value dimensions of pragmatist and moralist managers within each country. There is no statistical test for the significance of the difference between regression equations. As a substitute, two types of evidence are presented in Table 6. First, the findings indicate that six significant relationships were found among pragmatist managers, while these characteristics were unrelated to the value dimensions of moralist managers. More importantly, the results at the bottom of the table indicate that, on the

TABLE 2
(Continued)

Value	F2 Benev-olence Stability	F3 Power-Influence	F6 Personal Loyalty	F8 Effec-tive Social Change	F10 Personal Competence Indepen-dence
Authority	-0.11	.47	.10	-0.02	.04
Ambition	-0.12	.42	.28	-0.13	.27
Me	-0.11	.41	-0.02	.07	.29
My Boss	.10	.41	-0.01	.09	.29
Profit Maximization	.28	.41	-0.03	.00	-0.03
Honor	.02	.40	.31	-0.13	.06
Loyalty	-0.09	.06	.64	-0.03	-0.02
Trust	-0.07	-0.00	.62	-0.02	.11
Cooperation	-0.00	-0.07	.40	.18	.16
Obedience	-0.26	.05	.40	-0.08	-0.04
Compromise	-0.09	.02	-0.06	.64	-0.05
Leisure	-0.19	.19	.07	.43	.20
Achievements	-0.20	.09	-0.06	.40	.27
Change	-0.29	-0.08	-0.05	.40	.18
Skill	-0.02	-0.03	.04	-0.07	.52
Creativity	-0.02	-0.04	-0.01	.13	.49
Ability	.01	-0.14	0.12	-0.03	.49
Autonomy	-0.07	.28	.01	.11	.41
Tolerance	-0.19	-0.05	.23	.13	.41
Eigenvalue	2.631	2.511	1.761	1.333	1.243

TABLE 3

AUSTRALIAN MORALIST MANAGERS:
VALUE DIMENSIONS AND LOADINGS

	F1 Groups of Employees	F4 External Institu-tional Authority	F9 Employee Humanism-Socialism	F10 Org. - Individual Effective-ness	F11 Subordi-nate Certainty
Blue-Collar Workers	.85	.18	.07	.04	.01
Laborers	.78	-0.14	.23	.04	.08
Craftsmen	.71	-0.16	.25	.19	.01
Technical Employees	.70	-0.03	.07	.11	.07
My Co-Workers	.68	-0.13	.12	.35	.07
Managers	.55	-0.07	.02	.37	.05
Owners	.49	.05	.34	.02	.01

TABLE 3
(Continued)

	F1 Groups of Employees	F4 External Institu- tional Authority	F9 Employee Humanism- Socialism	F10 Org. - Individual Effective- ness	F11 Subordi- nate Certainty
Employees	.47	-0.02	.40	.16	.02
Stockholders	.47	.08	.00	.08	.11
My Subordinates	.42	.01	.21	.18	.61
Government	-0.05	.70	-0.06	.05	.02
Religion	.16	.68	.14	.00	.07
Authority	.26	.49	-0.24	-0.05	.19
Compassion	.00	-0.05	.65	.01	.10
Social Welfare	.02	.30	.55	.06	.10
Tolerance	.06	-0.01	.45	.07	.02
Employee Welfare	.13	.31	.44	.35	.13
Equality	.01	.03	.44	.15	.01
Liberalism	-0.06	.21	.40	-0.11	-0.10
Skill	.04	.04	.05	.66	.08
Ability	.15	-0.13	-0.13	.55	.18
Organization Efficiency	.21	-0.11	.00	.52	.14
Industry Leadership	.24	-0.07	.04	.42	.12
High Productivity	.21	.09	.05	.41	.03
Risk	.04	.25	.00	.01	-0.51
Eigenvalue	5.583	2.168	2.058	1.679	1.035

Value	F2 Authoritarianism	F3 Effectiveness- Competence	F8 Social Stability- Effectiveness
Conformity	.54	.04	.04
Conservatism	.49	.04	-0.04
Aggressiveness	.41	.19	-0.02
Honor	.41	-0.11	-0.10
Prejudice	.40	-0.10	-0.04
Organization Growth	.07	.60	-0.14
Ambition	.19	.55	-0.08
Competition	-0.04	.54	.01
Achievement	.12	.45	.12
Profit Maximization	-0.03	.41	-0.10
Equality	-0.02	.40	.13
Cooperation	-0.07	-0.05	.49
Leisure	.23	-0.11	.44
Success	.05	.30	.41
Rational	-0.05	-0.03	.40

	F2	F3	F8
	Authoritarianism	Effectiveness-Competence	Social Stability-Effectiveness
Eigenvalue	2.196	2.187	2.097

TABLE 4

INDIAN PRAGMATIST MANAGERS:
VALUE DIMENSIONS AND LOADINGS

	F1	F4	F5	F6	F7
Value	Pater-nalism	Organ-ization Individual Integration	Groups of Employees	Bene-factors of Org. Stability	Satis-faction-Harmony
Trust	.59	.11	.15	.12	.23
Obedience	.57	.14	.20	.00	.01
Loyalty	.46	.32	.09	.12	.21
Tolerance	.46	.06	.05	.10	.17
Caution	.43	-0.37	.04	.19	.16
Cooperation	.41	.24	.14	-0.03	.55
Conformity	.40	-0.27	.01	.00	.22
Security	.40	.07	.29	.34	.24
Creativity	-0.30	.59	.12	.08	-0.08
Organization Growth	-0.16	.52	-0.04	.17	-0.05
Organization Efficiency	-0.02	.51	.19	-0.27	.20
Industry Leadership	-0.07	.44	.10	.04	.01
Change	.00	.43	.07	-0.33	-0.21
Skill	.00	.40	.24	.02	.10
Blue-Collar Workers	.02	.06	.72	.15	.06
Laborers	.06	.02	.71	.18	.14
White-Collar Workers	.05	.18	.67	.11	.08
Labor Unions	.01	-0.59	.49	.21	-0.20
Employees	.11	.01	.40	.01	.07
Employee Welfare	-0.01	-0.10	.03	.64	.25
Organization Stability	-0.12	-0.15	-0.04	.46	-0.05
My Company	.24	.38	.06	.45	.08
Stockholders	-0.27	.02	.00	.41	.15
Job Satisfaction	.32	.21	.18	.23	.53
Conflict	-0.22	-0.20	.04	-0.04	-0.53
My Subordinates	.38	.19	.30	.04	.49
Eigenvalue	7.743	2.019	1.808	1.651	1.602

TABLE 4
(Continued)

Value	F2 Capitalism-Socialism	F3 Compassion-Equality	F11 External Institutional Influence
Prejudice	.60	-0.06	-0.07
Achievement	-0.55	.06	-0.10
Success	-0.44	-0.05	.02
Customers	-0.40	.05	.04
Social Welfare	.40	.15	.32
Compassion	.00	.47	-0.16
Risk	-0.14	.43	.10
Individuality	-0.12	.40	-0.17
Equality	.13	.40	-0.03
Religion	.04	.08	.55
Government	-0.07	.16	.54
Compromise	.12	-0.06	.42
Competition	-0.03	.17	.40
Conservatism	-0.03	.05	.40
Eigenvalue	2.890	2.390	1.006

TABLE 5

INDIAN MORALIST MANAGERS:
VALUE DIMENSIONS AND LOADINGS

Value	F1 Groups of Employees	F4 Organization-Individual Integration	F5 Paternalism
Blue Collar Workers	.61	-0.03	-0.13
Laborers	.61	-0.07	-0.04
White Collar Workers	.58	.05	.08
Labor Unions	.52	-0.06	-0.20
Employees	.47	-0.01	-0.02
Rationality	.18	.46	-0.11
Organization Growth	.07	.45	-0.15
Cooperation	.06	.45	.40
Ability	-0.11	.45	-0.26
Organization Efficiency	.01	.43	-0.28
Skill	.01	.42	-0.22
Creativity	.28	.42	-0.24
Achievement	.37	.42	-0.25

TABLE 5
(Continued)

Value	F1 Groups of Employees	F4 Organization-Individual Integration	F5 Paternalism
Job Satisfaction	.17	.42	.00
Obedience	-0.04	-0.09	.57
Loyalty	.04	.38	.55
Trust	.10	.25	.46
Security	.15	-0.12	.45
Tolerance	-0.10	.28	.44
Honor	.04	.19	.43
Caution	.00	.05	.43
Dignity	.13	-0.05	.40
Eigenvalue	7.811	2.106	2.106

TABLE 5
(Continued)

Value	F2 Personal-Social Concommitants of Change	F7 Social Concommitants of Organization Growth
Emotions	.60	-0.00
Autonomy	.54	-0.12
Religion	.48	.03
Compassion	.46	.33
Individuality	.40	-.00
Change	.40	.26
Conflict	.40	.20
Social Welfare	.04	.58
Employee Welfare	.02	.50
Compromise	-0.19	.43
Tolerance	-0.20	.41
My Co-workers	-0.20	.41
Liberalism	-0.29	.40
Organization Growth	-0.08	.40
Eigenvalue	2.568	1.104

TABLE 6

MULTIPLE CORRELATIONS, AVERAGE CORRELATION AVERAGE VARIANCE ACCOUNTED FOR AND PERCENT DIFFERENCE IN VARIANCE ACCOUNTED FOR IN WITHIN COUNTY COMPARISONS OF THE RELATIONSHIP BETWEEN OBJECTIVE JOB AND ORGANIZATION CHARACTERISTICS AND VALUE DIMENSION INTENSITY

	Group			
Value Dimension Number[1]	Australian Pragmatist (N=141)	Australian Moralist (N=141)	Indian Pragmatist (N=210)	Indian Moralist (N=275)
1	.392*	.387	.331*	.258
2	.315	.162	.354**	.179
3	.309	.354	.308	.276
4	.325	.220	.314	.252
5	.319	.348	.353**	.241
6	.226	.242	.266	.276
7	.411*	.316	.173	.256
8	.345	.241	.294	
9	.274	.291	.201	
10	.329	.255	.183	
11	.362	.310	.350**	
12	.313	.316		
13	.305	.250		
14		.216		
Average Correlation (Total / N Factors)	.325	.279	.284	.247
Average Variance Accounted for	10.6%	7.8%	8.1%	6.1%
Percent difference in Variance Accounted for	36%		33%	

1 Note: The pattern-magnitude of the factor loadings for values on each dimension for each group of managers differs greatly. Therefore, what determined the factor scores for each group of managers also differs greatly. As a result the dependent variables in this analysis differ from group to group. The relevant comparison is, therefore, between the average variance accounted for across all correlations.

*=p<.05
**=p<.01

TABLE 7

MULTIPLE CORRELATIONS AND BETA WEIGHTS IN RELATIONSHIPS BETWEEN ORGANIZATION VARIABLES AND VALUE DIMENSIONS STRENGTH FOR PRAGMATIST MANAGERS

Groups and value Dimension	R	Organization Variables and Beta Weights			
		Span of Control	Organization Size	Function[1]	Level of Responsibility
Australian Pragmatists					
F1. Groups of Employees (df=4, 139)	.39	.20*	-.10	1.18	.14
F7. Company Ownership	.41*	.07	-.18	1.28	.25*
Indian Pragmatists (df=4, 205)					
F1. Paternalism	.33*	-.20**	-.27**	1.35	-.07
F2. Capitalism-Socialism	.35**	-.21**	-.13	1.26	.02
F5. Groups of Employees	.35**	-.17*	-.22**	1.45	.15
F11. External Institutional Influence	.35**	.14	.27**	1.64	.13

* = $p < .05$
** = $p < .01$

[1] Figures in this column are t tests for the significance of the difference between multiple correlations with and without function entered in the equations. See Darlington (1968) for a discussion of this procedure.

While not central to this second hypothesis, the findings shown in Table 7 can aid in interpreting the significant relationships between objective job and organization characteristics and decision making found among pragmatist managers. Findings in this table indicate that all the objective characteristics made one or more significant contributions to these relationships with the exception of the position function of the manager. In addition, span of control was the most general contributor to relationships as indicated by significant beta weights in four of the six regression equations.

Hypothesis three proposes relationships between the time period between major career boundary passages and value dimensions of managers. Results in Table 8 show that these career passages relate to the value dimensions of managers in all four groups. Hypothesis three is therefore supported. The results in this table indicate more widespread significant relationships among Australian pragmatist and Indian moralist managers than the remaining managerial groups. In addition, the most crucial boundary passage, as indicated by the significant beta weights in all groups, is years of managerial exerience. This boundary passage made a significant contribution to relationships in all four groups and in six of the nine significant relationships observed.

While demographic variables in general were thought to relate to the value dimensions of managers, the fourth hypothesis concentrated on one such variable, similarity of fathers' occupation, because it represents a non-organization, early potential influence. Results shown in Table 9 support the expectation that demographic variables are significantly related to the value dimensions of managers in all four groups. In addition, these findings support the fourth hypothesis which proposes that fathers who were in similar occupations to their sons would have a greater influence on the degree of internalization of son's value dimensions than would be the case for fathers who were in dissimilar occupations. Similarity was coded 1 and dissimilarity 0 for this test. The signs for the beta weights for this variable are negative for Australian pragmatists and Australian moralists indicating that similarity reduces value internalization on Personal Loyalty and Social Stability-Effectiveness dimensions relative to their familial counterparts. In contrast, the positive sign of the beta weights for both Indian managerial groups suggest that similarity enhances value internalization on Benefactors of Organization Stability and Paternalism dimensions relative to their counterparts.

Hypotheses 5a and 5b proposed that each of the three sets of influences was significantly related to the intensity of different value dimensions. Table 10 summarizes the significant relationships for each group of managers. An examination of this table indicates that these hypotheses are completely

TABLE 8

SIGNIFICANT MULTIPLE CORRELATIONS AND BETA WEIGHTS IN RELATIONSHIPS BETWEEN CAREER HISTORY VARIABLES AND VALUE DIMENSION STRENGTH

Group and Value Dimension	R	CAREER HISTORY VARIABLES AND BETA WEIGHTS		
		Number of Years as a Manager	Time in Present Position	Time with Company
Australian Pragmatist (df=3, 140)				
F2. Benevolence-Stability	.25*	-.14	-.10	.26*
F3. Power-influence	.24*	-.24*	-.05	.09
F10. Personal Competence-Independence	.25*	-.14	-.15	-.12
Australian Moralist (df=3, 140)				
F2. Authoritarianism	.30*	-.30**	.20*	-.08
Indian Pragmatist (df=3, 206)				
F2. Capitalism-Socialism	.24*	-.25*	.23*	.01
Indian Moralist (df=3, 271)				
F1. Groups of Employees	.21*	.24**	.05	-.10

TABLE 8
(Continued)

Group and Value Dimension	R	CAREER HISTORY VARIABLES AND BETA WEIGHTS		
		Number of Years as a Manager	Time in Present Position	Time with Company
Indian Moralist (df=3, 271)				
F2. Personal-Social Concommitants of Change	.21*	.27*	-.03	-.10
F5. Paternalism	..19*	.16	.07	-.01
F7. Social Concommitants of Organization Growth	.24*	.23**	.10	-.08

* = p < .05
** = p < .01

TABLE 9

SIGNIFICANT MULTIPLE CORRELATIONS AND BETA WEIGHTS IN RELATIONSHIPS BETWEEN DEMOGRAPHIC CHARACTERISTICS AND VALUE DIMENSION STRENGTH

Group and Value Dimension	DEMOGRAPHIC CHARACTERISTICS AND BETA WEIGHTS				
	R	Education	Income	Age	Similarity of Father's Occupation
Australian Pragmatist (df=4, 139)					
F6. Personal Loyalty	.34*	.04	.21*	-.10	-.37**
F8. Effective Social Change	.33*	.03	.30**	-.06	.06
Australian Moralists (df=4, 139)					
F3. Effectiveness-Competence	.38**	.20*	.29**	-.15	-.04
F8. Social Stability-Effectiveness	.47**	.11	-.34**	.21*	.22*
Indian Pragmatists (df=4, 205)					
F6. Benefactors of Organization Stability	.33*	-.16*	-.19*	.11	.29*
Indian Moralists (df=4, 270)					
F5. Paternalism	.28**	.09	-.15*	-.12	.27*

* = p < .05
** = p < .01

TABLE 10

SUMMARY OF THE SIGNIFICANT RELATIONSHIPS BETWEEN OBJECTIVE JOB AND ORGANIZATION, CAREER HISTORY AND DEMOGRAPHIC VARIABLES AND VALUE DIMENSION INTENSITY

Independent Variable	Managerial Group and Value Dimension			
	Australian Pragmatist	Australian Moralist	Indian Pragmatist	Indian Moralist
Objective Job and Organization Variable	F1,F7	-	F1,F2,F5,F11	-
Career History Variables	F2,F3,F10	F2	F2	F1,F2,F3 F7
Demographic Variables	F6,F8	F3,F8	F6	F4

supported for Australian pragmatist and Australian moralist managers. Both objective job and organization, and career history variables were significantly related to the intensity of the Authoritarian dimension of Indian pragmatists. There were no overlapping significant relationships for the influences with the other four dimensions for Indian pragmatists. Both career history and demographic variables were significantly related to the Paternalism dimension of Indian moralist managers. There were no overlapping relationships for the remaining three value dimensions. While not completely supported, the findings do generally indicate that objective job and organization, career history and demographic variables relate to the value intensity of separate value dimensions.

Hypothesis six proposes that there are structure-content differences in the value dimensions of managers in the four groups that relate to their decisions. Evidence presented earlier indicated that only the Groups of Employee dimension for all groups and the Paternalism and Organization-Individual Integration dimensions of both groups of Indian managers were found to be similar using the coefficient of congruence as a critierion. Regression results shown in the top portions of Tables 11-13 indicate that of the twelve value dimensions making significant contributions to relationships between value dimensions and decisions, only the Paternalism factors among the Indian managers are similar. These findings support hypothesis six.

These value dimension-decision relationships also indicate problem specific influences of particular value dimensions within managerial groups. Only the Paternalism dimension of Indian pragmatists and the Employee Humanism-Socialism dimension of Australian moralists contribute to relationships with decisions on two separate problems. Even in this latter instance the signs of the beta weights are opposite. The general finding therefore supports a conclusion that value dimensions are problem specific in terms of their decision influences.

The question was raised in the introduction as to whether the value dimensions influenced by objective job and organization, career history and demographic variables, in turn, influence decisions. A comparison of the summary results presented in Table 10 with those in Tables 11 or 12 indicates that the answer is generally no. One of seven dimensions so influenced among Australian pragmatists; none of three dimensions so influenced among Australian moralist managers; two of five dimensions so influenced among Indian pragmatist managers, and one of four dimensions so influenced among Indian moralist managers, in turn, influence decisions.

TABLE 11

RELATIONSHIP OF VALUE DIMENSION, CONTEXT VARIABLES AND OWNERSHIP FORMS WITH DECISIONS FOR INDIAN MANAGERIAL GROUPS.

Managerial Group	Problem 1 R	Problem 1 Beta Wts.	Problem 2 R	Problem 2 Beta Wts.	Problem 3 R	Problem 3 Beta Wts.	Problem 4 R	Problem 4 Beta Wts.	Problem 5 R	Problem 5 Beta Wts.
Indian Pragmatists										
Values Dimensions	.22		.35*		.26		.26		.30*	
F1. Paternalism				.26*						.45**
F6. Benefactors of Organization Stability				.19*						
F7. Satisfaction-Harmony										
Context Variables	.21		.20		.33**		.20		.30*	
Level of Responsibility						.20**				
Span of Control										.18*
Ownership Variables	.19		.29**		.19		.28**		.28**	
Public Limited				-.19*				.25**		.18*
Indian Moralists										
Value Dimensions	.15		.15		.19		.16		.23*	
F5. Paternalism										.41***
Context Variables	.16		.14		.19		.20		.21	
Ownership Variables	.15		.31**		.24*		.27*		.16	
Proprietorship				.20*		-.14*				
Public Limited				-.19*		-.16*		.27**		

* = .05
** = .01
*** = .001

TABLE 12

RELATIONSHIP OF VALUE DIMENSION, CONTEXT VARIABLES AND OWNERSHIP FORMS WITH DECISIONS FOR AUSTRALIAN MANAGERIAL GROUPS

Managerial Group	Problem 1 R	Problem 1 Beta Wts.	Problem 2 R	Problem 2 Beta Wts.	Problem 3 R	Problem 3 Beta Wts.	Problem 4 R	Problem 4 Beta Wts.	Problem 5 R	Problem 5 Beta Wts.
Australian Pragmatists										
Values Dimensions	.37		.33		.35		.36		.39*	
F7. Company Ownership										-.25*
F11. Antecedents/Consequences of Subordinate Achievement										.29*
F13. Organizational Loyalty										.26*
Context Variables	.51**		.40*		.28		.38*		.46**	
Span of Control		-.37***		-.27*				-.21*		-.30**
Level of Responsibility				.22*						
Ownership Variables	.06		.10		.08		.21		.26*	
Public Limited										.29**
Australian Moralists										
Value Dimensions	.25		.42*		.48**		.35		.30	
F1. Groups of Employees				.22*						
F4. External Institutional Authority						-.21*				
F9. Employee Humanism-Socialism				.25*		-.27*				
F10. Organization-Individual Effectiveness						.28**				
F11. Subordinate Certainty						.20*				
Context Variables	.23		.38*		.32		.33		.36	
Span of Control				-.21*						
Ownership Variables	.16		.11		.16		.24		.15	

* = .05; ** = .01; *** = .001

In addition, there is no consistent support indicating that any of the three sets of influences on value dimensions is more powerful than the other two in working through values to affect decisions. Objective job and organization or demographic variables each relate to two of these value dimensions for Australian pragmatists (F7, F8) and Indian pragmatists (F1, F6) that affect decisions. Career history variables relate to the one dimension of moralists managers (F4) that affects decisions.

Hypothesis seven proposes a greater relationship between objective job and organization characteristics and decisions for pragmatist than for moralist managers. Results presented in Table 13 support this hypothesis. The bottom line in this table indicates that the average percent variance accounted for in these relationships is 70 percent greater for Australian pragmatist than Australian moralist managers, and 100 percent greater for Indian pragmatist than Indian moralist managers. Within country comparisons are appropriate in order to eliminate the confounding influence of national differences on these relationships.

TABLE 13

MULTIPLE CORRELATIONS, AVERAGE CORRELATION, AVERAGE VARIANCE ACCOUNTED FOR AND PERCENT DIFFERENCE IN VARIANCE ACCOUNTED FOR WITHIN COUNTRY COMPARISONS OF THE RELATIONSHIP BETWEEN OBJECTIVE JOB AND ORGANIZATION CHARACTERISTICS AND MANAGERS' DECISIONS

Problem	Australian Pragmatists	Australian Moralists	Indian Pragmatists	Indian Moralists
1	.51	.23	.21	.16
2	.40	.38	.20	.14
3	.28	.32	.33	.19
4	.38	.33	.20	.20
5	.46	.36	.30	.21
Average correlation	.41	.32	.25	.18
Average variance accounted for	.17	.10	.06	.03
Percent difference in variance accounted for	70%		100%	

Corollary hypotheses 7a and 7d propose that among pragmatist managers the nature of the problem will influence contributions of specific organization variables in relationships with decisions. Results bearing on these hypotheses are also shown in Tables 11 and 12. Hypothesis 7a proposes that organization size will make a significant contribution in relationships with decisions on problem four. This hypothesis is not supported since results show that organization size does not make a significant contribution to decisions of pragmatic managers. Results also show that function makes a significant contribution ($F = 4.11$, $p < .05$) in relationships to decisions only among Indian pragmatists on problem three. Hypothesis 7b is therefore only weakly supported.

Hypothesis 7c proposes that level of responsibility will make a significant contribution in relationships with decisions on problems two and three. Results indicate a significant contribution on decision two for Australian pragmatists and decision three for Indian pragmatists. Hypothesis 7c is therefore only partially supported.

Hypothesis 7d proposes that span of control will make a significant contribution in relationships with decisions on problems one and five. Results indicate that this hypothesis is supported among Australian pragmatists. However, span of control also contributed to relationships with decisions on problems two and four for this group. Results also indicate that span of control made a significant contribution to decisions on problem five for Indian pragmatists, but not on problem one. Hypothesis 7d is therefore only partially supported.

Hypothesis eight proposes a greater relationship between forms of ownership and decisions for Indian managers than Australian managers. The relevant comparisons are between managers in the two countries with the same value orientations. Results of these comparisons are shown in Table 14. These findings indicate that the average percent variance accounted for in these relationships is 300 percent greater for Indian pragmatist than Australian pragmatist, and 67 percent greater for Indian moralist managers than for Australian moralist managers. These results support the hypothesis.

Corollary hypotheses 8a through 8c also propose that the nature of the problem will moderate contributions of specific forms of ownership with decisions of Indian managers. Hypothesis 8a proposes that managers in public limited firms are more likely to choose a socio-emotional than a task oriented leader. Results in Table 11 show a positive sign for public limited among both groups of Indian managers indicating that this hypothesis is supported.

Hypothesis 8b proposes that public limited will have a negative sign, and proprietorship and partnership positive signs in

TABLE 14

MULTIPLE CORRELATIONS, AVERAGE CORRELATIONS, AVERAGE VARIANCE ACCOUNTED FOR AND PERCENT DIFFERENCE IN VARIANCE ACCOUNTED FOR WITHIN VALUE ORIENTATION COMPARISONS OF THE RELATIONSHIP BETWEEN TYPES OF OWNERSHIP AND DECISIONS

Problem	Australian Pragmatists	Indian Pragmatists	Australian Moralists	Indian Moralists
1	.06	.19	.16	.15
2	.10	.29	.11	.31
3	.08	.19	.16	.24
4	.21	.28	.24	.27
5	.26	.28	.15	.16
Average correlation	.14	.25	.16	.23
Average variance accounted for	.02	.06	.03	.05
Percent difference in variance accounted for	300%		67%	

relationships with decisions on problem two. Results indicate that public limited does make a negative contribution for both groups, but neither partnerships nor proprietorships make a contribution. This hypothesis is only weakly supported.

Hypothesis 8c proposes that public limited will have a positive sign indicating greater delegation on problem five, while proprietorships and partnerships will have negative signs indicating less delegation. Results show that public limited does have a positive sign with the decisions of Indian pragmatist managers, but that none of the other expected results were observed. Hypothesis 8c is not supported.

The model indicates no relationship between ownership types and value dimensions. Tests were made to determine if this was the case in order to validate the model, and to determine if the three major influence categories, make separate contributions to decisions. Results (not presented) indicate no significant relationship between ownership types and value dimensions of any of the managerial groups. When coupled with earlier results the indication is that the three categories of influence generally make separate contributions to managers' decisions.

Drawing back from these specific findings, the overall pattern of relationships between the three sources of influence and decisions differs for each managerial group. Results in Table

11 indicate no dominant influence for Indian pragmatic managers. Value dimensions (problem 2), objective characteristics (problem 3) and ownership types (problem 4) each play a slightly more prominent role on particular problems. Given hypothesis 7 either value dimensions or ownership could be more dominant for Indian moralist managers and results in Table 11 indicate that the latter generally is dominant. Results in Table 12 indicate that objective job and organization characteristics are the dominant influence on Australian pragmatist managers' decisions. Consistent with hypotheses 7 and 8 value dimensions tend to be the dominant influence on decisions for Australian moralist managers. Thus, each of four groups illustrates a pattern of relationships different from the other three.

DISCUSSION

These findings are important for their demonstration of results that can be brought to bear on several questions which have been widely voiced, but poorly integrated in the study of managers' values. One nexus of these questions centers around the properties of values influenced by intra-individual or extra-individual sources singularly or in combination; the distinguishing of values in terms of their particular sources of influence; and the range and power of influences on values which, in turn, influence decisions. A second nexus of questions centers around the comparison of values with other sources of influence on managers' decisions, and modifiers of the decisional impact of these influences.

Regarding the first nexus of questions, present results especially highlight findings that focus on the distinction between structure-content and intensity properties of value dimensions. The factor analysis results in Tables 2-5 show the complexity and diversity of the value dimensions of the four groups of managers. Comparisons of these value dimensions using the coefficient of congruence dramatically illustrate the powerful and pervasive influence of group cognitive differences on the structural organization of values. Taken jointly these findings indicate that the character of the value reasoning of managers in these four groups is enormously different. These results therefore support the argument advanced by the cognitive theorists (Endler and Magnusson, 1976). Specifically, individuals differ in the interpretation or meaning they assign to stimuli, and these differences have substantial structure-content consequences. These findings are also important because previous research suggests that indicators of meaning and interpretive differences, such as value orientations and nationality, yield highly stable effects on values (Goodenough, 1963; Lusk and Oliver, 1974).

The full implication of these differences in value dimension structure become clearer if comparisons are made between the decisions of managers in different groups on the same problem as shown in Tables 11 and 12. The paternalism and organization-social stability dimensions prominent in the reasoning on Indian pragmatist decisions on problem two reflect stability concerns from the point of view of the manager. Hence, retention and retraining decisions can stem from the association between an egoistic valuation of social stability, and the loyalty considerations embedded in the problem and alternatives. By contrast, the Australian moralist value reasoning stems from groups of employee and humanism-socialism dimensions reflective of more empathic considerations and humanism and employee perspectives on the rewards·for loyalty. Similarly, Australian pragmatist value reasoning that employee characteristics such as loyalty and achievement concommitants influence delegation decisions contrasts with the paternalism reasoning of Indian managers, which suggests a father-son type social arrangement as a primary delegation consideration. These findings provide a greater appreciation of how wide ranging different value orientations might be in terms of their ultimate impact on attentional processes (Bruner and Goodman, 1947). Perhaps, more directly, these contrasts underscore the large differences in the value reasoning or decision premises (Simon, 1947) of managers, thus their resulting varied decisions.

Shifting to the value dimension intensity (and intensity of value reasoning view) present findings initially support the position of others which collectively indicates that values are subject to a broad range of objective, experiential, social and familial influences (Porter and Lawler, 1965; Schein, 1971; England, 1976; Filley, et.al., 1976). However, having documented this range of influences on value dimension intensity, present findings hasten to add a number of important qualifications and distinctions.

First, the results presented in Table 6 support the second hypothesis which essentially says that even if all managers are subject to particular objective conditions, they are not equally influenced by these conditions. Rather, group cognitive differences in the form of pragmatic or success meanings moreso than moralist or right meanings, are critical to the impact of these objective influences on the intensity of some value dimensions. Why these differences occur is not fully understood, but may rest on attentional and information processing differences. Gross, et.al., (1957) suggest that pragmatists attend more to directly obtained factual information, while moralists attend more to socially mediated information. Driver and Mock (1975) go beyond attentional processes when they suggest that there are basic differences in the cognitive processing of factual and social information thus suggesting fundamental differences in thought processes.

The present findings, when coupled with these explanations suggest the following possibility. By themselves, objective job and organization characteristics are only potential influences on value dimension intesity, and as the results in Table 13 indicate, on the decision process. These objective characteristics become realized influences when they are interpreted as being conditions that signal individuals to adjust their relations to the environment in the form of value dimension intensity. If this interpretation is correct, then there are some important implications for theory that concentrates on value dimension or value reasoning intensity. At the very least it calls for a rejection of mechanistic models of the influence of organization context on value intensity. Instead it calls for a more active view of man which makes room for the role of interpretation and assigned meanings as prominent in any reorientation to the environment, or in establishing associations between objective contextual stimuli and their psychological consequences. Further, it requires a clearer specification of the nature of the value dimensions influenced once the role of interpretations is acknowledged, since any psychological consequences will undoubtedly be limited in scope.

Post hoc examination of the significant relationships in Table 7 for pragmatist managers provides some insight into the nature of the value dimensions that are influenced, and prominent sources of influences acknowledged by these managers. The span of control contributes to significant relationships with the intensity of Groups of Employees and Paternalism values. This association probably stems from changes in social interaction patterns and social influence processes that are contingent on objective characteristics like the span of control (Ouchi and Dowling, 1974). Contingent interaction patterns also probably underline the contributions that level of management or size of organizaiton make in relationships with the intensity of Company Ownership or External Institutional Authority value dimensions. More senior Australian pragmatist managers are likely to have greater contact with influential owners, while their Indian counterparts in larger firms are more likely to feel the brunt of powerful governmental and religious influences (Kerr, Dunlap, Harbison and Myers, 1962).

The boundary or career history results provide a second qualification to the documented wide range of influences on value dimension intensity. Results presented in Table 8 indicate that it is not career passages per se that are critical, but the continual change in degree of intensity over lengthy time periods. Continual change allows a wide array of influences to impact upon value dimension intensity. The most significant array of influences on value dimension would seem to result from the continual change that can be traced to occupational passages. Length of time as a manager makes the most consistant contribution to relationships between career variables and value dimension intensity. Others (e.g., Filley, et.al., 1976) too, have noted the impact that preparation for and entrance into an occupation can have on value dimension intensity. The dimensions on which time period as a manager makes its greatest contribution are decreasing intensity of some social influence values such as power-influence and authoritarianism; decreasing intensity of the philosophical dichotomy between capitalism and socialism; or increasing intensity of employees and personal-social consequences of change and growth. In essence the decreasing internalization of egoistic values and the increasing internalization of empathic values. Thus, what value dimension intensities are influenced varies widely between managerial groups. Hence, individualization rather than any commonality suggested by occupational socialization seems to be the outcome of this major career passage.

While career history results highlight the impact of occupation influences subsequent to entry, demographic results point to the impact of occupational considerations prior to entry into management. Specifically, similarity of father's occupation to the manager son provides a consistent contribution to significant relationships between demographic variables and value dimension intensity. This finding is important because it demonstrates the impact of nonorganization influences on value dimension intensity which is often absent in research on managers values.

It was thought that this early nonorganizational influence would signal a stability in value dimension intensity, this does not seem to be the case. Results in Table 9 indicate that similarity of father's occupation and income consistently have opposite signed beta weights. All the value dimensions involved where this pattern occurs are concerned with social stability. But where similarity of father's occupation depresses the intensity of these values as is the case among Australian groups, income as an indicator of presently attained organization status enhances the intensity. The opposite pattern occurs among Indian managers on social stability value dimensions suggesting some slight national differences. Thus, current degree of internalization on these values is function of conflict between the influence of early social models and current achieved status. This outcome is what Schein (1968) calls creative individualism where competing influences are the arbitor of current degree of internalization.

Further evidence of a pattern of individualization stems from a comparison of the modal category of influence on decisions. The modal category of influence based on the number of significant relationships (in parentheses) with value dimensions indicated in Table 10 are objective job and organization characteristics for Indian pragmatists (4), career history for Australian pragmatists (3) and Indian moralists (4), and demographic characteristics for Australian moralists (2). Additionally, intra-group comparisons in Table 10 indicate no overlaps in the three major categories of influence on any of the value dimensions of either Australian managerial group, and only one each in two Indian managerial groups. Overall, this limited range of impact and diversity provide a picture of balance, flexibility and continuity in the internalization of managers' value dimensions--conditions recognized as of major importance (Simon, 1947; Schein, 1969). Like others (e.g., England, 1976), the present results are also supportive of a view that the present internalization of managers' values are the product of multiple influences in a lifelong process.

What are the behavioral consequences of the value dimensions influenced in their internalization by the sources included in this study? The answer is very little. Comparison of the results in Table 10 with those in Tables 11-12 indicate that eight of the twelve dimensions that relate to decisions are unrelated to any of the major categories of influence. To a certain extent these findings may be due to other properties of the model such as problem content and the congruence explanation offered by others (Hage and Dewar, 1973; Nightingale and Toulouse, 1977). While this explanation seems to hold up in some instances it does not score well in others where the content of the value dimension and problem seems to have a congruence. As an example intensity on Groups of Employee and several stability-change dimensions would seem to share some congruence with problem content, but do not impact on decisions.

Values are also only one of the major influences on decisions recognized in the present model and in other models and theories (Festinger, 1954; Driver and Mock, 1975). Substitution of one of these other categories of decisional influence for value dimensions can occur, and indeed provides the underpinnings of Pondy's (1969) reasoning. Still this substitution explanation does not apply to the eight value dimensions whose intensity is uninfluenced by those sources thought to impact on them.

It would rather seem that the most general explanation can be traced to England's (1968) reasoning that those values which have a functional autonomy--that is, are unrelated to sources of influence--have the greatest impact on managers' decisions. These are values that are internalized to such an extent that they represent the central core of the constellation of value dimensions of managers. In a word, it is the closed system portion of managers constellation of value dimensions rather than the influenced and open system portion that plays the most prominent role in managers' decisions. The implications for practice of this finding are that value change strategies and programs are likely to have little impact in altering the intensity of those value dimensions that have the largest influence on decisions. Indeed, the research on the impact of such strategies just on value dimension intensity is very mixed (Campbell, Dunnette, Lawler and Weick, 1970). The implication for theory and research is that inferential leaps regarding the ultimate behavioral consequences of values are extremely tenuous in the majority of cases. The burden of proof is on the theoritician or researcher to make his case explicit and with empirical support.

The second major nexus of questions addressed in this study concentrated on inter and intragroup influences on decisions, and modifiers of the decisional impact of these influences. The findings in this regard consistently support the active, individualized view of managers that has been taken throughout this study. Four facets of this view are prominent in the decision findings: overall differences between groups, value orientations as moderators of situational impacts on decisions, national differences as moderators of ownership impacts on decisions and problem content influences.

By overall group differences, the intent is to compare the four groups of managers in terms of the modal category of influence on their stream of decisions. The three categories of influence included in the present model--objective, social and intrapersonal--share a common analytic structure with other models (Festinger, 1954; Driver and Mock, 1975). The decision diversity extends beyond that which was hypothesized as evidenced by the particular category with the highest correlations across the five problems for each group. Australian pragmatist and Indian moralist results indicate that the former was influenced by job and organization characteristics the most; while the latter was influenced by ownership characteristics the most. These findings support the objective-social distinction between pragmatists and moralists recognized by Gross, et.al. (1957). The Australian moralist results indicate a greater reliance on intrapersonal sources of influence or value dimensions, while Indian pragmatists show no dominant influence, thus suggesting flexibility depending on the problem content.

While not overwhelming these group differences do provide some interesting implications. First, undue concentration on one generic source of influence on decisions is not warranted since to do so is to constrain choice, thus, providing results with reduced external validity. For all groups it may be the initial individualized choice of what to be influenced by, and hence, how to economize on limited cognitive capacity, that is the most crucial, rather than subsequent choices which partially reaffirm this initial decision.

Second, these group differences speak somewhat to the issue of prescriptions for changing decision making. For Australian pragmatists the recommendation would be to change their objective mileau to change their decision making. For Australian moralists the recommendation is a pessimistic one since the value dimensions that are the dominant influence are functionally autonomous from any influences on their intensity. Perhaps international management experience would provide an avenue for changing their decision making by restructuring value dimensions. For Indian pragmatists the recommendation would be to change the mix of problems they must solve or the mix of issues imbedded in the problems. For Indian moralist managers the recommendation would be to change the social control processes which may be traced to other conditions beyond forms of ownership.

Endler and Magnusson (1976, p. 967) observed that "the meaning an individual assigns to a situation appears to be the most influential factor affecting his or her behavior." The moderating of relationships between objective job and organization characteristics and decisions by value orientations certainly bears out this observation, and extends the earlier similar moderator role when value dimension intensity was examined. A similar interpretation to that given for these earlier findings would therefore seem to apply to the present results. The cognitive element involved is the contrast between instrumental or success-failure interpretations and moralist or right-wrong interpretations of these objective conditions. For pragmatists the instrumental interpretation signals these managers to adjust relationships between these conditions and decisions. The moralist interpretation does not signal these managers to engage in a similar adjustment process.

Hence, the critical issue is as much one of the underlying differences in the characteristics thought processes involved, as it is one of whether or not the information is objective or not. A more critical test of this conjecture must await a study with perhaps a 2x2x2 design. Value orientations, type of information (objective, social) and whether the information was directly or socially mediated would be the sources of influence on both value dimension intensity and decisions. There is a dearth of research, to date, that does address the question of systematic differences in preferences for objective or social sources of information by those with different value orientations or values. But where this question has been examined results seem to suggest that there are large differences between people (e.g., Starck, 1973).

The specific objective characteristics that contribute significantly to relationships with decisions for pragmatist managers again support a contingent individual cognitive-social explanation. Span of control models makes room for personal cognition and interpretation (MacKenzie, 1974; Ouchi and Dowling, 1974). The latter model rests on a social distance explanation in which superiors' knowledge of subordinate needs, loyalty and performance diminishes with increasing spans. The negative beta weights for Australian managers in Table 12 indicate that under these conditions they opt for decisions reflecting lowered concern for human relations, loyalty and performance, choice of socially skilled subordinates and delegation of decision making. In addition to this being interpreted as a "successful" adjustment of decisions to existing conditions, a social distance explanation suggests that the price of acquiring extensive information about subordinates is viewed as being too high by Australian pragmatists. Since the objective characteristics compete with broad social influences stemming from ownership characteristics, span of control contributions may be attenuated in Indian pragmatist managers' decisions.

The inclusion of forms of ownership as a source of influence on decisions in the present model and research can be traced to the earlier thinking of Pondy (1969). According to Pondy's reasoning, managers' values substitute for forms of ownership as a greater relative influence on decisions when there is a separation of ownership and management, but not when there is no separation. Present findings support the hypothesized differences between Indian and Australian managers in ownership influences on decisions and thus Pondy's reasoning.

But the substitution explanation alone is inadequate since it provides a mechanistic basis for explaining relationships between ownership or values and decisions. How does a more active, individualized perspective enter like that adopted in the present model and study? Some insight can be provided by the additional finding in the present study that ownership and value dimension intensity are unrelated. In combination these findings suggest a cognitive social processes interpretation based on Kelman's (1958) distinction between compliance and internalization. Compliance is indicated when managers' decisions vary with surveillance, reward and punishment and social control process differences embedded in alternate forms of ownership in India. A lack of relationship between ownership and value dimension intensity suggests that surveillance, rewards and punishment and social control processes do not lead to an internalization of owner desires. Hence, ownership forms influence decisions in India due to a greater variation in compliance mechanism strength. Absent these variations in compliance managers' value intensity prevails, in a relative sense, because no internalization of ownership interest occurs. The individualized view based on the functional autonomy of the value dimensions influencing decisions is therefore once more reinforced.

Results among Indian managers do provide some insights into these compliance-social control differences in the forms of ownership even though they provide only mixed support for the hypotheses tested. Most apparent is the differences found between Indian moralist managers in proprietorship and public limited firms in their decisions to retain and retrain obsolete engineers. The positive sign of the beta weight for proprietorship (Table 11) indicates a greater concern for humanism, while the negative sign of the beta weight for public limited indicates a greater concern for economic costs. These differences within the Indian groups are consistent with the differences in social control and social climate observed between companies with these contrasting forms of ownership (Chowdhry, 1970; Baumgartel, 1971).

Other specific ownership influences are more scattered, but are consistent with the social control climate thought to exist in that type of organization. As examples, public limited has the same negative sign among pragmatist managers in decisions to retrain and retain engineers. Similarly, for both groups of Indian managers public limited has a positive beta weight on the staffing problem (number four) and is consistent with Baumgartel's (1971) observation that social control is more problematic in these firms. One further commonality for Indian moralist managers regardless of forms of ownership was found on problem three. The negative beta weights may be due to the nature of the problem hence the general unwillingness among managers with a right-wrong orientation to fund the R&D project proposed.

The intragroup differences from problem to problem provide the last brick in the edifice of dynamic, individualized view of managers and decision making. Examples are abundant in Tables 11 and 12 of specific and even generic categories of influence that vary from problem to problem in terms of their impact on decisions. Just for value dimensions alone the intragroup results call into question the interpretations of past studies that have used a congruence explanation of managers' decision processes (Hage and Dewar, 1973; Nightingale and Toulouse, 1977). The explanation would seem to first of all have limitations due to the assumption that all managers possess a particular value dimension and vary only in their intensity along this dimension. Second, these intragroup differences suggest the limitations of the congruence explanation which is often based on a single, single-issue problem culled out for special attention in order to maximize the possibility of finding expected relationships.

When multiple, multi-faceted problems are included the picture lent by intragroup results is rather one of an active, searching, flexible process in which the issues in the problem play a fundamental role in the final decision. To study managerial decision making is to acknowledge the whole stream of problems confronting them, and the complexities and variations in the decision process thus produced. This may be the most important contribution of this model and study.

When these complexities are modeled the congruence explanation for relationships between value dimensions or the other influences, and decisions is not viable precisely, as Arrow (1974) observes, because it is the warp and woof of a limited rational explanation of decision making. Rather, the present findings would seem to lie closer to the conflict process of decision making that Arrow proposes. That is, on any problem within a stream of problems the manager is confronted with, some conflict results between the wide and diverse constellation of value dimensions, tendencies toward one or the other generic influences with corresponding cognitive economics, and the value dilemmas inherent in the problem. Any decision, therefore, represents more the outcome of a highly individualized cognitive drama, than the conclusion of a harmonious and rational process.

APPENDIX A

BEHAVIOURAL MEASURES*

Instructions

Following are a set of five job incidents which a business manager may encounter in the daily performance of his duties. Below each incident are a number of statements of action that he could take to solve the problem presented in the incident. Read each incident carefully, then decide which statement of action you would take to solve the problem.

Job Incident 1

Assume that you are the owner-director of a small manufacturing company. Recently your employees have been complaining about the cafeteria and rest room facilities at the factory. These facilities were remodelled 25 years ago, and since then they have had only routine maintenance. Knowing that the anticipated profits for the year are $100,000 (about average for the company), which of the following actions would you take?

__4__ Installation of new equipment, complete repainting and cleaning--expected cost $30,000.

__3__ Partial installation of new equipment, complete repainting and cleaning--expected cost $12,000.

__2__ Major repairs, repainting and cleaning--expected cost $3,000.

__1__ Leave the facilities as they are.

Job Incident 2

Assume that you are the manager of the Research and Development Department. In your section are ten engineers who specialize in a phase of engineering in which there have been great breakthroughs in knowledge. As a result, it is only the engineers who have graduated in the last few years who are trained with respect to the new knowledge.

*Scale numbers are included for ease of reading, but were not included on respondent questionnaires in order to reduce response errors.

You, as the manager of this section, have been asked to make a recommendation about retraining the "obsolete" engineers or letting them go and hiring recent graduates. You have found that retraining would take about six months of full time study on the part of the "obsolete" engineers, and it is not certain that all would successfully complete training. You know that these ten engineers have made significant contributions to the company in the past and have an average tenure of seven years.

Which of the following would you recommend?

6 Retrain all the engineers and have the company pay all retraining costs.

5 Retrain all the engineers and have the costs of retraining shared equally by the company and the individual.

4 Retrain only those engineers who are judged to be "trainable" and have the company pay all retraining costs.

3 Retrain only those engineers who are "trainable" and have the company pay all retraining costs.

2 Retrain only those engineers who are "trainable" and have the cost of retraining shared equally by the company and the individual.

1 No retraining. Retain only those engineers who can continue to make significant contributions to the company.

Job Incident 3

Assume that you are the general manager of a manufacturing company. Your Research and Development Staff have been working on a project aimed at the development of an automated plant which will result in substantial reduction in the labor costs of production. It is expected that this plant can be made operational in five years if necessary funds are available for R & D.

The problem is securing the necessary funds for R & D. One alternative, which would represent the lowest cost to the company, is as follows. The production workers are union members. The union has been pushing for a retiring pension plan for its members and it is willing to accept a plan in which the benefits become available only after an employee has put in 20 years service with the company. The company has been opposed to the plan in the past because it felt that the potential costs of such a plan could not be accurately estimated.

Negotiations for a new industrial agreement or award are coming up in a few months. In view of the projected automated plant, the company will no longer need most of the current work force after five years, and therefore, the cost of accepting the pension plan would be relatively small. You have also ascertained that the union will accept a wage increase of about five cents per hour less than what would be the case if the retiring pension plan is not adopted. Assume that the total number of production hours per year are such that the required funds for R & D can be obtained through reduction in production costs in this way.

Indicate your willingness to obtain the R & D funds by putting an X at the appropriate place.

Not willing at all	1	2	3	4	5	6	7	8	9	10	Completely willing

Job Incident 4

Assume you are the administrative manager in a company and you are evaluating two senior clerks for a newly created position of assistant manager in your department. Both have worked for you for the past five years and are equally competent. However, the two men differ in the following way:

Robin Sharp is a very creative man who has been constantly making suggestions for improvement in office procedures. Although all his ideas are not practical ones you have, in the past, adopted some of his suggestions. Sharp is sincere and hard working, and he can be helpful to others, if he is asked for his help. He is, however, not a very popular man in the department, because other employees do not like procedural changes and extra pressures which they think are unnecessary at times.

John Roberts, equally efficient as Robin Sharp, is not a "man of ideas." He, on the other hand, is a very congenial and well liked person. He goes out of his way to help others whenever they have problems. He is definitely contributing to the good morale of your department. He enjoys the reputation of a kind man.

You are chairman of a ten member committee which is considering this question. Please indicate whom you would recommend:

Robin Sharp* 0 John Roberts* 1

*Local names used in India.

Job Incident 5

Assume that you are appointed as the manager of a recently reorganized personnel division of a middle sized manufacturing company. You have a personnel assistant in your division who directly reports to you and is of roughly similar background as yours. You are responsible for the total operation of your division. Given that you have to hire two technical employees for the Quality Control section of the company, which of the following functions would you delegate to your assistant?

Please note that the following functions are arranged in sequential order so that each subsequent function includes all the preceding functions.

___1___ Calling a placement office and placing orders.

___2___ Calling newspapers for placing advertisements, and composing same. (In addition to the preceding)

___3___ Screening the applications and selecting a list of candidates and, after selecting two persons, sending them to the supervisor of Quality Control for final approval. (In addition to the preceding)

___4___ Making an offer to those finally chosen. (In addition to the preceding)

___5___ Negotiating with the candidates, if the first offer is not acceptable, and making the final offer.

BIBLIOGRAPHY

Allport, G.W. (1966), Traits Revisited. In: American Psychologist 20: 1-10

Arrow, K. (1974), The Limits of Organization, New York: Norton

Bandura, A. (1974), Behavior Theory and the Models of Man. In: American Psychologist 29: 859-869

Baumgartel, H. (1971), The Penetration of Modern Management Technology and Organizaitonal Practices in Indian Business Organizations. In: Indian Administrative and Management Review 3: 1-13

Bem, D.J. (1970), Beliefs, Attitudes, and Human Affairs, Belmont: Brooks-Cole

Berger, C. and Cummings, L. (1979), Organization Structure, Behavior and Attitudes. In: Staw, B. (ed.) Research in Organization Behavior 1: 169-208, Greenwich: JAI Press

Bruner, J.S. and Goodman, C.C. (1947), Value and Need as Organizing Factors in Perception. In: Journal of Abnormal and Social Psychology 42: 33-44

Campbell, D. (1971), Handbook for the Strong Vocational Interest Blank, Stanford: Stanford University Press

Campbell, J.P.; Dunnette, M.D.; Lawler, E.E.; and Weick, K.E., Jr. (1970), Managerial Behavior, Performance, and Effectiveness, New York: McGraw-Hill

Campbell, D. and Fiske, D. (1959), Convergent and Discriminant Validity by the Multitrait-Multimethod Matrix. In: Psychological Bulletin 56: 81-105

Chattopadhyay, P. (1973), Corporate Personality. In: Neelameghan, S. (ed.) Management Development: New Perspectives & Viewpoints, Delhi: Kalyari. 142-166

Child, J. (1973), Strategies of Control and Organizational Behavior. In: Administrative Science Quarterly 18: 1-17

Child, J. and Kieser, A. (1977), Contrasts in British and West German Management Practice: Are Recipes for Success Culture-Bound? Honolulu: Conference on the Cross-National Functioning of Organizations

Chowdhry, K. (1970), Change-in-Organizations, Bombay: Lalvani

Clark, A.W. and McCabe, Sue (1970) Leadership Beliefs of

Australian Managers. In: Journal of Applied Psychology 54: 1-6

Connor, P. and Becker, B. (1975), Values and the Organization: Suggestions for Research. In: Academy of Management Journal 18: 550-561

Driver, M. and Mock, T. (1975), Information Processing, Decision Style Theory and Accounting Information Systems. In: Accounting Review 50: 490-508

Edstrom, A. and Galbraith, J. (1977), Transfer of Managers as a Coordination and Control Strategy in Multinational Organizations. In: Administrative Science Quarterly 22: 248-263

Endler, N. and Magnusson, D. (1976), Toward an Interactional Psychology of Personality. In: Psychological Bulletin 83: 956-974

England, G.W. (1968) Personal Value Systems of American Managers. In: Academy of Management Journal 10: 53-68

_________. (1976), The Manager and His Values: An International Perspective from the United States, Japan, Korea, India, and Australia, Cambridge: Ballinger

Festinger, L. (1954), A Theory of Social Comparison Processes. In: Human Relations 7: 117-140

Filley, A.; House, R.; and Kerr, S. (1976), Managerial Process and Organization Behavior (2nd. ed.), Glenview: Scott-Foreman

Goodenough, W. (1964), Explorations in Cultural Anthropology, New York: McGraw-Hill

Gross, N.A.; MacEachern, W.; and Mason, W.S. (1957), Exploration in Role Analysis: Studies of the School Superintendency Role, New York: John Wiley & Sons

Hage, J. and Dewar, R. (1973) Elite Values versus Organization Structure in Predicting Innovation. In: Administrative Science Quarterly 18: 279-290

Holland, J. (1973) Making Vocational Choices: A Theory of Careers, Englewood Cliffs: Prentice-Hall

Kaiser, H.; Hunka, S. and Bianchini, J. (1971), Relating Factors between Studies Based on Different Individuals. In: Multivariate Behavioral Research 6: 409-414

Katz, R. (1978) Job Longevity as a Situational Factor in Job Satisfaction. In: Administrative Science Quarterly 23

Kelman, H. (1958), Compliance, Identification and Internalization: Three Processes of Attitude Change. In: Journal of Conflict Resolution 2: 51-60

Kerr, C.; Dunlap, J.; Harbison, F.; and Myers, C. (1964), Industrialism and Industrial Man, New York: Oxford University Press

Kluckhohn, F.R. and Strodtbeck, F.L. (1961), Variation in Value Orientations, Evanston: Row, Peterson

Kohlberg, L. (1968), The Child as Moral Philosopher. In: Psychology Today 2: 24-30

Lawrence, P.R. and Lorsch, J.W. (1967), Organization and Environment: Managing Differentiation and Integration, Cambridge: Harvard University Press

Lusk, E. and Oliver, B. (1974), American Manager's Personal Value Systems-Revisited. In: Academy of Management Journal 17: 549-554

Mackenzie, K. (1974), Measuring a Person's Capacity for Interaction in a Problem Solving Group. In: Organizational Behavior and Human Performance 12: 149-169

March, J. and Simon, H. (1959), Organizations, New York: John Wiley

Merton, R. (1957), Social Theory and Social Structure, Revised Edition, Glencoe: The Free Press

Nightingale, D. and Toulouse, J. (1977), Toward a Multilevel Congruence Theory of Organization. In: Administrative Science Quarterly 22: 264-280

Ouchi, W. and Dowling, J. (1974), Defining the Span of Control. In: Administrative Science Quarterly 19: 357-365

Palmer, D.; Veiga, J.; and Vora, J.; (1979), Managerial Value Profiles Decisions in a Cross-Cultural Setting. In: Academy of Management Proceedings 133-137

Pondy, L.R. (1969), Effects of Size, Complexity, and Ownership on Administrative Complexity. In: Administrative Science Quarterly 14, 1: 47-60

Pondy, L. (1970), Toward a Theory of Internal Resource-Allocation. In: M. Zald (ed.) Power in Organizations, Nashville: Vanderbilt University Press

Porter, L. and Lawler, E. (1965), Properties of Organization Structure in Relaion to Job Attitudes and Job Behavior. In:

Psychological Bulletin 64: 23-51

Porter, L.; Hackman, R.; and Lawler, E., III (1975), Behavior in Organizations, New York: McGraw-Hill

Rokeach, M. (1973), The Nature of Human Values, New York: Free Press

Rummel, R. (1970), Applied Factor Analysis, Evanston: Northwestern University Press

Scheewind, K.A. and Cattell, R.B. (1971), Zum Problem die Faktor Identification Verteilungen und Vertrauensintervalle von Kongrung Koeffiguntten fur Personlichkeitsfaktoren im der Bereich Objektivanalytischer Text. In: Psykologische Beitrage, Sonderdrucke 12: 214-226

Schein, E. (1968), Organizational Socialization and the Profession of Management. In: Industrial Management Review 9: 1-16

Schein, E.H. (1971), The Individual, the Organization, and the Career: A Conceptual Scheme. In: Journal of Applied Behavioral Science 7: 401-426

Sewell, W.; Haller, A.; and Ohlendorf, G. (1970), The Early Educational and Early Occupational Attainment Process: Replications and Revisions. In: American Sociological Review 35: 1014-1027

Spearman, C. (1927), The abilities of Man, New York: MacMillan

Starck, K. (1973), Values and Information Source Preference. In: The Journal of Communication 23: 74-85

Taussig and Joslyn, R. (1932), American Business Leaders, Fortune

Thiagarajan, K.M. (1968), A Cross-Cultural Study of the Relationships between Personal Values and Managerial Behavior. In: Technical Report No. 23, Rochester: University of Rochester, Management Research Center

Thompson, J. (1967), Organizations in Action, New York: McGraw-Hill

Triandis, H. (1972), The Analysis of Subjective Culture, New York: McGraw-Hill

Tyler, L. (1956), The Psychology of Human Differences, New York: Appleton-Century-Crofts

Van Maanen, J. Breaking In. In: R. Dubin (ed.) Handbook of Work, Organization and Society

Wheelwright, E. (1957), Ownership and Control of Australian Companies: A Study of 102 of the Largest Public Companies Incorporated in Australia, Sydney: The Law Book Company of Australia

Whitely, W.T. and England, G.W. (1980), Variability in Common Dimensions of Managers Values Due to Value Orientation and Country. In: Personnel Psychology 33: 77-90

Wrong, D. (1961), The Oversocialized Concept of Man. In: American Sociological Review 26

Bureaucratic Structures in Cross-National Perspective: A Study of British, Japanese, and Swedish Firms*

Dezsö Horváth, Koya Azumi, David J. Hickson, Charles J. McMillan

ABSTRACT

Analysis of formal and perceptual measures of bureaucratic structures on thirty-six factories in three countries reveals dual influences - forces for similarities as well as differences - at work. Whilst contextual factors (size, technology, and inter-organizational links) exert common influences on formal structures of industrial units in all three countries, people tend to have different ways of living with bureaucracies in the societies studied. People appear to perceive and use bureaucracies differently due to deep-rooted cultural forces.

INTRODUCTION

It is now more than 15 years since Clark Kerr and his colleagues (1973) wrote Industrialism and Industrial Man. In the interim, the world has indeed shown many signs of the "total industrialization" which these authors foretold and the emergence of multinational corporations, satellite communications, and increasing economic interdependence have made the convergence thesis of industrial societies a major topic of study and debate. They state the convergence position as follows:

> The industrial society is worldwide. The science and technology on which it is based speak in a universal language. Science is non-rational, non-local and although one would not say non-cultural, singularly independent of the form of government, the intermediate tradition or the effective life of people..... The extreme discrepancies in the methods of production which now exist between more or less highly industrialized countries will tend to decrease over time, although significant differences in income levels and in the specialization of activity are likely to remain for a very long time (Kerr et al., 1973, p. 55).

---

* Grateful acknowledgment is made of financial assistance from the following sources: East Asian Institute, Columbia University; Joint Committee on Japanese Studies of the Social Science Research Council and the American Council of Learned Societies; Canada Council; Management Center, University of Bradford; Research Council, Rutgers University; Social Science Research Council, Sweden.

The arguments and issues surrounding the convergence thesis typically involve such questions as the process of modernization, the appropriateness or inappropriateness of certain "models" of development and the possibility of adoption or transfer of techniques from one country to another. All these issues carry certain assumptions. As Eisenstadt (1973, p. 15) puts it: "A crucial connecting point between the stress on such general categories and the evolutionary perspective, in which the unity of mankind was upheld, was the 'convergency' theory: all modern industrial systems will ultimately develop similar major industrial features. Behind this theory there loomed a conviction of the inevitability of progress towards modernity, be it political development or industrialization."

There are many features which appear quite different, yet the societies where they are located display the characteristics Kerr et al. (1973) discuss. So how different are they? Or beneath superficial and important differences, are there basic similarities? Differences and similarities! These are building blocks to cross-national research, and what is required are systematic means of studying them.

The convergence thesis debate has, to date, been largely confined to the societal level of analysis or to the level of individual values, career orientation and behaviour (Inkeles, 1960; Inkeles and Smith, 1974). For the most part, the debate has not touched on the mainstream issues of organization theory, even though the arguments and key variables overlap with organizational issues and center on the fundamental direction of theory building and methodology in organizational analysis (Hickson and McMillan, 1981; Lammers and Hickson, 1979). Yet comparative organizational research can help to identify how organizational features vary with national characteristics and how such characteristics give rise to culturally-based structures and processes.

Complex organizations are seen as products of modern, industrial societies, yet there remains the basic question of how similar or different they are across societies. This paper examines this question in the light of direct comparisons between organizations in three countries - Britain, Japan, and Sweden - which are at similar stages of industrial development, but which culturally and socially are perceived as different.

FRAMEWORK FOR ANALYSIS AND RESEARCH DESIGN

The three societies having been selected in such a way as to enhance the chances of divergent characteristics being apparent, with their industrialization and some other similar characteristics, then could organizations within them also be selected with the same aim in mind? What factors if any might be "controlled for" so as to maximize the chances of exposing societal differences in organizations?

The convergence/divergence argument hinges on industrialization, on the consequences which may or may not ensure from the spread of manufacturing technology. So factories become the primary situation in which to look for relevant evidence. If the convergence argument is right, then factories more than anything else, more than schools or stores or hospitals or villages or families, would be virtually identical whatever the society they happen to be in. If the divergence argument is right, then even factories should show some differences and if they do then other sectors of society may be presumed to do so much more.

This is why the research described here concentrated on factories. It focuses on what may be broadly termed the bureaucratization of factories. It does so partly because of the availability of methods for studying this, and partly because it is here in organizational analysis that the firmest base of established concepts has been built up with which clear comparisons can be made.

The meaning of the word bureaucracy stems from its definition by the German scholar Max Weber (1947); with a sweeping historical vision, he foresaw at the outset of the twentieth century that in time bureaucracy would become the dominant form of organization. By bureaucracy, he meant an organization whose activities had been broken down into defined sets of tasks allocated to the occupants of specialist offices or jobs. The work of those appointed to these offices, who would be selected for their potential competence, would be controlled by a hierarchy of successive layers of jobs in which each had authority over those below. All would be governed by rules and procedures. These rules and procedures would be stated in writing, and would apply impersonally to everyone. The assumption is that such a form of organization minimizes costs, acts consistently because precedents are noted and filed, treats all alike without personal favours, and continues even though individual employees come and go. Its success is evidenced by most people in industrialized societies taking it for granted and being unable to conceive of anything different.

Yet these descriptions of bureaucratic organizations are too simple. They are broad characterizations rather like describing people as having intelligence, emotions, and a distinctive human physique, when what is interesting are the infinite differences between individuals. Organizations differ in a myriad of ways, and probably no two have exactly the same degree of each of multiple bureaucratic characteristics. This has been demonstrated by empirical research, most notably that by Pugh and his associates (1968) in Britain and by Hall and associates (1967), Aiken and Hage (1968), and Blau and associates (1966) in the United States.

The question that instantly arises is why organizations should differ? What is it that may bring about this variety, and may push a given organization into changing this way or that? Is it growth to large size, or the product being made or service provided and its technology, or ownership by large public corporations, or what?

Here is the relevance of the convergence or divergence controversy referred to in previous section. If the structural characteristics of particular organizations are due directly or indirectly to their sizes, technologies, dependence on owning groups, and similar features of the context in which their structures function, then this favours convergence. Everywhere nations are industrializing so that organizations are growing in size, adopting modern technologies, linking contractually and by ownership with others, and so on; the presumption must then be that this has similar consequences for their bureaucratization. Everywhere the structures of organizations may hinge on these shifting contingent factors, which might be gradually edging all organizations in the same direction. These factors have to be examined in this study to test whether this is happening.

Relationship between (bureaucratized) structures and such contingent factors have been studied since the early 1960's by researchers, mainly in America and Britain, among whom those named above are prominent. They have been especially concerned with organizational context, such as size of organization and its parent organization, and technology; and environmental context, such as dependence on parent organization and other organizations, and nature of links to organizations in the environment or, as often referred to, environmental uncertainty. The pattern of relationships that is suggested is comparatively simple, as shown in Table 1.

Hence, there are two main groups of factors whose possible impact on organization may be compared with that of society itself - culture or nationality - to begin to see whether convergence or divergence is the most likely; namely organizational context (size and technology) and environmental context (dependence and uncertainty). These are critical contingencies in which may be found explanations for structural differences.

It follows that these main contingency factors could be made use of in the choice of factories within each country. For with the countries roughly matched as being industrialized, in order to maximize the chances of exposing differences which could be due to societal qualities, the research could be strengthened by doing the same with the organizations. If, for example, there was a certain kind of textile factory in Japan than equivalent Swedish and British factories would be selected, and so on for all organizations. There would then

TABLE 1

The Suggested Pattern of Relationships between Context and Structure

CONTEXT:	STRUCTURE: Formalization	Specialization	Centralization
Size[1)]	+	+	$\pm$ sometimes
Size of Parent Organization[1)]	+	+	
Technology[2)]	$\pm$ sometimes		$\pm$ sometimes
Dependence on Parent Organizations[3)]	$\pm$ usually		+
Dependence on Other Organizations[3)]			+
Environmental Uncertainty[3)]	-	-	-

1) Blau and Schoenherr (1971); Child (1972); Child and Mansfield (1972); Hickson et al. (1969); Hickson et al. (1974); Hinings and Lee (1971); Inkson et al. (1970); Pugh et al. (1969).

2) Child and Mansfield (1972); Hickson et al. (1969); Zwerman (1970); Woodward (1958 and 1965).

3) Greenwood and Hinings (1976); Jacobs (1974); Mindlin and Aldrich (1975); Hickson et al. (1974); Lawrence and Lorsch (1967); Pugh et al. (1969).

be a double strength to the research design. If clear differences were found even in matched sets of organizations in matched countries then such differences would most likely expose the cultural patterns due to their Britishness, Japaneseness, and Swedishness.

In this way then the research design of the project flows directly from the theoretical framework of organizational design. The attempt is to vary the range of contingency factors in each country but through direct matching of firms by country, hold for these contingency variables across the three samples to test for cultural differences and similarities.

SAMPLE, DATA COLLECTION, AND MEASURES

The sample for this study consists of 12 manufacturing firms each from Britain, Japan, and Sweden. Although the sample is small, it includes firms with a wide range of different products, with varying sizes, and with varying degrees of inter-organizational dependence.

Moreover, to the extent it has been possible, the set of firms for each country has been selected to match units in the other countries in the main contingency factors (size, technology, inter-organizational dependence and linkages). Selection had to be made on information available in official records and public directories before organizations were approached to sollicit collaboration and were visited to collect more complete data. For this purpose, the variables were represented as follows:

Size, by number of employees;
Technology, by type of product;
Dependence, by unit status.

In the case of dependence, previous research had established the close correlations of unit status with some aspects of dependence. Other aspects of inter-organizational dependence and linkages were not possible to control for. The resulting matching sets are given in Table 2.

Data have been collected from these sets of firms on standard schedules in structured interviews with chief excutives and, in some cases where the chief executive did not have full information, with other senior managers. When possible, the interviews were completed by an examination of company booklets, union contracts, advertising brochures, and organization charts. In order to ensure response and interpretation equivalance, with some exceptions, the relatively standardized methods for collecting and analyzing organizational and contextual data developed by Pugh and his colleagues (Pugh et al., 1968 and 1969; Hickson et al., 1969), and abbreviated by Inkson and associates (1970), are used in the study.

The organization structure has thus been made operational through formalization, functional specialization, and centralization. Formalization denotes the extent to which rules, procedures, instructions, and communication are written in the organization and (in some cases) the extent of their application and distribution; functional specialization refers to the degree to which the activities of an organization are divided into mutually exclusive sets; and centralization is the extent to which the authority for decision-making rests at the higher levels in the organization.

TABLE 2

Size, Main Product Lines, and Status of Organizations in the Three Countries

Firm No.	Country	Size - Number of Employees	Main Product Lines	Status
1	Britain	270	Meat	Branch
	Japan	229	Meat	Branch
	Sweden	238	Meat, sausages	Head branch
2	Britain	442	Textiles	Principal unit
	Japan	413	Yarn clothing	Branch
	Sweden	486	Textiles	Branch
3	Britain	280	Textiles	Principal unit
	Japan	270	Garments	Subsidiary
	Sweden	254	Fur goods	Principal unit
4	Britain	200	Publishing	Subsidiary
	Japan	161	Publishing	Principal unit
	Sweden	152	Publ., printing	Subsidiary
5	Britain	110	Chemicals	Principal unit
	Japan	110	Chemicals	Principal unit
	Sweden	126	Cosmetics	Subsidiary
6	Britain	400	Steel	Subsidiary
	Japan	350	Iron works	Branch
	Sweden	398	Steel	Branch
7	Britain	2,000	Copper plating	Principal unit
	Japan	1,672	Copper	Branch
	Sweden	1,657	Copper, lead	Branch
8	Britain	420	Eng.-works	Subsidiary
	Japan	450	Compr. springs	Principal unit
	Sweden	371	Eng.-works	Principal unit
9	Britain	700	Telephones	Principal unit
	Japan	712	Household appl.	Branch
	Sweden	552	Household appl.	Branch
10	Britain	1,050	Microphones	Subsidiary
	Japan	946	Transistors	Subsidiary
	Sweden	903	Comm. equipment	Branch
11	Britain	300	Road tankers	Principal unit
	Japan	290	Train cars	Principal unit
	Sweden	248	Steel-constr. cisterns	Principal unit
12	Britain	450	Paper	Subsidiary
	Japan	521	Paper	Branch
	Sweden	500	Paper	Branch

The contingency variables considered in the study are size, technology, and inter-organizational dependence and linkages. The aspect of size studied is the number of employees, both in the unit studied and in the parent organization - in both cases, after logarithmic transformation. The measure used for technology is what is referred to as production continuity; a tenfold categorization of the dominant method and style of production, which was originally developed by Woodward (1965) and refined and improved by Hickson et al. (1969). In the measures of inter-organizational dependence and linkages, however, modifications and extensions have been made. Instead of the overall scale dependence, as used by Pugh and associates (1968 and 1969), three main sets of measures of dependence and linkages were developed to tap the relationship of the focal organization to other organizations: (1) the dependence of the focal organization on its parent organization - a combined measure created from four scales on status, relative size, policy representation, and public accountability - referred to as internal dependence; (2) the dependence of the focal organization on other organizations, its suppliers and customers - a combined scale measuring the percentage of total purchase of the focal organization which comes from the largest supplier and the percentage of sales which the main supplier provides to the focal organization (and a similarly constructed scale with the main customer) - referred to as input and output dependence; (3) the nature and dynamics of the linkages between the focal organization and its suppliers and customers - a combined measure created from three scales on type and frequency of orders with suppliers and contractual links with customers - referred to as environmental uncertainty.

RESULTS

Patterns of Bureaucratic Structures Cross-Nationally

The major contingency factors influencing or shaping the characteristics of bureaucratic structures, as already noted in previous sections, are size, technology, and inter-organizational dependence and linkages. On the other hand, these influences are known to have certain effects, so they can be controlled in comparative analysis. This is the approach taken here.

The purpose of this section is to test the null hypothesis that there is no significant difference in bureaucratic structural features of work organizations across national boundaries. The subject for the analysis is the scale scores for the structural variables across the three national samples. Because the organizations within each sample vary considerably, but are at the same time matched across the national samples by size, technology, and inter-organizational dependence, any differences in the mean level of scores across the samples should expose country differences either in the overall pattern of scores or on the individual items in the scales themselves.

Table 3 gives the results on the structural data for the three national samples, providing the average score for each variable, the standard deviation and the range.

TABLE 3

Mean, Standard Deviation and Range for Structural Scores: Britain, Japan, Sweden

(N = 12)

COUNTRY OF ORIGIN:	STRUCTURE:								
	Formalization			Functional Specialization			Centralization		
	$\bar{X}$	SD	Range	$\bar{X}$	SD	Range	$\bar{X}$	SD	Range
Britain	27.9	7.2	14-37	7.5	3.2	3-12	118.5	12.6	103-141
Japan	32.1	9.4	16-41	8.3	2.9	0-11	121.7	25.0	66-162
Sweden	25.1	8.6	13-37	8.4	2.5	6-13	125.8	9.2	111-142

The wide number of variables and the choice of a range of different firms in each country allow the exposure of significant differences by country if they exist. Yet on the scales, the data show overwhelming similarities across the samples.

Taking the variables individually, on formalization, the three samples show negligible differences by country. However, the similarities outweigh these marginal variations, since the dispersion of scores on the plants within the samples are quite large, and the minimum degree of formalization is practically identical: 13, 14 and 16. On functional specialization, the three samples are very similar. On centralization, there is also some slight differences between the three samples. However, here again the differences must be kept in perspective, considering the range of scores in each country and the potential scoring range (0 to 185).

In summary, across the total samples the pattern of scores is clearly marked. The data reveal a consistent pattern of similar bureaucratic structural features which vary within the country much more than across the three samples, indicating the presence of identity of control for order, predictability, and rationality which Weber (1947) predicted; hence, there is no evident pattern of cultural variation.

Context and Bureaucratic Structures Cross-Nationally

As it has been demonstrated, the data by scale scores for the structural variables indicate an overwhelming similarity in the bureaucratic structures of each country. This section takes up this theme again and widens the spectrum of analysis to include the effects of size, technology, and inter-organizational dependence and linkages as predictors of bureaucratic structure. Whereas in the previous section, these organizational and environmental contextual variables were controlled to study the direct impact of culture on organization structure, here these variables are analyzed separately for each country to examine their impact on each sample. Theoretically this section tests the "bold hypothesis", advanced by Hickson et al. (1974), that the impacts of contextual constraints on structure are constant across societies.

An analysis of the product moment correlations between measures of contextual variables and structural variables for each of the three national samples suggests, as shown in Horváth et al. (1981), that the pattern of relationships is, for the most part, as hypothesized (cf. Table 1). The relationships between organizational contextual variables - size and technology - and corresponding hypothesized structural variables, although they vary in magnitude, point overwhelmingly to the existence of stable links across societies. However, for the environmental contextual variables, the correlations with organizational structure appear, at least at the surface, somewhat inconclusive across the three national samples.

In more detail, the hypotheses indicating a positive relationship between measures of size, both in terms of the focal organization and of its parent, and formalization and specialization are supported: in all three countries the correlation coefficients are positive and quite high. That is, in all countries, larger organizations will be more formalized and more specialized. Similarly, in all countries, organizations in a group adopt some of the procedures, rules, and habits of the group over and above any impact of being of a certain scale themselves; group size seems to have an effect on structure, as expected, which is more direct and tend to be explained with reference to the "miniature replica effect" (McMillan et al. 1973).

The evidenced strong relationship between technology (production continuity) and some aspect of structure, formalization, which also holds when the effect of size is partialled out, appears at first glance to contrast with previous studies using this measure (Hickson et al., 1969; Child and Mansfield, 1972). In these studies, production continuity did have some relationship to structural variables, but when the effects of size were partialled out, it was found that technology took second place to other variables. However, at a closer look, the findings seem consistent. Hickson et al. (1969) state that the smaller the organization, the more its structure will be pervaided by such technological effects; and the Hickson et al. (1969) and the Child and Mansfield (1972) studies both covered either a larger range on size of companies, or analyzed data from organizations across fewer industries, than in this study. Hence, the close technology-structure nexus demonstrated in the data in this study (and also in the Woodward study (1965)) is consistent with the Hickson hypothesis: in small organizations, technology does have a pervasive impact on structure. That is, in small organizations where everything is close to the workflow, the more firms have a continuous production process the more they have paperwork, written rules, and regulated work roles by formalized procedures.

With respect to internal dependence, that is the relationship of the focal organization to its owning group, the hypothesis is that membership in a group imposes structural demands because of the need for standardization of rules and operating procedures, but also for accountability - hence centralization. This line of reasoning receives support in this study. The correlations indicate that in Japan and Sweden, the two samples which are most heterogeneous in composition of internal dependence (i.e. independent units and dependent units), there is a strong positive relationship between dependence and centralization of decision-making and formalization; in Britain, however, due to the fact that the sample is more autonomous (cf. Table 2), the relationships are very weak and inconclusive. However, the strong zero order correlations should not be taken to obscure the pervasive impact of size, and to a limited degree technology, on the structural variables. In fact, the correlations between dependence and formalization are reduced somewhat when the scale effects are taken into account: the first order partials on size reduce the coefficients in all three samples; on group size, the coefficient becomes negative in Sweden. Hence, when the effects of size and technology are removed, internal dependence has its greatest impact on structure on the variable of centralization. That is, irrespectively of nationality organizations dependent within owning combines become more centralized. There is a tendency for dependent units also to be more formalized, but this is closely related to the impact of scale. Nonetheless, the results do show close conformity across the three samples so that there can be some confidence that the same control mechanisms are in operation.

The results, with respect to external dependence, that is dependence on external organizations for resources and exchange of finished goods, are somewhat mixed and appear to be only in partial support of the hypotheses. Taking the data on input dependence first, it appears that there is in all three countries a positive and, with the exception of Japan, strong impact of this aspect on centralization of decision-making, supporting the initial hypothesis. Also, as expected, input dependence has a mixed relationship to functional specialization. Unexpectedly, however, input dependence leads to more overall formalization; in all three countries the correlations are positive and quite strong after the effects of scale and technology are taken into account. These findings suggest that in dependent organizations control is exercised by formalized rules and procedures and also, especially in Britain and Sweden, directly by centralized decision-making at the senior echelons of the firm.

An examination of the correlations for output dependence reveals that output dependence does also relate to variables of structure, but in a more diverse way than does input dependence. In these cases, dependence on the major customers has a negative, although in some cases weak, correlation with formalization in all three countries; however, the relationship becomes mixed once the effects of scale and technology are taken into account. On the other side, in all three countries, output dependence is negatively related to functional specialization, but, with one exception, the coefficients are low. Unexpectedly, also the relationship with centralization that output dependence shows is somewhat different from that of internal dependence across the three national samples. In Britain, there is only a modest positive correlation with centralization; in Japan, the correlations are negative and quite high. It is in Sweden where output dependence leads to high centralization, just as it was the case of input dependence.

Notwithstanding some unexpected results on the relationships between external dependence and structural variables, under both types of dependence, centralization emerges as the variable most critically affected by these kinds of relationships with external organizations in the three countries studied.

It is only with respect to the last variable, environmental uncertainty, the results markedly deviate from initial hypothesis and do not show consistent patterns with the variables in the three samples. It is in Sweden where the results are most pronounced, especially on centralization and formalization. In Sweden high environmental uncertainty is associated with high centralization and high formalization - not decentralization and less formalization as the hypothesis predicts; however, partialling out scale and technology leads to weak but negative correlation with formalization. In Japan and Sweden, environmental uncertainty correlates positively with specialization, while in Britain, the correlation is negative, even so the correlation in each case is very weak. Hence, either the indicator itself is not a strong measure of the uncertainty of the environment, in which case the scales need to be improved in order to reduce measurement error, or uncertainty as such needs to be examined more closely as it relates to organizational structure. Certainly, the measure, environmental uncertainty, employed here does not produce strong evidence that demands of the environment impose such influence that the organization's structure itself must be congruent in every respect.

In summary, with the exception of environmental uncertainty, the hypotheses on contextual influence on structural variables are supported. Moreover, both organizational contextual variables and, to a lesser extent, environmental contextual variables do show stable linkages with variables of structure cross-nationally.

SUMMARY AND DISCUSSION

The previous section has focused on the relationships of organizational context (size and technology) and environmental context (dependence and uncertainty) with structure. The organizational context variables are the most influential predictors of organization structure consistent with the factors cited by the convergence theorists. The imperatives of scale and technology are thought by these theorists to overwhelm any effect of culture. In the data analyzed in this study, this hypothesis was basically upheld. It matters more for the control structure of an organization whether it is large or small, unit production or process, then whether it is British, Japanese, or Swedish.

However, neither size nor technology alone can be said to have a pervasive impact on structure: both variables influence certain aspects of structure, particularly the degree of formalization of rules and amount of paperwork; on other variables, either size or technology alone is a correlate, while on others, neither variable by itself predicts structure.

Centralization of decision-making, on the other side, is the main aspect of bureaucratic structure influenced by environmental contextual variables (dependence and uncertainty). In all three countries, dependence leads to centralization, while other variables such as formalization and specialization are less effected. Now this finding is basically consistent with the results in Pugh et al. (1969), who also found a strong positive association between dependence and centralization.

Contrary to dependence, as suggested by Aldrich and Mindlin (1978) and Lawrence and Lorsch (1967), uncertainty leads to decentralization of the decision-making authority. In addition, uncertainty is also influencing other aspects of bureaucratic structure; uncertainty leads to less formalization and, to a lesser extent, to less specialization. The pattern of findings in this study does not support the uncertainty model hypothesis.

However, the relationship of dependence and uncertainty to organization is difficult to divorce completely from the importance of scale and to some degree technology. With smaller organizations, almost every major variable becomes important, whether it is scale, technology or environment, simple because, as Hickson et al. (1969) argue in another context, everything is close to the workflow. As scale increases, however, this is not the case, and while this is easily overlooked it is worth emphasizing, precisely because reliance on one variable explanations are too readily put forward. The evidence in this study is that scale, either of the focal organization or of the group, influences organizational design across a wide sample of organizations; it is when scale is held constant that other variables become important predictors. In small organizations, technology is an important variable, not just for the workflow but for higher echelons of the administrative hierarchy. But in larger organizations, the all embracing impact of technology declines, and scale imposes further problems, including reliable supply lines and market sources. Dependence and uncertainty becomes a major issue, especially in the way it influences decision-making allocation.

A final point to be made is, that one of the complexities of organizational contextual (size and technology) and environmental contextual (dependence and uncertainty) analysis of structure is the many ways that each can be conceptualized and measured. Although size has a more consistent meaning among the many indicators - resources, sales, employees - organizational size and group size are best considered as separate indicators. Similarly, technology has several conceptual meanings, and while operations technology is the common basis of the measures employed, there are some inconsistencies in their application to structure. Dependence or uncertainty as a variable is, on the other hand, neither a monolithic entity, for as previously indicated, dependence and uncertainty can be of different types and they are not necessarily related. As a consequence, the inconsistencies in the measures get translated into inconsistencies across samples. Where the measures are clear and less ambiguous, they point to very strong similarities across the three national samples, as has been demonstrated above.

Indeed, the results of the organizational and environmental contextual analysis again show the patterns found in the section on overall patterns of scores of bureaucratic structures: there are common processes of rationality and decision-making which give rise to common structural features. Cultural differences are submerged by imperatives of scale, technology, and inter-organizational dependence and linkages. Hence, the case for the convergence thesis is supported.

THEORETICAL AND EMPIRICAL EXTENSIONS

Convergence and Individual Perceptions

The feature of the three country comparison in preceding sections is not the differences in their organizations, which are interesting, but the similarities in their organizations, which are overwhelming. With the possible effects of size and product technology largely ruled out of the comparison by the matching of the three sets of industrial units studied, societal differences in the formal structural characteristics of organization appear to be small. On the whole, though not entirely, a factory is a factory is a factory. It has everywhere a similar panoply of specialist departments, control procedures, and documentation; and even authorizes decisions at similar levels. Everywhere, nations choose bureaucracy as their form of organization, as Weber (1947) foresaw they would. They do so each constrained in much the same ways by the consequences of their decisions on that sizes of organizations they want, with which outputs and which technologies, and with what inter-organizational links. These factors appear to exert common contextual influences upon structure.

So similar organization structures under similar constraints should mould similar people. Or should they? Perhaps, but even though similar organizations mould people similarly, they may do so only slowly and only partially. A case for convergence need not stipulate that people will become similar in every respect, still less that they are similar here and now when obviously they are not. Moreover, somewhere ahead converging trends might come to some irreducible minimum of differences that cannot be erased.

For culture, a reservoir of differences, continues resilient. Child (1980, p. 54) summarizes the arguments in favour of persistent cultural differences:

> ..... it is noted that different societies exhibit distinct and relatively persistent cultures. This enduring strain of culture both reflects and is reflected in the social institutions which have evolved in each country, and here the way in which the major change entailed by industrialization has been handled seems to be a particularly significant historical point of reference. Cultural values and norms are internalized as each new generation passes through the process of socialization. People learn their own unique language, concepts and system of values, and they also learn to regard as legitimate certain modes of behaviour. Therefore, it is argued, even if organizations located within different nations do face similar contingencies and adopt similar modes of formal structuring, deep-rooted cultural forces will still tend to re-assert themselves in the way people actually behave and relate to one another. Structure will remain purely formal if it is not consonant with culturally derived expectations.

The difficulty is in knowing just how far to lean one way or the other. A balance has to be kept. Studies of Sirota and Greenwood (1971) and of Haire, Ghiselli and Porter (1966), for example, indicate that both workers and managers are subject to the converging effects of organization as well as to the differentiating effects of societal factors. What counts for more? What differences may be found between British, Japanese, and Swedish employees as against British, Japanese, and Swedish organization structures?

Some differences must be anticipated, for people have different ways of living with bureaucracy. They use it in different ways and experience it in different ways. This is, for example, clearly evidenced in a careful analysis by Aiken and Bacharach (1979) of the administrative staffs of 36 cities in Belgium - 24 in the Northern Dutch-speaking Flemish area of Belgium and 12 in the Southern French-speaking Walloon area. They find that between the same kinds of organizations within a single nation-state:

> ..... the Walloon organizations seemed to be characterized by greater rigidity and various characteristics that one associates with Weber's ideal type of bureaucracy while the Flemish organizations tend to be more flexible and less bureaucratic (Aiken and Bacharach, 1979, p. 240).

Cultural differences resistant to both the unifying efforts of the state and the uniform pressures of administrative structures cause these city bureaucracies to be operated very differently, conclude Aiken and Bacharach.

If even within a single European state across a set of the same type of institutions culture makes such an impression, it is not at all surprising to find differences between members of organizations in states whose peoples have contrasting elements of culture. Staying within Europe to illustrate this, there is a well-known humourism, of obscure origin, that to the Germans everything is forbidden except what is permitted, to the British everything is permitted except what is forbidden, to the French everything is permitted even what is forbidden! This has more than a grain of truth, as the saying goes. Hofstede (1977) reports unpublished studies by Stevens at INSEAD, Fontainbleau. To quote Hofstede (1977, p. 58):

> ..... (Stevens) let French, German, and British students individually analyze the same case study of an organizational conflict. The majority of the French tended to resolve the problem by referring to the hierarchy; the British, by horizontal negotiation; the German, by the establishment of procedures. The implicit model of a well-functioning organization for the French was a pyramid; for the British, a market; for the Germans, a well-oiled machine.

Maurice (1979) and Maurice et al. (1980) do indeed find that as between three trios of matched French, British and German firms the French are more hierarchical with more discipline-based authority, and a larger hierarchy of supervisory and managerial personnel. But as the joke says, the pyramid is not necessarily to be obeyed absolutely. In personal and status terms hierarchical echelons hold one another at arms length, and conformity may be rigid rather than real (Crozier, 1964). The British do not challenge the basis of authority, but nor do they always obey authority exactly as intended; they leave margin of ambiguity and doubt (Richardson, 1956). If the British defer but are disorderly then by comparison the German defer and are orderly; Child (1980) in a review of published work finds it consistent in its view of typical German ways of running bureaucracies.

The importance for the understanding of bureaucracies of the way authority is handled is made plain by Hofstede (1978 and 1979) whose work lifts the perspective from the intricacies of European examples to an unparalled world-wide vision. Across no less than 40 nations he shows in compelling fashion how differences in "power distance" form ethnic-linked patterns which seem to defy the pressures for sameness in a giant multi-national corporation. Comparing questionnaire responses by employees doing the same jobs in establishments of the same corporation dealing with the same products in every country, he reveals a range of responses which suggests that the views people hold of power and authority should be a key characteristic for cross-national comprehension. High power distance includes the acceptance of an autocratic exercise of authority, and an unwillingness to disagree with superiors; low power distance the opposite. The broad contrast it picks out is between Asian, Latin American and Latin European countries which show higher power distance, and Anglo, Germanic, and Scandinavian countries which show lower power distance. Of the three countries with which this study is primarily concerned, Japan is in the first set and Britain and Sweden are in the second.

Indeed, it is very apparent that bureaucracy can be applied in different ways when different peoples run the organization. So whilst in terms of formal control structure it may be that a bureaucracy is a bureaucracy is a bureaucracy, the people employed in it may make different things of it. The way it operates is very much affected by the society within which it is located. That much is clear from this brief and not at all exhaustive look at some illustrative research results.

However, while there is no doubting the extensive and fascinating differences brought to the running of bureaucracies by their employees in different societies, much more needs to be learned as to how far these go in countering organizational pressures for uniformity. This study raises this question but can hardly pretend to answer it. Perhaps it can contribute to future answers by examining in the following the differences brought to their industrial bureaucracies by the British, the Japanese, and the Swedish.

Design, Measures, and Sample

In previous sections, there is considerable evidence that there are few cultural patterns on organizational aspects of structure and control; the major influences are the scale and type of operations and linkages with other organizations. However, it must be remembered that the methodology of studying these relationships involves data gathered from relatively standardized, and objective instruments. The use of perceptual measures of attitudes and beliefs is an important one in organizational analysis, as the previous section indicated. This section explores the possibilities of cross-cultural influences in data gathered from individuals in the three countries; the aim is to test for differences in perceived bureaucratic structure and control.

For the purpose stated, an individual questionnaire was administered to a sample of managers, foremen, and rank and file workers in each of the 12 firms in each country. Included in the individual questionnaire were, among others, 12 of the 24 items from Hall's (1961) bureaucracy scale, as refined through factor analysis by Bonjean and Grimes (1970). This set of items is meant to cover two of the main dimensions of bureaucracy: division of labor and hierarchy of authority.

The stem question reads: "How well does each of the following statements describe your organization?" Five alternative answers are provided: "Very well", "Well", "Poorly", "Very Poorly", and "Undecided". The respondent chooses the alternative that applies in his case. The answers to the items provide the perceptions of the respondent about the two aspects of his organization. That perception is likely to vary depending on his job, his rank in the organization, and his personal characteristics. Moreover, given the complexities and idiosyncraises of man, it is plausible that people of the same rank performing identical tasks give different answers; or even that the same person gives different responses at different times when objective conditions remain the same. It is assumed nevertheless that there are patterns to perceptual responses that are no more than marginally unstable.

For this analysis, responses were aggregated by rank and organization; that is, for each respondent the mean was taken of his responses to the items dealing with one dimension, e.g. division of labor, to obtain his division of labor score. The division of labor scores of all respondents who are rank and file workers are then averaged to arrive at the rank and file division of labor score for the organization. Similarly, the division of labor score is obtained for the rank of foremen, and for the rank of managers. The three scores from the three levels are then averaged to arrive at the organizational division of labor score. Here the three levels are given an equal weight, standardizing the different distributions of personnel among the three levels observable across organizations. Each organization, then, has division of labor scores separated by rank, and one score for the organization as a whole.

The distribution of ranks among respondents varies by country but since controls for difference in levels rather than representativeness are being sought this is not important. The following gives the percent distribution of levels in the three nationality groups:

	Britain	Japan	Sweden
Managers	27.3	15.9	7.5
Foremen	18.0	16.8	26.0
Rank and File Workers	54.7	67.3	66.5
	100.0	100.0	100.0
(N)	(310)	(673)	(499)

Results

Division of Labor

As envisioned by Hall (1961) this dimension refers to the extent to which tasks are routine, and in our research is measured through the following six items:

1. There is something new and different happening almost every day.
2. Most jobs have something different happening from day to day.
3. Most jobs in this organization involve a variety of different kinds of activity.
4. No two days are ever the same in this job.
5. Every employee has a specific function which he is to perform.
6. We usually work under the same conditions from day to day.

Table 4 gives the results on division of labor for the whole organization and for each of the three ranks (managers, foremen, and rank and file workers) for the three countries, providing the average score for each variable (higher score meaning a greater degree of division of labor), the standard deviation and the range.

TABLE 4

Mean, Standard Deviation, and Range for Division of Labor: Britain, Japan, Sweden

LEVEL:	COUNTRY:	DIVISION OF LABOR: $\bar{X}$	SD	Range
Whole Organizations	B	3.13	.242	2.77-3.55
	J	3.59	.213	3.23-3.92
	S	3.01	.311	2.45-3.68
Managers	B	2.95	.421	2.25-3.63
	J	3.48	.278	3.07-3.93
	S	3.07	.513	2.11-3.75
Foremen	B	3.04	.181	2.82-3.42
	J	3.64	.209	3.28-3.94
	S	2.76	.451	1.92-3.51
Rank and File Workers	B	3.39	.280	2.98-3.86
	J	3.64	.276	3.11-4.04
	S	3.19	.372	2.77-4.02

Taking first the scores aggregated for organizations and comparing them by country, it appears that Japanese employees see themselves as having greater division of labor than their British and the Swedish opposite numbers. The difference between the Japanese and the other two countries are not so great that the ranges have no overlap, but are large enough to be statistically significant at 5% level.

Considering level specific scores, as perceived by managers, Japanese organizations again have the highest division of labor score; the British are lowest. The difference between the British and Japanese scores is statistically significant at 5% level but not the difference between the Japanese and the Swedish.

It would normally be expected that the division of tasks would increase level by level down the hierarchy, so moving down to foremen a higher score would be anticipated. That is foremen perceive their organizations and tasks to be more routinized than do managers. The data confirms this, except for Sweden, where foremen perceive a lower degree of division of labor than do managers. Once again, the Japanese score is significantly higher than the British and the Swedish.

The results show, that also for the rank and file level, the relatively high score for Japan persists, as does the trend for lower ranks to perceive a higher degree of division of labor. However, the rise is sharp for British and Swedish rank and file but for Japan the score remains the same as for foremen.

Hence, there seem to be a persistent tendency of the Japanese to experience their jobs as having a greater degree of division of labor than do the British and the Swedish. Regardless of rank, the Japanese employee tends to perceive his work to be more routine than does his counterpart in Britain and Sweden.

As suggested by the data, the perceived degree of division of labor varies by both country and rank. It may be that culture of industrialism has so pervaded these countries affecting most especially the rank and file workers that they share more in their perceptions with rank and file workers in other countries than they do with their supervisors and managers. Our interest here lies in the relative importance of rank and country as they influence one's perceptions of various facets of work life including attributes of the organization in which he works. In this instance we would want to know which of the two variables is more powerful as predictor of one's perception of the degree of division of labor.

An analysis of covariance with country as classification and rank as covariate and with the two variables affecting the dependent variable, division of labor, simulteneously finds that both variables are important together explaining 45.6% of the variance of division of labor ($R^2 = .456$), but country emerges as more important ($F = 25.41$, $p < .001$) than rank ($F = 11.14$, $p < .001$). In other words, in this the Japanese do differ markedly from the Europeans.

Hierarchy of Authority

Hierarchy of authority refers to the aspect of organizations characterized by chain of command and of obedience spanning the vertical line from top to bottom. The Aston group (Pugh and Hickson, 1976) called this aspect centralization and operationalized it in terms of the levels at which various decisions are made and executed. As conceived by Hall (1961), hierarchy of authority is here measured through the following items:

1. Any decision I make has to have the bosses' approval.

2. I have to check with my boss before I can do almost anything.

3. Even small matters have to be referred to some higher-up for the final answer.

4. A person who likes to make his own decisions would be discouraged here.

5. I feel I can act as my own boss in most matters.

6. Only persons in executive positions can decide how a job is to be done.

The scores of hierarchy of authority are presented in Table 5.

TABLE 5

Mean, Standard Deviation, and Range for Hierarchy of Authority: Britain, Japan, Sweden

LEVEL:	COUNTRY:	HIERARCHY OF AUTHORITY:		
		$\bar{X}$	SD	Range
Whole Organizations	B	2.43	.277	2.14-2.93
	J	2.81	.222	2.57-3.13
	S	2.19	.261	1.84-2.65
Managers	B	2.03	.550	1.42-3.00
	J	2.59	.319	2.13-3.17
	S	2.21	.628	1.45-3.33
Foremen	B	2.45	.324	2.13-3.15
	J	2.78	.252	2.42-3.15
	S	1.97	.222	1.50-2.30
Rank and File Workers	B	2.81	.427	2.08-3.50
	J	3.08	.219	2.63-3.41
	S	2.34	.408	1.89-3.34

Taking first the total organizational scores for all employees, the Japanese mean is significantly higher than the British and the Swedish, as it was on division of labor. The Swedish organizations are seen to have the lowest degree of hierarchy of authority with the British coming in between the Japanese and the Swedish (the difference between the British and Swedish, however, is not statistically significant).

Table 5 makes it clear that on each of the three levels, too, Japanese organizations have the highest hierarchy of authority score. Here again there is a measuring validation against the common sense of hierarchy, for as would be anticipated, the perceived degree of hierarchy of authority declines as one goes up the organizational ladder. Yet there is the same conspicuous exception in the case of the Swedish managers, who now not only see themselves as having more divided tasks than their foremen perceive, but see more hierarchy.

An analysis of covariance shows that rank and country account for 44.9% of the variance in hierarchy of authority (R^2 = .449). Most interestingly in this case, rank emerges as the more powerful predictor of hierarchy of authority (F = 31.246, p <.001); country, however, does remain important (F = 14.574, p <.001).

Hence, from our analyses of perceptual measures of bureaucratic controls an interesting and consistent picture emerges. Though rank appears as an important predictor of the differences found, so does nation or culture. In general, the Japanese experience of their working life is of a much more bureaucratic way of operating organizations than the British and the Swedes report. They see themselves as performing more specialized routine jobs and being careful to move only on the boss's instructions.

Summary

Employees in the three countries studied have been shown to differ. But not in the way in which the uniform mould of organizational hierarchy effects them. Whichever the country, people are shaped by this constant factor of hierarchy, a finding which supports the case that the contemporary form of organization exerts the same pressures on employees everywhere. That is, within each country, hierarchical rank affects perceptions basically in the same way.

Indeed, rank appears as an important predictor of the differences found. First, with one aspect of bureaucracy, that termed hierarchy of authority, it is the more powerful predictor. Not surprisingly, managers feel they have discretion to act independently much more than subordinates do, to a degree that outweighs national differences. But also on the other aspect of bureaucracy that was measured (division of labor), the division of tasks perceived consistently lessens as one goes up the ladder in all three countries. In general, rank and file workers see more bureaucracy than do their managers.

But the outstanding feature of the results is that societal or national differences are present. Individuals placed within very similar organizational frameworks of controls do not necessarily use them in the same way nor see them as the same. They use their organizations and perceive them in the ways they have learned to as British or as Japanese or as Swedish.

CONCLUSION

As initially noted, the convergence theorists put forward a number of reasons for the development of similar institutional, organizational and attitudinal patterns in modern societies. It is their view that the broad thrust of industrialization and its specific manifestation leads to common models. A number of other authors, on the other side, see major cultural differences across societies - indeed, some go so far as to claim some countries as culturally unique. Few authors use, however, explicitly an organizational framework to make their arguments. Fewer still are studies which try to make explicit why their way may be forces for similarities, and why their way may be forces for differences. By contrast, Webber (1977, p. 54), for example, argues that there may be such dual influences at work:

> For a long time at the least, cultural factors will exert a strong and differentiating influence upon managerial philosophy and practice: less on technological and production decision, less on the relations of man and job, less in the firm's relationship to its customers and society; but more on the methods of motivation, patterns of communication and styles of leadership.

In this study, there are considerable evidence that there are indeed few, if any, cultural patterns on organizational aspects of structure and control - the major influences are the scale of operations, technology, and inter-organizational dependence. Notwithstanding these results, in this study, there is also an overwhelming evidence that some nationally-bound differences are also operational in the organizational context; people have different ways of living with bureaucracy, they use it in different ways and experience it in different ways. So even though organizations cross-nationally face similar contingencies and adopt similar modes of bureaucratic structures, the people employed in it due to deep-rooted cultural forces make different things out of it. In this study, Webber's (1977) dual influence hypothesis is hence supported.

BIBLIOGRAPHY

Aiken, M. and S. B. Bacharach (1979), Culture and Organizational Structure and Process. In: C. J. Lammers and D. J. Hickson (Eds.), Organizations Alike and Unlike, London: Routledge and Kegan Paul

Aiken, M. and J. Hage (1968), Organizational Interdependence and Intraorganizational Structure. In: American Sociological Review 33: 912-930

Aldrich, H. and S. Mindlin (1978), Uncertainty and Dependence: Two Perspectives on Environment. In: L. Karpik (Ed.), Organization and Environment, Beverly Hills, California: Sage Publications

Blau, P. M., W. V. Heydebrand and R. E. Stauffer (1966), The Structure of Small Bureaucracies. In: American Sociological Review 31: 179-191

Blau, P. M. and R. A. Schoenherr (1971), The Structure of Organizations, New York: Basic Books

Bonjean, C. and M. Grimes (1970), Bureaucracy and Alienation: A Dimensional Approach. In: Social Forces 48: 365-373

Child, J. (1972), Organization Structure and Strategies of Control: A Replication of the Aston Study. In: Administrative Science Quarterly 17: 163-177

Child, J. (1980), Contingency, Culture and Other Problematics in the Cross-National Study of Organizations. In: B. Staw and L. Cummings (Eds.), Research in Organization Behaviour, Vol. 3, Greenwich, Connecticut: JAI Press

Child, J. and R. Mansfield (1972), Technology, Size and Organization Structure. In: Sociology 6: 369-393

Crozier, M. (1964), The Bureaucratic Phenomenon, London: Tavistock

Eisenstadt, S. N. (1973), Tradition, Change and Modernity, New York: Wiley Interscience

Greenwood, R. and C. R. Hinings (1976), Centralization Revisited. In: Administrative Science Quarterly 21: 151-155

Haire, M., E. E. Ghiselli and L. W. Porter (1966), Managerial Thinking: An International Study, New York: Wiley

Hall, R. H. (1961), An Empirical Study of Bureaucratic Dimensions and their Relation to Other Organizational Characteristics. Unpublished Ph.D. dissertation, Columbus: Ohio State University

Hall, R. H., E. Haas and N. Johnson (1967), Organizational Size, Complexity and Formalization. In: American Sociological Review 32: 903-912

Hickson, D. J., C. R. Hinings, C. J. McMillan and J. P. Schwitter (1974), The Culture-Free Context of Organization Structure: A Tri-National Comparison. In: Sociology 8: 59-80

Hickson, D. J. and C. J. McMillan (Eds.) (1981), Organization and Nation: The Aston Programme IV, Farnborough, Hampshire: Gower Publishing

Hickson, D. J., D. S. Pugh and D. C. Pheysey (1969), Operations Technology and Organization Structure: An Empirical Reappraisal. In: Administrative Science Quarterly 14: 378-397

Hinings, C. R. and G. L. Lee (1971), Dimensions of Organization Structure and their Context: A Replication. In: Sociology 5: 83-93

Hofstede, G. (1977), Cultural Determinants of the Exercise of Power in a Hierarchy. Working Paper 77-8, European Institute for Advanced Studies in Management, Brussels

Hofstede, G. (1978), Organization-Related Value Systems in Forty Countries. Paper presented at the World Congress of Sociology, Uppsala

Hofstede, G. (1979), Hierarchical Power Distances in Forty Countries. In: C. J. Lammers and D. J. Hickson (Eds.), Organizations Alike and Unlike, London: Routledge and Kegan Paul

Horváth, D., C. J. McMillan, K. Azumi and D. J. Hickson (1981), The Cultural Context of Organizational Control: An International Comparison. In: D. J. Hickson and C. J. McMillan (Eds.), Organization and Nation: The Aston Programme IV, Farnborough, Hampshire: Gower Publishing

Inkeles, A. (1960), Industrial Man: The Relation of Status to Experience, Perception and Value. In: American Journal of Sociology 66: 1-31

Inkeles, A. and D. H. Smith (1974), Becoming Modern, Cambridge, Massachusetts: Harvard University Press

Inkson, J. H. K., D. S. Pugh and D. J. Hickson (1970), Organization Context and Structure: An Abbreviated Replication. In: Administrative Science Quarterly 15: 318-329

Jacobs, D. (1974), Dependence and Vulnerability: An Exchange Approach to the Control of Organizations. In: Administrative Science Quarterly 19: 45-59

Kerr, C., J. T. Dunlop, F. Harbison and C. A. Myers (1973), Industrialism and Industrial Man, Middlesex, England: Penguin Books

Lammers, C. J. and D. J. Hickson (Eds.) (1979), Organizations Alike and Unlike, London: Routledge and Kegan Paul

Lawrence, P. R. and J. W. Lorsch (1967), Organization and Environment: Managing Differentiation and Integration, Boston: Division of Research, Graduate School of Business Administration, Harvard University

Maurice, M. (1979), For a Study of 'The Societal Effect': Universality and Specificity in Organizational Research. In: C. J. Lammers and D. J. Hickson (Eds.), Organizations Alike and Unlike, London: Routledge and Kegan Paul

Maurice, M., A. Sorge and M. Warner (1980), Societal Differences in Organizing Manufacturing Units: A Comparison of France, West Germany, and Great Britain. In: Organization Studies 1: 59-86

McMillan, C. J., D. J. Hickson and C. R. Hinings (1973), The Structure of Work Organizations Across Societies. In: Academy of Management Journal 16: 555-569

Mindlin, S. and H. Aldrich (1975), Interorganizational Dependence: A Review of the Concept and a Reexamination of the Findings of the Aston Group. In: Administrative Science Quarterly 20: 382-392

Pugh, D. S. and D. J. Hickson (1976), Organization Structure in its Context: The Aston Programme I, Farnborough, Hampshire: Saxon House

Pugh, D. S., D. J. Hickson, C. R. Hinings and C. Turner (1968), Dimensions of Organization Structure. In: Administrative Science Quarterly 13: 65-105

Pugh, D. S., D. J. Hickson, C. R. Hinings and C. Turner (1969), The Context of Organization Structures. In: Administrative Science Quarterly 14: 91-114

Richardson, S. A. (1956), Organizational Contrasts on British and American Ships. In: Administrative Science Quarterly 1: 189-207

Sirota, D. and J. M. Greenwood (1971), Understanding Your Overseas Work Force. In: Harvard Business Review 49: 53-60

Webber, R. A. (1977), Convergence or Divergence?. As reprinted in T. D. Weinshall (Ed.), Culture and Management, Middlesex, England: Penguin Books

Weber, M. (1947), The Theory of Social and Economic Organization, Glencoe, Illinois: Free Press

Woodward, J. (1958), Management and Technology, London: HMSO

Woodward, J. (1965), Industrial Organization: Theory and Practice, London: Oxford University Press

Zwerman, W. L. (1970), New Perspectives on Organization Theory, Westport, Connecticut: Greenwood

The Meaning of Working

MOW-International Research Team

ABSTRACT

The present paper describes a major comparative study in ten nations on the meaning, significance, importance and value of working. Although the project is in the early stages of data collection at the present time, we welcome the opportunity to present the theoretical rationale underlying our work and the methods by which we are obtaining data. Our work will shed light on a number of issues which are germane to the present conference and thus seems relevant even in its uncompleted form.

INTRODUCTION

The major thesis of this international research project is that the systematic and comparative study of major patterns of meaning attached to working (including the antecedents and consequences of these patterns of meaning) is essential to increased understanding of work as a life role. Support for this assertion is found in the absolute time commitment individuals make to work, the significance that working has for an individual's life, the social and economic consequences of work meanings to organizations and to society, and the active role that individuals and groups have adopted in structuring and changing their work, work institutions and societies.

In most industrialized societies, the average person spends nearly a third of his/her day's activities at work. In addition to that, the time one spends in training and preparation, and the time one spends worrying about being out of work or planning for a better work situation probably encompasses a major part of the adult's life. It seems that the very act of working fulfills basic human needs. In the 1977-78 Quality of Employment Survey conducted by the University of Michigan (1978), seventy-one percent of the national sample of employed persons replied that they would continue to work even if they "were to get enough money to live as comfortably as you'd like for the rest of your life." Similar results have been reported earlier by Morse and Weiss (1955), Jakubowski (1968), Tausky (1969), and Kaplan and Tausky (1974). Most respondents also indicated that "working gives them a feeling of being tied into the larger society, of having something to do, of having

---
[1] For list of members see p. 614

a purpose in life" (Morse and Weiss, p.191). The significance of work also is indicated by the impact of unemployment and retirement on people who have been productive and active all their lives (Friedman and Havighurst, 1954). If the retired person cannot find some other kind of involvement, work or a hobby, the effects of inactivity and idleness often are very demoralizing. Working, then, is significant to the individual in both an economic sense and in a socio-psychological sense and study of work meanings must include these possibilities.

The rather dramatic changes during the past twenty-five years in the legal and societal conceptions about "working rights" of women, racial minority groups, protected age categories, and a variety of disadvantaged groups have certainly altered employment policies and practices substantially. It seems highly likely that these legislated changes and the accompanying costs and benefits would impact over time on the significance and meaning attached to working by various segments of the population. The increasing levels of education in most industrialized countries and the sweeping developments that occur in the process of industrial development with reference to the possibilities of performing work in general and certain types of work in particular most certainly impact on the meaning and significance of working.

A likely consequence of these trends is that once certain patterns of "work meanings" have developed for individuals and groups of individuals, they will in turn affect organizations and society in areas such as mobility, conflict, productivity, dropping out, modifying organizations and creating new ones. For if we know anything about the world of work, we know that it is man made. It is man who is active; man who is the structurer of experience and meaning. This view of the "enacted environment" is certainly not new and in contemporary organization behavior is best represented by Weick (1969) and Silverman (1970). It is this sense of causality that we are hypothesizing; that man is the definer of reality as well as being defined by it, that social interaction, as an example, "is a process whose course is pre-defined yet one through which new definitions of reality emerge" (Silverman, p.213).

The implications of this view and the associated frame of reference are central to the research we seek to conduct. To view man as totally determined by external forces is to accept only positivistic explanations of causality. To accept man as one causal agent is to reject strict positivism and to recognize that man interprets the world subjectively and transcends subjective experience (Polanyi, 1962). We seek to study the meaning attached to working behavior as a totality whether it is attached to behavior retrospectively, concurrently or prospectively (Weick, 1969).

An additional implication of this view of man is that while

groups and organizations sustain meanings, the very fact that these collective structures develop in the first place, and endure, is likely the result of the overlaps in meaning structures of individuals that precede the collective structure (Allport, 1962). "Having first converged on shared meanings of how a structure can form, i.e. nationalization, worker councils, or whatever, the persons then activate a repetitive cycle of interlocking behaviors -- that is, they form an organization or community. The range of their behavior narrows before the environment is formed, not after; the environment is made possible by this initial narrowing and convergence" (Weick, 1969, p.44). If we want to know what man's environment will look like tomorrow in the world of work, we should start with the meaning of work today. Work meanings do have social and economic consequences to organizations and to society and it is important to conceptualize study of work meanings in both a present and a futuristic sense.

For all these reasons, it can be stated without exaggeration that the "meaning of working" forms one of the most relevant issues in the further development of the socio-economic structures of countries in the post-industrial era. For these same reasons, an international comparative project on the "meaning of working" was initiated in 1978. Tentative proposals and discussion papers were circulated and evaluated by research teams in fifteen countries during the latter part of 1977 and early 1978. Five project workshops have been held during 1978-1980 to initiate and develop the project:

February 28 - March 2, 1978 . . . . . Berlin
August 4 - 6, 1978 . . . . Munich
December 13 - 16, 1978 . . . . Berlin
September 10 - 14, 1979 . . . . Amsterdam
May 6 - 9, 1980 . . . . Berlin

During 1978-80, research teams from ten countries (Belgium, Federal Republic of Germany, Israel, India, Japan, the Netherlands, Sweden, United Kingdom, Unites States and Yugoslavia) have formed the core group of participants in the study. The bases of selection of these countries were: (a) representation of different work cultures and inclusion of a wide spectrum of potential work meanings as demonstrated by available country literature, (b) representation of different socio-economic systems for purposes of macro-variable hypothesis testing, and (c) availability of researchers and research institutes with experience in cross-national comparative research and interest in the present research topic. The set of ten countries obtained for the study closely approximates an ideal set for such a study when tested against major country clusters on related variables as reported by Hofstede (1977) and Gomez and Pettman (1978). The major shortcoming is omission of France and/or Italy, both of whom were solicited for the study but could not participate.

Country literature reviews have been exchanged by the ten research groups and agreement has been reached on central research questions, major variables of interest, research methods and procedures, and research phases and timing. It is indeed fair to say that the total study and proposals for its conduct are the product of the combined efforts of all ten research teams. In general, the basic focus of the comparative research project can be summarized as follows: the meaning, the significance and the value which individuals and groups attach to working is the central concept of the study. It is the concept that we are seeking to develop conceptually, to identify empirically and to understand in terms of its antecedents and its consequences.

Within this basic focus, the goals of the research are as follows:

(1) Identification of major patterns of meanings individuals and significant groups attach to working. The range of patterns identified obviously will be constrained by the possibilities inherent in our conceptualizations of work meanings, the instruments and methods of data collection, the range of countries involved and the groups we select to study. Considerable attention has been focused on these issues during project development and the design elaborated later indicates the conceptual development to date.

(2) To understand how individuals and groups have developed particular work meanings. This goal suggests that we seek to understand the developmental process involved in the work meanings we find. This is a complex task that requires analysis of personal and family variables, work and career history variables and macro-economic environment variables.

(3) To understand the consequences of meaning of work patterns to individuals, organizations, and society in general. Concern for these consequences is built into the primary data collection procedures but it is clearly recognized that alternative interpretations and professional debate or our findings are essential to this understanding.

(4) To estimate the proportion of the labor force in each country which "holds" each major pattern of meaning of work. Such a goal requires that we obtain data from representative samples of the employed population in addition to concentrated study of major target groups.

(5) To develop policy implications from our findings. Obviously, such implications must stem from the data and the country situations, but it seems reasonable to indicate major areas of possibility:

- --forecasting what changes seem likely to occur in meaning of work patterns for particular societal groups

--identifying possibilities and constraints concerning changes in the role of work in life (suggested by our data)
--identifying potential social problems that might arise because of work meaning pattern development
--identifying problems and opportunities for workforce management given certain meaning of work patterns
--evaluating the potential impact of normative values about working on organizational functioning
--identifying mental health implications such as occupational stress patterns associated with working in general and with particular target group membership.

(6) To compare work meanings, their developmental histories and their consequences across the countries involved in the study. This goal indicates that we are interested in both similarities (for generalization purposes) and differences (to capture group and/or country specific findings) concerning work meanings. We view this national comparative aspect of the research as a major requirement for fuller understanding of the phenomenon of meaning of working.

In short, we seek to assess and understand the variety of meanings individuals and groups attach to working in industrial societies; to understand how these meanings develop within and across national/cultural systems; to understand the consequences of different work meanings to individuals, organizations, and societies; and to provide policy suggestions and implications from our results.

RELATION TO THE STATE OF KNOWLEDGE

Work has not always been so important as it seems to be viewed today. Early Greeks and Romans viewed work as punishment and drudgery. The higher status class did not expect to work, and work was done primarily by slaves and the poor. "Manual labor was tiring, vulgar, degrading, and the enemy of the soul" (Heneman, 1973). Later, work took on some religious meanings, according to Tilgher (1962); Hebrew philosophers saw work as a way of punishment and conciliation for sins. Christians thought that work was good while loafing was bad. During the Protestant Reformation, work was considered as punishment for one's sins; work was a duty and not working was immoral.

The Nature of Work

The concept "work" is by no means an easy term to define. The American College Dictionary, for instance, gives forty-six noun and verb definitions of work! Other prominent dictionaries, such as the Oxford Universal Dictionary and the Webster's Third New International Dictionary, devote over a page of analysis to this topic. Probably as a result of this confusion, the International Encyclopedia of the Social Sciences doesn't even attempt to discuss the subject at all.

Part of the confusion in the definition of work results from the very fact that work does not have the same meaning and function for all people. For some it is an instrument through which they derive their basic maintenance and survival while for others it serves as a mechanism through which self expression and other social needs are fulfilled.

The authors of Work in America (1973) provide a "multi-dimensional" definition of work: "an activity that produces something of value for other people" (p.3). The authors claim that this definition is a comprehensive one that puts work within a social context and it suggests that work is purposeful. Two main functions that work serves are identified in Work in America. The first and the most dominating thought about work's meaning is its economic purpose(s). Less attention has been given to its second function, which is its social purpose(s) for the individual.

An empirical attempt to define "work" has been reported by Weiss and Kahn (1960). They selected a probability sample of working men -- aged 21 and over, living in Detroit -- and presented them with the question: "In your opinion what makes the difference between something you would call work and something you would not call work" (p.143). Over three fourths of the respondents defined work either as "activity one performed but did not enjoy" or as "activity which was scheduled or paid for."

Shimmin (1966) presented some of the criteria suggested by various authors who sought to define work. These are: (1) Work is purposeful activity; (2) It is instrumental; (3) It yields income; (4) It causes expenditure of effort; (5) It has some element of obligation or restraint.

Steers and Porter (1975) concentrate mainly on the importance and meaning of work for the individual from a psychological point of view. They see four main functions of work:

(1) Exchange -- each person receives some form of compensation in exchange for the services that he/she gives.
(2) Social function -- interaction with other people.
(3) Status -- work provides status and rank in society for workers.
(4) Personal meaning -- source of identity, self-esteem, self-actualization and fulfillment. On the other hand, work can also provide frustration, boredom, and a sense of alienation.

Friedman and Havighurst (1954), in an early study on the meaning of work and retirement, distinguished between functions of work for and individual and the relation of these universal functions to the meanings which the individual may assign to work as follows:

Function	Meaning
1. Income	a) Maintaining a minimum sustenance level of existence b) Achieving some higher level or group standard
2. Expenditure of time	a) Something to do b) A way of filling the day or passing time
3. Identification and status	a) Source of self-respect b) A way of achieving recognition or respect from others
4. Association	a) Friendship relations b) Peer-group relations c) Subordinate-superordinate relations
5. Source of meaningful life experence	a) Give purpose to life b) Creativity; self-expression c) New experience d) Service to others

Friedman and Havighurst claim that the meanings of work "vary as jobs vary and as people vary" (p.5). They conclude that in speaking of the meaning of work, one should look at the individual's life and also at "the type of effective response he has made to it" (p.6).

It seems clear that in defining work and in considering the nature of work, we are soon led into the topic of work meanings.

Work Meanings

Friedman and Havighurst (1954) studied steelworkers, coal miners, skilled craftsmen, sales people, and physicians. For all five groups, work was found to have meanings in addition to just that of economic gain. Some of the relevant findings were:

(1) The workers of lower skill and socio-economic status are more likely to see their work as having no other meaning than that of earning money . . .

(2) Work as a routine which makes the time pass is recognized about equally by all five groups.

(3) All groups discover self-respect and secure respect or recognition from others by means of their work.
(4) The physicians show a high awareness of the service to others meaning in their work. This may be characteristic of the "service professions."
(5) Work is important as a source of interesting, purposeful activity and as a source of intrinsic employment for all five groups (pp.173-174).

When occupational groups were examined according to their intentions of retirement, Friedman and Havighurst noted that people employed in higher occupational levels are less likely to desire retirement at age 65 even though they could more easily retire in an economic sense.

In another early and classic study of the function and meaning of work and the job, Morse and Weiss (1955) made the following observations from interviewing a national sample of working men:

1) Working is more than a means to an end for the vast majority of employed men;
2) . . . a man does not have to be at the age of retirement or be immediately threatened by unemployment to be able to imagine what not working would mean to him; and,
3) working serves other functions than economic ones for men in both middle class and working class occupations, but that the non-monetary functions served by working are somewhat different in these two broad classifications of occupations (p.191).

A survey of a national sample of employed blue-collar males, conducted by Tausky (1969) indicated that 11 percent worked mainly because they had no alternative; 22 percent were interested in work because of the income it provided; and 55 percent were interested in work for economic reasons but also indicated that such work must be acceptable by their friends and neighbors. Thus, Tausky concludes that three out of four men in the blue-collar category could be categorized as "consumer oriented and normatively tied to work as the acceptable source of income" (p.54).

These results are very similar to those reported 14 years earlier by Morse and Weiss (1955). When Tausky examined the meaning of work by educational level, education emerged as the single most important variable related to the meaning of work --men who had not completed high school were found to have an instrumental attitude toward work, while those with some college education valued more highly the prestige that was associated with work.

Dubin (1956) conducted a "central life interest" study, which was defined as: "the expressed preference for a given locale or situation in carrying out an activity" in three midwestern plants engaged in metal manufacturing and equipment assembly operation, industrial dress and novelty gloves and printed and novelty advertising items. Dubin's main finding is that "the industrial worker's world is one in which working, and the work place are not central life interests for a vast majority . . . Industrial man seems to perceive his life history as having its center outside of work for his intimate human relationships and for his feelings of enjoyment, happiness, and worth." Dubin concludes by pointing out that, although work was once a central life interest for employees, it is no longer true, and these interests are centered now in the community.

In an attempt to replicate Dubin's study, Orzack (1959) administered Dubin's "Central Life Interest" items to registered professional nurses, employed in public and private general hospitals and a state mental hospital in a midwestern city. In contrast to Dubin's findings, Orzack reported that "for four of every five nurses studied, work and the work place are central life interests" compared with Dubin's finding that almost 75 percent of the industrial workers responses indicated that work and the work place were not central life interests. In an explanation for these differences, Orzack maintains that the "Central Life Interest" inventory is a measure of values and by this comparison between the two groups, it seems obvious that the professional worker has a higher interest in work and also more pride and identification with it than the industrial worker.

Maurer (1968) studied a sample of first through third level supervisors employed by Michigan firms engaged in manufacturing and/or assembly operations. He found that for most of the bottom level and middle level industrial supervisors, the work place and the work itself <u>were</u> central life interests.

Guion and associates (1969) report several major conclusions from a series of studies in 53 organizations and encompassing over 1,400 workers concerning the meaning of work and worker motivation.

1) There are three major factors in the meaning of work (major in the sense that they apply in a wide variety of organizations, or occupations, and of job concepts). These are the <u>stimulus value</u> of the work or work aspect, the <u>autonomy</u> it provides or allows, and the demand it places for <u>accuracy</u> in work with details.
2) The greatest individual differences in meaning are in connotations of autonomy. Although most people consider autonomy an important feature of an ideal job, there are wide variations in degree and there are even many who do not consider autonomy desirable. There are also wide variations in autonomy within similar occupational groups. For example, nurses and bank tellers, on the average, want and have little autonomy on their jobs; nevertheless, there are individual nurses or bank tel-

lers who want and/or have very high degrees of autonomy.

3) Almost all people can be grouped in one of ten types or profile patterns of the meaning of an ideal job.

4) . . . some very general statements can be made. First, the semantic differential does in fact appear to be a promising tool for measuring the meaning of work. Second, measures of the meaning of work vary greatly from individual to individual, even when there are clear occupational or organizational influences on that meaning. Finally, the notion of typing people either in terms of common ideas about an ideal job or in terms of common perceptions of the jobs they have, is a potentially useful tool for seeking limited generality in making statements about satisfaction, motivation, and managerial actions.

In a recent study on the meaning of work to the hard core unemployed, Kaplan and Tausky (1974) surveyed individuals enrolled in a federal job training program designed to offset hard core unemployment. They found that 76 percent of respondents wanted jobs in order to get some economic rewards, little over one percent did not want work at all while eighty percent would continue to work even if they did not need the money. They concluded that "work as an activity was viewed in a positive light, but often with little commitment to the work normally engaged in when employed" (p.195).

Kaplan and Tausky (1974) suggested a useful typology of six meanings of work which include both expressive and instrumental meanings and are based on a review of several studies of the meanings and functions of work in the United States. It should be noted that this typology forms the basis for operationalizing "valued working outcomes."

Expressive

I. Work as an intrinsically satisfying activity. Enjoyment and a sense of accomplishment may be derived from performing a work task -- e.g., rendering a service to others. There may be a desire for new experience, to learn more, and to utilize and develop abilities in one's job -- to self-actualize. There may be a need for responsibility and autonomy.

II. Work as a status and prestige bestowing activity. A desire for status achievement in monetary or social terms. A job or type of work may be valued for the prestige accruing to the person performing such a task. Status or prestige may be sought from one's co-workers, friends, or relatives. The pursuit of money in this context is an outward sign signifying status achievement.

III. Work as a morally correct activity. Work is seen as an

activity that fulfills a prescribed role in society, carrying prescriptions about the "rightness" and "correctness" of working.

IV. Work as a source of satisfying interpersonal experiences. Satisfactions may be derived from association with others in work and during the course of one's work with clients, patrons, patients, or co-workers. The satisfactions are not from services rendered, but from affiliative relations in one's job.

Instrumental

V. Work as an economic activity, a means of survival. Work is sought for the money it provides. It is prized for the opportunities it provides for obtaining satisfaction away from one's job.

VI. Work as a scheduled or routinized activity which keeps one occupied. It consumes time and energy, and may be viewed as a vehicle for avoiding negative consequences associated with laziness and idleness -- e.g., hustling and illegal activities (p.186).

A set of general evaluative conclusions which we draw from studies conducted in the countries in the project are:[2]

(1) Meaning of work variables and patterns are measurable.
(2) There are occupational differences in several aspects of the meaning and significance of working and an occupational frame of reference for sampling purposes is suggested.
(3) Meaning of work is clearly a multidimensional construct although little systematic study of it as a multidimensional construct has been done.
(4) There is little systematic knowledge about how multidimensional work meanings develop or are altered in individual working lives and which work meanings are stable and which are dynamic.
(5) There is little systematic knowledge about the behavioral consequences of attaching different meanings to work and working.
(6) Most previous research has concentrated on meaning of work in a current perspective as opposed to either a past or future perspective and as such is relatively time bound.
(7) Most previous research is job oriented as opposed to working life oriented.
(8) There is no cross-national comparative research which focuses on the multidimensional meaning of working and which adequately deals with the often cited problems of comparative research such as: a) cross-national development of an adequate conceptual framework, b) cross-cultural and cross-linguistic comparability of research instruments, c) sampling

procedures and strategies which permit generalization of results, and d) combination of knowledge obtained from both ideographic and nomothetic approaches.

The research procedures outlined in the next section are a direct outgrowth of this literature evaluation and of our research goals.

RESEARCH STRATEGY AND DESIGN

Evaluation of literature in each country relevant to the topic of work meanings and consideration of the research goals of the project have led to the following research decisions:

1. Heuristic Model of the Major Variable Sets in the Study

It would be most desirable to have a well articulated theoretical model of Meaning of Working (MOW) which was transsituational, which included multiple levels of analysis and had the capability of yielding policy implications. The choice of variables would then be guided by a conception of what influences MOW and what, in turn, MOW influences and thus what is important to measure and relate. In the absence of any such generally accepted theory, it would seem unwise to allow any one theoretical position to specify all variables measured. Between these limits, the underlying model in the present study is based on the conception that MOW is determined by the choices and experiences of the individual and by the organizational and environmental contexts in which they work and live. The model which follows shows the major variable sets and the most direct and straightforward relationships that can be studied. The influence arrows in the model simply indicate that we shall attempt to determine the extent to which personal and work history data and macro-socio-economic environment (of the present) explain (in a statistical sense) presently measured meaning of work variables and patterns and the extent that presently measured meaning of work variables and patterns explain subjective expectations about future working situations and objective outcomes of working. It is clear that causal interpretation of such findings must take into account the probable developmental sequence of the studied variables in individuals' lives as well as the likely possibility that variable complexes may operate in more than one manner (e.g., certain life cycle variables may influence both the development of values about working and the extent to which these values influence later behavior). Our interpretive reference also changes when the analysis is within a particular target group, between target groups within a given country or between national samples in different countries.

As indicated in the model, there are three levels at which

Heuristic Research Model

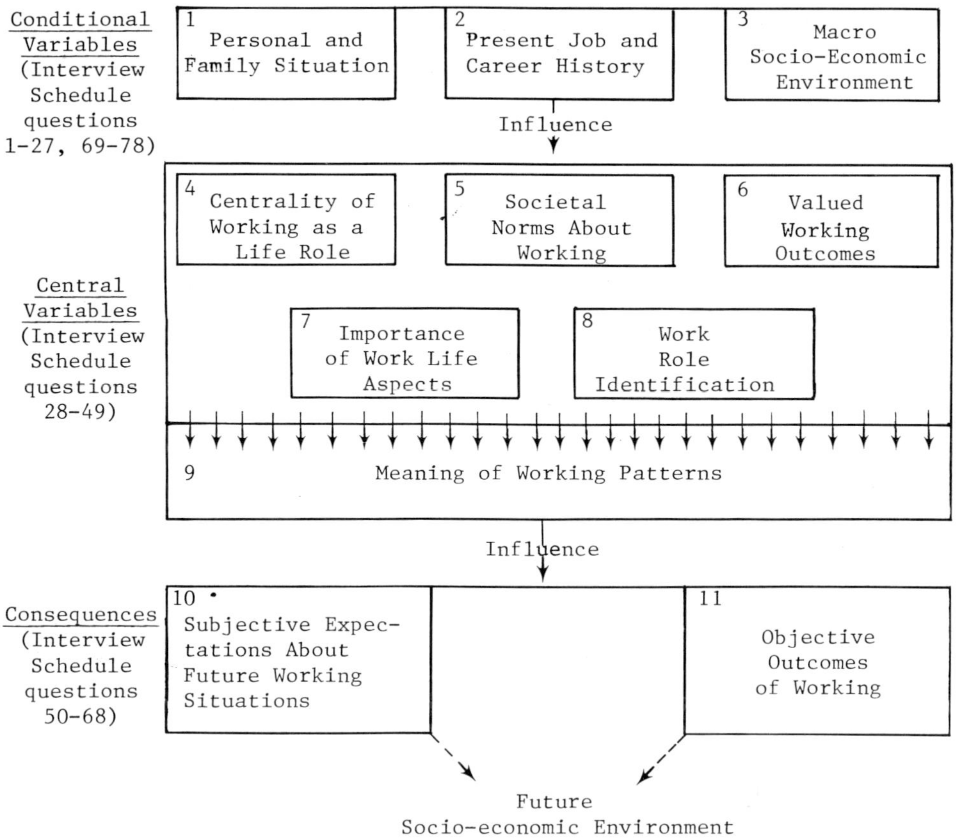

variables are being chosen and operationalized. The Interview Schedule to be used in data collection is presented at the end of the text.

(a) Conditional Variables

This level includes variables about personal and family circumstances (1) (numbers refer to numbered variable sets in the Hueristic Research Model) such as age, sex, family status, spouse's work situation, education, religious orientation, urban/rural upbringing, parents' education, similarity of parents' education to that of the respondent, individual and family income; variables concerning present job and career history information (2) such as present job situation, frequency and direction of changes in one's working career (stable versus erratic career patterns and occupational prestige or skill level changes), unemployment (frequency and duration), opportunities and factors which prompted job changes in one's career (desired versus forced changes), and variables concerning the social and economic environment (3) such as laws, industrial relations systems, labor force participation rates, educational systems and levels, unemployment levels and general level of wealth/affluence. This category of data will be used primarily to dimensionalize the variable country in seeking to understand observed country level differences in Meaning of Work patterns, their determinants and consequences and in testing specific hypotheses. Community level socio-economic environment variables will also be collected as it is a general hypothesis in the research that there is a relationship between community socio-economic indices and work meanings. There is general research support for such a relationship when job satisfaction is the dependent variable, e.g., Smith, Kendall and Hulin (1969); Wild and Kemper (1972); Roberts and Glick (1979). Of particular interest in the present research is a potential explanation for the above findings which has been termed the "frame of reference" hypothesis, Kendall (1973), Hulin (1966); Smith, Kendall and Hulin (1969). According to this hypothesis, individuals respond to work or their jobs in terms of available alternatives, community prosperity or decrepitude, labor market conditions, and past experiences. We would posit that the "frame of reference" which is appropriate to work meanings is considerably more complex than that suggested for job satisfaction.

(b) Central Variables

It should be noted that it is not meaning attributes related only to the present job or present work performed that is of interest, rather the concern is with the importance, the value, the significance and the meaning of having work and performing work in general. Meaning of working is defined conceptually in terms of five major domains and the resulting meaning of working patterns. The core notion being addressed in each of the domains is as follows:

Centrality of Working as a Life Role (4) -- How central is the role of working in one's life as compared to other life roles and in absolute terms?

Societal Norms about Working (5) -- A set of normative statements about work and working in terms of what one should expect from working (opportunities) and what should be expected from one in working (obligations). These norms have been defined as proscriptive or prescriptive standards involving relationships between a person category and a behavioral component in each of nine dimensions: Who should work, when during life stages should people work, competency in work, work career, time orientation, value of work, effort and success, work commitment and subordinate-superior relationships. The "opportunity" and "obligation" scores across dimensions will be most meaningful in developing meaning of working patterns.

Valued Working Outcomes (6) -- What are the outcomes one is seeking from working and what are their relative importances? Includes major expressive and instrumental meanings identified in the literature.

Importance of Work Aspects (7) -- What is the relative importance or significance to the individual of various aspects of working (e.g., autonomy, variety, skill utilization, promotional opportunity, security, physical working conditions)?

Work Role Identification (8) -- To what extent does one personally define and identify working in terms of various roles (e.g., task roles, company or organizational roles, product or service roles, occupational or professional roles)?

Meaning of Working Patterns (9) -- The logically and empirically determined patterns of the five meaning of work domains identified above (e.g., individuals who view working as very central to their life and want instrumental outcomes from working and identify strongly with their employing organization in role terms).

Measurement of these central variables (4-8) will take place through the use of partially open and partially closed response options to a series of structured questions in an interview format.

(c) Consequences

A third set of variables included in the study deals with (10) expectations, plans and aspirations for the future about working (e.g., with respect to future mobility, types of work, expected changes in work situations and meanings, retirement plans). This set of variables is future oriented and deals with aspirations or expectations. A related set of consequence variables also will be included which are more objective or behavioral in nature (11). These variables will be concrete steps currently being taken to achieve expected or aspired to work situations in the future (e.g., currently intending to change jobs, currently changing one's job training status, or currently changing the time one spends at work to reach some aspirational working situation).

2. The Samples to be Studied

The samples to be studied include a set of common target groups within each country and a representative sample of the labor force. There are three major and overlapping reasons for intensive study of comparable target groups within each country:

(a) The need to study groups which are critically important to policy concerns and policy-making within each country (e.g., increasingly important groups in the labor force such as women and part-time employees; current and potential problem groups such as the unemployed, drop-out groups or employees in declining industries).

(b) The need to map the domain of Meaning of Work Patterns in terms of different expected patterns because of attachment to the work force (reject employment, unemployed, temporarily employed, partially employed, fully employed, retired); in terms of the nature of work and/or career (skill levels and occupations-professions); and in terms of major personal and family, work and career history, and the socio-legal-economic variables.

(c) The need to deal with groups that are relatively homogeneous internally with respect to most variables identified above so that "causes" and "consequences" of meaning of work patterns can be better understood.

While career development per se is not the primary variable of concern in this study, we have been influenced in our selection of target groups and in stratification within groups to clearly cover the major adult career stages suggested by the research and theory of Super (1957), Erikson (1963), Levinson, et al. (1974), and Super and Hall (1978).

There are ten mandatory target samples to be studied in each country and the size of each target group will be approximately 90 individuals. Individual countries will add other groups which are particularly relevant to them to this mandatory set of target groups. The mandatory target groups are as follows:

- Unemployed - N = 90, 50% male, 50% female. Medium to low skill levels, all having been unemployed for at least the past six months. Do not include physically handicapped individuals or seasonal workers (construction and building, dock workers, and hotel workers).

- Retired - N = 90, 50% male, 50% female. Not presently working and of normal retirement age. If possible, select from among teachers, low skilled white collar workers and chemical engineers.

- Chemical Engineers - N = 90, all males. Graduates of university level training and currently doing professional chemical work (not managers) in companies of more than 200 employees. Do not select from food companies or from pharmaceutical companies.

• Teachers - N = 90, all females. Teaching 9-10 year-old students and in situations where they have the main teaching assignment for a whole class as opposed to teaching only one subject to many classes. Where appropriate, select teachers from both private and public schools in approximate proportion to their relative proportion in the industrial area (city) from which data is being collected.

• Self-employed businessmen - N = 90, all male. Select only those with less than eight employees. Select from among commercial, service and crafts type businesses. Do not use professionals such as lawyers, physicians or dentists. The intent is to take "small shopkeepers."

• Tool and die makers - N = 90, all male. This is a high skill level group which should be selected from the automobile industry or related industries.

• White-collar employees - N 90, 50% male, 50% female. The intent is to select low to semi-skilled, or lower service function employees whose occupations are being influenced by automation and technology. Select from the banking and insurance industry.

• Textile workers - N = 90, 60 males, 30 females. Low or semi-skilled job level such as "weaver."

• Temporary workers - N = 90, all female. Doing clerical work, non-skilled to low skill levels. They work for and are assigned to temporarily work somewhere by either private or governmental employment agencies. We do not want students but rather people whose present occupation is temporary clerical work through an agency.

• Students - N = 90, 50% males studying mechanical or machine trades or equivalent in vocational-technical schools, 50% females studying for clerical-secretarial occupations in full-time schools. These individuals may be employed part time but we are seeking individuals who are primarily students who will go directly into employment after their vocational-technical training. Do not select those who directly go on to university level education.

As indicated earlier, one of the study goals is to be able to estimate (within reasonable limits) the proportion of individuals within each country who have certain major patterns of work meaning. The rationale for this goal and for including the required national sample is three-fold: (a) it will provide a national picture of work meaning patterns for policy evaluation, for comparison with past studies, and as a reference point for future studies; (b) it will serve as a national reference group for evaluating and understanding critical target group data; and, (c) it will form the basis for cross-national comparisons and hypothesis testing about the impact of specified national dimensions upon meaning of work patterns. It is anticipated that this representative sample of the labor force will consist of 1,000 to 1,500 individuals in each country, that the amount of data collected from each individual will be held to the minimum required by our goals and that this data collection effort will be made at a late stage in the project.

3. Developmental Focus in the Study

We clearly recognize that in studying work meanings for any one person, we will be partially representing what is a complex developmental process depicted as follows:

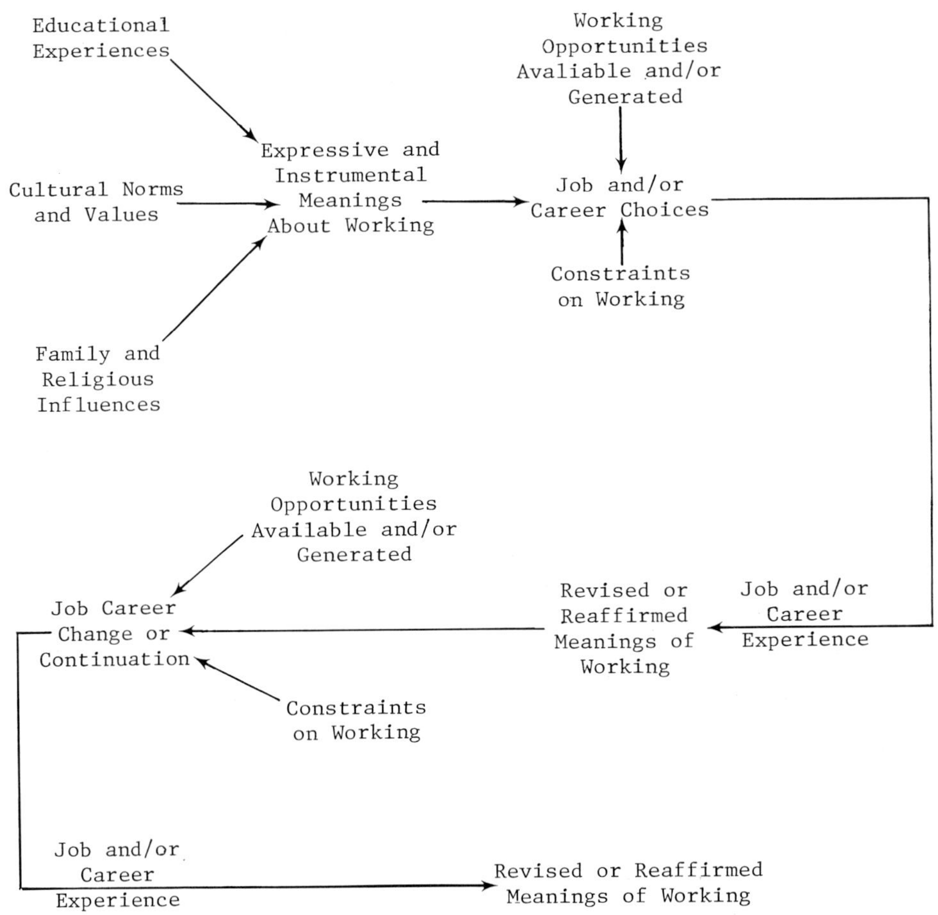

4. Time Perspectives in the Study

The study of the meaning of work should be at two time perspectives: meaning of work as it exists today and meaning of work in a futuristic sense. Both perspectives are important and complement each other, and by working at both perspectives our study will have increased policy relevance. A futuristic orientation to the research will be obtained in at least four ways:

(a) by simply extrapolating results about current patterns of work meanings into the future,

(b) by questioning our samples about their aspirations for work in the future,

(c) by selecting target samples to be studied which are presumed to be important in the future (this will get at the future through purposive sampling and selection of target groups),

(d) by employing methods such as the Delphi technique to have knowledgeable experts make futurological statements about work meanings in the future -- both in terms of how they think work meanings will develop, and how they think work meanings should develop for optimal societal benefit.

Alternatives (a) and (b) assume linearity between the present and the future in terms of work meanings while (c) and (d) allow for the possibility that the future is unlike the present because of basic societal change.

It will be useful to bring these alternative views into confrontation and to view how they differ and how they overlap with each other. A representation of these ideas is shown in the following diagram.

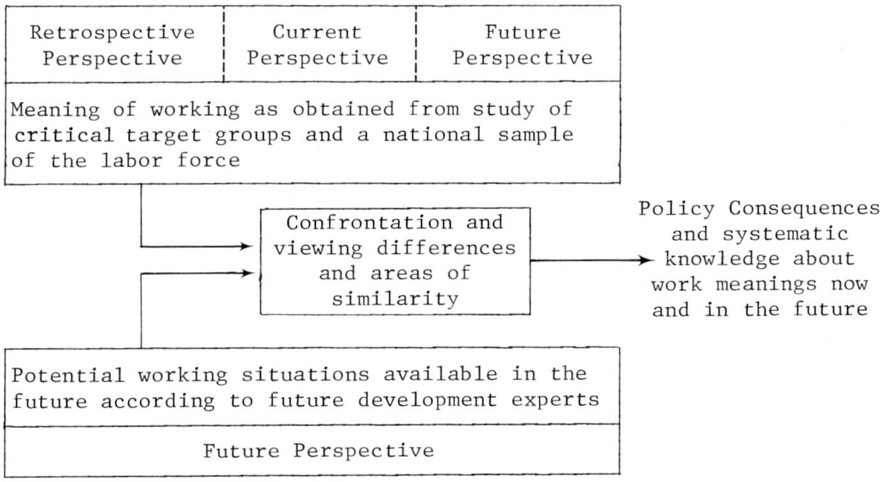

5. Analysis Plans

The data analysis techniques to be used will be determined by three major factors: (a) purpose of the analysis (e.g., identifying meaning of working patterns, explaining variations in MOW pattern distributions by work history and personal data, identifying potential national level problems because of meaning of work pattern development, testing specified hypotheses about national level dimensions as explainers of country level meaning of work pattern), (b) the measurement characteristics of the data being analyzed (e.g., appropriateness of treating the data at the ordinal or interval scale level), and (c) the appropriateness of aggregation procedures in light of our sampling procedures (e.g., comparing age groups within a given target sample within a given country, comparing target groups across countries, comparing national samples across countries). It seems likely that we shall use analysis techniques ranging from simple bivariate to multivariate covariation analysis, from simple non-parametric tests of significance to complex variance analyses designs, from simple mean difference comparisons to complex profile difference analyses.

While we are unable to completely specify all data analysis that will be conducted, the following outline is representative:

• The impact of developmental variables upon the major constitutive dimensions of work meanings. Using, for example, only the three major constitutive dimensions of work meanings (work centrality, valued working outcomes, and societal norms about working); past research and theorizing would lead us to hypothesize the following single variable developmental influences:

Developmental Variable	Impact on Meaning of Work Dimension
Sex	Males have higher work centrality than females.
	Females emphasize "obligations" in societal norms about working more than do males.
Educational Level	Higher educational levels lead to greater "expressive" components of valued working outcomes.
	Individuals with higher educational levels emphasize "opportunities" in societal norms about working more than do those with lower educational levels.
Urban-rural Upbringing	Rural upbringing leads to higher work centrality and to "obligations" being emphasized in societal norms about working.

(continued)...

Developmental Variable	Impact on Meaning of Work Dimension
Work History Patterns	Stable but ascending work histories lead to increased work centrality.
	Turbulent work histories or those with substantial periods of unemployment lead to higher "instrumental" components of valued working outcomes and to "opportunities" being emphasized in societal norms about working.

These and related developmental hypotheses will be tested (when possible and appropriate) within each target sample, across target samples within a country and between similar target groups and national samples across countries to assess the nature and generality of the hypothesized relationships. In addition, we will analyze all potential developmental variables (whether or not we have hypothesized a relationship) to determine what affects the variance of each constitutive dimension of work meaning. Correlational analyses, analysis of variance and regression analysis are the analytic methods that will be utilized for understanding the impact of developmental variables on meaning of working dimensions. The consistency of relationships between developmental variables and work meaning variables across samples and countries (as opposed to group and country differences on any given variable) will identify major developmental findings.

• The impact of the major dimensions of work meaning on subjective expectations about future working situations and objective outcomes of working. The basic conceptual hypotheses to be tested here can be stated rather directly:

--The more central work is to one's life, the more time and effort one spends working.

--The more one views societal norms about working in "obligation" terms, the more willing one is to accept structure in terms of authority and standards. Conversely, the more one views societal norms about working in "opportunity" terms, the less willing one is to accept structure unless it clearly provides opportunities.

--The more one views valued working outcomes in instrumental terms, the greater the relevancy of the present job and job situation in choosing future courses of action and the lower the relevancy of a work life or career orientation.

Each of these conceptual hypotheses can be tested by a wide range of data relationships. For example, the first hypothesis can be evaluated in terms of data relationship outcomes from our questionnaire such as the following:

Greater Work Centrality Leads to:

--working more hours
--greater stated willingness to continue working on the lottery question
--being unemployed less in the past 12 months and the past 5 years
--greater stated ease of finding work in the next 12 months if necessary
--greater stated intention to be promoted in the next 12 months
--less willingness to "cut down hours" in future situations
--higher evaluation of one's present job in terms of responsibility, participation and use made of one's skills and abilities
--higher scores on the importance of "upgrading and promotion" and there being a "good match between your job requirements and your abilities."

The basic data analysis procedures to be used in testing these hypotheses and those related to dimensions will be bivariate and multivariate covariation analysis.

• Development of Meaning of Work Patterns. This portion of the data analysis is largely a taxonomic effort and not one of hypothesis testing. We find no theoretical justification for expecting any substantial intrinsic relationship between the major dimensions of work meaning. This expectation has been partially substantiated empirically in a pre-pilot study of 600 working individuals where the highest correlation between centrality of work and valued working outcomes was .13. Indeed, a major reason for conducting this research is to systematically explore a reasoned multidimensional approach to the meaning of working. We expect to find individuals whose pattern of meaning of working is assessed to be almost any possible combination of the major variables. Such a finding will be interesting but hardly noteworthy. It will be noteworthy, however, if for example, we were to find that a high proportion of people who are currently working even though past retirement age and able to retire financially (real behavior) are predominantly individuals who view work as very central to their lives and have valued working outcomes that are more expressive than instrumental and emphasize obligations in terms of societal norms about working. Clearly, the significance of MOW patterns lies in their relative frequency in any population and in the kind of outcomes to which they are likely to lead. Our methodological approach to identification of MOW patterns will include both simple joint score classification of individuals based on levels (high, medium, low) of the major dimensions and relatively sophisticated classification based on factor and cluster analysis procedures. Joint probability statements will be used to express the descriptive incidence of each major pattern among any particular group of respondents.

● National Level Hypothesis Testing. As previously indicated, the collection of macro data (country level) is primarily aimed at dimensionalizing the variable country in seeking potential explanations of country differences in MOW patterns and relationships. A series of hypotheses are being constructed such as the following:

--Across countries, the level of guaranteed economic employment security is inversely related to the level of measured work centrality.

--Across countries, the average level of education is positively related to an emphasis on "expressive" components of valued working outcomes.

--Across countries, national cultural diversity (in terms of language, ethnic origin, religion, and political history) is negatively related to Meaning of Working pattern homogeneity.

--The average difference between countries on major meaning of work dimensions is larger than the average differences on the same dimensions between target groups within a country and between major industrial urban areas within a country.

These and related national level hypotheses will be tested individually and in combination where conceptually meaningful. It should be noted that some national level hypotheses also can be tested within a country and/or within target groups. Similar findings at different levels of analysis would obviously increase confidence in the intrinsic validity of the relationship.

WORK PLAN AND PROJECT ADMINISTRATION

Work Plan

The project will require 36 months for completion with a proposed starting date of September 1, 1980 and a completion date of August 31, 1983. Project phases and timing goals are as follows:

(1) Preparation Stage. Interview schedule translation and target group accessibility and identification will be completed during the Fall of 1980.

(2) Main Data Collection Phase.
   a. Study of the ten target groups will be completed by September 1981.
   b. Study of the national sample of the labor force will be completed by June of 1982.

(3) Confrontation of expert forecasts of future work availability with meaning of work data obtained in the present study and identification of potential social problems connected with work to be completed by March of 1983.

(4) Preparation and dissemination of national reports and

a cross-national comparative volume - to be completed by August 1983.

International Project Administration

The international comparative project on the Meaning of Working includes research teams from ten countries. Professor George W. England (USA) and Professor Bernhard Wilpert (West Germany) are co-coordinators of the project. The fact that nearly all of the project members have prior experience with cross-national comparative research studies suggests that we will be able to minimize administrative problems and expend our efforts on substantive research issues. The international research team has adopted the following policy guidelines for administration and governance of the project.

Governance of the project

Major decisions will be made by the total international research team, so that each country participating will have equal decision influence regardless of the size of their research team. England and Wilpert will serve as project coordinators to facilitate project development and coordination and to make interim project decisions when necessary. Workshops (we anticipate two during each year of the project) will be chaired on an ad hoc rotating basis according to topic requirements. The primary purposes of the above simple governance system are to provide full opportunities for participation in decision-making to all country teams, to reduce the amount of time taken in bureaucratic procedures and to allow more time for content-related work, and to move the project successfully and efficiently to its completion.

Data sharing

Project data is cooperatively owned by all of us and is available to any participating country research team. Access to project data by parties other than project participants must be approved in writing by the international research team through the project coordinators.

Data storage

One or more data banks will be established for the project for central data analyses and storage purposes. It is anticipated that each country will be provided tapes (insofar as it is practical) of all stored data and all major analyses.

Publication policies

Each country is free to publish data from its own country at any time and in any form it desires subject to two provisions:

(a) Prior to publication, the material should be sent to all international colleagues in the project through the coordinators for their information and comment.

(b) All publications should include a standard reference to the international study and its published research design.

Publication of any data and/or summary results statements from a different country than one's own requires the written permission of the research team of the second country.

Serious consideration will be given to the notion of publishing a joint set of all individual country reports as soon as is feasible.

Publication of the major comparative volume(s) on project results should be done by a group of authors who are selected by the international research team of the project.

After the comparative volume(s) is (are) published, each national team will be able to publish any project data as they see fit subject only to the circulation and acknowledgement procedures suggested above.

Funding arrangements

The desired funding strategy for the project consists of international funding which would be used for project coordination (secretarial assistance, data handling and processing, workshop expenses, including some travel facilitation, cooptation of experts on analysis issues, and some funding for the final comparative volume writing stage of the project). National funding will be obtained by each country individually to conduct the research in their country and to support their country research team as needed.

Work Completed To Date

Multi-national comparative investigations such as the present project require a major investment of time and effort in "preliminary" interest exploration, literature exchange, concept development, pre-pilot study tryout of data collection devices and methods, and instrumentation decisions. This necessary but time-consuming phase of the Meaning of Work Project has been successfully completed. The following points should be noted:

- Ten countries have continued their participation and contribution through the long developmental stage.

- A common conceptual framework has been developed and accepted by the ten countries.

- Several iterations of interview schedules have been empirically tested in pre-pilot study experiments and a common form was pilot-tested in seven countries during the first four months of 1980. Each country pilot-tested the schedule on a sample of 100 persons (ten individuals from each of five target groups and 50 from the labor force in general). Pilot-study data were evaluated in terms of translation problems, data collection difficulties, instrument sensitivity to individual differences and logically expected target group differences, time estimates of data collection, suggested instrument refinement and general feasibility of our procedures. The interview schedule shown represents a final schedule which has resulted from intensive empirical testing in several iterations.

- Every item in the final instrument is thus a product of conceptual requirements and of empirical trial in seven countries. Thus there is both theoretical and empirical justification for the items included in the final interview schedule. This instrument is currently undergoing translation-back translation into appropriate languages in preparation for the major data collection effort.

- Analysis plans have been sufficiently formulated to provide answers to the major research questions, but it is clear that data base development and particular national interests will produce a variety of analyses that are not visualized at present.

- Cooperative international agreement has been reached concerning project governance and administration, data sharing, data ownership and publication policies.

The Meaning of Work Project has clearly reached a stage of development which merits discussion by interested scholars.

INTERVIEW SCHEDULE

The following interview schedule (Form A) is for data collection among employed target group samples. A slightly altered version (Form B) is for data collection with retired and unemployed samples while Form C represents a version for student samples. Due to space limitations, the latter two versions are not presented.

FORM A
FOR EMPLOYED SAMPLES

MEANING OF WORKING
Study

This interview is about working. About what working means to you in general, about your specific working situation and about how you view working in the future.

The interview is anonymous. That is to say, no one will see or hear your answers except for the researchers who are conducting the study.

Many different types of people will be interviewed. Therefore it is possible that some questions do not apply exactly to your situation. If a question is not clear to you, or if you have any comment, please feel free to ask or tell the interviewer.

Many different types of questions are covered in this study. There are no "right" or "wrong" answers but it is important that you give us your opinion. You will answer some questions directly on the forms provided and the interviewer will record your answers on other questions.

These questions are being asked of about 2000 individuals in each of ten countries throughout the world to find out what working really means to people. The ____(country)____ portion of the study is being conducted by a research team from ______ ___(institution(s))_____. Your answers are important and we thank you in advance for helping us in this important study.

____
signed
country project director(s)

<u>First, some questions about your present work situation</u>.

1. What type of work (job) do you presently do? ____________
____

2. Is your position primarily:
   _______ Non-Supervisory
   _______ Supervisory
   _______ Managerial

3. Are you a member of the following types of organizations?

No	Yes	
_______	_______	Trade Union
_______	_______	Professional Association
_______	_______	Employers Association

4. On the average, how many hours a week do you work (including overtime)?
   _______ hours

5. On the average, how much time do you spend traveling to and from work (both ways) each day?
   _______ minutes

6. Now about your working schedule:

   a. Is your work schedule primarily:
      _______ day
      _______ night
      _______ swing shift (partly day, partly night)

   b. Are your work hours primarily:
      _______ regular
      _______ varied

   c. During the last 12 months, have you worked weekends at least half of the time?
      _______ no
      _______ yes

7. Have you been unemployed in the last 5 years?
   _______ no
   _______ yes

   If yes, for how many months in the past 5 years?
   _______ months

   If yes, for how many months in the past 12 months?
   _______ months

<u>Now, some questions about your present job</u>.

8. Which statement best describes your present job? (Check one statement.)
   _______ (a) I often do the same things over and over or use the same piece of equipment or procedure almost all the time.
   _______ (b) There is some variety in my job. I use different pieces of equipment or procedures.
   _______ (c) I do many different things, use a wide variety of equipment or procedures.

9. Which statement best describes your present job? (Check one statement.)
   _______ (a) There is hardly any room for me to make decisions about work and its procedures.
   _______ (b) I make some of the decisions about my work and some are made for me.
   _______ (c) I decide myself how to do my work.

10. Which statement best describes your present job? (Check one statement.)
   _______ (a) Mistakes in my work do not have serious consequences for the organization or for other people.
   _______ (b) Mistakes in my work may have somewhat serious consequences for the organization or for other people.
   _______ (c) Mistakes in my work may have serious consequences for the organization or for other people.

11. Which statement best describes your present job? (Check one statement.)
   _______ (a) Doing my job I really can't learn something new.
   _______ (b) Sometimes I can learn something new doing my job.
   _______ (c) My work gives me the opportunity to learn many new things.

12. Which statement best describes your present job? (Check one statement.)
   _______ (a) In fact, I do my work alone.
   _______ (b) I work with some other people, but this is not a big part of my job.
   _______ (c) Working with other people is a very big part of my job.

13. Which statement best describes your present job? (Check one statement.)

_______ (a) There is almost no chance during the work day to talk to other people about non-business topics.

_______ (b) Sometimes I do have the opportunity during the work day to talk to other people about non-business topics.

_______ (c) There is almost always an opportunity during the work day to talk to other people about non-business topics.

14. Do you sometimes have to do your work in dangerous circumstances?

_______ no
_______ yes

15. Do you sometimes have to do your work in unhealthy circumstances?

_______ no
_______ yes

16. Does your job require <u>too</u> much of you physically?

_______ It never does.
_______ It seldom does.
_______ It sometimes does.
_______ It often does.

17. Does your job require <u>too</u> much of you mentally?

_______ It never does.
_______ It seldom does.
_______ It sometimes does.
_______ It often does.

18. How much of your past experience, skills and abilities can you make use of in your present job?

_______ Very little.
_______ A little.
_______ Quite a lot.
_______ Almost all.

19. Which of the following statements best describes your relationship with your supervisor?

_______ He does not inform me at all about his decisions.
_______ He informs me after he has made his decisions.
_______ He usually asks for my advice before making decisions.
_______ We usually make decisions jointly.
_______ He allows me to make most decisions on my own.

<u>Now we would like to ask you some questions about jobs you have held in the past and about your work history</u>.

20. Is your present job your first job?
_______ no
_______ yes - If yes go to question 23.

21.* Let's start with your first full time job that lasted 12 months or longer.
(a) What type of job (occupation) was it?_______________
____
(b) What made you choose this job?_______________
____
(c) What was the name of the organization or company where you worked? _______________
____
(d) How long did you work in this job?
_______ years

22.* Now, for each job after your first job and up to but <u>not</u> including your present job, could you provide the following information:
(a) Second Job:
- Type of job (occupation)_______________
____
- Length of time on the job _________ years.
- Major reasons for leaving the job _______________
____

(b) - and following until job before present job:
- Type of job...
- Length of time on the job.....
- Major reasons for leaving........

23. Now considering your present job (occupation):
(a) What made you choose this job?_______________
____
(b) How long have you worked at your present job?
_______ years
(c) What is your monthly <u>net</u> income from your present job?
_______ dollars per month

*NOTE: For temporary workers, Questions 21 and 22 refer only to full time <u>steady</u> jobs that lasted 12 months or longer. If no steady job has been held, go to Question 23.

<u>Now, looking at your total working history as a whole, please describe it in the following aspects.</u>

24. Compared to your present occupational group (colleagues), where did you start your work career?
    _______ Lower than my occupational group
    _______ About the same as my occupational group
    _______ Higher than my occupational group

25. Would you describe your work career as having ups and downs (either large or small)?
    _______ no
    _______ yes - If yes, were the ups and downs:
        _______ small
        _______ large

26. Considering my whole work history until today in relation to where I started:
    _______ it is marked by some decline
    _______ it has remained approximately on the level where I started
    _______ it has improved somewhat
    _______ it has improved a great deal

27. On the whole, how satisfied are you with your work history until now?
    _______ very dissatisfied
    _______ somewhat dissatisfied
    _______ neutral
    _______ somewhat satisfied
    _______ very satisfied

For the next set of questions, we would like you to think about what <u>working</u> means to you at the present time. Please remember we are <u>not</u> referring only to your present situation. We are interested in knowing what beliefs and values you personally have regarding working as a result of your total working life.

- First of all, I would like you to tell me, in your own words, what is most important to you about working.

  ____
  ____

- Is there anything about working that really bothers you?

  ____
  ____

28. To help explain what working means to you, please assign a total of 100 points, in any combination you desire, to the following six statements. The more a statement expresses your thinking, the more points you should assign to it. Please read all the statements before assigning points.

_______ working gives you status and prestige.
_______ working provides you with an income that is needed.
_______ working keeps you occupied.
_______ working permits you to have interesting contacts with other people.
_______ working is a useful way for you to serve society.
_______ working itself is basically interesting and satisfying to you.

Total = 100

29. How important and significant is working in your total life?

One of the least important things in my life	☐ ☐ ☐ ☐ ☐ ☐ ☐	One of the most important things in my life
	Of medium importance in my life	

30. Assign a total of 100 points to indicate how important the following areas are in your life at the present time.

_______ my leisure (like hobbies, sports, recreation and contacts with friends)
_______ my community (like voluntary organizations, union and political organizations)
_______ my work
_______ my religion (like religious activities and beliefs)
_______ my family

Total = 100

31. When you think of your working life, which of the following aspects of working seems most significant and important to you? Could you rank these items from 1 = most significant to 6 = least significant.

_______ the tasks I do while working
_______ my company or organization
_______ the product or service I provide
_______ the type of people with whom I work
_______ the type of occupation or profession I am in
_______ the money I receive from my work

32. What about the nature of your working life? How important to you is it that your work life contains the following:

- -A lot of opportunity to LEARN new things
- -Good INTERPERSONAL relations (supervisors, co-workers)
- -Good opportunity for upgrading or PROMOTION
- -CONVENIENT hours
- -A lot of VARIETY
- -INTERESTING work (work that you really like)
- -Good job SECURITY
- -A good MATCH between your job requirements and your abilities and experience
- -Good PAY
- -Good physical working CONDITIONS (such as light, temperature, cleanliness, low noise level)
- -A lot of AUTONOMY (you decide how to do your work)

First, Look over the items above to get an idea of what they are.

Second, Determine which of the items is most important in your work life. Then write the capitalized portion of that item on the line of the rating scale which represents its importance in your work life.

Third, Cross the first item you selected off the list.

Fourth, Select the item which is least important in your work life. Decide how important it is in your work life and write the capitalized portion of that item on the line of the rating scale which represents its importance in your work life. Cross out that item.

Fifth, Now from the remaining list, select the item which is most important to your work life and repeat the process. Then select the item that is least important to your work life and repeat the process for that item. Do this until all of the items are written on the scale and all are checked off the list.

Note: You may choose to write more than one item on a line if you decide that they are of equal importance to your work life.

Extremely Important	15	______
	14	______
	13	______
Very Important	12	______
	11	______
	10	______
Important	9	______
	8	______
	7	______
Of Some Importance	6	______
	5	______
	4	______
Of Little Importance	3	______
	2	______
	1	______

Now, we would like you to tell us which choice you would make in the following situations.

33. Imagine that two jobs are available to you. Let's call them job A and job B. You have to take one of them.

JOB A	JOB B
If you take this job, you will have the same pay as you have now.	If you take this job, you will have the same pay as you have now.
You will decide yourself how to do your work.	There will be hardly any room for you to make decisions about your work and its procedures.

_______ It would be more or less the same to me to have either job.
_______ I would prefer job A.
_______ I would prefer job B.

*If job B is preferred, go to question 37.

34. Now let's say you have to take one of these two jobs:

JOB A	JOB B
If you take this job, you will have the same pay as you you have now.	If you take this job, you will have 10% higher pay than you have now.
You will decide yourself how to do your work.	There will be hardly any room for you to make decisions about your work and its procedures.

_______ It would be more or less the same to me to have either job.
_______ I would prefer job A.
_______ I would prefer job B.

*If job B is preferred, go to question 37.

35. Now imagine that you have to take one of these two jobs:

JOB A	JOB B
If you take this job, you will have the same pay as you have now.	If you take this job you will have 30% higher pay than you have now.
You will decide yourself how to do your work.	There will be hardly any room for you to make decisions about your work and its procedures.

_______ It would be more or less the same to me to have either job.
_______ I would prefer job A.
_______ I would prefer job B.

*If job B is preferred, go to question 37.

36. Now let's say you have to take one of these two jobs:

JOB A	JOB B
If you take this job, you will have the same pay as you have now.	If you take this job you will have 50% higher pay than you have now.
You will decide yourself how to do your work.	There will be hardly any room for you to make decisions about your work and its procedures.

_______ It would be more or less the same to me to have either job.
_______ I would prefer job A
_______ I would prefer job B

37. Now, let's say you have to take one of these two jobs:

JOB A	JOB B
If you take this job you will have the same pay as you have now.	If you take this job you will have the same pay as you have now.
In this job you will decide yourself how to do your work.	There will be hardly any room for you to make decisions about your work and its procedures.
You will fully use your skills and abilities.	There will be little opportunity for you to use your skills and abilities.
You will do something you really like.	You will not do something you really like.

_______ It would be more or less the same to me to have either job.
_______ I would prefer job A.
_______ I would prefer job B.

*If job B is preferred, go to question 41.

38. Now let's say you have to take one of these two jobs:

JOB A	JOB B
If you take this job you will have the same pay as you have now.	If you take this job you will have 10% higher pay than you have now.
In this job you will decide yourself how to do your work.	There will be hardly any room for you to make decisions about your work and its procedures.
You will fully use your skills and abilities.	There will be little opportunity for you to use your skills and abilities.
You will do something you really like.	You will not do something you really like.

_______ It would be more or less the same to me to have either job.
_______ I would prefer job A.
_______ I would prefer job B.

*If job B is preferred, go to question 41.

39. Now let's say you have to take one of these two jobs:

JOB A	JOB B
If you take this job you will have the same pay as you have now.	If you take this job you will have 30% higher pay than you have now.
In this job you will decide yourself how to do your work.	There will be hardly any room for you to make decisions about your work and its procedures.
You will fully use your skills and abilities.	There will be little opportunity for you to use your skills and abilities.
You will do something you really like.	You will not do something you really like.

_______ It would be more or less the same to me to have either job.
_______ I would prefer job A.
_______ I would prefer job B.

*If job B is preferred, go to question 41.

40. Now imagine that you have to take one of these two jobs:

JOB A	JOB B
If you take this job you will have the same pay as you have now.	If you take this job you will have 50% higher pay than you have now.
In this job you will decide yourself how to do your work.	There will be hardly any room for you to make decisions about your work and its procedures.
You will fully use your skills and abilities.	There will be little opportunity for you to use your skills and abilities.
You will do something you really like.	You will not do something you really like.

_______ It would be more or less the same to me to have either job.
_______ I would prefer job A.
_______ I would prefer job B.

41. Now let's say you have to take one of these two jobs:

JOB A	JOB B
This job will permit you to have as much leisure time as you have now.	This job will permit you to have less leisure time than you have now.
It will bring you the same pay as you have now.	It will bring you 10% higher pay than you have now.
There will be little opportunity for you to use your skills and abilities.	There will be little opportunity for you to use your skills and abilities.
You will not do something you really like.	You will not do something you really like.

_______ It would be more or less the same to me to have either job.
_______ I would prefer job A.
_______ I would prefer job B.

*If job B is preferred, go to question 43.

42. Now let's say you have to take one of these two jobs:

JOB A	JOB B
This job will permit you to have as much leisure time as you have now.	This job will permit you to have less leisure time than you have now.
It will bring you the same pay as you have now.	It will bring you 30% higher pay than you have now.
There will little opportunity for you to use your skills and abilities.	There will be little opportunity for you to use your skills and abilities.
You will not do something you really like.	You will not do something you really like.

_______ It would be more or less the same to me to have either job.
_______ I would prefer job A.
_______ I would prefer job B.

43. Now let's say you have to take one of these two jobs:

JOB A	JOB B
This job will permit you to have as much leisure time as you have now.	This job will permit you to have less leisure time than you have now.
It will bring you the same pay as you have now.	It will bring you the same pay as you have now.
There will be little opportunity for you to use your skills and abilities.	In this job you will fully use your skills and abilities.
You will not do something you really like.	You will do something you really like.

_______ It would be more or less the same to me to have either job.
_______ I would prefer job A.
_______ I would prefer job B.

*If job B is preferred, go to question 46.

44. Now imagine that you have to take one of these two jobs:

JOB A	JOB B
This job will permit you to have as much leisure time as you have now.	This job will permit you to have less leisure time than you have now.
It will bring you the same pay as you have now.	It will bring you 10% higher pay than you have now.
There will be little opportunity for you to use your skills and abilities.	In this job, you will fully use all your skills and abilities.
You will not do something you really like.	You will do something you really like.

_______ It would be more or less the same to me to have either job.
_______ I would prefer job A.
_______ I would prefer job B.

*If job B is prefered, go to question 46.

45. Now imagine that you have to take one of these two jobs:

JOB A	JOB B
This job will permit you to have as much leisure time as you have now.	This job will permit you to have less leisure time than you have now.
It will bring you the same pay as you have now.	It will bring you 30% higher pay than you have now.
There will be little opportunity for you to use your skills and abilities.	In this job you will fully use your skills and abilities.
You will not do something you really like.	You will do something you really like.

_______ It would be more or less the same to me to have either job.
_______ I would prefer job A.
_______ I would prefer job B.

46. And now the last choice about jobs A and B, you have to take one of these two jobs:

JOB A	JOB B
This job will permit you to have as much leisure time as you have now.	This job will permit you to have less leisure time than you have now.
It will bring you 30% higher pay than you have now.	It will bring you 30% higher pay than you have now.
There will be little opportunity for you to use your skills and abilities.	In this job you will fully use your skills and abilities.
You will not do something you really like.	You will do something you really like.

_______ It would be more or less the same to me to have either job.
_______ I would prefer job A.
_______ I would prefer job B.

47. Following are some work related statements that people might make. We would like you to decide whether you agree or disagree with each of these statements depending on your personal opinions. If you strongly agree with the statements, please mark the box on the far right; if you agree somewhat with the statements, mark the second box from the right; and so on.

	Strongly Disagree	Disagree	Agree	Strongly Agree
(a) If a worker's skills become outdated, his employer should be responsible for retraining and reemployment.	☐	☐	☐	☐
(b) It is the duty of every able-bodied citizen to contribute to society by working.	☐	☐	☐	☐
(c) The educational system in our society should prepare every person for a good job if they exert a reasonable amount of effort.	☐	☐	☐	☐
(d) Persons in our society should allocate a large portion of their regular income towards savings for their future.	☐	☐	☐	☐
(e) When a change in work methods must be made, a supervisor should be required to ask workers for their suggestions before deciding what to do.	☐	☐	☐	☐
(f) A worker should be expected to think up better ways to do his or her job.	☐	☐	☐	☐
(g) Every person in our society should be entitled to interesting and meaningful work.	☐	☐	☐	☐
(h) Monotonous, simplistic work is acceptable as long as the pay compensates fairly for it.	☐	☐	☐	☐
(i) A job should be provided to every individual who desires to work.	☐	☐	☐	☐
(j) A worker should value the work he or she does even if it is boring, dirty or unskilled.	☐	☐	☐	☐

48. Imagine that you won a lottery or inherited a large sum of money and could live comfortably for the rest of your life without working. What would you do concerning working?

___ (a) I would stop working.
___ (b) I would continue to work in the same job.
___ (c) I would continue to work but with changed conditions.

If (a), why would you stop working and what would you miss about working? ____________________

____

If (b), why would you continue working in the same job?

____

____

If (c), what are the changed conditions and why would you continue working? ____________________

____

49. Not everyone means the same thing when they talk about working. When do you consider an activity as working? Choose four statements from the list below which best define when an activity is "working."

___ if you do it in a working place
___ if someone tells you what to do
___ if it is physically strenuous
___ if it belongs to your task
___ if you do it to contribute to society
___ if, by doing it, you get the feeling of belonging
___ if it is mentally strenuous
___ if you do it at a certain time (e.g., from 8 until 5)
___ if it adds value to something
___ if it is not pleasant
___ if you get money for doing it
___ if you have to account for it
___ if you have to do it
___ if others profit by it

50. (a) If you were to start all over again, would you again choose your occupation or would you choose a different one?

_______ different occupation
_______ same occupation

(b) Would you recommend your occupation to your children for their work?

_______ no
_______ yes

Why would you make this recommendation? ____________________

____

51. Do you think that people's general attitude toward working will change in the next 10 years?

_______ no
_______ yes

If yes, what will be the nature and direction of change?

____

52. If you had to choose, which would you prefer? (Not applicable for self-employed or teachers.)

_______ stay in your present organization but with a different type of job.
_______ do the same type of job but with a different organization.

53. In your leisure time, how often do you do things that have nothing to do with work?

_______ never
_______ only occasionally
_______ sometimes
_______ often
_______ very often

54. If your company organized group activities outside of working hours, would you participate?

_______ no
_______ maybe
_______ yes

55. How often do you worry about work in your free time?

_______ never
_______ only occasionally
_______ sometimes
_______ often
_______ very often

Now some items concerning your plans about working in the future, about what you expect will happen in the future and what you would like to see happen in the future.

---

56. Do you intend to change jobs within the next 12 months?*

_______ no
_______ yes

If yes, what are you looking for in another job?_________

____

*For temporary workers, this means take a steady/fixed job.

57. Do you think it would be easy for you to find a similar job with another employer within the next 12 months?

_______ difficult
_______ not so easy
_______ somewhat easy
_______ easy
_______ very easy

58. Would you be willing to be retrained for a different job or occupation than you now have?

_______ under no conditions
_______ only if the economic situation forced me to
_______ under certain conditions, (please specify) _______
____

59. Do you intend to be retrained for a different job or occupation during the next 12 months?

_______ no
_______ yes

60. Do you intend to take part in further training related to your present job during the next 12 months?

_______ no
_______ yes
_______ I am already taking part.

61. Are you actively trying to be promoted within the next 12 months?

_______ no
_______ yes

62. Do you have any other significant plans regarding working during the next five years?

_______ no
_______ yes

If yes, what plans? ____
____

63. In the next 5 to 10 years, do you expect any societal developments which could endanger your employment?

_______ no
_______ yes

64. Are there any societal developments in the next 5 to 10 years which are likely to improve your employment situation or make it more secure?

_______ no
_______ yes

65. In the next few years, do you expect the level of pay for your job compared to pay for other jobs to:

_______ go down
_______ stay about the same
_______ go up

66. Compared to the present time, how important will work be to you in the next five to ten years?

_______ less important
_______ equal in importance
_______ more important

What are the reasons for this? ______________________________

____

67. Suppose people were able to work less hours for the same pay in the future, which alternative would be most preferable to you? (Pick one.)

_______ more holidays
_______ less working hours per day
_______ a free afternoon every week
_______ longer periods of education before beginning to work
_______ a year off for further study about every 10 years
_______ less working hours for older workers
_______ earlier retirement

68. If the general economic situation led to proposals to work less hours and earn proportionately less money, how would you feel about such proposals?

_______ I would be against them.
_______ I don't really care.
_______ I would be moderately in favor of them.
_______ I would be in favor of them.

Now, some final questions about you, about your background and about your family.

69. What is your age?

_______ years

70. What was the highest formal education which you completed? (Check one.)

_______ primary school
_______ secondary school or further vocational training
_______ some college or similar vocational training below university level
_______ university degree

71. Did you have a religious education?

_______ no
_______ yes

72. To what extent are you presently associated with a religion?

_______ no contact
_______ loose contact
_______ close contact

73. What was the highest formal education received by your parents?

(a) Father

_______ primary school
_______ secondary school
_______ some college
_______ univeristy degree

(b) Mother

_______ primary
_______ secondary school
_______ some college
_______ university degree

74. Concerning the community where you spent most of your childhood (to about age 14); was it primarily:

_______ city or big town
_______ village or small town
_______ rural

75. Concerning the community where you presently live; is it primarily:

_______ city or big town
_______ village or small town
_______ rural

76. Are you married and/or living with a partner in a joint household?

_______ no
_______ yes

If yes, is your partner:

_______ not employed and primarily a homemaker
_______ part time employment and homemaker
_______ employed full time
_______ other (specify) ______________________________

77. How many persons do you support financially (including yourself)?

_______ number

78. In general, how satisfied have you been with your life?

☐	☐	☐	☐	☐	☐	☐	☐	☐
Very Dissatisfied								Very Satisfied

- THE END -

THANK YOU VERY MUCH

INTERVIEWER CHECKLIST

To be completed for each respondent

Interviewer name ____________________

Date of Interview ____________________

Is respondent a citizen of this country? yes______ no________

City in which interview was done ____________________

Was interview conducted at: home___ workplace____ other _____

Sex of respondent: Male______ Female______

Target group to which respondent belongs____________________

If self-employed, check appropriate job type:
______craftsman
______service (non-craftsman)
______commercial (selling product)

Indicate nature and size of organization which employs the person:

______ public
______ private

Organization size at the location where person works:

______ under 100 employees
______ 100 - 299 employees
______ 300 - 999 employees
______ 1000 or over employees

Length of interview ______________minutes

To what extent did the respondent understand the questions?
___clearly understood, ___reasonably understood most questions, ___had difficulty with many questions, ___understood only a few questions.

Would you describe the respondent's cooperation in the interview as: ____high, ____ moderate, ____ low.

Interviewer comments about specific items in the interview (wording problems, understanding problems, resistance to answering)____________________

____

____

____

Interviewer comments about the respondent and/or the interview in general____________________

____

____

____

____

MOW - PROJECT MEMBER LIST

BELGIUM

Professor Pol Coetsier, State University of Ghent, Ghent;
Dr. Rie Spoelders-Claes, State University of Ghent, Ghent.

INDIA

Professor Sasi Misra, Indian Institute of Management, Ahmedabad.

ISRAEL

Dr. Itzhak Harpaz, University of Haifa, Mt. Carmel.

JAPAN

Professor Toshiko Futamura, Tokyo Metropolitan University, Tokyo;
Professor Juji Misumi, Osaka University, Suita, Osaka;
Dr. Makoto Takamiya, University of Tokyo, Tokyo, (Deceased).

NETHERLANDS

Dr. Erik Andriessen, IVA Institute of Social Research, Tilburg;
Professor Pieter J.D. Drenth, Free University, Amsterdam;
Dr. Rob van der Kooij, Free University, Amsterdam.

UNITED KINGDOM

Dr. Frank Heller, Tavistock Institute of Human Relations, London.

UNITED STATES

Professor George W. England, University of Oklahoma, Norman;
Professor William Whitely, University of Oklahoma, Norman.

WEST GERMANY

S. Antonio Ruiz Quintanilla, Technische Universitat Berlin, Berlin;
Professor Bernhard Wilpert, International Institute of Management, Berlin.

YUGOSLAVIA

Dr. Vojko A. Antoncic, University of Ljbublana, Cankarjeva;
Professor Veljko Rus, University of Ljbublana, Cankarjeva.

BIBLIOGRAPHY

Ajiferuke, M. and Boddewyn, J. (1970), Socioeconomic Indicators in Comparative Management. In: Administrative Science Quarterly 15: 453-458

Allport, F. (1933) Institutional Behavior, Chapel Hill, NC: The University of North Carolina Press

Allport, F.H. (1962) A Structuronomic Conception of Behavior: Individual and Collective. In: Journal of Abnormal and Social Psychology 64: 3-30

Andriessen, J.H.T.H. (1974) Veiligheid, een kwestie van motivatie

Asthana, H.S. (1956) Some Aspects of Personality Structuring in Indian (Hindu) Social Organization. In: Journal of Social Psychology 44

Azegami, H. (1953) The Development of the Concept of Occupation. In: I. Sakamoto, S. Nakano, K. Hatano and A. Yoda (Eds.) Educational Psychology Series 6, The Psychology of Occupational Guidance, Part 4: Kaneko Shobo (in Japanese)

Barker, R., and Schoggen, P. (1973) Qualities of Community Life, San Francisco: Jossey-Bass

Barzel, A. (1973) Der Begriff "Arbeit" in der Philosophie der Gegenwart, Frankfurt/M: Peter Lang

Becker, H., and Geer, B. (1966) Latent Culture: A Note on the Theory of Latent Social Roles. In: Administrative Science Quarterly 5: 304-313

Beehr, T. and Newman, J. (1978) Job Stress, Employee Health and Organizational Effectiveness: A Facet Analysis, Model and Literature Review. In: Personnel Psychology 31: 665-700

Bem, D.J. (1970) Beliefs, Attitudes, and Human Affairs, Belmont, CA: Brooks-Cole

Bhatnagar, Deepti (1977) Workers' Desire for Participation. In: Productivity 17: 579-590

Bishop, D., and Ikeda, M. (1970) Status and Role Factors in the Leisure Behavior of Different Occupations. In: Sociology and Social Research 54: 190-208

Bloom, W. (1961) Shift Work and the Sleep-Wakefulness Cycle. In: Personnel 38: 24-31

Blum, A. (1964) Social Structure, Social Class, and Participation in Primary Relationships. In: A. Shostak and N. Gomberd (Eds.) Blue-Collar World: Studies of the American Worker, Englewood Cliffs, NJ: Prentice-Hall 195-206

Buchholz, R. (1978) An Empirical Study of Contemporary Beliefs about Work in American Society. In: Journal of Applied Psychology 63: 219-227

Buckley, W. (1958) Social Stratification and Social Differentiation. In: American Sociological Review 23: 368-378

Burke, R.; Weir, T.; and DuWors, R. (1979) Type A Behavior of Administrators and Wives' Reports of Marital Satisfaction and Well-Being. In: Journal of Applied Psychology 64: 57-65

Campbell, D. (1975) On the Conflicts between Biological and Social Evolution and between Psychology and Moral Tradition. In: American Psychologist 30: 1103-1126

Caplow, T. (1954) The Sociology of Work, Minneapolis: University of Minnesota Press

Cattell, R. (1949) The Dimensions of Cultural Patterns by Factorization of National Characters. In: Journal of Abnormal and Social Psychology 44: 443-469

Champoux, J. (1976) Work and Non-Work: A Review of Theory and Empirical Research. In: Unpublished Monograph, University of California, Irvine

Chaudhuri, S.K. (1975) Internal vs. External Control: Attitudes Towards Work and Job Tension. In: National Labour Institute Bulletin 1: 14-19, New Delhi, India

Chinoy, E. (1955) Automobile Workers and the American Dream, Garden City, NY: Doubleday

Chowdhry, K.K. (1966) Social and Cultural Factors in Management Development in India. In: International Labour Review 94: 132-147

Coates, C. and Pellegrin, R. (1958) Executives and Supervisors: Informal Factors in Differential Bureaucratic Promotion. In: Administrative Science Quarterly 2: 200-215

Cottle, T. (1976) Perceiving Time, New York: Wiley

Dahrendorf, R. (1959) Class and Class Conflict in Industrial Society, Palo Alto, CA: Stanford University Press

Dam, van A. and Drenth, P.J.D. (1976) Hoger beroep; utikomsten over werk in inkomsten, COP/Vrije Universiteit

Davis, K. and Moore, W. (1945) Some Principles of Stratification. In: American Sociological Review 10: 242-249

Dayal, Iswar (1977) Change in Work Organization, Delhi: Concept Publishing

De, N.R. (1977) Participative Redesign of Work System and Enrichment of the Quality of Work Life. In: National Labour Institute Bulletin 3: 184-200 and 237-252

De, N.R. (1976) The Social Context of Work and Drop-out from Work. In: mimeo, National Labour Institute, New Delhi

De, N.R. (1977) Training Needs Assessment of Section Officers. In: mimeo, National Labour Institute, New Delhi

De, N.R. (1975) Work Commitment and Work Ethics in Public Enterprises. In: National Labour Institute Bulletin 1

De, N.R. and Tandon, Rajesh (1976) The Indian Elites: An Exploratory Study. In: Indian Journal of Industrial Relations 12

Doeringer, P. and Piore, M. (1971) Internal Labor Markets and Manpower Analysis, Lexington, MA: D.C. Heath

Domhoff, W. (1967) Who Rules America, Englewood Cliffs, NJ: Prentice-Hall

Dubin, R. (1956) Industrial Workers' Worlds: A Study of the 'Central Life Interest' of Industrial Workers. In: Social Problems 3: 131-142

Dubin, R. (1973) Work and Non-Work: Institutional Perspectives In: M. Dunnette (Ed.) Work and Non-Work in the Year 2001, Monterey, CA: Brooks-Cole

Dubin, R. (1973) Work in Modern Society. In: R. Dubin (Ed.) Handbook of Work, Organization and Society, Chicago: Rand-McNally 5-35

Dubin, R.; Champoux, J. and Porter, L. (1975) Central Life Interests and Organizational Commitment of Blue-Collar and Clerical Workers. In: Administrative Science Quarterly 20 411-421

Dunham, R. (1977) Shift Work: A Review and Theoretical Analysis. In: Academy of Management Review 2 624-634

Economic Planning Agency, Bureau of National Life (1977) Japanese Concept of Education and Occupation (in Japanese)

Education Ministry (1971) A Survey on the Guidance for Junior High School and Senior High School Students (in Japanese)

England, G.W. (1968)Personal Value Systems of American Managers. In: Academy of Management Journal 10: 53-68

England, G.W. (1976) The Manager and His Values: An International Perspective from The United States, Japan, Korea, India, and Australia, Cambridge, MA: Ballinger

England, G.W.; Harpaz, I.; and Horvath, I. (1977) Worker Satisfaction: Its Nature and Causes among Production Workers in Fifteen Countries. In: unpublished monograph

Erikson, E. (1963 2nd ed.) Childhood and Society, New York: Norton

Fasse, L. (1978) West Germany Work Humanization Projects Underway. European Industrial Relations Review 52: 20-21

Faunce, W. and Dubin, R. (1975) Individual Investment in Working and Living. In: L. Davis and A. Cherns (Eds.) The Quality of Working Life 1: New York: Free Press

Frankl, V. (1963) Man's Search for Meaning, New York: Washington Square Press

Friedman, E. and Havighurst, R. (1954) The Meaning of Work and Retirement, Chicago: University of Chicago Press

Frost, P. and Jamal, M. (1979) Shift Work, Attitudes and Reported Behavior: Some Associations between Individual Characteristics and Hours of Work and Leisure. In: Journal of Applied Psychology 64: 77-81

Fuji Film Labor Union (1962) The Sense of Labor and Existing Conditions of Fuji Film Labor Union Members (in Japanese)

Fujimoto, K.(1969) A Theory of Occupations. In: T. Ibukiyama (Ed.) The Method and Problem of Industrial Psychology, Chapter 2, Mineruba Shobo (in Japanese)

Fujiwara, K. (1950) The Concept of Occupation of Junior High-School Students. In: Adolescent Psychology 12 (in Japanese)

Geffen, van L.M.H.J. (1977) De keuze van werk, Culemborg: Schoolpers

Goldthorpe, J.; Lockwood, D.; Bechofer, F.; and Platt, J. (1968) The Affluent Worker: Industrial Attitudes and Behavior, Cambridge, MA: Cambridge University Press

Gomez, L.R. and Pettman, P.J. (1978) International and Domestic Differences in Work Values. unpublished manuscript

Guion, R.M. and Landy, F. J. (1972) The Meaning of Work and the Motivation to Work. In: Organizational Behavior and Human Performance 17: 308-339

Hackman, J. and Suttle, J. (1977) Improving Life at Work: Behavioral Science Approaches to Organizational Change, Santa Monica, CA: Goodyear

Hall, D. (1972) A Model of Coping with Role Conflict: The Role Behavior of College Educated Women. In: Administrative Science Quarterly 17: 471-486

Hall, D. (1976) Careers in Organizations, Pacific Palisades, CA: Goodyear

Hall, D. (1975) Pressures from Work, Self and Home in the Life Stages of Married Women. In: Journal of Vocational Behavior 6: 121-132

Hall, R. (1975 2nd ed.) Occupations and the Social Structure, Englewood Cliffs, NJ: Prentice-Hall

Hartmann, H. (1970) Codetermination in West Germany. In: Industrial Relations 9: 137-147

Hazama, H. (1970) Japanesque Management--Merits and Demerits of Group-Orientedness. Nikkei Shisho (in Japanese)

Hazama, H. (1967) The Sense of Labor among Automation Factory Workers. In: Bulletin of Faculty of Literature, Tokyo Educational University (in Japanese)

Heneman, H.G., Jr. (1973) Work and Non-work: Historical Perspectives. In: M. Dunnette (Ed.) Work and Non-work in the Year 2001, Monterey, CA: Brooks-Cole

Hoerning K.H. (Hrsg.) (1972) Der "neue" Arbeiter. Zum Wandel sozialer Schichtstrukturen, Frankfurt/M. Fischer Taschenbuch Verlag

Hofstede, G. (1973) The Importance of Being Dutch: National and Occupational Differences in Work Goal Importance. In: P.J.D. Drenth, P.J. Willems, and C.J. De Wolff: Arbeidsen organisatiepsychologie, Deventer: Kluwer

Hofstede, G. (1977) Within-Culture and Between-Culture Component Structures of Work Goals in a Heterogeneous Population, working paper 77-26, European Institute for Advanced Studies, Brussels

Hokkaido Development Bank (1976) A Survey on the Sense of Occupation Among Newly Recruited Employees in Hokkaido (in Japanese)

Holmstrom, M. (1976), South Indian Factory Workers, Cambridge: Cambridge University Press

Homans, G. (1961), Social Behavior: Its Elementary Forms, New York: Harcourt, Brace

Hoolwerf, G.; Thierry, H.K.; and Drenth, P.J.D. (1974), Ploegenarbeid en bedrijfspsychologisch onderzoek, Leiden: Stenford Kroese

House, J. (1974), Occupation Stress and Coronary Heart Disease: A Review and Theoretical Integration. In: Journal of Health and Social Behavior 15: 12-27

Hsu, F.L.K. (1963), Clan, Caste and Club

Huizinga, G. (1970), Maslow's Need Hierarchy in the Work Situation, Groningen: Wolters-Noordhoff

Hulin, C. (1971), Individual Differences and Job Enrichment: The Case against General Treatments. In: J.R. Maher (Ed.), New Perspectives in Job Enrichment, New York: Van Nostrand: 159-191

Hulin, C.L., (1966), Effects of Community Characteristics on Measures of Job Satisfaction. In: Journal of Applied Psychology 50: 185-192

Hulin, C.L. and Blood, M.R. (1968), Job Enlargement, Individual Differences, and Worker Responses. In: Psychological Bulletin 69: 41-55

Institute for Occupations (1976), Occupations and Life Cycle of Women -- A Report on the Survey Concerning Their Job Turnover (in Japanese)

Ishikawa, A. (1975), Social Change and the Sense of Labor -- Its Changing Process in Japan During the Post World War II Period: The Japanese Labor Association (in Japanese)

Iwauchi, R. (1975), The Sociology of Occupational Life: Gakubun sha. (in Japanese)

Jakubowski, T. (1968), Meaning of Work Among Middle Managers (unpublished), Amherst: University of Massachusetts

Japan Industrial Training Association (1972), The Problems and Sentiments of Japanese Workers (in Japanese)

Japan Productivity Center (1969-1977), The Survey Reports on the Sense of Working (in Japanese)

Japan Sociology Association (1957), A Stratified Structure of Japanese Society (in Japanese)

Japan Steel Federation (1974), A Survey on the Opinions of Young Steel Workers (in Japanese)

Kahn, R. (1972), The Meaning of Work: Interpretation and Proposals for Measurement. In: Campbell, A. and P. Converse (Eds), The Human Meaning of Social Change, New York: Russel Sage Foundation: 159-203

Kakar, S. (1974), Personality and Authority in Work, Bombay: Somaiya

Kalro, A., and Misra, S. (1973), Salience of Job Instrumentality Factors in Pre and Postdecision Organizational Choice. In: Indian Journal of Industrial Relations 8: 407-413

Kando, T., and Summers, W. (1971), The Impact of Work on Leisure: Toward a Paradigm and Research Strategy. In: Pacific Sociological Review 14: 310-327

Kanungo, R.N.; Misra, S.B.; and Dayal, I. (1975), Relationship of Job Involvement to Perceived Importance and Satisfaction of Employee Needs. In: International Review of Applied Psychology 24: 49-59

Kaplan, H.R., and Tausky, C. (1974), The Meaning of Work among the Hard Core Unemployed. In: Pacific Sociological Review 17: 185-198

Katz, E., and Gurevitch, M. (1976), The Secularization of Leisure: Culture and Communication in Israel, Cambridge: Harvard University Press

Kerr, C.; Dunlop, J.; Harbison,F.; and Meyers, C. (1964), Industrialism and Industrial Man, New York: Oxford University Press

Kesteren, Van (1977), Inventarisatie Arbeidsmarkt onderzoek, Amsterdam: SISWO

Krupp, S. (1961), Pattern in Organizational Analysis: A Critical Examination, New York: Holt, Rinehart and Winston

Kubo, K., and Meito, K. (1971), The Management of the Life Worth Living (in Japanese)

Kyushu Productivity Center (1977), The Sense of Working, (Newly Recruited Employees in 1977) (in Japanese)

Labor Ministry (1970), A Survey on Workers' Living (In Japanese)

Labor Ministry (1971), A Survey on Worker's Living (In Japanese)

Labor Ministry (1974), Laborers Overall Welfare Survey (In Japanese)

Labor Ministry Women's and Minors' Bureau (1975), The Progress of Women During the Past 30 Years (In Japanese)

Labor Ministry, Division of Statistical Information, Japanese Concept of Working (In Japanese)

Labor Ministry, Employment Stabilization Bureau (1958), Glossary of Occupational Terms (In Japanese)

Land, K., and Pampel, F. (1977), Indicators and Models of Change in the American Occupational System, 1947-1973. In: Social Indicators Research 4: 1-23

Lehr, U. (1969), Die Frau im Beruf, Eine psychologische Analyse der weiblichen Berufsrolle, Frankfurt/M. Bonn: Athenaum

Leisure Development Center (1974), Japanese Structure of Leisure, Diamond sha (In Japanese)

Levinson, D.J.; Darrow, C.; Klien, E.; Levinson, M.; and McKee, B. (1974), The Psychological Development of Men in Early Adulthood and the Mid-life Transition. In: D.T. Ricks, A. Thomas, M. Roff (Eds.), Life Span Research in Psychopathology 3, Minneapolis: University of Minnesota Press

Lipset, S., and Bendix, R. (1959), Social Mobility in Industrial Society, Berkeley, CA: University of California Press

Locke, E. (1976), The Nature and Causes of Job Satisfaction. In: Dunnette, M.D. (Ed.), Handbook of Industrial and Organizational Psychology, Chicago: Rand McNally: 1297-1350

Lodahl, T, and Kejner, M. (1965), The Definition and Measurement of Job Involvement. In: Journal of Applied Psychology 49: 24-33

Loether, H.J. (1964), The Meaning of Work and Adjustment to Retirement. In: A.B. Shostad and W. Gomberg (Eds.), Blue Collar World, Englewood Cliffs, NJ: Prentice Hall

Maccoby, Michael (1976), The Gamesman, New York: Simon and Schuster

Mannari, H. (1973), Automation and Workers' Alienation. In: H. Mannari (Ed.), A Study of New Workers -- The Innovation of Industrial Structure and Labor Problems: Hakuto shobo, (In Japanese)

Mannheim, B. (1975), A Comparative Study of Work Centrality, Job Rewards, and Satisfaction. In: Sociology of Work and Occupations 2: 79-102.

Mannheim, B., and Cohen, A. (1978), Multivariate Analysis of Factors Affecting Work Centrality of Occupational Categories. In: Human Relations

Mannheim, B., and Rein, J. (1975), Work Centrality in Different Age Groups: Paper presented at the Tenth International Congress of Gerontology, Jerusalem

Mannheim, B.; Chomsky, J.; and Cohen, A. (1972), Work Centrality, Rewards and Role Strains of Israeli Male Occupational Groups, Haifa: Israel Center for The Study of Man at Work, Technion Research and Development Foundation

Manpower Report of the President (1977), Washington, D.C.: U.S. Government Printing Office

March, J., and Simon, H. (1959), Organizations, New York: John Wiley

Mathur, Kuldip (1972), Bureaucratic Response to Development, Delhi: National

Maurer, J.G. (1968), Work as a 'Central Life Interest' of Industrial Supervisors. In: Academy of Management: 329-339

McGrath, J. (1976), Stress and Behavior in Organizations. In: Dunnett, M.D. (Ed.), Handbook of Industrial and Organizational Psychology, Chicago: Rand McNally: 1351-1395

Meade, R., and Singh, L. (1970), Motivation and Progress Effects on Psychological Time in Subcultures of India. In: The Journal of Social Psychology 80: 3-10

Mehta, Prayag (1977), Employee Motivation and Work Satisfaction in Public Enterprise. In: Vikalpa 2

Mehta, Prayag (1978), Work Motivation in Indian Public Sector. In: National Labour Institute Bulletin 4

Meissner, M. (1971), The Long Arm of the Job: A Study of Work and Leisure. In: Industrial Relations 10: 239-260

Mills, C. (1956), White Collar, New York: Oxford University Press

Misra, B.B. (1977), The Bureaucracy in India, Delhi: Oxford University Press

Miyazaki Prefecture Youth Problem Consultative Council (1976), A Survey on the Sense of Working Youth (In Japanese)

Momoeda, S., and Fujimoto, K. (1946), The Evaluation of Occupation by Junior High School Students. In: Japanese Journal of Psychology 2 (In Japanese)

Morris, R., and Murphy, R. (1959), The Situs Dimension in Occupational Structure. In: American Sociological Review 24: 231-239

Morse, N., and Weiss, R. (1955), The Function and Meaning of Work and the Job. In: American Sociological Review 20: 191-198

Motoyoshi, S. (1975), A Prospect of the Future Occupational Life -- Human Labor in Changing Society. In: R. Iwauchi (Ed.), The Sociology of Occupational Life, Chapter 9, Gakubun sha (In Japanese)

Munchow, U. (1973), Das Bild des arbeiters in der proletarischen Selbstdarstellung, Zur bedeutung der fruhen Arbeiterbiographie. In: Weimarer Beitrage, jg. 19: 110-135

Nagamachi, M. (1973), A Design of Job Enrichment, Diamond sha (In Japanese)

Nakamura, M. (1950), The Concept of Occupation of Junior High School Students. In: Occupational Guidance 7 (In Japanese)

National Life Research Institute (1968), A Survey on the Sense of Living (In Japanese)

NHK Broadcasting Public Opinion Survey Institute (1968), Japanese Concept of Occupation -- Based on the National Public Opinion Survey (In Japanese)

Nojima, C. (1950), The Problems of Adolescents about the Occupational Choices. In: Adolescent Psychology 12 (In Japanese)

Odaka, K. (1947), A Service to the Work. In: Ningen (In Japanese)

Odaka, K. (1973), Industrial Sociology, Revised, Diamond sha (In Japanese)

Odaka, K. (1941), Occupational Sociology, Iwanami shoten (In Japanese)

Odaka, K. (1953), Occupational Sociology, Revised, Futumura shoten (In Japanese)

Odaka, K. (1970), The Ethics of Occupation, Chuokoron sha (In Japanese)

Odaka, K. (1963), The Science of Human Relations in Industry, Yuhikaku (In Japanese)

Odaka, K (1970), Work and Leisure: The Case of Japanese Industrial Workers. In: Transactions of the Sixth World Congress of Sociology 3: 169-188

Okamoto, H. (1973), Occupational Society and Life Structure. In: H. Kaneko (Ed.), Work Place and Occupational Society, Chapter 1, Gakuyo shobo (In Japanese)

Orzack, L. (1969), Work as a 'Central Life Interest' of Professionals. In: Social Problems 7: 125-132

Parker, S. (1971), The Future of Work and Leisure, New York: Praeger

Parker, S., and Smith, M. (1976), Work and Leisure. In: R. Dubin (Ed.), Handbook of Work, Organization, and Society, Chicago: Rand-McNally: 37-62

Parker, S.R. (1965), Work and Non-Work in Three Occupations. In: Sociological Review 13: 65-67

Pillardy, E. (1973), Arbeit und Alter, Eine Soziologische Untersuchung uber die bedeutung der Arbeit nach der pensionierung, Stuttgart: Enke

Polayni, M. (1962), Personal Knowledge: Toward a Post-Critical Philosophy, New York: Harper

Porat, A., and Ryterband, E. (1974), Career Preference, Choice and Job Attainment for Members of Minority Groups. In: H. Fronkin and J. Sherwood (Eds.), Integrating the Organization, New York: Free Press

Porter L., and Lawler, E. (1968), Managerial Attitudes and Performance, Homewood, IL: Dorsey Press

Prime Minister's Office (1972), Survey on Senses of World Youth, (In Japanese)

Prime Minister's Office (1969), The Sense of Youth -- The Sense of Living, Society and Occupation (In Japanese)

Prime Minister's Office, Youth Affairs Bureau (1976), Survey on Young People's Sense of Solidarity, Etc., (In Japanese)

Rabinowitz, S., and Hall, D. (1978), Organizational Research on Job Involvement. In: Psychological Bulletin 85: 265-288

Radhakrishnan, S. (1948), Bhagavadgita, Britain: George Allen and Urwin

Rao, T.V. (1978), Psychology of Work: Individual in Organization. In: Indian Council of Social Science: Survey of Research in Psychology

Rao, V. Rukmini (1977), Attitudes Toward Quality of Work Life, Family Life and Change, mimeo, New Delhi: National Labour Institute

Riley, M., and Riley, J. (1954), Notes on a Comceptual Model. In: M. Riley, J. Riley, and J. Toby (Eds.), Sociological Studies in Scale Analysis, New Brunswick, NJ: Rutgers University Press

Roberts, K.H., and Glick, W.H. (1979), Missing Persons in Cross-National Research: Part-Time Workers. In: Academy Of Management Convention, Atlanta

Robinson, J.; Athanasiou, R.; and Head, K. (1969), Measures of Occupational Attitudes and Occupational Characteristics, Ann Arbor: Institute for Social Research, The University of Michigan

Rokeach, M. (1973), The Nature of Human Values, New York: The Free Press

Ruch, F. (1967, 7th edition), Psychology and Life, Glenview, IL: Scott Foresman

Sales, S. (1969), Organizational Role as a Risk Factor in Coronary Disease. In: Administrative Science Quarterly 14: 325-336

Schuler, R. (1980), Definition and Conceptualization of Stress in Organizations. In: Organization Behavior and Human Performance 25: 184-215

Sells, S. (1970), On the Nature of Stress. In: J.E. McGrath (Ed.), Social and Psychological Factors in Stress, New York: Holt, Rinehart and Winston

Seyle, H. (1956), The Stress of Life, New York: McGraw-Hill

Sharma, B.R. (1968), Commitment to Industrial Work. In: Indian Journal of Industrial Relations 4

Sharma, B.R. (1971), Company Satisfaction. In: Indian Journal of Industrial Relations 7

Sharma, B.R. (1974), The Indian Industrial Worker, Delhi: Vikas Publishing House

Sharma, B.R., and Dayal, Ishwar (1975), The Meaning of Work of Bank Employees. In: Management and Labour Studies 1

Sharma, K.N., et al. (1964), Job Satisfaction of Workers in Textile Mills. In: Productivity 5

Sheth, N.R. (1977), For a Sociology of Indian Workers. In: Social Action 27: 353-368

Shimmon, S. (1966), Concepts of Work. In: Occupational Psychology 40: 195-201

Silverman, D. (1970), The Theory of Organizations, London: Heineman

Singh, N.P., and Wherry, R.J. (1970), Ranking of Job Factors by Factory Workers in India. In: Personnel Psychology 81: 145-149

Sinha, J.B.P. (1978), Superior-Subordinate Relationship and Alienation. In: National Labour Institute Bulletin 4: 85-89

Smith, P.; Kendall, L.; and Hulin, C. (1969), The Measurement of Satisfaction in Work and Retirement, Chicago: Rand-McNally

Statistical and Mathematical Institute (1975), The Tertiary Japanese National Traits, Shiseido (In Japanese)

Steers, R.M., and Porter, L.W. (1975), Motivation and Work Behavior, New York: McGraw-Hill

Stichting Wetenschappelijk Onderzoek Vakcentrales (1975), De plaats der arbeid, Deel I., Utrech

Super, D.E. (1978), Career Development: Exploration and Planning. In: Annual Review of Psychology 29: 333-372

Super D.E. (1957), The Psychology of Careers, New York: Harper and Row

Sutaria, Rupande (1977), Motivation to Work. In: Indian Management 16

Swedish Labour Court Ruling on 'Sympathy' Strikes (1978). In: European Industrial Relations Review 52

Szalsi, A. (1972), The Use of Time: Daily Activities of Urban and Suburban Populations in Twelve Countries, The Hague: Mouton

Takeuchi, H. (1975), Man and Occupation. In: R. Iwauchi (Ed.), The Sociology of Occupation, Chapter 2, Gakubun sha (In Japanese)

Takezawa, S. (1975), Humanization of Labor, Overall Labor Institute (In Japanese)

Tandon, Rajesh (1978), Impact of Organizational Development on Underorganized Communities. In: Unpublished Ph.D. Dissertation, Cleveland: Case Western Reserve University

TASK Leisure Problem Research Association (1974), The Concept of Leisure and Entertainment of Blue-Collar Workers (In Japanese)

Tausky, C. (1969), Meanings of Work among Blue-Collar Men. In: Pacific Sociological Review 12: 49-55

Tausky, C., and Dubin, R. (1965), Career Anchorage: Managerial Mobility Motivations. In: American Sociological Review 30: 725-735

Thierry, H.K. (1968), Loont de prestatie beloning? Assen: Van Gorkum

Thompson, J.; Avery, R; and Carlson, R. (1962), Occupations, Personnel and Careers, Pittsburgh: Administrative Science Center, University of Pittsburgh

Thurman, J. (1977), Job Satisfaction: An International Overview. In: International Labour Review 117: 249-267

Tilgher, A. (1962), Work Through the Ages. In: S. Nosow and W.H. Form (Eds.), Man, Work and Society, New York: Basic Books

Tokyo Metropolitan Government Labor Bureau (1971), A Survey on the Occupational Training (In Japanese)

Triandis, H.; Kilty, K.; Shanmugan, A.; Tanaka, Y.; and Vassiliou, V. (1972), Cognitive Structures and the Analysis of Values. In: H. Triandis (Ed.), The Analysis of Subjective Culture, New York: Wiley: 181-261

Tsuzuki, A. (1954), A Study about the Formation of the Concept of Occupation (1). In: Bulletin of Faculty of Education, Nagoya Univeristy 1: 101-119 (In Japanese)

Tumin, M. (1963), On Equality. In: American Sociological Review 28: 13-26

Upjohn Institute for Employment Research (1973), Work in America, Cambridge, MA: MIT Press

Van Maanen, J. (1976), Breaking In: Socialization to Work. In: R. Dubin (Ed.), Handbook of Work, Organization and Society, Chicago: Rand-McNally: 67-130

Wallraff, G. (1970), Industriereportagen, Reinbek Bei Hamburg: Rowohlt Taschenbuch Verlag

Walton, R., and McKersie, R. (1965), A Behavioral Theory of Labor Negotiations, New York: McGraw-Hill

Weick, K. (1969), The Social Psychology of Organizing, Reading, MA: Addison-Wesley

Weiss, R., and Kahn, R. (1959), On the Evaluation of Work among American Men, Unpublished Manuscript

Weiss R.S., and Kahn, R.L. (1969), Definitions of Work and Occupation. In: Social Problems 8: 142-151

Wezel, J.A.M. van; Buckens, A.L.J. van; Vissers, A.M.C.: Wentink, A.A.L.G.; and Zanders, K.L.G. (1976), De verdeling en de waardering van de arbeid, Tilburg: IVA

Whitehill, A.M., and Takezawa, S. (1968), The Other Worker, Honolulu: East-West Center Press

Whitely, W.T. (1977), The Relationship of Managerial Values and Decision Making: A Cross-National Investigation. In: Unpublished doctoral dissertation, University of Minnesota

Wilensky, H. (1961), Orderly Careers and Social Participation. In: American Sociological Review 26: 521-539

Wilensky, H. (1964), Varieties of Work Experience. In: H. Bobrow (Ed.), Man in a World of Work, Boston: Houghton Mifflin: 125-154

Wilensky, H. (1960), Work, Careers, and Social Integration. In: International Social Science Journal 12: 543-560

Yagi, M. (1972), The Modern Occupation and Labor. In: Modern Sociology Research Series 14, Seishin sobo (In Japanese)

Yoshida, N., and Kanda, M. (1974), The Sense and Living of Modern Women, NHK Books (In Japanese)

Zanders, H.L.G.; Buckens, A.L.J. van; and Berkel, J.J.C. van (1977), Kwaliteit van arbeid, Tilburg: IVA

Zawadski, B. and Lazarsfeld, P. (1935), The Psychological Consequences of Unemployment. In: Journal of Social Psychology 6: 224-251

Zibler, E., and Child, I. (1969), Socialization. In: G. Lindzey and E. Aronson (Eds.), The Handbook of Social Psychology (2nd ed), Reading, Mass: Addison-Wesley: 450-589

Zweig, F. (1952), The British Worker, Baltimore: Penguin

Zweig, F. (1961), The Worker in an Affluent Society, New York: Free Press

NOTES

1. The present paper was written and presented by George W. England, Director, Center for Economic and Management Research and Professor of Management, College of Business Administration, University of Oklahoma, on behalf of the international team of MOW researchers and is really a product of the efforts of all of the team. Names of researchers and their institutional affiliations precede the reference section.

2. We have also reviewed the following bodies of literature but have found them less useful for our purposes: job satisfaction (e.g., Locke, 1976); job involvement or work orientation (e.g., Lodahl and Keyner, 1965; Goldthorpe, et al., 1968; Hulin, 1971; Rabinowitz and Hall, 1978); values and value systems (e.g. Rokeach, 1973; England, 1976; Whitely, 1977; Buchholtz, 1978); work, non-work and leisure (e.g., Parker, 1965; Kando and Summers, 1971; Champoux, 1976); the quality of working life (e.g., Davis and Cherns, 1975).

Social Responsibility of Business Firms and Social Reporting

Bikki Jaggi

ABSTRACT

The paper first examines social contract and quality of life arguments to determine whether enough justification exists to support the concept of corporate social responsibility. Different factors which led to the awareness of corporate social responsibility are discussed to identify the forces which played an important role in the development of corporate social responsibility in developed countries. The paper then evaluates various formats suggested to report social information to outside users. Finally, the goal orientation in social reporting is critically examined. Deutsche Shell's report is used for evaluation of this approach.

INTRODUCTION

Increasing public pressure through consumer groups and several legislative actions at federal, state and local levels have made corporations more aware of their social responsibility, especially environmental social responsibility. As a result of these pressures, economic growth is no longer the only objective which industrialized countries strive to accomplish. Along with economic goals, social goals have started receiving increasing attention and several issues related to the "quality of life" are being addressed by policy makers. This new social awareness at the corporate and society level has generated demand for information relating to the social impact of corporate activities. Several methods and techniques have been suggested to measure and communicate social information to users. This paper briefly discusses factors leading to the awareness of corporate social responsibility, and evaluates suggested social reporting models, especially those related to goal-oriented social reporting.

CORPORATE SOCIAL RESPONSIBILITY

Corporate social responsibility has been vigorously debated during the 1970s.[1] Those who believe in a policy of complete laisse faire, led by Milton Friedman[2], argued against business corporations getting involved in social responsibility-related activities. They consider the main purpose of businesses is to make profit and social issues do not fall within their domain. Governmental agencies are supposed to deal with social issues, when and where necessary. Thus, according to the opponents of corporate social responsibility, there is no justification for corporations to assume any social responsibility.

This 1970s debate, however, indicates that opponents' view represent minority views, which are not shared by society or even by a majority of businesses. Contrary to their views, social concerns have generated a considerable awareness, and corporations are recognizing that society expects greater socially responsible behavior from them. The expectation of socially responsible behavior from corporations can be justified on several grounds. The following two arguments have been especially used to support corporate social responsibility: (1) social contract argument and (2) quality of life argument.

Social contract argument

Though the social contract argument surfaced in several discussions relating to corporate social responsibility, it was formalized by Ramanathan.[3] Expanding on the idea of external diseconomies,[4] Ramanathan developed a comprehensive theoretical work on "social reporting", which uses the concept of a social contract.

The social contract argument is based on the notion that business firms do not exist in a vacuum, instead they are a part of society, which creates and supports them. Furthermore, corporations owe their existence to laws which have been developed by society. Thus, society's continued support for the existence of businesses may be dependent upon their performance which is considered socially desirable. These arguments imply that there is an implicit contract between businesses and society which requires socially desirable behavior from firms in return for rewards. If businesses engage in socially undesirable behavior, society may be forced to take steps to penalize such businesses. The steps may include boycott of their products and services, modification of existing laws or development of new laws to restrict activities of such businesses.

The contract argument requires development of certain criteria which can be used for evaluating corporate social performance to judge whether businesses' social behavior meets society's expectations. Social scientists have been attempting to develop "social goals", (also termed "social indicators") which would be analogous to economic indicators.[5] Once the macro level criteria are available, it is argued that micro level criteria applicable to a specific firm can be easily developed and adopted for social reporting. Unfortunately, despite sustained efforts, there has been no consensus of opinion with regard to social goals.

In the absence of social goals at the macro level, an alternative approach is to develop social goals at the micro level. Firms should establish their social goals depending upon the nature of their business and prepare social reports to show the degree of accomplishment of these goals. This approach however needs certain guidelines so that a comparative analysis can be made across different firms with regard to their social performance. Therefore, a general framework for social goals and social reporting would be desirable. The National Association of Accountants has suggested a general framework in this regard.[6] The proposal suggests the following general broad categories for social reporting: (1) Community involvement, (2) Human resources, (3) Physical resources and environmental contributions, and (4) Product and Service contributions.

At the practical level, several firms have attempted to develop social goals for social reporting. German Shell's approach in this regard can be considered to provide a better basis for the development of social reporting. Given the state of the art, an optimal approach for developing social goals at this time would be for each firm to establish socially desirable goals within the general framework suggested by the National Association of Accountants. These goals can then be used as benchmarks for evaluation of firm's social performance.

Despite the intuitive appeal of the social contract argument, the validity of the underlying assumption of this concept has been challenged. It has been asserted that the social contract notion is based on ambigious corporate legal rights and obligations which are not enforceable by law.[7] Furthermore, the notion is considered to be too narrow to capture the true nature of the relationship between businesses and society. The opponents of this concept believe that the firm as a social institution exists not as a matter of right, but as a matter of privilege. This relationship therefore cannot properly be depicted by the social contract concept. Since the social contract approach is not capable of explaining the true nature of the relationship between society and corporations, the concept is considered to be inadequate and unrealistic for development of social reporting objectives and reporting formats.

The above criticism is valid because this concept is not capable of depicting the true relationship between society and businesses and corporate rights and obligations are no where specifically defined. The concept is however useful because it provides a general framework to explain the relationship between society and businesses and it can serve as the basis for further research in this area.

Quality of life argument

Another argument which brought awareness of corporate social responsibility relates to the "quality of life". The social costs of economic development, which have been increasing at staggering proportions, started affecting different aspects of the quality of life. The increase in social costs and realization of quality of life issues resulted in a shift of society's attitude toward industrialization. Society started perceiving business as a villian, responsible for several social ills. Business was perceived to maximize profit by exploiting environmental and social systems. These perceptions and attitudes forced society to revaluate their expectations from business. It was realized that increased economic development at all costs would not be desirable. Only industrial development which does not reduce the quality of life should be encouraged.

Several factors contributed to the shift in society's attitude toward business. Some of them are as follows:

1. The power of labor unions resulted in inclusion of quality of life issues in labor negotiations during 1970s. These factors included safety in the work environment.

2. The emergence of the consumer movement in the United States led to a greater awareness of corporate social responsibility with regard to safety of products. This awareness resulted in several legislative actions designed to protect consumers from corporate abuse. Court cases have generally supported the consumer cause.

3. Damage to the physical environment in the form of air and water pollution alarmed society and resulted in a movement toward protecting the environment. In the early stages of industrial development, the impact of corporate activities on the environment was not so severe and was tolerated. The cumulative effect of these activities has been disastrous and environmental protection has become an important issue. These concerns have led to passage of several environmental protection laws.

4. Society started recognizing that natural resources are not unlimited and their unrestricted use will result in complete depletion soon. Thus, preservation of these resources assumed new importance.

5. The impetus to the movement of social justice in 1970s brought pressure on businesses to guarantee the right for equal employment opportunities, etc.

The debate of issues relating to the "quality of life" concern indicated that if businesses did not behave socially responsible, their activities will have a negative impact on society. This realization changed society's attitude toward business, and society demanded higher corporate social responsibility. As a result of this change, relations between society and business firms became strained. The change triggered a sense of frustration for corporate management in the early stages of this awareness, and created an uncertainty with regard to the role of business in the society. Later, recognizing realities, business feared extreme reaction from society if they did not address itself to the quality of life issues. In order to avoid confrontation with society, business firms recognized a need for a fresh start of cooperation with society. This realization encouraged firms to accept social responsibility.

SOCIAL REPORTING FRAMEWORK

An evaluation of corporate social performance requires availability of reliable information relating to social performance of the business. The availability of this information in turn will depend upon two factors - development of an appropriate data base and design of optimal reporting systems. Without development of an appropriate data base, relevant and timely social information is less likely to become available. Despite importance of the social information data base, not much theoretical work exists on its development. This being a pragmatic area, it is probably assumed that firms will be able to develop data bases according to their needs.

Most research in the English language literature relates to development of a framework for reporting social information. Several approaches have been suggested to develop a reporting format. Unfortunately, there is no concensus of opinion with regard to a wide acceptance of one particular format. A review of annual reports of U.S. Corporations would indicate that there is no standard format of social reporting. The social information, if reported, will be found in different places, such as the president's letter, annual financial statements, 10Ks, or sometimes in special reports.

An important reason for the lack of a generally accepted format probably lies in the absence of a theoretical framework. A general framework is desirable to identify the users of such reports, ultimate objective of preparing such reports, developing concepts and principles which will be useful in preparing such reports. The pioneer attempt to develop a theoretical framework has been made by Ramanathan.[8]

Theoretical framework for social reporting

Based upon the concept of the social contract, Ramanathan developed a theoretical framework for social accounting which proposes objectives and concepts. The following three objectives have been suggested:

1. To identify and measure the periodic net social contribution of an individual firm,

2. To help in determining whether a firm's activities are consistent with widely shared social priorities, and

3. To make available relevant information on a firm's goals, policies, programs, performance, and contributions to social goals.

In addition to these objectives, the following six concepts for preparing social reports are suggested: social transaction, social overhead, social income, social constituents, social equity and net social assets.

The author however recognized that there will be difficulties with regard to the measurement of various concepts, particularly social overhead, and social income. Despite weaknesses in the proposed theoretical framework for social reporting, its contribution is significant. This pioneer work for developing a theoretical framework should inspire other researchers to improve upon his framework and suggest alternative frameworks.

Corporate social reporting formats

Given the present need for social information, social reporting cannot wait until a theoretical framework is developed. Therefore, most research has been focused upon developing appropriate reporting formats.

Several formats have been suggested in the business and accounting literature in German as well as English language. This paper will critically review important formats suggested in the English language literature. The German Shell approach from the German language literature will be discussed in a separate section. In the absence of a theoretical framework, it will be difficult to closely examine strengths and weaknesses of each format. Therefore, the review contained in this paper will be general in nature.

Descriptive approach

The most common form of social reporting has so far been in the nature of narrative description of social activities undertaken by a firm. A firm attempts to highlight the positive aspects of its activities on the society. However, no special format is followed when this approach is used.

A review of most annual reports indicates that the president's letter in the annual report is the most favored place. This letter highlights all social activities undertaken by the firm. To illustrate narrative description of social activities, excerpts from the annual report of Republic Corporation are briefly reprinted below:

> Republic strives to be a good Corporate citizen in a number of other ways. Its' employees serve key roles in institutions and organizations that work to better their communities. They serve on hospital and school boards, head United Way and other community nonprofit organization drives and activities, and assis local cultural groups and governmental agencies.

Similar types of descriptions of social activities will be found in several annual reports; the details will however differ from company to company.

Another important format of narrative description is exemplified by a special social report of a firm. This format prominantly describes all social programs undertaken by a firm. An example of such a format is provided by Scovill Manufacturing Company. Scovill's social report provides a narrative account of its social activities as well as deficiencies, and presents this in the form of a balance sheet. This format however is not common.

The narrative description of social reporting cannot be considered a useful format for social reporting. The major deficiency of this format lies in its inability to provide the basis for evaluation of social performance by the firm. Furthermore, this type of social report will generally present the positive aspects only and the negative impact of corporate activities on social and physical environments will be ignored. Thus, such a report will not serve any useful purpose for evaluating a firm's real social performance, because a realistic appraisal of this performance should include negative as well as positive impacts.

Despite deficiencies and weaknesses inherent in the narrative description of social activities of a firm, this format cannot be ignored; it at least exhibits a degree of management's concern for social responsibility. Furthermore, this approach is simple, and it does not need any special accounting systems to keep track of the activities. An absence of a generally accepted social reporting format shows that several difficulties are being encountered in its development, especially difficulties relating to the measurement of the social impact of corporate activities. Until better measurement techniques become available, the narrative descriptive approach can serve a purpose.

Operating statement format approach

Another important approach which attracted several researcher's attention can be described as operating statement format approach. According to this approach, a firm should present not only social positive aspects but also the negative aspects of its activities. The positive aspects are broadly termed as "social benefits" and negative aspects as "social costs." Similar to operating statement, a net social contribution can be determined by taking the difference between social benefits and social costs.

The models suggested by Estes[9] and Linowes[10] relate to this approach. Since Linowes' model has received much attention in the literature, we will critically evaluate this model. Linowes suggested that a statement be prepared periodically which shows the expenditures made for improvements in social areas, offset against the cost of programs which were not undertaken but which would have made improvements. His concepts is based on the notion that a business gives something to the society and uses something of a society and this interaction can be presented in a statement format, which he terms as a socio-economic operating statement. A copy of this format is reproduced in Exhibit 1. In this statement, social programs are broken down into three major areas - relations with people, the environment, and product. Within each area, the voluntary expenditures made in developing and maintaining social programs are shown as benefits. For example, the costs incurred for installing pollution control devices or in maintaining a day care center for children of employees represents benefits. Any expenditures which were required by labor unions or by law are not included, since they are not voluntary.

Matched against benefits are the detriments to society for that period. These are the costs of those programs that were not undertaken but, that a reasonably prudent, but socially conscious management would have undertaken. The cost of not adding safety devices is seen as a detriment. The cost of any act required by the law which is not followed is included as a detriment. The benefits less the detriments in each category would result in a net improvement (deficit). The net results would then be summed, producing a total socio-economic improvement or deficit for the year.

The operating statement format approach has several advantages and disadvantages. A great advantage over many proposals lies in its inclusion of detriments. Linowes recognizes the need for dealing with those things a company could have done to further improve its social environment, but chose not to do. Most models based on other approaches deal exclusively with the positive aspects of a company's social responsibility programs. A second advantage lies in its inter-industry comparability. If a certain social concern is popular with the industry, such as conservation of energy, a firm could compare its outlays in this area, with those of other firms to determine if the company is keeping pace with the industry.

This approach has also several inherent weaknesses. The concept assumes that total cost measures total improvements or benefits of the program. This is not necessarily true. A company may be inordinately inefficient in a program, thus incurring more costs than an efficient business with a similar program. According to this model, the first business would be assigned larger benefits. Furthermore, it is perhaps inappropriate to deduct the detriments from the benefits. The cost of programs not developed has no relationship to costs actually incurred. Although Linowes considers comparability to be an advantage, it seems that the usefulness of the Statement is questionable in this area. Since the detriments are so subjective, it would appear that a comparison of bottom line figures would not result in meaningful information. In addition, the size of the firm is related to the amount of money it can afford to spend on social programs. Thus, comparison of firms of different sizes would not be meaningful.

A comprehensive approach

Another important approach which was developed and used by Abt Associates, is based on the concept of annual statements consisting of an income statement and a balance sheet. The objective of this approach is to determine the full impact of corporate activities on different constituents.[11]

The balance sheet part of the social statement contains information on social assets, social liabilities and social equity. The income statement provides monetary quantification for the corporation's social benefits. These benefits are defined as resources generated by company operations, having a positive impact, or increasing society's resources. The social costs are resources used in company operations at a "cost, sacrifice, or detriment to society." The net social income is the social gain or loss to society's resources due to the firm's operations. An equity figure is calculated for each separate category, and then these are summed to determine the net social income for the firm.

The strength of this approach lies in presentation of information in a quantitative form; additional information is provided in footnotes. Opportunity costs are also included where necessary. For example, the opportunity cost of total time worked has been estimated and recorded (a staff cost on the income statement).

This approach has been criticized on several grounds and its usefulness has been questioned. The main criticism relates to the quantification issue. In the absence of well accepted measurement techniques, valuation of social costs and social benefits will not be considered reliable. These weaknesses will lead many to question the credibility of information in the statements. Furthermore, there is no consensus of opinion with regard to the meaning of concepts used in the statements. Therefore, they are likely to be interpreted differently by different readers. In addition, the approach is highly complex. In view of difficulties involved in preparing such statements, tremendous practical difficulties will be faced. Consequently, this approach has not found favor with other firms.

Goal-oriented approach

Another important approach to social reporting relates to goal-oriented reporting. This approach was discussed by U.S. firms in early 1970s, but it was not fully accepted in the United States. Lately, this approach has found favor with German firms. Under the leadership and guidance of Prof.

Dierkes, several German firms have developed social reports on the basis of this concept.

According to this approach, annual reports first contain description of goals chosen by the firm depending upon the nature of its business and social demands of the society. Then detailed activities are enumerated and analyzed in pursuit of these goals. Where possible, a description of the activities is supported by data and graphs. This approach appears to be more pragmatic and capable of providing useful information. This approach is discussed in detail by analyzing German Shell's annual financial statements in the following section.

GOAL ORIENTATION IN CORPORATE SOCIAL REPORTS

The Social Program Management Report by the Bank of America and the Social Progress Plan by Quaker Oats are the examples of goal orientated approaches by U.S. firms in the early 1970's. But U.S. firms did not follow through with this concept. It is in Germany that this approach received special attention. The goal oriented corporate social report, which was first developed by the Deutsche Shell Company,[12] is becoming popular with other German firms. Furthermore, this report shows great potential for becoming a widely accepted social report. Although the report includes sections based on Social Accounts and Value-Added Concepts, only goal orientation aspects of the approach will be discussed.

Goal orientation in Deutsche Shell annual report

Deutsche Shell's management realized that changes in the social environment require an analogous change in the goals of the firm. In addition to achieving a reasonable return on investment, the firm recognized the need for other goals. The following goals have received special emphasis in the Deutsche Shell report:

1. Achievement of an adequate return on investment,
2. Meeting consumers' needs as determined by the market conditions,
3. Development of new processes and products,
4. Consideration of employees' interest, and
5. Regard for public concerns.

Each of these major goals is divided into subgoals. The first part of the annual report contains a discussion of the subgoals and the firm's important activities in pursuit of these goals. Although the major portion of the activities' description is narrative, the discussion is extensive and centers on specific objectives. This discussion covers approximately fifty-seven pages of the 1977 report. The highlights of the first section of the Deutsche Shell's 1977 report are summarized here.

The discussion on the objective of return on investment provides a summary of financial results for the 1968 to 1977 period, including a summary of the performance of its subsidiaries. The report also discusses the firm's policy to secure an adequate return on investment.

The section on consumers' needs comments on improvements in product safety and quality. The main emphasis, however, is on pricing policies and analysis of sales by product line, production, and exploration. In addition, comments are offered on the company's competitive position, tanker and chemical business, market research, exploration and diversification.

The discussion of goals for development of new products and processes deals with research and development issues which could save energy, reduce costs, improve the environment, and assure users' health and safety.

The goal relating to the consideration of employees' interest is especially emphasized and receives more coverage than other goals. It describes the firm's personnel structure in terms of age and sex, employees' training programs and associated costs, on-the-job accidents, expenditures on employee health plans, employee motivation, and reasons given by employees for leaving the firm.

The discussion of subgoals relating to public concerns provides information on the influence and interaction between the firm and (1) its natural environment, (2) the government, (3) economic/society/science, (4) people, (5) youth, and (6) workers belonging to under-privileged groups. This section also reports expenditure figures on investments relating to the improvement of the physical environment, such as air and water purification projects.

An evaluation of the goal orientation approach

This approach is more practical compared to other approaches. The description of social goals serves two purposes. First, these goals indicate the direction of the firm with regard to social performance, and these can be used to determine whether a firm is moving in the desired direction of social responsibility. Second, these goals serve as bench marks for evaluation of the firm's social performance. The actual social performance can be compared with the stated goals and the degree of achievement can be evaluated. Deutsche Shell's report shows that detailed social objectives can be stated by the management. Their report, however, emphasizes employees' related activities more than other social responsibility activities.

The approach is not without critics. The main criticism relates to the usefulness of this report. A general statement on management philosophy with regard to corporate social performance is not likely to provide enough information for evaluation of corporate social responsibility. In order to make the goal oriented statement useful, the goal description should be specific so that corporate performance can be compared with given targets. This type of evaluation is likely to provide useful information, which will help investors in their decisions. For example, a specific statement should be made with regard to the current level of pollution resulting from corporate activities and the goal of reducing this pollution to a certain level within a given time period. If possible, short term and long term effects of pollution abatement activities on the economic performance should be included.

Another criticism relates to the emphasis on activities involving employees. This emphasis will not provide detailed information on other corporate social activities. An emphasis limited to employees' concern will thus restrict the analysis of corporate social performance.

The approach is also criticized on the grounds of the omission of negative environmental impacts resulting from corporate activities. Analogous to other approaches, this approach primarily emphasizes the positive aspects of corporate activities, and makes no mention of negative impacts.

Despite the above criticism relating to the weaknesses of the report, the goal orientation approach cannot be ignored. The emphasis on goal description will inform the readers why certain activities are being undertaken by management and will enable readers to judge whether these activities are in the direction of desired social goals. Furthermore, inclusion of a description of the firm's goals in the annual statement is likely to encourage management to direct the firm's activities in a particular direction. In the absence of the established social goals, management philosophy and policies will remain obscure. Until social goals at the macro level are developed, this approach can serve a useful purpose. In order to enhance the usefulness of this approach, further research is needed to improve upon its present format.

CONCLUSION

The review of corporate social responsibility and social reporting practices indicates that some progress has been made in this regard but we are far from a solution to the problem of social responsibility and social reporting. Social information needs of users are highly divergent and any attempt to satisfy all needs of all users will result in a voluminous report which will lose its value because of its mere size. In order to develop a satisfactory and useful social report, it is important that information needs of users are critically examined and their legitimacy established. Once information needs are properly identified, these can then be grouped into meaningful categories. This process will enable us to develop a compact social report. However, this process is likely to take a long time and social reporting cannot be held up until then.

The intermediate solution would be for individual firms to establish their social goals within the general framework provided by social accounting and report detailed information in pursuit of these goals. These reports will be useful if they are systematic and consistent over time.

Despite problems associated with measurement of a firm's accomplishment in relation to the stated goals, the report will be more useful if it highlights firm's social responsibility activities in some quantitative form. For example, quantitative information on the degree of compliance with environmental laws can be developed. This information will be useful in evaluating risks of a firm associated with violation of pollution laws, etc.

REFERENCES

1. Sethi, S. P. (Ed.) (1975), The Unstable Ground: Corporate Social Policy in a Dynamic Society, Los Angeles: Melville Publishing Co.; Sethi, S. P. (1972/73), Getting a Handle on the Social Audit. In: Business and Society: 31-38.

2. Friedman, Milton, Social Responsibility is to Increase Profit. In: New York Times Magazine, September 13, 1970.

3. Ramanathan, Kavasseri V., Toward A Theory of Corporate Social Accounting. In: The Accounting Review, July 1976: 516-983.

4. For example, see Estes, Ralph W., Socio-Economic Accounting and External Diseconomies. In: The Accounting Review, April 1973: 284-290.

5. For example, see Bauer, Raymond R. (Ed.) (1960), Social Indicators, Cambridge, Mass.: MIT Press.

6. National Association of Accountants (1976), The Measurement of Corporate Environmental Activity, New York: NAA.

7. For example, see Tipgos, Manuel A. (1977), Toward A Theory of Corporate Social Accounting: A Comment. In: The Accounting Review October 1977: 977-983.

8. Ramanathan, ibid.

9. Estes, R. W. (1975), A Comprehensive Corporate Social Reporting Model. In: Seidler, L. J. and Seidler, L. L. (1975) (Eds.), Social Accounting: Theory, Issues and Cases, Los Angeles: Melville Publishing Company.

10. Linowes, D. F. (1974), The Corporate Conscience, New York: Hawthorne Books, Inc.

11. Abt Associates, (1976) Annual Report and Social Audit.

12. Deutsche Shell Company (1977). Annual Report. Also see Jaggi, Bikki (1980), An Analysis of Corporate Social Reporting in Germany In: The International Journal of Accounting, Spring 1980: 35-45.

Exhibit 1

JONES CORPORATION
SOCIO-ECONOMIC OPERATING STATEMENT
for the Year Ended December 31, 1971

I. RELATIONS WITH PEOPLE:			
A. Improvements:			
1. Training program for handicapped workers	$ 10,000		
2. Contribution to black college	4,000		
3. Extra turnover costs because of minority hiring program	5,000		
4. Cost of nursery school for children of employees, voluntarily set up	11,000		
Total Improvements		$ 30,000	
B. Less: Detriments			
1. Postponed installing new safety devices on cutting machines (cost of the devices)		14,000	
C. Net Improvements in People Actions for the Year			$ 16,000
II. RELATIONS WITH ENVIRONMENT:			
A. Improvements:			
1. Cost of reclaiming and landscaping old dump on company property	$ 70,000		
2. Cost of installing pollution control devices on Plant A smokestacks	4,000		
3. Cost of detoxifying waste from finishing process this year	9,000		
Total Improvements		$ 83,000	
B. Less: Detriments			
1. Cost that would have been incurred to re-landscape strip mining site used this year	$ 80,000		
2. Estimated cost to have installed purification process to neutralize poisonous liquid being dumped into stream	100,000	180,000	
C. Net Deficit in Environment Actions for the Year			($ 97,000)
III. RELATIONS WITH PRODUCT:			
A. Improvements:			
1. Salary of V.P. while serving on government Product Safety Commission	$ 25,000		
2. Cost of substituting lead-free paint for previously used poisonous lead paint	9,000		
Total Improvements		$ 34,000	
B. Less: Detriments			

1. Safety device recommended by Safety Council but not added to product	22,000	
C. Net Improvements in Product Actions for the Year		$ 12,000
Total Socio-Economic Deficit for the Year		($ 69,000)
Add: Net Cumulative Socio-Economic Improvements as at January 1, 1971		$249,000
Grand Total Net Socio-Economic Actions to December 31, 1971		$180,000

Part V
Value Changes and Conflict Management

The Relationship Between Changing Value Systems, Conflicts, and Conflict-Handling in the Enterprise Sector*

Günter Dlugos

ABSTRACT

On the basis of the assumption that non-material values are becoming ever more important, this paper discusses deducible interdependencies between value changes in the society and changes in goals, causes of conflict, areas of conflict, and conflict-handling in the enterprise sector. Furthermore, possible consequences for successful business management are examined along with some of their socio-political implications. A few of the problems pointed out in this paper will be elaborated in the three following articles.

INTRODUCTION

The results of empirical research into the essential criteria controlling human behavior in western societies seem to support the idea that values are changing and that more emphasis is being laid upon non-material values and less upon material ones. Without going into the empirical data interpretations that confirm or reject the fact of a change in values[1], we assume that non-material values are gaining considerably in importance. In this instance the substance of demands made and contributions offered in the enterprise sector will have to change accordingly. In this way the areas of conflict and consensus in the enterprise sector will change, too, and previously successful strategies for handling conflicts could become inefficient and will have to be modified. It is possible that changes in the value system could also have a direct and limiting effect on the arsenal of strategies for handling conflicts so that potentially successful strategies might not be used simply because the changes in the value system will have been internalized. Finally, a change in the nature of the causes of conflicts and in the methods of conflict-handling within the enterprise sector could affect other sectors of the society.

Analyzing these problems, we will discuss what the demands and contributions and the conditions for entering into and maintaining exchange relationships are, what causes conflict to develop, the forms of conflict-handling an actor can choose in principle, and what changes of effect must be anticipated. We will examine the sociopolitical implications of value changes on the basis of the assumption that there are interdependencies between the society as supersystem and the enterprise sector and that the supersystem dominates the enterprise subsystem. The main purpose of this article is to give some impulses for developing a conceptual framework as a first step toward empirical investigations on the field of research outlined.

THE ENTERPRISE AND ITS EXTERNAL AND INTERNAL EXCHANGE RELATIONSHIPS

In order to discuss the consequences that changes in societal values have in the enterprise sector, we must realize that enterprises are goal-oriented systems which are founded and organized to fulfill human objectives. They are dissolved if these objectives no longer apply or if the enterprises prove unable to fulfill them. Enterprises have no goals that are independent of the goals of those persons exerting an influence upon them. Neither do they have an immanent propensity to survive[2]. Therefore, the inter-relationship between value changes and changes in goals in the enterprise sector can never be a direct one; it must occur through the goal-systems of human actors.

The primary goals of an enterprise are to provide external actors with material goods/services and to entitle internal actors or members of the enterprise -- the staff (managers and workers) and shareholders (see below) -- to a share of the gross national product, which is represented by money in a money and credit economy. The goal of supplying the market with material goods and services as a way of meeting external needs coincides with the goal pursued by customers when they enter into an exchange relationship with the enterprise. Their demands to be supplied with factors of production are connected with monetary goods as their contribution. Supplying the members of the enterprise with monetary goods is in accordance with the goal system of the members of the enterprise. Likewise, their demand for monetary goods in an exchange relationship is connected with contributions of cooperation on meeting external needs. Supplying monetary goods is the central goal for members of private enterprises. Contrary to this, the goal of meeting needs is the priority for corporations participating in public utilities as shareholders. These enterprises fulfill a commitment to supply that in some circumstances makes it necessary for those supplied to subsidize production.

Members of the enterprise are people who have an internal func-

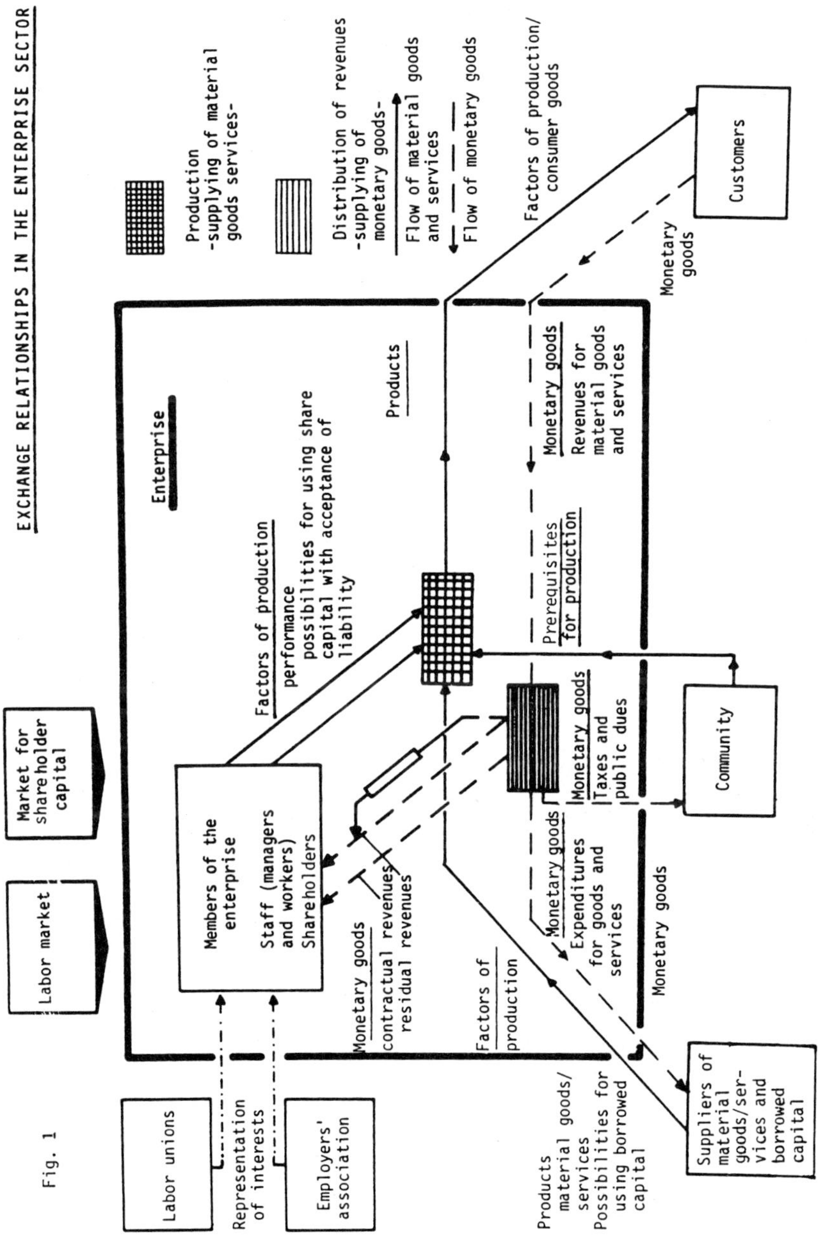
EXCHANGE RELATIONSHIPS IN THE ENTERPRISE SECTOR
Labor market
Market for shareholder capital
Production -supplying of material goods services-
Distribution of revenues -supplying of monetary goods-
Flow of material goods and services
Flow of monetary goods
Enterprise
Factors of production
performance possibilities for using share capital with acceptance of liability
Products
Monetary goods
Revenues for material goods and services
Prerequisites for production
Monetary goods
Taxes and public dues
Monetary goods
Expenditures for goods and services
Monetary goods
Members of the enterprise
Staff (managers and workers)
Shareholders
Monetary goods
contractual revenues
residual revenues
Factors of production
Factors of production/ consumer goods
Customers
Monetary goods
Community
Labor unions
Representation of interests
Employers' association
Products material goods/ services
Possibilities for using borrowed capital
Suppliers of material goods/services and borrowed capital
Fig. 1

tion (internal actors). One must differentiate the basic functions of "performance" and "provision of share capital with acceptance of liability".[3] The first function is the staff function, the second is the shareholder function. People having a staff function will be referred to in the following analysis as staff (S), and those fulfilling the shareholder function as shareholders (SH). The other functions that these people might have in life will not be included in this discussion. In terms of the authority to issue directives and the obligation to carry them out, staff functions can be divided into the superior's function and the subordinate's function (S_{sup} and S_{sub}). The staff can include both shareholder function and superior's function or shareholder's function and subordinate's function. In relation to a higher authority, managers represent the subordinate function; in relation to a lesser authority, they represent the superior function.

The exchange relationship between the enterprise and its suppliers of material goods/services and its suppliers of borrowed capital is characterized by the provision of material and non-material factors of production in the broadest sense in exchange for money. The contribution of products is connected with the demand for factors of production, which is derived from the production goal of the customer enterprise. Likewise, the customer enterprise's contribution of money meets the demand for monetary goods by the suppliers of material goods and services and the suppliers of borrowed capital.

In addition, there are reciprocal but not interconnected relationships between the enterprise and the community. The community prepares the production environment, subsidizes enterprises in special cases, and receives money from the enterprises in the form of taxes and dues. Furthermore, an exchange relationship can also exist between the enterprise and the community wherein the enterprise acts as supplier and the community as customer. Finally, the relationship between the management in its function as employer and the labor unions in their function of representing the interests of employees can be seen as an indirect exchange relationship (Fig. 1).

CONDITIONS FOR ENTERING AND MAINTAINING EXCHANGE RELATIONSHIPS

Exchange relationships in the enterprise sector are based on the exchange between material goods and services for monetary goods. Assuming rational behavior[4], exchange relationships are entered into and maintained if the contractors' demands at both the level of material goods and services and the level of monetary goods are reciprocally at least met by their contribution and if every contractors's demands and contribution are part of his/her optimal alternatives[5]. Whether the latter condition is perceived to be fulfilled is a question of the goal system, the alternatives, and the other variables influencing the goal setting process.

Rational goal setting (Fig. 2) is treated here as the product of a mental process[6] that begins (1) with the actualization of a desired but as yet unspecified goal conception (G_a) (general goal) and extends to the solution of subproblems and intervening feedback processes. The following are to be investigated in this context: (2) the search for and the recognition of alternatives fulfilling the conceived purpose and means, the establishment of the goal-specifying criteria which are considered important for the decision, the identification of each alternative's consequences for these goal criteria, (3) the evaluation of the specific consequences as seen from the individual value system of the goal setter and the amalgamation of the specific values that the consequences have for the alternative value, the use of the selected decision criteria to identify the optimal alternatives (specific goal) of the decision field so determined, and (4) the introduction and specific goal-oriented control of the realization process. Motivating situations, motivational structure, perception of the external world, thought processes with pragmatic, evaluative, and volitional function determine the specific goal as process result[7]. Motivation, perception, and information processing are influenced by external circumstances to which the societal value system also belongs.

The specific goal as a result of a rational goal setting process can be better described through the consequences which the selected alternatives have for the goal criteria that the decisionmaker perceives to be important. If the specific goal is tied to an exchange process, then the expected consequences represent, on the one hand, the contractor's fulfillment of a decisionmaker's demand as the purpose of the action and, on the other hand, the contribution to the contractor as a means of achieving the specific goal. In this case the goal criteria specify the demand on the one hand and the contribution on the other.

Demands and contributions as constitutive basic goal components (Fig. 3) define the enterprise's basic internal and external functions under the exchange aspect. Information about the specific interests of the function agents in the framework of their activity is contained in the goal criteria. If rational goal setting processes are assumed and if plausibility considerations are applied, the goal criteria of the basic functions (specified demands/contribution) can be derived from the demands and contributions of the function agents and can be considered as a heuristic framework for empirical research. Since the "staff" contributes performance, for example, to bring in revenues, and since they constantly need revenues, it can be assumed that the choice between job alternatives will

Fig. 2 PROBLEM COMPLEXES OF RATIONAL GOAL SETTING

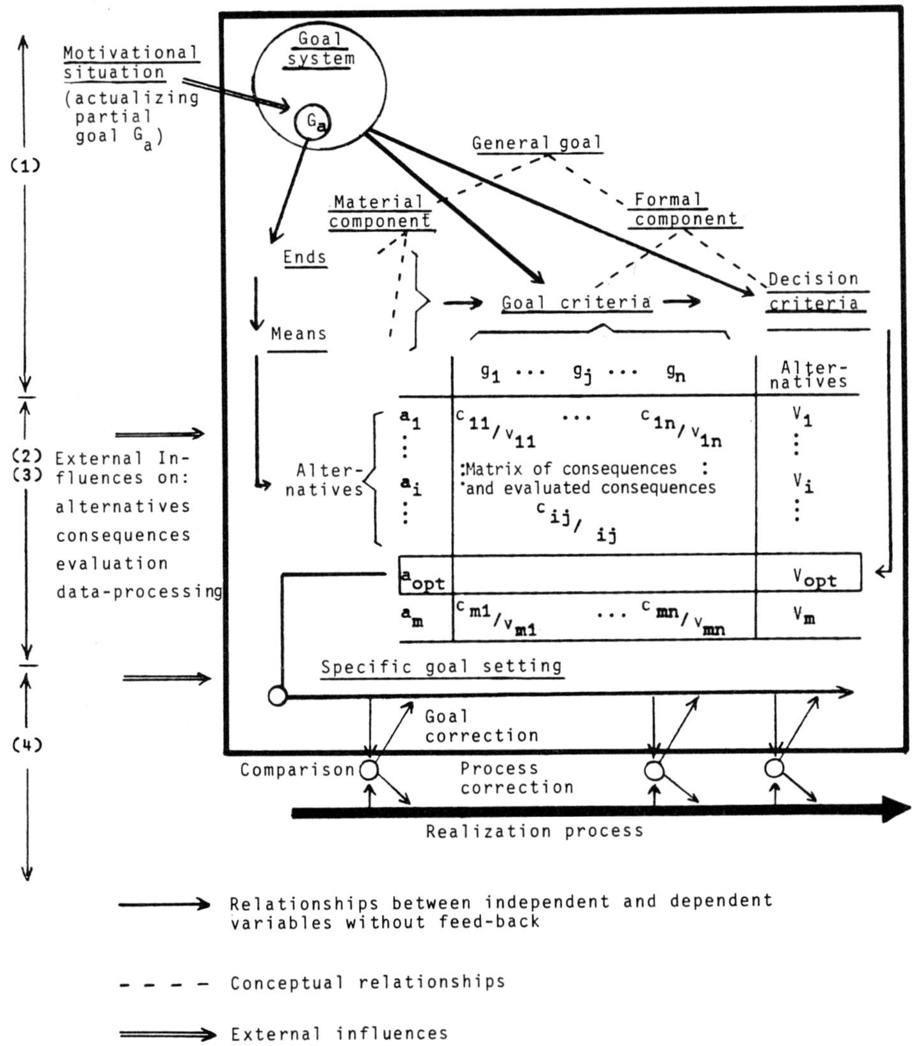

Fig. 3

BASIC FUNCTIONS AND BASIC GOAL COMPONENTS IN THE ENTERPRISE SECTOR

Basic goal components / Basic functions	Constitutive basic goal components: Ends (intrapersonal) / Demands (interpersonal)	Means (intrapersonal) / Contributions (interpersonal)	Goal criteria of the basic functions: Specified demands (D) and contributions (C)	
1. Internal to the enterprise Staff	Monetary goods	Performance	D D C D D	Revenues/net revenues Job security Performance Self-actualization/ participation Social conditions
Shareholders	Monetary goods	Possibilities for using share capital with acceptance of liability	D D C D D	Revenues/net revenues Capital security Possibilities for using share capital with acceptance of liability Participation in decision Informations
2. External to the enterprise Supplier of material goods/ services	Monetary goods	Products	D C D/C	Revenues/net revenues Products Contributions to the customer/supplier relationship
Supplier of borrowed capital	Monetary goods	Possibilities for using borrowed capital	D D C D	Revenues/net revenues Capital security Possibilities for using borrowed capital Information
Customer	Factors of production/ consumer goods	Monetary goods	D D/C C	Factors of production Contributions to the customer/supplier relationship Expenditures/gross expendit.
Member of the community	Prerequisites for production	Monetary goods	D C C	Prerequisites for production Expenditures/gross expendit. Contributions to general well-being

function: customer / function: supplier	C expenditures	D factors of production	D/C contributions to customer / supplier relationship
revenues D	D 11 \ C 11		
products C		C 22 \ D 22	
contributions to customer/supplier relationship D/C			D/C 33 \ D/C 33

Fig. 4

matrix format: exchange-relationship customer / supplier

function: employer / function: employee	C expenditures	C job security	D performance	C self-actualization /participation	C social conditions
revenues D	D 11 \ C 11				
job security D		D 22 \ C 22			
performance C			C 33 \ D 33		
self-actualization/ participation D				D 44 \ C 44	
social conditions D					D 55 \ C 55

Fig. 5

matrix format: exchange-relationship employer/ employee

be tied to the expected amount of net revenue as well as to job security. Performance involves obligations and stress; it can also contribute to self-actualization, and takes place in the enterprise within a social setting characterized by certain social conditions. These criteria will also determine the choice of alternatives and will thereby be relevant goal criteria.

Empirical investigations of expectations for the work process, particularly of conditions necessary for job satisfaction and job motivation, confirm the relevance of the goal criteria derived from the demands and contribution of the staff function[8]. Some of the goal criteria applied in these investigations correspond directly to this discussion so far; other goal criteria of the many-faceted question complex can be interpreted as subdivisions. The goal criteria of the other functions are still only partially documented empirically because similarly comprehensive investigations of the type that have been carried out in the field of staff interests do not yet exist. But since these goal criteria, too, can be plausibly derived from the corresponding demands and contributions, it will be assumed here that they largely correspond to the goal criteria established in a rational goal setting process. How much weight is given to the goal criteria -- an important question for the evaluation of consequences -- is still largely unanswered, however. The weight assigned by staff members, for example, can vary significantly, depending on each staff member's superior or subordinate function, and within these groupings, on his/her specific activity[9].

The condition established above for entering into and maintaining exchange relationships (assuming rational behavior) is that the contractors' demands at both the level of material goods and services and the level of monetary goods are reciprocally at least met by their contributions and that every contractor's demands and contributions are part of his/her optimal alternative. Based on the analysis of the problem complex of rational goal setting and the analysis of functional goal systems, the second part of the condition can be formulated more specifically: each contractor perceives as optimal the amalgamated value of the consequences expected for his/her actualized goal criteria. If these consequences accepted by each contractor are transferred to a matrix of goal criteria, then the demands and contributions can be specified. In each of the occupied cells (see Fig. 4), the respective demand (D) must at least be met by the corresponding contribution (C). Only the direct exchange values based on the consequences of the selected alternatives are entered in the exchange matrix (for example, "revenue" based on sales instead of "net revenue", a revenue reduced by transport costs, or other expenditures). If additional goal criteria are actualized in the framework of special exchange relationships, the matrix must be expanded accordingly.

Similarly, the matrix format can be applied to exchange relationships between staff with a superior function and staff with a subordinate function, a situation represented in Fig. 5 under the special rubric "Employer - Employee". In Fig. 3, the basic function "staff" is accorded goal criteria that determine the decision to work. Basically, these criteria apply to both the superior function S_{sup} and the subordinate function S_{sub}. In the present context, however, where the function S_{sup} becomes "Employer", the goal criteria of the employer function as contribution are based on the demands of the employee function and vice versa. The consequences expected for the employer's goal criteria in the framework of the exchange relationship are elements of the selected production alternatives to be pursued with division of labor. Depending on the division of power and assuming rational goal setting, a separation of the SH function and S_{sup} function is the optimal alternative for either the SH function, the S_{sup} function (manager authority), a SH/S_{sup} compromise, or a compromise integrating the S_{sub} function (participation in decision-making, codetermination). Here, too, the demands in each of the occupied matrix cells must be met by the contribution.

ORIGIN AND SHIFT OF CONFLICTS CAUSED BY VALUE CHANGE

The term conflict will be used in its broadest sense to refer to incompatibilities between individuals or groups[10]. The narrower version of Boulding's[11] concept of conflict has additional criteria -- that the parties are aware of the incompatibility of potential future positions (potential conflict) and that each party wishes to occupy the position (actual conflict). In order to investigate preventive third party conflict handling of a conflict that is still not apparent to one of the conflict partners, the restriction of the conflict concept to manifest incompatibility is not recognized; rather, Dahrendorf regards latent incompatibility as conflict, too.

Potential conflicts, contrary to Boulding, also include the situation in which only one of the parties involved perceives an incompatibility and knows how to handle it. Since the present investigation analyzes the actors of the enterprise sector only as agents of specific functions, all goal criteria and conflicts which are not derived from those functions (according to Dahrendorf such goal criteria and conflicts are not supra-individual) are not treated. Dahrendorf labels an incompatibility a "social conflict" if it can be derived from the structure of social units, that is, if it is supra-individual[12]. In this sense, the conflicts between agents of specific functions examined here can be called "functional conflicts" or, since the function agents can at the same time be considered structured social units, "social conflicts". The conflict concept is used below with this meaning and will be differentiated as latent, potential, or manifest (actual)[13].

On the basis of the aforementioned differentiation of the problem areas in rational goal setting (see Fig. 2), exchange relationships have two general causes of conflict generation. An exchange relationship that comes about through rational goal setting consists of an optimal alternative for each of the contractors that he/she regards as optimal on the basis of the evaluated and amalgamated consequences. The basis of the decision to enter into an exchange relationship is, on the one hand, the expected consequences and, on the other, their evaluation in view of each exchange partner's goal system. Within an exchange relationship the expected consequences refer to the reciprocal demands represented by a contractor's own contributions and the contributions of the exchange partner. As part of the optimal alternatives which are to be realized, the mutual contributions are at least accepted because of the evaluations made in the goal setting process. This does not mean, however, that every party has to feel its aspiration level has been fulfilled relative to its contributions.

The first cause for an exchange conflict can be seen in the disadvantageous realization of expected consequences. This can consist of the inadequate satisfaction of one's demands or the contractor's too-intensive use of one's own contribution. This disadvantageous realization of expected consequences can result from one's own inaccurate predictions or from a contractor's unfulfilled contribution. For example, a voluntary gratuity is not given in the expected amount or the performance required to receive a predetermined pay proves to be more intensive than expected. An alternative that the goal setting process excluded as not optimal would under certain circumstances now appear more advantageous. Indeed, there is in principle the opportunity to contract for the fulfillment of expected consequences, but such a form of limiting risks is not possible for all consequences. Incompatibilities of the type mentioned above cannot be excluded.

The second cause for an exchange conflict can be seen in the disadvantageous change of consequence values. This cause can also lead to an inadequate satisfaction of one's demands or to a too-intensive use of one's contributions. One reason for this, however, is an increased aspiration level. The second reason is a decrease in the value of the consequence, as when the contractor has a monetary claim in a situation of falling money value or when the contractor makes a monetary contribution before money value increases. Unlike the disadvantageous realization of expected consequences, the disadvantageous change of consequence values affects every alternative having such consequences. Therefore, the alternative selected as the most favorable remains the most favorable if the complex of consequences is otherwise unchanged. If, however, the consequence values of the individual alternatives are subject to various other influences or if the aspiration level increases as a result of shifting aspirations, then a different alternative can become the most favorable.

Disadvantageous realization of expected consequences and disadvantageous change of consequences values are identical for the affected actor when his demands are not met by the contractor's contribution, or when the contractor's demands are higher than the affected actor's contribution. If the exchange matrix's original data are updated, then a conflict matrix is created which expresses the exchange conflict numerically. If the exchange relationship is characterized not only by conflicting goal criteria but also by harmonized goal criteria, then the matrix is both a conflict matrix and a consensus matrix. As long as the cause of the exchange conflict lies in the disadvantageous realization of expected consequences, the contractor's negatively changed demands must be substituted into the matrix. In a disadvantageous change of consequences values, the change is determined by individual assessments and is subject to a certain degree of arbitrariness.

If it assumed that there is a value change toward placing more emphasis on non-material values, then it must be taken into account that the sensitivity toward a disadvantageous realization of non-material goal criteria is increasing, and that the aspirational level related to these goal criteria is also increasing, and will simultaneously precipitate a disadvantageous change of consequences values. This change can be at the expense of material goal criteria, but can leave the interest in material goal criteria unchanged in absolute terms, or perhaps only slightly retarded. To allow concrete statements about the implications between value change and conflict shifting in the enterprise sector, each internal and external exchange relationship would have to be examined to find out which goal criteria are affected and to what degree the value change is altering their importance. In the present context, only the exchange relationship employer/employee is to be discussed, and the overall assumption will be made that the possible changes just outlined affect the non-material goal criteria.

Non-material goal criteria of the employee function, which are expected to have a higher attraction if the assumed value change exists, are (see Fig. 5): Opportunities for self-actualization/participation, social conditions in the enterprise, job security as an extension of active participation in the societal production process, and performance, which here includes the negative quantitative and qualitative consequences for the private sector. If the interest in realizing these goal criteria increases because of a general value change, this increase will appear not only among staff with employee function, but also among staff with employer function.

For example, if opportunities for self-actualization through participation in decision making are restricted, then a bilateral exchange conflict is generated between both contractors, whose desire to fulfill non-material goal criteria is increased. In this case the increased employee demand conflicts with the employer's contribution, which has, in turn, been reduced by his simultaneously increased interest in self-actualization. Vice versa, if this change affects the employee's contribution of performance and the employer's demand for such performance (Fig. 5), the exchange relationship this time is endangered by a reciprocal and bilateral conflict. An additional complication of the conflict situation arises when more than two parties are interested in a good whose distribution is limited. For example, the employer is confronted by the demands of several employee groups. If the number of conflicting exchange relationships is n, there are generally unilateral or bilateral exchange conflicts which can be triggered by one or by both sides within a group of (n + 1) parties. A special case is the competition conflict. Competition conflict is defined as a conflict in which ($m \geq 3$) parties are involved of which (m - 1) parties having no exchange relationship are in a zero-sum conflict with each other over the good that is to be distributed by the remaining party[14]. In the context of the value change discussed here, this form of conflict can arise between staff who are not in an exchange relationship over the opportunities for self-actualization being distributed by a higher authority. This form of conflict can also arise between shareholders, the distributing authority, and staff if the shareholders have reason to fear that increased staff aspirations for self-actualization will cause material losses[15].

From the analysis of the implications between value change and conflict arises the question of whether a change of societal values should be regarded only as a general shift of values or also as a group-specific shift. The latter possibility could lead to a group-specific interest shift and to a unilateral or bilateral exchange conflict triggered by only one side[16]. Under these circumstances, the conflict matrix, which can at the same time be a consensus matrix, contains increased demands or reduced contributions for only one of the contractors; the demands and contributions of the other contractor remain unaltered. This difference between a general value shift and a desire, so to speak, for redistribution undoubtedly exists and must be taken into consideration and expressed clearly with various appropriate concepts. Another question is whether those non-material goods that are desired in greater amounts must always come from a limited pool of resources or if such a shift of interests cannot perhaps instead be directed to non-material goods whose quantity can be sufficiently augmented. Examples of such goods would be regard for one's individuality, recognition, understanding, collegial atmosphere as aspects of the goal criteria under self-actualization, and social conditions. The satisfaction of these aspects will not lead to redistribution.

The assertion that there is a change in values toward placing greater emphasis on non-material values must be specified if conclusions about the origins or shifts of conflicts are to be drawn. Such a change of values can, of course, occur without conflicts, or can provoke exchange conflicts and competition for realizing goal criteria that were either unimportant or non-conflicting before. In addition, a conflict caused by a change in values need not lead to a conflict shift; it can also lead to more conflicts. A special case of value change that has barely been analyzed is the change of distribution norms[17]. If such value change is internalized in general, one can expect conflicts to be defused as long as the requests for redistribution are oriented to the changed redistribution norms.

CONFLICT-HANDLING AS A DECISION PROBLEM

Latent and potential antagonism between persons or actors to be examined in the discussion are based on conflicting ranges of action, and manifest antagonisms are based on conflicting goals within these ranges of action. Conflict handling which includes preventive actions has the purpose of determining conflicting ranges of action. From the point of view of the involved actors, the conflict handling or the determination of conflicting ranges of action represents actions of safeguarding. These safeguarding processes are regarded as secondary actions. As such, they focus on setting and realizing safeguarding goals. To distinguish between these two goal categories, the concepts of primary goals and secondary goals or basic goals and safeguarding goals are useful[18]. Whereas the term "basic goal" is a collective term which, when applied to the business sector, includes such heterogeneous connotations as purchasing, production, sales, and financing goals, the term safeguarding goal is characterized by a homogeneous connotation. If the setting of basic goals and the setting of safeguarding goals proceeds rationally, then there is no formal distinction between the two. Both goal setting processes are formally identical and can be described by the aforementioned problem complexes (Fig. 2). Refining a general, as yet unspecified, goal conception (general goal) to a specific goal that controls the realization process proceeds in the case of safeguarding goals by linking the choice between specific alternatives to specific goal criteria. The multiplicity of safeguarding alternatives that are discussed in the literature as forms of conflict handling [19] can be traced to two basic processes of determination by differentiating those areas of the conflicting ranges of action that can be influenced (Fig. 6): the determination of the goal setting pro-

Fig. 6 BASIC FORMS OF DETERMINATION

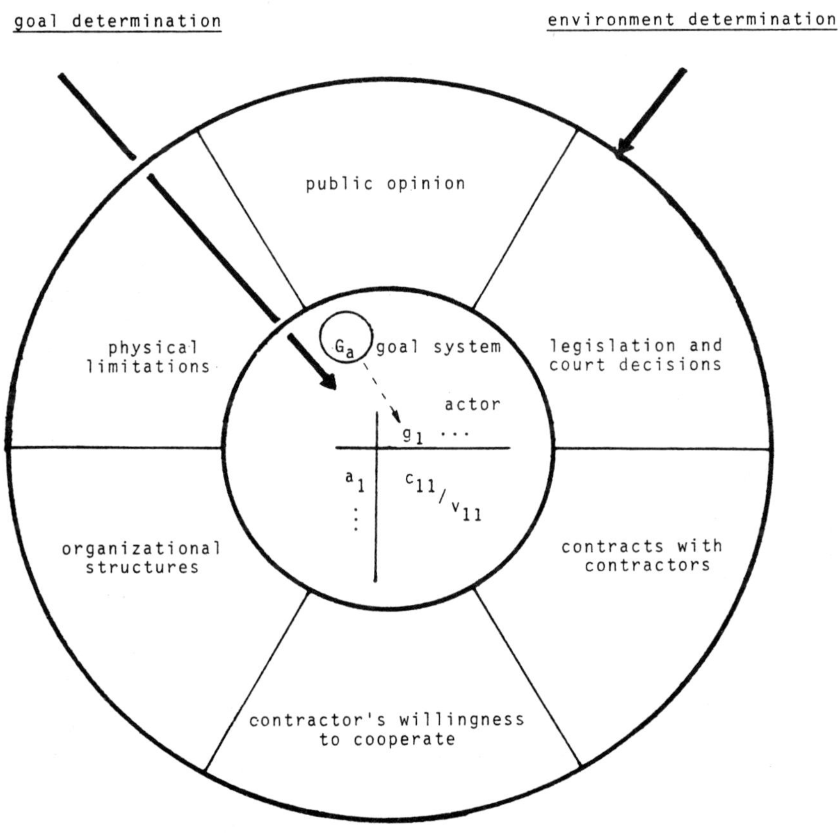

cess and the determination of the action environment of conflicting actors. The determination of a goal setting process takes place by communicative influence on that process with the aim of preventing and changing a conflicting goal. The determination of an action environment consists of the direct factual limitations on alternatives of action. Whereas attempts to change conflicting ranges of action by determining the conflicting goal setting processes cannot succeed unless the opponent agrees, the determining of the action environment, which is binding, becomes effective even without this compliance.

Alternatives of action inherent in goal determination (Fig. 7) are persuasion, manipulation, and the signalling of sanctions, either positive or negative. In the frame of persuasion, data are transferred according to one's best knowledge, which are appropriate for correcting the goal setting processes of the opponent in order to resolve the conflict in the interest of both parties. Attempts to manipulate are based on consciously selecting, overloading, distorting, or falsifying information[20]. By signalling sanctions, the attempt is made to offer the opponent improvements or to threaten deterioration of his situation. It is up to the opponent to consider or to ignore these sanctions as in cases of pure information transfer. Persuasion and manipulation can be directed to all phases or data complexes of the goal setting processes (see the explanation to Fig. 2). The use of sanctions aims only to correct the consequences expected by the opponent. Fig. 7 shows the opponent's compliance as a sixth area of influence which sometimes must first be won in order to be able to determine goals at all. The result of successful goal determination is a changed specific goal on the part of the opponent.

An actor's range of action is externally determined in a positive or negative way not least by public opinion, legislation, court decisions, contracts with his contractors, their willingness to cooperate, the organizational structure, and physical factors. If an actor's range of action determined in this way endangers the realization of his contractor's goal, the contractor can try to change the actor's action environment by influencing the limiting factors.

The actions of environment determination (Fig. 7) proceed either indirectly, by enlisting the goal setting process of a third party who then restricts the action environment of the opponent, or directly, by changing the opponent's range of action. Influencing public opinion, legislation, the structure of cooperation of, say, suppliers, customers, or workers at different levels of the hierarchy is a proven indirect action of environment determination for the purpose of safeguarding the realization of pursued goals. Such indirect influence can be achieved through persuasion, manipulation, and sometimes through the use of negative or positive sanctions.

Fig. 7 ALTERNATIVES AND RESULTS OF DETERMINATION

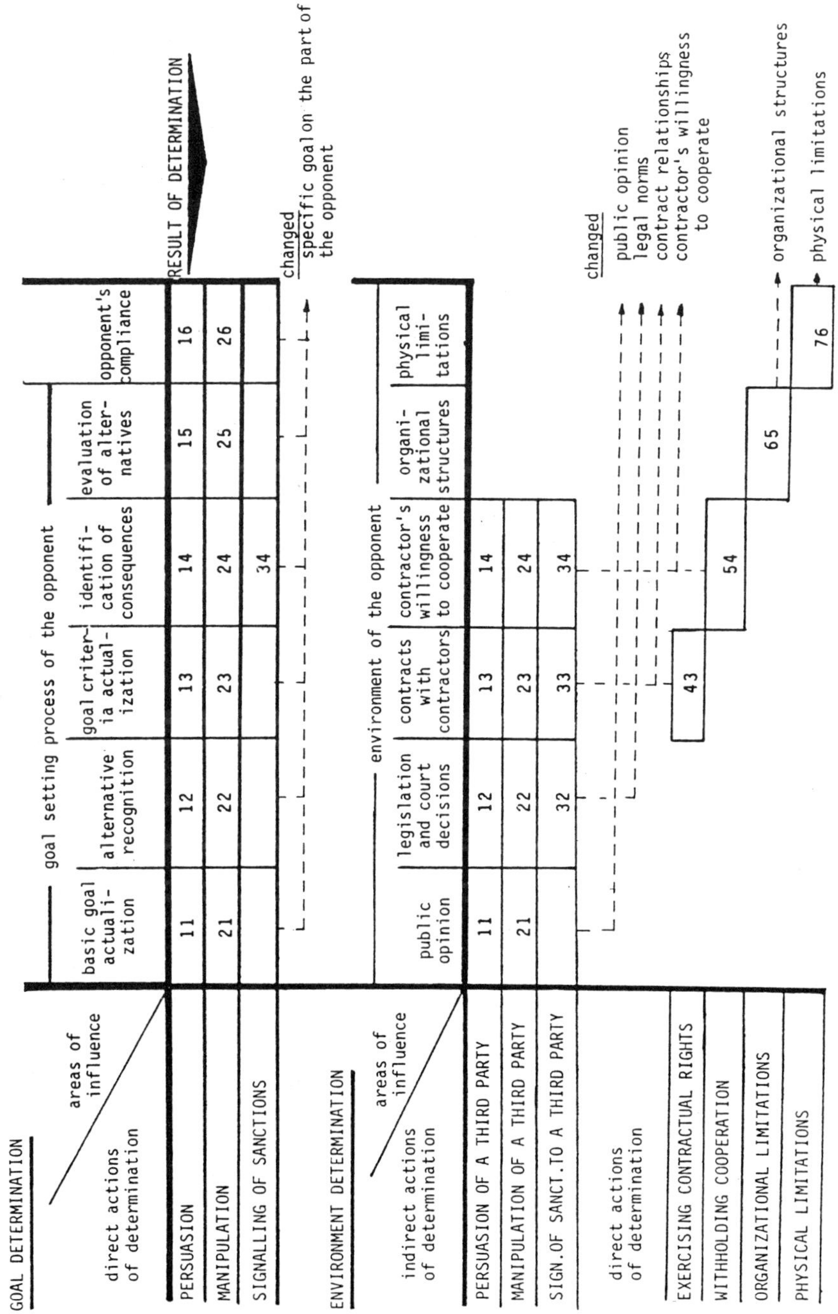

Direct actions of environment determination consist basically of shaping the opponent's range of action by exercising contractual rights, by withholding further cooperation, by setting organizational limitations and, lastly, physical limitations in such a way that the realization of one's own goals is safeguarded. In the framework of employment contracts, the latter three alternatives are already part of the employer's rights.

The possibilities for action in handling conflicts, differentiated according to areas of influence (the occupied fields of Fig. 7), form either singly or in combinations the determination alternatives or alternatives for setting safeguarding goals. Specific goal criteria needed in choosing between alternatives can be derived from the safeguarding goal, from the necessity of using resources, and from the consideration of side effects. In this light, the goal criteria for setting safeguarding goals can be seen as:

1) the extent of the change in the conflicting range of action,
2) the duration of the change's effect,
3) the costs incurred by the change,
4) complementary effects, and
5) competing effects.

In practice, the clusters of alternatives and goal criteria sketched here on the basis of special conditions must be expressed in exact terms. Then the consequences of each alternative and goal criterion are to be ascertained, evaluated, amalgamated. Lastly, the specific goal of the safeguarding action is to be determined by applying the chosen decision criterion[21]. The realization of this specific goal can lead to the determination results summarized in Fig. 7.

VALUE CHANGE AND CHANGES OF EFFECT IN THE FORMS OF CONFLICT-HANDLING

A change in societal values can have an impact on conflict handling either by rendering certain forms of conflict handling incompatible with the changed value system and thus in certain cases unusable or by altering their efficiency
The first case need not be treated in this context since the assumed change toward a heavier emphasis on non-material values would not have to exclude any of the safeguarding alternatives mentioned. In the second case, the value change will alter the efficiency of some forms of conflict handling in the enterprise sector. The following discussion of this problem complex will be restricted to employer/employee relations, which will be discussed as an example of other internal and external exchange relationships of the enterprise.

The efficiency of imposing indirect environment determination on an opponent depends on persuading the third party to enforce the desired limitations. If the societal value system changes and if the desired limitations are incompatible with the changed values, then the third party will not agree to enforce the desired limitations if it has already internalized these changes. The target groups for indirect means of determining have been cited already: public opinion, legislation and court decisions, the contractors, and other stipulators of the opponent (Fig. 7). If societal values change, then it can be assumed that this change will alter 1) public opinion, that is, majority opinion, 2) legislation, which in a democratic society expresses the will of the majority, and 3) court decisions. The other two target groups consist of actors with extremely different values.

For environment determination that aims at influencing public opinion, it can be assumed that its efficiency increases if it coincides with the trend of the value change and that its efficiency decreases if it runs contrary to that change. If one assumes that there is a change toward a heavier emphasis on non-material values, then the extension of the worker's self-determination and self-actualization can be regarded as a partial confirmation of this idea. Along the same lines are the attempts of the employers to influence public opinion against restricting their ranges of action, attempts which have been less than successful even when dangers for productivity and level of supply are pointed out.

For influencing legislation and court decisions as a further possibility of indirectly determining conflicting ranges of action, the same relationships will exist between value change in efficiency as exist for public opinion. In addition, it must be remembered that labor law in the second half of the previous century witnessed a continuous shift in the lines between the ranges of action that an enterprise's members have. The rights of the employers to determine the terms of a labor contract, which caused much social tension when combined at the beginning of industrialization with the preeminence of the shareholders, were gradually restricted by norms. Such norms concern in particular labor safety, vacation time, employee dismissal, codetermination, labor contracts, and the changed procedures of exercising labor law. That influence on legislation and court decisions which does not conform to the accepted value change will scarcely have a chance of success because it runs contrary to very long term development in the field of labor law. Probably the only way to defend the existing ranges of action used today by employers and capital owners is to test in court whether this development is compatible with other like or higher-ranking values.

A change in societal values will cause no change in the efficiency of the two other forms of indirect environment determination -- influencing the contracting parties and influencing the willingness of the opponent's other contractors to cooperate. It can only be assumed that the circle of third parties capable of enforcing limitations will change to the degree that their altered value concepts diverge from those of the determining actor and bar them from fulfilling the desired determination.

The forms of direct environment determination were listed above as exercising contract rights and, as far as these are not already included in this category, withholding cooperation and setting organizational and physical limitations (Fig. 7). In the framework of the employer/employee relationship, the employer has the right to organize the work flow and to determine the work relationship unilaterally on the basis of his right to issue directives. Major actions of this sort include transfers, regrouping, exclusion from certain benefits and promotion, and dismissal. The exercise of these inherent employer's rights has largely been curbed by the works council's rights to participation and co-determination. Under these circumstances the effects of the value change in the direction assumed here could be the obstruction of unpopular measures that still remain within the employer's range of action.

One can attempt to achieve goal determinations as a second basic form of determining conflicting ranges of action by persuading, manipulating, or by signalling sanctions. Threatening negative sanctions often represents a preliminary step toward directly determining the environment and, in the final analysis, is subject to the same limitations. Offering positive sanctions can refer to non-material goal criteria such as increased opportunities for personal development, improved chances for promotion, enhanced working conditions, or to material goal criteria. The problems associated with the limits on the distribution or redistribution of non-material goods have already been discussed. The assumed change in values will make an offer of material goods particularly problematic if non-material goods are at the core of the conflict. It can be assumed that the chance of solving such conflicts by monetary means in the form of wage rate increases or bonuses for compensation of overtime or particularly demanding physical work will increasingly diminish unless the offers are raised. For a society that is approaching the limits of economic growth, the monetary approach to conflict-handling thereby becomes a dual problem. It loses significance as an alternative and collides with ever narrower limits[22].

The last alternative for conflict handling to be discussed is pure information transfer, which aims to reduce the conflicting range of action through persuasion or manipulation. These possibilities were expanded for the employee by introducing rights to have a hearing, to advise, and to initiate (Labor

Management Act); they have remained unchanged for the employer. However, in view of the redistribution of opportunities for determination, particularly for determining the environment, these alternatives have basically become more significant for the employer and less so for the employee. Due to the restriction and neutralization of alternatives for determination, the employer has been forced to concentrate more on purely argumentative determination and to improve its efficiency. Since efficiency also depends on the other side's compliance[23], and since a long term relationship unquestionably causes a mutual reduction of this compliance if the argumentation subsequently proves to be manipulative, the increase in the efficiency of argumentative determination will be achieved by avoiding manipulation.

The renunciation of manipulation can enhance personal authority by providing the opportunity to exert influence on the basis of personal trust, personal integrity, and personal expertise[24]. The more complex the problem to be decided and the more specialized the expert knowledge needed in order to ensure a satisfactory problem analysis, the more important these personal qualities are to the persuasion approach. In spite of the significance of personal authority for the determining party, persuasion is not possible if there is no expertise, if the party to be persuaded has no capacity to process information, and if he/she is not willing to be influenced by relevant arguments. Since determination through persuasion cannot ignore the opponent's arguments, both parties in a long term relationship have an interest in establishing personal authority, expertise, capacity to process information, and a willingness to compromise. For the employer/employee relationship under discussion here, this means that these conditions must be fulfilled not only by the employer but also by the employee if conflicts of interest in the enterprise sector are to be reduced through, and in future be restricted primarily to, the persuasion approach.

SOCIOPOLITICAL IMPLICATIONS

The analysis of the relations between value change, conflict, and conflict handling in the enterprise sector indicates, first, that a change of societal values in the direction assumed here, can, at least within the enterprise sector, be expected to shift the focus of conflicts to non-material goods and in some circumstances to increase the number of conflicts in that area. Second, the persuasion approach will become more significant for conflict-handling. An adequate response to this development would be to improve the prerequisites for successful persuasion, that is, to establish personal authority, to increase expertise and the capacity to process information, and to forge greater willingness to make compromises.

Along these lines, the enterprise sector is already trying to expand cooperative forms of management while further developing and applying partnership concepts. Cooperative management necessarily reinforces dialogue and offers both sides the opportunity to demonstrate personal integrity, to deepen mutual trust, and to build personal authority. Constant discussion of the opponent's arguments and interests can also contribute to an improvement of specialized knowledge, especially that having to do with the function, and to a better assessment of the alternatives and limits that determine the other side's range of action, as well as a sound assessment of one's own alternatives. This can make the necessity for compromise all the more apparent. At present, the trend toward developing cooperative management has barely progressed beyond middle management, which means that the prerequisites for a successful synchronization of goals through persuasion have not yet been satisfied for the majority of the enterprise staff. Many of the staff do benefit in general from profit and capital sharing, but such material participation lacks the quality of personal involvement and development.

Achieving more participation in decision making within the framework of cooperative management increases the opportunities for including interests that focus on non-material goods and thereby keeps pace with the changes in societal values assumed above. Since there are interdependencies between the total societal system and its parts, and between the parts themselves, the development taking place in the enterprise sector will not only avoid discrepancies between this partial system and the total system changing in the same direction, but will stimulate impulses suitable to reinforcing a societal development along the lines assumed by this analysis.

In connection with the discussion of gaining acceptance for strategies of democratization, Naschold[25] refers to the thesis that reforming individual organizations without also reforming (revolutionizing) the whole society will not be successful. He supports this hypothesis with a theorem from systems theory which holds that the structure of the total system and the relations between the total system and its parts is more important than the structure of the parts. If this assertion of the primacy of the total system is correct, one could not expect the total societal system to be reinforced by parallel developments of its parts. Rather, these changes would have to be interpreted as the result of the development of the total societal system. In this case, the confirmed changes in the enterprise sector could be used to support the hypothesis that a change toward placing heavier emphasis on non-material values is taking place throughout the total system as well. Should empirical findings contradict such a development, however, the implications hypothesized here indicate that one can expect the workers to become increasingly indifferent particularly toward participation in decision-making, and that management will abandon measures concerning the issue as far as is legally possible. In view of the reduced number of alternatives in handling conflicts, such a turn would be more of a handicap than a help to successful business management.

NOTES

*The German edition of this contribution will be found in: Bedürfnisse, Werte und Normen im Wandel. Bd. 2: Methoden und Analysen. Hrsg. von H. Stachowiak zusammen mit T. Herrmann und K. Stapf, München, Paderborn, Wien, Zürich 1981 (im Druck)

1. R. Inglehart, original, p. 279: "Die Werte der westlichen Gesellschaften scheinen sich von einer beinahe ausschließlichen Betonung der materiellen und physischen Sicherheit in Richtung auf eine höhere Bewertung von immateriellen Aspekten des Lebens verlagert zu haben ..."
   F. Lehner (1979, p. 317 et seq.) argues that the "post-materialistic" attitude and behavior patterns pointed out by Inglehart have resulted not from a value change but from a differentiation of the value and attitude patterns characteristic for many members of society (p. 324). According to Lehner, a high standard of living leads to a shift in emphasis from material to non-material interests for only some of the citizens in western industrialized societies

2. S. Beer, original, p. 241: "... die Sprache beschreibt Systeme auf eine Weise, die nahelegt, daß es zweckorientierte Motivationen hinter diesen Systemen gibt, was in Wirklichkeit nicht zutrifft."

3. For a description of the work relation as a membership relationship in enterprise, see A. Söllner, 4th ed 1974, p. 210, reference to T. Raiser, 1969, p. 154

4. See H. Stachowiak, 2nd ed. 1969, p. 3

5. See J. G. March and H. A. Simon, 1958, p. 84, for a discussion of the problems of testing

6. See G. Gäfgen, 3rd ed. 1974, p. 101 (planning stages) in connection with p. 26 et seq. (formal rationality), C. Zangemeister, 4th ed. 1976, p. 324 et seq. (decisionmaking matrix)

7. See H. Stachowiak, 2nd ed. 1969, p. 8 et seq.

8. The reader is referred here to G. Ruehl, 1974, A. R. Bunz, R. Jansen, and K. Schacht, 1974, A. Bruggemann, P. Großkurth, and F. Ulich, 1975

9. G. W. England, 1976. E. Gabele, W. Kirsch, and J. Treffert, 1977

10. R. Dahrendorf, 1962, p. 201

11. K. Boulding, 1963, p. 5

12. R. Dahrendorf, 1962, p. 202

13. For a critical discussion with approaches of conflict theory and the concepts of conflict, see W. Dorow, 1978, particularly pp. 27 - 54

14. This form of conflict is also called distribution conflict. See the very thorough analysis of forms of conflict in Dorow, 1978, p. 147. In the present discussion, the term "competition" is preferred so as to avoid confusion with the intrapersonal conflict of the distribution and the fulfillment of higher demands, which can definitely be called re-distribution, the acceptance of reduced contribution in an exchange relationship

15. For a discussion of conflict-matrix shareholder/staff, see W. Dorow, 1978, p. 174 et seq., and 1979, p. 371 et seq.

16. This form would not correspond to the differentiations of value and attitude patterns which F. Lehner, 1979, p. 324, described as value change. See Note 1

17. K. Holm, 1970, p. 51 et seq.

18. The problems of setting and gaining acceptance for safeguarding goals in the enterprise sector (enterprise policy goals) are the focal point of enterprise policy conceived as an interdisciplinary field involving business management and political science

19. R. Dahrendorf, 1962, K. Boulding, 1963, W. Krüger, 1972, W. M. Esser, 1975, M. Deutsch, 1976

20. See M. Klis, 1970, for definitions

21. See notes to Fig. 2

22. See G. Dlugos, 1977, for implications

23. H. Ziegler, 1970, particularly p. 45 et seq.

24. H. Ziegler, 1970, p. 32

25. F. Naschold, 1969, p. 83

LITERATURE

Beer, S. (1967), Kybernetik und Management (Cybernetics and Management). Translated from the English, 3rd ed., 1959, Frankfurt a. M.: Fischer

Boulding, K. (1963), Conflict and Defense: A General Theory, New York: Harper & Row

Bruggemann, A., Groskurth, P., Ulich, E. (1975), Arbeitszufriedenheit, Bern, Stuttgart, Wien: Hans Huber

Bunz, A. R., Jansen, R., Schacht, K. (1974), Qualität des Arbeitslebens: Soziale Kennziffern zu Arbeitszufriedenheit und Berufschancen. In: Forschungsbericht des Bundesministeriums für Arbeit und Sozialordnung. Bonn

Dahrendorf, R. (1962), Elemente einer Theorie des sozialen Konfliktes. In: Dahrendorf, R.: Gesellschaft und Freiheit, München: Piper & Co.

Deutsch, M. (1976), Konfliktregelung: Konstruktive und destruktive Prozesse, Ed. H.-R. Lückert, München, Basel: Ernst Reinhardt

Dlugos, G. (1974), Unternehmungspolitik als betriebswirtschaftlich-politologische Teildisziplin. In: Wild, J. (Ed.), Unternehmungsführung, Festschrift für Erich Kosiol zu seinem 75. Geburtstag, Berlin: Duncker & Humblot

Dlugos, G. (1977), Gesellschaftspolitische Implikationen unternehmungsinterner Konflikthandhabung. In: Die Betriebswirtschaft 37: 465 - 474

Dorow, W. (1978), Unternehmungskonflikte als Gegenstand unternehmungspolitischer Forschung, Berlin: Duncker & Humblot

Dorow, W. (1979), Konfliktforschung aus unternehmungspolitischer Sicht. In Dlugos, G. (Ed.): Unternehmungsbezogene Konfliktforschung. Methodologische und forschungsprogrammatische Grundfragen, Stuttgart: Poeschel, 353 - 376

England, G. W. (1975), The Manager and His Values: An International Perspective from the United States, Japan, Korea, India, and Australia, Cambridge, Mass.: Ballinger

Esser, W. M. (1975), Individuelles Konfliktverhalten in Organisationen, Stuttgart, Berlin, Köln, Mainz: Kohlhammer

Gabele, E., Kirsch, W., Treffert, J. (1977), Werte von Führungskräften der deutschen Wirtschaft. Eine empirische Analyse, München: Planungs- und organisationswissenschaftliche Schriften

Gäfgen, G. (1974, 3rd ed.), Theorie der wirtschaftlichen Entscheidung. Untersuchungen zur Logik und Bedeutung des rationalen Handelns, Tübingen: Mohr

Holm, K. (1970), Verteilung und Konflikt. Ein soziologisches Modell, Stuttgart: Enke

Inglehart, R. (1979), Wertwandel in den westlichen Gesellschaften: Politische Konsequenzen von materialistischen und postmaterialistischen Prioritäten, In: Klages, H., Kmieciak, P. (Ed.), Wertwandel und gesellschaftlicher Wandel, Frankfurt, New York: Campus

Klis, M. (1970), Überzeugung und Manipulation. Grundlagen einer Theorie betriebswirtschaftlicher Führungsstile, Wiesbaden: Betriebswirtschaftlicher Verlag Dr. Th. Gabler

Krüger, W. (1972), Probleme und Instrumente der Konflikthandhabung in der Unternehmung, Berlin: Duncker & Humblot

Lehner, F. (1979), Die "Stille Revolution": Zur Theorie und Realität des Wertwandels in hochindustrialisierten Gesellschaften, In: Klages, H., Kmieciak, P. (Ed.), Wertwandel und gesellschaftlicher Wandel, Frankfurt, New York: Campus

Naschold, F. (1969), Organisation und Demokratie. Untersuchungen zum Demokratisierungspotential in komplexen Organisationen, Stuttgart, Berlin, Köln, Mainz: Kohlhammer

Raiser, T. (1969), Das Unternehmen als Organisation. Kritik und Erneuerung der juristischen Unternehmenslehre, Berlin: de Gruyter

Rühl, G. (1974), Menschengerechte Arbeitsplätze durch sozio-technologische Systemgestaltung, In: Schlaffke, W., Rühl, G., Weil, R., Qualität des Lebens am Arbeitsplatz, Köln: Deutscher Instituts-Verlag

Söllner, A. (1974, 4th ed.), Arbeitsrecht, Stuttgart, Berlin, Köln, Mainz: Kohlhammer

Stachowiak, H. (1969, 2nd ed.), Denken und Erkennen im kybernetischen Modell, Wien, New York: Springer

Zangemeister, C. (1976, 4th ed.), Nutzwertanalyse in der Systemtechnik. Eine Methodik zur multidimensionalen Bewertung und Auswahl von Projektalternativen, München: Verlagskommission Wittemannsche Buchhandlung

Ziegler, H. (1970), Strukturen und Prozesse der Autorität in der Unternehmung, Stuttgart: Enke

Values and Conflict Behavior. An Exploration of Conceptual Relationships

Wolfgang Dorow

ABSTRACT

Starting from Rokeach's basic assumption that values are the most central elements which guide actions, we will discuss the dependence of interpersonal conflict behavior on the value system of individuals. Values, attitudes, and intentions developed by individuals in conflict situations prove to be of special relevance for the explanation and prediction of conflict behavior. Deductions are made toward a formulation of conflict-theoretical and conflict-technological hypotheses.

Conflict research presumes that conflict handling decisions are strongly dependent on the actor's changing situational condition. Therefore, explanations and predictions of decisions on specific alternatives of conflict handling make it necessary to consider different situational conditions. But with the help of value theory it can be maintained that the basic pattern of conflict handling remains constant regardless of varied conflict situations. The integration of value research and conflict research is regarded as a way to overcome the adhocness of conflict-theoretical statements. As a step toward this scientific goal the Fishbein/Ajzen model is applied to the behavioral elements of conflict behavior. This contribution adds to the analytical framework of conflict research which has been described by Dlugos in the preceding article.

INTRODUCTION

Value research is very frequently regarded as a basic social science, capable of offering explanatory variables for many social phenomena. "Values are determinants of virtually all kinds of behavior that could be called social behavior." (Rokeach 1973,24). Values serve, according to Rokeach, as standards which guide actions, especially as they

(1) lead us to take particular positions on social and political problems

(2) predispose us to favor ideologies

(3) guide presentation of self

(4) guide evaluation and judgement, praise and blame

(5) guide our comparing ourselves with others

(6) are employed as standards to persuade others

(7) help to rationalize own actions.

Although likewise the behavior in social, i.e. interpersonal, conflict situations is more and more seen under the viewpoint of values and of value change, value and conflict research have hitherto scarcely endeavored to accomplish an integration of their theories. The reason for the largely unrelated development of both concepts can mainly be seen in that value and conflict research are still occupied with their scientific basal problems.

Meyer/Rüegg (1979,47) emphasize that on the part of value research it has not as yet been intended to gain progressive action-theoretical knowledge. In the foreground rather stands the indicator-movement which measures values and value change in various life-areas. This also includes numerous attempts to classify values (e.g. Morris 1956, Kluckhohn/Strodtbeck 1961, Rokeach 1973, Gabele/Kirsch/Treffert 1979). Also conceptual relationships must be established with such research areas as need-, motivation-, attitude-, interest-, and goal research (Kmieciak 1976, Hondrich 1979). Furthermore, the function of values in specific conflict situations remains a problem yet to be solved in the area of value and conflict research.

In the following, we will deal with the problem of interdependences of values and interpersonal conflicts. First, we will discuss some epistemological questions.

VALUES AS VARIABLES OF CONFLICT BEHAVIOR

Seen methodologically, values can have a very different function in an empirical theory of conflict behavior. They can have the function of a cause, an instrumental, an intervening, a dependent, or an independent variable in the frame of conflict behavior. If we study conflict behavior causal-analytically, values can be a cause of conflicts. Values cause conflicts, when actors perceive that their realization is incompatible. Whereas, if we study conflict behavior final-analytically in a way that the generation, reinforcement, or solution of conflicts is viewed as a goal, then the articulation and propagation of values may serve as a means or an instrument of behavior in conflict situations. In this case, the articulation and propagation of values can be regarded as an instrumental variable of conflict handling.

Moreover, values can have the function of an intervening variable. Let us assume the variable X_1 "hierarchic structure" has a negative effect on variable X_2 "satisfying working conditions" for a certain actor. Negative working conditions result in a conflict. Between X_1 and X_2 there may exist an intervening variable X_3, e.g. the actor's value "equality". X_1 would have a negative effect on X_3, and X_3 one on X_2, which together form causes of conflict generation between the actor and his superior.

Value research conceptualizes values primarily as dependent variables. Values and value change are viewed as depending on a variety of factors, such as culture, experience, education, and ideology (Rokeach 1973, 23). In the relation of conflict and value research the dependence of values and value changes on kinds of conflicts, conflict handling procedures, and structural conditions of conflict behavior are of special interest. For example, one has to examine the effects of co-determination in Germany or of workers' self-control in Yugoslavia on values of managers and workers. Another question could refer to the dependence of value generation or reinforcement on specific systems of pay and promotion within an enterprise.

Yet, conflict research primarily includes in its hypotheses values and value change as independent variables, using them as data out of value research. Conflict research analyzes the effects of value and value change on the generation of conflicts and the choice of alternatives of conflict handling. An important question is, which effects are caused by a change in the direction of immaterial values on conflict generation and conflict handling, that means which new types of conflicts result therefrom and whether the conflict handling is more forceful, or less forceful (see Dlugos).

In the following, we would like to enlarge on individual aspects of the relation of value and conflict research. In doing so, we analyze this relation from the perspective of conflict research. It is therefore necessary to give a brief survey on the structure of conflict research in order to point out conflict-theoretical statements towards the integration of values as explanatory factors.

THE STRUCTURE OF CONFLICT RESEARCH

Areas of conflict research

The empiric-theoretical analysis of conflicts primarily includes the following areas (Kamitz 1979):

- The development of a conflict-classification (frequently:

intrapersonal, interpersonal, intragroup, intergroup conflicts, manifest, latent conflicts).

- The description and explanation of the generation of conflicts of specific types in specific situations (e.g. conflicts of organizational structure, of wages, of leadership behavior).
- The description and explanation of the effects of conflicts on the behavior of the conflict partners (e.g. strikes as an effect of a wage conflict in a specific situation).
- The analysis and recommendation of means for handling conflicts in organizations (e.g. recommendations of methods of organizational change, of specific types of conflict-handling procedures, of structural determinants of conflict behavior).

Conflict Generation, Conflict Evasion and Conflict Handling

The differentiation of the research areas shows that one of the main questions of theoretical work on conflict behavior is to systematize the process-elements of conflict behavior. Numerous attempts of systematizing conflict behavior have been made, many of them unsatisfying, as they disregard methodological requirements of classification (see the discussion in Mack/Snyder 1957, Dorow 1978).
The solution for classifying conflict behavior here suggested is to differentiate between two general behavioral components: Conflict generation and reactions to perceived conflicts. Reactions to perceived conflicts are classified in conflict evasion and conflict handling processes.

The following set of properties characterize the social, i.e. interpersonal conflict behavior:

1. Social conflicts require at least two actors.
2. Social conflicts arise from "position scarcity" and "resource scarcity".
3. Social conflicts require the perception of a potentially or actually colliding goal-setting process (colliding range of action) by at least one of the involved parties.
4. Conflict generating behavior is a goal-setting process designed to safeguard or enlarge one's own range of action against colliding ranges of action.
5. Conflict handling behavior is a goal-setting process designed to determine colliding ranges of action by exercising power with the purpose of realizing the safeguarding or enlarging of one's own range of action against the colliding range of action.

6. Conflict-evading behavior is a goal-setting process designed to leave the conflictful relationship.

For the analysis of interpersonal conflict behavior it is useful to differentiate between goal-setting processes causing conflict situations and goal-setting processes which are the reactions to the perceived conflict situation (Dlugos 1974, Dlugos et al. 1979, Dorow 1978, Dorow/Grunwald 1980).
The essential point of this approach of analyzing interpersonal conflict behavior is to dissolve the conflict behavior into two goal-setting processes:

1. Goal-setting processes which cause the conflict between the actors and
2. Goal-setting processes which are reactions to the perceived conflict between the actors.

There are two general reactions to conflicts:

Firstly, the evasion of a conflict which includes several alternatives for evading the conflictful relationship.
Secondly, the handling of a conflict, comprising various alternatives of conflict suppression and conflict regulation.

Although in this contribution only the problems of conflict handling will be discussed, we would like to give a brief explanation of conflict evasion as a reaction to perceived conflicts. We can assume that actors choose to evade the conflict if they believe themselves unable to safeguard their jeopardized goal and do not want to accept a manifest loss situation. They give up their jeopardized goal without trying to safeguard their goal. Alternatives of conflict evasion are reduction, or termination, of exchange relationships, repression of the conflictful perception or ignoring the colliding behavior.

Conflict handling aims at a suppression or regulation of a conflict. The purpose of conflict handling is to safeguard own jeopardized goals with the aid of pwerbases. Alternatives of conflict handling are goal determination and environment determination. Goal determination aims straight at the opponent's colliding goal-setting process; environment determination aims at the opponent's goal-setting process via a third party, or it aims at re-structuring the opponent's environmental situation in such a way as to make it impossible for the opponent to pursue his colliding goal. The determining of an opponent means influencing, or predisposing, the course of action taken or intended by the opponent by blocking his goal-setting process, or by changing his environmental conditions (see the preceding article by Dlugos).

The following chart shows the various kinds of reactions of an actor to a perceived conflict situation:

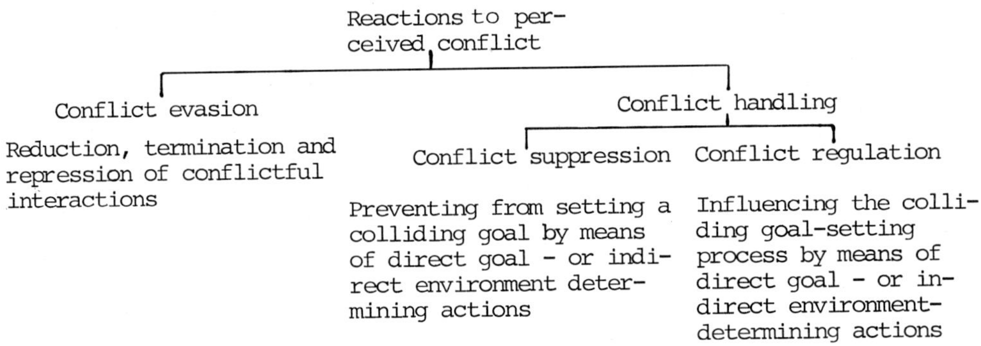

Figure 1: Alternatives of Conflict Reactions

A similar differentiation of conflict handling processes is discussed by Dahrendorf (1962).

The categories conflict evasion, conflict suppression, and conflict regulation are characterized by the purpose, or the general intention pursued by the actor in a conflict situation. The specific alternatives of conflict evasion (reduction, termination, repression), of conflict suppression and regulation (goal- and environment-determining) rather describe the pragmatic- technical procedure, how to evade, to suppress, and to regulate conflicts.

The purpose, or general intention of conflict evasion results from the actor's motive to avoid a manifest loss situation in his social relations.

The purpose, or general intention of conflict handling is the safeguarding of the jeopardized goal by actively influencing the opponent. Conflict suppression and regulation as categories of conflict handling differ, basically, from each other in their specific intentions.

The intention of conflict suppression is to prevent an actor from generating a colliding goal. Such an intention is primarily pursued by actors who evaluate conflict situations as dysfunctional. As is yet to be seen, this definition of conflict suppression has certain consequences for the formulation of hypotheses regarding the conflict suppression. The actor's intention to suppress the generation of a colliding goal means that the potential opponent must be placed in a situation in which he is incapable of developing and articulating colliding interests. Therefore, the prerequisites for a colliding behavior must be suppressed. For example, conflicts can be suppressed if the potential opponent is not supplied with relevant information which would enable him to develop colliding interests. Conflict suppression by filtering information is typical of the conflict handling policy of totalitarian governments (Dahrendorf 1962). Conflict suppression can also be based on a massive ideological influence. The main criterion of conflict suppression is the attempt to prevent a potential opponent from being capable of perceiving a conflict situation and developing colliding interests. Conflict suppression is, of course, not always effective. This is a question of power distribution between actor and opponent, but is not to be discussed here in detail. As long as a minimum of power bases are at the opponent's disposal, the attempts at suppressing the generation of colliding interests are no longer effective. Dahrendorf (1962) points out that conflict suppression cannot be durable and will result in violent upheaval.

It is not the purpose or general intention of conflict regulation to suppress conflict generation. The actor accepts that the opponent has a range of action which enables him to develop potentially or actually colliding goals. The conflict situation can even be desired, for it can be regarded as being functional. An example from the enterprise sector is the matrix organization which intentionally structures conflicts. Conflicts have to be solved, of course, for realizing the goals of the enterprise. It is not the purpose or intention of the conflict regulation to avoid a generation of conflict, but to regulate and solve the arisen conflict situation. This means that the conflict regulation must remove the expected or existent specific cause of the conflict. This definition of conflict regulation has also specific consequences for the formulating of the hypotheses. Conflict regulation means that new specific causes of conflict can be generated. By contrast, conflict suppression tends to solve conflicts for once and for all. Quasi-solution as a result of conflict-regulation processes does not in any way mean that a compromise is desired in every case. The result of conflict regulation processes depends, the same as with conflict suppression, on the power distribution between actor and opponent. According to the specific power distribution between actor and opponent the solution of a conflict regulation process may mean win, loss, or compromise for the actor.

Why do we stress the criterion of purpose or of general intention which is to be realized by the conflict handling ? In literature a number of approaches are discussed which systematize the conflict handling as per the criterion of results or the use of power. Win-lose struggles or strategies of compromise as well as processes of persuading, manipulating, and bargaining are discussed (Filley 1975, Tedeschi et al. 1972, Walton 1969, Thomas 1976, Oechsler 1979).

The analysis of the general intention of conflict handling is of major heuristic value for the integration of value and conflict research. This is based on the assumption that the relation between value system and the general intention how to react generally in conflict situations is more direct than the relation between value systems and an actual situation-specific behavioral process. The observable behavior is one of several alternatives of realizing a general intention of conflict handling. Structural and personal situation-specific variables influence the choice of these alternatives, such as the specific power-distribution, the costs of alternatives, the available period of time, social and legal norms and the actors' attitudes. The value system influences only indirectly the choice of a specific behavioral alternative, whereas the relation between value system and general intention of conflict handling can be considered as a more direct one. These relations have scarcely been explored.

The relations of value systems of actors, their actualization of general intentions of handling conflict situations and their actual behavior need to be explored. Intervening variables can, of course, also influence the relation of value system and general intention of conflict handling. An actor whose value system can be labeled authoritarian and repressive may develop the intention of conflict suppression in a conflict situation, but in view of social desirability he sets the intention of conflict regulation. In this case the actor experiences a conflict between his desired intention and the societally demanded intention of conflict handling.

The analysis of the relations "value system" - "intended conflict handling" - "actual conflict handling" requires further research, especially a refined frame of reference for the relevant variables. An approach to conceptualizing these relations is presented in chapter 4.

After this analysis of the conflict phenomenon we can discuss the scientific goals of conflict research.

Scientific Goals of Conflict Theory and Conflict Technology

The following is understood under conflict theory and conflict technology: Conflict theory is characterized by the theoretical scientific goal, conflict technology by the technological or instrumental scientific goal. The theoretic goal consists of the gaining of true, informative, and unbiased statements (theoretical hypotheses) on cause-effect relations in conflict behavior (Nagel 1961). The technological goal is based on the transformation of the theoretical statements, in a way that the effects of conflicts are regarded as goals, and the causes as means (technological hypotheses). (Popper, Poverty 1963, use the term 'social engineering'. See also the controversy on the scientific goals of social sciences in Adorno 1972.) Conflict-research, regrettably, does not differentiate in a sufficient manner between theory and technology. A scientifically founded conflict technology requires theoretical hypotheses on cause-effect relations.

Conflict technology has different tasks according to the actor's evaluation of conflicts. If conflicts are regarded as a threat to certain values, conflicts are evaluated as dysfunctional. It will then be the aim of conflict technology to inform about means for avoiding a generation of conflicts, in other words, means for conflict suppressing. For those categories of terminal values listed by Rokeach (1973), such as "a comfortable life", "a world at peace", "a world of beauty", "inner harmony" and "true friendship", conflicts can be dysfunctional, as they hinder the realization of these values. Conflicts, however, can also be evaluated as being functional, if they contribute to productivity, creativeness and organizational change. For terminal values such as "an exciting life", "freedom", "pleasure", and "self-respect", conflicts can be functional. In this case it would be the task of conflict technology to generate conflicts in social systems and to offer mechanisms of conflict regulation, in order to make an endangered value such as "self-respect" obvious and to propose a solution in such a conflict. It is in particular Dahrendorf (1962) who regards conflict technology as a means for piecemeal development of social systems.

Therefore, in addition to suppressing the generation of conflicts and the intended generation of conflicts, the third task of conflict technology is the recommendation of means for the regulation of generated conflicts. As we have seen, the mere existence of conflicting goals can be evaluated as functional or dysfunctional. However, whether or not functional conflicts end up being social-productive or social-destructive depends on the kind of conflict regulation processes. Actors who have the terminal value "an exciting life", will probably evaluate conflicts in a society as functional. But the kind of the conflict regulation process in a specific situation determines whether the conflict will end as win or loss for the actors, thus being social-productive or social-destructive.

A socially destructive conflict solution is reached, if both parties - compared with the initial situation - suffer losses. A socially productive conflict solution is reached, if both parties - compared with the initial situation - gain wins (integrative conflict-resolution). A distributive conflict solution is reached, if one actor gains what the other loses. It is the scientific goal of conflict-technological statements to inform actors how they might realize these alternatives of conflict solution.

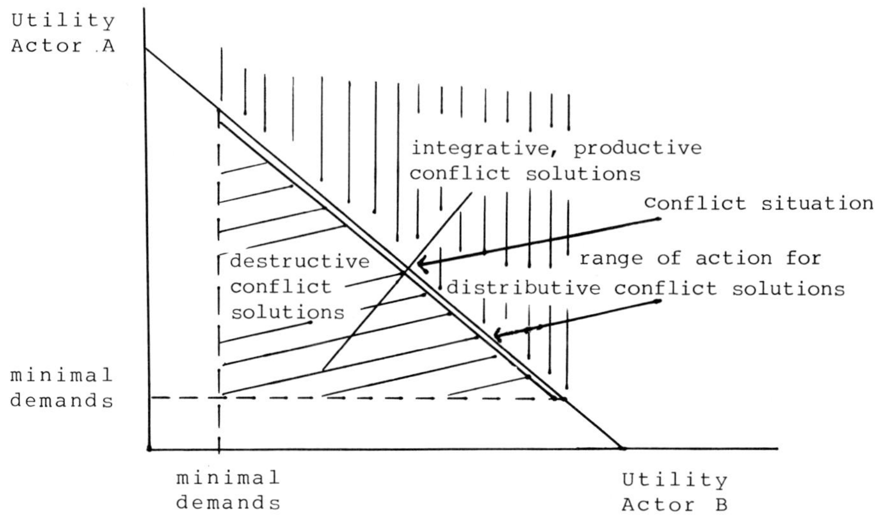

Figure 2: Social-productive, social-destructive, and social-distributive conflict solutions

After this brief review we can summarize the task of conflict technology as follows:

1. The recommendation of means for generating conflicts: - primarily actors are interested who regard conflicts as functional for the realization of their values.
2. The recommendation of means for suppressing the generation of conflicts: - primarily actors are interested who regard conflicts as dysfunctional for the realization of their values.
3. The recommendation of means for the regulation of conflict situations: - those actors are interested who want to solve generated conflicts distributively, social-productively or even--this is not to be excluded--social-destructively. (In many cases we can assume that a social-destructive conflict solution is not intended by the actors who regard conflicts as being functional, but that the social-destructive solution is the result of incapability of regulating the conflict situation in a social-distributive or social-productive way.)

The fulfilment of these technological aims or goals requires different conflict-theoretical hypotheses. It is of fundamental importance to differentiate the problems of

1. conflict generation
2. conflict suppression, and
3. conflict regulation

when formulating these hypotheses. In the following, we will deal with such hypotheses.

Theoretical and Technological Hypotheses of Conflict Generation

Conflicts are generated if actors pursue colliding goals and if at least one of the actors is conscious of the conflictful interaction process. Such actors will be interested in generating conflicts who evaluate conflicts as being functional. Is the specific cause of a conflict known, the realization of this cause induces the generation of a conflict situation. Let us assume the following theoretical hypothesis:

> "If employers and employees are represented in the supervisory board of a company, then colliding goals will be articulated openly."

Now if a society desires that conflicts in enterprises are not suppressed but can be openly formulated, the formation of such supervisory boards as a means for generating functional conflicts will be established as a law. The cause-effect statement of conflict theory will be transformed into an end-means statement of conflict technology:

> "If the aim of generating open goal conflicts is desired, then the formation of a supervisory board with employer's and employees' representatives is the suitable mean."

The institutionalization of such supervisory boards is obviously sufficient for generating open conflicts, but not necessary. Other causes or means of open conflict generation are also possible, e.g. actions of a powerful trade union. The generation of open conflicts would not be prevented by dispensing with the institutionalization of such a board.

The handling of conflicts by suppression or regulation is a further area of the theoretical and technological formulation of hypotheses. Let us at first regard the problem of conflict suppression.

Theoretical and Technological Hypotheses of Conflict Suppression

Naturally, in order to suppress conflicts, also the causes of conflicts must be known, which causes have to be prevented (Dahrendorf 1962). But the example just mentioned shows that the suppression of conflicts would necessitate the knowledge of all causes the appearance of which would have to be prevented. But it is hardly to be expected that we know of all specific conflict causes and can avoid conflicts in the supervisory board by preventing all these specific causes (Braun 1979). This problem can be solved by trying to find general causes or conditions which are necessary for all manifest conflicts. Therefore, we have to find the necessary conditions of conflicts, without which a generation of conflicting goals is not possible (Braun 1979). Let us assume that a necessary condition for the generation of all conflicts is that the actor has the ability or knowledge to set colliding goals and that at the same time he has the conviction of holding influencing power.

The theoretical hypotheses of conflict-suppression would then be as follows:

> "If actors do not have the ability or knowledge of setting colliding goals and are not convinced of holding influencing power, then the colliding goal-settings will not be openly articulated."

The technological hypotheses of conflict suppression would then be:

> "If it is the aim to suppress the open articulation of colliding goals, then the actors' ability or knowledge of setting colliding goals and their conviction of holding influencing power, is to be prevented."

We can therefore summarize that the conflict suppression is suitably reached by suppressing the necessary conditions. The conflict suppression is a special form of conflict handling. It serves the purpose to generally prevent the generation of conflicts. Therefore, we have to differentiate this type of conflict handling from the alternatives of conflict handling, which solely aim at the removal of sufficient but not necessary causes of conflict generation. In this case, conflicts are not suppressed but regulated by various processes of influence. Conflict handling processes of this kind are called conflict regulation processes. Therefore, we must also study the hypotheses of conflict regulation.

Theoretical and Technological Hypotheses of Conflict Regulation

As discussed before, conflict regulation is based on the attitude that conflicts are functional, justified and purposeful. Conflict regulation therefore means that actors do not try to suppress an opponent's ability to generate colliding interests, but it does not mean that they would not try to impede the realization of the colliding interest. The attempt of blocking the realization of a colliding goal may result in a win, loss or compromise for the actor, depending on the power relationship between actor and opponent. Conflict regulation aims at the blocking or determination of a specific colliding goal developed within the opponent's range of action. Theoretical hypotheses on conflict regulation inform about the actor's choice of a specific conflict regulation process and its consequences as an effect of the perception of a specific conflict situation. Such a cause-effect relationship is stated by the following theoretical hypothesis:

> "If, in a conflict situation, actors perceive beside limited colliding interests, also many facts of mutual interest valuable for both of them, then actors will only choose processes of goal-determining without any negative sanctions, which processes will improve faith in each other, improve future cooperation, and result in a social-productive compromise."

Another theoretical hypothesis of the effect of a specific conflict situation on the kind of the conflict regulation process and its solution could be:

> "If a wage conflict situation is perceived by actors as a situation of exploitation, then they will choose means of coercion for determining the opponent, which method will entail high conflict costs and lead to a break-down of cooperational relationships and to a solution which is socially distributive at best."

Depending on the kind of intentions actors may have regarding the way of handling conflicts, they will assign a different scientific goal to conflict technology. The hypotheses formulate two different cause-effect relationships, the transformation of which into end-means statements may result in extremely different recommendations. If actors pursue the aim that conflicts in organizations or in the society should be handled as much as possible free of coercion and in a social productive manner, then they will be interested in conflict-technological hypotheses of the first kind. We should not exclude that actors may themselves become interested in conflict-technological hypotheses, which inform them about the shaping of conflict situations, in order to cause vigorous forms of conflict handling in society or organizations. Actors who want to regulate conflicts in a society, primarily by means of coercion (prohibition, laws etc.), will demand conflict-technological recommendations on the basis of the second hypotheses, to exhibit wage conflicts as conflicts of aggression, exploitation or deprivation, if the aim of forceful conflict handlings is to be realized.

This review of the basal structure of conflict theory and technology will now be followed by the analysis of conceptual relationships between values and conflict behavior. In order to discuss the relationship between value and conflict research we shall at first elaborate the basic elements of the conflict-theoretical frame of reference. The relationships which are to be established between these conflict-theoretical elements and value research are simultaneously laid open.

LINKS BETWEEN CONCEPTUAL FRAMEWORKS OF CONFLICT AND VALUE RESEARCH

The Conceptual Framework of Conflict Research

The preceding discussion has shown that the conflict-theoretical framework is structured into the problem areas of conflict generation and conflict handling (in this discussion conflict evasion is excluded). Between value research and these still rather unspecified problem areas bridging theories are missing. In the following we will deal with this question of research.

Conflict Causes as a Conceptual Element

The analysis of Dlugos has worked out the dependences of the actors' contributions and demands on their internal and external functions in the enterprise sector. Since the participants of the firm as exchange partners can only achieve their goals if their contributions are mutually exchanged and/or their demands mutually fulfilled, they are in principle forced to cooperate (Jacobs 1971). However, since the goal-criteria, expectations of consequences and evaluations of the actors are not always homogeneous the exchange processes are permanently conflictful. Depending on the different interests and also on the factual possibilities of contribution, conflicts emerge within the exchange processes. The analysis of the actors' conflicting contributions and demands describes kinds and intensity of goal conflicts. Kinds and intensity of goal conflicts are strongly connected with the actors' ranges of action. The wider the actors' ranges of action, the more extensive their field of alternatives. The more heterogeneous the values, beliefs, attitudes, and intentions of actors, the greater the possibility that colliding alternatives of contributions and demands will be chosen. As mentioned above, the function of values and their specified beliefs, attitudes, and intentions as cause or intervening variables of interpersonal conflicts has to be clarified.

To gain explanations of a higher order conceptual links have to be established between conflict-theoretical analyses of conflicting goal-setting processes and value research. This interconnection can either effect an integration of value research results into conflict research or a genuine interdisciplinary exploration of problems of both approaches hitherto neglected.

Let us now consider the conflict-theoretical approach of analyzing causes of conflicting goals by breaking down the goal-setting processes into their structural elements (Dorow 1978, Dorow/Grunwald 1980):

Actor A		Actor B
Formal structure of the goal-setting process		Formal structure of the goal-setting process
1. Formulating a general goal conception		1. Formulating a general goal conception
2. Gathering alternatives	C	2. Gathering alternatives
3. Selection and evaluation of goal criteria	O	3. Selection and evaluation of goal criteria
4. Prediction of consequences	N F	4. Prediction of consequences
5. Evaluation of consequences	L I	5. Evaluation of consequences
6. Selection of a decision rule	C	6. Selection of a decision rule
7. Determination of the alternative to be realized	T	7. Determination of the alternative to be realized

Figure 3: Formal structure of conflicting goal-setting processes

The conflict is manifest in step 7. This step formulates the conflicting goals in terms of conflicting contributions and demands. The causal analysis of conflict generation has now to find the causes of such a goal conflict in the preceding steps of the goal-setting process. The phases 3 to 6 are especially conflictful, as here the different goal criteria, diverse expectations of consequences and diverse evaluations of goal criteria and consequences as well as the different choice of decision rules take effect on the conflict generation. Literature especially emphasizes conflicts regarding expectations of consequences and evaluations. Interpersonal conflicts due to incompatible expectations of consequences are also described as probability or belief conflicts. Evaluation conflicts refer to incompatible evaluations of goal criteria, consequences and decision rules. Statements on conflict generation will become more informative if, with the help of value research, the heterogeneity of expectations and evaluations of actors can be explained. Therefore, relationships have to be established between these conflict elements and the categories of value research such as values, beliefs, and attitudes.

After this brief discussion of conceptual elements of conflict generation we have now to turn to the sphere of conflict handling.

Conflict Handling as a Conceptual Element

In the sphere of conflict handling, the integration of value and conflict research aims at theories and technologies which refer to the question of choosing a certain alternative of conflict handling and to the question of achieving compliance in colliding goals. Value research has to supplement theories of power which also deal with these questions.

Conflict theory examines the question which individual goal criteria, expectations of consequences and evaluations determine the choice of a certain alternative of conflict handling, e.g. certain alternatives of conflict suppression and conflict regulation. Goal criteria of conflict handling, which are selected situation-specifically by the actors, are as follows:

1. Costs of conflict handling
2. Duration of conflict handling
3. Complementary effects of conflict handling
4. Competing effects of conflict handling
5. Degree of attainable safeguarding of one's own goal.

One of the technological tasks of conflict theory is to inform about methods of influencing the choice of conflict handling processes in the enterprise sector. This influence can be carried out by determining the goal criteria, the expectations and evaluations of conflict handling which are taken into consideration by the actors in the enterprise sector. It can be assumed that this technological task can essentially better be fulfilled by integrating value theoretical hypotheses. In the approach of Rokeach (1973) the instrumental values represent idealized modes of behavior. Instrumental values refer to actions which serve as means for achieving the terminal values. As conflict handling is a means for safeguarding jeopardized goals, conceptual relationships between goal-criteria - discussed in conflict theory - and instrumental values - discussed in value research - are to be assumed. Rokeach (1973, 15) points out that, for example, certain instrumental values concern the desirability of obedience, getting along well with others, politeness and self-control. For influencing the conflict handling processes employed in the enterprise sector it is necessary to obtain knowledge on the instrumental values of the participants of the firm which determine their situation-specific selection of goal criteria of conflict handling. If the kind of conflict handling is to be changed for a long period of time, influence must be taken directly or indirectly on values related to conflict handling decisions. For example, influence on conflict handling decisions can be exerted by encouraging, in a firm or society, such instrumental values as being courageous, broadminded, honest, or forgiving, polite, and obedient. An influence which is only directed at situation-specific goal criteria, expectations and evaluations, but not at the actors' instrumental values, is not likely to be of any lasting effect.

Conclusion

It was the purpose of this analysis to elaborate the basic elements of conflict situations which need to be interconnected with value research. The power of explanation and technological applicability increase if bridging theories between value and conflict research are developed. This, of course, raises basic questions of commensurability between primarily (social-)psychologically orientated value research and primarily economically orientated conflict research in the enterprise sector.

One of the problems deals with the question, whether the terms of both research conceptions are commensurable. The economic conflict research uses terms like contributions, demands, interests, goals, goal criteria, decision rules, expectations, and evaluations, whilst values, beliefs, attitudes, and intentions are central terms of value research. It is to be clarified, whether the terms of value and conflict research can be connected by definitions or whether they represent phenomena which have to be connected by hypotheses.

A further aspect concerns the question of reductionism. Can explanations of conflict phenomena which are characterized in the enterprise sector by economic goals be reduced to (social-) psychological explanations of value research ? But on the other hand we have to ask if (social-)psychological explanations of conflict phenomena in the enterprise sector can be reduced to economic explanations of conflicts (Nagel 1961, 336 pp.; Feyerabend 1962).

Being conscious of these unsolved problems we will now look at the conceptual elements of value research which are of importance for conflict theory.

The Conceptual Framework Relating Values, Beliefs, Attitudes, and Intentions to Behavior.

Let us again review the conceptual variables of conflict research and then discuss variables of value research. Conflict research dissolves conflict behavior into two goal-setting processes and explains them by the following variables:

1. Within the frame of limited ranges of action, the actors set specific goals of their functional contributions and demands. This goal-setting process induces or generates an inter-actor conflict which comprises the following explanatory variables:
   - the actors' goal criteria which are specifications of their functional contributions and demands, e.g. of stockholders, managers, workers, etc.;
   - the actors' expectations in respect of the degree of fulfilment of their goal criteria by the actions of the other actor,
   - the actors' evaluations of goal criteria and consequences.
2. Within the frame of limited ranges of action, the actors set safeguarding goals in order to safeguard their jeopardized contributions and demands. This goal-setting process is a conflict handling process which comprises the following explanatory variables:
   - the actors' goal criteria which are specifications of their general intention of safeguarding and of their employed power bases;
   - the actors' expectations in respect of the degree of fulfilment of their goal criteria by the various alternatives of conflict handling;
   - the actors' evaluation of goal criteria and consequences.

These explanatory concepts could be criticized by value research in that the variables taken into consideration by conflict research allow hypotheses of a low degree of explanation only. The goal criteria, evaluations, and expectations are only situation-specific and vary over time. Therefore, they are poor predictors. These variables are therefore less effective goals for conflict-technological purposes.

Explanation of conflict theory contain only those variables which cause behavior directly. More informative are explanations which state why actors pursue certain general intentions, specified goal criteria, predict certain consequences, and why they evaluate them in a certain way. The answer to these questions is the aim of value research and of its related concepts. The possibilities of predicting and structuring conflicts are therefore improved by an inclusion of value-theoretical hypotheses on goal criteria, expectations of consequences and evaluations by the actors.

In a recent paper, Rokeach (1979) analyzes the question of the relation between values, beliefs, attitudes, and behavior. Rokeach points out that "beliefs, attitudes, and values can be conceptualized as hierarchically-organized dispositions to respond preferentially, discriminatingly or differentially not only to objects and situations, but also to people in general, depending upon whether they agree or disagree with us and also to social controls, depending upon whether they are congruent or incongruent with our beliefs, attitudes, and values." Beliefs, attitudes, and values are regarded as central concepts of explaining behavior. The behavior towards persons and objects in various situations is not only a function of multiple attitudes towards the persons, objects, and situations, but also a function of related transcendental values that are activated by persons, objects, and situations. Put another way, the objects and situations we encounter have meaning for us not only because of the attitudes they activate within us, but also because they are perceived to be instrumental to realization (or to stand in the way of realization) of one or more instrumental values, and of one or more terminal values." (Rokeach 1979, 23). But not only instrumental and terminal values as well as attitudes, but also beliefs and intentions are behavioral determinants. These conceptual elements and their relation to the above mentioned variables of conflict research will be discussed in the following:

Beliefs. Beliefs are statements indicating a person's subjective probability that an actor, an object, or a situation have particular characteristics. Beliefs can be assumed to be numerous. They are formulated decision- and situation-specifically. If capital owners decide on investments, managers on production, workers on their places of work, and consumers on their purchases, they have to develop beliefs on their investment alternatives, on their production alternatives, on their alternatives of employment, and on their alternatives of purchasing. Beliefs represent the information an actor has about an object, a situation, and a person. Beliefs link objects, situations, and persons to certain attributes. For example, a statement like "a Volkswagen has a 37 mpg and costs $ 6.000,-" links the object Volkswagen to the goal criteria fuel consumption and purchasing price and to the consequences 37 mpg and $ 6.000,- to this alternative. "Thus the object of a belief may be a person, a group of people, an institution, a behavior, a policy, an event, etc., and the associated attribute may be any object, trait, property, quality, characteristic, outcome or event" (Fishbein/Ajzen 1975, 12) - or, as we might say, from the viewpoint of decision-making in conflict theory, beliefs describe alternatives in terms of goal criteria and expected consequences of alternatives for these goal criteria.

Attitudes. Attitudes refer to a person's favorable or unfavorable evaluation of an object, whereas beliefs represent the information he has about the object. Fishbein/Ajzen point out that this definition does not capture the full complexity of the attitudes concept, but that evaluation or feeling of favorableness or unfavorableness toward an object is the most essential part of the attitude concept. Attitudes interfere in a goal-setting process by weighing the considered goal criteria (mpg, costs, foreign product, service) and evaluating the believed consequences (low mpg is more important than high purchasing costs). Attitudes are the actors' likes and dislikes which determine the preferred alternative to be realized. According to Rokeach (1979), beliefs and attitudes are instrumental to the realization of values. Values, attitudes, and beliefs are congruent with one another and are hierarchically organized.

Values. Values are defined as being the most important and central element in a person's system of attitudes and beliefs. "They are ends rather than means; they are goals a person strives for and which help to determine many of his (her) other attitudes and beliefs." (Oskamp 1977, 13) Values like the acquisition of power, self-actualization, service to others, freedom, and equality determine via attitudes and beliefs the selection of behavioral alternatives. "One or more of such a relatively small number of values are implicated and activated whenever a person is required to act with respect to whatever the object in whatever the situation." (Rokeach 1979, 51). Rokeach (1973) proposes a list of 18 terminal and 18 instrumental values. Terminal values are structured in person-centered and societal-centered values, the instrumental values in moral and ego-centered values. Values as the most centered behavioral determinants take effect on behavior through beliefs and attitudes as well as intentions as specific expressions of terminal and instrumental values in concrete situations. Values are acquired institution-specifically, in educational, political, economic and legal institutions, and in the family. "Every human value, ..., is a 'social product' that has been transmitted and preserved in successive generations through one or more of society's institutions." "The values that one institution specializes in are not necessarily completely different from those in which other institutions specialize. They may overlap and share certain values in common and thus reinforce each other's values ... To the extent they do not overlap, however, they will compete with one another ...." (Rokeach 1973, 24).

This citation points out that the values which influence the conflict behavior in the enterprise sector reflect values which actors have acquired in other institutions. On the other hand, the enterprise sector, being one of the most important societal sectors can play an active rôle when forming values in a society (Etzioni 1968). This would be a task for the above discussed conflict technology within the enterprise sector.

Behavioral intention. Fishbein/Ajzen (1975) add a further variable to the relation of beliefs-attitudes-behavior which they call behavioral intentions. This variable is defined as indicating an actor's subjective probability that he will perform a particular behavior toward an object or person. If this variable is applied to the goal-setting processes discussed, we have to differentiate two kinds of behavioral intentions: General intentions and specific behavioral intentions. The general intention consists of a general idea how to solve a certain problem, whereas the specific intention consists of the selected alternative which is to be realized. General and specific intentions are determined by a hierarchy of general and specific beliefs and attitudes. If there are no conflicting ranges of action the specific behavioral intention may be realized, whereby the realization process may be observable as an overt behavior.

The framework discussed, relating beliefs-attitudes-intentions-and behavior, is illustrated by the following figure (Fishbein/Ajzen 1975, 15):

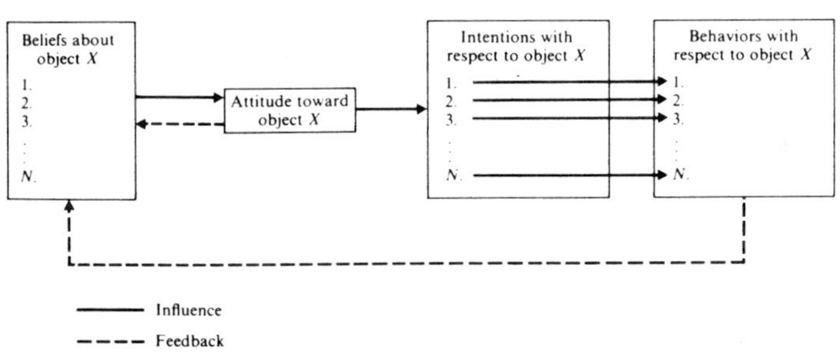

Figure 4: Conceptual framework relating beliefs, attitudes, intentions, and behaviors with respect to a given object.

After this analysis of conceptual elements of conflict and value research, some conclusions will be drawn for the development of an integrated research-design.

CONCLUSIONS FOR THE INTEGRATION OF VALUE AND CONFLICT RESEARCH

In this contribution we have dealt with the question of interpersonal conflicts and tried to analyze the rôle played by values in conflict generation and conflict handling. The aim was to elaborate the conceptual relationships between values and conflict behavior from two points of view: From the epistemological and from the empiric-theoretical perspective. The epistemological analysis dealt with values as variables within the frame of conflict behavior. The second aim of the epistemological part of this contribution was to show - with the examples of hypotheses - that empiric-theoretical conflict research requires a strict differentiation of the conflict generating and conflict handling problem areas. Conflict generation and conflict handling are to be understood as two different goal-setting processes. In the model of Fishbein/Ajzen we can insert these two goal-setting processes as differentiated "objects" which are subject to the behavioral components as explaining factors of conflict generation and conflict handling.

One of the main conclusions from this analysis is that value research is to be connected with conflict research by two hierarchies of behavioral components. The first hierarchy of values, beliefs and attitudes to be examined, is related to the formulation of intention and goal criteria of the conflict generating processes. The second hierarchy to be examined is related to the formulation of intentions and goal criteria of conflict handling processes.

For explanation, prediction, and technological influence conflict research requires two value-theoretical areas of results:

1. The first question is which values, beliefs and attitudes of actors cause the perception of certain conditions of interaction processes as conflicts ? The empirical investigation of these behavioral determinants and their change over time would inform us about the dynamics of conflict generation in the enterprise. The functional goal criteria stockholders, managers, workers and the other participants of the firm intend to realize are instrumental for the realization of their values. A bridging theory between value and conflict research within the range of conflict generation explains which self-concepts are pursued by the actors and which limitations of their ranges of action they perceive as conflicting with their self-concept. The technological use of such knowledge would enable us to influence the kinds of conflict generation. The possibility to influence the generation of conflicts presupposes the availability of still other power resources, for instance authority, in addition to necessary knowledge.

2. The second question which conflict research puts to value research refers to the effect of values, beliefs and attitudes on the decision of how a conflict is to be handled. From a conflict-theoretical view we assume that after the perception of a conflict situation a decision is made as regards the kind of conflict handling, whereby specific choice criteria, such as costs, duration of conflict handling procedures and so on are taken into consideration. But an integration of value and conflict research makes it possible to explain why actors have a certain predisposition to handle conflicts by processes of suppression or regulation. As discussed earlier, this predisposition depends on the actors' perception of conflicts as being functional or dysfunctional for the realization of their values. In both cases conflict handling processes aim at safeguarding their contributions which they are willing to perform and their demands they want to see fulfilled. For explanation, prediction and technological influence conflict research requires information about the values, beliefs and attitudes which induce actors to handle conflicts principally in a forceful, violent and uncompromising manner, or in a meliorative and compromising manner. A democratic society will assign to an integrated value and conflict research the technological task of actualizing values in the societal institutions in a way that conflict suppression is excluded from the field of conflict handling alternatives.

This discussion of an integrated value and conflict research proposes the investigation of interrelationships between values and conflict behavior in the distinct behavioral areas of conflict generation and conflict handling:

1. The investigation of interrelationships between values, beliefs, attitudes, intentions, and conflict generation.

2. The investigation of interrelationships between values, beliefs, attitudes, intentions, and conflict handling.

Finally we have to take into account that these interrelationships are influenced by specific functions performed by the actors in the enterprise sector. Each of these functions is in a different way instrumental in fulfilling the actors' values. We can expect that by analyzing the enterprise sector and its functions we will find not only conflicting but also harmonizing values, beliefs, and attitudes. With Rokeach (1973) we can assume that these values, beliefs, and attitudes within the enterprise sector can also collide or harmonize with those in other societal institutions. It is not only the task of conflict research related to the enterprise sector to reconcile conflicting values, beliefs, and attitudes within the enterprise sector, but also to reconcile conflicting values between the enterprise sector and its societal environment.

BIBLIOGRAPHY

Adorno, Th. W. et al. (1972), Der Positivismusstreit in der deutschen Soziologie, Neuwied und Berlin: Luchterhand

Braun, G. E. (1979), Das liberalistische Modell als konzeptioneller Bezugsrahmen für Konfliktanalyse und Konflikthandhabung. In: Dlugos, G. (Ed.) 89-114

Carnap, R. (1961), Introduction and Formalization of Logic, Vol. 1.2. Cambridge, Mass.: Harvard University Press.

Cyert, R. M., March, J. G. (1963), A Behavioral Theory of the Firm, Englewood Cliffs, N. J.: Prentice Hall

Dahrendorf, R. (1962), Elemente einer Theorie des sozialen Konflikts. In: Gesellschaft und Freiheit, München: Piper, 197-235

Dlugos, G. (1974), Unternehmungspolitik als betriebswirtschaftlich-politologische Teildisziplin. In: Wild,J.(Ed.), Unternehmungsführung, Berlin: Duncker u. Humblot, 39-73

Dlugos, G. (Ed.) (1979), Unternehmungsbezogene Konfliktforschung. Methodologische und forschungsprogrammatische Grundfragen, Stuttgart: Poeschel

Dlugos, G. et al. (1979), Business-Political Spectrum of Research, Work Paper 28/1979, Institute for Business Management, Free University Berin

Dorow, W. (1978), Unternehmungskonflikte als Gegenstand unternehmungspolitischer Forschung, Berlin: Duncker u. Humblot

Dorow, W. (1979), Konfliktforschung aus unternehmungspolitischer Sicht. In: Dlugos, G. (Ed.): Unternehmungsbezogene Konfliktforschung. Methodologische und forschungsprogrammatische Grundfragen, Stuttgart: Poeschel, 353

Dorow, W., Grunwald, W. (1980), Konflikte in Organisationen. In: Neubauer, R., Rosenstiel, C. von (Ed.), Handbuch der angewandten Psychologie, Band I, München: Moderne Industrie, 509-530

Etzioni, A. (1968), The Active Society, London: Collier-Macmillian

Feather, N. (1975), Values in Education and Society, New York: The Free Press

Feyerabend, P. K. (1962), Explanation, Reduction, and Empiricism. In: Feigl, H., Maxwell, G.(Eds.), Minnesota Studies in the Philosophy of Science, Vol. II. Minneapolis: University of Minnesota Press, 28-97

Filley, A. C. (1975), Interpersonal Conflict Resolution, Glenview, Ill.: Scott, Foresman

Fishbein, M., Ajzen, I. (1975), Belief, Attitude, Intention and Behavior: An Introduction to Theory and Research, Reading, Mass.: Addison-Wesley

Gabele, E., Kirsch, W. , Treffert, I. (1979), Die Messung von Werten in Unternehmen - Ein empirischer Versuch. In: Klages, H., Kmieciak, P. (Ed.)

Hondrich, K. O. (1979), Bedürfnisse, Werte und soziale Steuerung. In: Klages, H. Kmieciak, P. (Ed.)

Jacobs, T. O. (1971), Leadership and Exchange in Formal Organizations, Virginia: Human Resources Research Organization

Kahn, R. L., Wolfe, D. M., Quinn, R. P., Snoek, D. J. (1964), Organizational Stress: Studies in Role Conflict and Ambiguity, New York, London, Sidney: John Wiley

Kamitz, R. (1979), Wissenschaftslogische Probleme beim Aufbau einer Theorie der Konflikte. In: Dlugos, G. (Ed.), 33-44

Klages, H. Kmieciak, P. (Ed.) (1979), Wertwandel und gesellschaftlicher Wandel, Frankfurt, New York: Campus

Kluckhohn, F. R., Strodtbeck, F. L. (1961), Variations in Value Orientations, Evanston, Ill.: Row, Peterson & Co.

Kmieciak, P. (1976), Wertstrukturen und Wertwandel in der Bundesrepublik Deutschland, Göttingen: Campus

Mack, R., Snyder, R. (1957), The Analysis of Social Conflict Toward an Overview and Synthesis. In:Journal of Conflict Resolution. 1, 212-248

Meyer, R., Rüegg, W. (1979), Wertforschung im systematischen internationalen Vergleich. In: Klages, H. Kmieciak, P. (Ed.)

Morris, C. (1956), Varieties in Human Value, Chicago: University Press

Nagel, E. (1961), The Value-Oriented Bias of Social Inquiry. In: Nagel, E., The Structure of Science. New York: Harcourt, Brace, and World

Oechsler, W. A. (1979), Konfliktmanagement:Theorie und Praxis industrieller Arbeitskonflikte, Wiesbaden: Gabler

Oskamp, S. (1977), Attitudes and Opinions, Englewood Cliffs, N. J.: Prentice-Hall

Popper, K. R. (1960), The Poverty of Historicism, London: Routledge and Kegan Paul

Popper, K. R. (1963), Conjectures and Refutations, 2nd ed., London: Routledge and Kegan Paul

Rokeach, M. (1973), The Nature of Human Values, New York: The Free Press

Rokeach, M. (1979), Some Unresolved Issues in Theory of Beliefs, Attitudes, and Values. Paper presented on March 15, 1979 at the 1978-79 Nebraska Symposium on Motivation in the "Social Psychology of Beliefs, Attitudes, and Values".

Tedeschi, J. T., Schlenker, B. R., Lindskold, D. (1972), The Exercise of Power and Influence: The Source of Influence. In: Tedeschi, J. T. (Ed.), The Social Influence Process. Chicago: Aldine-Atherton, 287-345

Thomas, K. (1976), Conflict and Conflict-Management. In: Dunette, M. (Ed.), Handbook of Industrial and Organizational Psychology. Chicago: Rand McNally, 889-936

Walton, R. E. (1969), Interpersonal Peacemaking: Confrontations and Third Party Consultation, Reading, Mass.: Addison-Wesley

Dynamization of Employees' Goal Criteria

Jochen Wondracek

ABSTRACT

The difference between personal and organizational goals is one of the most important problems in organizational theory. This paper will attempt to elaborate on this difference by the use of sociological and psychological theories. Following this analysis, the impact of value change on the difference between personal and organizational goals in modern western societies will be assessed. Some consequences for the management process will be discussed.

TWO MAIN APPROACHES OF ORGANIZATIONAL THEORY

The study of the basic differences between individual goals and the so called "goals of the organization" is one of the most important areas of research of modern organization theory.

In this main stream of research we can differentiate between two major approaches:

On the one side there are students of organization theory who discuss the difference between personal goals and organizational goals as a human problem (alienation) or those who discuss it as an economic problem of organizational design (efficiency).

On the other side there are students, mainly in the tradition of Max Weber and especially for Germany Arnold Gehlen, who emphasize the immense advantage of this difference and praise it as one of the major invention of mankind in modern history.

My outline will discuss the second approach of organization theory. I will try to evaluate some consequences for the differences between personal goals and organizational goals caused by a change of values in modern western societies. Further I will discuss some probable implications of this development on management in modern corporations.

For the purpose of my discussion let me reformulate the basic idea of the difference between personal and organizational goals in terms of some different sociological and psychological theories with increasing complexity:

THEORETICAL RECONSTRUCTION OF THE DIFFERENCE BETWEEN INDIVIDUAL AND ORGANIZATIONAL GOALS

Functional Theory

As a first layer we use the functional theory of organization (Luhmann, 1973) to analyse the main advantages of the differentiation between personal and organizational goals.

In the view of this approach we can reformulate the goals of an individual as motives and the goals of an organization as ends. Between motives and ends there are only limited areas of consent. It is possible to develop a taxonomy of organizational types which varies in terms of the distance between motives and ends and the degree of necessary consent between the two variables.

Clerical organizations like protestant churches ask for a high conformity between their ends and the goals of their active members. This claim is weaker in the case of the Catholic church because of the central function of the ritual there and it is very weak in such secular organizations as clubs and the modern corporation (Gehlen, 1964). This short list of examples gives us a first hint of the main advantage of a weak congruence between motives and ends in organization. The ends of an organization can vary - caused by changes in the environment of the organization - without a comparable variation of the individual motives as long as this variation of organizational goals does not influence the area of partial consent between motives and ends. Chester Barnard has given us some interesting insights in the social-psychological processes which determine the area of general acceptance and the conditions of equilibrium between mutual contributions (Barnard, 1966). Another fruitful parallel to this basic idea is the taxonomy of Hirschman, especially his dichotomy of 'exit' and 'voice' (Hirschman, 1972). Members of organizations with a high congruence between individual goals and organizational goals will - in a case of conflicts between the goals - tend to use the mechanism of 'voice' and will then - if they have no success - leave their organization ('exit'). A good example of this process is the history of the Protestant church and the many different sects. Members of an organization with a medium congruence between motives and ends will tend to use 'voice', but, due to the flexibility of the organization, will seldom tend to leave the organization, even if they have no success (compare the relatively small number of schisms in the history of the Catholic church over 1500 years). Members of organizations with a low congruence of ends and motives will tend to leave their organization in a case of conflict instead of speaking out ('voice').

Of course, this level of analysis is too strongly macro-oriented because there are differences in the congruence between motives and ends even between members of the same organization. On the other side we sometimes have the problem to come to a higher congruence between motives of some members and the ends of an organization, for example, an increase in the overall efficiency by reducing the turnover.

Role Theory

As a second layer for the discussion of these and related problems we choose a more complex and more micro-oriented approach in the analysis of organizations, called role theory.

We can differentiate three major elements in the roles of organization members (Offe, 1973):

- instrumental rules
- regulative norms
- extrafunctional norms.

"Instrumental rules" are rules which are closely related to the duties of everyday work. They are predefined by the technological structures of the jobs in the organization.

"Regulative norms" are norms, which reflect the general expectancies in organizations, e.g. standards of behavior like punctuality, caution, cooperation with colleagues a.s.o.

"Extrafunctional norms" are not directly related to the situation at work. They stand for the degree of congruence between individual motives and ends, some may even call it 'ideology', of an organization. We can now distinguish between two types of typical roles of members in an organization:

(Diagram 1)

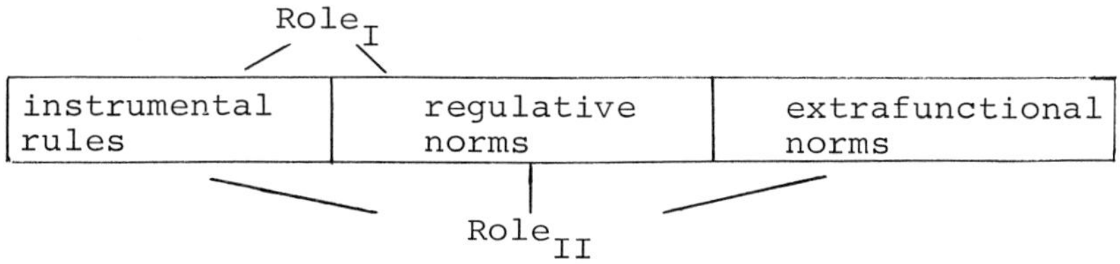

Normally we tend to say that the occurrence of role$_{II}$ is much higher in upper ranks on an organizational hierarchy while we usually find role$_{I}$ in lower ranks. This weak hypothesis would reflect a solution to the problem of the organization to differentiate requirements on its members under different circumstances like jobs, duties a.s.o.

In order to differentiate this simple picture of the two roles at the top and at the bottom on a hierarchy we must use a more complex approach, which we call "patterns of organizational integration". It reflects mainly some results of the field research in the area of industrial sociology. This will enable us to discuss some special problems of these two types of roles of organizational members concerning our main theme, the change of value systems.

Patterns of Organizational Integration

We will distinguish four different patterns of organizational integration (Türk, 1977; Duske/Wondracek, 1978):

(Diagram 2)

- instrumental integration
- bureaucratic integration
- professional integration
- political integration

"Instrumental integration" stands for an attitude of members who understand their organization mostly as a means of fulfilling their everyday needs. This does not coincide with the structure and the non-monetary gratifications offered by the organization (compare "calculative involvement", Etzioni, 1975; "instrumental orientation, Goldthorpe et al., 1976; "legal compliance", Katz, 1964).

"Bureaucratic integration" stands for a close relationship between the rules of an organization and the loyality of the members to its rules. This loyality is bound to the unique processes in organizational life and not to their motives or the ends of their organization (compare Kleman, 1958; "locals", Gouldner, 1969; "job bureaucrats", Reissman, 1949).

"Professional integration" stands for the behaviour of some members who actualize their internalized professional standards in their organization. For such a member the organization is only an interchangeable environment. If the organization is capable of providing the desired environment, professionally integrated members will accept some parts of the goal system of their organization (compare "cosmopolitans", Gouldner 1969; "specialists", Blau/Scott, 1962; "functional bureaucrats", Reissman, 1949).

"Political integration" stands for a special capability of some member to integrate their personal goals (motives) and the organizational ends but of course even this integration can always be only partial, with the exception of some pathological cases ("right or wrong, my corporation").

It seems reasonable to combine organizational hierarchy with these integration patterns in a way that the higher ranks correlate with the political integration pattern and the lower ranks with the instrumental pattern. If we consider the other two patterns and reflect them before the background of reality in modern corporations, we would run into difficulties.

Therefore we will leave the hierarchy - oriented analysis and will use a more sophisticated role theoretical approach which will give us much more insights in our problem.

The Problem of Variability in Role Behavior

For the purpose of our following analysis we will use a two dimensional scheme, proposed by Dreitzel (Dreitzel, 1968) in which the a-axis expresses the identification of an individual with his role, while the x-axis expresses the increasing strength of the ego. Every point in this diagram stands for a special degree of variability of role behavior of an individual or of a group of individuals.

(Diagram 3)

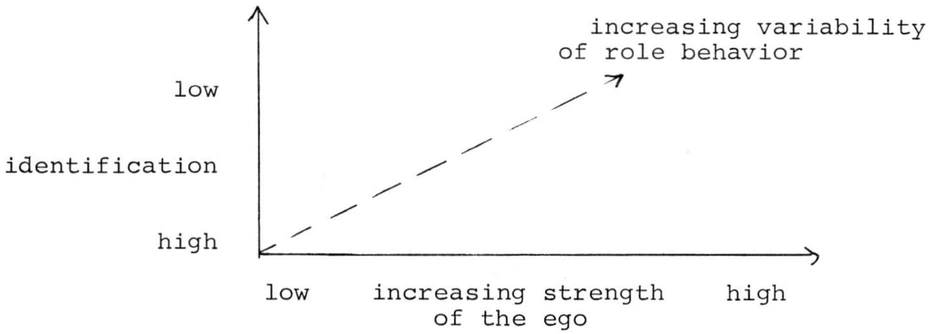

As a first step to clarify the intention of this approach, I will try to classify some well known social roles with the help of this scheme:

(Diagram 4)

low	participant in traffic game player	chairman of meetings student in examinations	neighbor host
identification	soldier prisoner	civil servant worker	politician actor scientist
high	children patient	parents priests	husband lover charismatic leader

low — increasing strength of the ego — high

If we analyse our integration patterns in terms of the basic scheme, we will find the following result:

(Diagram 5)

low	III instrumental integration		IV professional integration
identification			
high	I bureaucratic integration		II political integration

low — increasing strength of the ego — high

It is obvious that the dimensions of the x- and y-axis could be replaced with the dichotomy of Hirschman without changing the scheme: the y-axis would express the variable "exit", the x-axis the variable "voice" ("high" and "low" must be exchanged on the y-axis).

THE DYNAMIZATION OF INDIVIDUAL GOAL CRITERIA

We can now resume the results of our reconstruction of the problem of the difference between organizational goals and individual motives:

The mix of different integration patterns in one organization is a necessary postulate to preserve the unity of the organization and to provide the flexibility to react or to act in a changing environment. But we can also conclude that this mix is - at best - a very delicate equilibrium which is strongly exposed to more fundamental changes inside and mainly outside of the organization. We can also deduce that in a static analysis every integration pattern represents a specific but general set of individual goal criteria which is typical for this group and which is the main factor for forming it as a group. It is also possible - in a more integrated view as proposed by Prof. Dlugos in his outline - to analyse the members of every group in terms of a specific evaluation scheme concerning their goal criteria or concerning the consequences of different alternatives. The outline of Prof. Dlugos has very clearly shown which changes of internal structures and processes - especially conflict behavior - we have to expect under the conditions of a changing environment. I will discuss on the following pages a more specific question about consequences of the dynamization of individual goal criteria for the outside performance, especially flexibility of an organization under differing value systems. The question is, what will happen to these sets of individual goal criteria and their relation to another under the pressure of changes in the environment, for example:

what are the consequences for the organization

- if the members of group III will increase the strength of their ego ?
- if the members of group I will reduce their identification with the rules and structures of their organization ?
- if the members of group IV will tend to lower their already low identification with their organization ?
- if the members of group II will increase the strength of their ego ?

At first sight, we can expect that organizations will notice the consequences of this development in the form of some very "weak signals" (Ansoff, 1976) which will later force them to react at very high speed in a very short period of time.

From a scientific point of view, it therefore seems necessary to give some more precise and valid answers on the question, with which probability, which change will occur concerning goal criteria and the relative position of the groups to each other. Further, as we are involved in an applied science, we have to ask which strategic steps, and which new forms and instruments of organizational development, organizations should provide to solve the problems of a specific scenario of the near future.

THEORIES OF VALUE CHANGE IN MODERN CIVILIZATIONS

As a first step for a more systematic discussion of these questions, it seems interesting to analyze the results of some prominent and important contributions to a theory of value change in modern western civilizations, with the hope of finding some basic structures of a derived theory on the dynamization of individual goal criteria.

Rituals in Modern Cultures

Our main emphasis in this discussion will be on the work of Mary Douglas (Douglas, 1973) which was published some years ago as a comparative ethnological study with many important consequences regarding developments in modern cultures.
For the purpose of her analysis of very different societies, Mary Douglas has developed an analytical scheme in the tradition of Durkheim which consists of two social dimensions (Douglas, 1973, 77 ff): one dimension, called grid, is order, classification of the symbolic system and the way individuals see their world. The other dimension "group" is pressure, and the experience of having no option but to consent to the overwhelming demands of other people. We can draw the dimension of "grid" vertically up from zero towards more and more comprehensive articulation. The zero would represent a blank total confusion with no meaning whatever. Downwards from zero we can draw the world of private thought with the extreme case of a coherent but entirely private system of classification which would point eventually to madness.

On the x-axis we can draw pressure increasing from zero to the right. At zero, no demands are made on the individual. On the left side of zero we draw the degree of exerting pressure on other people. The result looks like this:

(Diagram 6)

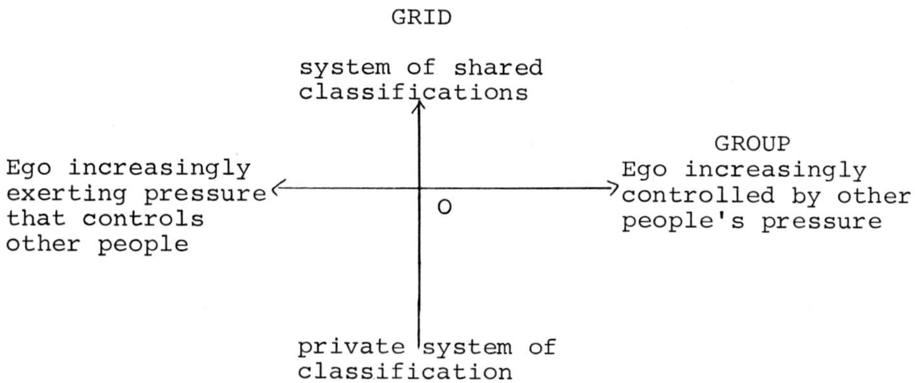

The parallels to our diagram 3 are obvious:

We can easily transform the dimensions "identification" and "increasing strength of the ego" to Mary Douglas' "group - grid" scheme.

If we map the four different integration patterns in the "group - grid" scheme, we will receive the result shown in diagram 7.

(Diagram 7)

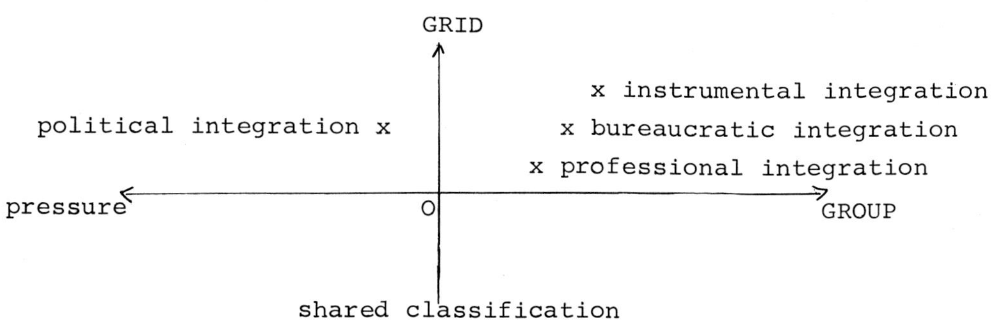

Mary Douglas' extensive analysis of the empirical findings of many different ethnological field researches has shown that every social system which is spread across the diagram from the highest point midway between the public grid and the group on the right and across to some high point at the top left can be called a stable but complex structure. As we can see this condition is fulfilled on our map of the different integration patterns in a modern corporation. Any significant shift downwards and/or leftwards will change the situation: A system that is spread across the diagram at a low level of classification is likely to become one that is continually subject to upheaval and a changing profile for the distribution of authority.

The "Bernstein-Effect"

Can we find such "downwards" tendencies in modern western cultures which would symbolize the kind of dynamization of goal-criteria which we are looking for ? One important and significant hint, given by Mary Douglas, for such a shift, is what she has called the "Bernstein-Effect".

Again, we can summarize Basil Bernstein's approach (Bernstein, 1971; Douglas, 1973, 44 ff.) in a two dimensional diagram.(Fig.8) The vertical line expresses his famous characterization of two different types of linguistic codes. One is called the elaborated code, which the speaker selects from a wide range of syntactic alternatives, which are flexibly organized. In the other, called restricted code, the speaker draws from a much narrower set of syntactic alternatives, which are more rigidly organized.

The x-axis expresses the system of family control. Bernstein distinguishes two extreme types, the positional and the personal control. The personal control system is determined by the idea of the autonomy and unique value of the individual. When the child asks a question, the parents feel obliged to answer it, by as full an explanation as they know. The child tends to be controlled by persons-oriented appeals and by abstract principles. ("Why can't I do it ? Because your father's feeling worried" or "How would you like it if you were a dog?" a.s.o.). In the positional family, the child is controlled by a continual internalizing of social patterns, of ascribed role categories. ("Why must I do this ? Because I said so" or "Because children always do" or "Because you are a girl.")

The structure of Bernstein's scheme looks like this:

(Diagram 8)

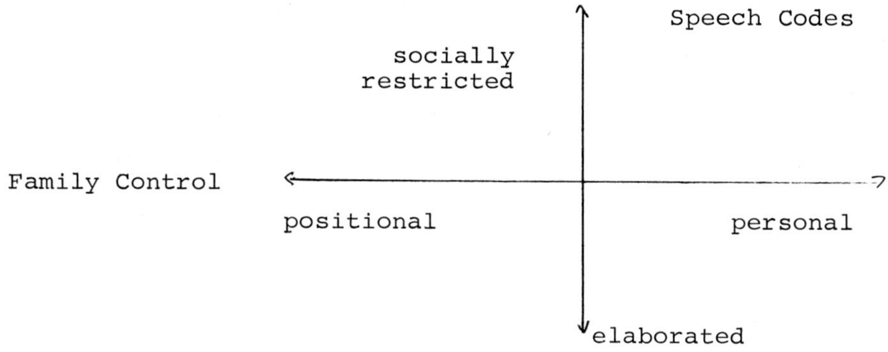

Mary Douglas, in collaboration with Basil Bernstein, has used this basic structure in a very interesting, but of course only impressionistic way. With Bernstein's help, Mary Douglas has differentiated four "cosmological ideas", and has analysed the actual constants of these four variables in every square of the scheme (Douglas, 1973, 50):

(Diagram 9)

(1) cardinal virtues

(2) cardinal sins

(3) the idea of the self

(4) art form

SPEECH

Socially restricted

A	C
(1) piety, honour (respect for roles)	(1) sincerity, authenticity
(2) formal transgression against social structure	(2) sins against the self, hypocrisy, cruelty, acceptance of frustration
(3) self, passive, undifferentiated element in a structured environment	(3) internally differentiated agent, attempting to control unstructured environment
(4) primitive; structural elaborations upon social categories, humans as cardboard allegorical figures	(4) romantic: triumph of individual over structure (escape, brief happiness, etc.)
	FAMILY CONTROL
positional	personal
(1) truth, duty	(1) personal success doing good to humanity
(2) cardinal sin is failure to respond to demands of social structure	(2) generalized guilt, individual and collective
(3) active agent, internally differentiated, responding to roles	(3) subject alone
(4) classical: triumph of structure over individual	(4) professional: overriding concern with techniques and materials of creative process
B	D

Speech elaborated

Empirical findings about the development in modern western cultures show a very significant tendency in the movement downwards and rightwards in this scheme, especially as a result of forms of primary socialisation of children in modern families. Mary Douglas has called the form of this upbringing "anti-ritualistic" and has summarized the consequences of this education as follows:

> "In this way the child is free from a system of rigid positions, but made a prisoner of a system of feelings and abstract principles. (48) ... It must be difficult for the child reared on abstract principles in the personal family to draw moral lines, to be bound by promises - for unquestioned boundaries have never been part of this upbringing. The child in the positional family grows in a set of unchallenged categories, which are expressed by non verbal symbols as well as by words. (54) ... The cause of antiritualism today in middle class European and American communities appears to be a predictable result of a process of socialisation in which the child never internalizes a pattern of social statuses and never experiences authoritative control which exalts the self evident property of a social system to command obedience. Symbols of solidarity and hierarchy have not been part of his education." (Douglas, 1973, 55)

CONSEQUENCES FOR THE MANAGEMENT PROCESS

What consequences can we draw from this development concerning our main theme, the management process ?

If we accept the empirical and analytical basis of Douglas' and Bernstein's contributions, we can expect that the attitude of the "new" organizational members will change in a way, which will strongly influence their ability to differentiate between personals motives and organizational ends. It is worthwhile to notice in this context that one of the central variables of traditional organizational analysis will change in quality: alienation will not be any longer the result of boring and assigned work in the firm, but the result of a deep frustration of an increasing number of organization members. This frustration is caused

- by a strong aversion against any kind of ritual, authority and hierarchy,
- by the unfulfilled claim to become involved into the organizational process with their personal motives,
- by their unused ability to analyze complex situations with the help of their elaborated speech code, which stands in sharp contrast to the number of standardized duties in the firm.

But the same analysis gives us some hints to positive implications of this development: the willingness to participate and to become involved and the ability for abstractions and for articulation, could be a great opportunity for management to realize a much more sophisticated kind of organizational structure.

This part of our analysis coincides well with the results of Inglehart's important studies about the outlines of a post-materialistic society in western cultures (Inglehart, 1977). Some consequences of this development have been discussed by Prof. Dlugos during this conference, especially the changes in conflict resolutions. We can add to this analysis our results about the decreasing flexibility of organizations to react to changes in their environment because of the diminishing difference between personal motives and organizational ends, because of the increasing danger of upheaval and changes in the profile for the distribution of authority in organizations, and because of a diminishing degree of shared classifications and the aversion to rituals.

All these aspects of consequences give an impression about the range of problems, corporations and their managers will face in a probable near future. Therefore we must ask whether it seems possible, that these corporations will be able to use the positive aspects of the development mentioned above. If we analyze this possibility against the background of some research results, it seems doubtful:

- if the technological development leads to situations at the working place (production and administration), where men have to deal in an environment whose "important events" are randomly occurring and unpredictable with all the consequences discussed by Davis and Taylor (Davis/Taylor, 1976, 388 f.),
- if the organization can provide all the opportunities for participation and involvement, because we learned out of Hirsch's studies that participation as a "good" belongs to the positional economy which means that it is impossible to multiply it without severe consequences on the quality of the good itself (Hirsch, 1977),
- if modern techniques of group-oriented organizational development (e.g. sensitivity training, team approaches) can have the expected effects, because of the diminishing capability of the organizational members to feel solidarity and group cohesion (Douglas, 1977).

Lastly, one could even be in doubt about the positive implications of Mary Douglas' analysis of the personal family. Reading the contributions of Christopher Lasch (Lasch, 1977; Lasch, 1979) about the "Besieged American Family" and the "American Life in an Age of Diminishing Expectations", we can even imagine a worse path of development:

His main thesis about the narcissistic individual - briefly, this is an individual who is unable to mourn or to accept old age and death, has lost belief in the meaningfulness and even the reality of the external world, lives for the moment without regard for tradition or posterity, and is anxiously concerned with appearances and fascinated with celebrities - has many important implications for modern corporations (Lasch, Part III, VII, 1979; Fischer, 1979).

Since Lasch uses a very different methodology influenced by Freud in his analysis, it is very difficult to integrate his results in our study without a thorough discussion of his analytical context. Nevertheless, it seems possible to represent Lasch's general idea of his findings by expanding our diagram No. 3, in which the left part of the x-axis could express a diminishing identity of the ego:

(Diagram 10)

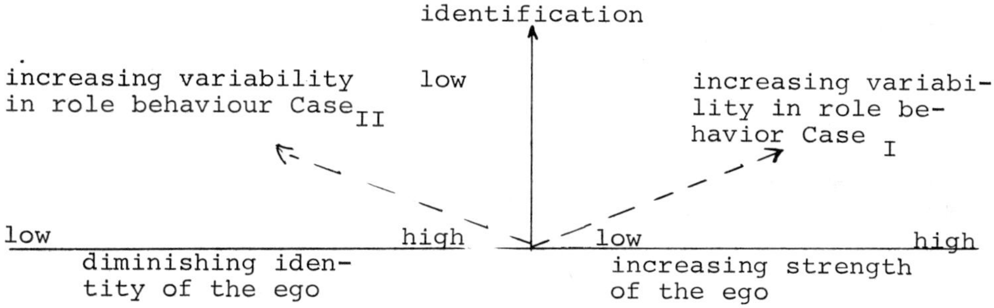

As a result we will get a second case of variability in role behavior, in which the identity and the identification of the individual is decreasing: in this case the corporation would have to deal with anti-ritualistic <u>and</u> uninterested, narcissistic members.

No matter if we accept Lasch's very pessimistic findings, or if we accept Mary Douglas' analysis, I hope that it has become obvious that from a theoretical point of view the dynamization of individual goal criteria is of central interest for research, if we try to discuss the implications of changing values for management. From a practical point of view we can deduce from our analysis that the strategic potential of corporations to handle the problems of value change we have discussed is relatively limited. In my opinion, there is still much work to be done in the social sciences before any substantial contributions on their part can be made towards solving the problems of value research still before us.

BIBLIOGRAPHY

Ansoff, I./Hayes, R.L. (Ed.) (1976), From Strategic Planning to Strategic Management, London: Wiley & Sons

Barnard, Ch. (1966) (17th ed. 1966), The Function of the Executive, Cambridge, Mass.: Harvard University Press

Bernstein, B. (1971), Class, Codes and Control Vol. 1, Theoretical Studies towards a Sociology of Language, London: Routledge & Paul

Blau, P./Scott, R.W. (1962), Formal Organization, Scranton: Chandler Publ.

Davis, L.E./Taylor, J.C. (1976), Technology, Organization and Job Structure. In: Robert, Dubin, Handbook of Work, Organization, and Society, Chicago 76: 379 ff.

Douglas, M. (1973), Natural Symbols. Explorations in Cosmology, New York: Random House, Vintagebooks

Dreitzel, H.-P. (1968), Die gesellschaftlichen Leiden und das Leiden an der Gesellschaft. Vorstudien zu einer Pathologie des Rollenverhaltens, Stuttgart 1972, original 1968: Enke Verlag

Duske, G./Wondracek, J. (1978), Kritische Analyse der Eignung motivations- und werttheoretischer Ansätze als basale Theorien einer betriebswirtschaftlichen Teildisziplin. In: Arbeitspapier 23/1978 des Instituts für Unternehmungsführung der Freien Universität Berlin

Etzioni, A. (1975), A Comparative Analysis of Complex Organizations, New York, revised and enlarged edition: The Free Press

Fischer, M. (1979), Criticizing Capitalist America, In: Salmagundi, Fall 79, p. 167 ff.

Gehlen, A. (1964), Urmensch und Spätkultur, Frankfurt-Bonn: Rowohlt Verlag

Goldthoppe, J.H. et al. (1970), Der "wohlhabende" Arbeiter in England, München, original 1968: The affluent Worker, Goldmann Verlag

Gouldner, A. (1969), Cosmopolitans and Locals. In: J.A. Litterer (Ed.) Organizations Vol. I, New York 67, p. 223 ff.: Wiley & Sons

Hirsch, F. (1977), Social Limits to Growth, London: Routledge & Paul

Hirschmann, A.O. (1972), Abwanderung und Widerspruch (Org. Exit and Voice), Tübingen 1974: J.C. B. Mohr (Paul Siebeck Verlag)

Inglehart, R. (1977), The Silent Revolution. Changing Values and Political Style Among Western Publics, Princeton, N.J.: Princeton Univ.Press

Katz, D. (1964), Die motivationale Basis organisationalen Verhaltens. In: Türk, K. (Ed.) Organisationstheorie, Hamburg 1975, p. 193 ff. (Org. 1964) : Hoffmann u. Campe

Kelman, H.C. (1958), Compliance, Identification, and Internalization. Three processes of attitude change. In: Journal of Conflict Resolution, p. 58 ff.

Lasch, Ch. (1977), Haven in a Heartless World The American Family Besieged : W. W. Norton

Lasch, Ch. (1979), The Culture of Narcissism: American Life in an Age of Diminishing Expectations, New York : W.W. Norton

Luhmann, N. (1973), Zweckbegriff und Systemrationalität. Über die Funktionen von Zwecken in sozialen Systemen, Frankfurt/M. (1st ed. 1968): Suhrkamp Verlag

Offe, C. (1973), Leistungsprinzip und industrielle Arbeit, Frankfurt/M. (3rd ed.): Europäische Verlags-Anstalt

Reissman, L. (1949), A Study of Role Conceptions in Bureaucracy. In: Social Forces 27, 1949, p. 305 ff.

Türk, K. (1977), Einbindungsmuster und ihre Wirkungen auf das Verhalten in Organisationen. In Gerhard Reber (Ed.) Personal- und Sozialorientierung der Betriebswirtschaftslehre Vol. 1, Stuttgart: Poeschel Verlag

Change of Leadership Style in German Enterprises: From Authoritative to Participative Leadership?

Wolfgang Grunwald and Hans-Georg Lilge

ABSTRACT

This study tries to determine empirically whether, and to what extent, a change in leadership style has occurred in West German enterprises. This is done by (a) a secondary analysis of selected questionnaire studies of values, attitudes, behavior, and expectations of managers and subordinates towards adequate leadership styles; and (b) a content analysis of 45 codified principles of leadership in major German enterprises.

To summarize the major findings of the study: a change in the predominant leadership style in West German enterprises towards a cooperative-participative form is evident. Still, there is a remarkable discrepancy between attitudes and behavior: the statements about the favoured leadership style are more progressive than is the actual behavior, from the the point of view of both leaders and subordinates.

INTRODUCTION

Since it has become evident in recent years that the traditional systems of leadership cannot react with sufficient flexibility and effectiveness to complex and dynamic technological and socio-cultural environments, bureaucratic-authoritative forms of leadership have increasingly declined in both actual practice and theoretical import.

New objectives and values, such as humanitarianism, internationalism, social welfare, quality of life, participation in the social articulation of will, and self-actualization, have obtained significant importance in the public and private minds (cf. Kmieciak, 1976; Klages/Kmieciak, 1979; Matthes, 1979). This process has - particularly in business life - been accompanied by a replacement of closed dogmatic systems of values in favour of pluralistic-relativistic principles of values. Those conventions that are more instrumentally oriented and

---

We would like to express our thanks to the numerous companies for their openness and willingness to cooperate. We also like to thank Linda van Esch and Hans-Jürgen Lebede for guiding us through the jungle of the English language.

based on consensus require new, cooperative-participative forms of leadership which should be able to connect and balance employees' individual objectives with the often diverging objectives of the organization itself.

In the past 30 years a rapid economic, technological and socio-cultural change has materialized in West Germany: Among other things, disposable income per capita has increased sixfold, with weekly working time falling to 40 hours average, and annual holidays rising to 4-6 weeks. On the other hand, signs of crises, such as new technologies, streamlining, with corresponding unemployment (averaging 5-6%), persistent recession, reduced economic growth, shortened product life cycles, new information technologies, increasing pressure from international competition and a shift from the sellers' markets of the sixties to buyers' markets, etc., indicate an increasingly turbulent environment.
Notwithstanding these tendencies towards a critical development the public is focusing on social, non-material requirements within the frame of quality of life.
The orientation toward non-material quality-of-life values is also reflected in new government regulations, e.g., the Works Council Act (1972), by which employers and works' council are obliged "to take into consideration the proven results about the humanitarian structuring of labor". The West German government's plan within HoL[1] has lead to comprehensive basic and field research, including model validation (cf. Gaugler et al., 1977; BMFT, 1978; Bartölke et al., 1978; Lilge/Grunwald, 1980).

This study aims to determine empirically whether, and to what extent, a change in leadership from authoritative-bureaucratic to cooperative-participative forms has in fact emerged in West Germany.

Specifically,
(a) the results of several relevant questionnaires which investigated managers' and subordinates' values, attitudes, expectations and behavior with regard to participative forms of leadership were reviewed,
(b) a qualitative-quantitative content analysis of 45 principles of leadership was conducted.

INDUSTRIAL DEMOCRACY AND PARTICIPATIVE LEADERSHIP: TWO COMPLEMENTARY DEVELOPMENTS IN WEST GERMANY

There are two interdependent and complementary developments in West Germany which determine the extent and intensity of cooperative-participative forms of leadership (Fig. 1):

(a) On the formal structural level, the "industrial democracy" with the Montan Law of Participation 1951; Works Council Act 1972; Worker Participation Act 1976 and numerous laws for the protection of labour.
(b) On the informal face-to-face level, "participative leadership" aimed at improving superior-subordinate relations.

In the US, the informal has dominated. In West Germany, the formal approaches have dominated, and only recently has management research and practice something like broadened its scope to include the informal aspects (Maslow, Herzberg, Michigan- and Ohio School, Tavistock-Group), influenced chiefly by Anglo-Saxon management research (cf. Neuberger, 1976; King/van de Vall, 1978; Bass et al., 1979; Grunwald/Lilge, 1980; Wunderer/Grunwald, 1980).

Hence our focus is "participative leadership" ("industrial democracy approach" cf. Brinkmann-Herz, 1975; Dlugos, 1980; Witte, 1980; Kirsch et al., 1980).

DEFINITIONS: LEADERSHIP, MANAGEMENT, LEADERSHIP STYLE, VALUE ORIENTATION, VALUE SYSTEM, PARTICIPATION, CO-DETERMINATION

In German literature, 'management' and 'leadership' are both used synonymously and subtly differentiated. The collective terms 'management' and 'leadership' have a number of different meanings, referring to: (a) group of people at the top of an organization, (b) knowledge, techniques and activities, (c) a mental attitude, a network of relations among formally authorized persons in a hierarchical system or functions such as deciding, motivating, planning, controlling etc. (cf. Bessai, 1974; Wunderer/Grunwald, 1980). The literature has frequently stressed that management and leadership are not congruent, since management always includes leadership but not vice versa; because, in contrast to a manager, a leader does not necessarily need exercise all the management functions required to motivate people or groups (cf. Miles, 1975). We do not endorse this view and consider both leadership and management or leader or manager to be synonymous with the idea of interpersonal influence. This report assumes the following working definition of "leadership" and "participative leadership" (Wunderer/Grunwald, 1980):

Fig. 1:

Forms of Change in Leadership in West Germany 1950 - 1980

Industrial democracy (Structural-formal level)	Participative leadership (Face-to-face level)
Origin: Second World War; negotiations between Trade Unions and employers' association.	Origin: Philosphy of humanism, theories of democracy; psychology of motivation; influence of US management research (Maslow, Herzberg, Likert)
Basic items/instruments: Legal and contractual norms, wage contracts, works agreements, company principles.	Basic items/instruments: Education and further education, role play, sensitivity training, job rotation, job enlargement, job enrichment, autonomous work groups, bargaining, conflict management.
Nature of participation Primarily indirect participation of employees through works' council, joint economic committee, supervisory board etc.	Nature of participation Primarily direct participation on the job.
Objectives: Balancing of power, proportional codetermination in the decision process concerning personnel, social and economic issues, individual wealth formation (accumulation)	Objectives: self-actualization, self-initiative, self-control.

1. Objective-oriented social influence to perform common tasks ...	→ Objective-performance aspect	Leadership in Enterprises
2. ... in a structured working situation ...	→ Structural aspect	
3. ... under mutual spheres of influence, initiative being symmetrical in tendency, ...	→ Participative aspect	Quality of cooperative-participative leadership
4. ... and within all-side-satisfying working and social conditions.	→ Pro-social aspect	

The term "leadership style" is vague and ambiguous. The German management literature and practice use it in the sense of (Wunderer/Grunwald, 1980):

1. Management philosophy or enterprise philosophy
2. Group climate
3. Leadership model or system (management by approaches)
4. A leader's enduring structure of needs
5. Management technique (management rules/principles)
6. Consistent behavior pattern of the leader towards subordinates.

The essential feature of leadership style is "leadership behavior". The former is a hypothetical construct, the latter an observation or description term: From repeatedly observed patterns of behavior in various situations a particular normative leadership style is inferred.

We define "leadership style" or "form of leadership" according to item No. 6 "as a temporary but enduring consistent pattern of behavior towards subordinates in reference to particular situations and guided by specific value orientations and value systems" (Wunderer/Grunwald, 1980). The terms 'value orientation' and 'value system' refer to the classic definitions of Kluckhohn/Strodtbeck and Rokeach.

> "Value orientations are complex but definitely patterned (rank-ordered) principles, resulting from the transactional interplay of three analytically distinguishable elements of the evaluative process - the cognitive, the affective, and the directive elements - which give order and direction to the ever-flowing stream of human acts and thoughts as these relate to the solution of "common human" problems." (Kluckhohn/Strodtbeck, 1973, 4)

"A value system is an enduring organization of beliefs concerning preferable modes of conduct or end-states of existence along a continuum of relative importance." (Rokeach, 1973, 5; 1979)

Further we distinguish between participation and co-determination. While participation primarily characterizes the subordinates' involvement in managerial decision process, co-determination refers to their formal and informal involvement, responsibility, and authority in that process.

Even though participation implies a multitude of dimensions (cf. Dachler/Wilpert, 1980; Witte, 1980) we are confining the present discussion aspect, according to the classic Tannenbaum/Schmidt scheme (1958; Likert, 1967; Heller, 1971; similar Vroom/Yetton, 1973; IDE, 1976; Wilpert, 1977; et al.):

Fig. 2: Continuum of management behavior according to Tannenbaum/Schmidt

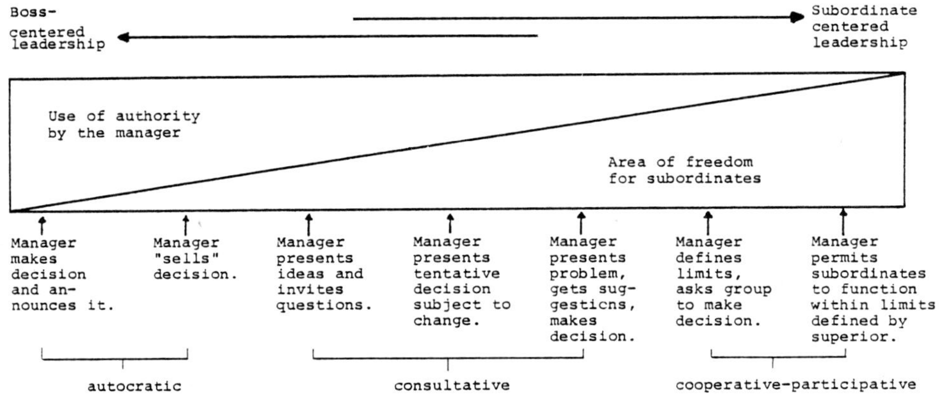

Co-determination is based on laws and/or treaties and refers to the institutionalized taking-part of employees or their representatives in the process of will-formation and decision-making in the enterprise as far as personnel, social, end economic issues are concerned.

Consistent with Tannenbaum/Schmidt's scheme, the right to participate can be differentiated into the following levels (see also Alewell, 1976; Chmielewicz et al., 1977; Dlugos, 1980):

Fig. 3:

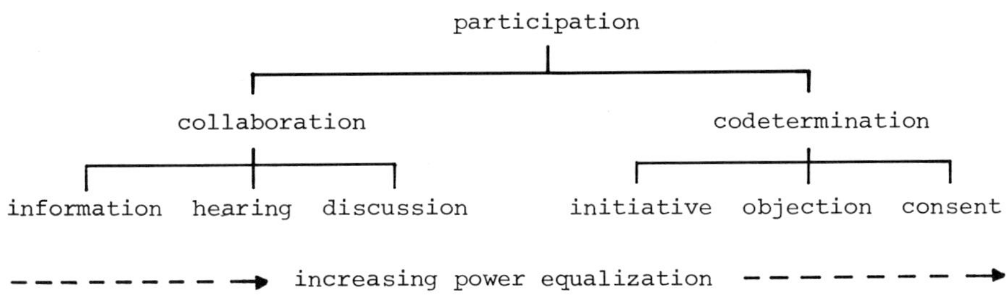

SELECTED EMPIRICAL FINDINGS

This section gives an overview of several selected opinion-polls which address the values, attitudes, expectations and to some extent actual behavior of managers and subordinates with respect to participative forms of management.

One basic problem of all questionnaire data is their insufficient predictive validity, since there is normally no 1:1 relationship between attitudes and behavior (cf. Fishbein/Ajzen, 1975; Rokeach, 1979).

As there is little valid behavioral data concerning the interaction between managers and subordinates in decision-making, we have to rely on their "verbal reports". Despite the 'self reports' being subjective and (still) relatively 'behavior remote', this method of questioning - beside the experiment and the systematic observation - is the best way to understand the leadership phenomenon (Friedrich, 1970, 25 f.):

"1. Verbal and practical (non-verbal) behaviour are the result of materialistic, more exactly: neuro-physiological processes; both are therefore equally objective.
2. Verbal and practical behaviour can change the objective (materialistic) world; e.g. they put social-personal processes of different kinds into operation; both are

therefore equally objective as influencing factors.

3. Verbal and practical behaviour are related to a subject, both are therefore equally subjective.
4. Verbal and practical behaviour can be equally "genuine", i.e. express correctly the inner condition, the subjective state of mind; but both can also (willingly or unwillingly) lead to opposite results.

For example purposeful deceptions (lies) may occur both in verbal and in practical behavior. The desire to be important can also be manifested verbally and practically. Moreover the motives underlying behavior cannot be derived with more certainty from practical behavior than from verbal behavior. It is therefore not possible to diagnose the personality more easily and more correctly through the practical behavior."

Socio-demographic characteristics of managers in West Germany

Regarding age, family background, education, and mobility there is a considerably closer affinity between German and American managers than between Northern and Southern European managers: The typical German manager comes from the middle- or upper-class, he is a protestant, has university education and is - compared to the personality profile of the average West-German male - more ambitious, risk-minded, self-conscious, self-controlled, team-oriented, "harder" and more masculine (cf. Haire et al., 1966; Pross/Boetticher, 1971; Biermann, 1971; Kruk, 1972; Booz-Allen/Hamilton, 1973; Gottschall, 1976, 65 f.; Lawrence, 1980, 56 ff.), as portrayed in Fig. 4.

Values, attitudes and behavior of German managers

Wilpert (1977) discovered, in interviewing 301 top managers of 17 major companies, that roughly every other decision was either coordinated with the subordinates or made jointly with them (cf. Fig. 5). This result is interesting in that it leads us to suppose the existence of congruent value structures. Nevertheless, much empirical research emphasizes that divergent, and to some extent conflicting, values, attitudes and expectations do exist between managers and subordinates.

Fig. 4: Personality profile of 507 German managers

Between 1973 and 1976 the personality profiles of 507 applicants for middle and top management openings were analyzed, using Cattel's 16-PF - Questionnaire (Manager Magazin, 1979, No. 6, pp. 66-72). Deviation from the middle line (scale value 5.5) indicates the strength of a characteristic compared with the average total male population in West Germany (standard sample N = 1.800).

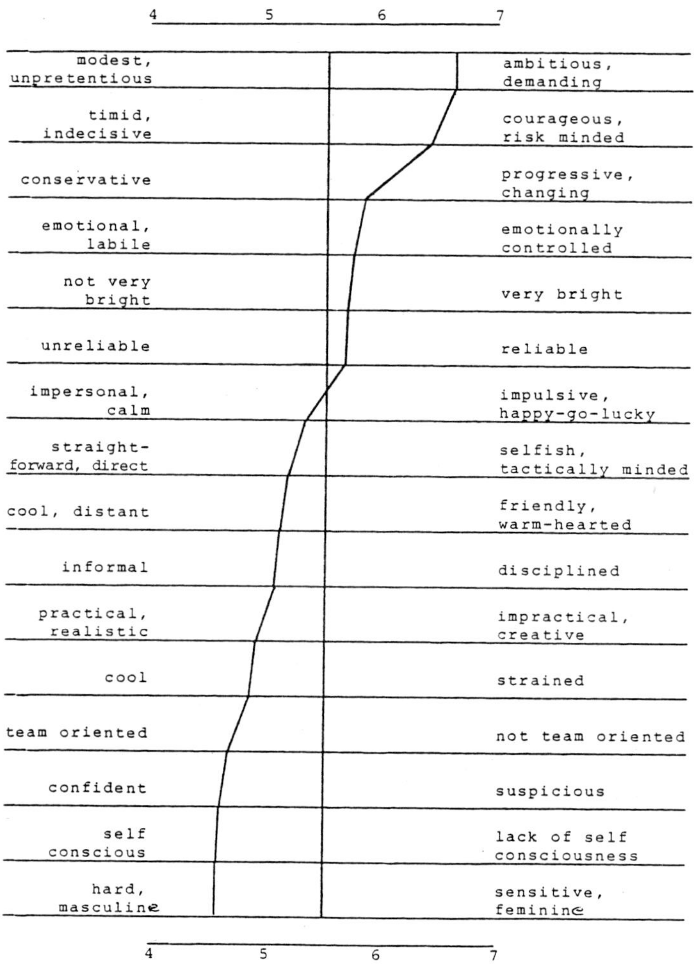

Fig. 5: General decision behavior: frequency of decision methods applied (in %) (N = 301)

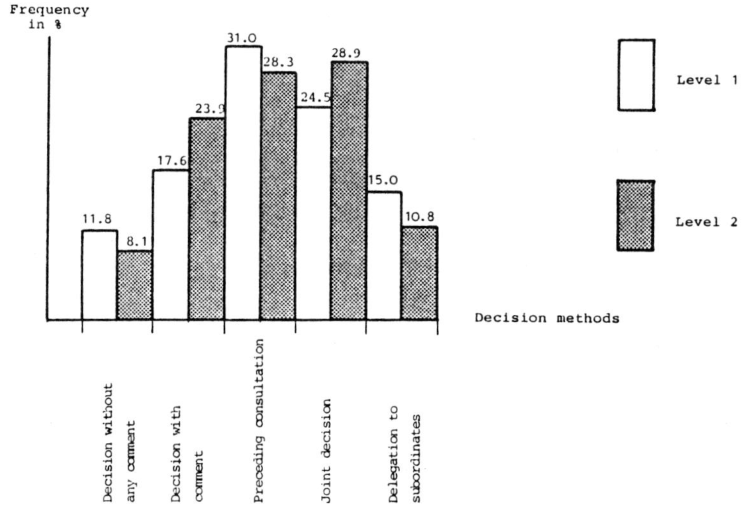

In this context the research findings of Kirsch et al. (1980) may be of interest, as they observed considerable differences in the value systems of 196 managers and 164 employee representatives (see Fig. 6). Zepf (1972) inquired into the management behavior of 194 managers at different hierarchical levels in 11 companies as regards their decision behavior and their opinion about manager-subordinate relations, and obtained the following results:

- Higher (lower) age and a longer (shorter) duration of employment correlated positively (negatively) with authoritative management.
- Qualified (little qualified) education correlated positively (negatively) with non-authoritative management.
- Managers on higher hierarchical levels tended to be more cooperative towards their subordinates in decision making than managers of lower hierarchical levels.

These findings have subsequently been confirmed by other studies (cf. Pross/Boetticher, 1971; Hartmann et al., 1973; VELA-study, 1976; et al.).

Fig. 6: Comparison of Value Systems of Managers (N=196) and Employees (N=164)

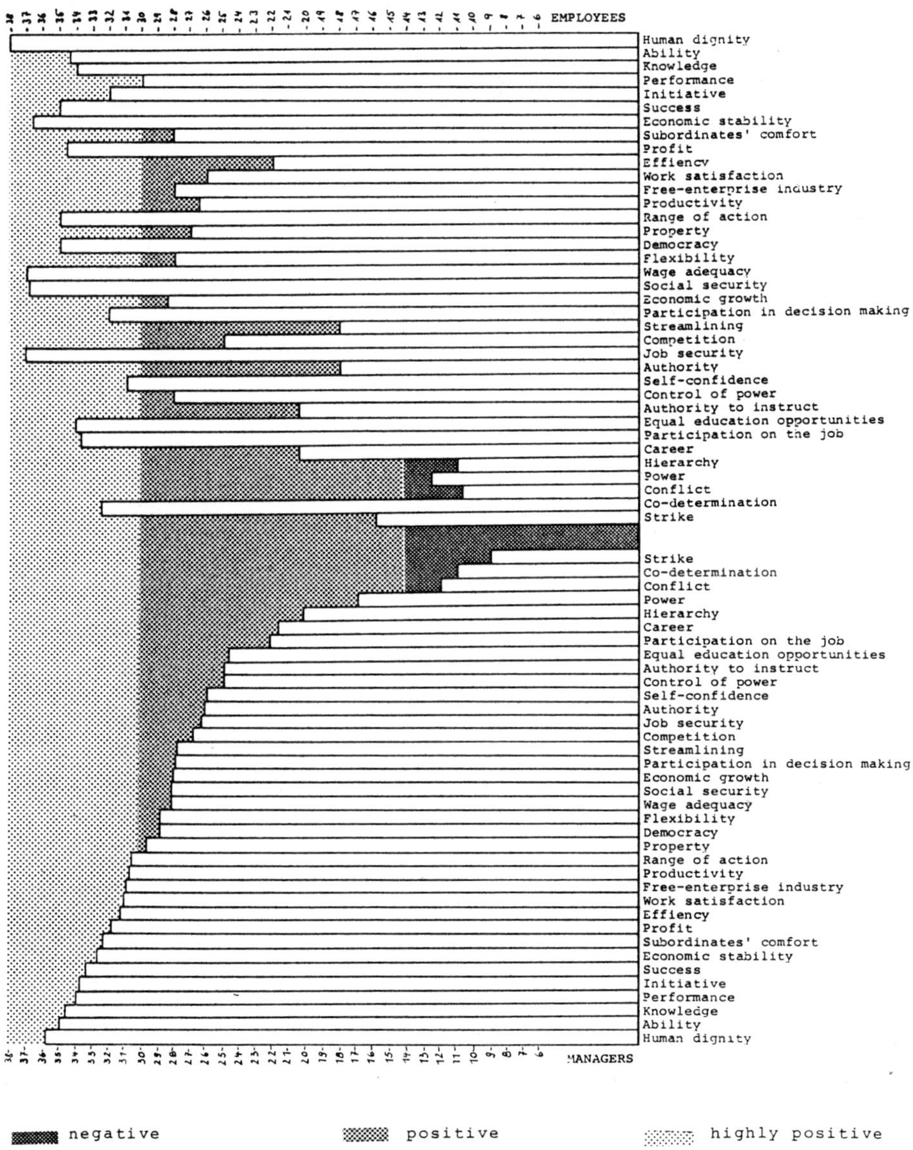

Fig. 7:

Leadership self-assessment (according to Koehne 1976, 107) (N = 454)

How do your (direct) subordinates assess you?	Total	Sex		Age			Property status		Company size			Employers Association		
		male	female	-35	36-45	46-	Owner	Non-owner	10-99	100-499	500-	Ideology	Function	without
	%	%	%	%	%	%	%	%	%	%	%	%	%	%
more authority	24,1	24,2	22,9	18,7	22,0	32,1	24,9	19,7	23,8	24,3	25,0	24,3	22,8	25,0
more colleague	63,7	65,0	51,4	70,9	69,5	49,1	61,2	73,2	62,9	63,9	61,8	59,7	67,6	67,9
other	10,8	9,2	25,7	9,7	6,8	17,0	12,5	5,6	11,2	10,4	13,2	14,4	9,0	3,6
no answer	1,4	1,5	0,0	0,7	1,7	1,8	1,4	1,4	2,1	1,4	0,0	1,7	0,7	3,6
Total	100,0	99,9	100,0	100,0	100,0	100,0	100,0	99,9	100,0	100,0	100,0	100,1	100,1	100,1

Leadership self-assessment (according to Koehne 1976, 108) (N = 454)

How do your (direct) subordinates assess you?	Total	Job identification		leadership style		Confession		
		very high	less high	authoritative	team	protestant	catholic	none
	%	%	%	%	%	%	%	%
more authority	24,1	24,5	23,7	31,6	20,0	19,9	27,9	28,6
more collegue	63,7	62,7	65,4	58,8	66,9	69,4	55,9	64,3
other	10,8	11,8	10,3	7,9	12,2	9,1	14,7	7,1
no answer	1,4	1,0	0,6	1,8	0,8	1,6	1,5	0,0
Total	100,0	100,0	100,0	100,1	99,9	100,0	100,0	100,0

In 1973 Koehne interviewed 181 "ideology-oriented" and 145 "function-oriented" members of employers' association, and 128 managers without such membership (see Fig. 7). He found that 1/3 of the managers interviewed opted for authoritative and 2/3 for cooperative forms of management (team idea). This attitude was congruent with their own personal identification in appendix to the question "How do your (direct) subordinate staff assess you?" (63,7 % are perceived as colleagues, and 24,1 % as so called authorities). A research study by Schmölders (cf. Koehne, 1976, 104) indirectly offers support that this self-portrait matches the factual behavior: He questioned West German workers about the leadershipstyle of their boss and found that 50 % regard their boss as "colleague", and 42 % as "authority".

The interviews which Lukatis (1972) carried out with 2.393 managers revealed that in 71 % of the cases, managers consulted their subordinates before deciding. 60 % of those managers would interfere in the subordinates' range of duties only if particular snags occurred and/or if they were asked by their subordinates for advice or assistance.

In a research study of the "Association of Executives" (German: VELA, 1976) the practiced leadership style was assessed in 1.152 questionnaires as follows:

Fig. 8: The VELA-results (N = 1.152)

Allocation of leadership style according to management levels (in %)

leadership style \ hierarchical level	top level	second & following level
authoritative	16	30
bureaucratic	2	16
cooperative	75	43
laissez-faire	7	10

In 1979 the Metal Workers' Union (IG Metall) carried out the most comprehensive survey to date in West Germany. A total of 100.000 questionnaires from about 500 companies of different branches produced the findings summarized in Figure 9.
If we sum up the Metal Workers' Union study, we can state that the range of decision-making has been increased for only 25,7 % of those interviewed and has remained unchanged or decreased for 67,5 %. Just 33,4 % of those interviewed answered that they were allowed to take part in decisions in connection with the structuring of work, with white collar workers participating

in decisions to a higher extent (59,5 %) than blue collar workers (22 %), and women still suffering disadvantages in working life.

The following section of this article summarizes the relevant findings from a representative poll conducted in 1972/73 by the Institute of Applied Social Science (German: Infas). 5.782 West Germans were interviewed about the problem of "Quality of work life" by order of the Ministry of Labour and Social Order, (the results reported here have different random samples) (see Fig. 10).

In 1975 the Bavarian Ministry of State interviewed 4.000 male and female employees aged 18-60 and working for 300 small companies (staff of up to 1.000) about their job situation. 16 % of those interviewed were white collar workers, 84 % blue collar workers (see Fig. 11).

In 1967, Pross/Boetticher found that "delegation of responsibility" was endorsed by 83 % of those interviewed (260 top managers), that this leadership form was accepted less with increasing age, but that 69,6 % of those interviewed still favoured team work. Despite these positive views, significant preference was given to "non-joint decisions after consultation of experts" (88,9 %) whereas the "joint decision with others" was opted for by only 7,3 %. These findings, which are contradictory in themselves, may be explained on the grounds that - according to type of task, time pressure, personal characteristics etc. - the complete spectrum from non-joint decision via consultative decisions to group decision is to be found in different frequency and configuration in practice, as the empirical studies of Wilpert (1977) and Heller/Wilpert (1977) have demonstrated (see Fig. 5).

Summary

We can sum up as follows: Authoritative leadership behavior based on the command - obedience principle has become atypical. Instead the leadership behavior that has been practiced in many major German companies (see Fig. 15) can be considered consultative-participative. The attitudes and expectations that have been demonstrated are even more cooperative-participative in mentation. Thus the actual leadership behavior may be called subordinate-oriented, but does not entirely satisfy the subordinates' expectations and wishes.

Fig. 9: Selected IG-Metall results (N = 100.000)

Question: My range of decision at work

	Total	blue collar workers	white collar workers	apprentices/ trainees	women	men	shift workers	non-shift workers
increasing	25,7	20,2	37,1	41,3	16,4	30,2	24,9	25,9
decreasing	15,7	16,4	15,5	1,6	11,8	17,5	16,8	15,5
unchanged	51,8	55,1	44,8	54,0	60,2	48,1	48,1	53,0
no answer	6,5	8,4	2,6	3,2	11,6	4,2	10,2	5,6

Question: Is your opinion how to structure the work flow requested?

Yes	33,4	22,0	59,5	34,9	18,3	40,5	23,0	36,0
No	58,0	67,9	35,0	65,1	69,2	52,8	66,3	55,9
no answer	8,6	10,2	5,5	0,0	12,5	6,8	10,7	8,0

Fig.10: Selected Infas results (N = 2.451; N = 982)

Question / Rating	very satisfactory	satisfactory	rather unsatisfactory	no comment
1. Question: How do you assess your cooperation and contacts with other subordinates? (N = 2.451)	27 %	65 %	4 %	4 %
2. Question: To what extent do you consider your boss satisfactory? (N = 2.451)	20 %	65 %	10 %	5 %
3. Question: What do you think about codetermination of employees in your company? (N = 2.451)	6 %	58 %	26 %	10 %

	improved	not improved	no answer	
4. Question: Do you think that the situation of employees will be improved when the codetermination is extended? (N = 982)	44 %	22 %	34 %	

5. Question:
What do you dislike, what bothers you most with your boss? (N = 2.451, multiple mentioning possible)

Lack of human open-mindedness	20 %
Lack of willingness to inform	18 %
Injustice (Unfairness)	12 %
Severe, constant control	11 %
Lack of competence	11 %
Exploits subordinates	10 %
Don't know, no comment	42 %

Fig. 11: Selected results of the Bavarian Ministry of State (N = 4.000)

Question / Rating	yes	rather yes	rather no	no
1. Question: Do you get along well with your boss?	69%	24,4%	5,2%	1,4%
2. Question: Does your boss stand up for you?	46,8%	33,9%	13,7%	5,6%
3. Question: Does your boss treat you fairly?	53,5%	35,2%	9,0%	2,3%
4. Question: Does your boss keep you sufficiently informed?	40,8%	29,6%	20,3%	9,3%
5. Question: Do you have problems in cooperating with your colleagues?	4,4%	7,1%	15,6%	71,9%
	no	moderately	highly	
6. Question: Do you feel strained because of the boss' behavior?	68,8%	26,1%	5,1%	
	always	often	seldom	never
7. Question: Does your boss tell you how he considers your performance?	13,8%	16,7%	29,9%	29,6%

QUALITATIVE-QUANTITATIVE CONTENT ANALYSIS OF 45 LEADERSHIP PRINCIPLES

Definition

The term "Leadership principles" as used here implies "Enterprise philosophy", "Guiding principles of cooperation", "Leadership directives" or "Rules of leadership and cooperation". Leadership principles are normative statements about socially requested, or not requested, formal and informal relations between managers and subordinates, as well as between peers. As opposed to leadership principles, company principles relate to the legal-organizational constitution of an organization.
Leadership principles function as frames of orientation for the members of an organization, implying among other things, must-, can- and target-expectations (cf. Lattmann, 1977 ; Fiedler, 1976; Paschen, 1977; Kossbiel, 1978). The importance of leadership principles as a regulator of behavior is reflected in that in 1977 only 30 out of 360 companies interviewed in West Germany had not considered implementing or applying leadership principles (Winter, 1978, 241).

In most cases, leadership principles are implemented by top management or central groups: In the early seventies it was discovered within 93 German companies that both the impulse and the drafting of leadership principles were initiated by the managing board or its subordinate personnel department (Fiedler, 1976, 315). This means that leadership principles show "towards what group of people the managing board orientate their corporate strategy above all and in whose interest they draft them" (Albach et al., 1977, 194). Thus leadership principles give an idea of top management's value orientation and value system.

Hypotheses

It was predicted that, within the past 20 years and particularly in major companies in West Germany, a change from a primarily instrumental (initiation structure) and less personal orientation in leadership relations towards an instrumental and increasing personal orientation has occurred.

This change may be described as a trend from an authoritative-bureaucratic to a cooperative-participative leadership style. Possible indirect indicators are the leadership principles which we are analysing. This hypothesis may be divided into four sub-hypotheses (Albach et al., 1977, 198):

a) Companies consider their staff to have come of age, to be self-responsible people, whose interests have to be respected.
b) Companies prefer to lead their staff not by command any-

more but by persuasion.

c) Companies have learned that being prepared to work and performing well do not necessarily follow from the employment contract; instead they are determined by the allocation of reasonable and responsible work.

d) Companies meet the demand for self-responsible work through increased decentralization of decisions, delegation and information.

We are now analysing 45 leadership principles from major German enterprises in different branches by means of a content analysis. These companies represent altogether a cumulated annual turnover of DM 446.6 bn and about 2.7 mill. of members of these organizations.

Methodological remarks

According to Berelson's classic definition (1952, 18), content analysis is "a research technique for the objective, systematic, and quantitative description of the manifest content of communication". But this does not sufficiently serve our pilot study, as we want to emphasize both the latent and the contextual "content of communication". The "non-frequency approach" and the "frequency approach" have both been considered:

> "We employ the term 'non-frequency' to describe the type of non-quantitative, non-statistical content analysis which uses the presence or absence of a certain content characteristic or syndrome as a content indicator in an inferential hypothesis. In contrast, a 'frequency' content indicator is one in which the number of times one or more content characteristics occurs is regarded as relevant for purpose of inference." (George, 1959, 7 f.)

The list of items, incorporated the essential features of participative leadership[2] (Wunderer/Grunwald, 1980; Grunwald/Lilge, 1980): decision participation, multi lateral information and communication, team work, open settling of conflicts, bargaining, self-actualization, power equalization, target- and performance orientation and personnel promotion. We analysed 45 leadership principles under the aspect, whether and to what extent these and further items which are not mentioned here, have been considered. A major problem with the collection of the items to be analysed is to determine what they have in common and what the distinctions may be, because the same items can often indicate different states of affairs and different items sometimes the same state of affairs.

Fig. 12 contains the 33 items which had a frequency of 5 or more. Those excluded were: equal opportunities (for men and women), equal interest (of capital owners and staff), loyalty (towards the company) and value ideas, this latter term having

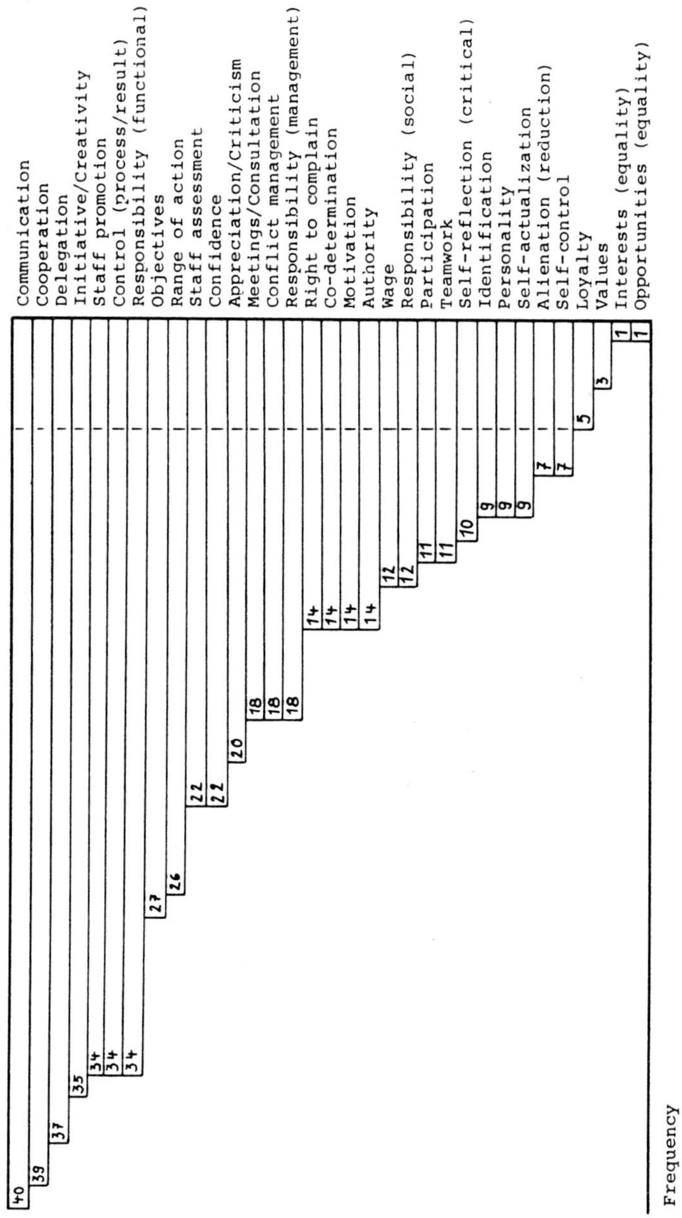

Fig. 12: Items according to order of options (N=45)

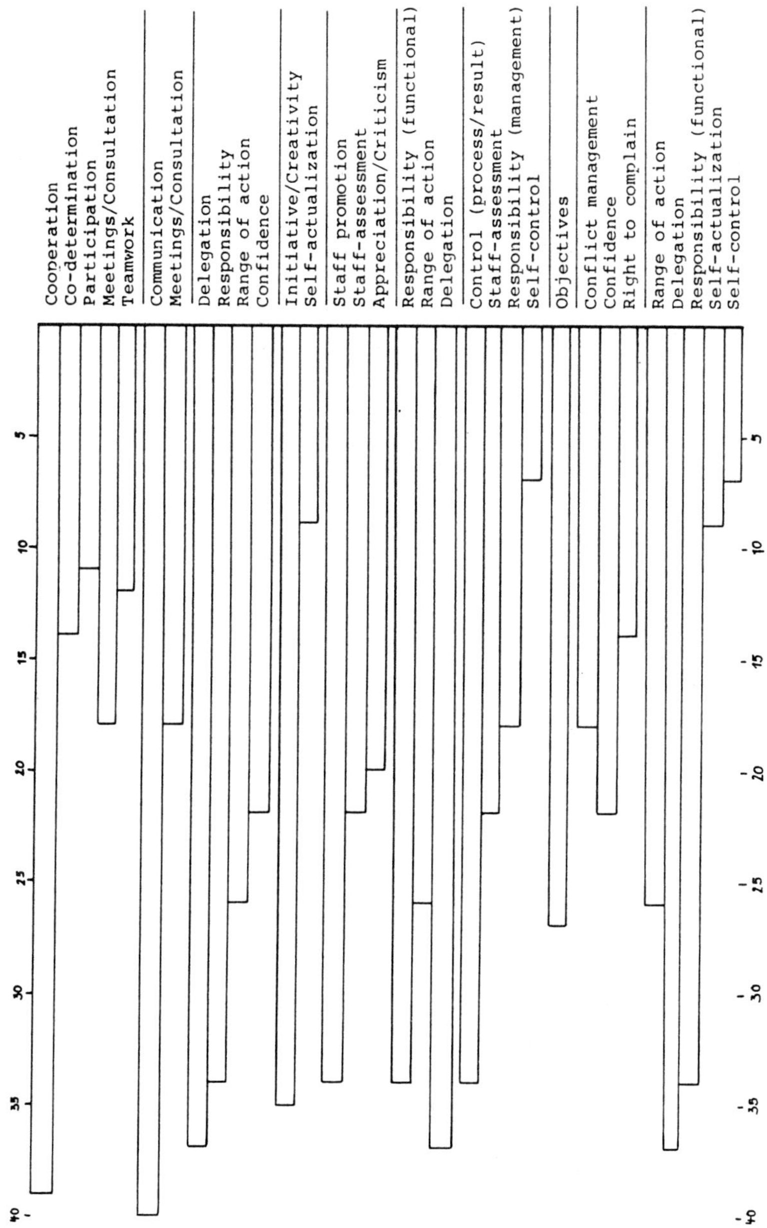

Fig. 13: Items condensed in classes and evaluated (N=45)

been used extremely vaguely and ambivalently.

Qualitative-quantitative evaluation

Fig. 12 and 13 give the quantitative evaluation. We assume that rank order also reflects the relevance of the single item. Certainly the individual items cannot be separated clearly - they overlap and/or are interdependent, thus complicating their interpretation (cf. Holsti, 1969). Those items that were opted for 10 times and more may serve as an important clue. They are: Communication, Cooperation, Delegation, Initiative/Creativity, Staff promotion, Control, Responsibility (functional), Objectives, Range of action, Staff assessment, Confidence, Appreciation/Criticism, Meetings/Consultation, Conflict management, Responsibility (management), Right to complain, Co-determination, Motivation, Authority, Wage, Responsibility (social), Participation, Teamwork, Self-reflection. For reasons of space, only the first 10 items are detailed in Fig. 13.

The analysis is concerned to fix a lead table by virtue of the absolute number of options. Semantic similarities, e.g. delegation range of action have not been considered here because of their transparency; but they will be addressed later.

The most frequently endorsed item was Communication (exchange of information), 40 times mentioned.It comprises both the "obligation to inform" and the "right to be informed". Thus the aspect of a balanced communication receives prominence with its realization being possible or required - as expressly stated - off the official channels.
Cooperation chosen 39 times ranked second. It refers to the basic pattern of a balanced, effective social structure. It is stressed that the individual can fully develop his/her capabilities only in cooperation with others, which may be seen on the one hand under the performance aspect of business administration, and on the other hand under the social-psychological behavior aspect. Nevertheless the importance of this item to leadership practice is not doubted.
Delegation was opted for 37 times. It means the passing on of competence from manager to subordinate, with the principal of being prepared or obliged to pass on rights and duties.
Item Initiative/creativity comes closely behind receiving 35 votes. This item covers initiative, the right to propose, active structuring, etc. The analysed leadership principles indicate that enterprises are increasingly looking for active staff who critically manage their field of operation.
Staff promotion, with a score of 34, also seems to be fairly important. By providing further education for their staff, the enterprises endeavour to have the subordinates grow in accordance with technological progress and to take them away from the passive consumer role.
Control and Functional responsibility (process/result) each

received 34 votes. Functional responsibility (to be separated from leadership responsibility and social responsibility) has to be seen as being dependent on delegation (and on range of action). It expresses the fact that the subordinate is responsible for the tasks and competences that have been delegated to him and that he may on the other hand be called to account for. The control of subordinates through the manager is understood to be an important aspect of the leadership principles. The range of responsibility of subordinates is reduced through the process- and output-control.
Objectives determined by the manager have a relatively high score of 27, which may reflect management's awareness of background of the "MbO" leadership style and the "Harzburg Model". 26 options each were taken for the range of action. The term "range of action" can be subdivided into the range of action, range of decision and range of freedom. Generally speaking, the range of action includes a limited number of actions with integrated decision competence.
The obligation and right to assess staff received a score of 22. These actions, of course, start with the manager, and are directed at the subordinates.

As we mentioned earlier, frequently the items overlap or are closely linked. These are not semantic overlappings, but follow from the context. A correct statistical record cannot do, indeed, without these interdependences but we are picking them up here in Fig. 13 and presenting them. Multiple options are permitted to enable better and more representative allocation.

CRITICISM OF PREVAILING LEADERSHIP PRINCIPLES

In general, leadership principles contain statements about
- Company philosophy
- Company objectives
- Delegation of tasks and responsibility
- Principles of behavior
- The information and communication structure
- Promotion opportunities for and systems of staff assessment
- Control mechanism
- Appreciation and criticism of staff

(cf. Zander, 1972, 186 ff.; Beckerath, 1976, 69).

Our content analysis of 45 leadership principles revealed that all the above requirements have been taken into consideration, with greater or lesser frequency.

Nevertheless, the analysis and interpretation must take into account that staff and the personnel department try to realize their own value expectations when they sit together to draft leadership principles or that the executive board may follow a fashionable trend towards participative leadership.

There is neither a common language nor a logical system of definitions (cf. Wistinghausen, 1977, 62). According to Gottschall the leadership principles seem often to be established without considering the economic, social, technological and political situation (1975, 78).

Contrary to this, our content analysis has shown that many leadership principles have been brought out unchanged in a third edition and so can claim transsituational and time invariant validity. Moreover, our analysis demonstrates that there is frequently a discrepancy between target expectation (leadership principles) and actual situation (leadership practice); thus one can agree with Albach et al. (1977, 206) who state that the leadership practice in enterprises does in principle differ from that described in leadership principles, and that leadership principles and leadership practice can never be brought to an agreement. Moreover, these principles do not seem to be relatively binding, because in very few cases do they make any statements about what would happen if someone did not comply with these principles. But this problem appears to be basic to any of the principles, as indicated by Winter (1978, 243), because they persist in requiring or stressing the socially requested only. An analysis of 75 leadership principles that were written down in West German companies provides additional supporting data (Fiedler, 1976, 213 ff.):

- the leadership principles belong to the tools of enterprise management;
- the leadership principles risk being dogmatic and artificial or simply serve as an alibi;
- in 70 % of all cases, the personnel department or the executive board initiated the working out of leadership principles;
- the committee to draft the leadership principles was in the first place made up of members of the personnel department/executive board and consisted in the second place only of other leading executives and staff representatives;
- about 6 to 18 months were required for the leadership principles to go from first impulse to final draft;
- the principles were worked out mainly in 1970 and 1974;
- the leadership principles take up about one binding half of employment contracts only, with the other half consisting only of recommendations with a "moral suasion" character;
- in 75 % of the cases, the implementation of new principles produced few or no difficulties at all;
- in 50 % of the cases, the implementation of leadership principles turned out to be positive as regards the behavior of managers and subordinates in management situations (fewer than 10 % of the leadership principles have

"come to nothing" after implementation);
- the principles that have been adopted least often are, in order of importance: delegation, information, staff assessment, appreciation and criticism.

CHANGE OF LEADERSHIP TOWARDS A PARTICIPATIVE STYLE?

We are now trying to find out with the help of comparing studies whether there has really been a trend in German enterprises from authoritative-bureaucratic to participative leadership.

Haire, Ghiselli and Porter's (1966) well-known international empirical leadership/management study, covering the period 1963-1965, may serve as a comparison study. German studies such as Braun/Fuhrmann (1970), Pross/Boetticher (1971), Lukatis (1972), Zepf (1972), Hartmann et al. (1973), Witte (1980) which are equally relevant, will, for space reason, be referred to only sparingly. Haire et al. investigated attitudes towards leadership behavior in 14 countries; our interest is confined to West Germany. Fig. 14 reveals that the German managers of 1963-65 had relatively little confidence in the capabilities of their subordinates, and were still less prepared to pass on information. On the other hand, it is amazing that the German managers in the mid-sixties accepted both material values and non-material values, and did not disagree with a participative leadership style; instead they took a rather indifferent stand. Internal control was determined through objective processes rather than through sanctions. A "carrot and stick policy" was rejected.
This observation led Haire et al. to conclude that a more authoritative leadership style was predominant in German enterprises: They found out that the German manager believed he could master his duties with severity, energy/strength, the capability to make his way/to dominate, infallibility and authority (cf. Haire et al., 1966, 50 ff.). That was 15 years ago. Today "the gap in leadership style" between the US and West Germany seems to have been bridged. (cf. the German literature on leadership/management and leadership practice Neuberger, 1976; Grunwald/Lilge, 1980; Staehle, 1980; Wunderer/ Grunwald, 1980). This thesis may be underlined by leadership principles which we filtered through a content analysis (empirical findings by Witte, 1980 and Kirsch et al., 1980; see also Lukatis, 1972; Zepf, 1972).

Fig. 14: Leadership behavior compared: 1966 and 1980

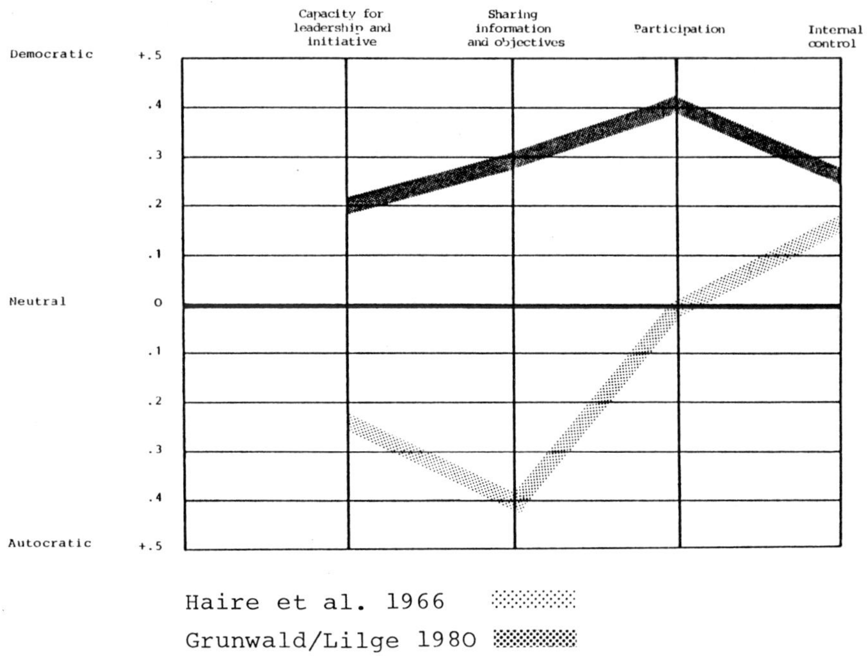

In Fig. 13 the single items have been condensed into classes and put into the following lead table according to their importance to a participative leadership style:

1. Cooperation, codetermination, decision participation meetings, teamwork
2. Communication, exchange of information, meetings
3. Delegation, functional responsibility, range of action, confidence
4. Initiative/Creativity, self-actualization
5. Staff promotion, staff assessment, appreciation and criticism
6. Functional responsibility, range of action, delegation
7. Control, staff assessment, management responsibility self-control
8. Objectives
9. Conflict management, confidence, right to complain
10. Range of action, delegation, functional responsibility, self-actualization, self-control

It has already become evident that the item-classes corresponding to participative leadership top the list. Thus, establishing a change towards a participative leadership style is met, in principle. A corresponding tentative curve would be almost completely in opposition to that of Haire et al. (cf. Fig. 14).

Despite many signs of a trend towards requested participative forms of leadership it must be remembered that writing down leadership principles does not say much about their realization in practice. This fact has been critically stressed by Albach (1976, 741 and 747) in his analysis of 36 leadership principles. However, if we accept the proposition that leadership principles often do describe the status quo of an organization, there is reason to be optimistic concerning the realization and further development of participative leadership in German enterprises. The central findings of all the leadership principles analysed produce the following model, as seen from the perspective of the participatively-extended variant of the MbO (Fig. 15).

Töpfer (1976; 1978, 1802 ff.) found empirically that three management models are characteristic of German companies: Management by Objectives (MbO), Management by Exception (MbE) and, above all, the Harzburg Model (HM) as one of management by delegation. Only 50 % of the 355 companies that were analysed were able to present a homogeneous leadership model. The MbO dominates (chiefly in large companies) the HM (mainly in small companies).

The fact that the evolution towards participative leadership on the personal level is not yet satisfactory may be demonstrated by the activities of the German Trade Union Confederation (German: DGB), attempting to extend, on an "industrial democracy" level (Fig. 1), a legal co-determination aiming at a parity of labour and capital. But even though the existing laws of co-determination evidence a lack of parity between employers and employees, some investors at home and from abroad (particularly from the Anglo-American area) consider them too far-reaching which makes them migrate to countries without any participation (cf. Der Spiegel, July 28, 1980).

Summing up, we can say that the investigations quoted demonstrate a change in leadership style in West Germany. In this context, the findings about leadership principles seem to be a step in the right direction. The majority of companies in our study may be put into categories 4 and 5 on the "continuum of leadership behavior" depicted in Fig. 16.

Fig. 15: A generalized model of management in German enterprises

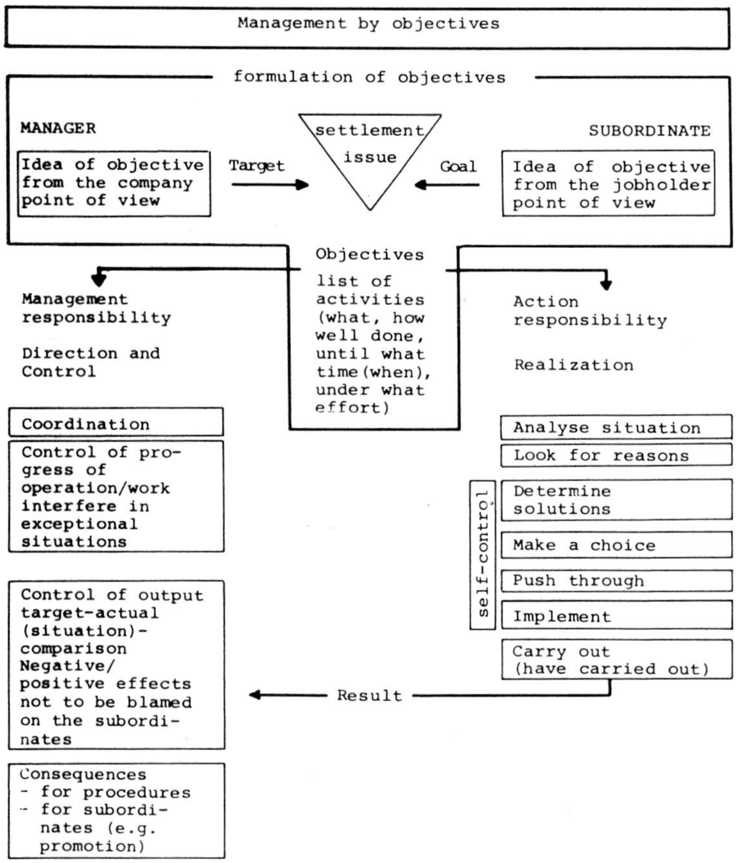

Fig. 16: The modified continuum of leadership behavior

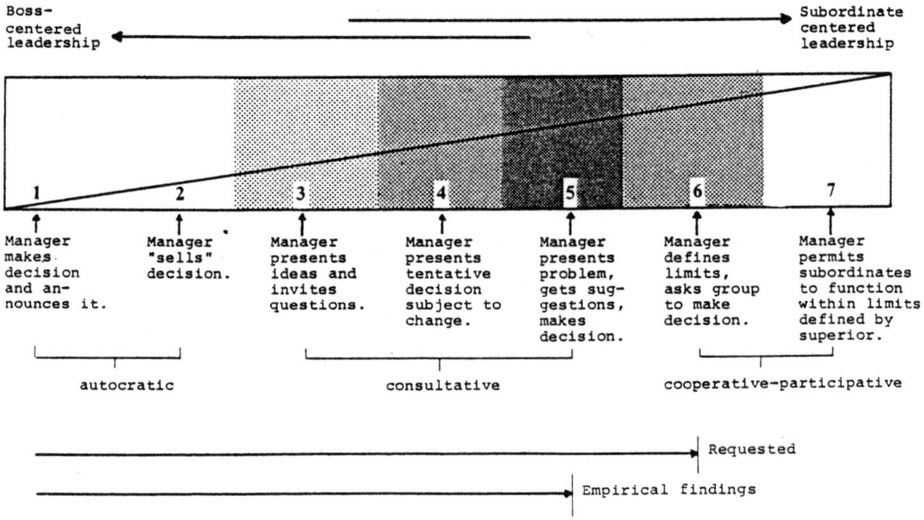

The magnitude of change in the value bases (Lilge, 1980, pp. 50- 72) cannot be definitively assessed. But it is safe to say that Haire, Ghiselli and Porter would no longer find their results confirmed in German enterprises.

The time seems to have come for intercultural comparisons of leadership style. These comparative studies might enable us to know whether our original proposition, that there is hardly any difference in leadership style between Germany and the U.S., or Canada, jibes with real-life leadership behavior.

Whatever the results, these studies could be the beginning of dialogue between North American and German researchers in the leadership field and contribute to a better understanding of reciprocal and mutual relationships.

NOTES

1. "HoL" stands for "Humanizing of Labour", a great research program sponsored by different organizations. Because of changing values, problems of motivation at work, problems of legitimation etc., researches of all faculties concentrate their interest on those problems of work organizations you cannot equalize in terms of money. Subjects as job rotation, job enlargement, job enrichment, autonomous work groups, co-determination on shop-floor level, participative leadership etc. were topics under the "HoL". This "full size research program" is still going strong and not only in West Germany but also in the states of the European Common Market. Some cross-cultural projects try to obtain results which perhaps offer chances to reach greater validity.

2. The development of the classification system and the distribution of the items resulted from a semantic analysis of leadership principles under consideration of the relevant leadership literature.

BIBLIOGRAPHY

Albach, H. et al. (1977), Mitarbeiterführung, Wiesbaden: Gabler

Albach, H. (1976), Welche Aussagen lassen Führungsgrundsätze von Unternehmen über die Auswirkungen gesellschaftlicher Veränderungen auf die Willensbildung in Unternehmungen zu? In: Albach, H., Sadowski, D. (Ed.) (1976), Die Bedeutung gesellschaftlicher Veränderungen für die Willensbildung in Unternehmen: 739-764, Berlin: Duncker & Humblot

Alewell, K. (1976), Veränderungen im Prozeß der betrieblichen Willensbildung bei Mitbestimmung der leitenden Angestellten. In: Albach, H., Sadowski, D. (Ed.) (1976), Die Bedeutung gesellschaftlicher Veränderungen für die Willensbildung in Unternehmen, Berlin: Duncker & Humblot

Bartölke, K. et al. (Ed.) (1978), Arbeitsqualität in Organisationen, Wiesbaden: Gabler

Bass, B. et al. (1979), Industrial democracy and participative management: what's the difference? In: International Review of Applied Psychology 28, 2: 81-92

Bayerisches Staatsministerium für Arbeit und Sozialordnung (Ed.) (1976), "Wo drückt uns der Schuh?" Reg. No. 10/76/12, München

Beckerath, G. v., (1976), Führungsgrundsätze - ein Instrument zur Bewältigung von Führungsproblemen im Arbeitsprozeß? In: Verwaltung und Fortbildung, 4. Jg. No. 2: 63-75

Berelson, B. (1952), Content analysis in communication research, Glencoe: Free Press

Bessai, B. (1974), Eine Analyse des Begriffs Management in der deutschsprachigen betriebswirtschaftlichen Literatur. In: Zeitschrift für betriebswirtschaftliche Forschung, 26: 353-362

Biermann, B. (1971), Die soziale Struktur der Unternehmerschaft. Stuttgart: Enke

BMFT-Leistungsplan (1978), Humanisierung des Arbeitslebens, Planperiode 1978-1982. Ed.: Der Bundesminister für Forschung und Technologie. Bonn

Booz-Allen & Hamilton (1973), Unternehmensberatung; Herausforderung des deutschen Managements und ihre Bewältigung. Göttingen: Schwartz & Co.

Braun, S., Fuhrmann, G. (1970), Angestelltenmentalität. Berufliche Position und gesellschaftliches Denken der Industrieangestellten. Neuwied: Luchterhand

Brinkamnn-Herz, D. (1975), Die Unternehmensmitbestimmung in der BRD. Köln: Kiepenheuer & Witsch

Bunz, A.R. et al. (1973), Qualität des Arbeitslebens. Bonn-Bad Godesberg: (Bundesministerium für Arbeit und Soziales)

Chmielewicz, K. et al. (1977), Die Mitbestimmung im Aufsichtsrat und Vorstand - Darstellung, Vergleich und Kritik der rechtlichen Regelung aus juristischer und betriebswirtschaftlicher Sicht. In: Die Betriebswirtschaft 37: 105-145

Dachler, H.P., Wilpert, B. (1980), Dimensionen der Partizipation. In: Grunwald, W., Lilge, H.-G. (Ed.), Partizipative Führung. Bern, Stuttgart: Haupt: 80-98

Dlugos, G. (1980), Mitbestimmung. In: Grochla, E. (Ed.), Handwörterbuch der Organisation. Stuttgart: Poeschel: col. 1343-1356

Fiedler, H. (1976), Führungsgrundsätze. In: Fortschrittliche Betriebsführung, Industrial Engineering. Vol. 25, No. 5: 313-317

Fishbein, M., Ajzen, I. (1975), Belief, attitude, intention, and behavior. London: Addison-Wesley

Friedrich, W. (Ed.) (1970), Methoden der marxistisch-leninistischen Sozialforschung. Berlin (DDR): Deutscher Verlag der Wissenschaften

Gaugler, E. et al. (1977) (2nd ed.), Humanisierung der Arbeitswelt und Produktivität. Ludwigshafen: Kiehl

George, A. (1959), Quantitative and qualitative approach to content analysis. In: de Sola Pool, J. (Ed.), Trends in content analysis. Urbana: University Press

Gottschall, D. (1975), Führungsrichtlinien - An Menschen vorbeigeschrieben? In: Manager Magazin, No. 2: 76-79

Gottschall, D. (1976), Merkmale des Erfolgs. In: Manager Magazin, No. 6:66-72

Grunwald, W., Lilge, H.-G. (Ed.) (1980), Partizipative Führung. Bern, Stuttgart: Haupt

Guserl, R., Hoffmann, M. (1976) (2nd elab. ed.), Das Harzburger Modell. Wiesbaden: Gabler

Haire, M. et al. (1966), Managerial thinking: An internation study. New York: Wiley & Sons

Hartmann, H. et al. (1973), Leitende Angestellte. Neuwied, Berlin: Luchterhand

Hartmann, H., Meyer, P. (1980), Soziologie der Personalarbeit. Stuttgart: Poeschel

Heller, F.A. (1971), Managerial decision making. London: Van Gorcum

Heller, F.A., Wilpert, B. (1977), Limits to participative management: Task, structure and skill as contingencies - A German-British comparison. In: European Journal of Social Psychology, 7: 61-84

Holsti, O.R. (1969), Content analysis for the social sciences and humanities. London: Addison-Wesley

IDE - International Research Group (1976), Industrial Democracy in Europe (IDE), an international comparative study. In: Social Science Information, 15: 177-203

IG Metall (1979), "Werktage müssen menschlicher werden!" Stuttgart: IG Metall

Inglehart, R. (1979), Wertwandel in den westlichen Gesellschaften: Politische Konsequenzen von materialistischen und postmaterialistischen Prioritäten. In: Klages, H., Kmieciak, P. (Ed.), Wertwandel und gesellschaftlicher Wandel: 279-316, Frankfurt: Campus

King, Ch.D., van de Vall, M. (1978), Models of industrial democracy. New York: Mouton

Kirsch, W. et al. (1980), Werte von Führungskräften und Arbeitnehmervertretern im Einflußbereich der Mitbestimmung. Published at Universität München

Klages, H., Kmieciak, P. (Ed.) (1979), Wertwandel und gesellschaftlicher Wandel. Frankfurt: Campus

Kluckhohn, F.R., Strodtbeck, F.L. (1973) (orig. 1961), Variations in value orientations. Westport Connecticut: Row, Peterson & Co.

Kmieciak, P. (1976), Wertstrukturen und Wertwandel in der Bundesrepublik Deutschland. Göttingen: Schwartz & Co.

Koehne, R. (1976), Das Selbstbild deutscher Unternehmer. Berlin: Duncker & Humblot

Kossbiel, H. (1978), Die Bedeutung formalisierter Führungsgrundsätze für die Verhaltenssteuerung in Organisationen. In: Sozialwissenschaftliche Annalen (vol. 2): 51-62

Kruk, M. (1972), Die großen Unternehmer. Frankfurt: Societäts-Verlag

Lattmann, Ch. (1977), Führung durch Zielsetzung. Bern, Stuttgart: Haupt

Lawrence, P. (1980), Managers and Management in West Germany. London: Croom Helm

Likert, R. (1967), The human organization. New York: McGraw-Hill

Lilge, H.-G. (1980), Wertgrundlagen partizipativer Führung. In: Grunwald, W., Lilge, H.-G. (Ed.), Partizipative Führung: 50-72, Bern, Stuttgart: Haupt

Lilge, H.-G., Grunwald, G. (1980), Humanisierung der Arbeit durch Job Enlargement und Job Enrichment. In: Neubauer, R., Rosenstiel, L.v. (Ed.), Handbuch der Angewandten Psychologie (vol. 1): 761-791, München: moderne industrie

The relatively high score of +.4 at 'participation' seems to be justified by the existence of several laws for participation (Montanmitbestimmungsgesetz 1952, Betriebsverfassungsgesetz 1972, Mitbestimmungsgesetz 1976) and labor laws.

Lukatis, I. (1972), Organisationsstrukturen und Führungsstile in Wirtschaftsunternehmen. Darmstadt, Frankfurt: Akademische Verlagsgesellschaft

Manager Magazin (1976), cf. Gottschall

Matthes, H. (Ed.) (1979), Sozialer Wandel in Westeuropa. Frankfurt: Campus

Miles, R.E. (1975), Theories of management. New York: McGraw-Hill

Neuberger, O. (1976), Führungsverhalten und Führungserfolg. Berlin: Duncker & Humblot

Paschen, K. (1977), Führungsleitsätze - eine modische Erscheinung oder eine Chance für eine effiziente Unternehmenssteuerung? In: Der Betriebswirt, No. 6: 168-171

Pross, H., Boetticher, K.W. (1971), Manager des Kapitalismus. Frankfurt: Suhrkamp

Reber, G. (1970), Vom patriarchalisch-autoritären zum bürokratisch-autoritären Führungsstil? In: Zeitschrift für Betriebswirtschaft, 40: 633-638

Ritsert, J. (1972), Inhaltsanalyse und Ideologiekritik. Frankfurt: Fischer

Rokeach, M. (in press), Some unresolved issues in theories of beliefs, attitudes, and values. Paper presented on March 15th, 1979, at the Nebraska Symposium on Motivation on the "Social psychology of beliefs, attitudes, and values"

Rokeach, M. (1973), The nature of human values. New York: Free Press

Staehle, W. (1980), Management. München: Vahlen

Steinle, C. (1975), Leistungsverhalten und Führung in der Unternehmung. Berlin: Duncker & Humblot

Steinle, C. (1978), Führung. Stuttgart: Poeschel

Tannenbaum, R., Schmidt, W.H. (1958), How to choose all leadership pattern. In: Harvard Business Review, 36: 95-101

Töpfer, A. (1976), Planungs- und Kontrollsystem industrieller Unternehmungen. Berlin: Duncker & Humblot

Töpfer, A. (1978), Das Harzburger Modell in der Unternehmenspraxis - Eine Bestandsanalyse. In: Der Betrieb, 31 ff., No. 38: col. 1892-1903

VELA-Untersuchung (unpublished manuscript), Der Führungsstil in den Unternehmen und die Gehaltsstruktur der Führungskräfte. Köln (1976)

Vroom, V.H., Yetton, P.W. (1973), Leadership and decision-making. Pittsburgh: University Press

Wilpert, B. (1977), Führung in deutschen Unternehmen. Berlin, New York: de Gruyter

Winter, R. (1978), Wegweiser zum Erfolg - Führungsgrundsätze in Wirtschaft und Verwaltung. In: Zeitschrift für Organisation, vol. 47: 241-243

Wistinghausen, J. (1977), Unternehmensgrundsätze - Entstehung, Form und Inhalt. In: Zeitschrift für Organisation, vol. 46: 61-66

Witte, E. (1980), Das Einflußpotential der Arbeitnehmer als Grundlage der Mitbestimmung. In: Die Betriebswirtschaft, 40, 1: 3-26

Wunderer, R., Grunwald, W. (1980), Führungslehre, vol. 1 and 2. Berlin, New York: de Gruyter

Zander, E. (1972), Führungssysteme in der betrieblichen Praxis. In: Zander, E. et al. (Ed.), Führungsmodelle. Leitbilder zur Unternehmensführung. Zürich: Sauer

Zepf, G. (1972), Kooperativer Führungsstil und Organisation: Wiesbaden: Gabler

Part VI
Values and Organizational Processes in Different Countries

Changing Business Values and Management Concepts - The German Experience

Meinolf Dierkes and Ariane Berthoin Antal

ABSTRACT

The changes in the socio-economic context for business activities have stimulated a reassessment of the role and tasks of the corporation in society on the part of researchers, managers, and the public. This article examines how business has approached the task of integrating social and financial considerations into decisionmaking. The model developed by Ackerman to describe the way firms deal with the concept of social responsiveness is applied to the experiences of West German firms, drawing on the results of longitudinal surveys and content analyses of social reports. Recommendations for the further operationalization of the concept are then elaborated.

THE CHANGED SOCIO-POLITICAL CONTEXT FOR BUSINESS

The past decade has been characterized by intensive discussions about the changes in the socio-political context for business in all highly industrialized countries. A growing awareness of the social costs of economic development has resulted in a more critical assessment of business activities. As the extent of environmental damages due to production processes and products became recognized, for example, concerned citizens and scientists alike demanded that business be held accountable for the negative impact of their activities. Consumer groups sprang up to criticize product quality, pricing, and marketing strategies. Labor representatives raised issues relating to the quality of life at the workplace. Investors started taking into consideration the social responsiveness of their companies (Longstreth and Rosenbloom 1973). Numerous studies have been conducted on the nature and sources of these changes. Some are of a broad nature affecting all sectors of society, while others stem more directly from specific business - society relations. To the first group belong, for example, changes in social values to what have been labeled "post-industrial" values, which have had a significant impact on the political and economic system (Inglehart, 1977; Strümpel, 1977). A further factor is that citizens are becoming increasingly critical of all major institutions, and have intensified demands for participation in planning and decisionmaking processes affecting all sectors of life - ranging from the workplace to community and national issues (Ellwein, Lippert, Zoll, 1975; Nelkin, 1978).

Two important changes belonging to the second group are the mounting distrust of business resulting from the increase in power and size of corporations, which have integrated vertically and diversified horizontally, and spread beyond national boundaries (CED, 1971, p. 18). In addition, the public has become sensitized by the mass media to the short and long term damages to the environment caused by uncontrolled and often unintended business activities.

The implications of these contextual changes for business are far-reaching. "The great growth of corporations in size, market power, and impact on society has naturally brought with it a commensurate growth in responsibilities; in a democratic society power sooner or later begets equivalent accountability." (CED, 1971, p. 21). Business activities are subjected to far more critical scrutiny than ever before - by more groups and in more areas (Corson & Steiner, 1974). The stakeholders to whom business must justify its actions have expanded from the traditional constituencies of shareholders, government, and employees, to consumers, environmentalists, and other groups in the interested public. Under public pressure, government regulation has spread to cover almost all areas of business activity, ranging from product safety to environmental standards in production processes, and hiring practices. Profitability is no longer accepted as the sole criterion for business decisions. Whereas the corporation was long judged in terms of individual contributions, it is being judged also increasingly in terms of its contributions to, and the costs it imposes on, society as a whole (Corson & Steiner, 1974, p. 17).

The criticism of business has stimulated a reassessment of its roles and tasks on the part of researchers, managers, and the public (Steiner, 1972, 1973; Dierkes & Bauer, 1973). It has gradually become clear that the business corporation can no longer be thought of as a purely economic institution, but that it also has an important socio-political dimension. An implication is that "every corporation has not only a legal charter, but a form of 'social charter', too - that is, the charter of public expectations of corporate performance. These expectations derive from the current set of social values and national goals; and, as these values and goals change, so too will the social charter of the corporation." (Williams, 1973, p. 26). Recognizing the complex interplay of the expanding nature of business activities and of the demands placed by the public, it is unrealistic to attempt to define a single role for the corporation in society in legal, economic or philosophical terms. More appropriate is a sociological approach to "the business firm as the central element of a role set in which a new pattern of relationships among the elements is evolving."

(Ackerman & Bauer, 1976, p. 16).

In view of the dynamic nature of the process of redefining the role of business in society, it is worthwhile to trace the development of the concept of social responsiveness in practice. How has business reacted to the challenge, and what has it done? A useful model in reviewing the developments over the past decade seems to be that developed by Ackerman to describe the response of individual firms to the need to define a policy integrating social and financial considerations in business decisionmaking (Ackerman, 1973, pp. 92-94). Reformulated to apply to the macro-level situation, the three stages of response are:

1. Recognition of the need for social responsibility by the CEO.
2. Development of broad social goals and establishment of an auditing function to review the social responsibility of the company in light of environmental demands and to encourage greater responsiveness.
3. Institutionalization of social responsiveness through changes in the management system.

In this paper we propose to examine the German experience with corporate social responsiveness by applying the Ackerman model to the business community as a whole. An examination of the progression from one stage to the next is intended to provide insights into the dynamics of the process in a highly industrialized society, and to reveal the level of responsibility actually achieved in the country today.

Phase 1: From Frustration to New Management Philosophies

Considering the mood which prevailed in Germany during the twenty years of the "Wirtschaftswunder", when the need to concentrate on economic goals and achievements determined the largely positive nature of the business - society relationship, it is not surprising that the business community was initially unprepared to understand the relatively fast and profound value change which became evident in the late 1960s. Leaders of the business community reacted at first with frustration and alienation, and they were unsure about the future role of the enterprise in society (Schmölders, 1973, p. 109). After this initial phase of frustration and lack of direction, leading corporations and later a growing segment of the business community began to accept the need for a redefinition of the role of business in society. They recognized the need to respond to the challenges it faced in order to preempt the imposition by government under public pressure of further regulatory measures which could threaten the very existence of the free enterprise system.

A survey conducted by the senior author, and Bernd Unger in 1975 among chief executives of the 400 largest companies in Germany reflected the various elements of this mood. (Fig. 1).

FIGURE 1

FUTURE GOVERNMENT INFLUENCE

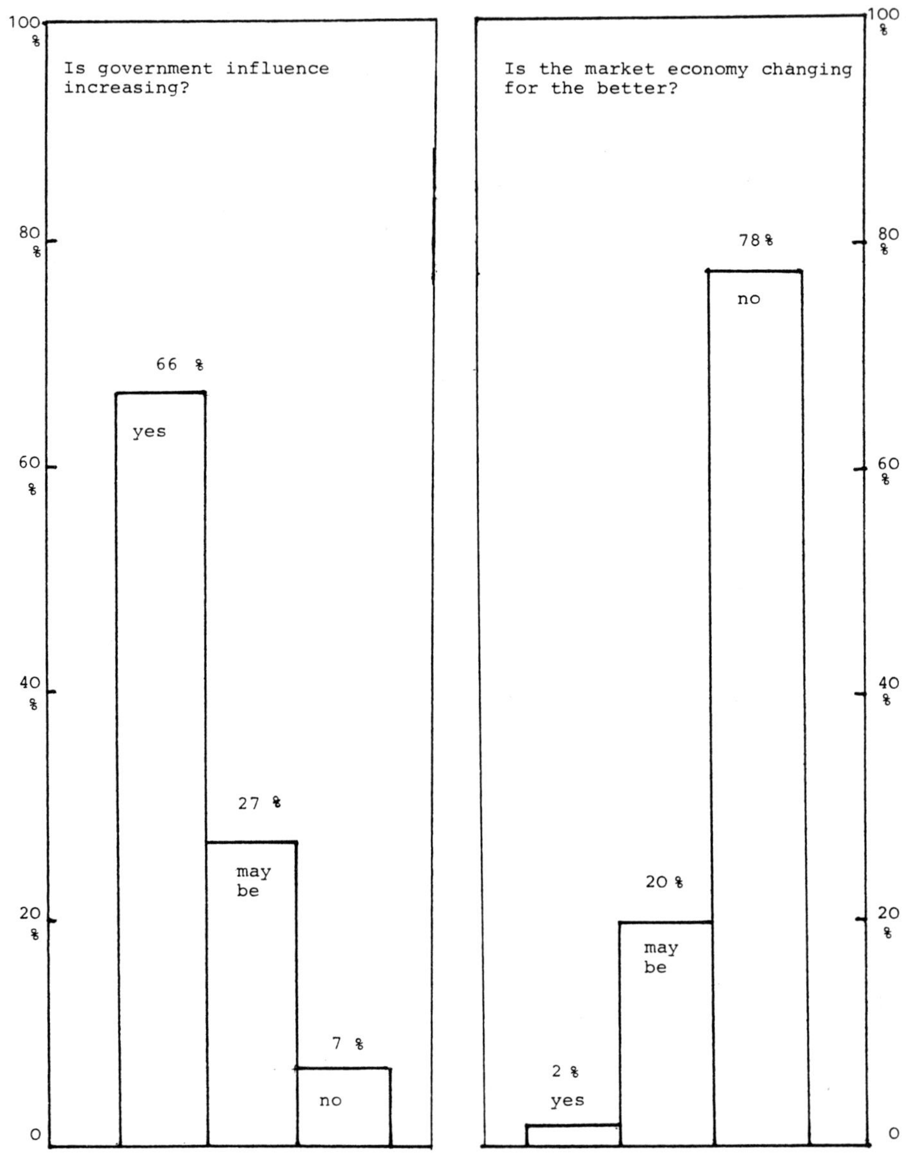

FIGURE 2

BUSINESS SOCIAL RESPONSIVENESS

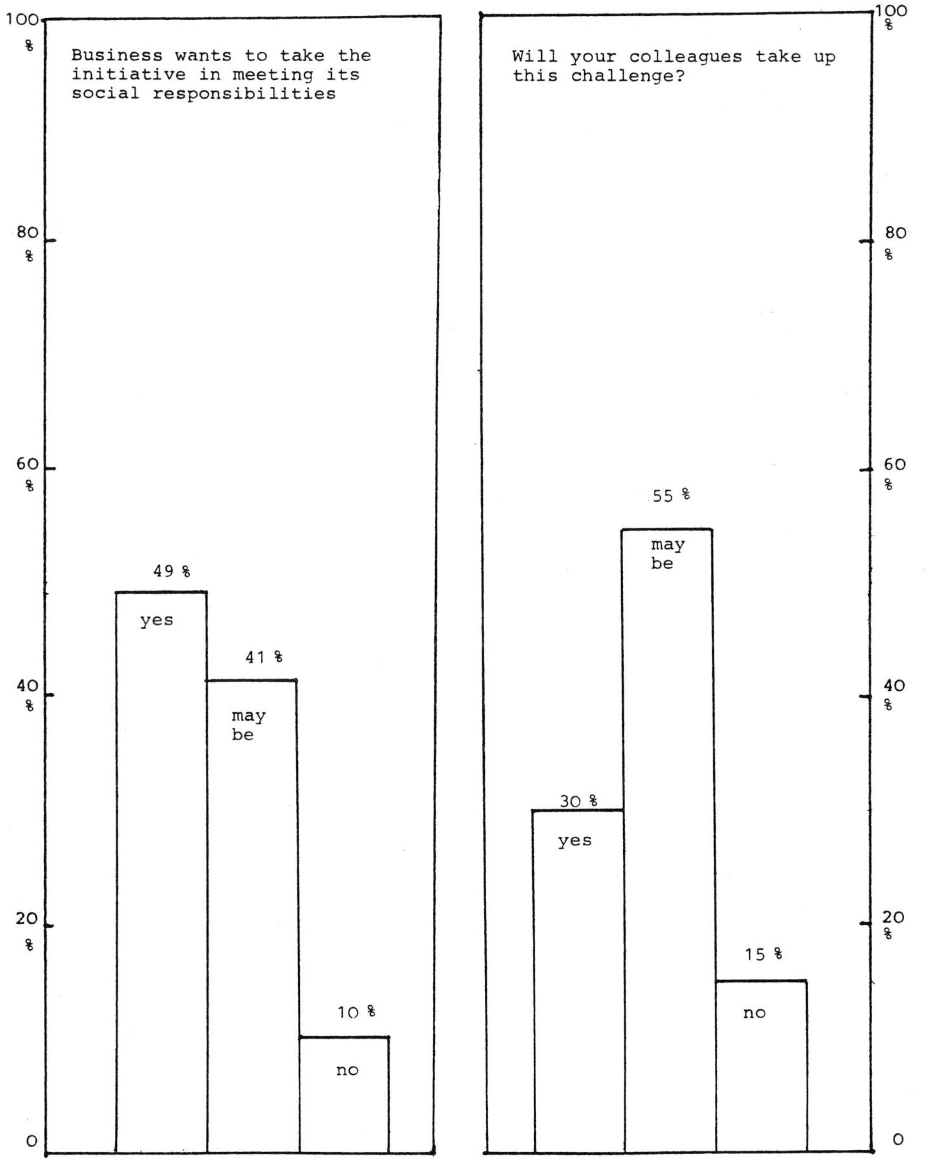

In the face of a perceived increase in government intervention (66 %) and an overwhelmingly negative assessment of the developments in the market economy (76 %), 49 % of the 198 top managers who participated in the survey responded that business was ready to take the initiative and assume social responsibilities (Dierkes & Unger, 1975). While they remained somewhat skeptical as to the degree of commitment of fellow managers to undertaking a fullfledged effort in assuming their social responsibilities, respondents indicated a growing conviction that a carefully designed, rigorous, and transparent policy of expanding the social responsiveness and accountability of the business corporation would be the optimal strategy under these circumstances. (Fig. 2).

On the one hand it would force business to take into consideration the social impacts of its activities, and on the other hand it could help to avoid detailed and often ineffective government intervention (Dierkes, 1979, p. 89).

These responses correspond closely to the description of behavior seen by Ackerman as characteristic of the first phase. The transition from frustration to supportive understanding among leading innovators in the business community is also reflected in the numerous publications and speeches on the subject, as well as the various institutions and organizations established in this area.

Phase 2: Defining Goals and Assessing Performance

While it is clear that the boundaries between one phase and the next are fluid, and that the exact nature and speed of transition must vary between firms, a number of indicators show that a significant portion of the largest German companies have moved beyond the first phase into the second; some can also be seen to be progressing to the third.

The two key elements identified by Ackerman as characteristic of the second stage in implementing corporate social responsibility is the definition of broad policy goals and the establishment of an auditing function to assess the company's current performance. A survey conducted by 'Manager Magazin' in Germany in 1976 revealed that approximately 200 of the largest corporations in this country had already developed formal statements integrating economic and social goals (Manager Magazin, 1976). As regards the second indicator, results from another survey conducted jointly by 'Manager Magazin', and the Foundation Business and Society in 1978 (Dierkes & Ullmann, 1979) on the extent of social reporting in Germany provide valuable insights. Companies were asked whether they were preparing any of the elements of a corporate social report recommended by the working group "Sozialbilanz-Praxis".[1]

1. Social report (Sozialbericht): verbal report of the goals, measures, achievements, and - as far as possible - the effects of societal activities, supplemented by statistical data;
2. Value added report (Wertschöpfungsrechnung): the value added by a firm in a given period; and
3. Social account (Sozialrechnung): account of all quantifiable, socially relevant expenditures and returns.

The preparation of a social report using one or more of these elements represents an attempt to obtain information about the company's social performance. Over half the respondents from industry and a quarter from retail indicated that they had compiled at least portions of a comprehensive social account (Sozialbilanz) according to this definition. An additional 15 % of industry and 25 % of retail businesses planned to prepare a social report for the following year. A more detailed analysis of the survey results for industry[2] provides the following picture of the practice of social reporting in Germany:

- Social reports together with a value added account were the most popular combination (28 %).
- An increasing number of companies (25 %) are preparing a verbal social report; it appears to represent a first step toward expanded reporting on socially relevant activities.
- 20 % of the companies prepared a separate value added statement.
- One fifth of the companies (13) prepared a combination of all three elements.

The survey revealed that firms perceive social reporting as a progression from a verbal report on socially relevant activities through the addition of a value added report, to the preparation of all three elements. There appear to be certain tendencies for blockage at each level, though. Only a few companies which are presently compiling verbal social reports intend to add value added accounts or prepare a comprehensive social account.

The results of this survey show that a significant number of major companies have established an internal auditing function to assess the social impact of business activities. As comparative studies show, German companies have been particularly creative and open to experimentation in designing ways of conducting such assessments (U.S. Department of Commerce, 1979).[3]

An Assessment of German Corporate Social Reports

Inspite if the numerous publications on the underlying theories and the results of the experiments with social reporting in Germany to date, no systematic analysis of these experiences has been conducted.[4] To meet this need at the end of the first decade of work in the area, the senior author and Andreas Hoff

Table 1: The Reports Analysed

AUDI NSU AUTO UNION AG:	Mitarbeiter - Unternehmen (1978)
BASF AG:	Menschen, Arbeit, Geschäft '77 (1978)
BATTELLE-INSTITUT e.V.	Battelle-Bilanz (1976)
BAYER AG:	Bayer in Wirtschaft und Gesellschaft (1976)
BBC AG:	BBC-Sozialbericht '77 (1978)
BERTELSMANN AG:	Geschäftsbericht/Sozialbilanz '77/78 (1978)
B. BRAUN MELSUNGEN AG:	Sozialbilanz (1978)
BUDERUS AG:	Buderus-Post (1978)
DEGUSSA:	Personal- u. Sozialbericht 77/78 (1979)
DEUTSCHE BP AG:	Sozialreport (1976)
DEUTSCHE SHELL AG:	Geschäftsbericht/Sozialbilanz (1979)
ETERNIT AG:	Geschäftsbericht '78 (1979)
HOECHST AG:	Hoechst '77 (1978)
KÖLNER BANK v. 1867 eG:	Geschäftsbericht '77--Sozialbilanz (1978)
LANDESFORSTVERWALTUNG DES LANDES BADEN-WÜRTEMBERG (MINISTERIUM FÜR LANDWIRTSCHAFT UND UMWELT):	Sozialbilanz 76/77 des Staatsforstbetriebs (1979)
MANNESMANN AG:	Mannesmann 1978: Mitarbeiter und Umwelt (1979)
E. MERCK AG:	Das Unternehmen und seine Mitarbeiter - Personelles und soziales Geschehen im Jahre 1977 (1978)
MIGROS-GENOSSENSCHAFTS-BUND:	Sozialbilanz (1978)
MOBIL OIL AG:	Geschäftsbericht 1977 (1978)
F. PIEROTH GmbH:	Pieroth-Sozialbilanz 75/76 (1977)
VEITH-PIRELLI AG:	Sozialbericht 1976 (1977)
RANK XEROX GmbH:	Geschäfts- und Sozialbericht 1976 (1977)
RHEINISCHE BRAUNKOHLENWERKE AG:	Rheinbraun Personal-u.Sozialbericht 1977 (1978)
RIEGER UND DIETZ GmbH&Co.:	RUD Sozialbilanz, 101. Geschäftsjahr (1976)
SAARBERGWERKE AG:	Sozialbilanz '77 (1978)
STADTSPARKASSE KÖLN:	Geschäftsbericht 1977 (1978)
STAHLWERKE PEINE-SALZGITTER AG:	Personal-, Arbeits- u. Sozialwirtschaft 1975/76, 1976/77 (1978)
STEAG AG:	Sozialbilanz '78 (1979)
STINNES AG:	Stinnes 1977 (1978)
VOLKSWAGEN AG:	Mitarbeiterzeitung d. Volkswagenwerk Aktiengesellschaft Wolfsburg: Sozialbericht 1978 (1978)

Source: M. Dierkes, A. Hoff; "Sozialbilanzen und gesellschaftsbezogene Rechnungslegung in der Bundesrepublik Deutschland" In: Hoffmann-Nowotny (ed.) Sozialbilanzen. Soziale Indikatoren VII. Campus Verlag 1980.

Table 2: Quantitative Analysis of the Reports According to Areas [1)]

	Total number of pages	Annual report	Social report: Total	Employees	Natural environment	Social environment	R+D	Suppliers	Competitors	Consumers	Value added statement	Social account	Goal catalogue
Audi	56	3	31	25	2	1	1.5				1		0.5
BASF	44	6	21	12	0.5	2	0.5				3	3	
Battelle	40	2	13	3.5		1	5			3			0.5
Bayer	68	6	42	20	5	5	8	1			3		
BBC	28		17	14.5							2.5		
Bertelsmann	104	37	13	8		2	1			1	1		
B.Braun	3	0.2	1.3	0.8								0.5	
Buderus	48	6	7	7									
Degussa	28	3	15	13.5	0.5						1		
Deutsche BP	48	1	15	9		1	0.5			0.5		4	
Deutsche Shell	62	8	25	7	3	5				6	1	2	1
Eternit	30	7	2.5	1							0.5	1	
Hoechst	72	44	7	1.5	1	0.5	2.5	1			0.5		
Kölner Bank	36	9.5	9.5	2.5		1.5				3.5	0.5	1	0.5
Landesforstverw.	24		11	5	2	1					1.5	1.5	
Mannesmann	24	1	13	10	1.5			0.5			1		
Merck	64		36	30		3					3		
Migros	90	5	34	8	3.5	10.5		1	1	8	1		1
Mobil Oil	40	13	4.5	1.5	1	0.5					1		
Pieroth	24	0.5	10.5	4		0.5					1	5	
Pirelli	20		6.5	4.5	0.5		0.5			0.5	0.5		
Rank Xerox	40	6	7	3		0.5					2	1.5	
Rheinbraun	40	1	14.5	13							1.5		
RUD	12		5	3.5		1						0.5	
Saarbergwerke	36		15	11.5							1.5	2	
Stadtsparkasse Köln	62	8	8.5	1.5		1.5				4	0.5		1
Stahl P.S.	48		36	36									
Steag	20	2	6	2	0.5	1	0.5				1	1	
Stinnes	60	29	3	1.5	1.5								
VW	12		6.5	5	0.5	0.5					0.5		

1) In pages; except for the first column, pictures are not included; graphics are included only where appropriate.

attempted the first such thorough study (Dierkes & Hoff, 1980). The purpose was to provide an empirical basis for a critical analysis of the state of the art of corporate social reporting in Germany today by conducting a content analysis of a broad spectrum of published social reports.[5] Table 1 presents the companies and their publications included in the study. A conscious choice was made to define social reporting in a very broad sense, in order to provide as large as possible an overview of the current activities in this field in Germany.[6] (See Table 1).
Among the publications used were:

- 6 annual reports (Geschäftsbericht) with a more or less detailed link to general societal considerations
- 12 social reports orientated largely to the internal sphere of reference (Sozialbericht)
- 3 integrated annual reports/social accounts (Geschäftsbericht/Sozialbilanz)

A breakdown by industrial sector reveals the following:

chemical, energy, oil	10
automobile, machine tool, metal	8
banks	3
retail, consumer goods	3
others	6
	30

The 30 reports in the study were subjected to a standard scientific and qualitative analysis to evaluate both the overall scope of the reports and their substantive treatment of areas of concentration.[7]

Quantitative Analysis

For the purpose of the quantitative analysis, the information included in the reports was first organized into categories and the amount of space devoted to each was tallied up (excluding empty space and pictures). The results in terms of pages are presented in Table 2. The general results of this part of the survey can be summed up as follows:

Of publications totalling an average length of 43 pages, the social report received a good third (43 %) of the space, and the annual report approximately 21 %. The remaining 45 % were taken up with pictures, graphics, or layout. Publications which included both an annual report and a social report were on the average half again as long as those dedicated exclusively to the social report (ca. 45 vs 30 pages). It is interesting to note that the often loose reporting style used in annual reports is usually not applied in the social report. There, the style is usually more concentrated and more information is provided. This is particularly noteworthy in view of the often heard accusation that social reports are little more than instruments of public relations. (Fig. 3).

FIGURE 3

The average space given to areas of social impact in social reports

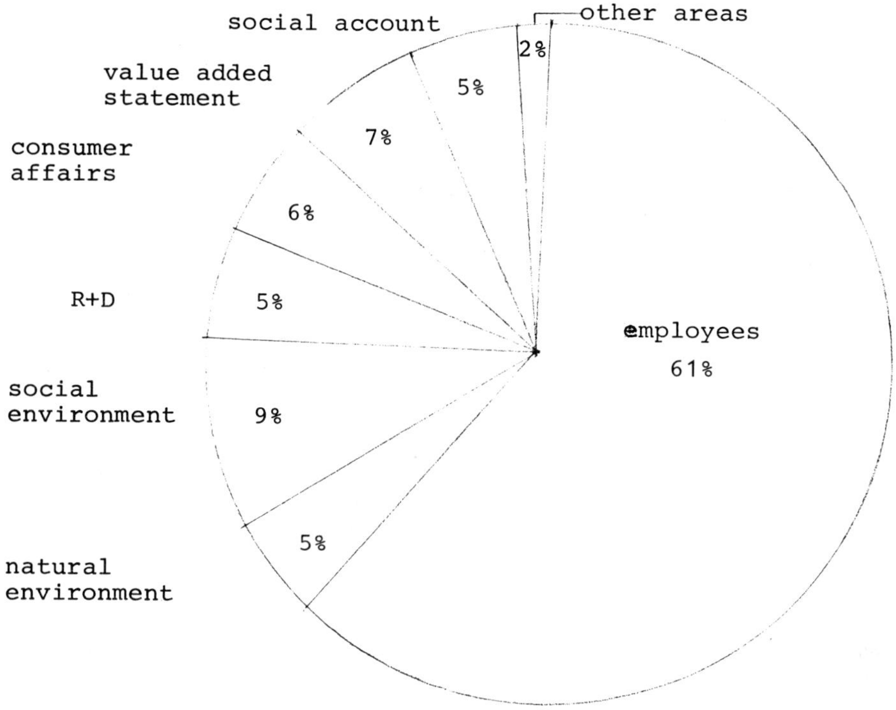

Source: M. Dierkes, A. Hoff; "Sozialbilanzen und gesellschaftsbezogene Rechnungslegung in der Bundesrepublik Deutschland" In: Hoffmann-Nowotny (ed.), Sozialbilanzen. Soziale Indikatoren VII, Campus Verlag, 1980.

Clearly, the areas of company - employee relations dominates the reports, particularly the value added statement (Wertschöpfungsrechnung) and social account (Sozialrechnung) also include information on this topic. Thus, almost three quarters of the social report format used today in Germany focuses on the employees and their interests. All other areas receive on the average less than 10 % of the total reporting space. When disaggregated, however, the picture changes somewhat. As indicated in Table 2, not all reports include all categories. The proportional distribution of space changes correspondingly. For example, those companies reporting on the natural environment dedicate an average of 10 % of the total space to this subject, which is about 11 % higher than the total volume reported above. Similarly, when the social environment is included, it receives 13 % of the space (also about 11 % more than the overall total). Further, companies reporting on R & D allocated 13 % of the total space to this area. The surprisingly high(21 %) attention paid to consumer affairs in those reports covering this topic is explained by the fact that most of the companies in this group are in the service sector.

A closer analysis of the scope of the efforts to monetarize social costs and benfits in various accounts (usually published as appendices) is also interesting. While the relative space (8 %) of the value added statement in those reports in which it is included is only a little higher than the average of all reports, the proportion of the social account at 18 % is accompanied by a reduction of 26 % in the total volume of the social report. Those reports including both of these two elements accord them 28 % of the total space, thereby reducing the overall volume of additional information given by an average of 18 %. This trend reduces the substantive section of the report, and is a source of concern especially when one considers the low quality of the measures usually applied in the social account. The exclusive reliance on input factors as indicators of social benefits is methodologically very weak. It mistakenly assumes a linear relationship between the input and output of a company, and therefore leads to a distortion in reporting and interpretation (Fischer-Winkelmann, 1980, p. 114).

Qualitative Analysis

There is no general agreement on the qualitative standards of measurement according to which social reports can be measured. The authors therefore followed a pragmatic approach in this part of the analysis. They developed a scale on the basis of the traditional "Principles of accounting" (Grundsätze ordnungsgemäßer Buchhaltung)[8]: truthfulness, completeness, clarity, comparability, care, and economic efficiency. These principles were added to the accepted modes of social reporting: verbal presentation, indicators, future orientation, and were then operationalized in the following scale:

1. verbal statements and/or low quality indicators with little or no comment;
2. verbal statement and indicators of average quality with some explanation;
3. detailed presentation using internal comparative data of high quality;
4. detailed presentation using internal and external comparative data of very high quality;
5. detailed critical treatment of the subject using internal and external comparative data; planning reference.

The results of this qualitative analysis are presented in Table 3.

In the qualitative analysis of the various areas reported on by the company it is necessary to distinguish between the structure of each subtopic and its substantive treatment. The structural analysis, as reflected in the number of subtopics used, corresponds roughly to the results of the quantitative analysis: the area of employee-related matters is by far the best documented, while in other areas usually only first steps have been taken. This fact can be attributed to three key factors. As stated in the BBC Social Report, "it is largely thanks to a thorough computer information system on personnel that it is possible to obtain and interpret a large amount of data on age, background, professional activity of personnel etc.". Further, such data, in contrast to much of the information from areas such as natural environment, products, and marketing strategies, belong primarily to the "non-sensitive" area of corporate activities; companies are therefore more willing to publish them. Finally, the methodological difficulties encountered in accounting for the other areas of corporate activity, with the possible exception of a natural environment, should not be underestimated. Whereas there appear to be certain implicit conventions on topics to be included in the area of company - employee relations and related indicators, their development in the other areas is still in the earliest stages.

Elements within the employee category are treated with varying levels of comprehensiveness. While the traditional indicators in the annual report - personnel structure, personnel expenditures including fringe benefits and training programs - are relatively well documented, topics such as working conditions, working environment and worker participation, are of relatively low quality. The general tendency to emphasize costs, i. e. inputs, is noteworthy. Subjective indicators are rarely used, although they would significantly improve those areas which to date are documented.

Social reporting: Achievements and Future Challenges

This content analysis shows that the social reporting of

Table 3: <u>Qualitative Analysis of the Reporting in the Various Areas</u>

Area	Number of companies	Quality Ø
EMPLOYEES		
<u>Personnel policy</u>		
Structure of personnel	30	2.37
Policy principles	19	1.63
<u>Personnel structure</u>		
Trainers	25	2.28
Status	24	1.88
Age structure	21	2.19
Women	18	2.00
Foreigners	16	2.31
Functional distribution	13	2.15
Handicapped	13	2.08
Regional distribution	12	2.33
Qualification	10	2.00
Part-time employees	8	1.88
Personal data	5	1.60
<u>Personnel expenditures</u>		
Personnel expenditures	21	1.81
Salaries and wages	30	2.40
Salary and wage structure	4	1.50
Pay principles	10	1.40
Additional personnel expenditures	12	2.42
Legally required social services	29	1.72
Contractually agreed social services	8	1.63
Other social services	10	1.20

Source: M. Dierkes, A. Hoff; "Sozialbilanzen und gesellschaftsbezogene Rechnungslegung in der Bundesrepublik Deutschland" In: Hoffmann-Nowotny (ed.) <u>Sozialbilanzen. Soziale Indikatoren VII. Campus Verlag 1980.</u>

Area	Number of companies	Quality Ø
<u>Other social services</u>		
Company pension plan	27	2.19
Savings plan	25	1.88
Cafeteria	23	1.48
Premiums	22	1.36
Accomodation	21	1.71
Finacial aid	20	1.45
Employee suggestion system	19	2.26
Vacation premium	18	1.28
Other leisure activities	15	1.40
Company health plan	15	2.57
Premiums for long services	13	1.38
Insurance plans	13	1.15
Sport	11	1.45
Social counseling	11	1.73
Non-monetary fringe benefits	7	1.29
Compensations/social plans	6	1.67
Other social services	(24)	1.42
<u>Training and education</u>		
Basic training	26	2.58
Additional training	25	2.08
General	10	1.40
<u>Working conditions</u>		
Accidents	21	2.62
Safety	22	1.68
Health	23	1.83
Psychological services	3	1.33
Structure of work-time	16	1.94
Shifts	7	1.43
Flexi-time system	4	2.00
Humanization measures	8	1.38

Area	Number of companies	Quality ∅
<u>Atmosphere and worker satisfaction</u>		
Length of service	17	2.18
Fluctuation	16	2.38
Health	15	2.27
Dismissals	13	2.23
Employee information	18	1.39
Employee surveys	6	1.83
Conflicts	3	1.67
Management principles	5	1.60
<u>Codetermination</u>		
Committees	22	2.22
Negotiation procedures	21	1.19
NATURAL ENVIRONMENT		
<u>Environmental protection department</u>	6	1.00
<u>Environmental protection equipment</u>		
Air	13	1.46
Water	12	1.75
Waste	9	1.44
Noise	6	1.17
Landscape	7	1.43
General	11	1.64
<u>Other measures</u>		
Recycling	8	1.38
Environmental research	4	1.50
Environmentally sound products	4	1.75
Energy conservation	3	2.33
Participation in development of legislation	3	1.33

Area	Number of companies	Quality Ø
SOCIAL ENVIRONMENT		
<u>Government</u>		
Taxes/Charges	20	1.55
Time off for public service	10	1.40
Infrastructural measures	6	1.83
Assistance to internal revenue service	6	1.00
<u>Public</u>		
Charity	17	1.47
PR	13	1.46
Publications	7	1.71
Social program	5	1.60
RESEARCH AND DEVELOPMENT		
Investments/Costs/Returns	7	1.43
Activities	13	1.54
Employees	7	1.14
Suppliers	10	1.40
CONSUMERS		
Quality of supply	7	1.71
Customer surveys	5	1.60
Marketing policy	5	1.80
Advisory services	4	1.50

German companies varies significantly as to length and quality, both overall and within the individual reporting areas. Some areas are relatively well covered, while others are treated only briefly, if at all, and are often of poor quality. The quality of the reporting also varies significantly between firms. Some reports come very close to meeting standards set by the research community in some areas, while others content themselves with verbal statements characteristic of the initial phases of development.

The constituencies at which these reports are directed vary equally greatly. They range from the traditional constituencies - whereby employees are often accorded a central role - to the general public and new stakeholders.

The survey also reveals the widely differing indicators used to describe similar phenomena. Whereas sometimes reports rely on ad hoc indicators based largely on verbal statements or expenditures, others use in depth measurements and a variety of sub-indicators, include comments on the problems of measurement, and refer to background material.

The great variety in the practice of social accounting in Germany brings to light the major challenges in this area for the next few years:

1. Continued development of indicators, particularly in the areas of the physical environment, consumer affairs, suppliers, and the social environment.
2. Schematization and condensation of data presentation, to be accompanied by more detailed discussions of goals and problems encountered in meeting them in a given period. Attempts should also be made to combine the three elements identified by the working group "Sozialbilanz - Praxis" into an overall matrix of societal costs and benefits resulting from business activity.
3. Further standardization of reporting in all areas, along the lines of consensus on reporting schemes and indicators already achieved in the area of company - employee relations.
4. Empirical research on information needs through the introduction of feed-back systems between the business and its various constituencies. Experiments along these lines are being conducted by such companies as Migros, Deutsche Shell, and Kölner Bank. This is particularly important for goal reporting as a means of aligning company goals and services with the needs of the different constituencies.

Phase 3: Has Social Responsibility Been Institutionalized?

Have German companies progressed beyond phase two and onto phase three? Have they done more than define social goals and establish auditing functions to evaluate their social performance? The increasing development and use of various approaches to corporate social reporting is a clear indicator that German companies are aware of their social responsibilities and are searching for concepts to integrate such considerations into their decision-making. But the acid test of the changes lies in the actual behavior.

In order to obtain insights into these developments, 'Manager Magazin' and the Foundation Business and Society have undertaken a longitudinal study of the behavior of leading German industries.[9] The stated purpose is

> to conduct a survey of all socially relevant activities of German industry, if possible in financial terms, to give management basic information and orientation for future social reporting and to stimulate the commitment of German industry to recognizing and taking into consideration the social impact of business activities (Manager Magazin, 1976/4, author's translation).

Thus far, two surveys have been conducted, the first in 1974 covering the years 1970-74 and the second in 1978 providing data on the period 1974-77. In 1974 questionnaires were mailed to 360 companies, including the 260 largest companies in German industry (each having a sales volume ranging from DM 30-250 million. Usable responses were received from 133 companies, representing a total sales volume of DM 240 billion, 29 % of the total industrial production of Germany and 20 % of all employees in German industry. The survey covered four areas of social commitment: employee relations, physical environment, social environment, and consumer relations.

In order to monitor changes in corporate social responsiveness over time, the survey was repeated in 1978. A few changes were made in the questionnaire on the basis of the experience in 1974: more qualitative indicators were integrated; 28 retail businesses were included to obtain insights into this field; and new areas were added, specifically, the development of business social policy using goal catalogues, the specification of tasks in the employee relations area, and the use of social reporting.

A comparison of the results of the two surveys conducted thus far produces interesting insights.[10] The first period 1970-74, was characterized by a signigicant expansion on the part of business into all areas of social responsibility, particularly, however, employee relations. This expansion was reflected in the high rate of growth of related expenditures and also in different sucesses at the achievement level. The second period, 1974-77, by contrast, reveals a very different situation: the social responsibility of business continued to grow, but at a far lower rate, and the overall pattern is less clear but more diverse.

While the first survey indicated that the large corporations were for more socially responsive than the smaller companies, and that chemical, petrochemical, and mining companies were far ahead of others, the second survey revealed that other branches of industry made up for lost time in practicing social reponsiveness, and size was no longer the determining factor. The key results can be summed up as follows:

- Social responsiveness focuses even more on employees (they accounted for 75.1 % (1974: 73.0 %) of value added).
- Both absolute and relative shifts were observed with respect to the fringe benefits provided by businesses largely due to increased legislation requiring services which heretofore had been provided voluntarily.
- Company pension plans continued to dominate fringe benefit expenditures.
- A further indicator of social responsibility are career opportunities for minorities: here no changes over the whole period 1970-77 were noted; only 3.3 % of management posts were held by women.
- Training and further education were recognized as central social responsibilities. Expenditures rose by 21 % in this area.
- Business intensified attempts to improve training opportunities: the proportion of apprentices to total employees rose from 3.0 % to 3.5 %.
- Job safety was given top priority. Expenditures rose by 32 % to DM 488 per employee, and the accident rate fell by 18.5 %.
- 50 % of the companies indicated that they were experimenting with ways to improve the quality of the workplace, particularly through job rotation. Job enrichment and job enlargement were also tried, but only few companies attempted introducing partially autonomous working groups. The importance of non-material incentives was given increasing recognition.
- Expenditures for environmental protection seemed to level off. In many areas running costs were already higher than investments. Noise pollution gained in importance, while water pollution received less funds.
- Two thirds of the businesses had already introduced energy conservation measures, and every tenth company responded such measures were planned. Results were already noticeable: energy consumption had fallen by 5 %.
- Outlays for charity and community involvement did not rise in the second period (taking inflation into account).
- Consumer affairs were still assigned relatively little importance. Only 12 industries had a consumer relations department.

Conclusion

The application of Ackerman's model in reviewing the development of corporate social responsiveness over the past decade has proven valuable. Applied in conjunction with the various survey data cited in this paper, it indicates that German companies have definitively progressed from an initial phase of frustration, to one of acceptance and active assumption of new responsibilities. A significant number of companies have clearly moved from the first phase to the second, defining social goals and establishing an auditing function to evaluate their social performance. An analysis of data on company behavior indicates that social responsibility is spreading; more companies are taking their social responsibilities into account in their business activities.

As Ackerman pointed out, in order for social responsiveness to be institutionalized, changes have to be made in the management structure. Incentive and decision-making structures have to be altered to take socially responsible actions into account. One of the most promising mangement tools for this purpose is goal-accounting. A company which defines its social goals along with its economic goals and then measures its performance according to these goals integrates the consideration of the societal impacts of its activities into every step of the planning and implementation process. By giving equal importance to its social and economic goals in policy formulation and in the evaluation of performance in the annual report, a company lays the groundwork for more responsible mangement decisions on a day to day basis. A number of companies are already experimenting with this concept. A careful analysis of their experiences should provide valuable insights into the advantages as well as problems involved in institutionalizing social responsiveness.

NOTES

1. Established in 1976 by 7 leading corporations to develop guidelines for social reporting in Germany; the group has since expanded to 15
2. A breakdown of data for retail was not possible
3. For more detailed discussions of the developments in this country see Dierkes 1979, 1979a, and 1980
4. A preliminary content analysis of 14 reports was conducted by the author and A. Hoff in 1978. For a discussion of the results see Dierkes 1979
5. The study was based only on published social reports; examples were not drawn from the estimated 200 social reports being prepared for internal purposes
6. Two Swiss companies (BBC AG and Migros-Genossenschaftsbund) were also included because they reveal new directions in the field
7. With reference to the procedure see W. Herkner, Inhaltsanalyse. In: J. van Koolwijk and M. Wieken-Mayser (Eds.), Techniken der empirischen Sozialforschung, Vol. 3, Erhebungsmethoden: Beobachtung und Analyse von Kommunikation, 1974: 158-191. Also R. Lisc and J. Kriz, Grundlagen und Modelle der Inhaltsanalyse, Reinbek bei Hamburg 1978
8. The application of these standards to social accounting was also suggested earlier by P. Eichhorn (Eichhorn 1974, pp. 19 -).
9. For reasons of comparability retail and service sectors were not included
10. For an international comparison of social responsibility among businesses see Preston et al., 1978

APPENDIX

Table 1: The Reports Analyzed

AUDI NSU AUTO UNION AG:	Mitarbeiter - Unternehmen (1978)
BASF AG:	Menschen, Arbeit, Geschäft '77 (1978)
BATTELLE-INSTITUT e.V.:	Battelle-Bilanz (1976)
BAYER AG	Bayer in Wirtschaft und Gesellschaft (1976)
BBC AG:	BBC-Sozialbericht '77 (1978)
BERTELSMANN AG:	Geschäftsbericht/Sozialbilanz '77/78 (1978)
B. BRAUN MELSUNGEN AG:	Sozialbilanz (1978)
BUDERUS AG:	Buderus-Post (1978)
DEGUSSA:	Personal- u. Sozialbericht 77/78 (1979)
DEUTSCHE BP AG:	Sozialreport (1976)
DEUTSCHE SHELL AG:	Geschäftsbericht/Sozialbilanz (1979)
ETERNIT AG:	Geschäftsbericht '78 (1979)
HOECHST AG:	Hoechst '77 (1978)
KÖLNER BANK v. 1867 eG:	Geschäftsbericht '77 Sozialbilanz 1978
LANDESFORSTVERWALTUNG DES LANDES BADEN-WÜRTTEMBERG (MINISTERIUM FÜR LANDWIRTSCHAFT UND UMWELT):	Sozialbilanz 76/77 des Staatsforstbetriebs (1979)
MANNESMANN AG:	Mannesmann 1978: Mitarbeiter und Umwelt (1979)
E. MERCK AG:	Das Unternehmen und seine Mitarbeiter - Personelles und soziales Geschehen im Jahre 1977 (1978)
MIGROS-GENOSSENSCHAFTS-BUND:	Sozialbilanz (1978)
MOBIL OIL AG:	Geschäftsbericht 1977 (1978)
F. PIEROTH GmbH:	Pieroth-Sozialbilanz 75/76 (1977)
VEITH-PIRELLI AG:	Sozialbericht 1976 (1977)
RANK XEROX GmbH:	Geschäfts- und Sozialbericht
RHEINISCHE BRAUNKOHLENWERKE AG:	Rheinbraun Personal- u. Sozialbericht 1977 (1978)
RIEGER UND DIETZ GmbH & Co.:	RUD Sozialbilanz, 101. Geschäftsjahr (1976)
SAARBERGWERKE AG:	Sozialbilanz '77 (1978)
STADTSPARKASSE KÖLN:	Geschäftsbericht 1977 (1978)
STAHLWERKE PEINE-SALZGITTER AG:	Personal-, Arbeits- u. Sozialwirtschaft 1975/76, 1976/77 (1978)
STEAG AG:	Sozialbilanz '78 (1979)

(continued)

Table 1 (continued):

STINNES AG:	Stinnes 1977 (1978)
VOLKSWAGEN AG:	Mitarbeiterzeitung d. Volkswagenwerk Aktiengesellschaft Wolfsburg: Sozialbericht 1978 (1978)

Source: M. Dierkes, A. Hoff; "Sozialbilanzen und gesellschaftsbezogene Rechnungslegung in der Bundesrepublik Deutschland". In: Hoffmann-Nowotny (ed.), Sozialbilanzen. Soziale Indikatoren VII. Campus Verlag 1980

BIBLIOGRAPHY

Ackerman, R. (1973), How Companies Respond to Social Demands. In: Harvard Business Review, July-August 1973: 88-98

Ackerman, R. and R. Bauer (1976), Corporate Social Responsiveness: The Modern Dilemma, Reston, Virginia: Reston Publishing Company

Committee for Economic Development (1971), Social Responsibilities of Business Corporations, New York: Committee for Economic Development

Corson, J.J. and G. A. Steiner (1974), Measuring Business's Social Performance: The Corporate Social Audit, New York: Committee for Economic Development

Dierkes, M. and R. Bauer (Eds.) (1973), Corporate Social Accounting, New York: Praeger Publishers

Dierkes, M. and B. Unger (1975), Die Zukunft der Elite. In: Manager Magazin, 6/1975: 36-43

Dierkes, M. (1978), Sozialbilanzen - Einige Gedanken zur konzeptionellen und politischen Entwicklung der letzten Jahre. In: Sozialbilanzen in der Bundesrepublik Deutschland; Edited by Elmar Pieroth, Düsseldorf: Econ Verlag: 202-221

Dierkes, M. (1979), Corporate Social Reporting in Germany: Conceptual Developments and Practical Experience. In: Accounting, Organization and Society, Vol. 4, No. 1/2, Pergamon Press

Dierkes, M. and A. Ullmann (1979), Wird die Offensive blockiert? In: Manager Magazin, 7/1979: 88-96

Dierkes, M. and A. Hoff (1980), Sozialbilanzen und gesellschaftsbezogene Rechnungslegung in der Bundesrepublik Deutschland. In: Sozialbilanzen. Soziale Indikatoren VII; Edited by R. Hoffmann-Nowotny, Frankfurt: Campus Verlag

Eichhorn, P. (1974), Gesellschaftsbezogene Unternehmensrechnung, Göttingen

Ellwein, T., E. Lippert and R. Zoll; with D. Bald (1975), Politische Beteiligung in der Bundesrepublik Deutschland, Kommission für wirtschaftlichen und sozialen Wandel, No. 89, Göttingen: Verlag Otto Schwarz

Fischer-Winkelmann, W. (1980), Gesellschaftsorientierte Unternehmensforschung, München: Verlag Franz Vahlen

Ingelhart, R. (1977), The Silent Revolution: Changing Values and Political Styles Among Western Publics, Princeton: Princeton University Press

Longstreth, B. and H. D. Rosenbloom (1973), Corporate Social Responsibility and the Institutional Investor, New York: Praeger Publishers

Manager Magazin (1976), Enquête über das soziale Engagement der deutschen Industrie, 1976/4

Nelkin, D. (1978), Technological Decisions and Democracy, Beverly Hills, California: Sage Publications

Preston, L., F. Rey and M. Dierkes (1978), Comparing Corporate Social Performance Germany, France, Canada, and the U. S. In: California Management Review, Vol. 20, No. 4: 40-49

Schmölders, G. (1973), Die Unternehmer in Wirtschaft und Gesellschaft, Essen: Girardet

Steiner, G. (Ed.) (1972), Contemporary Challenges in the Business - Society Relationship, Los Angeles: Graduate School of Management, UCLA (mimeographed)

Steiner, G. (Ed.) (1973), Selected Major Issues in Business' Role in Modern Society, Los Angeles: Graduate School of Management (mimeographed)

Strümpel, B. (1977), Die Krise des Wohlstands, Stuttgart: Kohlhammer

U. S. Department of Commerce (1979), Corporate Social Reporting in the United States and Western Europe, Washington, D. C.: U. S. Department of Commerce

Williams, H. M. (1973), The Challenge to Business. In: Selected Major Issues in Business' Role in Modern Society: 1-18; Edited by G. Steiner, Los Angeles: Graduate School of Management, UCLA (mimeographed)

Work Motivation and Canadian Bicultural Context

Rabindra N. Kanungo

ABSTRACT

Effective utilization of human resource in an organization requires an understanding of culture-based characteristics of its employees. The paper describes a study that identifies several culture-based motivational and attitudinal characteristics of Anglophone and Francophone employees in Canadian bicultural context. It has been argued that effective management of human resource requires an appreciation of the differences of the two culturally distinct groups of employees in Canada. Furthermore, it is suggested that organizational policies need to be formulated on the basis of the culture-based characteristics of the employees.

INTRODUCTION

An organization is a socio-technical system with a given structure defining the vertical and laterial relationships among its components. The way in which such a system has to be managed most effectively is determined by several factors located both outside and within the organization. Thus, broadly speaking the factors that influence managerial effectiveness can be grouped under two categories, the external and the internal factors. The factors in the external environment of the organization that have significant influence on the nature of management activities may refer to such things as the technological characteristics of the business operations, the type of government controls and legal frameworks that direct the operations, and the type and level of economic development surrounding the operation. The factors in the internal environment of the organization that have significant consequences for management operations may refer to the characteristics of the employees forming the organization, and the nature of their interaction with other organizational members and their jobs. Studying the nature of the external factors and their effects on organizational functioning has been the preoccupation of organization theorists of sociological, economic and legal persuasions, primarily interested in macroanalysis of organizational behavior (Khandwalla, 1977; Thompson, 1967; Woodward, 1965). Researching into the nature of internal factors and their effects however has been the main task of organization theorists of social psychological inclination, primarily interested in micro-analysis of individuals' behavior within organizations (Likert, 1961, 1965). This paper reports some recent research that clearly fall in the latter category. The research aims at understanding the nature of some factors in the internal environment of Canadian organizations that operate in a bicultural context.

Many Canadian organizations, particularly those that operate in French Canada (the province of Quebec) have a unique feature. Within these organizations, one finds two culturally distinct groups of employees, the English and the French Canadians. Very often managing these two groups of employees poses unique problems for management, the solution of which requires an understanding of the distinct characteristics of the two groups shaped by their own respective cultures. In order to find out what these culture-based characteristics are and how they can influence management operations, I have conducted a number of controlled field studies in several large Canadian organizations. For detailed description of these studies one might refer to my recent book on "Biculturalism and Management" (1980). In this paper however, I am just going to summarize the findings of one such study on the nature of work motivation among the French and the English Canadian employees of a large national corporation. The study was conducted as a consulting project, and it probed into the motivational profiles and attitudes of the two groups of employees in different areas of management concern as laid out in Table 1.

Table 1

Ares of Employee Behaviour Covered in the Study

1. Perceived importance of job outcomes
2. Satisfaction with job outcomes
3. Turnover potential
4. Degree of personal responsibility and commitment
5. Actual and ideal level of participation
6. Job enrichment potential or perceived ability in relation to job demand
7. Transfer readiness
8. Training programs
9. Job involvement
10. Recruitment practices

METHOD

The questionnaire for this study was prepared after consultation with the management of the organization where the study was conducted. The questionnaire was prepared both in English and in French language, and was distributed to 882 employees belonging to three different job categories, working in different branch offices in Quebec and Ontario. Of this total, 646 or 73.24% returned the filled in questionnaire. After eliminating 57 respondents who could not be classified as either English or French, we ended up with 379 French and 210 English respondents (see Table 2).

Table 2

Demographic Characteristics of the Sample Expressed in Percentages

	Francophones n = 379	Anglophones n = 210
SEX		
Male	83.9	81.9
Female	16.1	18.1
MARITAL STATUS		
Married	72.1	76.7
Single	27.7	23.3
AGE		
Less than 29 years	58.3	49.52
30-49 years	32.7	40.47
40-49 years	8.7	8.57
50 years and above	0.3	1.42
EDUCATION		
Less than High School	1.1	0.0
High School Graduate	37.0	38.6
College Graduate	61.9	61.4
INCOME LEVELS		
Below $10,000	29.0	20.1
$10,000 - $20,000	51.5	48.3
Above $20,000	19.5	31.6
TENURE WITH ORGANIZATION		
Less than 5 years	76.0	71.4
5-10 years	17.9	20.5
11-20 years	6.1	8.1
More than 20 years	0.0	0.0
TENURE WITH JOB		
1 year or less	37.7	32.9
2-5 years	51.7	52.9
6-10 years	8.7	11.0
11-15	.8	3.3
16-20 years	1.1	0.0

RESULTS

An examination of the demographic characteristics of the respondents revealed that the two groups were matched with respect to education, sex, age, marital status, tenure with the organization and tenure with the job. Only with respect to salary, the two groups differed ($X^2 = 17.56$, $p < .001$). In higher income brackets, there were greater percentage of anglophones relative to francophones. Past industrial practice of hiring anglophones for higher level and higher paying jobs (because of the importance of English language in commerce) mainly accounts for this discrepancy. Considering the fact that salary and sociolinguistic background of the respondents were not independent but related, in all subsequent analysis the confounding effects of the covariate (salary) were eliminated by using covariance analyses.

Perceived importance of job outcomes

The mean rankings of perceived importance of each of the 15 job outcomes were calculated for the two groups of employees and the main profiles are presented in Figure 1. Both groups consider interesting nature of their work to be the most important job factor, followed by adequate earnings. Both groups attach low importance to the nature of supervision and interpersonal peer relations at work. This pattern of results confirm our earlier findings (Kanungo, Gorn & Dauderis, 1976) that both English and French Canadian employees put the interesting nature of work in the highly important job factor category and the nature of supervision in the least important job factor category. So much for similarity between the two groups.

There were however several interesting statistically significant differences between the two groups observed in the present study. Francophone employees attached relatively greater importance to benefits, working conditions, opportunity for improving job skill, and equitable pay. The anglophone employees on the other hand, attached greater importance to earnings, company policy, recognition, and responsibility and independence at work. In our earlier study, we also found that francophones tend to attach relatively greater importance to fringe benefits and working conditions, where as anglophones tend to attach greater importance to recognition, responsibility and independence.

In general, if we consider the occupational values of the employees (see Figure 1), it seems that intrinsic motivation for both anglophone and francophone employees stems primarily from the interesting nature of work. But the differentiating elements in the intrinsic motivation of the two groups lie in the fact that francophone employees put greater emphasis on training opportunity to acquire higher level

Figure 1: Mean Perceived Importance Profile For Anglophone and Francophone Employees

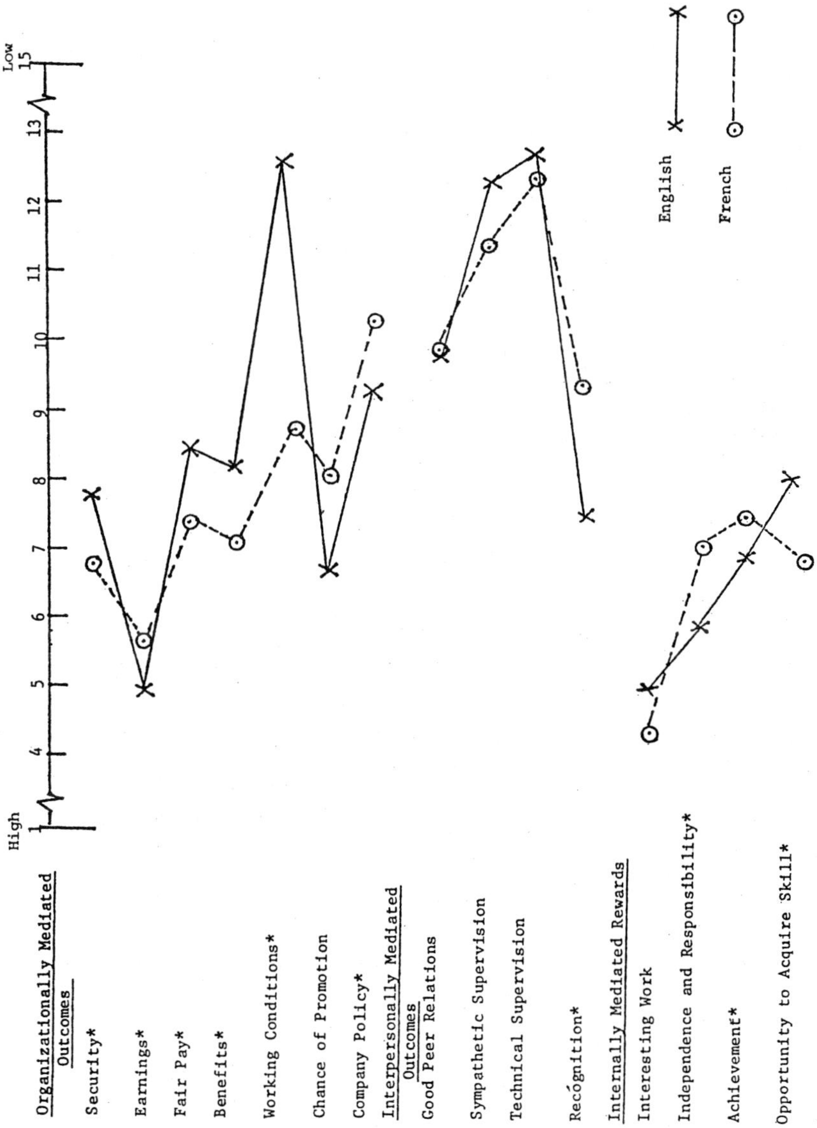

* $p < .05$

skills where as the anglophone employees emphasize more on autonomy, responsibility and recognition.

With respect to extrinsic motivation, both groups are looking for better earnings and promotions, but it is the anglophone employees that put greater emphasis on them relative to francophones. On the other hand, francophones relative to anglophones tend to put greater emphasis on fringe benefits, working condition and security. This pattern of motivational profiles of the two groups seems to support the notion that the saliency of the security needs and affiliative needs is somewhat greater among the francophone employees, where as the saliency of the personal achievement oriented needs for feedback, recognition and autonomy is relatively greater among the anglophone employees.

Satisfaction with job outcomes

The mean satisfaction score profiles of the francophone and anglophone employees for each of the 15 job factors on a 6 point satisfaction scale are presented in Figure 2. Inspection of the profile reveals that all employees show mild to moderate levels of satisfaction with their job outcomes. However, francophone employees seem to be relatively more satisfied with nine out of 15 job factors (security, company policy, promotion, fair pay, considerate supervision, recognition, interesting nature of work, autonomy and opportunity to acquire higher level skills). Francophone overall job satisfaction was also greater than anglophone overall job satisfaction. In five out of 15 job factors, there are no significant difference among the two groups (earnings, working condition, peer relation, technical supervision, and achievement). Anglophones compared to francophones were relatively more satisfied with benefits. These results are again consistent with the findings reported by us earlier (Kanungo *et al*, 1976) that given more or less the same job outcomes, the francophone employees express relatively greater degree of satisfaction than the anglophone employees. The reason for the more easily satisfied nature of francophone employees may lie in their lower level of expectation and a life style influenced by Catholic ethic and family orientation that emphasize enjoyment and contentment with existing life conditions.

Turnover potential

Since Francophone employees show higher levels of job satisfaction than do anglophones, it is expected that they will show lower turnover potential. In order to test this hypothesis, employees were asked to indicate on a four-point scale their chances of leaving the organization. The results are presented in Figure 3. The mean scores of the francophone group suggest that their probability of staying in the

Figure 2: Mean Satisfaction Profiles for Anglophone and Francophone Employees

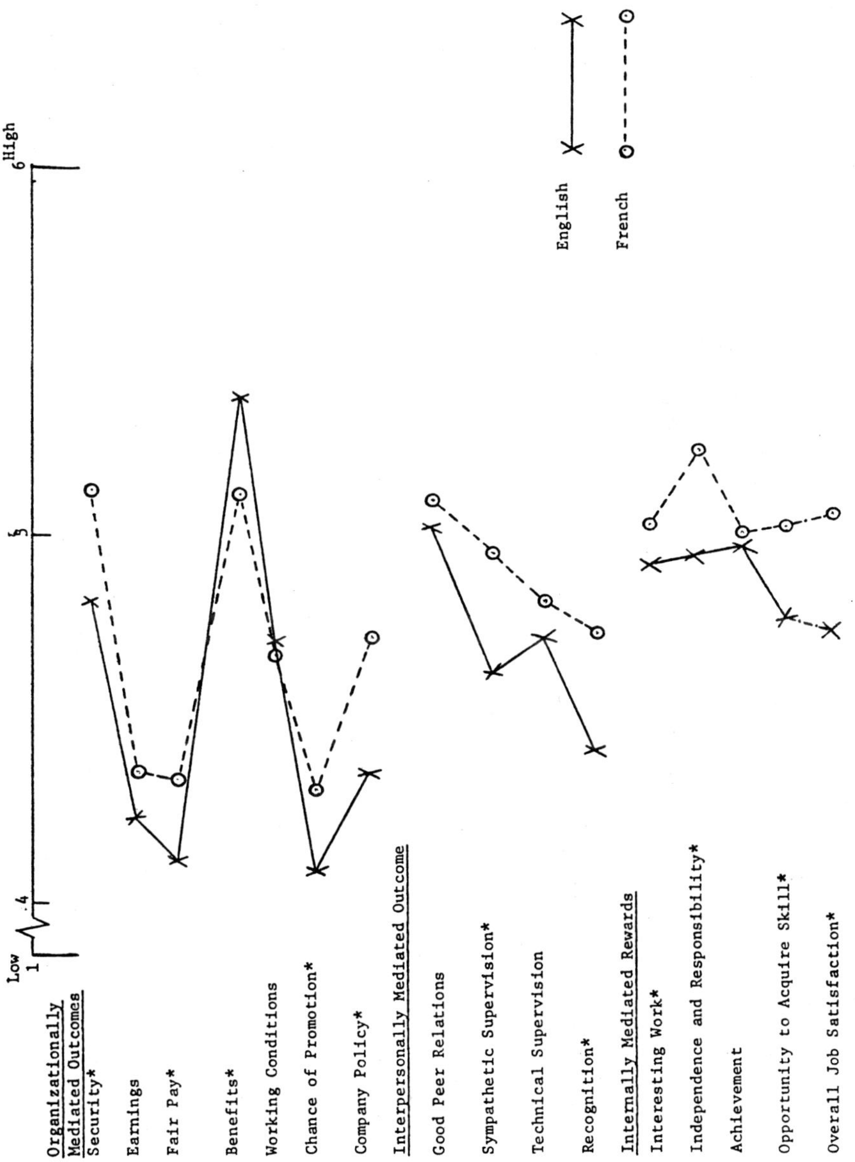

*p < .05

Figure 3:

Turnover Potential

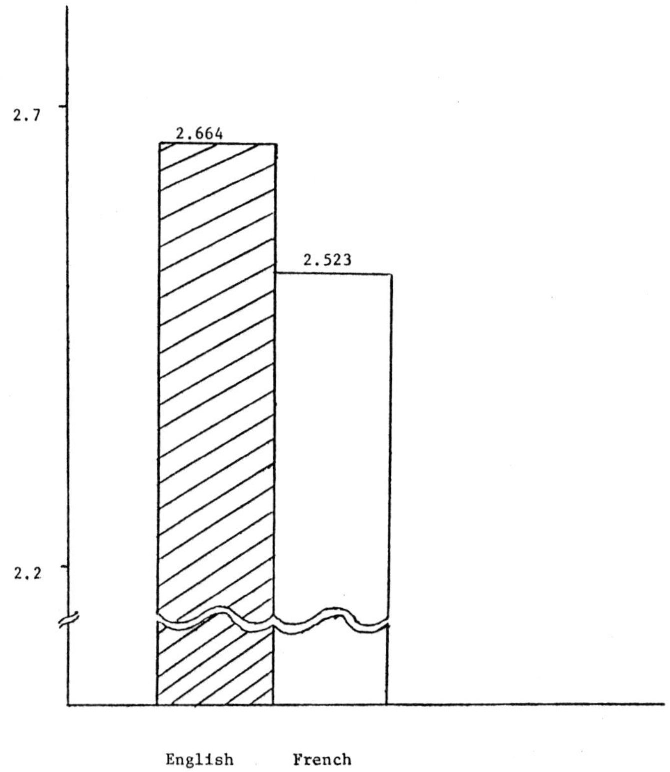

organization is significantly greater than that of the anglophone group ($p < .05$). This finding can be explained in three ways. First, the lower **turnover** potential of francophones may stem from their higher levels of job satisfaction. They are happier in their jobs than are the anglophones, and hence do not look elsewhere. The second reason for their lower turnover potential may be due to the fact that francophones find their choices of other jobs somewhat limited because of the language barrier. Anglophone employees do not face language problems, and thus find a wider job market in Canada and the United States. Francophone employees, on the other hand, may feel more secure staying in Quebec, since they will less frequently find a language problem at work where they will have francophone co-workers. In fact, francophone employees may feel that due to their language barrier they would be less effective outside Quebec, and such a feeling may discourage them from looking for work elsewhere.

Finally, higher turnover potential among anglophone employees could stem from the personal achievement of success orientation of the anglophones and the security and affiliative orientation of the francophones. It is likely that an anglophone employee would move from job to job or from one organization to another to seek his individual goals of autonomy and personal success. The more security conscious and affiliative francophone employees, on the other hand, will be less inclined to engage in job-hopping. Instead, they will be more prone to seek and settle in work surroundings which are stable and socially pleasant.

Degree of commitment

Degrees of personal responsibility and commitment in the job, in the department, and in the company as a whole were assessed for the two groups of employees. Their mean scores are plotted in Figure 4. Both groups of employees show a high degree of personal responsibility and commitment. However, two interesting observations can be made with respect to this variable. First, as one moves from job to department to company, personal commitment tends to decline. This is quite expected because of the fact that the employees have greater control over their actions in meeting job demands, whereas they may not feel the same way in achieving department or company goals. Because of the presence of other people working in the department and the company, there is a tendency for diffusion of personal responsibility and commitment. The second interesting observation from the data suggests that the anglophone employees tend to exhibit greater degree of personal responsibility and commitment to their job, department, and company than the francophone employees ($p < .05$ in each case). The latter observation is consistent with the findings mentioned earlier that the

Figure 4: Perceived Level of Commitment

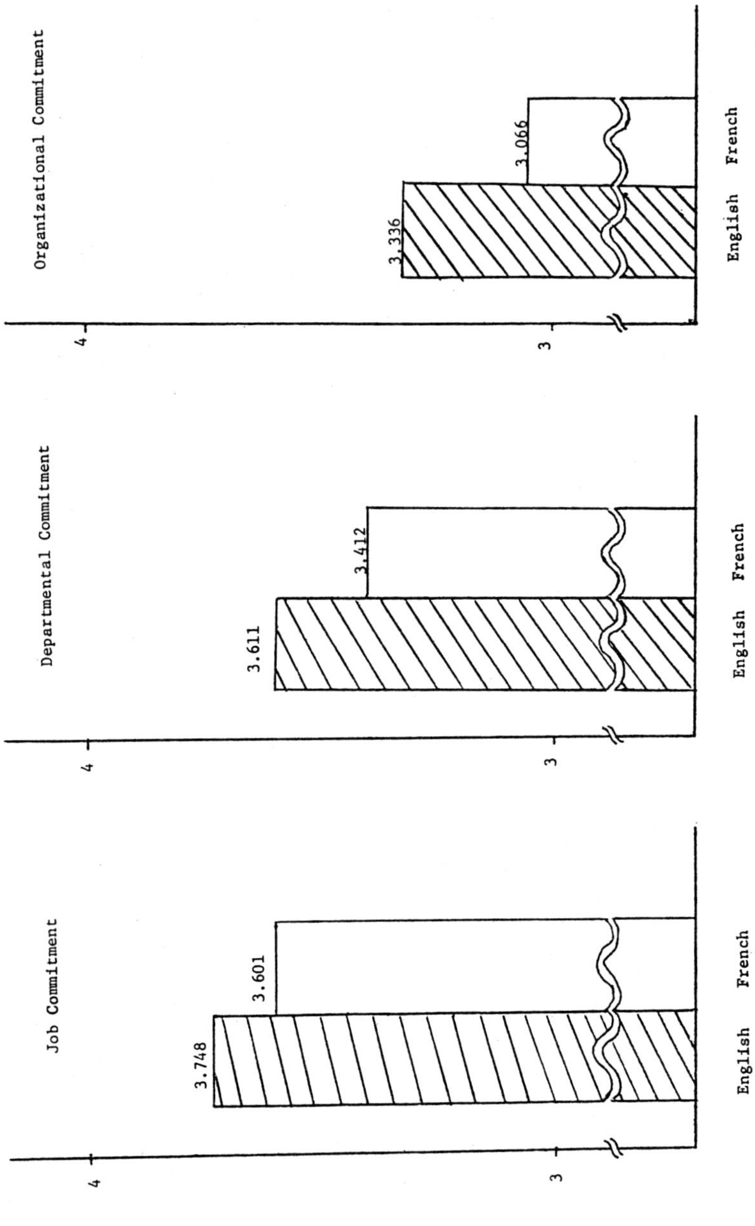

anglophone employees relative to their francophone counterpart, attached greater importance to responsibility and independence in their jobs. A possible explanation for the relatively lower degree of commitment among the francophone employees may stem from their perception of the organization as an essentially English institution with which they cannot identify as much as the anglophones. This explanation however, can be tested only if one is able to compare the two groups on this commitment variable in a comparable organization owned and dominated by French Canadians.

Level of employee participation

The mean scores on ideal and actual levels of participation for both the groups are presented in Figure 5. It may be observed that both the groups ask for high level of participation. They want that their opinions and suggestions be more often solicited by their superiors while decisions that affect them are made. As would be expected, the perceived ideal level of participation is significantly higher than the perceived actual level of participation for both groups of employees ($p < .05$ in each case). However, the francophone employees experience greater degree of discrepancy between the ideal and the actual levels of participation. This is because the francophone group perceives its actual level of participation to be lower than that of the anglophone group. Perception of relatively lower levels of actual participation among the francophone employees may result from two sources: the nature of supervisory practices, and the impersonal organizational climate created by rules and regulations. In the present study, most of the supervisors of the francophone employees were francophones, while most of the supervisors of the anglophone employees were anglophones. It is possible that the francophone supervisors may be perceived to be providing less opportunity to create a consultative atmosphere than the anglophone supervisors. Furthermore, there is some evidence to suggest that the impersonal rules and regulations tend to elicit greater compliance from francophone employees than anglophone employees. Since organizational rules do not dictate for consultative practice, the francophone employees will tend not to take any initiative to influence their supervisors with their suggestions and opinions. While francophone employees tend to be more 'role bound', the anglophone employees tend to be more 'person bound' with strong belief in the effectiveness of personal autonomy and initiative. Even in an impersonal organizational climate of rules and regulations, the anglophones are more likely to confront their superiors with their own work related opinions and suggestions regardless of whether their views are solicited or not.

Figure 5

Level of Employee Participation

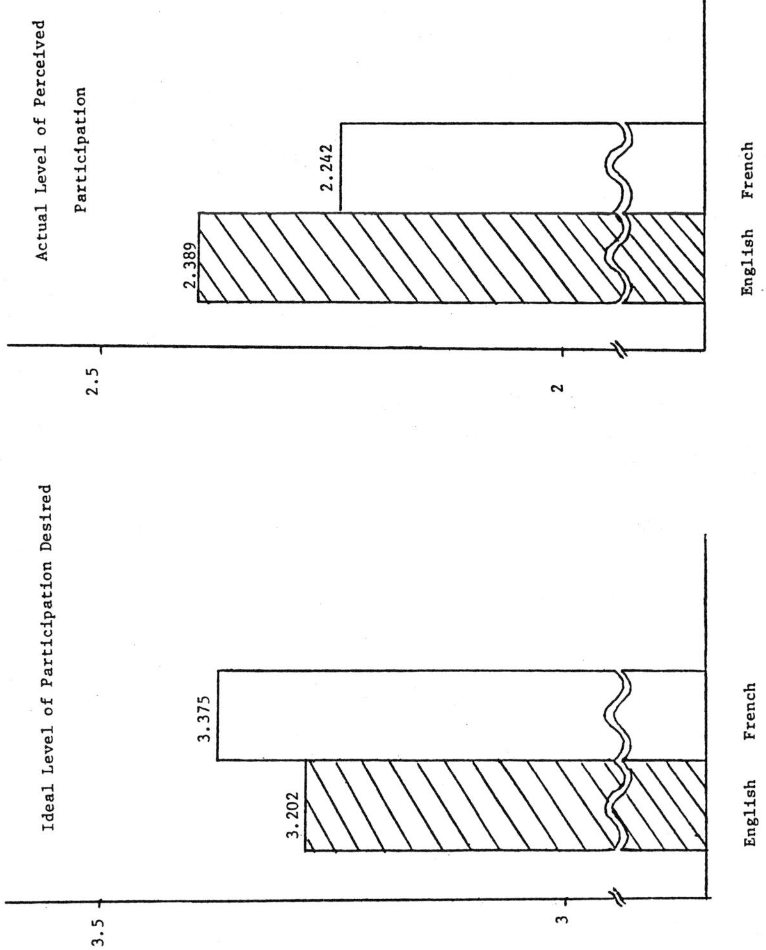

Job enrichment potential

Job enrichment potential of the employees was assessed by asking them to indicate the degree to which their abilities were utilized in their jobs. Thus, this variable measures employee's perception of his own ability in relation to his job demands. For example, if an employee feels that he is underutilised in his job, this means that he can handle a more enriched job of greater responsibility and complexity. This would mean that he has greater job enrichment potential. The mean scores of the two groups of employees plotted in Figure 6 suggest that the anglophone employees compared to the francophones consider themselves as more underutilised in their jobs, and hence have greater job enrichment potential ($p < .05$). Again this finding is consistent with the observation mentioned earlier that the anglophone employees consider responsibility and autonomy in their jobs to be more important than the francophone employees. The latter group however, tend to emphasize opportunity to acquire skills through training to be more important, presumably because of a sense of insecurity that they want to overcome through increasing their job skills.

Readiness to accept transfer

Employees were asked to indicate the degree of their willingness to accept transfer to a different location (different province or country). The mean scores of the two groups indicating their readiness to accept transfer are shown in figure 7. The results reveal that the anglophone employees express greater willingness to move out of their present location than the francophone employees.

In order to determine what factors influence the employee's decision to accept a transfer, two sets of questions were asked. One set of questions probed into the factors that are presumably responsible for the employee's reluctance to accept a transfer, and the other set of questions probed into the factors that might induce the employee to accept a transfer. The mean scores of the two groups on items relating to the reasons for reluctance and for acceptance are shown in figures 8 and 9 respectively. Figure 10 presents data on the preferences of the two groups for various locations where they would like to work.

Inspection of figure 8 reveals that for both the groups, satisfaction with their present job and possibility of financial loss are the two main reasons for their reluctance to accept a transfer. However, the two groups differ in that the francophone employees perceive transfer as having greater potential threat to the satisfaction of their security and affiliation needs. Transfer, to francophone employees means moving to strange environment, and consequently, it may

Figure 6:

Perceived Ability in Relation to Job Demand
(Job Enrichment Potential)

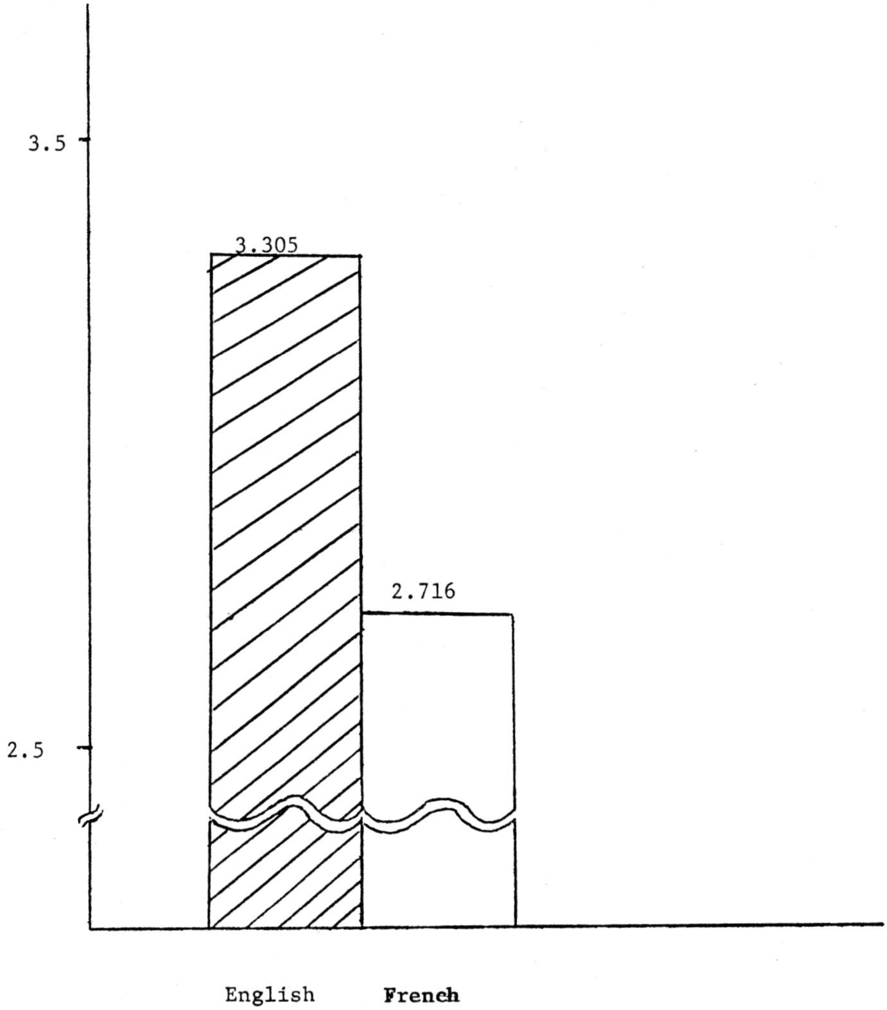

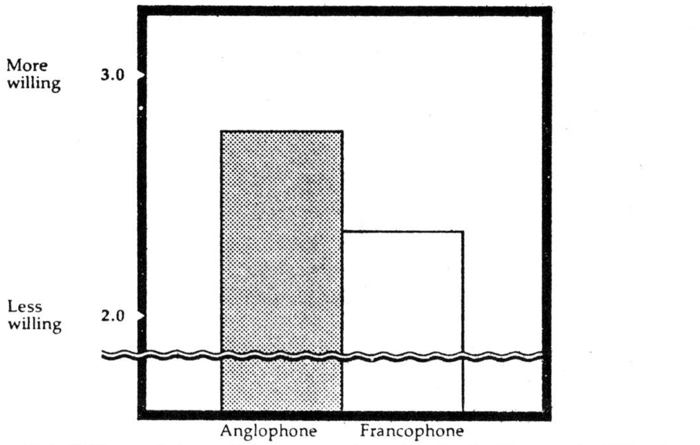

Note: Difference between the two groups is statistically significant at the .05 level.

Figure 7: *Willingness to Accept Transfer*

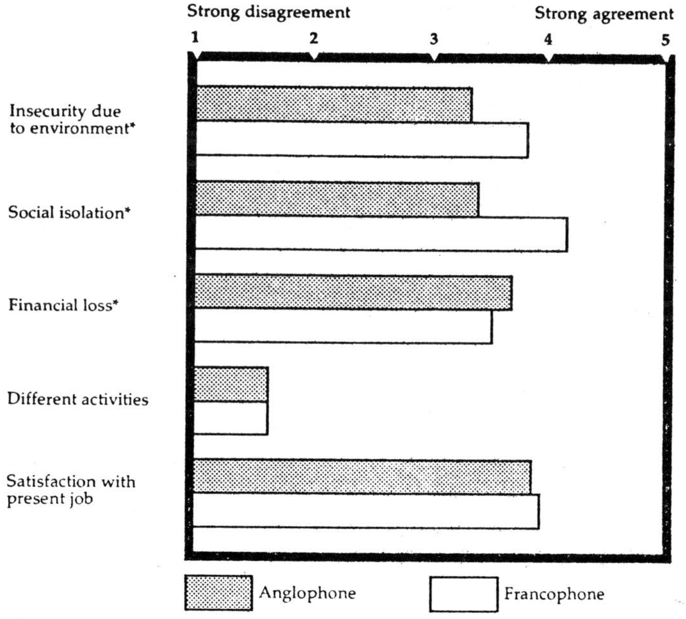

* Differences between the two groups are statistically significant at the .05 level.

Figure 8: *Reasons for Reluctance to Accept Transfer*

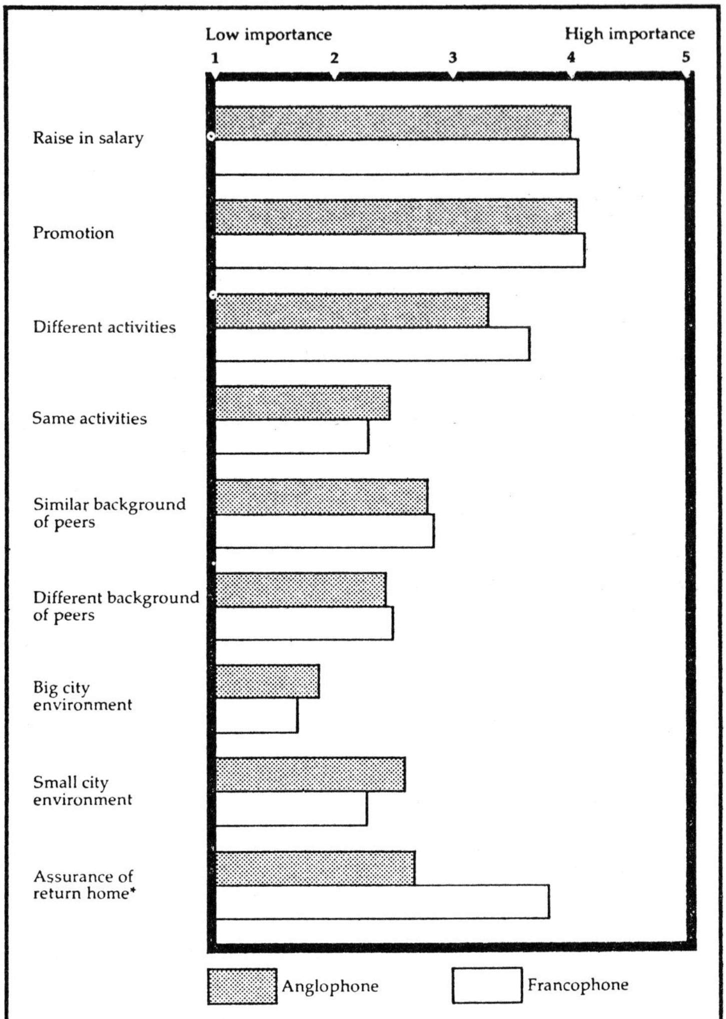

* Difference between the two groups is statistically significant at the .05 level.

Figure 9 : *Importance of Organizational Inducements to Increase Acceptance of Transfers*

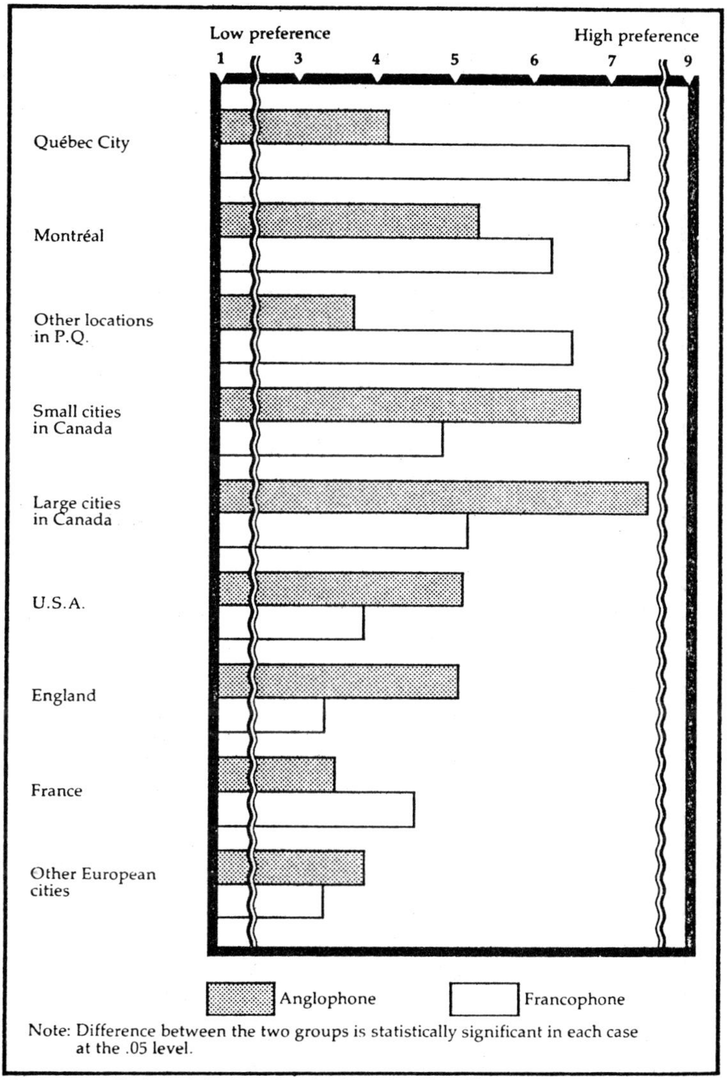

Note: Difference between the two groups is statistically significant in each case at the .05 level.

Figure 10 : *Preference for Locations in Accepting Transfers*

result in greater feeling of insecurity for them, and social isolation for their families.

With regard to the reasons for acceptance, both the groups consider a raise in salary, promotion, and different job activities as good forms of inducement to accept a transfer. However, here again the francophone employees consider another factor to be an equally important inducement. They want their organization to assure them that they can return home after a fixed period of service elsewhere. The results suggest that security and family oriented needs of the francophone employees are salient in determining their acceptance or rejection of a transfer.

The location preferences of the two groups as shown in figure 10, follow very much the linguistic line. When employees are asked to indicate their preferences for nine different locations to which they might be transfered for their own career progress, the following pattern emerges. The most preferred locations for the francophone employees are Quebec City, other areas in the province of Quebec, and Montreal in that order. The least preferred locations for them are the U.S.A., England, and European cities (even France is not preferred that highly by the francophones). For the anglophone employees on the other hand, the most preferred locations are large cities in Canada, small cities in Canada but outside Quebec, the U.S.A., and England. Their least preferred locations are the province of Quebec outside Montreal, and Europe outside England. Overall, the francophone employees seem to be reluctant to move out of the province of Quebec, and the anglophone employees seem to be reluctant to move into Quebec with the possible exception of Montreal.

Training programs

Employee attitude toward various aspects of orientation and training programs was assessed. The organization had training programs at six different levels. At each level, different materials and instructors were used. All materials and instructions were in English.

The questionnaire used to assess employee attitude toward the programs included two sets of items. The first set was designed to indicate whether the employees faced any difficulty at each of the six levels. Specifically, the employees were asked whether they faced difficulty due to (a) use of English in training materials, (b) use of Anglophone trainer, and (c) the presence of Anglophone co-trainees. The second set was designed to determine employee preference for (a) use of French in training materials, (b) use of unilingual or bilingual trainers, (c) use of culturally homogeneous co-trainee groups, and (d) suitable location for training.

The responses of the employees to each item in the questionnaire were recorded on five-point scales.

Training difficulty due to English materials

Employees were asked to indicate whether they had difficulty in comprehending and assimilitating information presented to them in English in each of the six training situations. The mean scores of anglophone and francophone employeed calculated separately are presented in Figure 11.

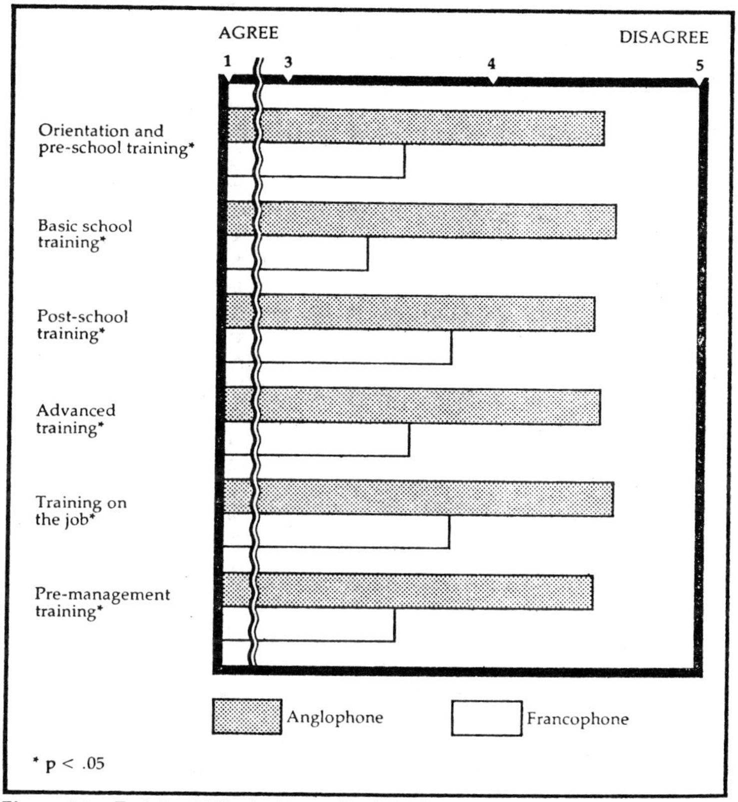

Figure 11 : *Training Difficulty Due to English Materials*

Comparison of the two groups reveals that both manage adequately with English materials. Their mean scores fall on the "disagreement" side of the scale. However, the mean scores also indicate that, relative to anglophone employees, francophone employees face significantly greater difficulty in comprehension and assimilation because of the use of English materials. Furthermore, for anglophone employees, different training situations made no difference with respect to the ease of handling materials. For francophone employees, however, the basic school training in the United States caused relatively greater difficulty in comprehension of materials. Difficulties in comprehension during training increase as francophones move out from their local branch office in Quebec. While they are in the branch office, the francophone employees are able to seek assistance in matters of comprehension and assimilation from their more experienced bilingual peers. Such benefits from peer consultation are substantially reduced during training in the United States.

Training difficulty due to anglophone trainer

When employees were asked to indicate whether trainers who spoke only in English caused difficulties for them, the two groups responded much as they did with respect to English training materials. The mean score comparisons are presented in Figure 12. Both groups found the anglophone trainer

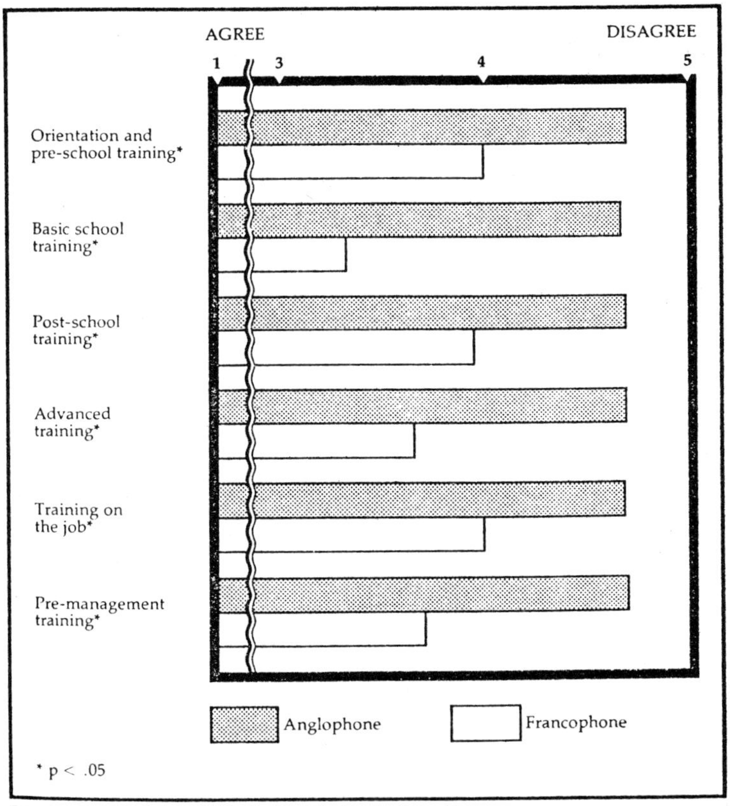

Figure 12 : *Training Difficulty Due to Anglophone Trainer*

acceptable, but the francophone trainees faced greater difficulty in understanding and communicating with the trainer than the anglophone trainees. The difficulty was greater for the francophone trainees at the basic school in the United States than it was at the local branch office.

Training difficulty due to anglophone co-trainees

Because of the international character of the company's operations, very oftne the training situations involve large numbers of anglophone co-trainees. Their presence may cause some difficulties for francophone trainees. Since English is not the first language of the francophone trainees, they may feel reluctant to express themselves freely in English, particularly when anglophone co-trainees are present. To avoid embarrassment in front of their colleagues, they may prefer to take the passive role of a listener rather than to actively participate during the sessions. In order to explore this possibility, employees were asked to indicate whether they felt uncertain and uneasy interacting with anglophone co-trainees during training sessions. Comparison of the mean scores of the two groups is presented in Figure 13. Here again, the pattern of results is similar to those described in the preceding sections. Francophone employees faced more difficulty than did anglophone employees in expressing themselves and interacting freely with others during training (classroom interaction, role-playing situations, etc). Furthermore, these difficulties were manifested to a greater extent during basic school training in the United States than in other training situations at local branch offices.

Employee preference for French training material

The employees were asked to indicate whether the company should make all the training material available in French. Results in Figure 14 clearly shows that the francophone employees considered the availability of French materials more desirable than did the anglophone employees ($p < .05$).

Employee preference for unilingual or bilingual trainer

The trainee's attitude towards the trainer or instructor will influence how well and how much he learns. If the attitude is favorable, the trainee will probably benefit more from the program than he will if the attitude is unfavorable. In a bicultural context, the attitudes of trainees may be largely determined by the perceived similarity or difference in the cultural and linguistic backgrounds of themselves and the trainers.

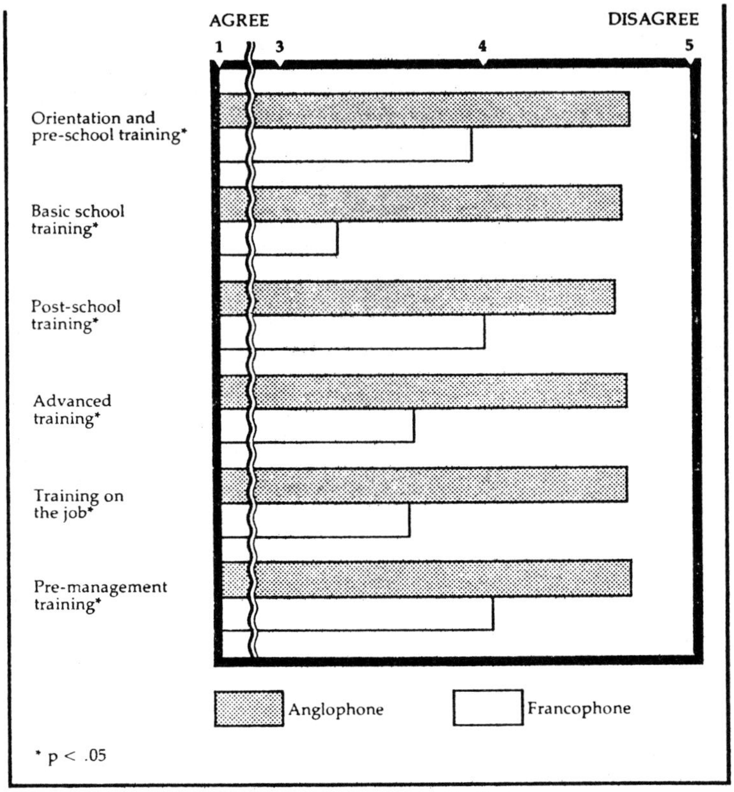

Figure 13: *Training Difficulty Due to Anglophone Co-Trainees*

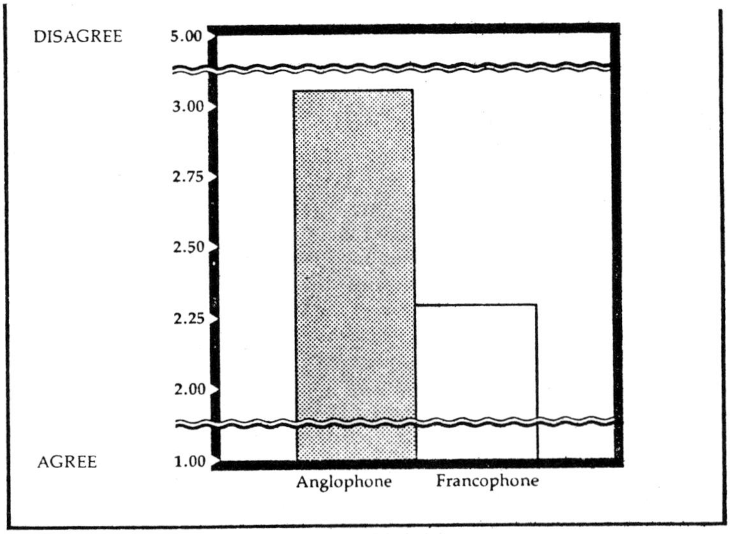

Figure 14 : *Preference for French Training Materials*

In the context of the present study it was expected that the employees would prefer trainers belonging to a cultural background similar to their own. Employees were asked to indicate the desirability of four types of trainers (unilingual anglophone, bilingual anglophone, unilingual francophone, and bilingual francophone) in two locations (basic school and branch office). The mean scores of anglophone and francophone employees are presented in Figure 15. In general,

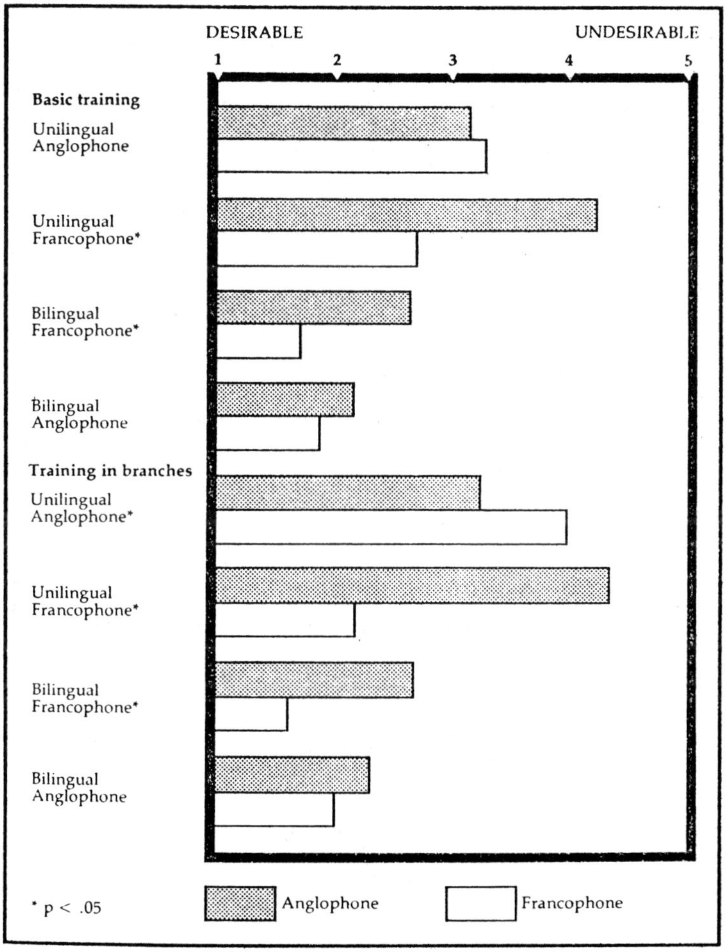

Figure 15 : *Preference for Unilingual or Bilingual Trainer*

employees did not consider it desirable to have a unilingual anglophone trainer. A unilingual francophone trainer, on the other hand, was favored by francophone employees, but was considered undesirable by anglophone trainees; bilingual trainers were favored by both groups. Within each group, however, francophone bilingual trainers were considered most desirable by francophone employees and anglophone bilingual trainers were considered most desirable by anglophone employees.

Employee preference for homogeneous francophone co-trainee at basic school

The composition of the trainee groups may affect the degree to which a trainee can benefit from the training program. Very often trainees learn a great deal from other trainees through mutual interaction, disucssion and clarification sessions both inside and outside the classroom. In organizations with both anglophone and francophone employees, training programs can be offered either to mixed or homogeneous groups of francophones and anglophones. In order to determine employee preference, employees were asked to indicate on a five-point scale the desirability of mixed versus homogeneous trainee groups at the basic school training in the United States. The mean scores presented in Figure 16 show that

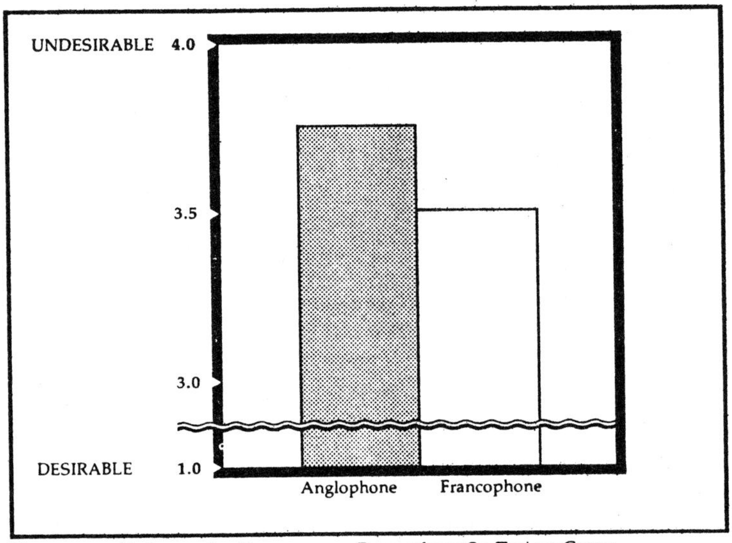

Figure 16 : *Preference for Homogeneous Francophone Co-Trainee Group*

homogeneous francophone co-trainee groups were generally considered undesirable by both groups, although francophone trainees felt such groups were less undesirable than did the anglophones. This indicates the possibility of some benefits from mixed-group training situation. Working with anglophone co-trainees during training may create some difficulties in classroom participation for francophones, but it also helps the trainees to understand each other better and to acquire ways of anticipating and adapting to difficulties arising out of similar situations in their jobs.

Employee preference for location of basic school training

Where should a large corporation with anglophone and francophone employees and branches all over the country locate its basic training school? Employees were asked to indicate their preference for having the training school in (a) the province of Quebec and (b) in Canada. The francophone employees were very much in favour of having basic school training located in Quebec. However, the anglophone employees opposed this idea. Both groups were in agreement with the idea that the basic training school should be located in Canada and not in the United States. It seems that home-based training schools are preferred to training schools abroad. In a bicultural context, perhaps two training schools catering to the cultural needs of the two groups of employees would be more appropriate.

Job involvement

What is the nature of the difference in the job involvement attitudes of the two groups of employees? The question can be addressed from two theoretical stand-points. The sociological and psychological approaches that emphasize the importance of autonomy and control for developing job involvement, will suggest that, in the Canadian bicultural context, anglophone employees, being products of a socialization process based on the Protestant ethic, will tend to value autonomy and achievement and show involvement on the job to a greater extent than do francophone employees. On the other hand, the motivation approach to work involvement (Kanungo 1979) will suggest that the two groups may or may not differ in their job involvement. Francophone employees would be expected to show greater job involvement when they perceive that the job leads to greater satisfaction of their salient needs for security and affiliation. Anglophone employees, on the other hand, would be expected to show greater job involvement when they find that the job meets their saient needs for autonomy and control. In order to verify such expectations, job involvement of employees was measured in this study by a questionnaire developed by Lodahl and Kejner (1965).

The mean involvement scores of the two groups are presented in Figure 17. In the case of fifteen out of twenty items, the mean scores of francophone employees are higher than those of anglophone employees. Statistically significant differences between the two groups are revealed in the case of fourteen items. In ten of these, francophone employees showed greater job involvement than did anglophone employees. More francophone employees say that their major satisfaction in life comes from work. Furthermore, the francophone

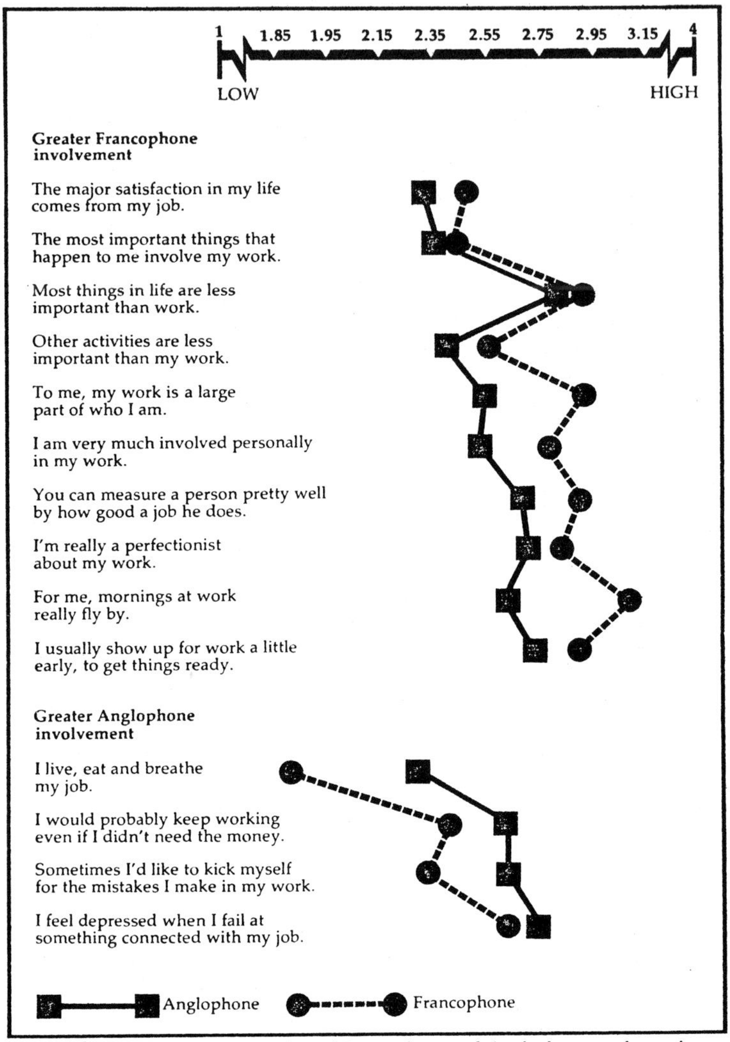

Figure 17: *Job Involvement Profiles of Francophone and Anglophone employees in an Industrial Setting*

employees consider work more important and more central to their life. They are personally more involved in their work and consider themselves as perfectionists at work. They also show stronger agreement with items such as "For me, mornings at work really fly by" and "I usually show up for work a little early to get things ready".

The anglophone employees, on the other hand, show significantly stronger agreement on four of the items. They live, eat and breathe their jobs and are prepared to work even if they do not need more money. They seem to feel more responsible for their own mistakes and more depressed about their own failures.

Overall, it would appear that francophone employees show a greater degree of job involvement than anglophone employees. The reason for this may stem from the fact that they perceive their jobs to have greater potential for satisfying their salient social and security needs. Anglophone employees, on the other hand, may find that their jobs have less potential to satisfy their salient autonomy and achievement needs.

Thus, the motivational basis of job involvement for the anglophones lies in their emphasis on personal autonomy and achievement at work. For francophones, the basis for job involvement lies in their emphasis on social and security needs, which are easily met on the job; it is easier to provide security and comfortable social surroundings at work than it is to provide a job that has autonomy and achievement opportunities. This may explain why francophones identify more with their jobs and derive greater satisfaction from them than do anglophones. Because of their achievement orientation, anglophones may find their jobs relatively less satisfying and consequently may regard other activities as more important and central to their lives than work.

Recruitment programs

To assess the effectiveness of recruitment efforts of the organization the employees were asked to indicate the frequency of noticing publicity of job openings in newspapers and college campuses. Besides, the employees were also asked to indicate the source of information of job opening for which they got selected by the organization.

Job opening were seen less frequently in French newspapers by most employees (both francophone and anglophone), where as, they were noticed with greater frequency in English newspapers. Both low frequency of inserts in French as opposed to English newspapers, and greater exposure of employees to English newspapers than to French newspapers accounts for this trend.

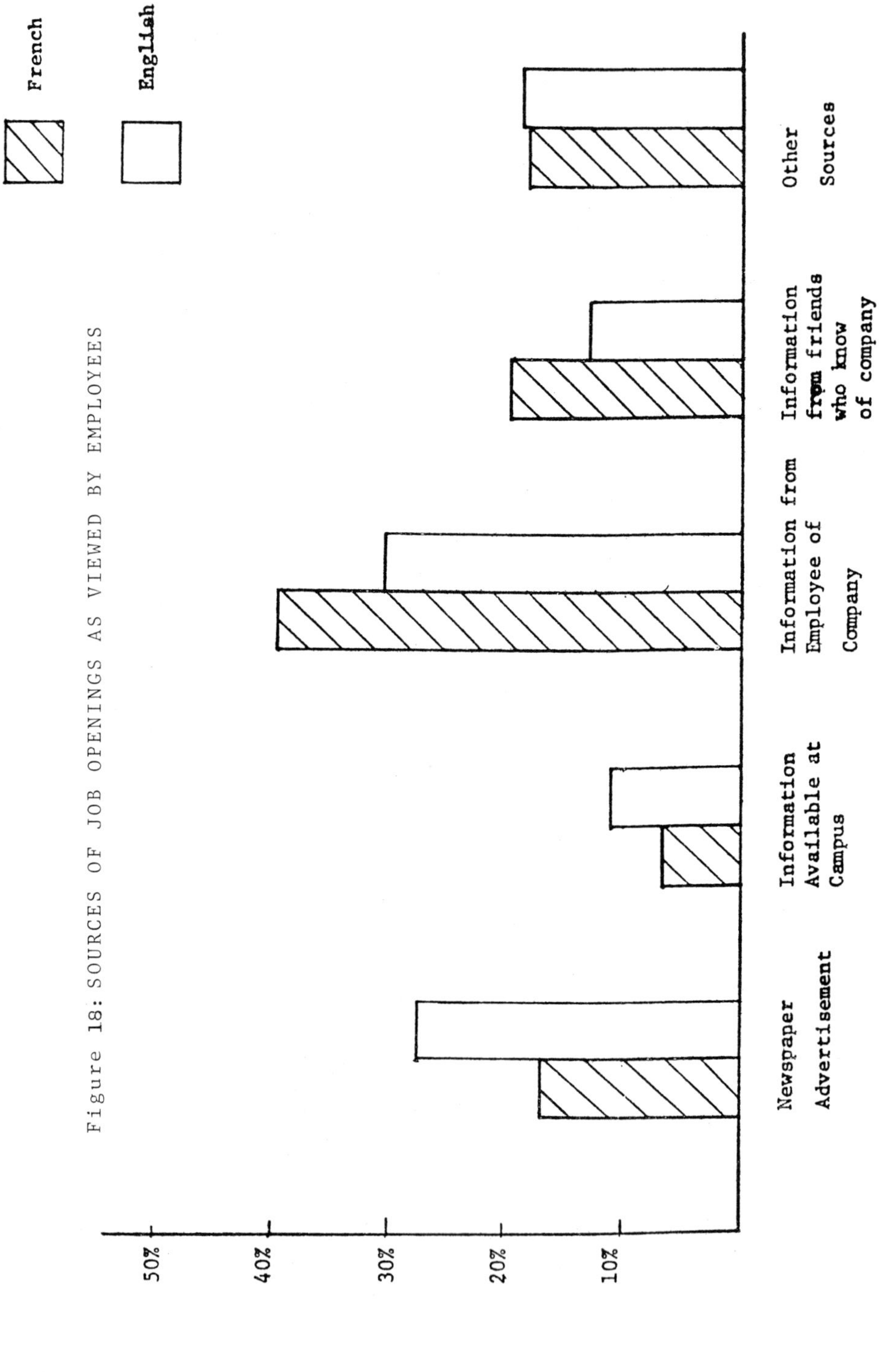

Figure 18: SOURCES OF JOB OPENINGS AS VIEWED BY EMPLOYEES

Publicity in college campuses however were less frequently noticed by anglophone employees than francophones. This indicated that for francophones, recruitment efforts were seen in college campuses more than in newspapers. The reverse is the case for anglophone employees.

Information source of own job

Employees were asked to indicate how they got information regarding the job for which they applied and got selected. Such information indicated the nature of the organizational practice. There are five sources of such information for the employees and percentages of employees using each of these sources are presented in Figure 18. For both anglophone and francophone employees, very small percentages know of their jobs through information available at college campuses. The francophone employees knew about their jobs primarily through personal information provided by other employees in the company and friends who knew of the company. The anglophones on the other hand knew of their jobs through newspaper advertisements and information from employees of the organization. It seems that anglophone employees used more impersonal sources (newspaper and campus information) relative to francophones who tend to use more personal sources. It may be pointed out that while the francophone employees noticed college campus publicity more often than the anglophone employees, the former group used such publicity less for their own entry into the organization than the latter group.

CONCLUSION

The study provides interesting profiles of anglophone and francophone employees working in the same organization. From the point of view of work motivation, the two groups differ with respect to their intrinsic as well as extrinsic sources of motivation and involvement at work. With respect to intrinsic motivation, both the groups consider interesting nature of work to be the most important job factor. However, what makes work more interesting for one group may not be the same for the other group. This is a question that needs further exploration in the future. The results of the study strongly suggest that the nature of the intrinsic motivation in the two groups are different. The anglophones seem to have a relatively stronger need for autonomy, personal responsibility, and feedback (all signs of personal achievement orientation at work as McClelland defines it) than the francophones. On the other hand, the francophones seem to possess a relatively stronger need for improving their abilities through training (signs of a need for professional growth and competence). With regard to extrinsic motivation, the anglophones seem to have a relatively stronger need for higher earnings and recognition for their work (which presumably meet their need for feedback on how well they are progressing at work), while the francophones seem to reflect a relatively stronger need for security and affiliation. Such differences in motivational orientation between the two groups explain other differences in their job behaviors and attitudes. The reasons for the differences in the motivational profiles of the two groups have been elaborated elsewhere (Kanungo 1980). At this point it may suffice to mention that both the socio-cultural (influences of family, religion, education, etc.) institutions and historical events (past industrial practice, political forces etc.) have shaped the nature of work motivation of the two culturally distinct groups of employees in Canada. Management may be well advised to take note of such differences in work motivation of the two groups and develop appropriate organizational policies that are compatible with the culture-based characteristics of the two groups.

REFERENCES

Kanungo, R.N. (1980), Biculturalism and Management, Toronto: Butterworth & Company

Kanungo, R.N. (1979), The Concepts of Alienation and Involvement Revisited. In: Psychological Bulletin 86: 119-137

Kanungo, R.N., Gorn, G.J., and Dauderis, H.J. (1976), Motivational Orientation of Canadian Anglophone and Francophone Managers. In: Canadian Journal of Behavioral Science 8: 107-121

Khandwalla, P.N. (1977), The Deisgn of Organizations, New York: Harcourt Brace Jovanovich

Likert, R. (1961), New Patterns of Management, New York: McGraw-Hill

Likert, R. (1967), The Human Organization, New York: McGraw-Hill

Lodahl, T.N., & Kejner, N. (1965), The Definition and Measurement of Job Involvement. In: Journal of Applied Psychology 54: 305-312

Thompson, J.D. (1967), Organizations in Action, New York: McGraw-Hill

Woodward, Joan (1965), Industrial Organization: Theory and Practice, London: Oxford University Press

Social Values and Management Innovation: The Case of Japan

Charles J. McMillan

ABSTRACT

"In hierarchical Japan there is greater Eqalitarianism in the workplace than in the eqalitarian United States."

- U.S. Comptroller General

INTRODUCTION

Japan's phenomenal growth and development as an economic superpower have now reached the point where even Americans and Europeans - whom Ballon (1978) singles out as having an attitude and anxiety to teach the rest of the world - are having to accept the role of student in the face of Japanese managerial efficiency. This startling change in position seems to pose a paradox, in that many Japanese view their own society as culturally unique, owing, for example, to its feudal history, geographical isolation, and religious traditions. Perhaps the best known position of this kind is Nakane's (1973) concept of the vertical principle and its corresponding "frame" and "vertical links". This cultural uniqueness, manifested in a variety of behavioural and organizational phenomena, allegedly persists as an enduring characteristic of Japanese society despite economic growth, post-industrialism, and advanced technology.

At another extreme, a number of writers argue for a form of social and economic convergence, which Kerr et. al. (1973) see in the logic of industrialism: "Industrial systems, regardless of the cultural background out of which they emerge and the path they originally follow, tend to become more alike over an extended period of time...move towards 'pluralistic industrialism.'" A notion in the convergence thesis is the direction of change towards uniformity, but this therefore gives rise to categories of such change such as Harbinson and Meyers (1959) distinction between "transitional" and "pluralistic" industrialization or, more recently, Marsh and Mannari's (1976) "traditional" and "modern" management practices.

Invariably, there is an implicit, if not explicit, assumption in the Japanese case that the directional path is towards a uniformity with the West and, most explicitly, the United States. To cite one example, the so-called individualism of the United States, contrasted to the groupism of Japan, is much more favourable to social and economic development, according to Talcott Parsons:

> It is indispensable that conditions should favour the continual extension of "individualism" in the fundamental sense - a situation where the individual can become emancipated from the pressure of the particularistic group solidarities which have been so prominent in traditional Japanese society. By far the most favourable conditions are those of the westernized type of urban society with occupational roles of the type best exemplied in urban industry (Parsons, 1954).

The sizeable debate on convergence/divergence involves arguments about similarities and differences at one or more levels of analysis, such as societal, organizational, and the individual (McMillan et. al., 1980). Two variations on this theme have been provided by Cole (1973) and by Dore (1973). Cole (1973), for example, argues for the notion of functional alternatives to indicate the potential for varying responses to common industrial problems. Dore (1973) turns the convergence thesis on its head, and argues that rather than the West being the model of direction for Japan, Japan, in fact, is the model for such Western societies as Britain, especially in industrial relations policies.

From the perspective of management and organization, the debate over values and industrialization has two serious defects, particularly when making policy judgements on cross-cultural comparisons. In the first place, there is simply no way in any of the social sciences to disentangle the vast web of interrelationships and interdependencies linking societal characteristics, industrial structures, and organizational features in any clear causal model, let alone in any credible time perspective. For example, while Dore (1973) argues that Japan, like Germany, is a late developing country, compared to Britain, Japan's industrialization now spans over 100 years. Or put differently, Japan's past generation of economic growth, say from 1950-1980, covers an era when her per capita income was less than one-fourth of Britain's to a state where it is now more than double (JERC, 1977). Even if one were to accept the proposition that industrialism and its inexorable logic produce a convergence in industrial and organizational structures and practices, there seems simply too much unexplained variance in the resulting managerial and economic performance.

The second consideration, and the one to be amplified in this paper, is this: many of the parameter variables underlying the logic of industrialization, for example, machine technology, economies of scale, and information are themselves policy choices which offer a greater range of possibilities than any converging determinism would allow. Indeed, in the case of Japan, not only have the forces of resource scarcity (food, energy, and raw materials) coincided with extreme land density to accompany very rapid growth, but so have the persistence of basic social values and leadership norms which appear on the surface to be antithetical to Western logic. This linkage has rarely been studied.

Consider the case of resource scarcity and physical density. Japan's extreme dependence on virtually all major types of raw materials, energy and food stuffs have been extensively documented. Not only does Japan differ from virtually all major industrial countries in this respect, but also the physical environment of scarcity raises a social awareness of the fact which is truly surprising to a visitor from, for example, resource abundant Canada or the United States. Given the geography of Japan during the last century of industrialization, it is not surprising that various institutions and social behaviours have sprung up to counterbalance the extreme costs of this economic weakness. Externally, Japan's outward investment policies, government foreign policy, and scientific thrust have all been aimed at the goal of reducing external dependence on any one source country (including the United States), and of maximizing flexibility on payment terms and securing long term contracts (e.g. the ABC policy - Australia, Brazil, Canada). Internally, the Japanese government and political leaders have been particularly adept at using this notion of dependency and scarcity for maximum effect for social ideology. The average high school graduate is probably more aware of Japan's relative standing in the international pecking order than any other country. The two most important economic events of the past decade - Nixon shock and oil shock - have reinforced the well inculcated values of living with scarcity and the need for constant social innovation in their aim of catching up with the West.[1]

From a purely managerial perspective, such values have enormous significance. Japanese managers have developed policies on such issues as material handling, transportation, quality control, cutting out waste, energy conservation, and energy convertibility which go far beyond programs elsewhere, even in the United States. In part, of course, luck has been on the side of the Japanese. Faced with geographical isolation from major Western markets just at a time when the energy balance between oil and coal were changing and when major new technologies were being introduced (oxygen blast furnaces in steel, micro circuitry in electronics and telecommunications, and machinery in agriculture), Japan could make startling social innovations in several industries which improved her competitive position. For example, not only did the steel plants built in the fifties have more than double the economies of scale which American engineers thought feasible, they were located on deep water seaports adjacent to steel customers, just when Britain and the United States found themselves with land-locked steel facilities of smaller scale located near low grade raw materials rather than near customers. To add further insult, Japan then turned its military technology in shipbuilding, mostly acquired from Britain (which had fifty percent of the world market in 1950 and most of the best welding technology) to revolutionize global transport systems and long-range bulk carriers. In other words, a physically-imposed problem of scarcity has been seen as a major policy threat and a whole series of managerial actions have been a direct consequence - ranging from Japan's record as the most energy efficient industrial structure and highest expenditure on energy R & D to its energy efficient products in radial tires, small cars, and commercial motors.

Consider briefly, the second issue, physical density. Historians of ideas will know that Frederick Jackson Turner established his themes of American history around the notion of conquering geography and expanding frontiers. It is no accident that one of the few recent American presidents with any sense of history, John F. Kennedy, used the New Frontier as his slogan and conquering space as his legacy. The geographical theme of Japan's physical structure has received much less attention among writers who dwell on its managerial practices. Yet Japan is one of the most densely populated countries of the industrialized world and certain areas, the Tokyo-Osaka conurbation, for example, puts it in a league with New York City. Japan's density is not only the pressure of so many people among its four main islands, but the problem that so much of its land area is mountainous, volcanic, or otherwise unusable.[2]

The impact of Japan's population density shows in several ways, many of which have enormous managerial implications. Severe land density makes housing enormously expensive and, aside from any tax law absurdities, communter time for workers is considerable (often up to two hours). Expensive housing reduces the per capita/square meter housing ratio and encourages multiple use of rooms and combined inter-generational families. The high cost of housing - opinion polls consistently show that owning a house is the main goal of young people - affects the pattern of savings, the percentage of income spent on housing (Japan is twice, for example, that of Britain) with a consequent loss of income for other products. It is little wonder that the average Japanese consumer is in no mood to buy a car which has too many defects, a consumer product which doesn't last, or a personal toy which isn't price competitive.[3]

In this respect, Japan's physical and geographical characteristics give enormous reinforcement to its social history of groupism, interdependence, and sense of on and giri - debt and obligation. The fact is, Japanese citizens have been forced to cope with social interdependence and close living for centuries. In Japan, there has been great capacity to transfer rural values to urban living. By contrast, what has existed in some societies as agrarian or rural interdependence gets lost in urban industrialization - the sense of belonging, social togetherness, and mutual interdependence. According to Phillip Hauser (1969), and more recently Ezra Vogel (1979), this is precisely the problem of American forms of industrialization and transformation to urban values in a post-industrial age.

Again, however, Japan has turned a necessity into a virtue. Since Meiji (1868), the notion of ie (household) has been the predominant form of small firm and farm, and this is extended to the dozoku (confederation of households by kin, or "tribe") with consequent notion of exclusion/inclusion, and consequent loyalties and supportive belief systems. Today this basic system remains intact, with Japanese management placing far greater emphasis on human resource management and the ideological belief so common in North American public relations that "our workers are our most important asset." It is somewhat ironic that the humanistic models of work developed in the behavioural sciences in the West find so little practice of text book theory. According to Takezawa (1976:31),

> The behavioural science model of management however, is not perceived as an antithesis of the organizational reality, as it might be in the United States. Instead, Japanese managers tend to accept the model as an idealized goal which essentially lies in the same direction as their own behavioural orientation. Often they are puzzled to find out that American management in practice fits the scientific management model far better than that of the behavioural sciences.

In this respect, there can be some appreciation for Dore's (1973) view that Japan may indeed be a model for Western countries. Not only has there been a clear attempt, at least in big firms, to reconcile the economic advantages of scientific management with the human conditions requisite in the social side of work behaviour, the movement for such conditions has been led by prominent Japanese industrial leaders and business groups. True there is a clear element of self-interest in the approach, but the prominently displayed slogans in such factories as Matsushita, Sony, Toyota, and Hitachi as "Make Every Man a Manager" (Cole, 1979) or "Make Every Worker a Quality Control Inspector" have succeeded in making some dent in the general armoury of theory-oriented engineering systems and managerial decision-making.

In point of fact, Japanese industrial relations and managerial personnel policies have recently been examined not so much in terms of the traditional cultural arguments, resting as they must on a complex interplay of anthropological, sociological, and historical arguments, but rather on a newer tradition of human capital theory in economies (Becker, 1962); clan, team or family behaviour in organizations (Ouchi, 1980); or human relations and internal labour markets in industrial relations (McMillan, 1980a, Jacoby, 1979).

Such themes leave little doubt that in many areas, Japanese management's appreciation and understanding of humanistic principles have led to interesting social and organizational innovations, which, while generally widespread in Japan, are relatively or virtually unknown in Europe or North America. (Parenthetically, Japan's media-press, radio, T.V. and journals have no parallel at describing and explaining managerial and economic facts to the average Japanese citizen, such that James Abegglen of the Boston Consulting Group describes Japanese citizens as the most economically literate people in the world.)

JAPANESE WORK INNOVATIONS

The aggregate outcome of Japan's managerial success can be shown by such indicators as total GNP, trade surpluses, and currency reserves; by output of specific industries competing against once healthy foreign sectors - German cameras, Scotch whiskey, American cars, steel, and televisions, and British almost everything. Relatively less attention has been given to the micro aspects of managerial behaviour as a contribution to Japan's productivity success. Yet much of Japanese management practice in the past twenty-five years has owed far more to American text books than any esoteric thesis on cultural values (McMillan, 1980b). On such factors as balancing short run profitability with long run investment and market share decisions, on replacing and upgrading technological hardware, or keeping abreast (and building on) technological trends in basic industries and exploiting commercial applications, the Japanese have learned their lessons from the Americans in general, from other countries where appropriate in certain sectors.

The theme of Japan as learner in management should not lead to the conclusion that Japanese management hasn't pioneered technologies in the areas of organization and job design. Indeed, the opposite is the case. As will be shown in this section, two examples will illustrate them from the Japanese automobile industry, now the world's largest. The first innovation is Toyota's policies in product planning and control - Kanban. The second is the confederate structure of assembly and suppliers.

THE KANBAN SYSTEM

What does a modern supermarket and an auto assemblyline have in common? In many factories the probable answer is lemons! At Toyota, the Kanban system is a novel approach to reduce inventory costs, reduce waste, and use blue collar ingenuity for quality control. Like the supermarket, Toyota's assembly line is a system of flows centered around particular functions or services. In the same way that shelves are quickly restocked when supply run low, Kanban is a system of supplying a particular assembly stage just as the products are needed, i.e. 'just in time'. When gear boxes are needed for motor assembly, the parts arrives just in time for the motor assembly crew. If more than enough gear boxes arrive, there is excess inventory (i.e. waste). If fewer arrive, there is a break in the flow (i.e. down time) and the line stops.

Traditional assembly line production is a classic example of what Thompson (1967) classifies as long linked technology with sequential dependence, that is, where work completed at one phase moves in planned sequence to the next and subsequent phases. Sequential dependence is more complex than pooled dependence (i.e. sharing of some common resources) and includes some measure of it. By contrast, sequential dependence is less complex than reciprocal dependence, which includes pooled and sequential linkages. Reciprocal dependence is the most costly to manage, because of its high information and coordination costs. From the perspective of decision engineering, it generally pays managers to use various techniques to reduce such transaction costs and shift reciprocal dependencies to sequential or pooled dependence by gaining control over variations in quality, volumes, or output rates. Such techniques as duplicate equipment, buffer stocks between sequential phases, and added supervision are examples in point. But bear in mind that the main idea in such design approaches is to shift the direct control of costs to where management has increased discretion or flexibility, not necessarily to a reduction in costs per se (Galbraith, 1977; Miller, 1981).

Kanban is a technique which in fact increases the rigidity of the assembly line. Rather than increasing the lead time available between entry of materials to their use (by building inventories), the Toyota system attempts to eliminate them altogether. Instead of developing production schedules from Phase 1 to Phase N, Kanban works from the quantity and timing of parts needed at Phase N and works backward, to Phase N-1,

N-2, etc.. When coupled from finish to start, the process produces a chain where the entire line is locked into a flow where each phase must deliver to the next "just in time." In this way, the traditional long linked assembly line is converted into a continuous process system requiring great stability in input supplies, much like a chemical plant (Woodward, 1965).

The system is inflexible for management in several ways. In its ideal format, each phase will produce only one unit, convey one at a time to the next phase, and keep no surplus stock in inventory. Second, quality control must be of a sufficient level either to assure problem detection and correction at a very fast rate or have the whole production line stop even for a small error. Third, the capacity to plan ahead for a required volume of output of a product involving so many parts and phases as automobiles requires a style of management willing to assume the risk of failure and uncertainty. The sheer number of separate parts greatly increases that something will go wrong even under ideal conditions. Fourth, in its extended form, Kanban involves not only the delivery of parts and sub-assemblies between and among phases, but also between external suppliers and Toyota plants. Kanban, in short, is a system of placing extraordinary faith in the capacity of blue collar workers to cope with speed, feedback, autonomy, and multiple jobs. At Toyota, any blue collar worker can stop the entire line in the plant a) when he finds a defect; b) when he runs out of parts; c) when he is over-burdened.

In the conventional assembly line, only an extreme cause would merit stopping the entire line, and indeed, any unwarrented stoppage would potentially lead to worker dismissal. At Toyota, a red cord runs the length of the assembly line and any worker can stop the entire line. The usual causes for stoppage are equipment problems, shortage of parts, or discovery of defects. In the center of the line in a Toyota factory is an enormous number board, something like a stadium score board. This board indicates the specific spot where the line has been stopped, the area of the problem, and the time involved. In this way the system reinforces the basic aims of eliminating waste and reducing inventory.

The Jidoka system of allowing workers to stop the line serve as a method of pinpointing the source of errors and directing resources to the exact trouble spot. All workers and foremen are fully aware of the impact of a line stoppage, hence the possibility of such a clear detection system acts as a deterrence to slipshod work or careless behaviour. The origins of the idea are clearly traceable to the textile weaving equipment at Toyota Automatic Loom Works. In the same way that the loom stops when wool runs out from a spindle, the line stops when a defect is discovered or an excess or shortage of parts occurs.

The managerial consequences of this system should not be misunderstood. Where the conventional production system with its buffer stocks and decoupled production stages gives a premium to managerial flexibility and control, the Japanese system makes different tradeoffs. The line is almost totally inflexible, with minimal buffer stocks and greater reliance on workers for inspection and quality control. Yet the high risk which at first glance appears to be a feature of the Toyota system also raises the awareness level of individual workers and the need to perform to standards. Even though one line at Toyota moves more slowly than some US plants (60 cars per hour, compared to 100 at GM's Lordstown plant,) there are also lower defects and lower injury rates.

The extent of Toyota's capacity to develop its Kanban system for its internal operations is greatly fostered by its open consultation across functions, its decentralized planning among work groups, and top management's willingness to challenge conventional assumptions of hierarchical control. In this respect, the Kanban system's general application is limited only to management's willingness to make it work. For example, one Japanese company with no experience in the Kanban system, had stocks for work in process and finished products equipment to 36 days. Within four years the company introduced the Toyota Kanban system and lowered its recorded stocks to a 5.8 yield (McMillan, 1981).

CONFEDERATE ORGANIZATIONS

The more extensive form of Kanban, however, involves the application of inventory control and delivery to the parts supplier. Here the principles of Kanban are applicable to any country but, in practice, there are important obstacles. In Japan, the linkages between suppliers and the parent company goes far beyond a simple buyer - seller relationship common in North America and Europe. The popular conception of corporate competition owes much to the macro economic view of the economy comprised of atomistic firms in battle for consumers using price as the main tool. The notion of oligopolistic markets, wherein a few giants compete with differentiated products, goes a long way to correct this deficiency. Unfortunately, it still is inadequate to explain the reality of Japanese organizational structure and micro competition.

Reference was made earlier to the Japanese idea of dozoku, or confederation of households. For westerners, the image of Japanese firms connected by kinship and contacts raises the spectre of Japan Inc. and the conglomerage structure of zaibatsu (business groupings). As Drucker (1981) lucidly argues, this image is largely a Western fiction.

Figure 1 gives a view of organizational competition in the United States, as contrasted with Japan. In the former case, competition is organized around the large legal entities, say Ford and GM. In high technology products used as components, there may be common suppliers (because of patents, as in the case of Bendix), dealing at arms length. For highly standardized products, which can fit almost any model or make, there may be common suppliers where economies of scale offer price advantages. The supplier-firm relationship is purely an economic transaction, which may be substituted for vertical integration. For example, car plants in North America are vertically integrated for almost 75% of parts, where the figure in Japan is only 30 per cent.

For Westerners, the Japanese auto industry illustrates a clear misunderstanding of the underlying social reality of supplier-firm relationships and the strength of competition among the main manufacturers. It is extremely misleading to think, for example, of Toyota as Toyota alone (like GM), without taking into account its seven major subcontractors (where Toyota has some equity, ranging from eight to forty-eight percent and one of which, Daihatsu Motors, is a car manufacturer in its own right), and its minor suppliers which serve one company only. In addition, there is the bank relationship, which serves as a major lender and which, when things go badly, as with Toyo Kogo can move in and clear out all top management. Like the U.S., there may be some common major suppliers, usually Japanese firms which have licensing arrangements with U.S.A. or European companies for high technology parts. Finally, there are the trading firms of each family group which acts as the marketing arm both in Japan and abroad.

To say then that real competition in Japan is between these "household" groupings doesn't do justice to the extent of cooperative behaviour and innovation between manufacturer and supplier. There is often detailed two-way discussion on such issues as equipment design, product quality, and even packaging quite beyond the normal negotiations on price, delivery dates, volume, and the like. In the case of Kanban, for instance, Toyota held protracted discussions with its suppliers and subcontractors on the system and despite the many years to implement fully the total process, it now serves as the prototype model for Japan. Toyota's forward planning extends over a five-year horizon and Toyota management deals with its more than 200 suppliers as imputs to that decision process.

Indeed, in many industries in Japan, this confederate form of organizational design has become a prototype and it is one explanation for the persistence of the dual economic structure between large and small firms. In a less sympathetic vein, this confederate form acts as a buffer or cushion for the principal manufacturer to the vagaries of the business cycle,

Figure 1

North American Oligopoly Competition

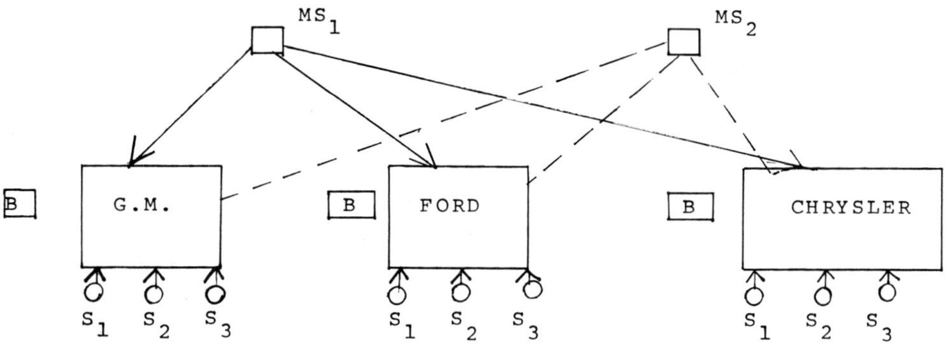

B Bank MS - Major Supplier ○ - Minor Supplier

Japanese Oligopoly Competition

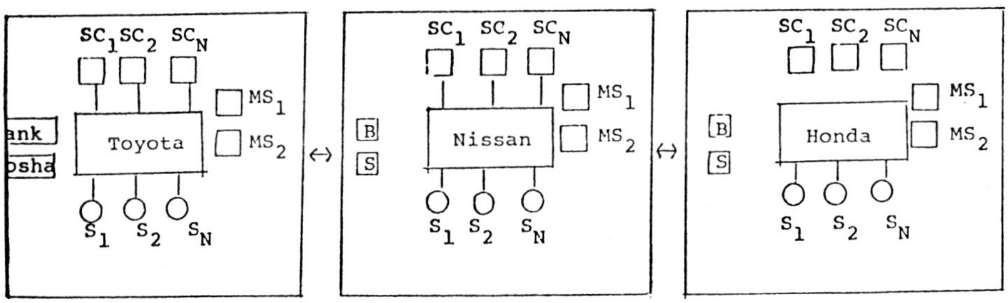

SC - Sub-contracors

$\bigcirc_S$ - Minor supplier

B - Bank

S - Trading firm

MS - Major suppliers

by allowing the principal to transfer many of its costs to the allied suppliers. For the latter, wages and profit levels are likely to be lower than the principal and the immediate and direct effects of sales decreases will be felt by them. Conversely, however, the confederate form allows a more rapid and pervasive diffusion of new organizational and knowledge technologies, a more direct stake in the advantages of rapid sales growth, and probably a larger production economic base to face interational competition. For example, Suzuki Motors, an independent manufacturer, exported in 1979, 14.2 per cent of its output of 341,000 vehicles. By contrast, Hino Motors and Daihatsu, both affiliates of Toyota's confederate structure, exported 23.7 and 21.7 per cent respectively in 1979.

The Japanese parent company is not just a buyer of parts and components: it provides credit, equipment, machinery, technological know-how and managerial experience (often by transferring "retired" senior managers as board directors of supplier forms.) More directly, parent firms also hold shares in the suppliers, even when the suppliers are also quoted separately on the stock exchange. As shown in Table 1, all of Japan's auto manufacturers have a number of such "captive" suppliers in the group, and the linkage extends to product planning and process developments in long range strategy. Not only does this system strengthen the competitive edge of Japanese manufacturers, by providing the parent firms with virtually guaranteed delivery schedules and assured product quality, it acts as a clear barrier to supplier firms, such as those from overseas, who want to break into the close family circle. It also goes a long way to explaining the almost defiant reluctance of the Japanese manufacturers to enter North American markets via direct foreign investment. The reason is simple: Their family group structure would be difficult to replicate on foreign soil.

SUMMARY AND CONCLUSIONS

This paper has focused the analysis of Japanese managerial innovations in one sector, the automobile industry. The automobile industry is the epitome of mass production assembly-line technology, or what Thompson (1967) called long linked technology. The social innovations in this industry are startling from the perspective of organizational theory and the analysis of organization design, and from the perspective of organization strategy.

From the perspective of organization design. The social innovations at Toyota confront the design theorists with a number of paradoxes. .A basic premise of traditional design theorists is to cope with environmental uncertainty by inter-

Table 1

Group Structure of Japanese Auto Manufacturers

Group	Group Affiliates	Number Listed on Stock Exchange	1979 Market Share
Toyota	32	14	30.6
Nissan	35	17	25.0
Honda	25	4	10.3
Mitsuhishi	9	0	10.0
Toyo Kogyo	10	2	8.1
Isuzu	18	8	4.2
Hino	16	2	3.5
Fuji Heavy Industries	4	1	3.7
Suzuki	10	0	3.4
Daihatsu	6	0	0.8
Nissan Diesel	6	0	0.4

TABLE 2

INTERNATIONAL COMPARISONS OF STOCKTURN

COUNTRY	ALL MFG (1969-75)	AUTOMOBILES	METAL PRODUCTS
Japan	3.1	5.6	4.3
West Germany	3.0	---	7.9
U.S.A.	2.3	4.4	3.1
U.K.	1.8	1.8	1.6

SOURCE: Adapted from Ray (1980)

nal structural configurations which buffer or shield the organization from unpredictable forces. Buffer stocks, delivery requirements, and decoupling are well known devices for coping with uncertainty. Such devices are common practice in American and European organizations (see Figure 2) and provide management with large discretionary control (Galbraith, 1977).

In the case of the Japanese firms, such devices are secondary. The Kanban system as analyzed in this paper is a design device of intentionally increasing the "inflexibility" of the assembly line by reducing decoupling and lowering buffer stocks. Where American and European firms diffuse the element of design disturbance, the Japanese firms increase it - to the point where no surplus stock is on hand or where a single worker can stop the entire line. The aim is to substitute uncertainty which is environmentally imposed to a flow where it is not substituted but internally managed.

The success of the Kanban system can be recognized not only in the spectacular growth of the Japanese sector in only a decade, or in the desire of foreign firms to emulate the Kanban system, but also in the impact it has on very specific organizational policies. Consider the case of stock control. At the company level, stock control is a function of inventory management control of raw materials, work in process and finished goods. The national indicator of inventory management in the aggregate is stockturn, an index of how frequently stocks are moved and converted into cash via sales.

As shown in Table 2, there are not only enormous differences by country but also even more startling figures by specific sectors. Stockturn for all manufacturing, calculated by dividing GDP by book values of inventory stock of the manufacturing sector for certain years (Ray, 1980), indicates that Japan leads the major industrialized countries in median stockturn performance. As argued earlier, the social values of scarcity, import dependence, and frugality are an important influence on managerial practice and behaviour. Yet for specific sectors, the Japanese performance on stockturn is even more impressive. Calculations by Ray (1980) on such sectors critical to export and employment as motor vehicles, metal products, shipbuilding and textiles, British industry trails the major industrial rivals by as much as 200 per cent. with Japan consistently near the top. Even assuming that all other factors bearing on competitive performance were equal, such as wage levels, interest rates, productivity and the like, superior inventory management techniques can give as much as ten per cent advantage on cost structures in international competition.

Figure 2

Organizational Contrasts In Auto Manufacturing

	American	Japanese
Competitive Strategy	Brood Product Range, Options	Price Strategy and Economies of Scale
Production Planning	Sequential Stages	Backwards from Final Assembly
Systems Architecture	Decoupling of Flows	Coupling of Flows
Production Continuity	Intermittent	Continuous
Uncertainty Absorption	Buffer Stocks Down time	Stable Delivery Multiple Work-shifts
Managerial Control	Centralized	Diffused

The analysis of the Japanese system of organization design and production system at Toyota points to the specific role of managerial work innovations in the explanation for Japan's recent success. Brood cultural arguments used by many authors writing on Japan fail to do justice to the success of very basic practices which are basically rationale and non-culturel in their use. Indeed Japan's management and work organizations in recent years are remarkable less for their uniquesness and particularities from a theoretical and cultural perspective. Rather the major factor seems to be the pervasive adoption of such innovations across big and small firms alike. Cultural values may help explain Japanese groupism and consensus decision-making at a very abstract level. Beyond that explanations for the success of specific organizational policies and design practices can be found in the system of management thinking and ideology. Seen in this light, Japanese management is remarkably similar to Western managers and there is a convergence of thinking around a common core of basic premises.

REFERENCES

Becker, Gary, 1962 "Investment in Human Capital: A Theoretical Analysis," Journal of Political Economy, 70: 9-44.

Cole, Robert, 1973 "Functional Alternatives and Economic Development: An Empirical Example of Permanent Employment in Japan," American Sociological Review, 38: 424-435.

____________, 1979, Work, Mobility and Participation (Berkeley: University of California Press).

Dore, Robert, 1973, British Factory - Japanese Factory, Berkeley: University of California Press.

Drucker, Peter F., 1981, "Behind Japan's Success." Harvard Business Review (January, February), 83-90.

Galbraith, Joy. 1977, Organization Design (Don Mills, Ontario: Addison Wesley).

Hallen, Lars, 1980, "Stability and Change In Supplier Relationships" in Lars Engwell and Jan Johnson (eds.). Some Aspects of Control in International Business (Uppsala: Borgstroms Tryckeri,).

Hauser, Philip, 1970, "The Chaotic Society: Product of Social Morphological Revolution." American Sociological Review: 34, 1: 1-18.

Hilton, John, 1980, "Report from the Assembly Line," Newsweek (June 30, p. 11).

Kerr, Clark, et. al. 1973, Industrialism and Industrial Man. (Hammersmith, U.K.: Penguin).

Jacoby, Sanford, 1979, "The Origins of Internal Labour Markets in Japan," Industrial Relations, Vol. 18 (Spring), 184-196.

Japanese Economic Research Center, 1976, The Japanese Economy In 1985 (Tokyo, Japan).

Kahn, Herman and Thomas Pepper, 1979, The Japanese Challenge: The Success and Failure of Economic Success (New York: Harper and Row).

Krause, Lawrence B. and Sueo Sekiguchi, 1976, "Japan and the World Economy" in High Patrick and Henry Rosovsky (1976).

Marsh, Robert and Hiroshi Mannari, 1976, Modernization and the Japanese Factory. Princeton, N.J.: Princeton University Press.

McMillan, C.J. et. al., 1980, "National Culture and the Convergence Thesis." Unpublished manuscript, York University, Faculty of Administrative Studies.

____________. 1980a, "Human Resource Policies, Labour Markets, and Unions: Canada-Japan Comparisons" in Keith Hay (ed.), Canadian Perspectives on Economic Relations with Japan (Montreal: IRPP).

____________. 1980b, "Is Japanese Management Really So Different?" The Business Quarterly (Fall).

____________. 1980c, "Kanban - Managerial Innovation in Assembly-Line Technology in Japan," unpublished manuscript, York University, Faculty of Administrative Studies.

Nakane, Chie, 1973, Japanese Society, Hammersmith, U.K.: Penguin.

Ouchi, William, 1980, "Markets, Bureaucracies, and Clans." Administrative Science Quarterly, Vol. 25 (March), 129-141.

Parsons, Tolcott, 1954, "Population and Social Structure of Japan" in Essays in Sociological Theory (New York, 1954).

Ray, D.L. 1980, "Assessing U.K. Industry's Inventory Performance," International Journal of Production and Operations Management, Vol. 1, 12-26.

Sugisawa, Hideo and Kazuo Hirose, 1977, "'Jishu Kanri' Activities in the Japanese Steel Industry," International Journal of Production Research, Vol. 15: 523-538.

Takeuchi, Hiroshi, 1978, "Keys to Corporate Resilience" Asahi Shibun Sho.

Takezawa, Shin'ichi, 1976, "The Quality of Working Life: Trends in Japan," Labour and Society, Vol. 1: 29-48.

Thompson, J.D., 1967, Organizations in Action, New York: McGraw-Hill.

Vogel, Ezra, 1979, Japan As Number One: Lessons For America (Cambridge, Mass.: Howard University Press, 1979)

NOTES

1. Consider the following comment: "Japanese consumers are choosier than their foreign counterpart. When purchasing a bucket, for instance, a Japanese will examine it from every angle, even scrutinizing the underside of the bottom plate, and will not buy it if there is the slighest dent in any part of it...

There is an experimental device that consists of a steel cylinder about 50 cm in length, inside which is a steel ball of such an exact fit that when water is poured in the top of the cylinder not a drop will leak through to the bottom. Moreover, the ball is made to move slowly downward in the cylinder at such a speed that it reaches the bottom in 24 hours. A study has shown that only Japan and West Germany have technicians capable of producing this precision cylinder and ball." (Takeuchi, 1978).

2. According to Krause and Sekiguchi (1976:450), "Part of the Japanese economic miracle, however, may be the result of an inherent weakness - the Japanese learned to make the best of adversity...The lesson the world might learn from the Japanese example is not, of course, to seek adversity, but to recognize that most difficulties can lie transformed in such a way as to advance society."

3. By way of comparison, certain density figures for selected areas are as follows (population per sq. kilometer) from Kahn and Pepper, 1980:92:

Japan	- 299	Tokyo	- 9,499
Holland	- 374	New York City	- 10,162
Taiwan	- 472	Paris	- 8,455

Since much of Japan is mountainous and forested, a more relevant measure is habitable land. The following table, adopted from the Japanese Economic Research Center data, gives Japan-Europe comparisons:

	People/Km^2	GNP/Km^2	Energy Consumption*
Japan	928	787m.	299
Britain	248	213m.	134
W. Germany	351	502m.	190
Italy	227	139m.	63
France	127	164m.	53

* tonnes of coal equivalent of energy consumed/area of habitable land.

Ambiguity of Managerial Values in Self-Management

Eugen Pusić

ABSTRACT

In Yugoslav self management the group traditionally associated with the concept of "management" still often has a dominant position due to their monopoly on the technologically required knowledge, though it is ultimately dependent in all essential decisions on the working collectivity and the organs of self management. This ambiguity is reflected in their value orientation defining progress as material improvement, equality as equality of opportunity, autonomy and participation as initiative, work as an end in itself rather than as means and stressing remuneration according to work.

SOCIAL VALUES DETERMINING THE ENTERPRISE SECTOR: YUGOSLAVIA

There are two crucial concepts in the discussion of the theme "Management under differing value systems": values and management. Both raise a number of questions. What is the value of values as predictors and regulators of behavior? and what is management in Yugoslav self management?

I

The term "values" will be used to denote those states of mind about what is desirable or what is to be desired that are linked to behavior by affective loads and that confer positive or negative affective accents upon a choice or a course of action. As such, values should be expected both to predict human behavior and to regulate it. But do they actually do that?

The slight ambiguity in the above definition between "what is desirable" and "what is to be desired" contains more then a semantic pitfall. The debate between "values as goods" and "values as criteria" is as old as the concept itself and is still going strong,[1] even if the difference is sometimes excalated, in my opinion, beyond what is reasonable.[2] Research on human reactions to disonant psychological states has demonstrated convincingly that people can show surprising ability in reconciling what they want with what someone in authority has told them they should want. The same behavior, after all, can be regarded as resistance of the free personality against stultifying and dehumanizing work pressures, and as plain laziness. Values, like goods and criteria, are linked to human behavior in at least three ways: as integrators of interests, as orientation in choice and action, past or contemplated. In the complexities of human situations, however, the values needed to achieve these various effects are not necessarilly identical or even compativle, logically or morally.

Values are a social phenomenon. They are born in human interaction, transmitted through various processes of socialization, and sanctioned by reactions of one's social environment. Society itself, however, is an abstraction. In any human population there are various social groups tending toward different values because they have different interests to integrate, different actions to justify; they are confronted with different choices. Again, these differences are not absolute. The value-universa are by no means hermetic, but values of one group are often reflected in the consciousness of another even when those values are against the "objective" interests of its members. This happens in a complex and subtle process of adjustment, of changing status and power, of ambiguity stemming from small discrepancies below the level of conscious attention to fully developed "double-thought."[3]

Values can harden and petrify into the ideational superstructure of an institution, an organization, an enterprise, a state. In this case they can lose their affective load, be emptied of their emotional content, and still be used for integration, orientation, and legitimation by various actors on the strength of institutional mechanisms of enforcement and sanction without any motivational effectiveness of their own. Again, the question remains how long a period of stability an institution needs to inculcate these quasi-values and transform them into experienced values in the minds of their members and dependents. The important point to note is that "role values" (Jacob, 1971, p. 10) will tend to influence the behavior of role-bearers in an enterprise long before they are internalized, and can be identified as values by survey techniques.

II

The self management system in Yugoslav enterprises approximates the theoretical model of a participatory economy, or rather the theoretical model follows the normative system which evolved in Yugoslavia.[4]

All people working in an enterprise elect a workers' council for a two-year term, the same members being eligible for re-election only once. The workers' council in turn appoints one or several directors for a four-year term without limit to reappointment, and elects a number of bodies with general or specialized roles in management such as a management board and personnel commission. Important decisions have to be made by all through a referendum held in the enterprise. Decisions on the "inalienable rights" of the participants, which are related to personal income and similar matters, have to be ratified by each participant individually in writing. Larger enterprises are subdivided into "basic organizations of associated labor" in order to make the situation in each of them overseeable by all their members. The system, thus, operates with concentric management circles, the widest circle being responsible for the most far-reaching decisions. As the circles get narrower -- from the workers' council, possibly a management board and other management bodies created by the workers council, technical experts, appointed administrators, and middle managers, down to the individual or collective directors -- so do the responsibilities,which move from long-range key decisions towards day-to-day management.

Effective participation in management and decision making in Yugoslav enterprises, however, falls short of this normative model. The reasons for the discrepancy could be inferred a priori from existing technological and structural determinants of the Yugoslav organizations. Predominantly, enterprises employ technologies corresponding to the stage of "large batch and mass production" (Woodward 1965, p. 69) implying concentration of necessary knowledge and information near the apex of a hierarchical pyramid and leaving information-poor routine and manual operations to the rank and file. A technology based on simplifying complex work by dividing and subdividing it into progressively narrower and simpler actions implies a hierarchical structure and makes superordinate and subordinate relationships difficult to avoid at work. People with higher education made up only 2.62 per cent of the participants in Yugoslav enterprises in 1977 (Pusić 1977, p. 39), indicating an exceptionally high degree of concentration of expertise.

Some groups in Yugoslav enterprises have effective decison-making participation disproportunate to their numerical strength in the total work force. This seems to hold for wider issues of business policy, and, to a somewhat lesser degree, for issues of personal income distribution as well. The relevant data were published by Obradović (1972, 1978, pp. 240, 255) and were collected by observers in 20 enterprises over a period of three years (see table I).

The results are somewhat different, but not too different, on issues concerning the distribution of personal income, an "inalienable right" of the workers, presumably of the highest significance to each individual (see table II).

TABLE I: Participation in Market Issues According to Professional Qualifications

(1966–1969)

Dimensions of Participation	Faculty	Polytechnical High School	Lower Technical Administrative	Highly Skilled Blue-Collar Workers	Skilled Blue-Collar Workers	Semi-skilled Blue-Collar Workers	Without Qualifications
Frequency of Discussions	50.2	33.2	1.2	9.2	5.2	1.0	0.0
Length of Discussions	73.6	17.8	0.7	3.9	3.6	0.4	0.0
Number of Presentations	68.4	20.3	7.6	1.3	2.5	0.0	0.0
Number of Proposals	49.7	41.0	4.0	1.3	2.0	2.0	0.0
Number of Proposals Accepted	50.7	36.6	4.2	4.9	2.1	1.4	0.0
Percent Employed	6.4	11.0	4.2	10.9	28.6	17.2	21.6

Source: Josip Obradovic, Participation in Enterprise Decision-Making, in: Workers' Self Management and Organizational Power in Yugoslavia, ed. Josip Obradovic and William N. Dunn, Pittsburgh: University Center for International Studies, 1978, pp. 240 and 255.

TABLE II: Participation in Personal Income Distribution Issues According to Professional Qualifications

Dimensions of Participation	Faculty	Polytechnical High School	Lower Technical Administrative	Highly Skilled Blue-Collar Workers	Skilled Blue-Collar Workers	Semi-skilled Blue-Collar Workers	Without Qualifications
Frequency of Discussions	48.0	26.2	0.5	18.9	4.3	1.5	0.5
Length of Discussions	60.1	20.9	0.3	13.7	3.4	1.0	0.7
Number of Presentations	67.7	17.4	0.0	7.2	5.8	1.2	0.7
Number of Proposals	42.8	33.9	0.0	16.6	4.4	1.8	0.4
Number of Proposals Accepted	42.0	45.0	0.0	8.0	3.1	1.9	0.0
Percent Employed	6.4	11.0	4.2	10.0	28.6	17.2	21.6

Source: Josip Obradovic, Participation in Enterprise Decision-Making, in: Workers' Self Management and Organizational Power in Yugoslavia, ed. Josip Obradovic and William N. Dunn, Pittsburgh: University Center for International Studies, 1978, pp. 240 and 255.

A similar tendency is apparant when the various groups in the enterprise are ranked according to their power in the organization. The rankorder in table III was computed by Rus (1978) on the basis of eight analyses made prior to 1971.

TABLE III: Average Power of Organizational Groups in Yugoslavian Enterprises before 1971

Organizational Group	Average Power Rank
Collegium[a]	1.0
Technical Departments	2.2
Supervisors of Economic Units[b]	3.1
Management Board and Workers' Council	3.8
Skilled Workers	4.7
Political Organizations	6.0
Highly Qualified and Qualified Workers	6.4
Semi-qualified and Non-qualified Workers	7.3

Source: Veljko Rus, Enterprise Power Structure, in: Workers' Self Management and Organizational Power in Yugoslavia, Josip Obradovic and William N. Dunn, Pittsburgh: University Center for International Studies, 1978, p. 203.

a. The collegium is "an executive group normally composed of heads of departments and presided over by the director" Veljko Rus, Enterprise Power Structure, in: Workers' Self Management and Organizational Power in Yugoslavia, Pittsburgh: University Center for International Studies, 1978, p. 199.

b. The Economic Units are an embrion form of the later Basic Organizations of Associated Labor.

How much these data reflect the situation today is an open question,[5] for major reforms, including the introduction of "basic organizations of associated labor" mandated by the Associated Labor Act of 1976, have since been undertaken in order to increase participation by the rank and file. The whole situation is fluid and quickly changing. The institutions of self management are radically new and are certainly entitled to a longer period of gestation before anything more definite can be said about them. The situation is different in organizations where the necessary knowledge and information are more evenly distributed; in non-industrial organizations, managed according to the same model of self management, an average of 16,69 per cent of the participants have a university education, and in some branches such as research and the chambers of commerce the average is around 40 per cent.

With all these reservations, however, the conclusion seems warranted that at present there exists in Yugoslav enterprises a group of managerial and technical experts whose overt contribution to managerial decisons is greater disproportionately than their numerical share in the work force would justify. The operative word in this statement is "overtly." The managerial group that initiates most of the proposals, talks longest about them, and in a significant majority of cases, has them accepted by the rank and file in their referenda and individual declarations of consent, is for that matter not free to decide as it pleases. The members of that group are severely restricted by the one-man-one-vote principle, by the knowledge that certain proposals are simply not going to be accepted by the rank and file, as well as by the further knowledge that if they try to force an issue they may jeopardize their own jobs. This ambiguity between technological dominance and ultimate dependence in matters of interest is the fundamental characteristic of the present position of that group in Yugoslav enterprises that can still be called "management."

This is also the main feature of management's position in the field of values. Managers are part of the Yugoslav society, products of her system of socialization and education, and therefore share the main convictions and ideational representations that dominate this society.[6] In subscribing to values of their time and place, however, they tend to accent the institutional values of their enterprise and the role-values of their position in it, and interpret the same values differently when encountered in other social groups.

Like value systems in other societies, the values dominating Yugoslavia today must integrate diverse interests, must reconcile widely divergent situations, and must justify incompatible actions. They must thus be, if not actually inconsistent, sufficiently general to give enough scope for interpretations that suit specific and varying situations.

There are, first, the values of progress, a better life, material improvement, and development on the one hand and the value of equality on the other.[7] It is one of the fundamental tenets of the Marxian interpretation of history that any betterment of the human condition, improvement in social relations, the general movement of the human race towards liberty, dignity, and greater humanity must be based on the growth of productive forces and an escape from want and poverty. In a country where poverty was endemic and the example effect of neighboring developed European countris was penetrating these theories acquire an immediate practical significance and urgency sufficiently potent to move considerable masses of people, to focus their aspirations, and to justify radical action.

The overiding assumption, however, was of a firm commitment to equality, containing the promise that the better life shall not be preempted by the few but shared by all under conditions of equality.

Both values offer sufficient latitude for intepretations that are divergent in more than details. One group may emphasize the means to progress: industrialization, modernization, efficiency, responsibility; on other on the results: higher living standards, material security, the acquisition of durable goods, mobility (particularly from rural to urban areas) and moderate work pressures. As a matter of fact, both interpretations could be, and were, adhered to by the same individuals and groups with the priority shifting according to situations. Furthermore equality is open to a range of meanings. It can mean primarily the reduction or abolition of class differences,[8] or an equal position for all national groups living in Yugoslavia (see footnote 9). It can be understood as actual equality of economic position, or merely as equality of opportunity to achieve this position.

Managers together with other groups in Yuguslav society tend to subscribe to these values, stressing the instrumental aspects of progress and equality of chances. In his empirical findings Zupanov (1978) illustrates these differences explicit (see table IV).

One of the major practical implications and controversial points about equality is the equalization of income. Zupanov's study reveals attitude differences on this point as well (see table V).

The second relevant pair of complementary values is the value of <u>autonomy</u> and the value of <u>participation</u>. The ultimate autonomy of the human person is the deepest aspiration of a self-management world view. It is rooted in the actual social transformations that have occured in Yugoslavia during and after the war. The basis of economic domination by the owners of the means of production has been destroyed by the nationalization of these menas. Hierarchical domination of all kinds in organizations has been essentially mitigated by the structural arrangements of self-management. Political domination has been reduced, first, by the adoption of a federation making it more difficult for any one of the Yugoslav nationalities to establish its hegemony over the others, and then by general political decentralization and liveralization from 1950 onward. The feeling of individual autonomy generated by theses developments seems to be widespread.[9]

People, however, spend most of their waking life working with others. Autonomy under these conditions cannot mean individual isolation but should mean participation in deciding the vital questions, together with other members of one's working collectivity on a footing of equality, that affect one's inter-

Table IV: Desired Direction of Development of Yugoslav Society by Qualification Level and Position (in percentages)

Direction of Development	Non-qualified and semi-qualified workers	Qualified and highly qualified workers	Clerical workers	Immediate Supervisors	Experts	Managers
Ever-increasing equality in income and standard of living	44.3	39.8	28.6	20.8	12.7	11.5
Equal chances	42.0	53.2	67.4	75.8	85.9	86.5
Ever-increasing inequality	2.8	1.6	0.9	0.7	0.1	0.3
No response	10.9	5.4	3.1	2.7	1.3	1.7
N = 2,957	(212)	(671)	(674)	(413)	(710)	(304)

Source: Josip Tupanov, Egalitarianism and Industrialism, in Workers' Self Management and Organizational Power in Yugoslavia, ed. Josip Obradovic and William N. Dunn, Pittsburgh: University Center for International Studies, 1978, p. 70.

Table V: Attitudes toward Wage Equalization as an Explicit Values by Qualification Level and Position (in percentage)

Group	Support Equalization	Oppose Equalization	Don't know	No response	N
Non-qualified and semi-qualified	54.5	36.4	8.6	0.5	(221)
Qualified and highly qualified	22.2	70.6	5.9	1.3	(222)
Administrative Employees	11.4	84.1	3.7	0.8	(246)
Immediate Supervisors	6.9	88.8	2.7	1.6	(188)
Experts	3.3	96.1	0.6	-	(154)
Managers	0.9	97.3	-	1.4	(110)

Source: Josip Zupanov, Egalitarianism and Industrialism, in Workers' Self Management and Organizational Power in Yugoslavia, ed. Josip Obradovic and William N. Dunn, Pittsburgh: University Center for International Studies, 1978, p. 73

ests in that setting. In this sense participation is indeed complementary to autonomy.[10]

Bolcić (1972) found empirical differences among workers as to their readiness to assume the wider social responsibilities of participation, versus an equally pronounced desire to participate. To the question "Do you consider it your obligation to reflect on how some problems in your environment should be solved?" the percentage of positive answers differed between manual (76.1) and non-manual workers (including the group of managers, 91.7) as well as between more educated (95.7) and less educated workers (78.3). The ratio of desired to actual influence in their organization was higher for manual (141.5) than for non-manual workers (139.4) and for less educated (145.1) than for more educated workers (137.7) because perceptions of their actual influence were smaller (241 : 251 and 2.37 : 2.72) (pp. 104-105).

Finally, there is the value of work complementary to the value of solidarity, meaning the readiness to assist one's fellows in need beyond the claims to which their work would entitle them. Work can be valued as a means of achieving desired ends or as a value in itself. Opinion surveys of youth show interesting differences in this respect (see table VI).

Among adult workers Bolcić (1972 found a crasser instrumental attitude toward work, but with differences indicating a possible nuance in the attitude of more educated and managerial groups. Among 916 respondents in 16 enterprises the response to the statement: "People do not work much on the job, for they consider that they are not sufficiently paid for the work they perform" was measured on a scale from 1 to 4. The average response for all had the value of 2.81 approaching a value corresponding to the verbal reaction "I agree." The average for manual workers, however, was 2.90 and for non-manual workers, 2.61; for less educated workers, 2.81, and for more educated workers, 2.63 (p. 107).

The most controversial aspect of work values is the tenet that everybody should be paid according to work. Generally lip-service is paid to it in principle, but the attitudes differ widely as to practical implications. As to desirable income differentials in enterprises Zupanov (1978) figures are shown in table VII.

The value of solidarity is in this context a necessary complement of the rule "to each accordint to his work".[11] It is institutionalized in a number of ways from the "Fund for Common Consumption" in each enterprise to the social security system. Actually, it is the point where work as a general criterion is transcended and the rule "to each according to his needs" begins.[12]

Table VI: Relation of Yugoslav Youths Towards Work (in Percentages)

Type of Orientation	Village youth	Laboring youth	Young White Collar Workers	Young Technical Experts	Youth in School
Work is a means	51.3	46.4	22.4	33.3	11.1
Work is a value in itself	37.0	48.2	68.9	66.7	84.2

Source: Vladimir Arzensek, Participacija zaposlenih u jugoslavenskoji industriji (Moderna organizacija br. 2, 1971), p. 195

Table VIII: Perceived and Desirable Differential Between Lowest and Highest Income by Qualification Level and Position (in Percentages)

Differentials	Non-qualified and semi-qualified		Qualified and highly qualified		Clerical		Immediate Supervisors		Experts		Managers	
	Perceived	Desirable	Perceived	Desirable	Perceived	Desirable	Perceived	Desirable	Perceived	Desirable	Perceived	Desirable
Low (1:2,1:3)	32.6	78.5	26.6	74.4	23.2	61.8	22.7	43.2	23.4	52.6	29.3	25.9
Medium (1:4)	23.4	13.5	31.5	18.2	30.5	25.5	32.2	16.7	34.3	27.8	42.0	32.5
High (1:5-1:10)	44.0	8.0	41.9	7.4	40.2	12.7	44.1	50.1	42.3	19.6	28.7	44.0
N	(212)		(671)		(647)		(710)		(413)		(304)	

Source: Josip Zupanov, Egalitarianism and Industrialism, in Workers' Self Management and Organizational Power in Yugoslavia, Pittsburgh: University Center for International Studies, 1978, p. 77

In their total value spectrum, managerial groups differ from those of workers with low levels of skill at least in emphasis and priority. Bolčić (1972) found the following ranking orders for both groups:

Table VIII: Value Systems of Unskilled and Semi-skilled Workers and Managers in Yugoslav Industry

Managers	Unskilled and semi-skilled workers
1. Personal freedom	1. Equality
2. Equity	2. Equity
3. Honesty	3. Personal freedom
4. Payment according to work	4. Security
5. Standard of living	5. Standard of living
6. Security	6. Honesty
7. Equality	7. Solidarity
8. Self management	8. Self management
9. Solidarity	9. Payment according to work

Source: Silvano Bolčić, The Value System of a Participatory Economy, in: Participation and Self Management, ed. Eugen Pusić, Vol. 1, Zagreb: Institute for Social Research, 1972, p. 111.

In case of conflict the two groups are likely to be on different sides. Investigating strikes in Yugoslav industry, Arzenšek (1978) found the following attitudes:

Table IX: Behavior of Social Groups During Strikes As perceived by striking Workers (in percentages)

Groups	Supported	Opposed	Neutral
Management	17	61	22
Blue-Collar Workers	62	13	25

Source: Vladimir Arzenšek, Managerial Legitimary and Organizational conflict, in: Workers' Self Management and Organizational Power in Yugoslavia, Pittsburgh: University Center for International Studies, 1978, p.382.

Managers in Yugoslav enterprises are, thus, in an ambiguous value position. Embracing consciously the new values of an egalitarian and participatory future, they are nevertheless tied by their positions and functions in the enterprise to the old values of leadership and authority, expressing them overtly as an accent on efficiency, stimulation to hard work, and equality of chances that have to be utilized. This should be the background for value conflicts of tragic proportions in Yugoslav managers. But there is no evidence that this is the case. It is difficult to avoid coming to the conclusion, as another contempory investigation on the values of local leaders (Jacob and Teune 1971) did, "that the dynamics of developmental change is not universally and systematically predictable from the values espoused by the leadership" (p. 315).

SELECTED BIBLIOGRAPHY

Arzenšek, Vladimir (1971), Participacija zaposlanih u jugoslovenskoji industriji. Moderna organizacija br. 2

Arzenšek, Vladimir (1978), Managerial Legitimacy and Organizational Conflict. In: Workers' Self Management and Organizational Power in Yugoslavia. Edited by Josip Obradović and William N. Dunn. Pittsburgh: University Center for International Studies, pp. 374-389

Bolčić, Silvano (1972), The Value System of a Participatory Economy. In: Participation and Self Management. Vol. 1, Zagreb: Institute for Social Research, pp. 97-112

Džinić, Firdus (1973), The Perception of Socialism and the Value Systems in Yugoslav Society. In: Participation and Self Management. Vol. 6. Zagreb: Institute for Social Research, pp. 151-158

Jacob, Philip E. (1971), Values and Public Vitality: The Political Dynamics of Community Activeness. In: Values and the Active Community, New York: The Free Press, pp. 3-9

Jacob, Philip E. and Henry Teune (1971), Values, Leadership, and Development. In: Values and the Active Community, New York: The Free Press, pp. 313-320

Jovanov, Neca (1972), Definition Théorique de la notion et de lèssence de l'autogestion en Yugoslavie. In: Participation and Self Management. Vol. 1. Zagreb: Institute for Social Research, pp. 9-17

Obradović, Josip (1978), Participation in Enterprise Decision-Making. In: Workers' Self Management and Organizational Power in Yugoslavia. Edited by Josip Obradović and William N. Dunn. Pittsburgh: University Center for International Studies, pp. 232-262

Pusić, Eugen (1977a), Vrijednosti i drustvena regulacija. In: Vrijednosti i drustveni sistem, Zagreb: Biblioteka "Covjek i sistem," sv. 4, pp. 11-34

Pusić, Eugen (1977b), Neki nacelni problemi udruzivanja rada u odnosu na tecnologiju. In: Samoupravni odnosi i udruzeni rad u teoriji praksi, Zagreb: "narodne novine," pp. 31-50

Rescher, Nicholas (1969), Introduction to Value Theory. Englewood Cliff, New Jersey: Prentice Hall, p. 2

Rus, Veljko (1978), Enterprise Power Structure. In: Workers' Self Management and Organizational Power in Yugoslavia, Pittsburgh: Institute for Social Research, pp. 199-217

Soergel, Wolfgang (1973), Die jugoslawische Arbeiterselbstverwaltung im Bewußtsein der Arbeiterschaft -- am Beispiel eines ausgewählten industriellen Großbetriebes, Berlin: Freie Universität Berlin

Vanek, Jaroslav (1971), The Participatory Economy; An Evolutionary Hypothesis and a Strategy for Development, Ithaca: Cornell University Press

Woodward, Joan (1965), Industrial Organization: Theory and Practice, London, Oxford University Press, pp. 85-86

Zupanov, Josip (1978), Egalitarianism and Andustrialism. In: Workers' Self Management and Organizational Power in Yugoslavia, Pittsburgh: University Center for International Studies, pp. 60-96

NOTES

1. See for example, Rescher (1969) quoting George Lundberg, Robert Park, E. W. Burgess, Howard Becker, and Stuart C. Dodd on the "values as goods" side, and Clyde Kluckhohn, Philip E. Jacob, and James J. Flink for the "values as criteria" party

2. "The phenomenon we identify as "value" is a standard, or principle, used by human beings in justifying or opposing a course of action .... It must be clear that what we are talking about here is something quite different from a body of desired or wanted things. People's wants, likes or preferences may be completely devoid of "value" in the sense in which we are defining it." (Jacob 1971, pp. 3-9).

3. It is, of course, very difficult to do anything with so elusive a reality. People studying it understandably resort to simplifications and aproximations of all sorts in order to gain some hold on the value situation. Dzinic (1973) thinks that value systems in Yugoslavia "can be roughly classified as follows: traditional bourgeois (which is characteristic of the older generation and smaller social groups which are remnants of the pre-revolutionary society in the economic or psychological respect); traditional socialist (with different social protagonists, egalitarianistically oriented); modern bourgeois (in which material values and spiritual values of a lower level are

dominant); and modern socialist whose basic characteristic are: instrumental relationship toward material values and a free authentic personality that makes the best of its human possibilities - as the highest value" (p. 156).
An example of a more generalized simplification is the relationship between the dominant values in a population (meaning the values of the dominant social group) and the actual interests present in the population at a given time. Four typical situations are relevant.
- The dominant values adequately express the existing interests of a stable dominant group whose position is still largely unquestioned.
- The dominant values no longer adequately express the interests of any significant social group but continue to influence people's consiousness out of a sort of social inertia. The conflicts created by this situation are resolved by reinterpreting values by means of a vague reformulation at a higher level of generality or by simple voluntary value-blindness.
- In the absence of an effective system of dominant values, say, after a radical change in the relative position of various groups in the population, the dominant group will tend to orient its choices and actions pragmatically by considering their actual interests.
- Finally, values may cease tc function through a process of erosion or because of other factors, and at the same time the interest relationships among social groups may not be sufficiently clear for any interests to serve as an orientation. This should result in an increase in anomic behavior if other orientation patterns are not available (see Pusić, 1977/I).

4. The model of Vanek (1971) is an example. In the interpretation of Bolcić (1972) it contains the following points:
"1. a 'participatory economy is one based on, or composed of, firms controlled and managed by those working in them. This participation in management is by all and on the basis of equality, that is,on the principle of one man one vote'.
"2. The second characteristic is incom sharing: 'the participants of the labor-managed firm, after they have paid for all material and other costs of operation, share in the income of the enterprise'.
"3. The working community, which has the exclusive right to control and manage the affairs of the enterprise, does not have, however, full ownership in the traditional sense of the word 'ownership' over the means of production that it uses. It has the right to enjoy the fruits of the use of these means.
"4. A participatory economy is a market economy. This implies and is the condition of it being completely decentralized.
"5. Since the 'human factor' is no longer only a 'factor of production', but above all a 'decision-making factor' carrying out the entrepreneurial function, a participatory economy implies freedom of employment, i.e. mobility of the labor force" (p. 98).

5. Wolfgang Soergel (1973) finds that in three large Yugoslavian industrial enterprises not a single unskilled worker has been elected to the workers' council, though this group was significantly represented in the work force.

6. Dzinić (1973) finds that "series of research results indicate the process of forming the self-managing character in a significant part of the population, above all, in urbanized and workers' environments .... The feeling of self-management has spread, is deeply-rooted and has become transformed into a basic stance for one's own political behaviour and evaluation of the behaviour of others" (p. 155).
One important breeding ground of the values that dominate Yugoslav society is the League of Communists. Obradović (1978), upon finding that members of the League predominate in discussions in enterprises on all issues in a proportion of two to one (or, better, they represent only 12,9 per cent of the work force), attributes this finding to the likelyhood that frequent participants are managers: "A majority of these managers are concurrently members of the League of Communists" (p. 241).

7. "Two values were present and dominant in the consciousness of all social groups: economic and cultural progress and the national liberation - or equality. The fulfillment of these two values was promised by the revolutionary movement almost from the very beginning" (Dzinić 1973, p. 153).

8. "Dans ce sens, l'autogestion est le mouvement révolutionnaire de la classe ouvrière qui élimine les fondements de toute nouvelle polarisation, de toute nouvelle division de la société en propriétaires des moyens de production et en détenteurs du pouvoir, d'une part, en salariés et en administrés d'autre part" (Jovanov 1972, p. 11).

9. "L'autogestion c'est avant tout la possibilité pour chacun de dédider lui-même, de constituer la société, d'y définir sa condition, de se déterminer souverainement dans le temps et l'espace" (Jovanov 1972, p. 17).
"Submissiveness and yielding to manipulation is constantly decreasing particularly among the generations who have experiences the process of political socialization in self-managing relations. The consciousness of one's own rights and obligations, e.g. of one's own social position is very present among them" (Dzinić 1973, p. 155).

10. "Above all, the most important place in a real value system should belong to that value which defines the basic organizational principle of the economy, and that is participation .... After all, people can experience participation as a value, for it is not a mere means for attaining self-determination but also a direct expression of self-determination" (Bolcić 1972, p. 101).

11. "Le principe" de chacun selon ses possibilités, a chacun selon son travail' dont les rśultats son verifiés sur le marché est immanent à l'autogestion. La répartition selon les besoins' attenue la rigeur de ce principe" (Jovanov 1972, p. 12).

12. "In conjunction with the whole value orientation toward collectivism, one should expect on the one hand great emphasis on equity and on the other hand on solidarity ...." (Bolcić 1972, p. 102).

Societal Values Affecting the Level of Leadership Creativity in Polish Economic Organizations

Tomasz Wielicki

ABSTRACT

This chapter aims to explain the limitations upon Polish enterprise in leadership creativity as it relates to the accepted values and management system of a national economy. Changes in the societal value system and subsequent stages of the system's development for management of the national economy in Poland are summarized. The distinction is made between two major attitudes of innovative activity, a "progressive" attitude and a "protective" one. The "protective attitude" has been emphasized as the result of an inappropriate correlation between the societal values as they are, and a highly centralized management system which has led Poland into a period of deep unrest and societal conflict.

INTRODUCTION

The Polish enterprise sector has been functioning within a socialist economy for 35 years. The socialist economic system in Poland has developed through a number of stages, dealing continuously with differing social and economic circumstances, internal as well as external. The basic principles of the socialist system, which have totally changed the mechanism of national economic performance, also had a considerable influence on various spheres of social life, especially on the accepted societal value system that shapes the motivation processes and the management system of the national economy as a whole.

The present stage of national development is referred to as "the stage of advanced socialist society". Its characteristic features are the high level of industrialization and the considerable acceleration in satisfying the people's growing social needs as well as aspirations. This stage entailed - apart from substantial improvement in the social living standard - some unexpected and disturbing phenomena linked mainly with management processes of economic organizations under the differing value system within socialist society.

DIFFERING SOCIETAL VALUE SYSTEM IN SOCIALIST POLAND

Though its intuitive meaning is obvious, the notion of "value" can be interpreted in a variety of ways. "The value can be considered as a psychical representation of the whole of needs categories, primary goals or systems of occasions."[1] One can also understand "social values" as health, sense of safety, social position, children's good, family, work, homeland, acceptance by one's associates, art, leisure, and erotics. We should remember, however, that value as an attribute of human personality is subjective. In discussing the problem of a societal value system we are taking under consideration the reasonable generalization based on the investigation of values commonly accepted by society.

The succeeding stages in the development of the socialist system were followed in Poland by modifications in the accepted societal value system. During the first stages of the national economic development, which were based on the principle of common ownership of the means of production, material goods did not play an overly important part in the accepted value system. The primary places within the hierarchy of societal values were occupied by prosperity of homeland, prosperity of the firm, satisfaction gained by the performance of assigned tasks, sense of usefulness, among others. There are at least three reasons for that kind of hierarchy in the value system:

1. The historical - emotional reason: Actual enthusiasm united the whole society in the work for the reconstruction of the free but destroyed country after the Second World War;
2. The psychological - societal reason: People's aspirations and the scope of their needs were very limited after World War II;
3. The economic reason: The real possibilities of satisfying needs by means of money were very limited. (The distribution of goods was under rigorous control)

The next stages of economic development in Poland had considerable influence on modifications in the value hierarchy.

Despite the system's principles rejecting the direct causal nexus between material goods, possession, and societal position Polish society did not avoid the natural process of commercialization. Satisfying the material needs of individuals became increasingly important while values like the satisfaction of executing tasks and contributing to the prosperity and good of firm or country were discredited. The values linked to the satisfying of an individual's material needs, or his or her family's, emerged in the center of the society interests. Sociological investigations proved that the main object of individual identification is one's family and its prosperity. However, in contradiction to capitalist countries, possession of material goods cannot constitute a value in itself. The socialist economy in Poland accepts private ownership of the means of production to a very small extent, which has caused the inseparable connection between the promotion of values linked with satisfying material needs and the promotion of values constituted by societal position. Societal position is here understood as position within the organizational hierarchy of an enterprise or of an institution. Societal position is not secondary relative to material goods possessed by an individual. On the contrary, it constitutes the primary value in the system of societal promotion. One might say that any societal position is demarcated by the scope and value of common property at one's disposal. It is only when an appropriate societal position is attained that there is a chance of getting and using material goods.

We should remember that the set of convictions and societal values accepted by the whole of society plays a part more or less similar to the set of axioms in geometric systems. That is, it embodies established assumptions which are never proved and/or are accepted on the basis of confidence or intuition. The substantial feature of this set is that it distinguishes between desired and not desired, good and bad states.[2] Constantly modifying and changing of the societal value system is an unavoidable attribute of the human being. This attribute makes it necessary for the system of management to keep up with the changing value system. If the management system does not keep up with these changing values, deep societal and economic conflicts are inevitable.

DYNAMICS OF NATIONAL ECONOMY MANAGEMENT SYSTEM

Changes within the accepted societal value system should not take place without linkage to changes in the system of manageing the economy. These two elements ought to be connected by motivation processes that constitute the substantial function of management and that are consistent with the value system.

The socialist system, however, is constantly on guard against a strong inclination to centralize management systems without regard for the existing value system. That inclination is caused by the character of the principles in the socialist system and, above all, by the common ownership of the means of production. The main element of the centralized management system is the central planning of the national economy. In such a model the procedures of multi-level decentralization of national, societal, and economic goals are used.

Five main stages can generally be identified in the development of the system for managing the national economy in Poland over the last 35 years.

The first stage was characterized by the high centralization of the management system. It resulted in the dominance of central economic plans and a lack of independence for economic organizations, which was required by the need to protect the new societal system, especially, the common ownership of the means of production.

The second stage aimed at considerable development of the intermediate level of the management system, created to mediate between the center and various individual economic organizations, whose growing number began to cause difficulties in central planning and decision making processes in Poland during the 1960s. It was obvious that the establishment of an intermediate managerial level did not contribute to decentralizing the management system because this level's only function was to transmit directives from the center to economic organizations. Moreover, by creating, in some cases, new additional directives, it restricted what independence the economic organizations had left.

The third stage took place in the beginning of the 1970s when the rapid and high increase of people's aspirations and the needs of Polish society confronted the Polish economy with the necessity of a general turn from the extensive to the intensive ways of economic development. The theoreticians and most practitioners have concluded that the management systems established in the Soviet Union and other socialist countries in the 1930's,'40's and '50's are not appropriate at present as they wasted considerable material, capital, and manpower.

The situation in the beginning of the 1970s, mentioned above, created a strong tendency to organize a big and specialized concentration of equipment, manpower, and energy within so-called "big economic organizations". This kind of solution created much better technical and economic conditions for pursuing economic tasks while simultaneously creating a good opportunity for decentralizing the management system.

The center was not able to control the whole of the huge and complicated national economy directly, so traditional, centralized management proved useless in many respects. The independence of the big economic organizations consisted primarily in deciding how to achieve the general goals previously established by the center, an approach that greatly increased the efficiency of planning and decision making processes, because it reduced the directives to the country's economic units to two factors: profit and production value. These modifications, however, did not solve another problem which seems to be very important - the problem of people's motivation. As it was rightly noticed by E. F. Schumacher, survival usually becomes the basic need of the people involved in the huge structures of economic organization.[4] This need predisposes managers to take "the protective attitudes" which allow them to avoid taking risks. This attitude considerably reduces the likelihood of their creative participation in achieving the organization goals.

The fourth stage, which took place in the second half of seventies, consisted of re-embracing the idea of centralization. It resulted in a considerable, progressive increase of number of directives (from two to about one hundred directives annually), reducing the independence of economic units. The main reasons for this situation had to do with the world recession. The inclinations toward centralization have always increased in Poland when there is an emergency. This time the emergency was the unexpected economic recession, which compelled the Polish economy to lower national economic and social goals substantially. It turned out to be impossible to achieve many of them under the pressure of new external and internal circumstances. There is no doubt that the return of the centralized management system was caused to some extent by the traditional reluctance of central agencies to resign their power and competencies despite their awareness that they are not able to use those competencies properly.[5] Consequently, centralization reduced the scope of participation by lower and middle-level leadership in economic decision making, theoretically divesting them of responsibility for their economic organizations. In practice, however, the highly formalized system of controlling and reporting left this part of the leadership responsible for the performance of the economic units. This situation reflected the evident lack of balance between the leadership's competence and its responsibility on each level of the managerial hierarchy. People's need for real participation in decision making that affected the future of an enterprise, district, or of the whole country grew considerably. Inappropriate correlation between values at that time and centralized management greatly restricted the motivation processes and dragged Poland to serious internal social and economic conflicts.

The many strikes in Poland during the summer of 1980 were an index to the general unrest. Nation-wide discussion is now focusing on the necessity for far-reaching changes in the Polish system of managing the national economy. This is undoubtedly the beginning of the unexpectedly sudden fifth stage of development in this system. The new solutions are still being discussed rather than introduced, so all considerations below concerning the fourth stage are still very relevant.

MOTIVATION PROCESSES: "THE PROGRESSIVE ATTITUDE" AND "THE PROTECTIVE ATTITUDE"

The problems with motivation are rooted in a great many issues. It seems reasonable for the purposes of this paper to concentrate solely on external motivation to execute professional tasks.[6]

The economic motivation seems to be a major element of external motivation and is based on the economic needs of society. Another substantial need affecting external motivation is an individual's need to control his situation. It frequently appears in the form of preference for an independent position or for protection against emergencies, including the loss of the societal position.

The same need can be satisfied by means of two different attitudes, the offensive attitude (steering towards autonomy) and the defensive attitude (steering towards the protection of the status quo).

Economic needs and the need to control play a very important part in the societal value system accepted by Polish leadership staff members in economic organizations. These needs are very close to the lower, basic physiological needs and needs of safety as distinguished by Maslow.[7] Satisfying them consitutes a worker's primary motivation.

The activity of the human being involved in the complicated mechanism of societal and economic activity cannot be adequately explained with the traditional "stimulus - response" model. It is necessary today to use a more complex approach based on the "system - personality - activity - effect" model in which the existing societal value system and the management system in use are the primary parts in the vast range of activities of economic organizations. More precisely, the most substantial part of the model shown in Figure 1 is the process of correlation between the value system and the management system.

The notion of correlation suggests the existence of relationships and interdependencies between those two elements, and it can be assumed that it actually works in this way.

The subsystem of motivative procedures will be considered as the whole system of wages, rewards, privileges, penalties, and rules of professional and societal promotion. This subsystem (together with the whole management system) undoubtedly has a considerable influence on the societal value hierarchy. On the other hand, commonly accepted societal values must be taken into account while the motivative pro-

Fig. 1

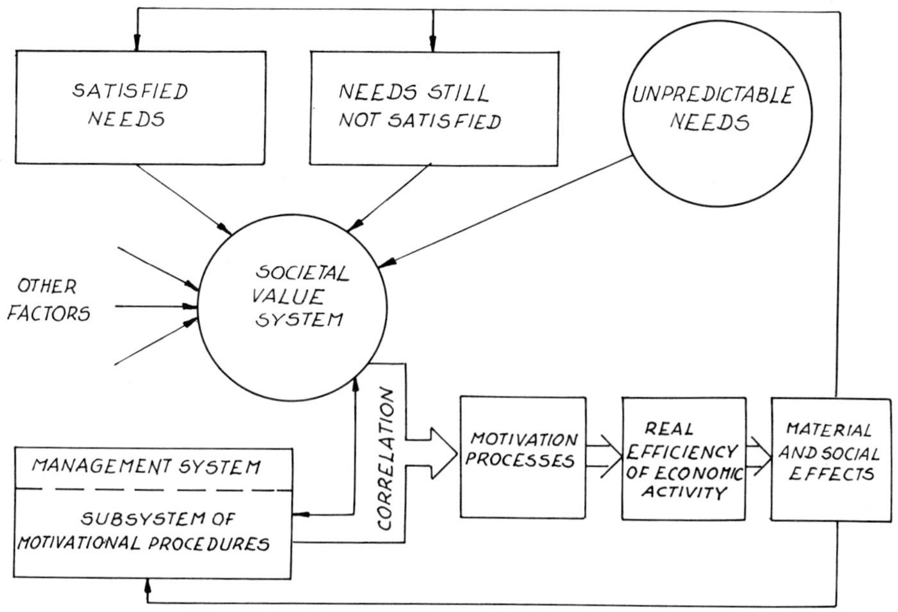
SATISFIED NEEDS
NEEDS STILL NOT SATISFIED
UNPREDICTABLE NEEDS
OTHER FACTORS
SOCIETAL VALUE SYSTEM
CORRELATION
MOTIVATION PROCESSES
REAL EFFICIENCY OF ECONOMIC ACTIVITY
MATERIAL AND SOCIAL EFFECTS
MANAGEMENT SYSTEM
SUBSYSTEM OF MOTIVATIONAL PROCEDURES

Fig. 2

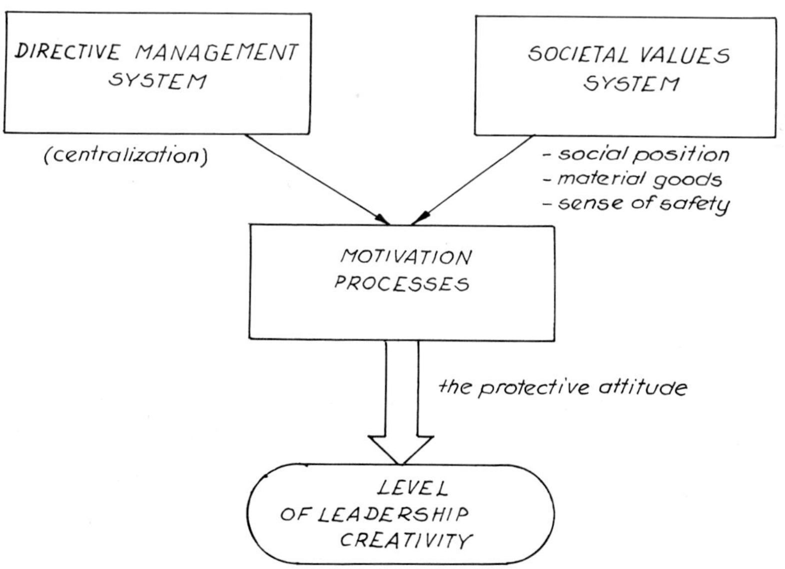
DIRECTIVE MANAGEMENT SYSTEM
(centralization)
SOCIETAL VALUES SYSTEM
- social position
- material goods
- sense of safety
MOTIVATION PROCESSES
the protective attitude
LEVEL OF LEADERSHIP CREATIVITY

cedures are being set because it determines their efficiency. However, the correlation of these two elements cannot be a mere compromise. It must be achieved under the assumption that the system of preferred societal values performs the primary function because, in fact, it is uncontrollable. One can attempt to shape this correlation, but it is not possible to control this system while the motivative procedures are fully steerable and formed by the group of regulations and principles set by a centralized management. Hence, the management system's disregard for the actual value system when attempting to play the primary part in the process of correlation usually reduces motivation and leads to societal tension and conflict.

Such was the case with Poland's leadership in the seventies. The creative leadership and innovative activity of those in charge declined as motivation was reduced. There are two major attitudes recognizable in the leadership of the Polish enterprise sector. The first one is "the progressive attitude", which manifests itself in the tendency to innovate, continue developing and improving the quality of one's own work and the work of subordinates, take high risks whenever it is required for the sake of improvement. This attitude prevails in the full application of the principles of creative leadership, the utilization of one's inventiveness and the inventiveness of subordinates, and competence in taking risks. The dynamics of such attitudes are derived from a constant open-mindedness to situations and problems while simultaneously aspiring to an acceptable degree of autonomy within the management system. In fact, this is the offensive attitude.

The second frame of mind recognizable in the Polish economic leadership is "the protective attitude", which is, of course, the antithesis of the first. The main aspiration of the leader who has taken the protective attitude is the maintenance of the situation's stability, which is supposed to ensure his position. The principle of cancelling innovations and changes enables a leader to avoid risk. The creative thinking aimed at constant technological and organizational progress is replaced by straightforward fulfilling of directives from superior agencies. This is naturally a kind of defensive attitude.

THE LIMIT OF LEADERSHIP CREATIVITY AND THEIR RESULTS IN NATIONAL ECONOMY

The level of creativity among the members of Poland's leadership is a very important matter for the whole national economic system, for Poland has very great industrial potential (10th - 11th in the world) which is still not sufficiently utilized even though the needs of Polish society are still unsatisfied. An alternative would be to intensify economic development at the national scale. However, this can only be done through technological and organizational progress, and that requires the full utilization of the leadership's creative abilities at every level of management.

In the meantime, however, the inappropriate correlation between the centralized management system and the societal value system created the very dangerous tendency of Polish economic leaders to take the "protective attitude" in the second half of seventies. Allowing societal position to determine the access to material goods intensified people's safety needs, understood as the need to maintain one's position in the managerial hierarchy. This very need has not yet caused any deviation in motivational processes. As shown earlier, it can be satisfied by taking the offensive attitude (struggle for autonomy) or by taking the defensive attitude (aspirations towards maintaining status quo). Only the confrontation of the value system with the rigid, centralized management system implies that the leaders who have no choice usually adopt the defensive attitude, "the protective attitude" (see Figure 2).

As matter-of-fact people, leaders usually act in accordance with the principle of profitability, but in the present situation this steers them towards cancelling any innovative activites.[8]

It is one of characteristic peculiarities of the centralized management system that the leaders' creativity does not create the necessary condition for the survival. The procedures of evaluating leaders in centralized management system do not include the consideration of their creativity. Hence, leaders treat their positions as an important value, and they are interested mainly in the fulfilling of directives coming to them from the center. In daily life within an economic system, this omission results in the fact that an average of 90 % of all innovations implemented in enterprises lie between only the first and fourth degree of a seven degree scale of innovation depth. It means that most innovations are simple adjustment and little improvement. There is a substantial lack of deep innovation in the technology of organization. These kinds of barriers limiting the creative leadership are smothering the invention of both leaders and their subordinates. Their useful ideas will never be heard if other members of the leadership never listen. This is one of the main causes of the considerable waste of materials, manpower, and energy in Poland.

CONCLUSIONS

Since the socialist system, as a model and an idea, can be considered a just system, even stronger feelings of injustice are felt at every point where it is inappropriately and inadequately correlated to the value system developed by a given society, i.e. values originating in the history, traditions and mentality of a people.

The system for managing the national economy must be constantly adjusted to the societal value system if otherwise serious social and economic conflicts at the level of enterprise are to be avoided.

Those conflicts can considerably reduce leadership creativity and block emerging of the innovative activity within economic organizations.

It seems necessary to seek equilibrium between the processes of centralization and decentralization of the system for managing the national economy, a balance that would allow harmonious control of economy development while preserving a specific level and range of independence for economic organizations. Only then can the Polish economic leadership begin to see "the progressive attitude" as indispensable to the process of independent problem solving.

In order to take advantage of the importance attached to societal position (in the sense of position occupied in the institutional hierarchy) in the societal value system it is necessary to make holding a given position more dependent on the evaluation of a leader's creativity, on his competence in taking risks, and much less dependent on correct and straightforward execution of directives handed down by superiors. The potential increase in creativity among Polish leaders can become a decisive factor in the intensive development of the national economy.

BIBLIOGRAPHY

1. T. Kocowski (1978), Potrzeby człowieka: Koncepcja systemowa, Ser. Monografie, Wroclaw, Prace Naukowe OBP Politechniki Wroclawskiej

2. K. Koźmiński and M. Zawiślak (1979), Pewność i gra, Warsaw: PWE

3. W. Morawski (1980), Management as a Factor of Social and Economic Development under Conditions of the Technological Acceleration, paper presented at the International Sympos ium on Management Problems Under Conditions of Advanced Scientific-Technical Revolution, Warsaw

4. E. F. Schumacher (1980), Małe jest piekne, Warsaw: TIW

5. J. Pajestka (1980), Zmienić sposób działania, Polityka 35

6. Various authors usually recognize two major kinds of motivation within this scope, internal motivation and external motivation, whereby external motivation is understood as the motivation stimulating an individual to achieve goals which are indirectly useful for him, and internal motivation is understood as the motivation stimulating an individual to achieve goals which are directly useful for him. See J. Reykowski (1979), Teoria motywacji a zarzadzanie, Warsaw: PWE

7. A. Maslow (1954), Motivation and Personality, New York: Harper

8. Z. Pietrosiński (1975), Twórcze kierownictw, Warsaw: PWN

Subject Index